English Writing and Language Skills

Fifth Course

Critical Readers and Contributors

The authors and the publisher wish to thank the following people, who helped to evaluate and to prepare materials for this series:

Charles L. Allen, Baltimore Public Schools, Baltimore, Maryland
Kiyoko B. Bernard, Huntington Beach High School, Huntington Beach, California
Sally Borengasser, Rogers, Arkansas
Deborah Bull, New York City, New York
Joan Colby, Chicago, Illinois
Phyllis Goldenberg, North Miami Beach, Florida
Beverly Graves, Worthington High School, Worthington, Ohio
Pamela Hannon, Kirk Middle School, Cleveland, Ohio
Carol Kuykendall, Houston Public Schools, Houston, Texas
Wayne Larkin, Roosevelt Junior High School, Blaine, Minnesota
Nancy MacKnight, University of Maine, Orono, Maine
Catherine McCough, Huntington Beach Union School District, California
Lawrence Milne, Ocean View High School, Long Beach, California
Al Muller, East Carolina University, Greenville, North Carolina
Dorothy Muller, East Carolina University, Greenville, North Carolina
John Nixon, Santa Ana Junior College, Santa Ana, California
Jesse Perry, San Diego City Schools, California
Christine Rice, Huntington Beach Union School District, Huntington Beach, California
Jo Ann Seiple, University of North Carolina at Wilmington, Wilmington, North Carolina
Joan Yesner, Brookline, Massachusetts
Seymour Yesner, Brookline Education Center, Massachusetts

Classroom Testing

The authors and the publisher also wish to thank the following teachers, who participated in the classroom testing of materials from this series:

David Foote, Evanston High School East, Evanston, Illinois
Theresa Hall, Nokomis Junior High School, Minneapolis, Minnesota
Carrie E. Hampton, Sumter High School, Sumter, South Carolina
Pamela Hannon, Proviso High School East, Maywood, Illinois
Wayne Larkin, Roosevelt Junior High School, Blaine, Minnesota
Grady Locklear, Sumter High School, Sumter, South Carolina
William Montgomery, Hillcrest High School, Jamaica, New York
Josephine H. Price, Sumter High School, Sumter, South Carolina
Barbara Stilp, North High School, Minneapolis, Minnesota
Joseph Thomas, Weymouth North High School, East Weymouth, Massachusetts
Travis Weldon, Sumter High School, Sumter, South Carolina

Teachers of the Huntington Beach Union High School Writing Program:

Cassandra C. Allsop
Eric V. Emery
Michael Frym
Barbara Goldfein
Joanne Haukland
Don Hohl
Sandra Johnson
Carol Kasser
Patricia Kelly
Stephanie Martone
Lawrence Milne
Richard H. Morley
John S. Nixon
Catherine G. McCough
Kathleen C. Redman
Christine Rice
Michael D. Sloan
S. Oliver Smith
Glenda Watson
Dorothy Augustine, District Consultant in Writing

English Writing and Language Skills

Fifth Course

W. Ross Winterowd

Patricia Y. Murray

HARCOURT BRACE JOVANOVICH, PUBLISHERS

Orlando   New York   Chicago   San Diego   Atlanta   Dallas

THE SERIES:

English Writing and Language Skills, First Course

English Writing and Language Skills, Second Course

English Writing and Language Skills, Third Course

English Writing and Language Skills, Fourth Course

English Writing and Language Skills, Fifth Course

English Writing and Language Skills, Complete Course

A test booklet, teacher's manual, and workbook are available for each title.

W. ROSS WINTEROWD is the Bruce R. McElderry Professor of English at the University of Southern California. Since 1975, Dr. Winterowd has traveled widely as a writing consultant for numerous schools in North America.

PATRICIA Y. MURRAY is director of the writing program and the writing laboratory at the University of Michigan—Flint. Dr. Murray taught junior and senior high school English in the Los Angeles city schools. She is also a consultant in curriculum development and teacher training.

Design: Michael Rogondino

Photo Credits   8, Evan Johnson, Jeroboam, Inc.; 9, Werner Hiebel, Alphapress, Jeroboam, Inc.; 13, © Louise Dahl-Wolfe; 46, Kent Reno, Jeroboam, Inc.; 46, Lee Youngblood; 188, © Ivan Massar from Black Star; 189, Al Giddings, Ocean Films Ltd.; 324, Steve Malone, Jeroboam, Inc.; 325, © Elizabeth Crews, Stock, Boston; 385, Gaylord Herron, Archive Pictures; 404, Kent Reno, Jeroboam, Inc.; 413, © Paul Fortin, Stock, Boston; 483, Peter Vilms, Jeroboam, Inc.

Part- and Chapter-Opener Photographs by Lee Youngblood

Illustrations by Pat Rogondino

Photo Research by Lindsay Kefauver

Printed in the United States of America

ISBN 0-15-311554-8

Contents

3 Writing the Paragraph 47

4 Writing Exposition: The Composition 74

5 Writing from Sources: the Research Report 94

2 Resources for Writing

3   Reading

12   Reading Social Studies Materials   232

4   Sentence Combining

13   Joining Sentences   248

14   Inserting Sentences   259

5   Language

6   Using Grammar

7   Mechanics

8 Speaking/Listening

9 Testing

1 Writing

1 Writing the Journal and Personal Narrative

Learning About Personal Writing

Many people enjoy keeping souvenirs, such as posters from favorite movies, scout badges, letters, or trophies, to provide memories of special times and places. Souvenirs are also called *mementos*, from a Latin word meaning "to remember."

Personal writing—writing about your own life—is another kind of memento. It gives you the opportunity to capture special and everyday experiences, thoughts, feelings, events, and moods that you might otherwise forget. Personal writing ranges from private journals to informal essays, including personal narratives, anecdotes, and autobiography, all of which emphasize the life of the writer. Your personal writing re-creates impressions and experiences that are important to you.

Personal writing is in a natural voice.

Whether you write for an audience of one in a private journal, for an audience of friends, or for the general audience addressed by a personal essay or an autobiography, the basic style of personal writing changes very little. It sounds natural and conversational, as if you were sitting down to have a talk with friends; the descriptions are lively and colorful.

In this chapter you will read about two types of personal writing: the journal and the personal narrative. You will learn ways to improve your skills of observation and self-expression, and you will discover how personal writing can help you become more perceptive about your own life.

Reading Personal Writing

The following passages are from the essay "The Hawk Is Flying" by Harry Crews. As you read, notice how the passages sound almost as though the writer were speaking. Also, try to identify the specific details with which he makes his description of the scene come alive for the reader.[1]

Palmetto is a type of palm tree. *Attitude* here means "position of the body."

> I was jogging between Lake Swan and Lake Rosa on a ridge full of blackjack oak when I saw the hawk, tail feathers fanned and wings half spread, beside a clump of palmetto about twenty yards off the dim path. From the attitude of her wings and tail I first thought she was sitting on a kill, maybe a rabbit or a rat, but then she turned her wild dandelion eyes toward me and I knew that she was there in the sand not because of something she had killed but because she herself had almost been killed. Blood was dark and clotted on the trailing edge of her right wing. Someone had brought her down with a gun and then not had the decency to find where she fell.
>
> I stood there in the path for a long time, deciding whether or not to kill her. I knew the chances of keeping her alive were slim after she'd been hurt. But leaving her wing-shot in the dirt like that would take more meanness than I thought I could manage. At the same time, though, I knew the right thing to do would be to step quickly across the sand and kick her to death. I watched her where she sat quietly, feathers ruffled now and unafraid, and I knew I was not going to find it in myself either to leave her or kill her. There was nothing to do but take her up and try to save her.

For Discussion

1. In the excerpt from "The Hawk Is Flying," Harry Crews writes about his train of thought as he finds the hawk. For example, he says, ". . . I first thought she was sitting on a kill, maybe a rabbit or a rat, . . ." What other thoughts pass through his mind about the hawk? What do you learn about Harry Crews as you follow his train of thought?

2. Vivid descriptions, such as the "wild dandelion eyes" of the hawk, help the reader visualize the scene. What other descriptive details play an important part in the scene? For example, how does Crews describe the setting? How does he describe his feelings about the hawk?

Writing Practice 1

Use the Discovering Ideas for Writing section that follows to help you with ideas for this assignment.

Take a moment to recall an experience that was important to you in some way, perhaps an event from your childhood or something that happened more recently. It can be a solitary experience, such as the one Harry Crews described, or a shared one. On a separate sheet of paper, write your memory of this experience, including as many specific details as you can recall. Tell the reader about the sights, sounds, smells, and tastes of the experience, as well as your reaction to what happened.

Discovering Ideas for Writing

In the excerpt from "The Hawk Is Flying" on this page, Harry Crews writes about a memorable experience. He recalls just what he saw, how he felt,

---

[1] Excerpt from "The Hawk is Flying" by Harry Crews from *Esquire* Magazine, June 1977. Copyright © 1977 by Harry Crews. Reprinted by permission of Paul R. Reynolds, Inc.

and what he was thinking as it happened. For your first assignment you will also write about an important experience.

One theory of memory states that your brain stores images of everything that has ever happened to you. To discover some of these stored memories, clear your mind of all other thoughts but the event you want to write about. Sit for a few moments, perhaps with your eyes closed, and remember. Imagine the event again as it took place, step by step. The following questions will help shape the experience in your mind. As you ask yourself these questions, write down the most important details you recall.

1. Where are you?

    Imagine looking carefully at your surroundings. Focus on something far away from you and then look at something nearby. Is the place familiar or unfamiliar? How is this setting important to your memory of the event?

2. Are you with someone?

    Is someone else sharing the experience with you? Visualize exactly what this person looks like. Does he or she react in the same way you do? If you are with strangers, how do they seem to you? If you are alone, do you feel uneasy, or do you feel comfortable being by yourself?

3. What time is it?

    The time of day and year when events happen are often important to an experience. Is it early morning or evening? Does the time of day affect your reactions, perhaps making you feel alert and energetic, or sleepy? What season is it? In what ways does the time influence how you feel about the experience?

4. What kind of mood are you in?

    Are you anticipating the experience, or does it come as a surprise? Do you feel suspenseful? Bored?

5. Are you an actor or a bystander in this event?

    Are you the central figure in the experience, or is your role more that of an observer? (You can be both participant and observer.)

6. What are your reactions during the event?

    What do you think and feel about what is happening? If you are with others, how do they react? Do you feel close to the others, or do you feel apart? Do your reactions surprise you?

As you go through questions such as the preceding ones, you will discover how much you remember about the experience. You may also think of other questions to help refresh your memory.

Thinking in specific details will help you to remember accurately. When you are ready to write, describe the experience in simple words, using *I*, *my*, or *we*. Relate the memory as if you were talking with a friend.

The Journal

A *personal journal* is similar to a diary but is usually more elaborate. The English words *diary* and *journal* derive from words meaning "daily" because both are daily records of events, impressions, and ideas.

Journal writing helps you to remember events and to reflect on them. It can give you a perspective on your life that you might otherwise lose. With a journal you can look back when you are older and read what an ordinary day in your life at a certain age was like. You can recall the experience of getting your drivers license, remember your impressions of an exciting concert, or relive the feelings of preparing for your first date.

A personal journal is often private, like a diary, but other journals are written to be shared. As you work on the journal entries in this chapter, write each one as you would for a public journal so that you can share it with your teacher and classmates. If you wish to write about private thoughts and feelings, consider keeping a second journal at home on your own. Your teacher will tell you what form the journal will take. You may use a looseleaf or spiral notebook or perhaps a collection of pages in your English notebook.

The Trained Observer

An essential skill in journal writing is *observation*, the art of paying attention.

When scientists make observations during an experiment, they frequently pay attention to one particular thing, such as the growth of a cell, the reaction of a chemical, or the behavior of an organism. Sometimes, writers observe in a similar way. They know exactly what they want to examine, and they focus all their attention on it.

However, when detectives make observations during an investigation, they frequently do not know exactly what they are looking for. Anything might be a clue, so they train themselves to notice things in general: times, places, appearances, and people's actions and reactions. Sometimes, writers observe as detectives do, taking in everything around them for future use.

Writing Practice 2

For this observation experiment you will focus on one item. You may select an object in the classroom, in the library, or in any other place where you can sit and observe without interruption for about ten minutes. Focus your attention on the item you have selected, perhaps a swinging door, clock hands slowly moving, the nub of an eraser, or a globe. On a separate sheet of paper, make a list of details that thoroughly and exactly describe the object—its location, shape, size, color, weight, dimensions, density, texture, smell, sounds that it makes, and so on. Next, list every detail, down to the most minute features, that distinguish this item from others of its sort. For example, if you describe a door, look for unusual marks, perhaps scars in the wood or paint coming off around the handle. Allow sufficient time for this exercise so that you observe and describe the object completely.

Writing Practice 3

In the following experiment you will test and try to expand your powers of general observation. As you observe, try to make yourself aware of everything around you and use all your senses, not just your power of sight. You will need a pad of paper and about ten minutes.

First, choose a room for the setting of your experiment—your classroom, the library, a room in your house or apartment, or any other room that appeals to you. Imagine that this room is the scene of a crime and that you are the detective called in to investigate. Everything that you observe is a possible clue.

Label your paper with the following columns: SIGHTS, SOUNDS, TASTES, TEXTURES, and SMELLS. Record your observations under each column, including as many details as possible.

Example

Basement room

SIGHTS

Concrete floor with stain in middle
Maze of pipes overhead
Dusty wooden shelves in cupboard
Basket of apples

SOUNDS

Clinking in pipes
Creaking floor overhead—people walking?
Scurrying sounds in corner

TASTES

Dry throat—dusty taste
Metallic taste of water from old faucet

TEXTURES

Rough edge of basement door
Smooth handle of water tap
Skin of soft apple in roughly woven basket
Damp slickness of floor

SMELLS

Sharp smell of apples
Musty smell of damp floor and old boxes

Reading About Observation

Scientists are trained to observe in order to solve the mysteries of the physical world; detectives are trained to look for clues so that they can solve mysteries surrounding crimes. The mysteries you explore when you write in a journal are personal. They concern your relationship to others and to the world around you, and your attitudes about yourself. In a journal you observe the world around you and also yourself—your own emotions, beliefs, and reactions.

The following excerpt from a memoir titled *An Unfinished Woman* by the well-known writer Lillian Hellman concerns a place from her childhood that took on a special meaning in her life. As you read, notice how Lillian Hellman combines an exact description of that place with the emotions she felt there.[1]

Following this selection is a For Discussion activity.

There was a heavy fig tree on the lawn where the house turned the corner into the side street, and to the front and sides of the fig tree were three live oaks that hid the fig from my aunts' boardinghouse. I suppose I was eight or nine before I discovered the pleasures of the fig tree, and although I have lived in many houses since then, including a few I made for myself, I still think of it as my first and most beloved home.

I learned early, in our strange life of living half in New York and half in New Orleans, that I made my New Orleans teachers uncomfortable because I was too far ahead of my schoolmates, and my New York teachers irritable because I was too far behind. But in New Orleans, I found a solution: I skipped school at least once a week and often twice, knowing that nobody cared or would report my absence. On those days I would set out for school done up in polished strapped shoes and a prim hat against what was known as "the climate," carrying my books and a little basket filled with delicious stuff my Aunt Jenny and Carrie, the cook, had made for my school lunch. I would round the corner of the side street, move on toward St. Charles Avenue, and sit on a bench as if I were waiting for a streetcar until the boarders and the neighbors had gone to work or settled down for the post-breakfast rest that all Southern ladies thought necessary. Then I would run back to the fig tree, dodging in and out of bushes to make sure the house had no dangers for me. The fig tree was heavy, solid, comfortable, and I had, through time, convinced myself that it wanted me, missed me when I was absent, and approved all the rigging I had done for the happy days I spent in its arms: I had made a sling to hold the school books, a pulley rope for my lunch basket, a hole for the bottle of afternoon cream-soda pop, a fishing pole and a smelly little bag of elderly bait, a pillow embroidered with a picture of Henry Clay on a horse that I had stolen from Mrs. Stillman, one of my aunts' boarders, and a proper nail to hold my dress and shoes to keep them neat for the return to the house.

Henry Clay was a United States orator and statesman (1777–1852).

It was in that tree that I learned to read, filled with the passions that can only come to the bookish, grasping, very young, bewildered by almost all of what I read, sweating in the attempt to understand a world of adults I fled from in real life but desperately wanted to join in books. (I did not connect the grown men and women in literature with the grown men and women I saw around me. They were, to me, another species.)

For Discussion

1. In the preceding excerpt Lillian Hellman writes about a place that was her "first and most beloved home": a fig tree. In describing her favorite place, Lillian Hellman uses specific details of sight when she writes that "to the front and sides of the fig tree were three live oaks that hid the fig

---

[1]Excerpt from *An Unfinished Woman* by Lillian Hellman. Copyright © 1969 by Lillian Hellman. Reprinted by permission of Little, Brown and Company and the Harold Matson Company, Inc.

from my aunts' boardinghouse." What are other details of sight the writer uses to describe her home in the fig tree? Of smell? Of texture?

2. Lillian Hellman also writes about her reaction to the fig tree then and now: ". . . I still think of it as my first and most beloved home." What are other instances of the writer describing her thoughts and feelings?

Writing Practice 4

Use the Discovering Ideas for Writing section that follows to help you with this assignment.

Imagine that you are taking part in the scene shown in one of the photographs on this page and page 9. Examine the scene closely and then write a journal entry describing what it is like to be there. Include sensory details of what

you observe and what you do, as well as your impressions of how the place makes you feel.

Discovering Ideas for Writing

In this writing assignment you will describe your reactions to a specific place. One way to begin is to ask yourself questions about the sights, sounds, tastes, textures, and smells you observe in the scene. After you have thought about your physical surroundings, ask yourself questions about your thoughts and feelings. The following questions are suggestions that may help you. Use them or ask yourself similar questions.

1. Do I feel calm or ill at ease here?

2. Do I feel comfortable or am I an intruder?

3. Does this place make me recall memories of other places?

4. What is my first reaction to this place?

5. What do I like or dislike about being here?

As you decide on your responses to questions such as the preceding ones, remember to be specific. If you simply write, "This is a nice place, and I like it here," you do not help the reader understand your experience. Describe *what* you see, *how* it affects you, and *why* you feel as you do.

Writing Practice 5

Use the preceding Discovering Ideas for Writing section for help with this assignment.

This exercise is similar to the preceding writing practice, but here you will write a journal entry about an experience in a place you have really been.

Take a moment to think of a place that was significant to you in some way. It can be a place of recent memory, such as the gym where your team won a game, or a distant memory of the lake where you first learned to swim. It can be a public place or a private place, a place you visit frequently or a place you saw only once. As you write, remember that your purpose is to give your reader a picture of the place itself, your impressions and feelings about it and reasons why the place affects you this way.

Using Vivid Details

When you observe an object or a person or a place, you have specific impressions. Think for a moment about a person you know well. You do not simply think of this person as *male* or *female*, *child* or *adult*; instead, you are aware of such details as his or her age, height, coloring, and length of hair. You probably remember the *smell* of a favorite cologne, the *texture* of an often-worn sweater, and the *sound* of his or her voice.

Vivid details are ones that re-create sights, sounds, tastes, textures, and smells for readers.

As a writer your purpose is to "translate" what you observe into words that give the reader a precise description. In the two passages that follow, the writers chose vivid details to translate their impressions into words. As you read, try to visualize the subject being described.

In the first selection, by Anne Rivers Siddons, the writer recalls her memories of fall. What details of sight, smell, sound, and texture help you to share the experience?[1]

> As the fall wore on, mornings were born silver, and bleeding sunsets came earlier, and rumbling furnaces came alive in basements. We melted, with a winter-long stench, the soles of our saddle oxfords, standing over hot-air registers. The Southeastern Fair wheeled by in a technicolor blur of sawdust and

---

[1] Excerpt from "Fall Comes in on Roller Skates" by Anne Rivers Siddons from *Atlanta* Magazine, October 1969. Reprinted by permission of *Atlanta* Magazine and the author.

cotton candy and forbidden midway shows where, the big kids said, ladies took their clothes off. Halloween smelled of the wet, burnt insides of pumpkins and was terrible with an atavistic terror in front of the fire in our living room, where my father read me the witches' speech from *Macbeth*. I remember one magic night in October when I was plucked up out of sleep, wrapped in a quilt, and taken outside in our back yard to watch a meteor shower. Warm on my father's shoulder, but with everything strange and too big and not like our back yard at all, I watched as the very sky above me wheeled and arced and bloomed. It was, I thought, something God arranged for me because He knew my father.

Atavistic means "reverting to a much earlier or primitive type."

In the following paragraphs the writer Robert Penn Warren relates his memories of his grandfather. What details of sight and sound help you to see and hear this man?[1]

When I think of my maternal grandfather, I see an old man with white hair and a rather pointed beard, wearing blue-jean pants, with a black tie hanging loose from a collar open at the throat—for in that memory it is an unchanging summer. He is sitting in a sturdy, split-bottom chair, with its arms broadening to wide, rounded ends—the kind of chair that in the old days appeared here and there among rockers of similar design on the verandas of summer hotels in the South, called springs, where people went to avoid malaria. But my grandfather's chair is under a cedar tree, propped back against the trunk, and blue smoke from his cob pipe threads thinly upward into the darkness of the cedar.

I am a small boy sitting tailor-fashion on the unkempt lawn, looking up at the old man, and then, beyond him, at the whitewashed board fence, and then at the woods coming down almost to the fence. If it was getting toward sunset, the uncountable guinea fowl would be coming in from foraging to roost near the house, making a metallic and disgruntled but halfhearted clatter, not the full, outraged racket of morning. I would be waiting for the old man to talk. Or even to sing, in his old, cracked voice, one of the few songs that might rise from his silence, sung only for himself.

By using vivid details, the writers of the preceding passages re-create their subjects. Details such as "Halloween smelled of the wet, burnt insides of pumpkins" make Anne Rivers Siddons' impressions meaningful to her and to her readers. Similarly, Robert Penn Warren's readers can see his grandfather when he describes him "propped back against the trunk" as "blue smoke from his cob pipe threads thinly upward into the darkness of the cedar."

What other vivid details do these writers use?

Writing Practice 6

Each of the five sentences that follow attempts to describe a person in a setting, but each needs to be improved by the addition of vivid details. Rewrite each sentence, adding details of sight, sound, taste, texture, and smell that make the person and scene come to life.

---

[1] Excerpt from "Jefferson Davis Gets His Citizenship Back" by Robert Penn Warren. Copyright © 1980 by Robert Penn Warren. Reprinted by permission of the University of Kentucky Press.

Example

a. The woman sat on her front porch, looking into the street.

a. *The elderly woman leaned back in her front porch swing, gazing into the street, which was filled now with noisy groups of children from the nearby school.*

1. The boy looked around, an unusual expression on his face, and then ran down the alley.

2. The girl sat at her desk in the empty classroom, not doing anything.

3. He had an interesting face for a child; occasionally a strange expression appeared on it as he sat alone in the darkened theater.

4. The woman ate her supper alone in the restaurant, stopping to wipe her mouth with the napkin.

5. The man sat by the seashore with a nice expression on his face.

Writing Practice 7

In a journal entry describe the French writer Colette in the photograph on page 13 or someone who stands out in your mind. Use vivid details to re-create your subject for readers.

Reading Journal Writing

The following journal entry by Anne Morrow Lindbergh recalls her first meeting with the famous aviator Charles Lindbergh, her future husband, when she attends a reception in his honor. As you read, notice the writer's attention to details. What does she observe? How does she portray Colonel Lindbergh? How does she portray herself?[1]

Following this selection is a For Discussion activity.

Odious means "hateful."

"Colonel Lindbergh was there*—a very nice boy, very nice, but he and Daddy were going out tonight." We hardly took it in, or at least were a little annoyed—all this public-hero stuff breaking into our family party. What did I expect? A regular newspaper hero, the baseball-player type—a nice man, perhaps, but not at all "intellectual" and not of my world at all, so I wouldn't be interested. I certainly was *not* going to worship "Lindy" (that *odious name,* anyway). We drove through the streets and honked loudly before an iron gate with eagles above on the crest; the gates opened; we drew up. A wall covered with geraniums to our right, a great movie-scene door and staircase to the left, stone steps, red "velvet" rolling up, like a wedding, in between palms. Officers stood on the steps at attention. We tumbled out dazed and peered up the red plush stairs between "lines" of officers. What a movie! How ridiculous, was all I could say. Elisabeth sat down on the steps exhausted. We went up at last.

*Colonel Lindbergh had flown the "Spirit of St. Louis" nonstop from Washington, D.C., to Mexico City on December 13–14, 1927. The flight was planned at the suggestion of Ambassador Morrow and made in response to an invitation issued by President Calles of Mexico.

[1]From *Bring Me a Unicorn,* copyright © 1971, 1972 by Anne Morrow Lindbergh. Reprinted by permission of Harcourt Brace Jovanovich, Inc., the author, and Chatto & Windus Ltd.

At the top another line of celebrities. Elisabeth went first. Mother hurried up: "Colonel Lindbergh, this is my oldest daughter, Elisabeth." I saw standing against the great stone pillar—on *more* red plush—a tall, slim boy in evening dress—so much slimmer, so much taller, so much more poised than I expected. A very refined face, not at all like those grinning "Lindy" pictures—a firm mouth, clear, straight blue eyes, fair hair, and nice color. Then I went down the line, very confused and overwhelmed by it all. He did not smile—just bowed and shook hands.

A bright fire in the fireplace, great calla lilies on the stone mantelpiece, red tapestry on the stone walls, rich priest's robes, and the intoxicating scent of something. Chinese lilies? Gardenias? They were tuberoses.

It was all unreal.

Baronial means "grand, in the manner of a baron."

Supper that night in a regular baronial hall: stone pillars, stone mantelpiece, etc.

We explored the rooms—high-ceilinged and Nassau-ish. I felt in Nassau, or Panama. I had to run in to Mother every three seconds to feel sure it was true. Daddy, I realized, belonged to so many people now. I was utterly confused.

Later Daddy came home, with Colonel L. Daddy told us to come into the little sitting room. "Is there anyone there?" (With *great* pride, restrained.) "Oh no, just Colonel Lindbergh." Elisabeth and I went out. Why is it that attractive men stimulate Elisabeth to her best and always terrify me and put me at my worst!? We sat around the fire stiffly: Colonel L. stood awkwardly by the desk, shifting from one foot to another. Elisabeth talked.

He is very, very young and was terribly shy—looked straight ahead and talked in short direct sentences which came out abruptly and clipped. You could not meet his sentences: they were statements of fact, presented with such honest directness; not trying to please, just bare simple answers and statements, not trying to help a conversation along. It was amazing—breath-taking. I could not speak. What kind of boy was this?

"How did he like the bullfight?" He blushed a little and shifted his position. "Well, I have seen things I enjoyed more," he blurted out abruptly. "Would he show us the cape and hat—Mexican—presented to him?" "I would be very glad to," and he wheeled out of the room (with evident relief), returned with richly embroidered cape and sombrero, which he passed around with dry impersonality. It did not touch him, all this, and neither did we. It embarrassed him to have to talk to us. He was asked a question about the crowds here and in London. They were not half as bad here as in Paris and London, he said with a dry, simple-statement-of-fact statement. Suddenly the picture of that mad crowd, that whole *nation* surging around his plane in Paris, came into my mind. And it was this *boy*—this shy, cool boy—and he describes that tremendous mad scene in a few dry matter-of-fact words. My Lord!

Daddy said we must go to bed. Abruptly, the Colonel announced, "Well, as the Ambassador's orders are such, I will say good night," and he shook hands quickly without looking at us (girls) and wheeled out of the room, leaving a perfectly amazed stillness inside of me.

For Discussion

1. One way that Anne Morrow Lindbergh makes her journal entry interesting is by weaving many elements into the description; she writes about the mansion where the reception is held and about the reactions of the guests. She also conveys how she *feels*. What are her primary reactions during this episode? What specific words or phrases indicate the writer's reactions?

2. The writer's first meeting with Colonel Lindbergh is a surprise, as he is quite different from what she expects. She first describes him as "a tall, slim boy in evening dress," who does not smile as he greets the guests. What other specific details does the writer give about his appearance and behavior? How does he surprise her?

3. Anne Morrow Lindbergh uses lively descriptions to involve the reader in her experience. For example, she tells how her sister and she came to the receiving line for Colonel Lindbergh: "We tumbled out dazed and peered up the red plush stairs between 'lines' of officers." These details give a sense of the sisters' hurry and their anticipation. What are other descriptive passages that involve you in the story? What specific details help you to visualize the subjects of these passages?

Writing Practice 8

Write a journal entry about meeting someone who makes an impression on you, perhaps in a first meeting or a meeting that stands out in your memory for some other reason. The person you met may have made either a favorable or an unfavorable impression.

The use of descriptive details in writing is discussed on pages 24–25.

Convey your thoughts and feelings about this person through description as well as statements. Explain *what* you did or did not like about the person, *why* he or she made an impression on you, and *how* you reacted. Include a description of your surroundings as part of the journal entry. Write in a natural tone of voice, as if you were telling the incident to a friend.

Revising Your Journal Entry

When writers submit their personal journals for publication, they frequently rework them first.

Revision is the process of making changes to improve a piece of writing.

When revising, some journal writers delete entries that are too private to be published or that would not be interesting to a wide audience. More often, however, they add details to make the manuscript easier for the general reader to understand, and frequently they make changes in style as well.

Writing Practice 9

Using the following guidelines, revise one of the journal entries you have written in this chapter.

1. The entry is written in a natural, conversational style.
2. The entry is interesting to the general reader.
3. The entry gives exact, lively descriptions of the people and places involved.
4. The writer uses vivid details to convey his or her impressions.

When you are satisfied with your revision, you are ready to proofread your composition.

Proofreading Your Journal Entry

Proofreading is also discussed on pages 16–17.

Proofreading is a word of American origin and means, specifically, "reading and correcting *proofs*, or sample pages, from a printer before the final production of a book."

Proofreading has also come to mean reading and correcting a manuscript before submitting it to another reader.

When you proofread, you scan each line carefully for any errors in grammar, style, spelling, or punctuation. Because these errors are easy to miss, many proofreaders advise using a ruler and reading up from the bottom of the page and from right to left. This backward manner of reading forces you to look at each word separately, giving you a better chance of finding any mistakes.

To make corrections on a manuscript, proofreaders use a set of symbols so that they do not have to write out corrections by hand each time. The following list shows some commonly used proofreading symbols and their meanings.

The checklist on page 17 reviews features of Edited Standard English. Copy it into your notebook and refer to it when you have completed a writing

Symbol	Meaning	Example
Cap ≡	Capitalize	*Cap* justice Sandra O'Connor ≡
lc /	Lowercase letters	*lc* a new /Justice
¶	New Paragraph	¶ ∧Justice Sandra O'Connor is the first woman to be appointed to the Supreme Court of the United States.
no ¶	No new paragraph	*no* ¶ In addition to having been a representative in the Arizona State Legislature, Justice O'Connor also served as a federal judge.
∧	Insert letter, word, or phrase; called a *caret*; also used to indicate where a change is to be made	Justice∧O'Connor has a reputation as *Sandra* being a highly qualified judge.
stet	Leave as is (from the Latin phrase meaning "let it stand"); used to indicate that a marked change is not to be made.	*Stet* Justice ~~Stewart~~ Potter resigned, leaving the vacancy that was filled by Justice O'Connor.
∾	Transpose	Justice S∾n∾dra O'Connor's swearing-in ceremony was not open to the public. After the ceremony her fellow justices and Justice O'Connor posed for an ⁀photograph⁀ historical⁀.
‿	Close up space.	Justice O'Connor appeared in news‿papers once again when she announced that she would begin an exercise program in the gymnasium of the Supreme Court building. The new Justice invited other women who
#	Insert space.	worked in the building to join∧her. #

assignment that should conform to ESE. Check your writing carefully against each item on the list. If you can make corrections neatly on your finished draft, do so; if not, copy your paper over correctly.

Following the Checklist for Proofreading is a section titled For Extra Help. Page numbers in that box refer to sections in the textbook that will give you help with specific problems.

Remember that proofreading is the final stage in the process of writing.

Checklist for Proofreading

1. The paper is carefully written or typed and is not marred by smears, messy smudges, or crossed-out words.

2. Sentence structure is accurate. There are no fragments or run-on sentences. Punctuation is used correctly in forming compound sentences.

3. Singular verbs are used with singular subjects, and plural verbs with plural subjects.

4. All pronouns have clear antecedents. Plural pronouns are used to refer to plural nouns, and singular pronouns are used with singular nouns.

5. Pronouns are in the correct subject or object form.

6. Singular pronouns such as *either, each, anybody, everybody,* and *nobody* are used with singular verbs.

7. The writer uses verb tense consistently and accurately.

8. The writer avoids unnecessary shifts in pronouns, such as *I* to *you,* or *they* to *you.*

9. Confusing verbs such as *lie/lay, sit/set,* and *leave/let* are used correctly.

10. The endings *-s, -'s, -ing,* and *-ed* are used correctly with nouns and verbs.

11. To avoid misunderstanding, participial phrases, prepositional phrases, and dependent clauses are clearly attached to the words they modify.

12. Capitalization is used correctly at the beginning of sentences and with proper nouns and adjectives.

13. Each word is spelled correctly.

14. Punctuation is used correctly throughout the writing.

15. Contractions such as *they're, it's,* or *you're* are not confused with possessive pronouns.

16. Confusing words such as *farther/further* and *fewer/less,* or sound-alikes such as *desert/dessert* and *since/sense* are used and spelled correctly.

17. Dialogue is punctuated and capitalized correctly.

18. Slang and other words or phrases not a part of Edited Standard English are used only when they are appropriate.

For Extra Help

Writing Practice 10

Using the Checklist for Proofreading, proofread a journal entry that you have revised. (Your teacher may wish to look at your revision before you begin proofreading.) Use the proofreading symbols in the previous section to mark your manuscript for corrections. Then rewrite your entry, making the changes you have marked.

Continuing Your Journal Writing

In the remaining chapters of this textbook, you will find suggestions for journal entries. In addition, you may wish to use the writing practice assignments that follow as the basis for further journal writing.

Writing Practice 11

It may help you to continue journal writing by focusing on a general idea or theme. For example, the writer Barbara Brenner combined her interest in writing with her interest in snakes and produced *The Diary of a Snake Lover*. If you have a hobby or special interest, you may want to keep a record of it. For a series of journal entries on one theme, use one of the following suggestions or write on an interest or a hobby of your own.

1. Journal of a Hiker
2. Journal of a Sports Fanatic
3. Journal of a Music Lover
4. Journal of a Science Fiction Fan
5. Journal of an Actor

Writing Practice 12

Another idea for journal writing is to concentrate your attention on the area where you live—its seasons, natural beauties, and your favorite places there. Many journals, such as *Walden* by Henry David Thoreau and *Pilgrim at Tinker Creek* by Annie Dillard, center around observations of nature in a particular place. Write a series of journal entries encompassing your observations over the period of one month in the place where you live.

Writing Practice 13

Journals often record impressions of people: their habits and conversations, their thoughts, and their lives in general. You may want to use your journal as a way of recording observations of people. Write a series of journal entries focusing on the people in your life, both those you see daily and those who play only a brief part in your life, such as strangers you observe or friends you see only rarely.

Writing Practice 14

Even within your lifetime and the lifetime of your relatives, many changes will occur. For example, if you ask your grandparents or older relatives, perhaps they will be able to relate experiences from their childhood that are no longer a part of daily life. They might remember the trucks that delivered ice before electric refrigerators became popular or recall the days before television, when the family gathered in the evening by the radio.

Write a series of journal entries about the habits and customs of your daily life. Remember that these customs do not have to be unusual; it is the usual, ordinary sights and sounds and daily events that you want to record. By keeping such a record, you may someday be able to look back with a new understanding of what it was like to grow up during the last half of the twentieth century.

Writing Practice 15

Use your journal as a place to record interesting or unusual observations and experiences that might later become the basis for other kinds of writing. These entries might come from your direct experience with people and places, or they might be drawn from your reading, television viewing, or similar kinds of experiences.

The Personal Narrative

The *personal narrative* is a form of personal writing in which the writer relates and comments on an incident in his or her life or focuses on a single theme in the life of the writer.

The *personal narrative* presents an experience partly in narrative form, as if it were a story, and partly by discussing the significance of the experience.

Writing a personal narrative is similar to writing a journal: both record personal ideas and experiences and both are written in the natural language of the writer. Personal narratives rely on many of the same skills you use in journal writing: keen observation and vivid re-creations of scenes and characters. In fact, your journal will be an excellent source of ideas to develop as personal narratives.

Central Theme and Action

A personal narrative incorporates five elements: the *central action and theme*; the *chronology*; the *narrator and characters*; the *descriptive details* of setting, action, and characters; and the *commentary*.

Each personal narrative incorporates the five elements in a different and unique way.

Unlike journal entries, which can follow the flow of the writer's thoughts from one idea to another, the personal narrative always focuses on one particular incident or idea that functions as the *theme* of the narrative.

Since the personal narrative is usually a short composition, from two to three pages, the opening paragraph often introduces the theme. The following excerpt is the introduction to a personal narrative by Lorraine Hansberry titled "On Summer." The title gives you a general idea of the theme. What is the writer's basic attitude toward summer?[1]

> It has taken me a good number of years to come to any measure of respect for summer. I was, being May-born, literally an "infant of the spring" and, during the later childhood years, tended, for some reason or other, to rather worship the cold aloofness of winter. The adolescence, admittedly lingering still, brought the traditional passionate commitment to melancholy autumn— and all that. For the longest kind of time I simply thought that *summer* was a mistake.

Writing Practice 16

Use the Discovering Ideas for Writing section that follows to help you with ideas for this assignment.

On a separate sheet of paper, write three sentences stating the themes of personal narratives you would like to write. For example, the sentence "It has taken me a good number of years to come to any measure of respect for summer" tells the theme of "On Summer." The topic for each sentence should be different and should include an expression of your own point of view or feelings about the topic.

Discovering Ideas for Writing

The following examples show how to divide your experience into categories to find ideas for writing a personal narrative. Since a personal narrative draws on individual experience, try to relate the suggestions to activities and ideas of your own.

---

[1]Excerpted from "On Summer" by Lorraine Hansberry. Copyright © 1960, by Robert Nemiroff as Executor of the Estate of Lorraine Hansberry.

1. *Patterns of behavior*

    Is there some habit or other pattern of behavior in your life that stands out in your mind? Think of comments that others make about you: are you considered generally punctual or tardy, messy or fastidious, serious or comic? What event or series of events best illustrates this behavior?

    Example

    The only way I can make myself get up in the morning is by setting three alarm clocks around my bedroom to go off at five-minute intervals.

2. *Relationships*

    Do you have a close friend or relative who is special to you? How has this person affected your life? Think of an incident or related incidents that illustrate your relationship with him or her.

    Example

    Because of my Aunt Dinah I was the first girl in school to know how to clean a fish and tell a mushroom from a toadstool.

3. *Ownership*

    Do you own or would you like to own something that you see as making an important difference in your life? (Ownership can apply to pets as well as objects.) Why is this possession important, and how does having or not having it affect your life? What event or series of events demonstrate your attitude toward it?

    Example

    I used to think I could never be happy without a lightweight, ten-speed European touring bicycle, but now that I own one, I've had to change my mind.

4. *Places*

    Is there a particular place that has a special meaning for you? Perhaps it is a place where you learned something or did something that is still important in your life. What incident or series of incidents do you associate with this place?

    Example

    For most people airports are busy, exciting places of arrival and departure, but for me airports have always meant one thing: boredom.

5. *People*

    Is there some person or persons you have observed or shared something with who are important to you? They can be people who have played a part in your life without being personally involved with you, such as childhood idols, distant relatives, or groups you join. Think of an incident or series of incidents that demonstrates how these people have affected you.

Example

Until I was twelve years old, when I had to start studying more and going to movies less, the most important man in my life was Paul Newman.

Chronology

Chronology means "order in time."

The story-telling part of a personal narrative, the part that relates the incident or experience, relies on chronological order. For a discussion of chronological order, see page 64.

The Narrator and Characters

A *narrator* is one who tells, or narrates, the events of story.

In fiction the narrator can be the writer of the story or one of the characters within the story. In a personal narrative, however, the narrator is always assumed to be the writer.

Often the narrator is the only character or the most important character in a personal narrative. Other characters are described when they play an important part in the narrative as a whole. Writers present their characters in many different ways. One method is to make direct statements about the character, as Lorraine Hansberry does in the following description of her grandmother from "On Summer."[1]

> I remember being startled when I first saw my grandmother rocking away on her porch. All my life I had heard that she was a great beauty and no one had ever remarked that they meant a half century before. The woman that I met was as wrinkled as a prune and could hardly hear and barely see and always seemed to be thinking of other times. But she could still rock and talk and even make wonderful cupcakes which were like cornbread, only sweet. She was captivated by automobiles and, even though it was well into the Thirties, I don't think she had ever been in one before we came down and took her driving. She was a little afraid of them and could not seem to negotiate the windows, but she loved driving. She died the next summer and that is all that I remember about her, except that she was born in slavery and had memories of it and they didn't sound anything like *Gone with the Wind*.

In the preceding passage the writer gives a physical description of the grandmother and also tells the reader what kind of person she was. What physical details does Lorraine Hansberry notice about her grandmother? How does she illustrate her grandmother's character?

The following description uses a different method of presenting a character. In this excerpt from *I Know Why the Caged Bird Sings*, Maya Angelou

---

[1]Excerpted from "On Summer" by Lorraine Hansberry. Copyright © 1960, by Robert Nemiroff as Executor of the Estate of Lorraine Hansberry.

portrays her grandmother. As you read, try to decide what makes this description different from the preceding one by Lorraine Hansberry.[1]

> "Thou shall not be dirty" and "Thou shall not be impudent" were the two commandments of Grandmother Henderson upon which hung our total salvation.
>
> Each night in the bitterest winter we were forced to wash faces, arms, necks, legs and feet before going to bed. She used to add, with a smirk that unprofane people can't control when venturing into profanity, "and wash as far as possible, then wash possible."
>
> We would go to the well and wash in the ice-cold, clear water, grease our legs with the equally cold stiff Vaseline, then tiptoe into the house. We wiped the dust from our toes and settled down for schoolwork, cornbread, clabbered milk, prayers and bed, always in that order. Momma was famous for pulling the quilts off after we had fallen asleep to examine our feet. If they weren't clean enough for her, she took the switch (she kept one behind the bedroom door for emergencies) and woke up the offender with a few aptly placed burning reminders.
>
> The area around the well at night was dark and slick, and boys told about how snakes love water, so that anyone who had to draw water at night and then stand there alone and wash knew that moccasins and rattlers, puff adders and boa constrictors were winding their way to the well and would arrive just as the person washing got soap in her eyes. But Momma convinced us that not only was cleanliness next to Godliness, dirtiness was the inventor of misery.

Clabbered milk is thickly curdled sour milk. Maya Angelou calls her grandmother *Momma*.

In the preceding passage Maya Angelou tells about her grandmother's belief in cleanliness and what she made her grandchildren go through to attain it. While Lorraine Hansberry describes her grandmother by direct statement, Maya Angelou gives facts about her grandmother and lets the readers draw their own conclusions. Also, Maya Angelou includes no physical description of her grandmother because she is more concerned with focusing on one trait: her grandmother's love for cleanliness. What do you learn about Maya Angelou's grandmother from this passage? Does the grandmother have a sense of humor?

Characters can be described by direct statement or by letting their actions and beliefs speak for them. Whichever method you choose, remember that it is important to describe only the central characters in the narrative. Other characters can be mentioned briefly or left out of the narrative entirely.

Writing Practice 17

Imagine that you are going to write a personal narrative with one central character and yourself, the narrator. You may choose to describe the character directly, as in the example by Lorraine Hansberry, or indirectly, as in the example by Maya Angelou. Select one experience you had with this character and write one or two paragraphs describing the character and the experience.

---

[1] Excerpt from *I Know Why the Caged Bird Sings*, by Maya Angelou, 1969. Reprinted by permission of Random House, Inc.

Descriptive Details

Descriptive details help make personal writing come alive for the reader.

Specifics about people, places, feelings, and states of mind all make descriptions more vivid and help the reader share in the writer's experience.

The following excerpt from *Pilgrim at Tinker Creek* by Annie Dillard describes the writer's finding a snakeskin in the woods. As you read, notice the descriptive details the writer uses to help you visualize the scene and experience it with her.[1]

> Yesterday I set out to catch the new season, and instead I found an old snakeskin. I was in the sunny February woods by the quarry; the snakeskin was lying in a heap of leaves right next to an aquarium someone had thrown away. I don't know why that someone hauled the aquarium deep into the woods to get rid of it; it had only one broken glass side. The snake found it handy, I imagine; snakes like to rub against something rigid to help them out of their skins, and the broken aquarium looked like the nearest likely object. Together the snakeskin and the aquarium made an interesting scene on the forest floor. It looked like an exhibit at a trial—circumstantial evidence—of a wild scene, as though a snake had burst through the broken side of the aquarium, burst through his ugly old skin, and disappeared, perhaps straight up in the air, in a rush of freedom and beauty.
>
> The snakeskin had unkeeled scales, so it belonged to a nonpoisonous snake. It was roughly five feet long by the yardstick, but I'm not sure because it was very wrinkled and dry, and every time I tried to stretch it flat it broke. I ended up with seven or eight pieces of it all over the kitchen table in a fine film of forest dust.

Unkeeled means "unridged."

In the passage from *Pilgrim at Tinker Creek*, Annie Dillard describes the experience of finding the snakeskin—where she found it, what it looked and felt like, and how she imagined it got there. To understand how descriptive details help make the scene come alive, go back through the passage and be prepared to discuss each specific sensory observation. First the writer tells where she was: "by the quarry." The snakeskin is "lying in a heap of leaves." How else does she describe its location? If you were to touch the snakeskin, how would it feel?

Writing Practice 18

Write the beginning one or two paragraphs of a personal narrative, paying special attention to descriptive details. These details can focus on a place, a person, or an object, or can include all of these. You may want to think of an incident when you encountered something unusual like the snakeskin Annie Dillard found in the forest. Perhaps you were walking down a street in your neighborhood and came upon something that held your attention; perhaps you too were walking in the woods and found something there that made

---

[1]Specified excerpt from pp. 72–73 in *Pilgrim at Tinker Creek* by Annie Dillard. Copyright © 1974 by Annie Dillard. Reprinted by permission of Harper & Row, Publishers, Inc. and Blanche C. Gregory, Inc.

you stop and observe. As you write, remember to pay attention to chronological order when it will help your readers follow the action of the scene.

Commentary in the Personal Narrative

Commentary is the writer's direct comments, reflections, and observations in a personal narrative.

Commentary is essential to the personal narrative; it is the element that makes this type of writing closer to an essay than to fiction. In fiction the characters speak for themselves, and readers draw their own conclusions about significance and meaning. In a personal narrative, however, it is the job of the narrator to share ideas and feelings with the readers by commenting directly.

Because the personal narrative focuses on one central action or theme, the commentary also has a single focus. The following paragraphs are the concluding paragraphs of Lorraine Hansberry's "On Summer." (You may want to reread the introductory paragraph on page 20.) Lorraine Hansberry introduces her theme by stating that she never used to appreciate summer and continues throughout the narrative with memories of summers spent in different places. In the concluding paragraphs notice how Lorraine Hansberry comes back to the original theme of her attitude about summer. She is talking about an older woman dying of cancer, whom she has just met; the writer describes the woman as courageous and filled with life.[1]

> The last time I saw her she was sitting surrounded by her paintings with her manuscript laid out for me to read, because, she said, she wanted to know what a *young person* would think of her thinking; one must always keep up with what *young people* thought about things because, after all, they were *change.*
>
> Every now and then her jaw set in anger as we spoke of things people should be angry about. And then, for relief, she would look out at the lovely bay at a mellow sunset settling on the water. Her face softened with love of all that beauty and, watching her, I wished with all my power what I knew that she was wishing: that she might live to see at least one more *summer.* Through her eyes I finally gained the sense of what it might mean; more than the coming autumn with its pretentious melancholy; more than an austere and silent winter which must shut dying people in for precious months; more even than the frivolous spring, too full of too many false promises, would be the gift of another summer with its stark and intimate assertion of neither birth nor death but life at the apex; with the gentlest nights and, above all, the longest days.
>
> I heard later that she did live to see another summer. And I have retained my respect for the noblest of the seasons.

Apex means "highest point."

Lorraine Hansberry learns to see summer through the eyes of a dying woman. What does this teach her about her own feelings for summer? How does Lorraine Hansberry comment on her feelings and thoughts to the reader?

---

[1] Excerpted from "On Summer" by Lorraine Hansberry. Copyright © 1960, by Robert Nemiroff as Executor of the Estate of Lorraine Hansberry.

Writing Practice 19

Select one of the sentences you wrote as a theme sentence in Writing Practice 16 or use a new theme topic. Remember that your theme should be illustrated with an incident or incidents from your own experience. Write one or two paragraphs of a personal narrative on this theme, paying special attention to the commentary. Your comments should let the reader know your feelings and reactions to the theme of the personal narrative. (As you write, remember to include character description when appropriate, to follow chronological order, and to use descriptive details.)

Reading the Personal Narrative

Following this selection is a For Discussion activity.

The following personal narrative was written by Loren Eiseley, an anthropologist, writer, and poet. It deals with an unusual animal, named Maddy, and the lesson he learned from her. As you read, notice how Eiseley combines the narrative, or storytelling parts, with the commentary.[1]

A *prima donna* means, literally, "first lady."

Maddy was what we called her familiarly. Madeline was her real name and she was a prima donna and a cat—in that order. Maddy was a cat that bowed, the only one I have ever encountered. She is part of my story, what one might call the elocution or stage part. We patronized each other. Maddy performed her act, and I assumed the role of her most ardent admirer. In discharging this duty I learned a great deal from Maddy, my patroness, whom I here acknowledge.

I have known a good many cats in my time—some that scratched, some that bit, some who purred, and even one who, by my standards at least, talked. I liked Maddy, I suppose, because we had so much in common. Maddy was an isolate. Maddy lived with three other more aggressive and talented animals, who took the major attention of my host. Maddy, by contrast, was not so much antisocial as shy, when you came to know her. She wandered a little forlornly in back rooms and concealed herself under furniture, or in a recess above the fireplace.

Maddy, in short, wanted a small place in the sun which the world refused to grant her. She was at heart simply a good-natured ginger cat in a world so full of cats with purrs less hoarse that Maddy, like many of us, had learned to slink obscurely along the wall and hope that she might occasionally receive a condescending pat. Nothing was ever going to go quite right for Maddy. In this we reckoned without poor Maddy's desperation. She discovered a talent, and I, at least, among her human friends, was appalled at how easily this talent might have gone unguessed, except for a chance episode and an equally uncanny tenacity on Maddy's part. Maddy learned to bow.

Perhaps you may think, as a human being, that this is a very small accomplishment indeed. Let me assure you that it is not. On four feet it is a hard thing to do and, in addition, the cat mind is rarely reconciled to such postures. No one among us in that house, I think now, realized the depths of Maddy's need or her perception.

---

[1] From Loren Eiseley, *All the Strange Hours: The Excavation of a Life.* Copyright © 1975 by Loren Eiseley (New York: Charles Scribner's Sons, 1975). Reprinted with permission of Charles Scribner's Sons.

Ensconced means "comfortably settled."

The *Sun King* is the French ruler Louis XIV.

It happened, as most things happen, by accident, but the accident was destined to entrap both Maddy and ourselves. She was ensconced in her favorite recess upon the mantel of the fireplace, watching us, as usual, but being unwatched because of the clever gyrations of one of her kindred down on the floor. At this point, Mr. Fleet, our host, happened to stoop over to adjust a burning log in the fireplace.

Easing his back a moment later, he stood up by the mantel and poked a friendly finger at Maddy, who came out to peer down at the sparks. She also received an unexpected pat from Mr. Fleet. Whether by design or not, the combination of sparks and the hand impinging upon her head at the same time caused Maddy to execute a curious little head movement like a bow. It resembled, I can only say, a curtsey, an Old World gesture out of another time at the Sun King's court.

Maddy both hunched her forefeet and dropped her head. All she needed to complete the bow was a bonnet or a ribbon. Everyone who saw applauded in astonishment and for a few moments Maddy, for once, was the center of attention. In due course that would have been the end of the matter, but a severe snowstorm descended over our part of the state. We were thus all housebound and bored for several days. This is where Maddy's persistence and physical memory paid off; on the next night upon the mantel she came out of her own volition, and bowed once more with precisely similar steps. Again everyone applauded. Never had Madeline received such a burst of affectionate encouragement. If there were any catcalls they could only have come from her kin beneath the davenport. Her audience was with her. Maddy seized her opportunity. She bowed three times to uproarious applause. She had become the leading character in the house. The event had become memorable. Maddy, no more than a dancer, would forget the steps and the graceful little nod of the head. It became an evening routine.

I have said that in the end both Maddy and her audience were entrapped. It happened in this way: finally the snow went away and we, all except Maddy, tried to resume our usual nocturnal habits—the corner bar, the club, the book. But the bow had become Maddy's life. She lived for it; one could not let her down, humiliate her, relegate her unfeelingly to her former existence. Maddy's fame, her ego, had to be sustained at any cost, even if, at times, her audience was reduced to one. That one carried, at such times, the honor of the house. Maddy's bow must be applauded. Maddy would be stricken if her act began to pall.

To me the act never did pall. More than once I gave up other things to serve as a substitute audience. For, you see, I had come to realize even then that Maddy and myself were precisely alike; we had learned to bow in order to be loved for our graceless selves. The only difference was that as a human being living in a more complex world it had taken me longer to develop the steps and the routine. I talked for a living. But to talk for a living, one must, like Maddy, receive more applause than opprobrium. One must learn certain steps.

Opprobrium means "scorn."

I was born and grew up with no burning desire to teach. Sea captain, explorer, jungle adventurer—all these, in my childhood books, had been extolled to me. Unfortunately my reading had not included the great educators. Thus upon completing my doctorate I had no real hope in those still depressed times of 1937 of finding a university post. While I was casting about for a job among newspaper folk of my acquaintance, word came that I had been proffered a position at the University of Kansas.

Most of the midwestern universities of that period had joint departments of sociology and anthropology, or at best one tame anthropologist who was expected to teach in both fields. When I appeared that fall before my first class in introductory sociology I realized two things as I walked through the door. I did not dare sit down. I did not dare use my notes for anything but a security blanket to toss confidently on the table like a true professor. The class was very large. A sizable portion of the football squad was scattered in the back row. I was, I repeat, an isolate like Maddy. If I ever lost that audience there would be chaos. The class met every day in the week.

Each night I studied beyond midnight and wrote outlines that I rarely followed. I paced restlessly before the class, in which even the campus dogs were welcome so long as they nodded their heads sagely in approval. In a few weeks I began to feel like the proverbial Russian fleeing in a sleigh across the steppes before a wolf pack. I am sure that Carroll Clark, my good-natured chairman, realized that a highly unorthodox brand of sociology was being dispensed in his domain, but he held his peace. By then everything from anecdotes of fossil hunting to observations upon Victorian Darwinism were being hurled headlong from the rear of the sleigh. The last object to go would be myself. Fortunately for me, the end of the semester came just in time.

At the close of the first year I had acquired, like Madeline the ginger cat, some followers. I had learned figuratively to bow and I was destined to keep right on bowing through the next thirty years. There was no escape. Maddy had taught me how necessary it was that one's psyche be sustained. An actor, and this means no reflection upon teaching, has to have at least a few adoring followers. Otherwise he will begin to doubt himself and shrink inward, or take to muttering over outworn notes. This is particularly true in the case of a cat who has literally come out of nowhere to bow under everyone's gaze on a fireplace. Similarly I had emerged as a rather shy, introverted lad, to exhort others from a platform. Dear Maddy, I know all you suffered and I wish I could think you are still bowing to applause. You triumphed over your past in one great appreciative flash. For me it has been a lifelong battle with anxiety. . . .

The steppes *are the great plains of southeastern Europe and Asia.*

To exhort *is to urge.*

For Discussion

1. "Madeline" is the account of a personal learning experience. In your own words explain the theme Loren Eiseley is writing about. For example, what does the writer learn about himself from Maddy's behavior? Be prepared to discuss specific references he makes in comparing himself to Madeline.

2. The narrative in "Madeline" is skillfully woven in with Loren Eiseley's commentary on his experience. Go carefully through the description of Maddy's bowing act and be prepared to discuss the specific details the writer uses to help the reader visualize the scene. How does he introduce, or lead into, the scene?

3. One place that "Madeline" uses chronological order is in the account of the evening that Maddy learns to bow. Where else does Eiseley use chronological order to help the reader follow his story?

4. The two basic characters in "Madeline" are Loren Eiseley and Maddy. What characteristics do they share? What is the writer's attitude toward Maddy? What are specific references that demonstrate his attitude?

5. "Madeline" is full of descriptive details that help the reader visualize each scene. For example, reread the paragraphs where the writer describes his first classroom experiences. What details help the reader share his nervousness and fear of not holding the students' attention? What details describe how he did hold the students' attention?

Writing Practice 20

Use the Discovering Ideas for Writing section on pages 20–22 for help with this assignment.

Using a theme sentence you have already written or one you write for this assignment, write a personal narrative. You may want to review the five elements of the personal narrative before you begin writing.

Revising the Personal Narrative

The process of revision is discussed on pages 52–53.

Use the following checklist to revise your personal narrative. (Your teacher may wish to see your first draft before you begin your revision.)

Checklist for Revising the Personal Narrative

1. The personal narrative is written in a natural, informal style.
2. The personal narrative is developed around one central action or theme.
3. The narrative, or storytelling part, of the writing is presented in chronological order.
4. The important characters are sufficiently described so that their behavior is understandable to the reader.
5. Descriptive details about people, places, and feelings help readers share in the writer's experience.
6. The writer comments and reflects on the central action in the narrative.

Writing Practice 21

Using the preceding checklist, revise your personal narrative. Proofread the narrative for errors in usage and mechanics by using the Checklist for Proofreading on page 17.

2 Gathering Information for Writing

Finding What to Write About

For many writers, finding what to say about a subject is as difficult as deciding how to say it. This is true for professional writers of all kinds: journalists, novelists, poets, and playwrights. It is often true for student writers as well.

This chapter provides approaches and techniques to help you develop ideas for writing. It will help you discover what you already know about a subject and show you how to question, observe, and analyze information.

Brainstorming: Discovering What You Know

Brainstorm is an American word meaning "a sudden idea or inspiration."

Brainstorming is the process of trying to arrive at a new idea by letting your mind wander freely over a subject.

Brainstorming can be done as a group activity with members sharing thoughts about a subject as quickly as they come into their minds. This freedom to say whatever comes immediately to mind helps stimulate everyone's thinking and frequently brings about fresh ideas and solutions.

You can use the technique of brainstorming to find ideas for your writing. Brainstorming helps you to explore what you already know or feel about a subject, so it is a good starting place for gathering information. Often you will find that you know more about a subject than you thought.

To begin group brainstorming, decide on the general subject, idea, or problem. Imagine, for example, that you have been assigned an American history project and that your group has chosen the subject *Oral history*. As the group members focus their attention on the subject, thinking of everything they have heard or read about it, ideas begin to come as words, phrases, or even longer statements. In a group brainstorming session assign one member to record ideas.

Oral history is historical data consisting of personal recollections.

If you brainstorm alone, try to sit in a quiet place with pencil and paper in front of you. Sometimes, it helps to write your subject in large letters in the center of the page. Clear your mind of all other thoughts and let your mind roam freely over the subject. As ideas come, jot them down on paper.

A list of ideas gathered on the subject of oral histories might look like the following one.

Tape recorders

Studs Terkel

Merle Miller—on President Lyndon Johnson

Foxfire

Tell stories in their own words

American Mosaic

Interviews

Make list of questions to ask

Interviews about working

How did you choose your job?

What do you like or dislike about your job?

I Wish I Could Give My Son a Wild Raccoon

Interviewing relatives

Could interview my great-uncle about life in Armenia

Why did you come to this country?

How was life in your old home different from here?

Interviews about life in the Great Depression

Aunt's life on maple sugar farm

What garbage collectors think about their jobs

Custodians look at their work

Life as a principal

Make commentary on interviews

Interview each other

Brainstorming shows you how much you know about a subject and what you need to research before you can begin writing. Also, it can often help you decide how to limit the subject. For example, after brainstorming about oral histories, you may decide to focus your project on the specific topic of your great-uncle's oral history of life in Armenia or perhaps on the lives of workers on the maple sugar farms.

Because it helps you call up memories and impressions, brainstorming can be especially helpful as a way to gather ideas for a character sketch or other kind of description. Suppose, for example, that you have decided to write about the woman who runs your neighborhood grocery store. In brainstorming you can let your mind focus on details of her appearance, behavior, and your experiences with her. Your notes might look like the following ones.

MRS. TANAKA

Brown, weathered skin and bright eyes

"Say hi to your mother for me"

Looks like she spends a lot of time outside,
but she doesn't seem to

Blue apron; thin, short black hair

Very strong—I've seen her lift heavy boxes

Has two children

Quiet

Likes to have things in order—always rearranges
the shelves every Monday morning

Never loses her temper

Loves fruit

When I was little, she gave me a huge apple once
when the bigger kids were teasing me.

"You will be big some day, too"

Hums to herself as she works

From these recollections of Mrs. Tanaka, you can select the ones you want for your character sketch.

Writing Practice 1

The following list suggests subjects for brainstorming. Choose one of them or substitute a similar subject of your own. In a group (if your teacher requests) or alone, brainstorm the subject and record your ideas on a sheet of paper. Remember to write down *all* the ideas that come to you or to members of your group. You can select the ones that seem most appropriate after you have finished brainstorming.

1. Life on other planets
2. Ideas for a new comic strip
3. An oral history project for your class
4. Curriculum for the ideal school
5. A major problem facing the United States today

Writing Practice 2

For this writing practice you will brainstorm alone to discover information for description. You may describe what you like—a person, location, or specific experience—but it should be something that you have actually seen or done. Clear your mind of other thoughts and let the memory of that person, place, or experience come back to you. Jot down your impressions and thoughts as they come to you.

Writing Practice 3
Using the details you gathered for Writing Practice 2, write a description of your subject.

Asking the Right Questions: The Pentad

Discovering ideas is often a matter of asking the right questions about a topic. Questions can show you how to examine and explore material, and (like brainstorming) questioning can help you find out how much you already know about a subject and how much you need to learn before you write.

There are many different kinds of questions you can use to investigate your subject. Part of your task in gathering information for writing is learning what approach and which kinds of questions are most appropriate. The questioning system you are probably most familiar with is the *who? what? where? when? why?* and *how?* list of questions used by journalists. These questions are helpful because they provide a formula for gathering basic information about an event.

A second questioning approach used to gather information is called the *Pentad.*

Pent- is the prefix meaning "five." The Pentad, or five-questions approach, resembles the basic *who? what? where? when? why? how?* system, but there is an important difference: The Pentad helps you to investigate a subject in greater depth. The Pentad questions can be formulated in the following way.

1. What is the *action?*
   What is happening, has happened, or will happen?

2. Who are the *actors?*
   Who are the people involved in the action?

3. What is the *scene?*
   Where and when does the action happen?

4. What is the *method?*
   By what method is the action performed?

5. What is the *purpose?*
   Why does the action happen?

Writing About Action

The first Pentad question focuses on *action.*

In the Pentad, *action* is defined as any physical or mental activity that has happened or is in the process of happening and any creative work or product resulting from those activities.

Events, such as a volcano erupting or a person driving to work, are actions. Thoughts—the result of mental activity—are also actions. Any work of art or craft (such as writing, music, movies, or handicrafts) is the result of physical and mental activities and so is classified as an action. Questions such as the following ones will help you explore the action.

1. What is it?
2. What happened?
3. What is happening?
4. What will happen?
5. What could happen?

Always ask yourself Question 1, even though the answer may seem obvious. It will help to formulate the action in your mind.

For actions in the past, ask Question 2. For example, if you write about an event from American history, you would need to know exactly *what happened*. For present actions ask Question 3. Questions 4 and 5 deal with future actions or the result of actions. To see how an action has changed over time or is in the process of changing, ask yourself all five questions.

Imagine, for example, that you have decided to write a paper about Ellis Island, the most famous immigrant-receiving station in American history. You want to gather as much information as possible to help decide on a specific topic for your paper. To do this you will read about Ellis Island and, if possible, talk with people who know something about it from personal experience. Imagine that you can consult your great-grandmother about her experiences there.

The following notes show one way to apply the action questions to the subject of Ellis Island.

1. What is it?

> Ellis Island is a small island off the New Jersey shore in the state of New York. From 1892 until the late 1920s, it was the site of the largest immigrant-receiving station in the U.S.

2. What happened?

> Ellis Island was selected as the site of a new receiving station in 1890 by the Federal Bureau of Immigration. The old station, Castle Garden, lost its contract with the government after a public investigation of corruption and terrible conditions there.

3. What is happening?

> Ellis Island is currently a part of the Statue of Liberty National Monument (by decree of President Johnson in 1965). Visitors are free to tour the site, and every year thousands go to Ellis Island for the first time or return to their place of entry into the United States. Grandmother Killian went back to visit in 1980

with her son and daughter. She said it brought back many memories of coming through there in 1920.

4. What will happen?

Ellis Island will probably continue as a national monument.

5. What could happen?

In 1954, when Ellis Island closed forever as an immigration station, it was put up for sale, and the government considered many proposals for new use: as a hotel, an orphanage, a trade fair center, or a cathedral. None of these were accepted then, and it is not likely that anything will happen to change the status of Ellis Island as a national monument. However, one possible change for the better could be that Congress would appropriate more funds to maintain and repair Ellis Island.

Writing Practice 4

Select one of the following physical or mental actions or substitute a similar one of your choice. Then ask yourself the *action* questions on page 34 that apply to your topic. Write the questions and your answers on a sheet of paper.

1. _____ has been a major influence in my life.

2. _____ was a turning point in American history.

3. The most (courageous/difficult/disastrous) thing I have ever done was _____ .

4. The President I most admire is _____ .

5. _____ , a character in a (book/movie/play/television show), taught me something important about myself.

6. Prejudice can take many forms.

7. I clearly remember the time my (father/mother/other relative) taught me to _____ .

8. _____ is the most serious problem facing the United States.

9. Affluent nations (should/should not) be more responsible for combating starvation in the world.

10. If someone were to make a movie of my life, the opening scene would be _____ .

Writing About Actors

In the Pentad, *actors* are defined as "people responsible for and involved in the action," or *actors* are defined as "other causes of the action" (not necessarily people). The following set of questions relates to the actors.

1. Who or what is responsible for the action?

2. Who are the people involved in the action, or what are the other factors causing the action?

3. What are the actors like?

Applying the *actor* questions to the subject of Ellis Island leads to the following information.

1. Who or what is responsible for the action?

In 1890 President William Henry Harrison signed into law a bill approving Ellis Island as the site for the new immigrant-receiving station.

2. Who are the people involved in the action, or what are the other factors affecting the action?

The main people involved in the action were the immigrants themselves. They came in such numbers, approximately 8 million through Castle Garden (1855–1890), that the Bureau of Immigration was forced to find new facilities to accommodate them. Widespread corruption at Castle Garden was another factor in the selection of Ellis Island as the new site. The Bureau felt that an island would be a self-contained unit, relatively easy to oversee.

3. What are the actors like?

From 1900–1914 just under 13 million immigrants entered the country, with an average of 5,000 a day passing through Ellis Island in the peak year of 1907. This new wave shocked immigration officials, who had thought that the numbers of immigrants would decline. The new immigrants were predominantly from southern and eastern Europe: Italians, Russians, Poles, and Austro-Hungarians instead of the Scandinavians, Irish, British, and German immigrants who had made up the first enormous wave.

Some came because of famine, some came for religious or political freedom, and some came for the free land available under Homestead Acts. My grandmother came because of persecution by the Turks, who tried to exterminate the Armenians during World War I. She and her sister were the only members of her family who survived.

Famous immigrants included such people as Knute Rockne, the legendary football coach of Notre Dame; Emma Goldman, political activist and radical; Irving Berlin, songwriter; Felix Frankfurter, Justice of the Supreme Court; Samuel Goldwyn, film producer; Albert Einstein, physicist; and Thomas Mann, novelist.

Writing Practice 5

Using a topic from the list on page 41 or a similar one you select, ask yourself the *actor* questions that apply to the topic. Write the questions and answers on a sheet of paper.

Writing About Scene

Questions about the *scene* focus on the time and place where the action occurs.

Questions about scene, such as the ones that follow, ask for descriptive details about the scene.

1. Where is the action happening?
2. Where did the action happen?
3. Where will the action happen? (for future action)
4. What is the place like?
5. When is the action happening?
6. When did the action happen? (for past action)
7. When will the action happen? (for future action)
8. What is the historical background of the action?

Applying the *scene* questions to the subject of Ellis Island produces the following information:

1. Where is the action happening?

   Ellis Island, now a national monument, stands in view of the Statue of Liberty in New York Harbor.

2. Where did the action happen?

   Ellis Island was just a small sandbar of an island when it was selected by the Federal Bureau of Immigration. It had been called Koshk (Gull Island) by the Native Americans who first owned it.

3. What is the place like?

   The first main building on Ellis Island was a wooden structure two stories high containing the inspection hall and baggage rooms. A hospital, electric power plant, kitchens, and bath house flanked the main building. When these structures burned in 1897, they were rebuilt in brick to follow the original layout. The new construction was grander than the original, with ornamental corner towers, arches, and a three-story central building. My grandmother said that she and her sister gasped when they saw it because it was the largest building they had ever been inside. She laughs when she tells the story that they thought all buildings in America would be that size and how disappointed they were when they reached New York City.

4. When did the action happen?

   Ellis Island opened officially on January 1, 1892, and continued operation through the late 1920s as an immigrant-receiving station. Intermittently during that time it was also used as an internment center for what the government called "undesirable" aliens and as a port of expulsion for deportees. During World War II it became an official prison for enemy aliens. Then in 1954 it closed permanently, and its fate remained uncertain until Lyndon Johnson declared it a national monument in 1965.

5. What is the historical background for the action?

   The primary period of activity at Ellis Island, from 1892 through the late 1920s, spans the Spanish-American War, World War I, and the beginnings of the Great Depression. In terms of immigration law, it covers a period of little regulation and general acceptance of immigrants and periods of extreme fear and hostility that led to highly restrictive immigration laws. Three years before my grandmother immigrated, a controversial immigration law had been passed to keep out all sorts of "undesirables." This law included a literacy requirement, which fortunately my grandmother and her sister could pass. She was also lucky because in 1921, the year after she immigrated, the First Quota Law was passed. This set an annual ceiling of immigrants, with certain numbers set for each country. This discriminatory law was not abolished until 1965.

Writing Practice 6

Using a topic from the list on page 41 or a similar one you select, ask yourself the *scene* questions that apply to the topic. Write the questions and answers on a sheet of paper.

Writing About Method

The fourth Pentad question asks, *What methods are used to bring about the action?* It applies whether the actors causing the action are people or not.

Applying the *method* questions to the subject of Ellis Island led to the following information.

1. What methods were used to process immigrants through Ellis Island?

    Immigrants were examined for sickness by doctors from the U.S. Public Health Service. Anyone with a serious communicable disease was sent back or quarantined. Inspectors checked records to identify criminals trying to enter the country, and immigrants were routinely questioned about their skills, destination, finances, job prospects, ability to read and write, and family connections in the United States. After these examinations the immigrants were helped to change their currency and to buy tickets to their destinations. My grandmother said that she heard people on the boat discussing whether or not to try bribing officials at the port, but she and her sister thought this would cause trouble. They both passed through with no difficulty, except that their luggage was lost and they never saw it again. This loss made them sad, but it wasn't as terrible as it could have been, since everything they really treasured was lost when they had to flee their town in the middle of the night.

2. Did methods change? What other factors were involved?

    The methods used to process immigrants changed according to many factors. When the influx of people was at its height, the sheer numbers made it impossible to check on every immigrant thoroughly. Corruption played a part, with some officials accepting bribes to speed the admission process or to admit those who would otherwise be deported. When immigration laws tightened, many were deported for mental deficiency, illiteracy, or political views.

Writing Practice 7

Using a topic from the list on page 41 or a similar one you select, ask yourself the *method* questions that apply to the topic. Write your questions and answers on a sheet of paper.

Writing About Purpose   The final Pentad question asks, *What is the purpose of the action?* For some kinds of writing, this is a crucial question because it asks about the *reason* for the action. For others it is relatively unimportant because the action may have occurred in an unplanned or accidental way.

The following information was gathered by applying the *purpose* question to the subject of Ellis Island.

1.   What was the purpose of Ellis Island?

> Its purpose was to provide a large, safe, and comfortable immigration station. This purpose was not always fulfilled, due mostly to miscalculations about the numbers of immigrants who were to arrive. Furthermore, its purpose changed during the times when the facility was converted to a detention center.

2.   What was the purpose of establishing an immigration receiving station?

> The original purpose was to screen immigrants in order to prevent people with serious communicable diseases, criminals, or people likely to become wards of the state from entering the country. This purpose also changed in later years when attitudes toward immigrants became fearful and prejudicial. The purpose under the quota system was to ensure that a predetermined balance of ethnic minorities be admitted into the country and to keep out political activists.

Writing Practice 8

Using a topic from the list on page 41 or a similar one you select, ask yourself the *purpose* questions that apply to the topic. Write your questions and answers on a sheet of paper.

For Your Journal

Perhaps you have a relative or acquaintance who moved to the United States from another country or who moved to your area from another place. For a journal entry write this person's feelings about changing homes. Was it a pleasant experience? Was there one incident in particular that he or she recalls about the move? What does this person miss most from the former home? If this person has not already spoken with you about this subject, take time to ask questions to find information for your journal entry.

Further Uses for the Pentad   The Pentad questions can be used for many different kinds of writing assignments—the personal essay, exposition, research reports, and creative writing. If, for example, you want to write a short description of an incident, the Pentad questions will help you re-create the event in your mind and make clear what you need to tell about what happened.

The following example shows one way to generate information using the Pentad questions.

Incident: My parents grounded me for coming in late.

ACTION

I had come in late the night before, well after the time I promised to be in. The next morning my father said he wanted to talk with me before I went to school. I knew he was angry, so after he said a few words, I just handed him the car keys.

ACTORS

I could tell that my mother agreed with my father by the way they looked at each other before he said he wanted to talk with me. My father is a fair person, but for him a rule is a rule. If you break it, you take the consequences.

MEANS

I knew that my punishment would be grounding because I was given the same punishment once last year. This time I was grounded for the weekend. It meant I wouldn't be able to go to the football game Saturday night, but I knew better than to ask my father not to ground me. A rule is a rule. It could have been worse.

SCENE

The living room. I always feel more formal in there, I guess, because we're usually there only when we have company, and I associate it with having to get dressed up and be on good behavior. I think my father wanted to talk with me in the living room because he knows we both feel more formal in there.

PURPOSE

My father has always had strict ideas on discipline. He thinks that if you know what you can do and what you can't do, you'll be a better person. He wants me to be responsible for myself, I guess.

The following description shows one way to use the information gathered about the incident. In this example the writer focuses on one of the actors, the father.

My father stood looking at me with unsmiling gray eyes. He rubbed his cheek thoughtfully and then clasped his hands behind his back.

"I don't like having to say this, son," he began.

I knew what was coming. He always stuck by his rules, and the night before I had come in at 11:00 after promising to be back by 9:30. Automatically I fished the car keys out of my pocket and set them down on the living room coffee table. They reflected dully in the morning light. I sighed.

"For the weekend," he finished and then hesitated slightly. "You know better."

He looked at me and shook his head, but before leaving the room he tousled my hair like I was ten years old again.

This piece of writing begins and ends with attention on the father. It is possible to write about the same incident by directing more attention to the son or to one of the other Pentad components: the action itself, the method, the scene, or the purpose.

Writing Practice 9

Using the incident described on page 40, select another Pentad component and rewrite the incident by changing the emphasis. You can do this by focusing attention on what happens between the father and son, by focusing attention on the scene, or by focusing attention on their motives or on the reasons for their action. Feel free to add any details you wish or to begin or end the scene differently.

Writing Practice 10

Using the Pentad questions to help you gather information, write notes for the description of an event that has happened to you. Before you begin writing, decide which Pentad element you will focus on in the description. Next, select details and other information from your notes to write a descriptive account of the incident. Choose one of the following suggestions for the incident or substitute one of your own.

1. A discovery you made or were involved in making
2. A surprise
3. A loss that you experienced
4. A disappointment that you experienced or observed
5. An argument that you had with another person
6. A trick that someone played on you or that you played on someone
7. A routine from your daily life or a special routine that has to do with a job or vacation
8. An incident that occurred during a trip somewhere
9. An incident that made you realize something about yourself or about someone else
10. An incident in which you did something you are proud of

Using Different Points of View

When scientists discover a new planet, insect, or animal, one of their first tasks is to decide on its proper classification. An animal, for example, can be classified according to its bone structure, diet, or circulatory system. Deciding on the proper classification gives scientists a framework for further investigating their discoveries.

Classification also applies to gathering information for writing.

When you need to discover ideas for subject matter, a system of classification can help you to arrange your ideas by providing a framework for them. There are many different ways to classify subjects, and the system of classification you will learn about here uses three separate categories. The first category looks at the subject by "freezing" it in time and space; the second looks at how the subject alters through the passing of time; the third examines the composition of the subject—how all its parts fit together—and how as a whole it fits into a larger background.

Each of these different categories presents a different point of view on the subject. You can think of each viewpoint as asking a question.

FIRST CATEGORY

What is it? (What are the features, qualities, or characteristics of the subject?)

SECOND CATEGORY

How does it change or vary? (In what way does the passage of time affect the subject?)

THIRD CATEGORY

What are its relationships? (How do its parts work together, and how does it relate to a larger background?)

When you need to write about a subject, you can apply each of these categories to help decide which viewpoint best suits your purpose.

What Is It? The *What is it?* question focuses on the appearance, identity, or definition of your subject.

Suppose that your subject is a person—for example, the poet Gwendolyn Brooks. Using the *What is it?* question, you imagine that you are able to see this person "frozen" in time and space, as if you were looking at her in a photograph. From this viewpoint you would describe the poet's physical characteristics, for example, what she does, and what she writes.

Comparison is another aspect of this category. By comparing and contrasting your subject with similar subjects, you will learn more about its distinct features. For example, how would you compare Gwendolyn Brooks with other poets of her generation, with other women poets, or with other black poets? Are the themes she writes about similar to theirs? Does the style she uses group her in a school with other poets? Comparison points up similarities and differences between Gwendolyn Brooks and other writers, enabling you to deepen your understanding of her.

The *What is it?* question also applies to ideas and concepts. Suppose that your subject is the concept of capitalism. The first step in describing this concept is to give a definition; most dictionaries define *capitalism* as "an economic system with most means of production and distribution privately owned and operated for profit." You can describe your concept further by examining one economic system based on capitalism, that of the United States, to study its specific features.

Comparing your subject with other similar subjects will also expand your understanding of what it is. For example, you could make a comparison between capitalism and other economic systems, such as socialism or communism. To make your comparison more specific, you would compare capitalism in the United States with socialism in Great Britain or with communism in China. Your comparison would turn up similarities among the systems, but it would most likely concentrate on the differences. For example, in contrast to capitalism, socialism is a doctrine that emphasizes collective ownership and profit sharing among workers.

Writing Practice 11

For this assignment think of someone you know, perhaps a person in the news or someone from history whom you have studied in school. Then use the following *What is it?* questions to help you gather information about the subject. When you have finished, use the ideas you discover to write a paragraph describing the person.

1.   What are the physical characteristics of your subject?

2.   What feature of your subject is most striking or interesting?

3.   What does your subject do?

4.   What is your subject known for (if the person is from the news or history)?

5.   How does your subject compare to similar subjects? (Be sure to compare your subject to a *specific* group.)

Writing Practice 12

For this assignment select one of the following ideas or concepts or a different one you have in mind. Then ask yourself the following *What is it?* questions to help you discover ideas about your subject, answering them on a sheet of paper. Finally, use the information you gather to write a detailed description of the idea or concept that you have explored from this viewpoint.

IDEAS AND CONCEPTS

Democracy	Religion
Fad	Dictator
Integrity	Loyalty
Recycling	Reincarnation
Poetry	Diesel engine

1.   How is the subject defined? (First write your own definition and then check the dictionary definition.)

2.   How is the subject close in meaning to similar subjects?

3.   How does the subject differ in meaning from similar subjects?

4.   What are specific examples or illustrations of the subject?

How Does It Change or Vary?

The *How does it change or vary?* question asks you to view your subject as it changes with time.

For example, using this category you would view the subject Gwendolyn Brooks as she grows as a person and writer. You would ask how her interests have changed since she began writing. You would examine the ideas she writes about and the language she uses to see how they alter as she matures.

This viewpoint also applies to how an idea or concept can change over time. For example, in studying capitalism, you would learn that today's capitalistic societies are not fully competitive due to recently imposed regulations and other conditions. You would want to know how this change has affected people's views of capitalism. It will be helpful with some subjects for you to look at change within a specific time framework: changes that occur, say, from 1850 to 1950, or during the Great Depression, or any other framework that makes sense to you.

When your subject is abstract—an idea or a concept—you can also ask how it can vary without losing its identity. For example, if in the United States the means of production and distribution were to be controlled by two large corporations, would we still have a capitalistic system?

Writing Practice 13

Select one of the following subjects or use one of your own choice. Apply the *How does it change or vary?* question to gather information, and then write a paragraph describing how your subject changes or has changed over time. If appropriate, include information on how it can vary without losing its identity. Before you begin, ask the following specific questions about your subject.

SUBJECTS
Hockey
Sports cars
Freedom of speech
Muhammad Ali
Your (town/city/farm)

1. How has the subject changed over time?
2. Is this change caused by natural or internal forces?
3. Is this change caused by outside forces, such as the influence of other people or natural disasters?
4. To what extent can this subject vary without losing its identity?

What Are Its Relationships?

When you ask *What are its relationships?* you examine the different parts of the subject and how they interrelate, and also how the subject itself relates to a larger background of subjects.

For example, to understand the subject Gwendolyn Brooks, you would ask questions about her different interests, the various influences on her as a child and young woman, her different occupations, and even her different concerns as a writer. Then you would look at how these factors interrelate in her life and her writing. To study the system of capitalism from this viewpoint, you would need to know how it works: How do competition and private ownership coordinate to produce all the necessary means of production and distribution?

This category also examines the subject as it fits into a larger background. Using the *What is it?* category, you noted that Gwendolyn Brooks could be studied by comparing her with other similar writers. The *What are its relationships?* category would place her in the larger context of women writers through the centuries or minority writers who write at a time of social crisis.

Capitalism itself is an abstract idea applied to a complicated economic system. How does this idea fit into the history of ideas about economics? How does it fit into one specific economic system?

Writing Practice 14

For this assignment select a subject from the following list or use one of your own. (You may want to continue with subjects from previous writing assignments.) First, ask yourself the following *What are its relationships?* questions and write the answers to them on a sheet of paper. Then write two paragraphs, one describing how the parts of the subject work together and another explaining how the subject relates to a larger background.

SUBJECTS

Hologram	Congress
A shark	Snow
The penal system	DNA
Radio	Sap
The heart	The Everglades

1. What are the different parts of the subject?
2. How do these parts work together or interrelate?
3. How does the subject fit into a larger system?
4. How do these other systems work with the subject?

Writing Practice 15

Choose one of the following categories as a way to gather information about one of the photographs on page 46. Ask yourself the questions appropriate to the category you selected and then write a complete description of the subject.

1. The subject itself
2. How the subject changes over time
3. The relationships of the subject

3 Writing the Paragraph

The Paragraph   A *paragraph* is a group of related sentences.

The purpose of dividing your writing into paragraphs is to set each idea or subject apart from the rest. One basic rule to remember is to begin a new paragraph each time you introduce a new idea or subject. Paragraph divisions will help make your writing clear and easy to follow.

Good writers use various types of paragraph development. In this chapter you will learn about one basic model for constructing paragraphs and about several other methods of paragraph development. Even though there are many different kinds of paragraphs, they all share certain traits. Well-written paragraphs concentrate on one main idea or subject; they are clear; their organization is easy to follow; and they are interesting. In this chapter you will also learn how to write paragraphs that reflect these characteristics.

The TRI Paragraph Model

Expository writing, or *exposition*, is writing that explains.

Exposition is the writing you use most often, both in school and out, for essays and reports of all kinds. In this section you will learn a method of paragraph development frequently used in expository writing called *Topic-Restriction-Illustration* (TRI).

The *Topic* of the TRI pattern is the sentence that states the general topic of the paragraph. The *Restriction* is the sentence limiting the general topic to the specific idea to be dealt with in the paragraph; it restricts, or narrows, the subject matter. The *Illustration* sentences develop the main idea of the paragraph by giving examples, reasons, data, or descriptive details.

In the following example of a TRI paragraph from *The Indian Heritage of America* by Alvin M. Josephy, Jr., the topic sentence comes first.[1]

> In America ignorance and misconceptions about Indians are still common.

The preceding topic sentence states that the general topic of the paragraph is American beliefs about Indians.

The restriction sentence follows:

> This is due largely to the fact that many Indian traits, which are centuries old, conflict with traits considered important in white culture.

The restriction sentence limits the general subject to a specific reason for American beliefs about Indians.

The illustration sentences come next.

> Many Indians, for instance, still do not understand or cannot accept the concept of private ownership of land.
>
> Many do not understand the need to save for the future, a fundamental requirement of the economies of their conquerors.
>
> Many find it difficult, if not impossible so far, to substitute individual competitiveness for group feeling.
>
> Many do not see the necessity for working the year-round if they can provide for their families by six months of work or the reason for cutting the earth-mother with a plow and farming if they can still hunt, fish, and dig roots.
>
> Many yet feel a sacred attachment to the land and a reverence for nature that is incomprehensible to most whites.
>
> Many, though Christian, find repugnance in the idea that man possesses dominion over the birds and beasts and believe still that man is brother to all else that is living.

The six illustration sentences discuss ways in which Indian values differ from values important in white culture.

Written in an essay, the paragraph would have the following form.[1]

> In America ignorance and misconceptions about Indians are still common. This is due largely to the fact that many Indian traits, which are centuries old, conflict with traits considered important in white culture. Many Indians, for instance, still do not understand or cannot accept the concept of private ownership of land. Many do not understand the need to save for the future, a fundamental requirement of the economies of their conquerors. Many find it difficult, if not impossible so far, to substitute individual competitiveness for group feeling. Many do not see the necessity for working the year-round if they can provide for their families by six months of work or the reason for cutting the earth-mother with a plow and farming if they can still hunt, fish, and dig roots. Many yet feel a sacred attachment to the land and a reverence for nature that is incomprehensible to most whites. Many, though Christian, find repugnance in the idea that man possesses dominion over the birds and beasts and believe still that man is brother to all else that is living.

---

[1] Adapted from *The Indian Heritage of America* by Alvin M. Josephy, Jr. Copyright © 1968 by Alvin M. Josephy, Jr. Used by permission of Bantam Books, Inc. All rights reserved.

The preceding paragraph begins with a sentence stating that erroneous beliefs about Indians are widespread in America; this is the general topic of the paragraph. The restriction sentence limits the general subject to one important reason for the erroneous beliefs: White culture and Indian culture value different kinds of behavior. By restricting the topic in this way, the writer can then present specific examples of cultural differences between whites and Indians. There is no rule about the number of illustration sentences in a paragraph. Use as many as you need to make your point clear.

Writing Practice 1

Each of the following sentences is a topic sentence for an expository paragraph. Select two of these or write two of your own. Then on a separate sheet of paper, write a restriction sentence and three or four illustration sentences for each topic sentence.

Use the Discovering Ideas for Writing section that follows to help you find ideas for this assignment.

1. Pollution is a problem for everyone.
2. My attitude about myself is changing.
3. Everyone should have a robot.
4. Peer pressure isn't necessarily bad.
5. People have always dreamed of utopias—societies where everything is perfect.

Discovering Ideas for Writing

The chapter "Gathering Information for Writing" discusses other methods to use for discovering ideas.

One way to gather information for paragraph writing is to draw on your own experience. Your experience includes anything you have done, thought about, investigated on your own, or studied in school. Writing from your own experience gives you a unique point of view because no one else has had exactly the same experience as you have had.

If, for example, you plan to write on the topic sentence "Pollution is a problem for everyone," your strong interest in a specific kind of pollution may have led to your reading books or articles about it. If you live in the city, your interest may be in noise pollution; if you live in the country, you may be more concerned with strip-mining or with the spraying of pesticides. Any of these specific types of pollution could be used to restrict the general topic of your paragraph. You could illustrate the restricted topic by giving information about specific actions people have taken or should take to help solve the problem. Take time to let your mind wander over your various experiences, jotting down the ideas that come to you on a piece of scratch paper. When you have finished, choose the area that most interests you or that you know most about as the topic of your paragraph.

Variations on the TRI Pattern

Many expository paragraphs use *variations* of the basic Topic-Restriction-Illustration pattern.

One variation combines the topic and restriction parts into one sentence.

When you combine the topic and the restriction sentences into one, you present your general topic and restrict it in the same sentence and then devote the rest of the paragraph to illustrations. This type of paragraph development is called the *Topic-Illustration* pattern.

The following paragraph from an essay by Michael Arlen titled "Prufrock Aloft; Prufrock Before the Television Set" uses the Topic-Illustration pattern. The topic and restriction are stated in the first sentence, "Aggressive behavior is not actively prohibited, but it is discouraged." The general topic is behavior among television viewers; the restriction is that television discourages aggressive behavior. The remaining sentences are illustrations of the restricted topic. What specific examples does the writer use to illustrate that aggressive behavior is discouraged?[1]

> Aggressive behavior is not actively prohibited, but it is discouraged. There are almost no viewer phone-in programs, as on radio. Live audiences are few. Real audience participation is almost nonexistent, save for the inflated hysteria of a few game shows. Indeed, even some of the new game shows have become quite stylized and remote, with earnest, sedate couples trying to guess the authorship of "Hamlet" in the company of a lonely host and much electronic paraphernalia. On what are described as comedy or drama or adventure programs, there remains scarcely any nourishment of the viewer's active participation, in the form of emotionally involving stories. Thus, a middling detective series such as "Baretta" becomes oddly noticeable, as if it contained a certain gritty substance that somehow spoke to the still-awake part of the viewer's mind—that part persistently untouched by the noisiest bang-bang of cop-show revolvers or even by the sight of artillery explosions in foreign lands. In recent years, many news programs have taken steps toward greater informality and a semblance of involvement on the part of the newscasters. But the involvement of these newsmen has been mostly with each other. The audience continues voyaging, buckled into its Barcaloungers, attending no longer to the voice of a single, solemn captain but to the equally distant, cheery chitchat of two or three of them.

Writing Practice 2

For help with ideas, use the Discovering Ideas for Writing section on page 49.

Each of the following sentences is a combination topic and restriction sentence. Select two of these or substitute two of your own choice and on a separate piece of paper write out three or four illustration sentences for each combined topic-restriction sentence. Use the standard paragraph form, beginning with the topic-restriction sentence.

1. Most good suspense stories have three basic qualities in common.

2. Being an athlete isn't as glamorous as people think.

3. Having a garden has taught me a lot.

4. Everyone should learn to play a musical instrument.

5. The season when I feel most alive is (spring/winter/autumn/summer).

---

[1]Excerpt from "Prufrock Aloft; Prufrock Before the Television Set" in *The Camera Age* by Michael J. Arlen. Copyright © 1976, 1981 by Michael J. Arlen. Reprinted by permission of Farrar, Straus and Giroux, Inc. and Deborah Rogers Ltd.

For Your Journal

After reading the paragraph by Michael Arlen on page 50, perhaps you have an opinion about the effects of television on Americans. Do you feel that television has any other detrimental effects? How would your life be different if there were no television? Would you spend more time exchanging ideas with family and friends? Would you devote more time to more productive activities, such as reading or participating in a sport? Use your journal as a place to respond to the powerful medium of television.

The Reverse TRI Pattern

Another common variation on the Topic-Restriction-Illustration pattern is called the *Reverse TRI pattern.*

The *Reverse TRI pattern* inverts the order of the topic and illustration sentences: The illustrations come first and the topic, which is often a topic-restriction sentence, comes last. The following paragraph from Jacques Cousteau's *The Ocean World* uses the Reverse TRI pattern.[1]

Immune means "unaffected by." *Navigational sense* is the ability to find directions.

> Due to the high salt content of seawater, birds must be able to cope with the effect of chemicals in the ocean. (ILLUSTRATION) Some seabirds need a third eyelid to protect their eyes and to help them see clearly while they are diving in search of food. (ILLUSTRATION) They must remain immune to the effects of constant motion as they ride the waves for hours and days at a time. (ILLUSTRATION) And they require an astonishingly accurate navigational sense to migrate over an environment where there are no landmarks to guide them on their long overwater flights. (ILLUSTRATION) In many ways, birds must adapt to life in the sea. (TOPIC AND RESTRICTION)

The topic of the preceding paragraph is the many ways in which birds must adapt to life at sea. Each illustration is a specific example of how birds do adapt.

Writing Practice 3

For help with ideas, use one of the methods discussed in Chapter 2.

Select one of the following topic-restriction sentences or write one of your own. Then write a paragraph with that topic-restriction sentence and four or five illustration sentences, using the reverse TRI pattern. Remember that your topic-restriction sentence will be the last sentence of your paragraph.

1. We knew at once that the creature wasn't human.
2. Some people are just lucky.
3. I could hear the quiet sounds of the forest all around me.
4. Learning a foreign language is important.
5. Americans spoil their pets.

---

[1]Excerpt from *The Ocean World* by Jacques Cousteau. Reprinted by permission of Harry N. Abrams, Inc.

Revising Paragraphs

Revision means, literally, "seeing again." When you revise your writing, you read it again carefully, making corrections and improvements as needed.

How you choose to revise your writing is up to you. Some writers like to write a first draft of a whole paragraph or essay before rereading; some revise as they go along. This means that as they write, they reread each sentence, examining how the sentence sounds by itself and how it fits into the paragraph as a whole.

The first step in revision is to examine each sentence separately.

Each sentence, by itself, should make a clear statement about the topic. Remember that only the topic sentence should give general information; the other sentences must be specific. For example, consider the following topic sentence from a paragraph about unidentified flying objects.

> Popular belief in unidentified flying objects, or UFOs, seems to be growing.

The restriction sentence narrows the subject by giving more information about it and is always more specific than the topic sentence.

> Most UFOs, however, have natural causes and are not the "flying saucers" from other planets that many people believe.

The illustration sentences are the most specific of all; each one presents a new piece of information:

> For example, some reported UFOs investigated by the Air Force have turned out to be nothing more than weather balloons.
>
> Most UFOs that are observed at night are really fireballs, meteors, or falling stars.
>
> Many investigators believe that UFOs sighted during the day are really beams of sunlight reflected off airplanes.

Each of the preceding three sentences gives a specific example of a natural cause for a UFO.

When you revise your paragraph, keep in mind that you should be moving from the general to the specific as you proceed from topic to restriction to illustration sentences.

The second step is to examine each sentence in relation to the paragraph as a whole.

Each sentence in your paragraph should have something unique to contribute. If you find two sentences that repeat the same information, combine them or take one out when you rewrite. If you find an illustration sentence that does not contribute specific information, rewrite it or remove it from your paragraph.

The third step is to examine your paragraph as a whole.

Each paragraph is a separate unit of information; it presents and develops a topic. When you reread your paragraph, make sure that it gives enough specific information to support the topic. If you do not include sufficient examples, details, data, or other illustrations, your ideas will not be clear to the reader.

The following checklist for revising paragraphs covers all of the items on paragraph development discussed in this chapter. For now, check your writing only against those items you have studied; as you work through the chapter, refer back to the checklist for help in revision, adding those points you have included in your study. When you have finished revision, proofread your paragraphs for features that are not a part of Edited Standard English by using the Checklist for Proofreading on page 17.

Checklist for Revising Paragraphs

1. The paragraph has a clear central idea. If appropriate, this idea is expressed in a topic sentence.

2. The central idea is sufficiently restricted to be developed in a paragraph; if appropriate, the restriction is expressed in a separate sentence or combined with a statement of the topic in a topic-restriction sentence.

3. The central idea is adequately developed with illustration sentences giving specific information about it.

Development through definition is discussed on page 54.

4. A paragraph developed through definition defines the term by discussing general and specific meanings, giving examples of meanings, explaining the term's history, or explaining what the term is not.

Development with data is discussed on pages 55–56.
Development with comparisons is discussed on pages 56–57.

5. A paragraph developed with data contains a sufficient number of facts, figures or statistics, and dates to make the point clear; contains only data that relate to the main point of the paragraph; and contains data that have been checked for accuracy.

6. Paragraphs developed through comparisons are organized either by a block or a point-by-point method; the points of comparison are similar.

Unity in paragraphs is discussed on pages 60–64.

7. The paragraph has unity. The main idea is apparent; every sentence in the paragraph supports or develops the main idea; a "clincher" sentence, if there is one, focuses the reader's attention back on the main idea.

Coherence in paragraphs is discussed on pages 64–70.

8. The paragraph is coherent. Sentences are arranged in some sort of orderly progress; transitional devices, connecting pronouns, paraphrase, and repetition are used to link ideas.

Improving Paragraph Development

In the TRI pattern each paragraph is built with three parts: Topic, Restriction, and Illustration. Each paragraph makes a statement with the topic sentence, becomes more specific with the restriction sentence, and develops its main idea with the illustration sentences. In the following sections you will study methods of illustrating the restricted topic of a paragraph: definition, data, comparison, and a combination of methods.

Developing Paragraphs with Definition

When you define a word or term, you explain its meaning. Some words need to be defined because they are difficult or unfamiliar to your readers; others need to be defined because they have many general meanings and you want to be specific about which one you are using.

Two types of definition are common in expository writing. The first is a brief definition, usually no more than a phrase or sentence, as in the following brief definition of the word *masonry*.

> Masonry, the art of building in stone or brick, has been practiced for thousands of years.

Use a brief definition when the word or term you need to explain is simple.

In the preceding sentence the word *masonry* can be defined in a simple phrase.

Still another way to develop a paragraph of definition is to provide an example that readers will recognize.

In the following paragraph the writer explains what is meant by "gratitude" by telling the fable of the lion and the mouse.

> When a person shows gratitude, he or she shows thankfulness for a favor or good deed. You probably know the Aesop fable about the mouse who returned a favor to a lion. The mouse, who had run over the sleeping lion, was seized and about to be eaten. The mouse pleaded with the lion to save his life, promising to repay the favor someday. The lion was amused to think that a mouse could ever do a lion a favor but let the mouse go anyway. Some time later, hunters caught the lion and bound him with a rope. Fortunately, the mouse heard the lion's cries for help and gnawed through the rope, setting him free. "You smiled at me because you didn't see how one so small could ever repay one so great," said the mouse, "but now you know that even a mouse can show gratitude."

Two other ways that the writer might have developed the paragraph are by explaining the term from a historical viewpoint or by explaining what the term is *not*.

When defining a term by explaining its history, the writer shows how meaning has changed over time.

For example, in the early 1900s the word *lady* meant "a woman who behaved according to strict social conventions." *Ladies* were expected to have social graces and housekeeping skills. Obviously the definition of the term has undergone a great change.

Stating what a term is not is also a common way to explain a definition.

The word *love*, for example, was defined in a popular movie and song of the 1970s as "never having to say you're sorry." *Love* might also be defined as "not being possessive," "not finding fault," "not being afraid to trust someone."

Writing Practice 4

To revise your paragraph, use the Checklist for Revising Paragraphs on page 53.

For this assignment select one of the following terms to define in a paragraph or use one of your own. Begin by writing a topic or combined topic-restriction sentence. Then develop the paragraph by discussing general and special meanings of the term, giving examples of these meanings, explaining the term's history, or explaining what the term is not. You might want to use a combination of these methods.

1. Lady
2. Gentleman
3. Hero
4. Coward
5. School spirit

6. Failure
7. Reward
8. Faith
9. Courage
10. Student

Developing Paragraphs with Data

The term *data* includes facts, figures or statistics, and dates: information that has been proven to be true.

Develop a paragraph with data when you make a statement that needs to be supported with facts.

While you can use different types of data in your paragraphs, remember that the facts, figures or statistics, and dates must all relate to one main idea. In the following paragraph from *The Black Almanac*, notice how all the data support the general subject of the paragraph.[1]

The *libertarian* and *egalitarian spirit* is the spirit of liberty and equality.

> The great increase in the free black population in America came after the Revolutionary War. In appreciation of the service of some 5,000 blacks in the War for Independence and as a result of the libertarian and egalitarian spirit that the Declaration of Independence and the war inspired, many masters, especially Northerners, freed their slaves. Soon individual states in the North decreed the gradual abolition of the institution, beginning with Vermont's action in 1777. In 1776 the population of the United States was about 2½ million, more than 500,000 black slaves and approximately 40,000 free blacks. More than one half of these free blacks lived in the South. The Revolutionary leaders, including Washington and Jefferson, anticipated a continuation of the trend toward emancipation until eventually slavery would disappear from the land. This expectation was to be drowned, almost literally, by the whirring noise of Eli Whitney's cotton gin. The invention of this native of Massachusetts made cotton production increasingly profitable and caused rapid and substantial increases in the slave population, so that on the eve of the Civil War there were 4 million black slaves in the South.

The first fact presented in the preceding paragraph is that after the Revolutionary War the free black population in America increased greatly. What is the first figure or statistic given in the paragraph? What is the first date that is mentioned?

---

[1] Reprinted by permission of Barron's Educational Series, Inc. © copyright 1977. From *The Black Almanac* by Alton Hornsby.

When you develop a paragraph with data, remember to use as many facts, figures or statistics, and dates as needed to make your point. Do not include any data that do not directly relate to the main idea of your paragraph. Another important point to remember about using data is to check them for accuracy. *Accuracy* means "correctness." You can check data in such reliable sources as encyclopedias, atlases, almanacs, dictionaries, and history books.

Writing Practice 5

To gather ideas for this assignment, use one of the methods discussed in the chapter "Gathering Information for Writing."

Select one of the following general subjects and develop a paragraph with data on this subject. First, limit the subject to a restricted topic. Next, use a dictionary, an encyclopedia, or other reference works to find at least four facts, figures or statistics, or dates to support your topic. On a separate sheet of paper, write a paragraph using the information you have gathered.

1. Fish hatcheries
2. Sports cars
3. Solar power
4. Unemployment
5. The electoral college

Developing Paragraphs with Comparisons

Development through comparison is also discussed in the chapter "Reading Social Studies Materials."

A *comparison* points out ways in which items are the same and ways in which they differ.

When you develop a paragraph with comparisons, you liken and contrast ideas, points of view, experiences, people, places, and things.

Comparison paragraphs give information by showing two items in relation to one another. When you write a comparison, it is important to make the points of the comparison similar. For example, if you compare alternative energy sources and discuss the environmental effects of one, you must also discuss the environmental effects of the other.

You can develop a paragraph with comparisons by two basic methods: the *block method* and the *point-by-point method* of comparison.

The *block method* of comparison separates the two items being compared. It is called the block method because ideas about each part of the comparison appear together in a group, or block. In general, use the block method when you are contrasting the two parts of the comparison, as in the following paragraph by Bruce Catton.[1]

Burgeoning means "rapidly growing."

> So Grant and Lee were in complete contrast, representing two diametrically opposed elements in American life. Grant was the modern man emerging; beyond him, ready to come on the stage, was the great age of steel and machinery, of crowded cities and a restless burgeoning vitality. Lee might have ridden down from the old age of chivalry, lance in hand, silken banner fluttering over

---

[1]From Bruce Catton, "Grant and Lee: A Study in Contrasts," from *The American Story*, ed. Earl Schenck Miers, © 1956 by Broadcast Music, Inc. Used by permission of the copyright holder.

his head. Each man was the perfect champion of his cause, drawing both his strengths and his weaknesses from the people he led.

The first sentence in the preceding paragraph states that the generals Grant and Lee "were in complete contrast." Catton believes that both men represented opposing elements in American life. What did Grant represent? How does this contrast with the way of life that Lee stood for? What descriptive details does Catton use to emphasize this comparison?

A second type of comparison you can use in paragraph development is called the *point-by-point method* because the items are compared point by point. In general, use the point-by-point method when you are emphasizing the similarities between the two parts of the comparison, as in the following example.

> Theodore Roosevelt and Franklin Delano Roosevelt had more in common besides their name. Both came from wealthy and distinguished families. Both would later be called traitors to their social class due to liberal political beliefs. Beginning first with careers in law, both served as Assistant Secretary of the Navy (though Franklin Roosevelt took the job at age thirty-three, six years younger than Theodore Roosevelt when he accepted the post). The governorship of New York was the next stepping stone for each man. Theodore Roosevelt had lost the election once, in 1886, and when he won in 1898, it was by a slim margin. Franklin Roosevelt also won by a small plurality, but the year was 1928 and his win was considered a triumph since the Democrats had lost badly nationwide. Both men were popular governors. In terms of character, the two Roosevelts were vigorous, compelling, personable men known for their intellectual interests. As Presidents both were active conservationists and reformers. Though Theodore Roosevelt was a Republican and Franklin Roosevelt a Democrat, historians agree that both worked to strengthen and reshape the power of the Presidency.

The preceding paragraph begins with a general statement about the similarities between the two Roosevelts: "Theodore Roosevelt and Franklin Delano Roosevelt had more in common besides their name." Then the similarities are discussed point by point: that both men came from "wealthy and distinguished families," that both Presidents were thought of as traitors to their social class, and so on. The paragraph continues to list further points in common between the two men. Name other specific ways in which the writer shows that Theodore and Franklin Delano Roosevelt were similar. Name the ways in which they were different.

Writing Practice 6

For help with this assignment, use the Discovering Ideas for Writing section on page 49.

The following five sets of ideas suggest topics for paragraphs to be developed with comparisons. Select one or write a similar comparison topic of your own. Your paragraph can focus on the similarities or the differences between the two parts of the comparison. Before you write, decide whether you will use a block or a point-by-point method of comparison.

1. Compare the characteristics of those born under two different astrological signs.

2. Compare your experience of a holiday when you were young with your experience of a vacation now.

3. Compare two musicians or musical groups, two writers, painters, or sports stars.

4. Compare two makes of bicycles, automobiles, boats, skateboards, or any other means of transportation.

5. Compare two jobs or careers or other plans you have for the future.

Developing Paragraphs with a Combination of Methods

Many of the expository paragraphs you will read, especially longer paragraphs, use more than one method of development. As you learn to use the different methods of development in your own paragraphs, you will find that combining two or more of these methods can help make your writing interesting and varied.

The following paragraph combines definition, examples, and data in its development. Its general subject is the sound pollution created by the supersonic transport (SST). As you read, try to identify each different method of development.[1]

> In the United States the most dramatic struggle against sound pollution has centered around the sonic boom of the projected supersonic transport, the SST. A sonic boom is the sharp, loud noise, very similar to an explosion, that is produced when a plane flies faster than sound, popularly called "breaking the sound barrier." This popular expression is misleading because the plane doesn't break the barrier once, the noise is not created once, but is continuous throughout the flight. A sonic boom lays down a noise carpet of very high intensity that can shatter windows and crack plaster, walls, building foundations, tiles, and masonry. It can shatter fragile antiques and art objects in homes and museums. It can also trigger rock slides. In 1966 a boom from an Air Force plane caused 80,000 tons of rock to fall on ancient cliff dwellings in Arizona, causing irreparable damage. In 1968 a sonic boom loosened 66,000 tons of rock in Mesa Verde National Park in the Rocky Mountains. Because of these experiences, ecologists have been up in arms at the idea of building a supersonic transport plane, the SST, designed to fly at 1,800 miles an hour. Its development is estimated to cost $2 to $3 billion. Nearly all of it would come from federal funds—that is, taxpayers' money. Proponents of the SST argue that this money would be repaid when the plane is in production, but many observers are highly skeptical. The SST is an excellent example of private gain overcoming the public good, they say. Present jet planes fly at 600 miles per hour and thus take five or six hours for transatlantic flights. The SST would do the trip in two hours. But because of the normal delays in getting to and from airports, it is estimated that the present eleven hours of door-to-door transatlantic flights would be reduced to eight hours, a gain of only 27 percent to be measured against the cost, the discomfort, and the hazards of the SST.

---

[1]Excerpt from *The Wounded Earth* by Carl Marzani, A Young Scott Book, Addison-Wesley, 1972. Reprinted by permission of the author.

The preceding paragraph defines a sonic boom. Why is this definition placed early in the paragraph? In describing the effects of a sonic boom, the writer gives examples of windows shattering and plaster cracking. What other examples does the writer give of possible consequences of a sonic boom? What other examples does the paragraph present?

The SST paragraph also uses different kinds of data to support its main idea. For example, one fact given is that the SST is designed to fly at 1,800 miles per hour. What other facts does the writer present about the SST? What dates and figures are important to the main point of the paragraph?

Writing Practice 7

For help with this assignment, use the Discovering Ideas for Writing section that follows.

Select one of the following ideas for a paragraph to be developed with a combination of methods or use a similar idea of your own. Combine *examples* with at least one other method of development and write a paragraph using those methods. If necessary, use a dictionary, an encyclopedia, or other reference sources to gather information for your paragraph. You may want to begin by writing either a topic sentence or a combined topic-restriction sentence.

1. The changes in major league baseball (or in any other sport)
2. The most important environmental problem today
3. The causes of a historical event
4. The reason I enjoy a type of music (book, movie, etc.)
5. The difficulties of student life

Discovering Ideas for Writing

The chapter "Gathering Information for Writing," on pages 41–45, discusses classification in detail.

On page 49 you read about how to use your own experience as a source for ideas in paragraph writing. Another method of gathering information is called *classification*.

Classifying a topic means looking at it from a specific point of view.

You use classification in your daily life to think about or discuss people, objects, ideas, and concepts. If, for example, you are having a discussion about cars, you might look at them from the viewpoint of appearance, cost, speed, or handling ability. To use classification as an aid to information gathering, think of your topic in terms of three specific points of view. Each point of view can be expressed as a question. The first question asks *What is it?* (What are the special features or qualities of the topic?); the second question asks *How does the topic change or vary?* (In what way does the passage of time affect it?); and the third question asks *What are its relationships?* (What are the separate parts of the topic, and how does the topic as a whole fit into a larger category?).

1. What is it?

     Suppose that your general topic is the automobile, and you have decided to use the classification approach to discover information about it. Using the *What is it?* question, you would ask about the physical appearance of the automobile. What are the shapes and colors that are popular? What kinds of engines are used? You can compare different types of cars to produce information as well. How does the design of a racing car differ from the design of a standard car? What types of engine produce the most fuel efficient cars?

2. How does it change or vary?

    When you ask *How does it change or vary?* you look at your topic from the viewpoint of change through time. With the general topic of the automobile, you could ask how designs have changed since the first car was on the road. How has their physical appearance altered? How has the engine design, other mechanical design, or the fuel altered?

    You can also use this viewpoint to consider how much the basic automobile can change and still remain an automobile. For example, if at some point automobiles no longer run on petroleum-based fuel, if they float above the road instead of riding on it, or if their shape is no longer angular but circular, will they still be considered automobiles? This question asks *How much can the topic change or alter and still remain itself?*

3. What are its relationships?

    Relationships for a topic apply to the parts that make up the topic and to the ways in which the topic fits into a larger category. First, imagine that you have a diagram of the workings of an automobile. This question asks *How do all the parts of the automobile work together?* (If this question seems too broad, you can narrow it. For example, you could focus on how one part of the engine works, or how the brake system works.)

    Second, this question asks you to see the automobile as it relates to a larger category. The automobile is used for transportation, so you could ask what role it plays in the general transportation system of the United States. In terms of the car-manufacturing industries, you could ask what role the automobile plays compared with their other products. You could also consider the automobile in a social category as one of many factors producing changes in American life during the twentieth century.

    As you think about your topic from different points of view, jot down the questions and answers that come to you. Then for any one paragraph, decide which point of view most interests you. To develop your paragraph, use the information you have gathered about your subject by looking at it from that viewpoint.

Unity in Paragraph Writing

Unity means "oneness," an important quality in a well-written paragraph.

You can improve the unity of your paragraph in three ways: first, state the main idea in one clear sentence; second, relate each sentence to that main idea; and third, use the final sentence to tie the paragraph together.

The Topic Sentence

The *topic sentence* states the main idea, or topic, of the paragraph.

Not all paragraphs have directly stated topic sentences; experienced writers often write paragraphs in which the main idea is implied rather than explicitly stated in one or two sentences. Even so, however, the writer keeps this main idea in mind and relates other sentences to it. For beginning writers it is usually easier to write a topic sentence that can be used as a way to ensure the unity of the paragraph.

The topic of the following paragraph from the book *A History of Women in America* is that women played an essential part in settling America. As you read, notice how each sentence develops that idea.[1]

Women were an integral part of all permanent settlements in the New World. When men traveled alone to America, they came as fortune hunters, adventurers looking for a pot of gold; such single men had no compelling reason to establish communities. Women acted as civilizers for men living alone in the wilderness. Where there were women, there were children who had to be taught. There was a future—a reason to establish laws, towns, churches, schools. The organizers of Virginia understood as much when they sought to attract women to their colony so that the men who came "might be faster tied to Virginia." The labor provided by a wife and children also helped transform the forest into farmland. In the early days of the Georgia settlement the proprietors advertised for male recruits with "industrious wives."

The preceding paragraph is unified because each sentence develops the topic of the part women played in settling America. Suppose the paragraph had been written in the following way. Why are the *italicized* sentences out of place in the paragraph?

Women were an integral part of all permanent settlements in the New World. When men traveled alone to America, they came as fortune hunters, adventurers looking for a pot of gold; such single men had no compelling reason to establish communities. Women acted as civilizers for men living alone in the wilderness. *In fact, some people believe that women were responsible for developing the early arts of civilization, such as cultivating crops, making eating vessels, and even inventing writing.* Where there were women, there were children who had to be taught. There was a future—a reason to establish laws, towns, churches, schools. The organizers of Virginia understood as much when they sought to attract women to their colony so that the men who came "might be faster tied to Virginia." *Virginia was one of the original colonies of the United States.* The labor provided by a wife and children also helped transform the forest into farmland. In the early days of the Georgia settlement the proprietors advertised for male recruits with "industrious wives." *Georgia was inhabited by the Creek and Cherokee Indians before the English and Spanish empires made their claims.*

The first *italicized* sentence relates to the general idea that women act as civilizers, not to the specific topic of the role they played in the New World.

---

[1]From *A History of Women in America* by Carol Hymowitz and Michaele Weissman. Copyright © 1978 by the Anti-Defamation League of B'nai B'rith. By permission of Bantam Books, Inc. All rights reserved.

Remember your journal as a source of ideas for writing.

What information do the second and third *italicized* sentences give? Why do they prevent the paragraph from being unified?

After writing a paragraph, check to see that each sentence gives information directly relating to the topic sentence. Delete any sentences that do not support the main idea of the paragraph.

Writing Practice 8

Choose one of the following topic sentences or write a similar one of your own. Using the topic sentence you have chosen, write a paragraph developed with examples, definitions, data, comparison, or a combination of these methods. Pay special attention to unity in your paragraph by making sure that each sentence in the body relates directly to the main idea expressed in the topic sentence. Be prepared to explain how each sentence develops the main idea.

1. The elderly are not valued enough in today's society.
2. Too much organization can take the fun out of sports.
3. By studying nature you can learn a lot about yourself as well.
4. Education means more than what you learn in school.
5. My grandparents (or parents) grew up in a world that was very different from mine.

The "Clincher" Sentence

A *"clincher" sentence* sums up a paragraph.

You will not always need a "clincher" sentence, but it often serves a useful purpose in reminding the reader of the main idea of the paragraph. It helps improve the unity of a paragraph by focusing attention back to the main idea, by stating the topic sentence in a new way, or by giving a final piece of information about the topic.

The following paragraph from *Forty American Biographies* closes with a "clincher" sentence that sums up the main idea of the paragraph. The paragraph tells of an incident in the life of Harriet Tubman, a black woman born in slavery who became famous for her efforts to free other slaves.[1]

> One of the strangest adventures that Harriet Tubman had occurred when she decided it was time to rescue her aging parents. Her biggest problem was that they were too old to travel on foot all those weary miles without rest and often without food. Finally, she decided to take a great risk. She bought an old, worn-out carriage and an ancient horse just before she crossed into the slave states. Meeting her parents at the appointed place, she put them in the carriage and boldly made her way to the nearest railroad station across the Maryland state line. There she discovered she did not have enough money for their train fare. She left the old couple overnight at a safe station on the Underground Railroad and went back into Maryland to sell the horse and carriage. Then, walking through the woods to avoid the roads, she went back to the train

[1] Excerpt from "Harriet Tubman" from *40 American Biographies* by Helen Miller Bailey. Reprinted by permission of Harcourt Brace Jovanovich, Inc.

station, bought tickets, and sent her father and mother safely to Canada. The bold scheme had worked.

The subject of the preceding paragraph is Harriet Tubman's efforts to free her parents from slavery. The "clincher" sentence, "The bold scheme had worked," sums up the main idea of the paragraph. Notice that the paragraph is complete even without the "clincher" sentence but that this final sentence helps to make the paragraph more unified by directing the readers' attention back to the main idea.

The "clincher" sentence in the following paragraph by Edward T. Hall gives a final piece of information to interest the reader. The subject of the paragraph is *olfaction*, the sense of smell.[1]

> Most Americans have cut themselves off from a powerful communication channel: olfaction. Our cities lack both olfactory and visual variety. Anyone who has walked along the streets of almost any European village or town knows what is nearby. During World War II in France I observed that the aroma of French bread freshly removed from the oven at 4:00 A.M. could bring a speeding jeep to a screaming halt. The reader can ask himself what smells we have in the U.S. that can achieve such results. In the typical French town, one may savor the smell of coffee, spices, vegetables, freshly plucked fowl, clean laundry, and the characteristic odor of outdoor cafés. Olfactions of this type can provide a sense of life; the shifts and the transitions not only help to locate one in space but add zest to daily living.

The topic sentence of the preceding paragraph is "Most Americans have cut themselves off from a powerful communication channel: olfaction." The body of the paragraph gives examples of a culture with a variety of smells. The "clincher" sentence provides a general statement about the importance of olfaction in daily living. By making this general statement, the "clincher" sentence reminds the reader of the main idea the paragraph expresses, helping to unify the paragraph as a whole.

Writing Practice 9

To revise this paragraph, use the Checklist for Revising Paragraphs on page 53.

Choose one of the following five suggestions for a paragraph topic or write one of your own. On a separate sheet of paper, write a clear topic sentence based on the topic you have chosen. Then write a complete paragraph using that topic sentence. Develop your paragraph with examples, definitions, data, comparisons, or a combination of these methods. As you write, pay special attention to unity by relating each sentence in the body of the paragraph to the topic sentence. Close your paragraph with a "clincher" sentence.

1. Compare a book you have read with the movie that has been made from it.

2. Describe ways in which you are a different person now than you were a year ago.

3. Explain why people do (or do not) need laws.

---

[1]Excerpt from *The Hidden Dimension* by Edward T. Hall. Copyright © 1966 by Edward T. Hall. Copyright © 1966 by Edward T. Hall. Reprinted by permission of Doubleday & Company, Inc., the author, and the author's agents, Blassingame, McCauley & Wood.

4. Relate your views on an important consumer issue, such as warning labels on products or another issue of your choice.

5. Define what success means to you.

Coherence in Paragraph Writing

Coherent writing is clear writing. A paragraph is *coherent* when the sentences follow an orderly progress and when the connections between the sentences are made clear to the reader.

You can improve the coherence of your writing by paying attention to the order of your sentences in a paragraph and by using transitions to make the order clear.

Types of Paragraph Order

Sentences in a paragraph may be arranged in several ways: by order of chronology, by order of spatial arrangement, or by order of importance.

Sentences organized by *chronological order* present events as they happen in time.

You use chronological order in any paragraph that explains a process or the sequence of an event. When you organize your paragraph according to chronological order, you help your reader follow step by step through a process or an event. The process you describe can take place over a short period of time or over large time spans. The sample paragraph on pages 62–63 is organized in chronological order.

Sentences organized by *spatial order* present things as they are placed in relation to one another.

You use spatial order when you need to show the location of people, places, or objects. When you want to describe where things are in a scene so that your reader can imagine the setting clearly, use spatial order to organize the paragraph. In the following paragraph from *A Childhood: The Biography of a Place*, the writer Harry Crews describes himself as a child waking up in front of his house. As you read, notice which sentences help you to imagine the scene as Harry Crews describes it.[1]

> I awoke in the middle of the morning in early summer from the place I'd been sleeping in the curving roots of a giant oak tree in front of a large white house. Off to the right, beyond the dirt road, my goats were trailing along in the ditch, grazing in the tough wire grass that grew there. Their constant bleating shook the warm summer air. I always thought of them as my goats although my brother usually took care of them. Before he went to the field that morning to work, he had let them out of the old tobacco barn where they slept

[1] Specified excerpt from page 47 in *A Childhood: The Biography of a Place*. Copyright © 1978 by Harry Crews. Reprinted by permission of Harper & Row, Publishers, Inc. and Paul R. Reynolds, Inc.

at night. At my feet was a white dog whose name was Sam. I looked at the dog and at the house and at the red gown with little pearl-colored buttons I was wearing, and I knew that the gown had been made for me by my Grandma Hazelton and that the dog belonged to me.

The first way Harry Crews uses spatial organization is by telling the reader his location: "in front of a large white house." How does the next sentence give you a sense of location? What other sentences in the paragraph help show the way things are placed in relation to one another?

Sentences organized by *order of importance* rank things by their order of significance.

You may use order of importance to rank the ideas, facts, reasons, and any other illustrations that you present in a paragraph. The most common way to use order of importance is to move from the least important to the most important point. Order of importance is sometimes called *climactic order* because when you progress from the least to the most important point, the paragraph builds to a climax.

The following paragraph, from *The Eternal Bliss Machine* by Marcia Seligson, organizes its information by order of importance.[1]

> Every culture, in every time throughout history, has commemorated the transition of a human being from one state in life to another. Birth, the emergence into manhood, graduation from school at various levels, birthdays, marriage, death—each of these outstanding steps is acknowledged by a ceremony of some sort, always public, the guests in effect becoming witnesses to the statement of life's ongoingness, of the natural order of history. To insure the special significance of the rite of passage, its apartness from any other event of the day, these rituals usually require pageantry, costumed adornment, and are accompanied by gift-bearing and feasting. We wear black to funerals, bring presents to christenings and birthday parties, get loaded at wakes, eat ourselves sick at bar mitzvahs. Birth, marriage, and death, to be sure, are the most elemental and major steps, and as there is only one of these ritual commemorations for which we are *actually*, fully present, the wedding becomes, for mankind, its most vital rite of passage. And for this reason it is anchored at the very core of civilization.

Marcia Seligson notes that important steps in life are marked with special ceremonies or observances. What important rites of passage does she list? Why does she call marriage the "most vital rite of passage"?

Writing Practice 10

The following topics are suggestions for paragraphs to be organized by chronological order, spatial order, or order of importance. Select one or write a similar topic of your own. On a separate sheet of paper, write a complete paragraph based on your topic, paying special attention to the organization.

1. Training (for a sports event, for a performance, or training an animal) is not easy.

---

[1]Excerpt from *The Eternal Bliss Machine* by Marcia Seligson. Copyright © 1973 by Marcia Seligson. By permission of William Morrow & Company and the author.

2. Getting ready (for school, to go out with friends, or to go on a trip) is a ritual for me.

3. When I think of everything I do during the course of one day, I amaze myself.

4. There are several qualities I value most in another person.

5. I have very good reasons for believing in the future of this country.

6. I will always remember one special day from my childhood.

7. My room may look disorganized, but I know where everything is.

8. As we cruised over planet XJ117 in the Double-M Galaxy, strange new sights met our eyes.

9. When I go for a walk, I always seem to follow the same path.

10. I remember (the house where I grew up or the town where I used to live) very clearly.

For Your Journal

Because he believes so strongly in the effect that place has on a person's life, Harry Crews titled his autobiography *A Childhood: The Biography of a Place.* Think about the place where you have spent most of your life. What effect do you think this place has had on the kind of person you are now and the kind of person you will someday become? In your journal write about the influence of the city or area where you live on your life.

Using Transitions to Improve Coherence

A *transition* is a word or phrase that helps to link the sentences of a paragraph together.

You may see transitions referred to as *transitional devices,* or as *linking expressions,* or as *connectives.* These are other labels for transitions.

Transitions help the coherence of paragraphs by indicating the connection or relation between sentences. These connections help the reader follow the writer's thoughts from one point to another. There are many different kinds of transitions. The following paragraph from *Sports Illustrated* magazine uses three common transitions: *but, however,* and *although.* As you read, notice how these transitions help your understanding of the paragraph.[1]

> The bear is a classic and enduring American symbol for the benevolent wild. We tend to think well of bears, viewing them as large, powerful, stubborn creatures capable of mischief but somehow vaguely humorous and, like defen-

---

[1] Excerpt from "Bearing Up Under the Strain" by Bil Gilbert. Reprinted courtesy of *Sports Illustrated* from the June 5, 1978 issue. © 1978 Time Inc.

sive tackles, essentially good-hearted. However, when it comes to direct dealings with bears, our behavior has not been especially benign. For better than three centuries we have been hunting them, trapping them, setting dogs on them, clearing and leveling their natural habitat. With the notable exception of griz-zlies, bears have held up under this harassment better than many less con-spicuous, more mobile creatures. Although there are fewer bears in the U.S. than there were when Europeans first came to the continent, they still remain reasonably numerous. Bears now exist in population pockets scattered through-out most of their former range, which was just about all of the wooded parts of the country.

In the preceding paragraph, transitions help make the writing easy to follow. The first transition, *but*, introduces a contrasting statement that bears are large and mischievous *but* at the same time they are humorous and good-hearted. The second transition, *however*, contrasts the idea of bears as humorous and good-hearted creatures with the fact that Americans have not behaved kindly toward them. The third transition, *although*, indicates that even though there are fewer bears than there once were, they have survived. By linking and connecting ideas within a paragraph, transitions help the reader understand its meaning.

Select your transition according to its use.

The following list of transitions is organized according to use. Some transitions are used for paragraphs written in chronological order, spatial order, or order of importance; some are used to introduce or add ideas or to present contrasting ideas. Refer to this list as you write your own para-graphs until you are familiar with all the transitions included. As you read, be aware of the many other transitions that writers use.

TRANSITIONS	USES
for example, for instance	to introduce illustrations
and, also, in addition, besides, another, moreover, furthermore	to add details, facts, examples
but, nevertheless, on the other hand, however, on the contrary, yet, still, despite, similarly, in the same way	to show contrasting statements or comparisons
first, second, third, then, next, now, then, later, meanwhile, eventually, finally	to show chronological order
at the top, above, below, behind, near, far, far away, on the right, on the left, about	to show spatial order
least, most, least important, most important	to show order of importance
so, for this reason, thus, in conclusion, therefore, finally	to make a conclusion

Writing Practice 11

To find ideas for this assignment, use one of the methods discussed in the chapter "Gathering Information for Writing."

The following topic sentences indicate which type of organization they would require in a paragraph. Select one of these sentences or write a similar one of your own, indicating what type of organization or development it would require. Write a paragraph based on the topic sentence of your choice, paying particular attention to your list of transitions.

1. When we started to pitch camp for the night, I didn't realize it would take so long. (chronological order)

2. My (brother/sister) and I have developed the art of getting in each other's way. (spatial order)

To revise this paragraph, use the Checklist for Revising Paragraphs on page 53.

3. I have some bad habits that I would like to break. (order of importance)

4. Compared with (football or another sport), (baseball or another sport) is much less exciting. (comparison)

5. High school is very different from what I thought it would be. (examples)

Other Methods to Improve Coherence

Other methods to improve coherence include the use of connecting pronouns, paraphrase, and repetition.

Pronouns are words that act or substitute for nouns: *he, she, they, them, this, that, those,* or *it*.

By referring to nouns in a previous or later sentence, pronouns emphasize the connection in thoughts from one sentence to the next and help the reader follow the point of the paragraph.

In the following sentences taken from an interview with Walter Lindstrom, a Swedish immigrant who came to the United States in 1913, notice the pronouns that are *italicized*.[1]

> The place where my ancestors lived was on a small island off the coast of Sweden. *It* was a little farm surrounded by dark pinewoods.
> My father often told me there were trolls in those woods, *who* crept out at night to do mischief to us. I had no reason to doubt *him* because the bowl of milk that we put out for *them* every night was always empty in the morning. Of course we had plenty of barn cats, too.

Using the pronoun *it* instead of "The place where my ancestors lived" connects the first two sentences and also avoids unnecessary repetition. What nouns do the pronouns *him* and *them* replace? What sentences do these pronouns connect? You will find that substituting pronouns for nouns is one of the most widely used methods of improving coherence in writing.

Paraphrase is the rephrasing of a word or a phrase.

Paraphrase improves the coherence of your writing by linking ideas from one sentence to the next.

Paraphrase reminds the reader of a previous idea by stating it in another way, thereby avoiding unnecessary repetition. In the following paragraph

---

[1] Excerpt from *American Mosaic* compiled by Morrison & Zabusky. Copyright © 1980 by E. P. Dutton, Inc. Reprinted by permission of E. P. Dutton.

from Daniel Mannix's *All Creatures Great and Small*, which tells of a visit with Grace Wiley, a snake and reptile collector, the paraphrases are *italicized* and explained.[1]

Feinting means "moving to throw an opponent off guard."

> Grace advanced her hand toward the nearest cobra. *The snake* [paraphrase of *the cobra*] swayed like a reed in the wind, feinting for the strike. Grace raised her hand above the snake's head, *the reptile* [paraphrase of *the snake*] twisting around to watch her. As *the woman* [paraphrase of *Grace*] slowly lowered her hand, the snake gave that most terrible of all animal noises—the unearthly hiss of a deadly snake. I have seen children laugh with excitement at the roar of a lion, but I have never seen anyone who did not cringe at that *cold, uncanny sound* [paraphrase of *hiss*]. Grace deliberately tried to touch the *rigid, quivering hood* [paraphrase of *snake*]. The cobra struck at her hand. He missed. Quietly, Grace presented her open palm. The cobra hesitated a split second, *his reared body* [paraphrase of *cobra*] quivering like a plucked banjo string. Then he struck.

Notice how the paraphrases in the preceding paragraph make the progression of events easy to follow.

Repetition can also be used as an aid to linking ideas within a paragraph.

Although you use connecting pronouns and paraphrases to avoid unnecessary repetition, in some cases the repetition of a word or phrase helps to emphasize an important point. Using repetition well takes careful thought. When a writer is not careful, the repetition of a word or phrase can seem pointless, or the paragraph can seem monotonous. Select your repeating word or phrase by making sure that the repetition improves the sense of the paragraph. For example, the following paragraph is the conclusion of an essay on friendship in American, French, German, and English culture by anthropologists Margaret Mead and Rhoda Metraux. Notice how the *italicized* words *friend* and *friendship* repeat to give the paragraph coherence.[2]

> What, then, is *friendship*? Looking at these different styles, including our own, each of which is related to a whole way of life, are there common elements? There is the recognition that *friendship*, in contrast with kinship, invokes freedom of choice. A *friend* is someone who chooses and is chosen. Related to this is the sense each *friend* gives the other of being a special individual, on whatever grounds this recognition is based. And between *friends* there is inevitably a kind of equality of give-and-take. These similarities make the bridge between societies possible, and the American's characteristic openness to different styles of relationship makes it possible for him to find new *friends* abroad with whom he feels at home.   [*italics* added]

By repeating the words *friend* and *friendship*, the writers emphasize the theme of their paragraph and make their thoughts easy for the reader to follow. Repeating a key word is usually more effective than paraphrase if there is not a suitable word that can be substituted. For example, although

---

[1] Excerpt from *All Creatures Great and Small* by Daniel P. Mannix. Copyright © 1963 by Daniel P. Mannix. Reprinted by permission of the Harold Matson Company, Inc.

[2] Excerpt from "On Friendship—August 1966" from *A Way of Seeing* by Margaret Mead and Rhoda Metraux. Copyright © 1966 by Margaret Mead and Rhoda Metraux. By permission of William Morrow & Company.

the words *buddy* and *chum* are slang paraphrases for the word *friend*, they would have been out of place in the preceding paragraph.

Writing Practice 12

To find ideas for this paragraph consider using the Pentad approach discussed on page 33–41.

Choose one of the following suggestions as a topic for a paragraph or substitute a similar topic of your own. Before you write, decide which method of development you will use in the paragraph. As you write, pay special attention to connecting pronouns and paraphrasing. When you finish, underline the connecting pronouns and paraphrases you have used.

1. The effect of television on your life
2. An experience that taught you something about yourself
3. The characteristics of the ideal movie hero or heroine
4. Three steps you would take to improve your high school
5. How you see yourself ten years from now

Writing Practice 13

For help with revision, refer to the section Revising Paragraphs on pages 52–53.

The following five sentences can be used as topic sentences for paragraphs made coherent through repetition. In each sentence the word to be repeated throughout the paragraph is *italicized*. Choose one of these sentences or write a similar sentence of your own with an underlined repeating word. Then write a paragraph developed from your sentence, repeating the underlined word *at least four* times.

1. The difference between (my sister, brother, friend) and me is that I suffer in silence but (he/she) always *complains.*
2. The *moon* landing is the most exciting event of recent history.
3. I was seven before I overcame my fear of the *dark.*
4. *Honor* is a misunderstood word.
5. Some people believe that *astrology* can help guide their lives.

For Your Journal

The interview in the preceding section is from the book *American Mosaic*, a collection of interviews with immigrants to the United States. What is your family's country of origin? If you have a grandparent, aunt, uncle, or other relative who came to the United States from another country, consider interviewing him or her to find out about important memories of the country that has been left behind. Then write about the interview in your journal.

If you have moved to the United States from another country yourself, you might want to write in your journal about some early memories you have of your country of origin or about some thoughts you have on the United States—its people, land, or customs.

Writing a Précis

A *précis* is a written summary.

You are probably already in the habit of making summaries in your daily life. For example, when you read a detailed newspaper article and want to tell someone about it, you summarize the information you have read. Many times in school you are asked to give a summary, or brief account, of a book or article you have read. In written form this summary is called a *précis*.

A précis can be a valuable study aid. When you learn how to pick out the most important points in an article and record them, you will find it easier to remember them or to refer to them when studying. In fact, some students use précis instead of taking notes on articles.

Précis is both the singular and plural form.

The first step in précis writing is to read thoroughly the article you are going to summarize.

As you read the following paragraphs from Dorothea Dix's Memorial to the Legislature of Massachusetts, try to identify the most important points. Miss Dix presented this paper in 1843, after spending eighteen months gathering evidence on the treatment of the insane in the state of Massachusetts.

> I come to present the strong claims of suffering humanity. I come to place before the legislature of Massachusetts the condition of the miserable, the desolate, the outcast. I come as the advocate of helpless, forgotten, insane, and idiotic men and women; of beings sunk to a condition from which the most unconcerned would start with real horror; of beings wretched in our prisons and more wretched in our almshouses. . . .
>
> *Injustice* is also done to the *convicts:* it is certainly very wrong that they should be doomed day after day and night after night to listen to the ravings of madmen and madwomen. This is a kind of punishment that is not recognized by our statutes, and is what the criminal ought not to be called upon to undergo. The confinement of the criminal and of the insane in the same building is subversive of that good order and discipline which should be observed in every well-regulated prison. I do most sincerely hope that more permanent provision will be made for the pauper insane by the state, either to restore Worcester Insane Asylum to what it was originally designed to be or else make some just appropriation for the benefit of this very unfortunate class of our "fellow beings."
>
> Gentlemen, I commit to you this sacred cause. Your action upon this subject will affect the present and future conditions of hundreds and of thousands. In this legislation, as in all things, may you exercise that "wisdom which is the breath of the power of God."
>
> Respectfully submitted,
> D. L. Dix

The second step in précis writing is to make a list of the most important points in the article.

A précis must always be written in your own words, so do not quote or copy from the article you are summarizing. The preceding excerpt contains three paragraphs, so it would seem likely that a list of its most important points should contain at least three points, one for each paragraph. However, because the document is more than a hundred years old, the language and style of writing differ from our modern use. The third paragraph in the excerpt is merely a formal closing to the document.

The most important points in the excerpt from Miss Dix's "Memorial to the Legislature of Massachusetts" are the following:

1. The insane men and women in Massachusetts are being miserably treated.

2. They are housed in almshouses and in prisons, where convicts are forced to listen to their ravings.

3. This is unfair and unjust to the convicts.

4. The insane in Massachusetts should be housed in special asylums, such as the Worcester Insane Asylum.

5. Money needs to be appropriated to improve the treatment of the insane.

The preceding list of points is sixty-four words long. In general, a précis should be no longer than one third the size of the original article. To make your summary of important points even more brief, take out any illustrations or examples and make sure that you state each point clearly and simply.

The third step in précis writing is to write down your final version in paragraph form.

> The insane men and women of Massachusetts are being miserably treated. They are housed in almshouses and in prisons, where convicts are forced to listen to their ravings. This is unfair and unjust to the convicts. The insane in Massachusetts should be housed in separate asylums, such as the Worcester Insane Asylum, and money needs to be appropriated for this purpose.

The preceding précis, which is 61 words long, contains only the most basic points in the 262-word excerpt.

Writing Practice 14

The following article from *The Book of the Eskimo* by Peter Freuchen is to be used as the basis for a précis. Read the article carefully and, on a separate sheet of paper, make a list of the most important points. Check the points against the original to make sure you have included correct information and have not left out a basic point. Then write out your précis in paragraph form on a separate sheet of paper.[1]

> The familiar igloo is used by the Polar Eskimos only as a temporary shelter during travels. Most of the winter they live in permanent winter houses made of stones and peat. Permanent, that is, for the winter, for each spring they are left by the inhabitants and automatically become public property the next fall.
>
> You enter the winter house through an entrance tunnel, usually about fifteen feet long so as to provide both ventilation and protection against the outside cold. Since the house usually faces the sea, it is on a hill which the horizontal tunnel cuts into. The floor of the tunnel is laid with flat stones, the

---

[1]Excerpt from "The Eskimo Way of Life" from *The Book of the Eskimo* by Peter Freuchen. Copyright © 1961 by Peter Freuchen. Reprinted by permission of the Harold Matson Company, Inc.

walls are piled up stones, and the ceiling is made of flat stones covered with peat or turf. It is low, so that you have to crawl in on your hands and knees.

In the tunnel, you will find a strange little instrument, a little saber of wood or bone, called a *tilugtut.* When snow is falling or drifting outside, thousands of snow crystals will be lodged in the long hair of your skin clothes. If you enter the warm house like that, they will melt and make your clothes wet and heavy. Moreover, if you soon have to go out again, they will freeze. The tilugtut is used to beat the clothes free of snow while still in the entrance tunnel. During this procedure, it is a good idea to call out a few remarks, like: "Somebody comes visiting, as it happens!" so that the people inside are prepared to see you. It is true that an Eskimo home is open to visitors at almost any time of day or night, but there are strained relationships everywhere in the world, and it is neither wise—nor polite—to show up in the house without a word of warning!

Revising a Précis

To proofread your précis use the Checklist for Proofreading on page 17.

To revise a précis use the following checkpoints.

1. Each important point in the original article is expressed in one clear sentence.

2. The précis does not include any illustrations, such as examples, data, or details, that are given in the original article.

3. The précis is no longer than one third the length of the original article.

4. The précis is a complete paragraph in itself.

4 Writing Exposition: The Composition

Exposition:
A Definition

Expository writing, or *exposition*, presents and explains information.

Exposition is the writing used most often in school, daily life, business, and professions. When you write a book report, an essay examination, or a research paper, you use expository writing; directions, recipes, instructions, and business reports are other examples of exposition.

Since its purpose is to present and explain information, exposition must be *clear* and *easy to follow*. It must also be *thorough*—presenting sufficient information and explaining it completely.

In this chapter you will study the qualities of good exposition. You will also learn how to find topics for expository papers, how to organize your information, and how to write an informal outline. Finally you will practice writing two kinds of expository compositions: a paper of opinion and a paper of classification.

Writing an Expository Composition

The Audience
for the
Expository
Composition

In school your expository writing is often aimed at a *general audience*, sometimes called the "universal" audience because it can include everyone.

Always keep your audience in mind when you write.

With a general audience you cannot assume that the person reading your composition will have any knowledge of its subject. When you write for a limited audience, you can make these assumptions. For example, if you write instructions on how to make a soufflé for a friend who knows how to cook, you can assume that you will not need to explain basic cooking terms. If you write a report on class activities to be read only by class members, you can assume that they will have a basic knowledge of these activities. When you write for a general audience, however, you will need to be certain that your composition can be understood by everyone.

The general audience of expository writing also determines the type of "style" you will use.

Your *writing style* is your manner of expressing yourself with words. When you write to friends, your writing style is casual; the style you use for expository writing, however, is more formal. This does not mean that expository writing should be stiff, but it does mean that slang and casual expressions that you use with friends are not appropriate here. (Most exposition is written in Edited Standard English.) As you write your expository composition, imagine speaking it to your teacher or in front of an audience. This will help you to find the appropriate style.

Writing Practice 1

This exercise will give you practice writing for a specific audience. Write an expository paragraph explaining an important decision you had to make and why you made it. First, write the paragraph for a friend who attends the same school. Next, write an expository paragraph on exactly the same subject, this time for a general audience. Be prepared to discuss how the two paragraphs are different and why.

Finding Subjects for the Expository Composition

An *expository composition* is a group of related paragraphs that present and explain information.

Keeping in mind the purpose of an expository composition will help you to find an appropriate subject. Since the purpose is to present and explain information, you know first of all that you should choose a subject familiar to you or one that you can easily learn about. For example, suppose that your teacher has assigned a paper on the general topic of student government. You have just run for a student government office, so you have information about how your own school elections are conducted.

Approach your subject in a way that is appropriate to expository writing. A paper describing your feelings about the election would be descriptive rather than expository writing; a paper telling about your experience of running for office would be narrative rather than expository writing.

To present and explain information, you could write a paper explaining your opinion about the fairness or effectiveness of elections at your school, or you could make a comparison between elections at your school and those at another school. Another possibility would be to explain how the student government itself works by subdividing the different offices according to their function or their importance.

The information you present and explain in expository writing comes from two sources: what you already know and what you learn through further investigation.

When you decide on a subject, think about whether or not you have or can gather sufficient information before beginning your paper.

In some cases what you already know from your experience or your reading will be sufficient; in other cases you will need to explore the subject further.

When you are asked to choose your own subject, remember that many of your experiences can be used as general subjects for expository compositions. Your experiences include anything you have done, read, or studied, as well as your observations about life. A good place to begin looking for source material is in your journal, where you have recorded significant observations and events.

Writing Practice 2

Thinking about your own experience, write down at least three possible subjects for an expository composition. If you have kept a journal, read through it for possible ideas.

Limiting the Subject

Limiting the subject means "narrowing a subject to the specific topic of your composition."

Once you have a subject, the next step is to limit it to a topic that you can explain clearly and thoroughly in the space of a composition. *Developing a topic* means "making a decision about the kind and amount of information you will present in your paper." Be sure to ask your teacher if there is a length requirement, since the length helps determine the amount of material you can treat effectively. If, for example, you are asked to write a five-paragraph essay, you will know to limit your topic to what you can discuss in that amount of space.

There are three important points to remember when selecting a topic for an expository composition:

1. The topic should be interesting to you.

   In order to interest your readers, you must find the topic interesting yourself.

2. The topic should not be too general for the length of the composition.

   When you think of a possible topic, write down your basic ideas about it on a piece of scratch paper. If you feel that it will be difficult to fit them all into one paper, limit your topic further.

3. The topic should be broad enough to include interesting information.

   If, when you write down your basic ideas, you feel that you will have to use unimportant information to make your paper long enough, re-evaluate your topic. Broaden it so that you do not need to pad material or stray from the topic to include unimportant information.

Imagine that you are asked to write about the general subject *Education* in a five-paragraph composition. *Education* is a large subject: it includes classroom education and unusual learning experiences, new approaches to education, and the effects of television on education. *The value of grades in education* is a narrower subject than *Education* but is still too broad for a short composition. To limit this topic further you could narrow it to your own opinion about the importance of grading in secondary school. The following examples show other general subjects and the specific topics developed from them.

Subject: *Superstitions*
Topic: *How a common superstition began*

The preceding topic limits the general subject *Superstitions* to the development of a particular superstition.

Topic: *Different types of good luck charms*

The preceding limited topic is *Good luck charms*. The writer will classify the different types of *Good luck charms* by dividing them into specific groups.

Subject: *Ecology*
Topic: *Why noise pollution is harmful*

The preceding topic limits the general subject *Ecology* to the specific ecological problem of noise pollution. The writer will present his or her reasons for believing that noise pollution is harmful.

Topic: *Long- and short-range goals of the Green Earth group*

The preceding topic is limited to a classification of the goals of a specific ecology group.

Writing Practice 3

The following five subjects are too general and need to be limited for use in writing an expository composition of about five paragraphs. On a separate sheet of paper, write a limited topic for each subject.

Example
Subject: *Natural foods*
Topic: *The benefits of eating organically grown foods*

1. Space exploration
2. Politics
3. Astrology
4. The prison system
5. Comedy

Gathering Information

Choosing a subject and limited topic are the first two steps in writing an expository composition.

Gathering information is the third step. Because the information you gather for your topic forms the basis of your whole composition, always allow sufficient time to investigate your topic thoroughly.

The Pentad is discussed in the chapter "Gathering Information for Writing."

The following example shows how to use the Pentad to gather information for an expository composition. The Pentad is a five-question approach to finding ideas for writing.

Act:	What is the main action, plot, or idea?
Actors:	Who or what is involved in the action?
Scene:	What is the general setting, or background, of the event or idea?
Method:	How or by what means is the action performed?
Purpose:	What are the reasons (personal, social, or historical) for the events or ideas?

For example, the general subject *Popular literature* is too general for an expository composition. Even narrowed to *Detective novels*, the subject remains too broad for a suitable topic; however, a classification of the *types* of detective novels would be an appropriate topic. Using the Pentad questions approach, you could develop the following ideas about this topic.

Act:	What is the basic action of all detective novels? A mystery has to be solved: some mysteries have to do with stolen money, others with missing persons, murder, or foreign intrigue.
Actors:	What kind of people are actors in detective fiction? The actor can be a mastermind on the wrong side of the law, an intelligence agent of a foreign power, and sometimes a seemingly ordinary citizen. The agent on the side of the law can be a detective or other police agent, a private investigator, or a private citizen somehow involved in the events.
Scene:	What is the setting, or background? Settings are usually of two general types: the exotic or foreign setting when the crime involves the very rich; or the drab, heart-of-the-city setting of police detective stories.
Methods:	What methods are used to produce the action? The agent can cause events by acting alone, by collaborating with a gang or other organization, or by forcing others or tricking them into being a part of the crime. The agent on the side of the law causes events to take place—solves the crime—by superior intelligence or force.
Purpose:	What are the reasons for the events of detective fiction? Some criminals are motivated by private reasons of greed or revenge, some by political belief, and some by the desire for power. The agents on the side of the law are usually motivated by the desire to do their job, by the desire to earn money for their job or as a reward, by the desire for justice, or by a political belief.

The Pentad approach will help you to discover ideas and to find your main area of interest.

For example, after exploring the topic *Detective fiction* using Pentad questions, the writer might decide to focus the paper on an idea discovered through the Pentad. The topic could be further narrowed to one of the following.

1. A classification of three common mysteries: foreign intrigue, underworld crime, and murder (act)
2. The character of the criminal mastermind (actors)
3. Why setting is important in detective stories (scene)
4. Conspiracy: how it works in the plots of two detective novels (method)
5. An examination of motive: three honest detectives and why they stay that way (purpose)

You could also write on a combination of the preceding topics, depending on the length of your composition.

Writing Practice 4

Select one of the following subjects to explore with the Pentad questions approach or use any of the other information-gathering approaches from Chapter 2. (You may write a similar subject of your own if you prefer.) On a separate sheet of paper, write out the questions you ask and the information you gather by answering them.

1. Popular heroes or heroines
2. Contemporary American poetry
3. Computers in daily life
4. Endangered species
5. How teenagers are portrayed on television

Writing Practice 5

Using your subject from Writing Practice 4 or a new one you select, write two topics for expository compositions based on material that interests you.

Recording Information

Note taking is the simplest and most effective way of recording information for your composition.

When you take notes, use a note card or separate slip of paper for each thought. As you think about how to deal with your topic, make notes of your thoughts, ideas, and observations as they occur to you. Imagine, for example, that you are assigned to write a paper on the general subject of politics. You have narrowed this subject to the topic of voting rights for women. Your first note might look like the one on page 80.

You can write notes in whatever form is most helpful to you—words and phrases, complete sentences, or whole paragraphs.

> *History of suffrage*
>
> *The 15th Amendment, passed in 1870, gave suffrage to blacks; women did not win suffrage nationwide until 1920.*

Organizing Your Notes

The information you record in your notes can form the basis of your expository composition.

To make the best use of your information, organize it well at the beginning. Remember that a good expository composition presents information that is interesting, clear, and easy to follow. A review of your notes will tell you whether or not your information is interesting, but it is the organization—the sorting and ordering of your notes—that helps make your composition clear and easy to follow.

When you are at the organizing stage, you probably will have a pile of notes arranged in the order that you wrote them; the next task is to find the most effective way to order your notes.

Look for ways in which the ideas relate and then separate your notes by ideas into different groups.

There is no general rule about the number of groups you should have; it depends on the length and topic of your composition.

The following list of notes was collected for an expository composition on the idea of evil in horror films. The writer has developed a limited topic: *A comparison of the evil characters in the horror films* Dracula, The Wolfman, *and* Dr. Jekyll and Mr. Hyde. The notes are as yet unorganized. As you read through them, look for ways to categorize the ideas. Decide in what general ways the ideas connect and how you would separate them into different groups.

NOTES

1. Dictionary definition of word *evil:* "morally bad or wrong" (from an ancient word meaning "up from under")

2. Basic horror film plot involves struggle between good and evil

3. Dracula wants to control a world full of vampires, so he turns his victims into vampires who must obey him.

4. Vampire Dracula returns to his coffin at night.

5. Wolfman differs from Dracula—did not want to become evil as Dracula did.

6. Dracula supreme evil

7. *The Strange Case of Dr. Jekyll and Mr. Hyde* is the title of an original work by Robert Louis Stevenson.

8. Dracula rises from his coffin at night. Relates to original meaning of word *evil*—"up from under"—he comes up from under the ground

9. Quotation from Wolfman film: "Even a man who is pure of heart, and says his prayers by night, can become a wolf when the wolfbane blooms, and the autumn moon is bright."

10. Wolfman represents evil in conflict.

11. Unlike Dracula and Wolfman, Dr. Jekyll does not become evil through magic; he uses science.

12. What makes the monsters evil? They destroy lives. More than that, however, they go against the idea of life by turning their victims into creatures like themselves. This is true even for Dr. Jekyll, because he has created the potion that can release the evil in humans.

Writing Practice 6

This assignment will give you step-by-step practice in choosing a subject, narrowing it to a topic, finding ideas, and taking notes for an expository composition. Use the following procedures: (a) *Select an interesting subject.* Go through your journal, previous writing practices, and any other sources to find a subject that interests you: the Olympic Games, vegetarianism, the theater, conservation, or any subject you enjoy. (b) *Limit the subject to a topic that you can cover in a brief expository paper.* From the preceding subjects you could develop topics such as *Why I think the Olympics should be above politics; How to be a vegetarian; Two types of theatrical experiences;* or *Practical conservation measures.* (c) *Gather information about your topic.* As you gather information, record your ideas and impressions on 3 × 5 note cards or on similar-sized slips of paper.

Writing Practice 7

Study the notes on the horror film in the preceding section until you can decide on four or five general headings under which to group them. Then write these headings on a sheet of paper and write the notes beneath them that fit into each category.

Writing Practice 8

Divide the notes that you have made for your own expository composition into stacks by subject headings. On a separate note card, write the heading for each stack. Put this card on the top of the stack and secure it with a rubber band or large paper clip. Save the notes for later use.

**Making an
Informal
Outline**

An *outline* is a guide, or plan, to follow for your composition.

After you have sorted and ordered your notes, the next organizing step is to make an outline. Making an outline shows you in detail how your ideas fit together and helps you decide on the most effective way of presenting them. If you are not familiar with outlining, it may seem like an unnecessary step, but by focusing your ideas and making you plan how one thought will lead to another, outlining will save you time and help to make your writing well organized.

The two basic kinds of outline are the *formal* and the *informal outline.*

In the chapter "Writing a Research Report," you will study the *formal outline*; in this chapter you will learn how to prepare an *informal outline* for an expository composition.

When you put your notes in order, you separate them into groups, or categories, of related ideas. (For a brief composition you will probably have four or five categories of ideas.) Now look for ways in which the categories relate to one another and decide in what order you want to present these general headings in your composition. Once you have decided on the order of major headings, you can begin ordering the supporting details. Arrange and rearrange your notes until their order makes sense to you, discarding those that do not fit into the general framework of your paper. As you organize your notes, new ideas will probably occur to you. Feel free to add any new information that will strengthen your composition.

Notice that the following informal outline uses *phrases* to convey its ideas; some informal outlines use *complete sentences* instead.

This outline is based on the notes on pages 80–81.

Evil Characters in Three Horror Films

Evil and the horror film
    Definition of evil
    Evil and basic plot

Dracula
    Represents supreme evil
    Freely chooses evil
    Turns good into evil

Wolfman
    Represents evil in conflict
    Made evil through curse
    Can create evil

Jekyll and Hyde
    Represents evil within us
    Chooses to explore evil
    Turns good into evil

Evil nature of three characters
    Causes destruction of lives
    Causes destruction of good
    Punished with destruction

The preceding outline shows one of many ways to organize the information presented in the horror film notes. Some of the information from the notes was omitted, and a few new ideas not mentioned in the notes were added. There is no absolute right or wrong way to organize information. What is important is that the outline you write makes sense to you and that it presents information in a way that is clear and easy for you to follow.

The order and arrangement of ideas in the preceding outline correspond to the way they will be presented in the composition.

Each group of ideas represents a new paragraph or paragraphs, depending on the length of the paper. The points listed under each new heading are given in the order the writer plans to use them.

After you prepare your informal outline, you are ready to begin writing the composition. Remember that the purpose of an informal outline is to help you organize information. Once you begin writing, you may decide that the plan of ideas you made in your outline needs to be altered. Do not hesitate to make changes as you write. Your informal outline should serve as a guide to help you, not as a restriction on your writing.

Writing Practice 9

For this assignment use one of the following suggested subjects or another one of your choosing. Then narrow the subject to a specific topic for an expository composition of about five paragraphs. Next, write an informal outline using the following suggestions: (a) Organize your thoughts into separate groups. (b) Give each group a major heading. (c) Indent the points you make under each group. (d) Use either phrases or sentences in your outline, not a combination.

1. The Civil Rights Movement
2. Learning a foreign language
3. Life on other planets
4. Fads in music
5. Peer or group pressure

Writing a Thesis Statement

The *thesis statement* is the main idea, or thesis, of an expository composition.

The purpose in writing a thesis statement is to clarify the central idea of the paper for yourself and your readers. A thesis statement summarizes the central idea and lets the reader know how you are going to approach it in the composition. Before you begin writing, you should formulate a thesis statement.

Write your thesis statement in the form of a simple, declarative sentence.

This sentence can simply express the main idea that is the basis of your paper, or it can present a summary of ideas you will use to develop the topic. For example, suppose that you have been assigned to write an expository composition on the subject of unusual learning experiences. You have narrowed down this subject to the topic, *What acting teaches*; the main idea is that the study of acting has many benefits. One thesis statement would be a simple, declarative sentence that states this idea: "The study of acting has many benefits." Another kind of thesis statement both states the idea and gives the major points to be covered: "The study of acting has many benefits, such as improving public-speaking ability, posture, and powers of observation."

Remember that the purpose of your thesis statement is to tell the reader in clear and simple terms what to expect from your paper. Do not begin with prefatory remarks, such as "My purpose is . . ." or "The main idea of this paper is. . . ." Although these remarks are clear and simple, they are unnecessary additions to your thesis statement.

Writing Practice 10

The following subjects are suggestions for expository compositions. For each subject write a specific topic and a thesis statement. If you prefer, you may substitute five subjects of your own choice.

Example

a. Subject: *Advertising*
a. Topic: *The changing role of women in ads*
   Thesis Statement: *The way women are presented in advertisements has changed significantly over the last several years.*

1. New careers for the 1980s
2. Women's rights
3. Current events
4. Youth culture
5. Hobbies

Writing an Introduction

Many expository compositions share the same basic structure: introduction, body, and conclusion.

The purpose of the *introduction* is to give interesting background information about the topic and to present the thesis statement.

A well-written introduction engages the reader's attention with descriptive details, a quotation, a question, an unusual piece of information, or with some other idea. You may also begin your introduction with the thesis statement itself. In the following introduction notice the descriptive details, the definition of a key term, and the presentation of the paper's main idea.

> Sally's eyes opened wide, her heart beat faster, perspiration dampened her palms, her legs froze, and she tried to scream, terrified by what she saw. What Sally saw was a cat. Like Sally, millions of people are subject to irrational and uncontrollable fears, better known as *phobias*. A phobia is not just any fear. Derived from the Greek word *phobus*, meaning "flight," it is more accurately defined as "an inappropriate, intense fear of a perfectly natural situation or object." Although hundreds of phobias exist, they can be generally categorized into four main types: fears of places and things, interpersonal and social fears, internal fears of thoughts, and derivative fears.

In the preceding introduction the thesis statement is the final sentence of the paragraph. It tells the reader that the purpose of the paper is to present information about the classification of phobias. For other examples of introductory paragraphs, see the expository compositions on pages 87 and 92.

Writing Practice 11

Using a topic you have already selected or a new one you choose for this assignment, write an introductory paragraph for an expository composition. To make your paragraph interesting, use one of the methods discussed in the preceding section or one of your own devising. If you have not already decided on a topic, you may wish to develop it from one of the following subjects.

1. Advertising
2. Effects of television
3. The United Nations
4. School regulations
5. World hunger
6. Popular music
7. Presidential elections
8. Hypnosis
9. Atlantis
10. Fraternities and sororities

The Body of the Composition

The *body of the composition* consists of all the paragraphs between the introduction and the conclusion.

The paragraphs of the body fulfill the purpose stated in the introduction by developing the topic with illustrations.

Illustrations—the examples, facts, figures, and reasons that support the writer's ideas and opinions—are essential to good expository writing. Illustrations not only make a composition more interesting to read, but they also make the paper more understandable. In addition, proper use of illustrations makes a topic come alive for the reader. There is no rule about the exact number of illustrations to use in a composition; this depends on the nature of the topic and the length of your paper.

The paragraphs of the body should be unified.

A composition has unity when the reasons for its organization are apparent and when each detail in the paper clearly supports or develops the thesis statement. If you have grouped your notes under major headings and each of these headings is developed in a separate paragraph, your paper should have a logical organization.

The paragraphs of the body should be coherent.

Transition devices in paragraphs are discussed on pages 66–67.

When an expository composition is coherent, readers can easily move from one idea to the other because the writer has provided transitions. These transitions may be the same as those used to develop paragraphs: transition words, connecting pronouns, paraphrases, and repetitions of key words. For example, the following two paragraphs are (1) the introduction to the paper on phobias discussed in the previous section and (2) the first paragraph of the body. Notice how the repetition of the *italicized* words helps the reader make the transition from one paragraph to another.

Sally's eyes open wide, her heart beats faster, perspiration dampens her palms, her legs freeze, and she tries to scream, terrified by what she sees. What Sally sees is a cat. Like Sally, millions of people are subject to irrational and uncontrollable fears, better known as *phobias*. A phobia is not just any *fear*. Derived from the Greek word *phobus*, meaning "flight," it is more accurately defined as "an inappropriate, intense *fear* of a perfectly natural situation or object." Although hundreds of *phobias* exist, they can be generally categorized into four main types: *fear* of *places and things*, interpersonal and social fears, internal fears, fears of thoughts, and derivative fears.

As the elevator door closes, John's chest tightens and his breathing becomes difficult. John is suffering from claustrophobia, an example of the *places and things phobia*. This type of phobia (which includes the *fear* of being in *places* like elevators, tunnels, or small rooms; the *fear* of conditions such as fire, thunder, or heat; the *fear* of animals and insects; and the *fear* of transportation such as planes, trains, or buses) is the most common and easily recognizable.

Writing Practice 12

Using a topic you have already developed or one you select for this assignment, write the body for an expository composition.

Writing a Conclusion

The purpose of the *conclusion* is to reinforce the main idea of the composition by summarizing the most important points or by restating the purpose of the composition in a new way.

A good conclusion gives the reader a sense of completion.

Many writers refer directly to the thesis statement of the paper as a way of concluding it. You may also end your paper with a quotation or a final statement of opinion.

The following paragraph is the conclusion to an expository paper on phobias. The phrase "these phobic reactions" refers to the different types of phobias dealt with in the body of the composition. In this conclusion the writer presents the negative effects of the phobias she has described and ends with a final thought about the topic.

While these phobic reactions may be amusing to some, phobias can ruin lives, destroy careers, and even drive a phobic to suicide. There is still a great deal to learn about these illnesses, but their treatment has been very successful. Recent publicity of this topic has helped the phobic to realize that millions share this form of illness and has helped the nonphobic to appreciate the depth and complexity of the disease.

Writing Practice 13

Using a topic you have already developed or one you select for this assignment, write a concluding paragraph for an expository composition. If you have completed Writing Practice 12, write a conclusion for that essay.

Writing a Title

A *title* is an important part of any expository composition. It is treated last here because many writers prefer to compose a title after finishing the paper.

A good title informs the reader specifically about the topic and purpose of the composition.

Some titles are simple statements of purpose: "How Bats Communicate," for example, tells you that the purpose of the composition is to give information about bat communication. Some titles are derived from a phrase used elsewhere in the paper; this is why some writers prefer to add the title last. For example, in the paper on phobias discussed in the preceding sections, the title "Not Just Any Fear" is taken from the introduction; it tells you that the topic of the paper is a special kind of fear. Some titles try to engage the reader's attention with humor or to make the reader want to read more. From the title "Saga of the Barefoot Bag on Campus," an essay by John Riley, the reader wonders what the bag is and what it is doing on a campus.

Essay of Opinion

Expository compositions can be divided into *types* according to the purpose of the essay. The purpose may be to explain a process, define a concept, make an analysis, clarify an opinion, or make a classification. The two kinds of expository compositions you will learn about in the following sections are the *paper of opinion* and the *paper of classification.*

A *paper of opinion* not only states an opinion but also presents information, explains it, and supports the opinion with facts and observations.

"A Simplified Alphabet" by Mark Twain discusses three methods of spelling: (1) the traditional method that we use today, (2) Simplified Spelling based on our present alphabet, and (3) the spelling of words as they are pronounced based on Isaac Pitman's phonographic alphabet (used in shorthand). As you read, determine which system Twain is advocating, and look for the reasons and evidence he gives to support his opinion.

> I have had a kindly feeling, a friendly feeling, a cousinly feeling toward Simplified Spelling, from the beginning of the movement three years ago, but nothing more inflamed than that. It seemed to me to merely propose to substitute one inadequacy for another; a sort of patching and plugging poor old dental relics with cement and gold and porcelain paste; what was really wanted was a new set of teeth. This is to say, a new *alphabet.*
>
> The heart of our trouble is with our foolish alphabet. It doesn't know how to spell, and can't be taught. In this it is like all other alphabets except one—the phonographic. That is the only competent alphabet in the world. It can spell and correctly pronounce any word in our language.
>
> That admirable alphabet, that brilliant alphabet, that inspired alphabet, can be learned in an hour or two. In a week the student can learn to write it with some little facility, and to read it with considerable ease. I know, for I saw it tried in a public school in Nevada forty-five years ago, and was so impressed by the incident that it has remained in my memory ever since.

I wish we could adopt it in place of our present written (and printed) characters. I mean *simply* the alphabet; simply the consonants and the vowels—I don't mean any *reductions* or abbreviations of them, such as the shorthand writer uses in order to get compression and speed. No, I would *spell every word out*. . . .

What should we gain?

First of all, we could spell *definitely*—and correctly—any word you please, just by the *sound* of it. We can't do that with our present alphabet. For instance, take the simple, every-day word *phthisis*. If we tried to spell it by the sound of it, we should make it *tysis*, and be laughed at by every educated person.

Secondly, we should gain in *reduction of labor* in writing.

Simplified Spelling makes valuable reductions in the case of several hundred words, but the new spelling must be *learned*. You can't spell them by the sound; you must get them out of the book.

But even if we knew the simplified form for every word in the language, the phonographic alphabet would still beat the Simplified Speller "hands down" in the important matter of economy of labor. I will illustrate:

> *Present form*: through
> *Simplified form*: thru
> *Phonograph form*:

To write the word *through*, the pen has to make twenty-one strokes.

To write the word *thru*, the pen has to make twelve strokes—a good saving.

To write the same word with the phonographic alphabet, the pen has to make only *three* strokes. . . .

[Twain goes on to compare the number of strokes required for the words *laugh*, *highland*, and *phonographic alphabet*, and the letter *m*.]

It has taken five hundred years to simplify some of Chaucer's rotten spelling—if I may be allowed to use so frank a term as that—and it will take five hundred more to get our exasperating new Simplified Corruptions accepted and running smoothly. And we sha'n't be any better off then than we are now; for in that day we shall still have the privilege the Simplifiers are exercising now: *anybody* can change the spelling that wants to.

But you can't change the phonographic spelling: there isn't any way. It will always follow the *sound*. If you want to change the spelling, you have to change the sound first.

Mind, I myself am a Simplified Speller; I belong to that unhappy guild that is patiently and hopefully trying to reform our drunken old alphabet by reducing his whisky. Well, it will improve him. When they get through and have reformed him all they can by their system, he will be only *half* drunk. Above that condition, their system can never lift him. There is no competent, and lasting, and real reform for him but to take away his whisky entirely, and fill up his jug with Pitman's wholesome and undiseased alphabet.

One great drawback to Simplified Spelling is, that in print a simplified word looks so like the very nation! and when you bunch a whole squadron of the Simplified together the spectacle is very nearly unendurable.

The da ma ov koars kum when the publik ma be expektd to get rekonsyled to the bezair asspekt of the Simplified Kombynashuns, but—if I may be allowed the expression—is it worth the wasted time?

. . . To see our letters put together in ways to which we are not accustomed offends the eye, and also takes the *expression* out of the words.

La on, Makduf, and damd be he hoo furst krys hold, enuf!

It doesn't thrill you as it used to do. The simplifications have sucked the thrill out of it.

But a written character with which we are *not acquainted* does not offend us—Greek, Hebrew, Russian, Arabic, and others—they have an interesting look, and we see beauty in them, too. And this is true of hieroglyphics, as well. There is something pleasant and engaging about the mathematical signs when we do not understand them. The mystery hidden in these things has a fascination for us; we can't come across a printed page of shorthand without being impressed by it and wishing we could read it.

Very well, what I am offering for acceptance and adoption is not shorthand, but longhand, written with the shorthand alphabet unreduced. You can write three times as many words in a minute with it as you can write with our alphabet. And so, in a way, it *is* properly a shorthand. It has a pleasant look, too; a beguiling look, an inviting look. . . .

You have probably noticed that the introduction to "A Simplified Alphabet" does not contain a thesis statement in the form of a single simple, declarative sentence. Experienced writers sometimes use what is called an *implied thesis statement*, meaning that the main idea of the paper is so clear that it is *implied* by other statements in the introduction. (The writer has the thesis statement firmly in mind while writing; but it is not written into the paper as a simple, declarative sentence.)

In the preceding essay the introduction prepares the reader for a discussion of Simplified Spelling and the traditional alphabet and also for a discussion of Mark Twain's other ideas about writing English words. If Twain had included a thesis statement in the introduction, it might have been similar to this: "I propose that we use the Pitman phonographic alphabet to spell all English words."

For Discussion

1. What is the main opinion expressed in this essay? What lines express the main opinion most fully?

2. Twain gives two reasons for replacing our traditional alphabet with the phonographic (shorthand) alphabet. What are these reasons?

3. What specific evidence does Twain give that writing words in the phonographic alphabet is less work than writing in the traditional alphabet? According to Twain, how many times faster can writing be accomplished using the phonographic alphabet?

4. What examples does Twain give of the Simplified Spelling system? Can you write these sentences in the traditional way?

5. According to the author, what are the disadvantages of the Simplified Spelling system?

6. Find at least one analogy in the essay. What purpose does the analogy serve?

7. This essay was first published in 1917. Why do you think we are still using the traditional alphabet and method of spelling—and not the system that Twain advocates?

8. In his essay, Twain says that only the sound (pronunciation) of words would govern their spelling under his proposed system. However, he does not account for the differences in pronunciation that would result from regional dialects and foreign accents. How do you think Twain would reply to this objection?

9. Do the ideas presented in this paper follow a logical order? Does the order make sense to you?

10. Are there any ideas or points made in the paper that do not relate to the main idea? If you were writing this paper, is there any part you would leave out?

11. Is this paper made coherent through the use of transitions? Give examples the writer makes of connecting words and phrases, repetition, paraphrase, and connecting pronouns. What phrases help connect one paragraph to the following paragraph?

12. What does the title tell you about the essay? Does it help you know what to expect from the paper?

Writing Practice 14

Use the Discovering Ideas for Writing section that follows to help you with this assignment.

Using a subject of your choice, write an expository composition that presents an opinion. To do so follow the steps you studied in this chapter about planning and writing a composition: (a) Narrow the subject to a limited topic. (b) Gather information about the topic. (c) Take notes on the topic. (d) Make an informal outline based on your notes. (e) Write a thesis statement before you begin writing the composition. (f) Write the composition, using the informal outline as a guide. As you write, pay special attention to logical organization, sufficient illustrations, a unified approach, a helpful title, and coherence through the use of transitions. Before you begin, read the Discovering Ideas for Writing section that follows.

Discovering Ideas for Writing

When you write a paper of opinion, you express your ideas about a particular issue or event. In "A Simplified Alphabet," for example, Mark Twain explores the issue of spelling reform. Twain believes that Simplified Spelling may be an improvement over traditional spelling but that it is not the best reform. He gives reasons why the phonographic alphabet—his own choice—is superior to both Simplified Spelling and our traditional system.

Papers of opinion are more interesting when the writer presents a belief that he or she feels strongly about. Using Twain's "A Simplified Alphabet" as a model, you might start looking for a subject by making a list of books you have read over the last year. As you compile your list, perhaps you will recall a book with which you agreed or disagreed. If so, you can use the central issue of the book as the basis for your paper of opinion (This technique can also be applied to movies or television programs you have seen, school projects you have participated in, and other subjects.)

Another way to find subjects for a paper of opinion is to look through newspapers, current events magazines, and similar sources. When you find an interesting article, decide what the central issue is and what opinion you have of it. Then decide whether or not you have enough information on the subject for a whole composition.

Finally, your opinion paper can deal with an issue that you encounter in your daily life. To help you recall this kind of issue, you might make a list of the many different roles you play in your life: high school student, employee, member of a church or youth group, sports fan, family member, hobbyist, art student, social group member, movie fan, club member, community volunteer, and so on.

Each of the different roles you play is a source of issues and your opinions about them. As a high school student, for example, you may have an opinion about school issues, such as the role of student government, community attitudes toward high school students, or academic pressures. After each role that you list, write out an issue that applies to that role. When you finish, select an issue that interests you and that you feel strongly about as the subject of your opinion paper.

Revising an Expository Composition

Use the following revision checklist as a guide to revising your expository composition.

Check your composition by using the Checklist for Proofreading on page 17.

Checklist for Revising an Expository Composition

1. The purpose of the composition is clearly stated in the introduction.
2. The introduction presents interesting background information about the topic.
3. Each paragraph presents new information about the topic.
4. The composition is well-organized.
5. The composition presents sufficient information about the topic to make it interesting and understandable.
6. Each paragraph in the composition supports or develops the thesis statement.
7. The composition includes transitions to help coherence.
8. The conclusion reemphasizes the main idea of the paper or restates it in a new way.
9. The title helps explain the topic of the paper.
10. A composition explaining an opinion uses sufficient illustrations to support the writer's opinion.

Essay of Classification

A *paper of classification* presents and explains its topic by dividing it into smaller parts. Its purpose is to help the reader understand the topic by sorting it into related groups.

The paper of classification in this section, "See You in the Funny Papers," explains the popularity of the "Peanuts" comic strip by examining its comic characters. As you read this paper of classification, read also the notes in the margin. These explain the structure of the essay.

Following this essay is a For Discussion activity.

See You in the Funny Papers

Introduction: gives background information and makes thesis statement

Of the many popular comic strips today, "Peanuts" is perhaps the most loved. The enormous popularity of Charlie Brown, Lucy, Snoopy, and the other characters is partly due to the charm and gentle humor of the strip. On a deeper level, however, the comic world of Charlie Brown fascinates because it shows us our own world in miniature.

First paragraph of the body: presents information and illustrations about the character of Charlie Brown

Charlie Brown reflects qualities we have sometimes felt in ourselves; he is perpetually trusting, tenderhearted, and vulnerable. When Lucy promises once more not to move the football he is about to kick, we know that she will, and that Charlie Brown will end up on his back in a pile of leaves. We sympathize with his wanting to believe her, with his optimism and naiveté. When we relate to Charlie Brown, we acknowledge that we too sometimes feel besieged by the world. We become the batter who could save the team at the last moment but who strikes out, the only kid who gets no valentines, the boy who cannot even fly a kite. Good grief. We love Charlie Brown because he helps us put those failures in perspective with the positive qualities that go with them. We know that Charlie Brown tries so hard because he wants to be loved.

Second paragraph: presents information and illustrations about the character of Lucy

Lucy is the aggressor. She is vain, conceited, selfish, peremptory, and downright nasty at times. We see her as the antagonist and root for Charlie Brown or Linus or even Snoopy to win out against her, but we also identify with her single-mindedness. Lucy is a winner. She takes what she wants, and something in us warms to her angers, her explosions. "You Blockhead," she screams at the top of her lungs, just as we would sometimes like to do. Lucy also stands for the reality principle. She is the one who always deflates Snoopy, informing him that he really is not a rhinoceros charging for the attack. She brings everyone back to the real world. We are all too literal-minded at times, too harsh and pragmatic. We step all over the Charlie Browns with no afterthought or apology. Through Lucy we can acknowledge this side of ourselves.

Third paragraph: presents information and illustrations about the character of Snoopy

Snoopy is our fantasies. His only occupations are eating and sleeping. His favorite pastimes are dancing and playing make-believe, and he does both with an immense concentration that transforms his world totally. When he dances through frame after frame with an ecstatic, absorbed grin on his face, Snoopy stands for joy. When he slinks through the grass like a boa constrictor, or flies to meet the Red Baron from the top of his dog house, Snoopy is our imagination. Fantasy is not an escape for Snoopy; it is his mainstay. He is the child in us that never grew up, who wants to sleep all day or invent other selves to be. We identify with his creativity and recognize our own fantasies through his.

Conclusion: rephrases thesis statement and makes concluding points about the main idea of the paper

Charlie Brown, Lucy, Snoopy, and the many other "Peanuts" family members reflect back to us our admirable and sometimes less than admirable ways of moving through the world. We may feel with Lucy that the negative traits are not ours but belong to our neighbors: "*I* am humble, but *you* are wishy-washy," as she tells Charlie Brown. Nonetheless, in "Peanuts" we find characters that we recognize, laugh at and with, and find wholly sympathetic. This is the goal of the best kind of comedy: to enlighten us about ourselves and our world in a way that makes us laugh. In "Peanuts" we find this kind of humor.

For Discussion

1. What sentence in the introduction serves as the thesis statement of the composition?

2. What background information about the comic strip "Peanuts" do you learn from the introduction?

3. What is being classified, or divided into different groups, in the paper?

4. What examples does the writer give to illustrate the characters of Charlie Brown, Lucy, and Snoopy? Are there sufficient illustrations to make each character clear?

5. Do you agree or disagree with the characterizations the paper makes of Charlie Brown, Lucy, and Snoopy? Why?

6. How does the writer restate the thesis statement in the conclusion? What other information do you learn from the conclusion?

7. Are the ideas presented throughout the paper in an order that is easy to follow? What is the order?

8. Are any of the ideas presented in the paper unrelated to the thesis statement? If you were rewriting this paper, would you add or delete any material?

9. Does this paper use transitions effectively? Give examples of how the writer uses connecting words or phrases, repetition, paraphrase, and connecting pronouns as transitions. What words or phrases help connect one paragraph to the following paragraph?

10. What does the title tell you about the composition? Does the title help you know what to expect from the paper?

Writing Practice 15

Using a subject of your choice, write an expository composition that makes a classification. Follow the steps you have studied in planning and writing a composition: (a) narrow the subject to a limited topic, (b) gather information about the topic, (c) take notes on the topic, (d) make an informal outline of the composition based on your notes, (e) write the thesis statement before you begin the composition, and (f) write the composition, using the informal outline as a guide. To help develop ideas for writing, use any of the suggested methods in the chapter "Gathering Information for Writing" on pages 30–45.

When you have finished your first draft, use the Checklist for Revising an Expository Composition on page 91 to help you with revision but substitute the following point for Number 10 on the checklist: A composition of classification includes sufficient illustrations about each category to make it clear to the reader. Proofread your composition by using the Checklist for Proofreading on page 17.

5 Writing from Sources: The Research Report

Writing the Research Paper

Why do teachers ask students to write research papers? Because it requires the student to initiate and carry out a complex assignment within a specific time limit, the research paper promotes mature, responsible study habits. Also, the research paper involves finding and evaluating information.

The *research*, or *term*, *paper* is a long, formal essay that presents specific information from a variety of sources.

Writing a research paper involves the same skills used in writing an expository essay but also requires using library resources and identifying those sources in footnotes and a bibliography. There are two ways to write a research paper: Some research papers pull together and summarize the existing information on a topic; others answer a specific question or draw conclusions from the gathered information.

In this chapter you will learn the basic steps in the research process: choosing and limiting a topic, finding and evaluating sources of information, taking notes, making an outline, writing a rough draft and footnotes, and preparing the final draft with a bibliography.

Be sure to schedule enough time for each step. You will find the paper easier to write if you plan carefully and follow the procedures suggested in this chapter.

Choosing and Limiting a Topic

Try to choose a topic from your own interests; your paper will be more successful if you genuinely enjoy working on the topic. As you consider possible topics, remember that your research topic should be general enough to include interesting and pertinent information and limited enough so that you can discuss ideas in depth. If your teacher indicates a certain length for the assignment, that guideline will influence how you limit the topic.

To decide whether or not your topic is adequately *limited*, check references about that topic in your local library. If whole books have been written on your topic, it is probably too general for a research paper. If you find very little information, your topic may be too limited for a research paper. For example, a topic that covers many years (the history of American poetry) or many categories or groups (famous writers) is probably too general.

Suppose you have been assigned a research paper dealing with American literature. You have enjoyed reading poems by Robert Frost and know that he is a famous American poet. You could write about his life, or you might explain a technique used in some of his poems. When you check the library, you discover that works by and about Frost occupy half of one card catalogue drawer! As a result you decide that you will find out more about Frost's poetry and write about a single aspect of his work.

Writing Practice 1

Divide a sheet of paper into two columns with the headings SUBJECTS and LIMITED TOPICS. List five general subjects that appeal to you in the first column. In the second column write five good topics for a short research paper that you have developed from the subjects in the first column. You may use subjects from the following list.

1. Invention of the bicycle
2. History of science fiction
3. Migrant workers in America
4. The development of alternative fuel sources
5. The search for utopia in American history
6. Recent space exploration
7. History of a major business or industry in your area
8. Legends about werewolves
9. History of television
10. Famous Black American writers
11. Discovery and development of nuclear energy
12. The growth of the railroad in the U.S.
13. Theories about the aging process
14. Patents for unusual inventions
15. Famous women in politics

Using the card catalogue and the *Readers' Guide* is discussed in the chapter "Library Resources."

Writing Practice 2

Use the card catalogue and the *Readers' Guide to Periodical Literature* in your library to find at least two books and two articles that have information about your research topic. On a separate sheet of paper, write the titles of the books and articles and the names of the writers.

Getting an Overview

Once you have decided on a topic, the next step is to get a general idea, or *overview*, of what is involved in that topic. If you have decided to write about some aspect of Robert Frost's poetry, for example, you might read the introduction to Frost's poetry in your textbook and the entry for Frost in a general reference work, such as *Twentieth Century Authors*.

The *Readers' Guide* and encyclopedias are also good places to locate general background information on your topic. You will need to skim through several general references that analyze Frost's poetry, sort out the viewpoints of different critics, and gain a general understanding of the poetry.

Gathering Information

The next step in the research process is to *gather information* for your paper from books and magazines, personal interviews, pamphlets, and other resources. You will probably use both *primary* and *secondary sources* in your paper. *Primary sources* are firsthand documents: an entry in Frost's journal, a poem by Robert Frost, a letter by his wife, or an interview with Frost. A *secondary source* is one that is written about some aspect of the primary source. For example, an essay about Frost's poems or a biography of Frost is a secondary source.

The Bibliography Card

At the end of the research paper, the writer attaches a list of sources, called a *bibliography*, to show the origin of the information used in the paper. Preparation of your final bibliography will be much easier if you keep a separate note card for each source you use. Each card records the information about that source's title, author, publisher, and details of publication that you will need later to compile the bibliography.

The order in which title, author, publisher, and publication details are presented in a bibliography card (and later in a bibliography) and the marks of punctuation that separate these items follow a standard form. The form used by most research paper writers is the one found in the *MLA Handbook*, published by the Modern Language Association. Although the MLA form is used in this chapter, your teacher may ask you to use one of the many other acceptable forms, instead.

The bibliography card on page 97 shows the form for a book; magazines, newspapers, pamphlets, and personal interviews have a slightly different form.

The circled number in the upper-right corner of the bibliography card identifies Poirier's book as source Number 1.

Numbering each reference work will save time later when you take notes from that source.

The following list, composed of fictitious authors and titles, shows the format for other kinds of bibliography entries.

①

*Poirier, Richard. Robert Frost: The Work of
Knowing. New York: Oxford Univ. Press, 1977.*

BOOK BY ONE AUTHOR
Nero, Caesar. *Country Fiddling.* Rome: Myth Press, 1969.

BOOK BY MORE THAN ONE AUTHOR
Straight, Samuel, and Mary Narrow. *The Perfect Pear.* Boston: Brahmin Books,
    1929.

ESSAY WITHIN A COLLECTION OF PIECES BY DIFFERENT AUTHORS
Apfel, Addams. "Moonlight Walks." In *Exercise Around the Clock.* Eds. Ichabod
    Crane and Horace Hyde. London: Fog Publications, 1898.

EDITION OF A WORK OF LITERATURE
Brunte, Charlotte. *Withering Looks.* Ed. Jane Austere. Paris: Lowe Classics, 1945.

ARTICLE IN AN ENCYCLOPEDIA OR OTHER REFERENCE WORK
Bunyan, Paul. "Raising Cattle." *Encyclopedia Animalia.* 1976 ed.

ARTICLE FROM A MONTHLY MAGAZINE
Dinmont, Dandy. "Dog Days." *Veterinarian News,* May 1980, pp. 5–10.

ARTICLE FROM A NEWSPAPER (NO AUTHOR GIVEN)
"Income Tax Reduced." *Athens Evening Star,* 14 Feb. 1981, p. 6.

REVIEW OF A FILM, BOOK, OR PLAY
Dawn, Aurora. Rev. of *Sleeper, Awake!* by I. E. Lidd. *Morpheus,* 23 Jan. 1944,
    p. 37.

INTERVIEW
Sprat, Jack. Personal interview. 11 Mar. 1983.

RADIO OR TELEVISION PROGRAM
"Touching Scenes." *Soap Opera Preview,* NBS, 12 Jan. 1979.

PAMPHLET
U.S. Cong. House. *Report on Sea Mishaps.* By Captain Ahab. Washington, D.C.:
    GPO, 1973.

If some information about a source is not available, record that fact by
writing *no author, no date of publication,* or *no place of publication* on the
bibliography card. Later, when you organize the bibliography, you will know
you did not forget to record this information.

Writing Practice 3

Prepare a bibliography card for each source you will use in your research paper or select a topic for this assignment and prepare five bibliography cards, using sources from your library.

Taking Notes

Unfortunately some students still try to write a research paper by stacking their books and magazines in front of them and writing directly from these sources. This time-consuming method usually results in a disorganized, haphazard paper since careful organization frequently requires the writer to zigzag from source to source. *Taking notes* that summarize and rephrase information from reference works is a more efficient process. With each item of information recorded separately on a small card, the writer can easily rearrange the cards into one or another order to create the best possible arrangement.

Reading Selectively

A student who tries to read and take notes on every word in every source can easily become bogged down and discouraged. Learn to read selectively and use your preliminary outline questions to decide what information is important. Examine chapter headings in the table of contents and the topics listed in the index at the back of a book to locate those sections that provide information on your topic. Scan magazine articles and chapters of books for the main idea, noticing headings, subheadings, and *italicized* words, before you read in depth. Always read the material before you take notes rather than recording as you read, since you may discover that the writer's first explanation of a term is not the best one or that the entire chapter is quickly summarized in the last few pages.

Adding Source Numbers

Before you begin to take notes on a card, place the circled bibliography card number for that source in the card's upper-right corner. For example, if *Robert Frost's Poetry and Prose* is source Number 2, every note card with information from this source should have the circled number 2 in the upper-right corner. Under the source number, place the page number(s) from which your note is taken. You may also want to put a topic heading in the upper-right corner of the card.

Writing the Note

Usually a note card summarizes or paraphrases information. *To paraphrase* information read the source several times and then write a version that restates the ideas in your own words.

Taking notes in your own words and marking all quotations carefully will ensure that you do not plagiarize an author's words or ideas. In its original Latin form, the word *plagiarism* referred to theft or kidnaping. To *plagiarize*—that is, to present another person's ideas or words as your own—is a form of theft, a dishonest practice you should conscientiously avoid.

Using your preliminary outline as a guide, record specific information related to your questions on the note card but avoid taking notes on unrelated information. For example, you may discover intriguing facts about Robert Frost's experiences as a farmer, but if your topic is limited to Frost's ideas about marriage in certain poems, you will not need this information.

You may want to write your notes in phrases rather than complete sentences or use abbreviations and symbols (*ex.* for "for example"), but be certain your notes are complete enough to understand later.

Quoting Directly from the Author

If an author's exact words are important or especially well-chosen, you can quote them on the note card. Do this sparingly, however, remembering to record the author's words exactly and to put quotation marks around them.

Notice the location of the source number, page number, and topic heading on the sample note card at the bottom of this page.

Writing Practice 4

Write note cards on the information you find in at least three sources. You may use your research paper topic, or you may want to select another topic for this assignment.

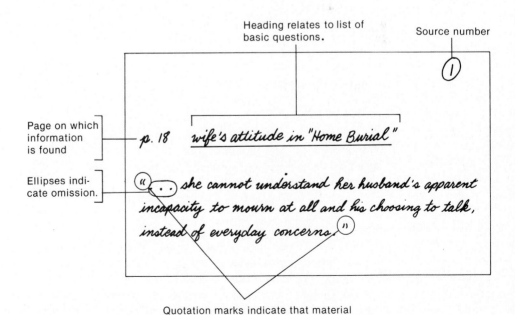

Heading relates to list of basic questions.

Source number

Page on which information is found

Ellipses indicate omission.

p. 18   *wife's attitude in "Home Burial"*

"... *she cannot understand her husband's apparent incapacity to mourn at all and his choosing to talk, instead of everyday concerns.*"

Quotation marks indicate that material is quoted directly.

Reevaluation   After reading and taking notes on all your sources, *reevaluate* your research project before you begin writing. If you have too much or too little information, it will be easier and less disappointing to revise your topic and preliminary outline or to add more specific source materials now than it will be once you have written the rough draft.

1. Have you discovered new information that changes the emphasis of your paper? Will you need to modify your topic to reflect this emphasis or add another heading to your outline?

2. Is there a question in your outline that is not answered by your note card? Should you eliminate the question, changing your emphasis slightly, or locate more information to develop the question adequately?

3. Have you recorded information unrelated to your topic? If so, set these note cards aside; perhaps you can use this information in your introduction but avoid using it where it does not fit.

The Formal Outline   Once you have reviewed your note cards and put them in stacks corresponding to your basic questions, you can prepare a *formal outline*. The *formal outline* uses Roman numerals (I, II, III), capital letters (A, B, C), and Arabic numbers (1, 2, 3) to show the order, relationship, and relative importance of the ideas in the paper.

The headings in a formal outline share a similar grammatical structure. An outline in which all the headings are stated as complete sentences is a *sentence outline*; one in which only words and phrases are used is called a *topic outline*. These two forms should not be mixed in the same outline.

The following topic outline is for a research paper on marriage relationships in three poems by Robert Frost.

I. Frost as poet of marriage
   A. Differences between male and female personalities
   B. Delicate balance necessary for good relationships
   C. Best poems about marriage
      1. "A Servant to Servants"
      2. "Home Burial"
      3. "The Death of the Hired Man"

II. Marital tensions in three poems
   A. Differences in emotional make-up
      1. Husband's strength and lack of sympathy
      2. Wife's sympathy thwarted
   B. Differences in perception of nature
      1. Husband's view
      2. Wife's view
   C. The ideal marriage

III. "A Servant to Servants"
  A. Wife
      1. Anguish over husband's indifference
      2. Sensitivity to nature
      3. Morbid fantasies
  B. Husband
      1. View of nature as way to wealth
      2. Insensitivity to wife's breakdown
  C. Wife as speaker
      1. Submission to husband evident in words
      2. Inability to communicate

IV. "Home Burial"
  A. Wife
      1. Refusal to accept child's death
      2. Anger at husband's attitude
      3. Negative attitude toward nature
  B. Husband
      1. Work as salve for grief
      2. Attempts to reach out to wife
      3. Acceptance of death as part of nature
  C. Husband as speaker
      1. Dialogue to wife
      2. Rejection by wife

V. "The Death of the Hired Man"
  A. Attitudes toward Silas
      1. Husband's attitude
         a. Silas's responsibility
         b. Expense of boarding Silas
         c. His skill in loading hay
      2. Wife's attitude of mercy and compassion
  B. Definition of *home*
      1. Husband's definition
      2. Wife's definition
  C. Delicate balance in relationship

Notice in the preceding sample outline that there are always two or more divisions under a heading or none at all. The divisions (or subheadings) are only used when a broad topic is broken down into smaller topics; when the major topic cannot be divided into two or more parts, there is no reason for a subheading.

The following example shows the second division in sentence form.

II. Marital tensions are depicted in the three poems.
  A. There are differences in the emotional make-up of husbands and wives.
      1. The husband has strength and a lack of sympathy.
      2. The wife's sympathy seems thwarted.
  B. There are differences in the way the men and women perceive nature.
      1. The husband's view is more practical.
      2. The wife's view is more sensitive.
  C. The ideal marriage requires a delicate balance.

Writing Practice 5

Write either a formal sentence outline or a topic outline for a research paper on your research topic, using information from your note cards.

The Rough Draft

Qualities of good exposition are discussed in the chapter "Writing Exposition: the Essay."

The next step is to write a *rough*, or *first*, *draft* of the research paper, using the formal outline and note cards.

Since a research paper is a longer essay, it should possess all the characteristics of a well-developed expository essay. The introduction, which should engage and hold the reader's attention, should also introduce the central idea, or thesis statement.

Each paragraph in the body of the paper should be restricted to one idea. This central idea should be adequately and clearly developed with examples, facts and statistics, the steps in a process, or other methods of paragraph development.

Transition devices should be used between sentences and paragraphs to help the reader move from idea to idea and to show the relationships between these ideas.

The conclusion should restate the paper's central idea in an interesting way and reveal the significance of the research.

The term *rough* indicates that this draft will not be a polished, flawless product. At this stage you will want to focus on presenting your ideas in clear, well-organized sentences and paragraphs. In the final draft you can concentrate more carefully on spelling, punctuation, grammar, and the reorganization of weak sentences or paragraphs.

Writing your rough draft will be easier if your note cards are organized to correspond with your outline. You may find that some of your notes do not fit the final organization of your paper or that you need more details to develop your topic. Do not be afraid to omit or add information to improve the quality of your paper.

Two important parts of writing the rough draft for a research paper are incorporating the quoted material you plan to use and adding footnotes.

Using Quotations

If you plan to use an author's exact words in your research paper, you will need to know the procedures for inserting quotations in the paper. Long quotations, usually more than three lines of poetry or five lines of prose, are set apart from the body of the paper. Rather than dropping the quotation into the paper abruptly, introduce it with a short statement followed by a colon. Any of the following statements could be used to introduce a quotation.

1. The following comment by President Ronald Reagan appeared in *Time* magazine:

2. In *The Age of Innocence* Edith Wharton wrote these words:

3. Commenting on Twain's use of dialect in *Huckleberry Finn*, Fadiman makes this observation:

4. A noted critic of Dickinson's poetry makes the following statement:

The long quotation is then indented ten spaces from the left-hand margin. If you write your paper in longhand, be certain that your reader knows you are quoting directly by making the indentation obvious and by introducing the quotation. Because this special form indicates that the passage is a quotation, the quotation marks at the beginning and end of the passage are omitted.

In addition to the similar narrative structure, Thompson also notes:

> . . . there is the subtle indirection of Frost's dramatic method. So much more is suggested than is stated. Somehow the thoughts and emotions are embodied in a context of words which suggest not only a physical setting—a room, a road, a garden, a farm, a grove, a hill—but also a psychological setting.

Short quotations of fewer than three lines are not indented; quotation marks at the beginning and end of such a passage indicate that the words are a quotation. A short quotation should not upset the smooth flow of the sentence or paragraph to which it is added, as the following example shows.

It has been noted that "Frost's families are man and wife units" and if something complicates the relationship "special things happen."[1]

Adding Footnotes

Footnotes were originally placed at the bottom, or foot, of the paper to tell readers where to locate important information or exact quotations used in the paper. However, today they are often added on a separate page at the end of the paper. Regardless of where your footnotes appear, remember that all quoted material, unusual facts, and authors' original ideas must be footnoted. Unique information developed by a particular author is footnoted even if you do not quote that information word for word. However, when several sources mention the same facts or ideas, the information is considered general knowledge and does not require a footnote. For example, it has been generally acknowledged that Robert Frost is one of the great American poets, so that information would not be footnoted. You also need not footnote the dates of Frost's birth or death, since that information is undisputed fact.

As you write your rough draft, you can add the footnote immediately after the information to which it refers or put it on a separate card or piece of paper and number it. Later, the footnotes can be moved to the bottom of the page or assembled at the end of the paper, according to which style is being used. Remember the following important points.

1. Footnoted material in the paper is numbered consecutively (1, 2, 3, etc.).

2. A footnote with the corresponding number appears at the bottom of the page on which it occurs or at the end of the paper.

3. The *superscripts*, or slightly raised numbers in front of the footnotes, identify the material footnoted, telling the reader which footnote to consult for the source of that information.

4. Four lines of space separate the last line of text and the first footnote on the page.

5. The first line of the footnote is indented five spaces.

6. The footnote numbers are raised by half a line.

7. One space separates the raised footnote number and the footnote itself.

8. Information within the footnote is single-spaced; the footnotes are separated from one another by a double space.

9. An abbreviated form is used for the second and all later footnotes referring to a source already footnoted.

The following sample footnotes show the MLA form for various sources of information; your teacher may ask you to use this form or another one. Notice that the order and punctuation used in footnotes differ from that used in a bibliography.

BOOK BY ONE AUTHOR
[1] Caesar Nero, *Country Fiddling* (Rome: Myth Press, 1969), p. 2.

BOOK BY MORE THAN ONE AUTHOR
[2] Samuel Straight and Mary Narrow, *The Perfect Pear* (Boston: Brahmin Books, 1929), p. 69.

ESSAY WITHIN A COLLECTION OF PIECES BY DIFFERENT AUTHORS
[3] Addams Apfel, "Moonlight Walks," in *Exercise Around the Clock*, eds. Ichabod Crane and Horace Hyde (London: Fog Publications, 1898), p. 1200.

EDITION OF A WORK OF LITERATURE
[4] Charlotte Brunte, *Withering Looks*, ed. Jane Austere (Paris: Lowe Classics, 1945), p. 21.

ARTICLE IN AN ENCYCLOPEDIA OR OTHER REFERENCE WORK
[5] Paul Bunyan, "Raising Cattle," *Encyclopedia Animalia*, 1976 ed., p. 99.

ARTICLE FROM A MONTHLY MAGAZINE
[6] Dandy Dinmont, "Dog Days," *Veterinarian News*, May 1980, pp. 5–10.

ARTICLE FROM A NEWSPAPER (NO AUTHOR GIVEN)
[7] "Income Tax Reduced," *Athens Evening Star*, 14 Feb. 1981, p. 6.

REVIEW OF A FILM, BOOK, OR PLAY
[8] Aurora Dawn, rev. of *Sleeper, Awake!* by I. E. Lidd, *Morpheus*, 23 Jan. 1944, p. 37.

INTERVIEW
[9] Personal interview with Jack Sprat, 11 March, 1983.

RADIO OR TELEVISION PROGRAM
[10] "Touching Scenes," *Soap Opera Preview*, NBS, 12 Jan. 1979, p. 64.

PAMPHLET
[11] U.S. Cong. House, *Report on Sea Mishaps*, by Captain Ahab, Washington, D.C.: GPO, 1973, p. 3.

Since your first footnote for a source gives complete information, the second and all later references to that same source use an abbreviated form. Usually this abbreviated form includes only the author's last name and the page number for the information you are footnoting. If you use two books by the same author, add a shortened form of the book's title after the author's last name. The following fragment from a footnote page shows how this abbreviated form is used.

[1] David A. Sohn and Richard H. Tyre, *Frost: The Poet and His Poetry* (New York: Bantam Books, 1967), p. 44.

[2] Sohn, p. 48.

[3] Lawrance Thompson, *Fire and Ice: The Art and Thought of Robert Frost*, 2nd ed. (1942 rpt., New York: Russell and Russell, 1961), p. 48.

[4] Lawrance Thompson, ed., *Selected Letters of Robert Frost* (New York: Holt, Rinehart and Winston, Inc., 1964), pp. 158–159.

[5] Thompson, *Fire and Ice*, p. 20.

Writing Practice 6

Use your note cards and formal outline to write the rough draft of your research paper. Add footnotes to your paper wherever they are needed and be certain to insert quotations correctly.

The Bibliography

The final *bibliography* includes only those sources you consulted for your research paper. Before you begin to write, check to be certain that the information on your bibliography cards is accurate and complete. Then arrange your cards alphabetically by the author's last name. If no author is listed for a source, alphabetize it by the first major word in the title. Sometimes, sources are subdivided by types (books, articles, films, pamphlets) each alphabetized under a separate heading. This format is only used if there is an extensive bibliography.

Taking the information directly from your cards, write the bibliography on a separate sheet of paper. If an entry requires more than one line, indent the second and all other lines five spaces. If you use two sources written by the same author, do not rewrite the author's name in the second listing; instead, use a long dash in place of the name for all other sources by that author. The following example shows the listings for two books by Lawrance Thompson.

Thompson, Lawrance. *Robert Frost*. Minneapolis: University of Minnesota Press, 1959.

———. *Robert Frost: The Early Years* 1874–1915. New York: Holt, Rinehart and Winston, Inc., 1966.

Look closely at the sample bibliography on page 113. Notice that only the listings for magazine and newspaper articles indicate the page numbers on which the article can be found; no page numbers are listed for books.

The bibliography form in this section conforms to the MLA style, but your teacher may prefer that you use another accepted style.

The Final Draft

Before you begin the final draft of your research paper, revise your rough draft carefully. Read it through several times. Have you covered all the important points about your topic? Are you satisfied that you have arranged the information in the best possible order? Take out any details that do not relate to your major outline points.

The following is a rough draft of a paragraph in the research paper "Robert Frost's Poetry of Marriage" on pages 107–113. As you read it, notice the deletions and corrections the writer has made. The notes in the left-hand margin explain the changes.

Combining the first two sentences eliminates repetition.

Nice is too vague. Details unrelated to the main idea of the paragraph are removed.

Beginning with a prepositional phrase creates sentence variety.

Sentence fragment is corrected.

> Perhaps more than any other poet, Robert Frost is associated with the beauty of the New England landscape. ~~He is associated~~ with swinging birches, mending walls, apple-picking, the woods on a snowy evening. However, there is another Frost, the poet not of nature, but of marriage. The marriages in Frost's poems are rarely as ~~nice~~ tranquil as his New England landscapes. ~~Three of Frost's best poems about marriage appear in his early collection North of Boston.~~ Often, though not always, the husbands and wives in these poems are emotionally separate and lonely even though they live in the same house. ~~The husbands and wives~~ In his poems of marriage Frost examines the differences between the male and female personalities, and he reveals his ideas about the delicate balance of the two ~~N~~ecessary for a successful relationship.

In revising the preceding paragraph, the writer decided to remove several pieces of information. Even though this information relates to the topic, it detracts from the paragraph as a whole by breaking up the flow of ideas. While it is difficult to take out details you have carefully researched, in revision it is important to think of the general organization of ideas and delete any information that does not contribute to the paragraph's main idea and the paper as a whole.

Writing Practice 7

Using the Checklist for Revising the Research Report that follows and any suggestions your teacher may add, revise your rough draft and write a final version of your research report. Remember that revision is not a patchwork process. In your final draft readers should not be able to tell where you have made changes. As a final step proofread your paper, using the proofreading checklist on page 17.

Checklist for Revising the Research Report

1. The subject is limited to a topic that can be developed in a research paper.

2. The topic is adequately developed with factual information from outside sources.

3. Each item of information in the final paper explains or develops the topic in some way.

4. Important theories, unusual or specific facts, and quotations are footnoted.

5. Information in footnotes is ordered correctly, and footnotes follow a standard form, such as MLA.

6. Information in the bibliography is ordered correctly according to a standard form.

7. If quotations are used, they are placed correctly in the paper.

As a further aid, use the Checklist for Revising an Expository Composition on page 91.

Reading a Research Paper

Robert Frost's Poetry of Marriage

Perhaps more than any other poet, Robert Frost is associated with the beauty of the New England landscape—swinging birches, mending walls, apple-picking, the woods on a snowy evening. There is another Frost, however, the poet not of nature but of marriage. The marriages in Frost's poetry are rarely as tranquil as his New England landscapes. Often, although not always, the husbands and wives in these poems are emotionally separate and lonely even though they live in the same house. In his poems of marriage Frost examines the differences between the male and female personalities, and he reveals his ideas about the delicate balance of the two necessary for a successful relationship.

Three of Frost's best poems about marriage appear in his early collection *North of Boston*, which was first published in 1914, when Frost was forty. The poems are "A Servant to Servants," "Home Burial," and "The Death of the Hired Man." These poems reveal married couples in conflict, but they also convey Frost's ideal of marriage as a harmony. The first two of these poems, "A Servant to Servants" and "Home Burial," emphasize the misery of marriage partners who cannot communicate their emotional needs to each other. The third poem, "The Death of the Hired Man," also explores a situation of domestic discord. In this poem, however, conflict leads not to paralysis but to resolution, as Frost beautifully evokes an ideal of perfect understanding and sympathy between husband and wife.

All three poems dramatize marital tensions arising out of the differences between the sexes. The husband in each poem is strong in being self-reliant and hard-working. However, there is a negative side to this strength; the husbands are considerably less sensitive and imaginative than their wives. The sensitivity of the wives, however, has in most instances been thwarted in marriage. Except in the last poem, "The Death of the Hired Man," the women have had their spirits broken by the loneliness, poverty, and physical hardship of their lives. It is notable that none of the wives in these three poems have children or jobs that take them out of the home. They are obliged to adapt to their loneliness and isolation.

Frost also reveals a powerful difference in the way his men and women perceive the landscape. Frequently, the sensitivity of the wives is shown in their poetic awareness of nature's beauty. The husbands, on the other hand, tend to view the landscape in purely economic terms. For them the land is the way they make their living. The men are unimaginative and blunted in their relation to nature as, for the most part, they are in their relation to their wives.

Frost's purpose, however, is not to portray one sex as superior to the other. Rather, his ideal is a reconciliation of the differences that separate men and women. He portrays the delicate balance and harmony of relationships in which these differences are respected, and the discord that results when either the male or female personality dominates the other. Discussing the female-male attitudes in Frost's poetry, Elaine Barry points out that the poet does not seem to take sides in presenting these two attitudes. Rather, Frost sees the male and female attitudes as one aspect of the tension and opposition that exists throughout nature and human society.

> . . . he often dramatizes (this polarization and tension) through separate voices. Often the two opposing voices are those of a man and a woman, sometimes creative, sometimes destructive in their opposition. At their best, they are complementary rather than opposing principles.[1]

In "A Servant to Servants" the wife has been driven nearly mad by isolation, drudgery, and her husband's indifference. Her speech expresses her anguish:

> . . . It seems to me
> I can't express my feelings any more
> Than I can raise my voice or want to lift
> My hand . . . .
> It's got so I don't even know for sure
> Whether I *am* glad, sorry, or anything.
> There's nothing but a voice-like left inside
> That seems to tell me how I ought to feel
> And would feel if I wasn't gone all wrong.[2]

As Elizabeth Isaacs writes, the woman has become "a mere mechanism no longer able to think coherently, feel sensitively, or act defensively."[3]

This is not to say, however, that the wife of "A Servant to Servants" was not once sensitive and imaginative. Even now her imagination lives, although

Footnotes may also be numbered in sequence, beginning with 1 on each page. Use the style your teacher prefers.

[1] Elaine Barry, *Robert Frost* (New York: Frederick Ungar, 1973), p. 76.

[2] Robert Frost, *Complete Poems of Robert Frost* (New York: Holt, Rinehart, and Winston, 1964), p. 82. All further references to this work appear in the text.

[3] Elizabeth Isaacs, *An Introduction to Robert Frost* (Denver: Alan Swallow, 1962), p. 131.

directed to morbid and grotesque fantasies. Once, too, with her sensitivity to nature she thrilled to the beauty of the lake five miles from her home. Even now "I see it's a fair, pretty sheet of water, / Our Willoughby!" But her capacity for response to the beauty of nature has been dulled as she has been crushed by her lack of love and by over-work, "doing/Things over and over that just won't stay done."

Her husband Len takes a different view of nature. He has built tourist cabins along the lake's edge and sees "Our Willoughby" as a way to get rich if only the two of them will just keep working at it. Elaine Barry characterizes him well:

> Len is the archetypal Yankee, pragmatic and self-reliant ("He looks on the bright side of everything/ Including me"; "He says the best way out is always through"; "He's into everything in town"). But he is also insensitive . . . to his wife's incipient breakdown ("He thinks I'll be all right/ With doctoring").[4]

These quotations, and everything else the reader learns about Len, are learned from his wife's words. Her submission to his iron will is shown in the fact that what she speaks of most frequently are *his* dreams, opinions, and attitudes rather than her own:

> Len says one steady pull more ought to do it.
> He says the best way out is always through.
> And I agree to that, or in so far
> As that I can see no way out but through. . . .

(p. 83)

Readers of the poem learn a good deal about Len even though he is not a speaker. As in most of Frost's marriage poems, however, more is revealed about the wife. That is because hers is the only voice in the poem. In "A Servant to Servants" the wife is speaking to a group of people camping on land rented out by her husband. The campers are a silent audience. Although the woman's speech is addressed to them, as if to open a dialogue, she speaks as if to herself alone, expressing her most secret thoughts. The wife is unburdening herself of pent-up feelings, but she no more truly communicates with the campers than with her husband.

In another study of a marriage, "Home Burial," the husband and wife have the same male-female traits as in "A Servant to Servants." The husband is realistic, practical, and less emotionally vulnerable. The wife is emotionally charged, sensitive, and directed entirely by her feelings. "Home Burial," how-ever, reverses the situation of "Servant to Servants." Now it is the husband who senses the conflict and tries to heal the relationship, and the wife who resists communication.

The wife in "Home Burial" is deeply disturbed. Her suffering grows out of her continuing grief over the early death of her child. The child had been the first-born, and there is no sign in the poem that this couple has had other children to replace the lost one. Rather, the death of the first child has driven them apart so that they can hardly talk to each other.

The wife's coldness to her husband—she "stiffens and shrinks" at his approach—expresses her bitter conviction that he has not really cared about the child's death:

[4] Barry, p. 64.

'If you had any feelings, you that dug
With your own hand—how could you?—his little grave;
I saw you from that very window there,
Making the gravel leap and leap in air,
Leap up, like that, like that, and land so lightly
And roll back down the mound beside the hole.
I thought, Who is that man? I don't know you. . . .'

(p. 71)

As Elizabeth Isaacs says about these lines: "The fact that his spade could leap and leap and turn over with its usual dexterity a carefully piled little grave is for her a pure desecration of the love that once created the child and now buries it."[5]

The wife's interpretation is ungenerous, because the husband by no means is uncaring. Instead, he repeatedly reaches out to his wife:

'Let me into your grief. I'm not so much
Unlike other folks as your standing there
Apart would make me out. Give me my chance.'

(p. 71)

Despite his appeals, he is repeatedly rebuffed. When he says to his wife, "There's something I should like to ask you, dear," she replies, "You don't know how to ask it."

The wife is convinced that her husband has not truly grieved. For her a grief that passes away is no grief at all. She cries out, "I won't have grief so/ If I can change it. Oh, I won't, I won't!" Elaine Barry rightly observes that the wife is being self-pitying in not acknowledging that grief can have many expressions and that the husband's grim concentration on the routine of physical work is one of them.[6]

That grim concentration mirrors the husband's general attitude to nature. He has the healthy, matter-of-fact view of a man who lives close to the soil. He accepts death as a part of life and turns to hard physical labor to soften the pain of his loss. His attitude toward his child's death, like his attitude toward nature, may be limited, even unimaginative, but it is healthier than his wife's unwillingness to surrender her grief.

The perversity of the wife in "Home Burial" is reflected in her attitude toward nature. Her voice is filled with revulsion and horror as she describes the gravel that leaped in the air as her husband dug the child's grave. She speaks of the fresh earth that "stains" his shoes, and she concludes that "the world's evil." In perceiving nature as evil, however, she is blind to the ordinary cycles of nature. That blindness may be seen in the way she reproaches her husband for his apparent lack of response to their child's death:

'I can repeat the very words you were saying.
"Three foggy mornings and one rainy day
Will rot the best birch fence a man can build."
Think of it, talk like that at such a time!
What had how long it takes a birch to rot
To do with what was in the darkened parlor. . . .'

(p. 72)

[5] Isaacs, p. 144.
[6] Barry, p. 77.

In fact, it has a great deal to do. The wife willfully misunderstands her husband's grieving and what his words signify. Richard Poirier clarifies that significance:

> With (the wife's) desire to stop everything in the interest of mourning the death of an infant, she cannot understand (her husband's) apparent incapacity to mourn at all and his choosing to talk, instead, of everyday concerns. She does not see that this is his only way of managing grief, ...[7]

Thus, as Poirier suggests, there is poetry after all in the grieving of this most unpoetic of men. The husband's poetry is the poetry of the possible, of the acceptance of life in all its changes.

"A Servant to Servants" is in its form a personal confession. The wife's monologue is conditioned by the presence of the campers, but she is talking mostly for and to herself. "Home Burial" differs in being an invitation to dialogue, the husband's invitation to his wife. The invitation, however, is rejected. At the end the wife walks out the door despite her husband's begging her to stay and talk some more.

In the last of these poems, "The Death of the Hired Man," there is a joining rather than a leaving, and a husband and wife achieve perfect harmony. "The Death of the Hired Man" is about the different attitudes of a husband and wife toward Silas, an old farmhand who has worked for them in the past. Silas had been very irresponsible in his comings and goings, but now, sick and possibly unable ever to work again, he has come back to them. The question is whether to let him stay.

At first, the husband, Warren, seems unshakeable in his decision not to take Silas back. He says flatly: "I'll not have him back." Warren remembers that Silas left him in the middle of haying season, breaking the agreement between them. Also, he points out practical reasons why Silas is not welcome: Silas has relatives he can turn to, and Warren doubts that Silas is capable now of enough work to justify the expense of room and board. As with Frost's other males, Warren's response to nature is linked to his work. This is the basis of Warren's grudging praise for the hired man's "one accomplishment," his skill in loading hay:

> He bundles every forkful in its place
> And tags and numbers it for future reference,
> So he can find and easily dislodge it
> In the unloading. Silas does that well.
> He takes it out in bunches like big birds' nests.

(p. 52)

Warren's wife, Mary, has a very different relation to nature and to Silas. She expresses the same sensitivity and heightened emotion as Frost's other female characters. In the first line she is pictured "musing on the lamp-flame." Later, she spreads her apron to the moonlight, touches the morning glory strings, and contemplates whether a "small sailing cloud/ Will hit or miss the moon." Correspondingly, if Warren's attitude to Silas emphasizes justice,

---

[7]Richard Poirier, *Robert Frost: The Work of Knowing* (New York: Oxford University Press, 1977), p. 130.

Mary's emphasizes mercy and compassion. She intercedes with Warren on the old man's behalf without, however, making for an ugly confrontation, as in the preceding poems.

Masculine fairness and strength, feminine tenderness and diplomacy: here these differences complement each other. Mary's tone is gentle and sympathetic, toward Warren as well as Silas, as she seeks to make Warren share the pity she feels:

> . . . he hurt my heart the way he lay
> And rolled his old head on the sharp-edged chair-back.
> You must go in and see what you can do.
> I made the bed up for him there tonight.
> You'll be surprised at him—how much he's broken.
> His working days are done; I'm sure of it.
>
> (p. 54)

While husband and wife disagree, their conversation never suggests the harshness of "Home Burial" or the despair of "A Servant to Servants." Disagreeing with Mary, Warren only "mocks gently." As in "Home Burial," the couple's conversation occurs on a set of steps. These, however, are not the steps of a claustrophobic house, but porch steps that link them to the beauty of a summer night. They sit side by side, Mary drawing Warren down beside her. Gently, also, she draws him away from his definition of home as "the place where they have to take you in" toward her more generous definition of home as "something you somehow haven't to deserve."

There is something almost magical about the wife's gentleness, her ability to soften the man's rigor. Mary's tenderness recalls William Dean Howells' observation, in 1915, that Frost is "manliest in penetrating to the heart of womanhood."[8] Perhaps Howells had this poem in mind, for out of conflict the wife is able to create harmony. Frost symbolizes this harmony, and the wife's effect on her husband, in musical terms:

> . . . She put out her hand
> Among the harp-like morning-glory strings,
> Taut with the dew from garden bed to eaves,
> As if she played unheard some tenderness
> That wrought upon him beside her in the night.
>
> (p. 52)

"The Death of the Hired Man" is the fulfillment of Frost's study of marriage. In "A Servant to Servants" and "Home Burial" the differences between wife and husband make for polarization and isolation. The marriage partners stand to each other as strangers. They are static, trapped in their respective prison-houses. "The Death of the Hired Man" suggests a happier possibility for reconciling the differences between the sexes. The wife proceeds by way of gentle persuasion. She is able to escape from the cage of her own personality to reach out both to a sick old man and to her well-meaning but skeptical husband. Warren, for his part is able and willing to be touched, emotionally and physically, by his wife. Her difference is precious to him as his difference is precious to her. They achieve a remarkable harmony, a unity of opposites.

[8] Quoted in Lawrance Thompson, *Robert Frost: The Years of Triumph* (New York: Holt, Rinehart, and Winston, 1966), p. 57.

Bibliography

Barry, Elaine. *Robert Frost.* New York: Frederick Ungar Publishing Company, 1973.

Brooks, Cleanth and Robert Penn Warren. *Conversations on the Craft of Poetry.* New York: Holt, Rinehart & Winston, Inc., 1961.

Cook, Reginald. *Robert Frost: A Living Voice.* Amherst: The University of Massachusetts Press, 1974.

Frost Centennial Essays. The Committee on The Frost Centennial of the University of Southern Mississippi. Jackson: University Press of Mississippi, 1974.

Frost, Robert. *Complete Poems of Robert Frost.* New York: Holt, Rinehart & Winston, Inc., 1964.

Frost, Robert. *Robert Frost Reads His Poetry.* New York: Caedmon Records, Inc. TC 1060, 1957.

Greiner, Donald J. ed. *Robert Frost: The Poet and His Critics.* Chicago: American Library Association, 1974.

Hughes, Robert and Charlotte Zwerin. *Robert Frost: A Lover's Quarrel With the World.* New York: Holt, Rinehart & Winston, Inc., and WGBH Education Foundation, Boston, 1963.

Isaacs, Elizabeth. *An Introduction to Robert Frost.* Denver: Alan Swallow, 1962.

Poirier, Richard. *Robert Frost: The Work of Knowing.* New York: Oxford University Press, 1977.

"A Portrait in Sound," Writ. William Pritchard, *A Question of Place.* Sound Portraits of 20th Century Americans. NPR, 26 Oct. 1980.

Sohn, David A. and Richard H. Tyre. *Frost: The Poet and His Poetry.* New York: Bantam Books, 1967.

Thompson, Lawrance. *Fire and Ice: The Art and Thought of Robert Frost.* New York: Russell and Russell Publishers, 1961.

———. *Robert Frost, The Years of Triumph, 1915–1938.* New York: Holt, Rinehart & Winston, Inc., 1970.

———. ed. *Selected Letters of Robert Frost.* New York: Holt, Rinehart & Winston, Inc., 1964.

6 Logic and Writing

Experts who study human thought identify two types of logical thinking: *inductive* and *deductive*. In this chapter you will study the principles of inductive and deductive reasoning. You will also learn some of the ways in which thinking can be illogical, so that you can recognize faulty reasoning in arguments directed toward you and in your own thinking and writing. The ability to "think straight"—to arrive at logical or sound conclusions on which you can base your actions—is a skill that you can use for the rest of your life.

Inductive Reasoning

Inductive reasoning begins with a series of specific facts or data and moves to a general statement or conclusion based on the evidence.

Suppose that on three different occasions you tried to take a photograph indoors without a flash. When your film was developed, you found that no pictures resulted from these shots. You can summarize the data in the following way.

Evidence: Photo A taken indoors without a flash did not come out.
Photo B taken indoors without a flash did not come out.
Photo C taken indoors without a flash did not come out.

You might go on indefinitely taking photographs without a flash, or you might make the following conclusion based on your experience.

Conclusion: All photographs taken indoors without a flash will not come out.

In making the preceding conclusion, you have made what is known as *the inductive leap*—moving from a series of specific facts (about particular events, objects, or people) to a general statement (about a whole class of events, objects, or people). If it were not for the inductive leap, you might go on gathering evidence forever without reaching a conclusion.

Consider another example of inductive reasoning. Suppose that you had made the following observations.

Evidence: Robins have feathers.
              Sparrows have feathers.
              Ostriches have feathers.
              Owls have feathers.
              Hummingbirds have feathers.

From this series of data about specific kinds of birds, you can make the inductive leap and arrive at the following conclusion.

Conclusion: All birds have feathers.

Defining Terms

At this point you need to understand some important terms associated with inductive reasoning.

An *argument* is a logical presentation of ideas.

In an inductive argument a *population* is the whole class of events, objects, or persons being studied.

Any population—not just people—may be the subject of inductive reasoning. For example, you may be stating an argument about taking photos without flashbulbs, or about scuba divers, living in high-rise apartment buildings, peace treaties, tulips, or people who own poodles. The evidence in your argument must be restricted to the population under study. This means that if you are gathering information about the habits of migrating wild ducks, any evidence that you gather about domesticated ducks will not be meaningful or useful in your argument.

The *sampling* consists of the specific cases out of the entire population that you are able to observe.

Two things are important about the sampling: its size and its randomness. The larger the sampling, the more likely you are to arrive at a sound conclusion. As far as possible, a sampling should be chosen at random without any previous selection or grouping. For instance, if you were surveying a group of twelfth-graders to see how they felt about the draft, a random sampling (perhaps every fifth student on your class list in alphabetical order) would give you a much more accurate sample of the opinion of twelfth-graders than would a sampling of all of your friends, who are likely to have similar opinions.

A *generalization* is the conclusion in an inductive argument.

A generalization makes a statement about the whole population based on the specific data or facts.

How the Evidence Supports the Conclusion

In inductive reasoning the specific facts or evidence can never be considered absolute proof that the conclusion is true. You could, for example, continue taking unsuccessful photographs indoors without a flash for fifty days, or you could examine every single bird in the United States to see if it has feathers; yet theoretically you could not deny with *absolute* certainty that on the fifty-first day you might take a successful photograph without a flash or that there might be a featherless bird somewhere in Australia or the Philippines. While the evidence in an inductive argument may not *prove* the conclusion, however, the evidence does *support* the conclusion—to a greater or lesser degree. If the evidence is very strong, the conclusion is a sound one. If the evidence is weak, the conclusion is not sound.

Consider the following example. How sound is the conclusion?

A wealthy widow with a reputation for being extremely unpleasant has been found murdered on her estate. In trying to find her murderer, Detective Kronowitz is, for the moment, thinking about the butler.

Evidence: The butler had no known motive for murdering the widow. In fact, with the widow dead the butler would be likely to lose his job—a situation that could be considered a motive for keeping her alive.

The butler was seen by many witnesses in the village at the established time of the murder.

The murderer apparently entered the house by way of a narrow chimney, which the butler, who weighs 250 pounds, could not possibly have squeezed himself through.

Conclusion: The butler did not murder the wealthy widow.

Based on the evidence, Detective Kronowitz's conclusion seems sound; he is probably right in looking for another suspect. Remember, however, that the evidence cannot be said to *prove* that the butler is not the murderer. Rather, it lends support and probability to the conclusion that the butler did not commit the murder.

The Inductive Method

Much of what you learn about life you will learn inductively, drawing general conclusions on the basis of your own experiences and observations. Scientists, too, use inductive reasoning. Many of the laws that help us to understand how the natural world works were arrived at inductively. Most research scientists today follow the inductive method, which scientists used hundreds of years ago to discover how our solar system works and what elements make up our world. The inductive method involves making countless specific observations before formulating a conclusion based on the evidence.

In the *inductive method*—the method of discovery—three basic steps can be identified:

1. Gather the data.
2. Weigh the evidence carefully.
3. State the conclusion.

Evaluating an Inductive Argument

Suppose that someone tried to persuade you to a course of action by means of an inductive argument. How could you judge whether or not the argument was sound? Remember that reasons in an inductive argument are the evidence presented to support the conclusion. Your first task is to identify both the evidence and the conclusion. In a long argument or speech, it is not always easy to spot the reasons or to identify the conclusion. Reasons are often introduced by words such as *since, because, for,* and *as shown by.* Words such as *therefore, hence, in conclusion, indicates that,* and *consequently* signal that a conclusion will follow. It is helpful to outline the argument, listing each reason separately.

The following paragraph, for example, is a sample argument.

> Community leaders have been trying to drum up support for the $2.5 billion mass transit bond issue, which will come before the voters in November. Unfortunately the election occurs at a time when most economists agree the country is deep in a recession. No matter what benefits the community leaders claim the transit system will bring the city, experience has shown that during times of recession, voters almost invariably defeat measures they consider "excess government spending." Inflation and unemployment are the voters' main concerns according to a *Tribune* poll of 300 adults published in this week's newspaper. Sixty per cent of those polled said they were against the bond issue; only twenty per cent supported it, and another twenty per cent were undecided. It seems likely, therefore, that the bond issue is doomed.

The following is an outline of the argument.

Evidence: Most economists agree that the country is in a recession.

In a recession voters almost invariably defeat "excess government spending" measures.

Inflation and unemployment are the voters' main concerns according to a poll of 300 adults.

Sixty per cent of those polled were against the bond issue; twenty per cent supported it, and twenty per cent were undecided.

Conclusion: The bond issue will be defeated.

Before you decide whether the conclusion is sound or not, some further questions might occur to you: What is the source of the statement that "most economists" agree that the country is in a recession? How many economists agree, and how many disagree? What does "almost invariably" really mean? Exactly what are the statistics on the defeat of bond issues during times of recession? How were the 300 people polled by the newspaper selected? Was it a random sampling? Were different racial, ethnic, and socioeconomic groups adequately represented in the sampling? In short—do not believe everything you read or hear. Every reason given in an argument should be examined critically.

The following guidelines may be helpful to you in evaluating an inductive argument and in trying to write one.

1. What is the conclusion of the argument?
2. What evidence is offered to support the conclusion?
3. How much evidence has been gathered?
4. What is the source of the evidence?
5. Is the conclusion carefully worded to reflect the evidence or does it attempt to make a statement for which there is no adequate evidence?
6. Does the argument contain any fallacies? (See pages 124–131.)

Exercise 1

For each of the following situations, write a conclusion based on the specific evidence presented.

1. For the past three years you have grown tomatoes in your vegetable garden. Each year you have planted six tomato plants and have watered, fertilized, and sprayed them equally. The only difference has been that three of the plants were grown in full sunlight and three in partial sunlight. You have noticed that the plants in full sunlight produced significantly more tomatoes than the plants in partial sunlight.

2. Your neighbors' newspapers have been piling up in front of their door for the past two days, and you can see a light on all day and all night in their window. Their dog, who is normally quiet, has been howling and barking for two days. No one answers the door or the telephone.

3. You have been having a great deal of trouble memorizing dates for your American history class. During the past three weeks, however, you have tried a new technique. You have studied for three hours on the evening before the exam. You have written down the dates and practiced saying them aloud. On the past three weekly tests your grades have gone up from a *C* to two *B*'s and a *B* + .

Exercise 2

For each of the following generalizations, add one of the following limiting words to make the generalization sound. Think about the evidence you would need to support each generalization. (Note that some of the items state opinions, not facts.) Write your answers on a sheet of paper numbered 1–10.

All   Most   Few   No   Some

1. _____ swimmers can float.
2. _____ men are good cooks.

3. _____ human beings can live underwater for extended periods of time without artificial apparatus.

4. _____ elected government officials are sincerely dedicated to serving the public.

5. _____ human beings live to be 185 years old.

6. _____ birds can fly.

7. _____ two-year-old children are able to learn a second language.

8. _____ women want to marry and have children.

9. _____ twelfth-graders know what careers they want to follow.

10. _____ human beings have basic needs, such as food, shelter, clothing, and love.

Exercise 3

Each of the following is a conclusion in an inductive argument. For each generalization tell what data you would need as evidence to support each conclusion. If you disagree with the conclusion, reword it to your satisfaction.

1. Women are as intelligent as men.

2. Young men under the age of twenty-five are the cause of more car accidents than any other group of drivers.

3. Cigarette smoking is a major cause of lung cancer.

4. Too many cooks spoil the broth.

5. Water freezes at a temperature of thirty-two degrees Fahrenheit.

6. In order to develop into mentally healthy adults, children need to have a positive self-image (think of themselves as worthy, good people), which comes mainly from their parents.

7. In this community the average rainfall is greatest during March.

8. People who live in cities are less inclined to help a stranger than are people who live in rural areas.

Deductive Reasoning

Inductive reasoning begins with specific facts and then moves to a general conclusion.

Deductive reasoning begins with a general or universal statement and moves to a specific, more limited statement.

The following is an example of a deductive argument.

> Premise: All eleventh-graders must take English.
> Premise: JoAnn is an eleventh-grader.
> Conclusion: JoAnn must take English.

The differences between inductive and deductive reasoning are shown in the following diagrams:

DEDUCTIVE REASONING	INDUCTIVE REASONING
Generalization	Specific fact
+	+
Related fact	Specific fact
↓	+
Conclusion (specific instance)	Specific fact
	+
	Many more specific facts
	↓
	Generalization

Defining Terms

The reasons leading to the conclusion in a deductive argument are called *premises.*

A *premise* is a general or universal statement asserted to be true.

A premise in a deductive argument may even be the conclusion of an inductive argument. For example, on page 115, the generalization "All birds have feathers" is presented as the conclusion of an inductive argument. In the following deductive argument the same statement is used as a premise.

> Premise: All birds have feathers.
> Premise: An osprey is a bird.
> Conclusion: An osprey has feathers.

Both the osprey example and the one about JoAnn taking English are *syllogisms.*

A *syllogism* is a three-part form of deductive reasoning.

In a syllogism the first statement is called the *major premise.* The second premise, which states a fact or truth related to the major premise, is called the *minor premise.* The third statement is called the *conclusion.*

Truth and Validity

Consider another example of a deductive argument:

> Premise: All green plants contain chlorophyll.
> Premise: The aloe is a green plant.
> Conclusion: The aloe contains chlorophyll.

In a deductive argument two conditions must be met in order for the conclusion to be true: (1) Both of the premises must be true, and (2) The argument must be logically valid.

A *valid argument* is one that follows the rules of reasoning.

Notice what happens to the conclusion when one of the premises is not true:

Premise:	All cows can fly.
Premise:	Beulah is a cow.
Conclusion:	Beulah can fly.

The conclusion in the preceding argument is not true because the major premise is false. Cows cannot fly. Even though this conclusion is false, the argument is said to be valid because it follows the rules of logical reasoning.

There is an important distinction between truth and validity. An argument—such as the one about Beulah the cow—may still be valid even though its conclusion is untrue. Similarly, even when both premises are true, the conclusion may be untrue because the argument is not valid, as in the following example.

Premise:	Some twentieth-century novels are based on ancient Greek myths.
Premise:	*My Ántonia* by Willa Cather is a twentieth-century novel.
Conclusion:	*My Ántonia* by Willa Cather is based on an ancient Greek myth.

The conclusion is false because the argument is not valid. The major premise says that *some*, not all, twentieth-century novels are based on ancient Greek myths. One would have no way of knowing—on the basis of deductive reasoning alone—whether *My Ántonia* is one of these "some novels" or whether it is one of the other group of twentieth-century novels that are not based on Greek myths. Therefore, the argument is not valid.

In a deductive argument the major premise must make a universal statement. That is, it must be true of *all*, *every*, *no*, or *none* of the persons, objects, or events that are the subject of the generalization. In a valid argument a major premise can never contain a limiter, such as *some*, *most*, or *many*. The following example uses the absolute word *no* in the major premise. Is the argument valid? Is the conclusion true?

Premise:	No players on Wilson High's basketball team are taller than seven feet.
Premise:	Pedro is a player on Wilson High's basketball team.
Conclusion:	Pedro is not taller than seven feet.

In the preceding argument the conclusion is both true and valid.

Evaluating a Deductive Argument

In a deductive argument the premises must be true, and the argument must follow the laws of reasoning in order to arrive at an acceptable conclusion. Yet how can you know if the premises are true? Suppose the premises lie outside your experience. If you had never read *My Ántonia*, for example, how could you tell that the conclusion is not true? If you had never heard of the novel, how could you know whether it is indeed a twentieth-century novel, as the minor premise states? You might even be unsure whether the major premise in this argument is true.

In evaluating a deductive argument, you can try to check the truth of a premise you are not sure about by consulting reference books. You might also discuss the premise with friends, relatives, and teachers to see whether they agree that the premise is true.

In some arguments—especially in long, written arguments and in speeches—the premises are not clearly stated. Sometimes, they are left out altogether, and you must discover the unstated assumptions that the writer or speaker makes. Assumptions, too, must be carefully examined to see whether or not they are true.

Use the following questions to evaluate deductive arguments. You may also find these questions helpful as guidelines in preparing your own deductive arguments.

1.   What is the conclusion?

2.   What are the reasons offered to support the conclusion?

3.   Are all of the reasons true? (How can they be checked?)

4.   If the reasons are true, must the conclusion necessarily be true? That is, does the argument follow the laws of reasoning?

5.   Does the argument contain any fallacies? (See pages 124–131.)

Exercise 4

For each of the following pairs of statements, write the conclusion that follows logically from the premises. If no valid conclusion is possible, write "No conclusion possible."

Example

a.   All Eskimo artists depict daily events and myths of their culture.
Kenojuak is an Eskimo artist.

a. Conclusion: *Kenojuak depicts daily events and myths of her culture.*

1.   All lawyers must pass a bar exam.
Barbara Vicevich is a lawyer.

2.   Alan is allergic to all foods containing wheat.
Spaghetti contains wheat.

3.   Carey's dog only barks when it is hungry.
Carey's dog is barking.

4.   Five to ten per cent of all men are colorblind.
Jerry is a man.

5.   The ancient Chinese believed that objects carved from jade had supernatural qualities.
This ancient Chinese deer is carved from jade.

6. Elderly people who have friends and lead active lives are healthier and happier than those who are inactive.
   Grandmother Benjamin, who is seventy-six, rarely sees people or goes out of her house and has been complaining about not feeling well.

7. When awakened during a period of REM sleep (when they have "rapid eye movement" beneath closed lids), people in a sleep laboratory invariably report that they are dreaming.
   Baby Jana's eyes are moving rapidly under closed lids.

8. Many Pueblo women have produced excellent pottery.
   Maria Martinez of San Ildefonso is a Pueblo potter.

9. Nutritionists say that Americans should eat more chicken and fish because eating too much red meat is associated with coronary-artery disease.
   I eat beef at least once a day—sometimes twice a day.

10. A *noun* is a word or words that name a person, place, or thing.
    Hailey High School names a place.

Exercise 5

In this exercise you are to do two things. First, write the logically valid conclusion that can be drawn from the premises. Then, decide whether the conclusion is true or not. If the conclusion is not true, examine the premises to see whether one or both of the premises are not true.

Example

a. All eighteen-year-olds are eligible to vote if they are registered.
   Rick Griselda will be eighteen in October.
a. *Conclusion: Rick Griselda is eligible to vote in the November election if he is registered.*
   The conclusion is true.

1. All energy sources are in short supply.
   Sunlight is an energy source.

2. All mammals live on land.
   Porpoises are mammals.

3. All insects have six legs.
   The praying mantis is an insect.

4. All workers should retire at the age of sixty-five.
   The distinguished senator is sixty-eight.

5. Every parallelogram has four sides.
   A square is a parallelogram.

Exercise 6

For each of the following situations, tell whether inductive or deductive reasoning is being used.

1. A legislator studies hundreds of case histories of child abuse and talks to many social workers before writing a report on recommendations for legislation dealing with child abuse.

2. An office manager looks up the company policy in the employees' manual before deciding whether or not Rosemarie can take two extra weeks of vacation without pay.

3. Over a period of several months, Mrs. O'Keeffe has been trying to create a recipe for the oatmeal raisin bread she remembers from her childhood. Each time she bakes the bread, she changes one ingredient slightly to see if the bread is improved. Finally, after many months, she writes down a recipe that reproduces exactly the remembered bread.

4. Before the jury goes out to deliberate, the prosecuting attorney summarizes the evidence he has presented in court against a person accused of smuggling drugs into the country. He concludes his argument by saying that the evidence makes it clear that the person is guilty of the crime.

5. A psychology student has learned in class that children's behavior is shaped more effectively by rewards and praise than by punishment and criticism. The student decides to apply this principle the next time he baby-sits with three-year-old Wendy, who has frequent temper tantrums.

6. A student is given a definition of a gerund and is then asked to identify all the gerunds in a passage from a short story.

7. An astronomy teacher assigns the following homework: at 9 P.M. every night for two months, see which constellations are visible in the eastern sky. Report your findings to the class.

Errors in Logical Reasoning

An error in reasoning is called a *fallacy*.

You should be able to recognize the following errors in the speeches that you hear and in the newspaper articles, editorials, and ads that you read. Your ability to detect fallacies in the reasoning of others will also sharpen your own reasoning powers and will help you to avoid errors in your own thinking and writing.

Hasty Generalization

No generalization can be made on the basis of a single experience.

Suppose you had a chance to talk with a young man from Argentina named Pablo. What could you tell about Argentineans in general after your conversation? Nothing. You would have no way of knowing whether what you observe about Pablo is true only of Pablo himself or of Argentineans in general.

Suppose you were asked to evaluate the following argument. What is wrong with it?

Evidence:	Rattlesnakes are poisonous.
	Coral snakes are poisonous.
	Water moccasins are poisonous.
Conclusion:	All snakes are poisonous.

The preceding argument contains the error in reasoning called a *hasty generalization*, or an *oversimplification*. Out of a population of more than 2,500 species of snakes, only 3 were sampled before the conclusion was made that all snakes are poisonous. (Actually, about four fifths of all snakes are not poisonous.)

The following are other examples of hasty generalizations.

My cousin broke her leg while she was on her first skiing trip, so I'm never going to go skiing because it's too dangerous a sport.

The old sea captain nodded his head wisely and said, "When Anya's father died, she decided to captain his fishing boat. The boat was wrecked off the coast last year during a hurricane. Women just don't know the ways of the sea as well as men do. Women should stay ashore."

In an inductive argument how much of a sampling is enough before a generalization can be reached? The larger the sample, the better chance there is that you will have an accurate understanding of the population being studied. If the person studying snakes, for example, had gone on to sample a dozen or so more species, she would probably have turned up several that were not poisonous and would not have reached her hasty conclusion. When the subject you are dealing with is extremely complex—such as nations or wars or human nature—you will need a great deal of evidence to support your generalization.

Stereotypes

A *stereotype* is a particular kind of hasty generalization—a fixed idea about the characteristics of certain groups of people.

Jane, who is a Martian, worked as a teller at Sun City Bank. She embezzled $30,000 dollars and disappeared. Now all the people in Sun City are going around saying that Martians just can't be trusted.

On the basis of one bad experience, you cannot generalize about a whole group of people. It may be that only Jane is not trustworthy and that most Martians are. (Perhaps the reason Jane came to Sun City in the first place is that she was so dishonest and untrustworthy that the Martians made her leave Mars!)

We have all heard some of the racial or ethnic stereotypes that exist in our culture, even when they are not blatantly expressed. Psychologists and social workers know that when people have the opportunity to get to know and work with others who are different from themselves, they learn to see each person as an individual human being. Perhaps in this way stereotypes can be eliminated from our thinking.

Dependence on Unqualified Authority

One of the pitfalls of inductive reasoning can be shown in the following paid political announcement.

Evidence: Billie the Kid is a famous, successful movie star.

Billie the Kid is voting for Candidate X.

Billie the Kid must know what he is doing, or he wouldn't have become famous and successful.

Conclusion: Therefore, Candidate X is the best candidate because Billie the Kid is voting for him.

The fallacy in the preceding argument is called *dependence on unqualified authority*. What does Billie the Kid know about whether or not Candidate X is the most qualified candidate? Is he thoroughly familiar with each candidate's history? Does he have a real understanding of the issues? Probably he does not.

When you cannot gather evidence for yourself in an inductive argument, you must depend on data gathered by someone else, but be careful whom you choose. Your authority should be an unbiased expert in the field, someone with respected credentials. For example, a professor at an esteemed university who specializes in Mideast policy is much more likely to produce an accurate, unbiased history of American-Iranian foreign relations than is a person who has invested heavily in Iranian oil. It is a good idea never to depend on a single authority for data for conclusions. In writing a research paper, for example, never depend on a single source, for it might be biased in some way that you cannot detect unless you compare it with other sources. You are much more likely to gather accurate evidence when you consult several reliable sources.

False Analogy

Comparisons can be useful in an argument and are frequently entertaining, but they never prove anything.

An *analogy* is a comparison in which two dissimilar things are shown to have at least one quality in common.

Usually in an analogy, more than one similarity is pointed out, as in the following example from Anne Morrow Lindbergh's *Gift from the Sea:*[1]

A good relationship has a pattern like a dance and is built on some of the same rules. The partners do not need to hold on tightly, because they move confidently in the same pattern, intricate but gay and swift and free, like a country dance of Mozart's. To touch heavily would be to arrest the pattern and freeze the movement, to check the endlessly changing beauty of its unfolding. There is no place here for the possessive clutch, the clinging arm, the heavy hand; only the barest touch in passing. Now arm in arm, now face to face, now back to back—it does not matter which. Because they know they are partners

---

[1]Excerpt from "Argonauta" from *Gift from the Sea* by Anne Morrow Lindbergh. Copyright © 1955 by Anne Morrow Lindbergh. Reprinted by permission of Pantheon Books, the author, and Chatto & Windus Ltd.

moving to the same rhythm, creating a pattern together, and being invisibly nourished by it.

The writer's analogy is simple and beautifully written: marriage partners are like dance partners—free to move apart and together.

An analogy may never be offered as proof in an argument. Sometimes, even the analogy itself makes a false comparison.

Consider the following *false analogy*.

> Being a parent is like having a full-time job. The responsibilities are enormous, and the work week is long. Doing a good job requires a tremendous amount of time, energy, and expense. Therefore, parents should be paid by the government for caring for their children.

The analogy is a false one because being a parent is *not* like having a full-time job. No one has hired you, you cannot quit, and you are not paid for your work. If anything, being a parent is like having an extraordinarily demanding *volunteer* job.

Cause-and-Effect Fallacies

Human beings seem to have an innate need to look for causes, a tendency that leaves them vulnerable to two common fallacies. The Latin name for one of these fallacies is *post hoc, ergo propter hoc*, which means, "After this, because of this." Post hoc reasoning, as it is called, can be seen in the following argument.

Evidence:	Yesterday it rained.
	Yesterday I failed my math test.
Conclusion:	Every time it rains, I am going to fail my math test.

Even if you failed four or five math tests in a row on rainy days, you would still be committing the post hoc fallacy by concluding that the rain was the cause of your failure. Just because one thing happens right after (or even soon after) another event does not mean that the first was the cause of the second. The two events may be entirely coincidental. Scientists know that it takes a great deal of careful experimenting to establish a cause-effect relationship. So whenever you see something attributed as a cause, make sure that the cause-effect relationship has been reliably and thoroughly established and that you are not witnessing a post hoc fallacy, which is based on coincidence.

Another cause-effect fallacy is the naming of a single cause in a complex situation that, in reality, has many causes. This is known as the *only-cause fallacy*. Wars, social unrest, crime, economic problems, even love—none of these has a single cause. Whenever you hear someone claiming to have a simple solution to a complex issue, look to see if the argument contains the only-cause fallacy.

Exercise 7

Identify the fallacy in each of the following arguments. You may find that in some arguments two fallacies occur. Write them both.

Hasty generalization	False analogy
Stereotype	Post hoc
Unqualified authority	Only-cause

1. Jason gave me a ball cactus plant, but it died from over-watering. Cactuses are too difficult to grow.

2. Ali McGraw, the movie star, drives a Superwheels car, so it must be a good car.

3. English men and women are unfriendly.

4. I've had a good time whenever I've worn this T-shirt. This must be my lucky T-shirt. Whenever I want to have a good time, I'm going to wear it.

5. Dr. Olin, my dentist, tells me to vote for Ellen Flintstone for senator because she is a patient of his.

6. People who oppose nuclear power plants are just like people who opposed the first railroads. You can't stop progress.

7. My brother's friend went to Ohio State University and didn't like it because he said it was too big. So I'm not planning to apply to any state universities because the classes are too big.

8. Every time I call Maria, someone in her family answers and says she isn't home. Maria must be avoiding me because she doesn't like me.

9. The problems of this city are like the growing pains of an adolescent. Problems of housing, development, and transportation are inevitable in any city just as problems of independence and responsibility are inevitable during the teenage years. But as with the problems of adolescence, nothing drastic needs to be done; urban problems will solve themselves with time, understanding, and patience.

10. The reason for the soaring divorce rate is the liberalized divorce laws. If we change the laws back the way they used to be, the divorce rate will drop to what it was in the early part of this century.

Faulty Premises

In a deductive argument the premises must be true in order for a true conclusion to be possible. (See pages 120–121.) Also, the major premise must not contain a limiting word, such as *some*, *many*, or *few*, or the conclusion will not be valid, as in the following argument.

Major Premise:	Many teenagers are in conflict with their parents.
Minor Premise:	Carol is a teenager.
Conclusion:	Carol is in conflict with her parents.

In the preceding argument the conclusion is not valid because the major premise contains the limiting word *many*. You cannot know whether Carol is one of the many who are in conflict or one of the other group who are not in conflict.

In a deductive argument examine the premises carefully to make sure that they are true and that the major premise does not contain a limiting word.

Exercise 8

Each of the following sets of premises is true. Which ones can lead to a valid conclusion? Which ones cannot?

1. Every worker in America must have a Social Security number.
    Marc Linson is an American worker.

2. Many cities have consumer affairs departments.
    Minneapolis is a city.

3. Many nations are represented in the United Nations.
    Tanzania is a nation.

4. Some diseases are caused by viruses.
    Typhoid is a disease.

5. All employees of Justin Industries are vested in the pension plan after ten years of employment.
    Annette Valentino has worked for Justin Industries fifteen years.

Begging the Question

The fallacy of *begging the question* is also called *circular thinking*. It occurs in arguments in which reasons are not given to support the conclusion, but in fact, the conclusion is exactly the same as the premise. Look, for example, at the following arguments.

> Jack is the best candidate for president of the student government because he is better than all of the other candidates.

> The law giving preference to veterans of the armed forces for government jobs is unfair because it gives veterans a slight advantage in applying for any government job.

What are the reasons in the preceding arguments? There are none. In each argument the writer has simply restated the initial premise after the word *because*. What sounds like a reason is found to be, on careful examination, simply repetition.

In any valid argument reasons or evidence *must* be given to support the conclusion. When you are presented with an argument that tries to persuade you to take action or to change your mind, always look first for the conclusion (that which the writer or speaker is trying to prove) and then look for the reason. Usually two or three reasons are offered. If you find that the reasons say the same thing as the conclusion, you have discovered a case of circular thinking (or begging the question).

Exercise 9

Restate the following arguments so that they do not contain the fallacy of begging the question. Make up two or three reasons to support each of the conclusions.

1. Brand X is the best brand of laundry detergent because it is better than any other brand on the market.

2. The city should provide recreational programs for young people because young people in this city need recreational programs.

3. My grade in physical education is unfair because I deserve a better grade.

4. According to the Homeowners' Association, the airport's traffic patterns must be changed because the present traffic patterns are unacceptable.

5. Capital punishment should be outlawed because it is not right for human beings to take the lives of other human beings as a punishment for a crime.

Attacking the Person and Not the Issue

The Latin name for the fallacy of attacking the person and not the issue is *ad hominem*. A speaker or writer commits an ad hominem fallacy by attacking the person who offers the argument rather than facing the issues squarely and replying to the reasons of the argument. Suppose, for example, a speaker has just presented a list of reasons why a nuclear arms limitation treaty should be approved by Congress. The following response by her opponent contains the ad hominem fallacy.

> Obviously Ms. Speaker supports an arms limitation treaty because she is a pacifist. She has a long history of work in the peace movement. You can't believe what she says about an arms limitation treaty because she is vehemently prejudiced against war.

The following are two other examples of ad hominem arguments.

> The recommendations for candidates supported by the *Daily Gazette* should not be taken too seriously because we all know that the *Daily Gazette* is controlled by its advertisers. After all, the newspaper depends on its advertisers for its continued existence; therefore, it can't possibly make unbiased recommendations.

> In its advertisements, which are skillfully produced by highly paid advertising agencies, the oil company tells us why we should conserve fuel. But the oil company is a profit-making concern, and it will tell us anything in order to justify its price increases. How can we believe anything the ad says when we know that the purpose of the ad is to improve the oil company's image?

Either-Or Fallacy

An argument that offers only two alternatives may contain the *either-or fallacy*. Such an argument ignores the possibility of alternative solutions or choices.

The county prison is dangerously overcrowded. It contains 1,800 prisoners in a building designed to hold a maximum of 1,100. Either we must build a new prison in this county, or we must release at least 700 prisoners.

The preceding argument contains the *either-or fallacy*, for it admits of only two courses of action. A sounder conclusion to this argument would be, "We must find some way of relieving this overcrowding."

In any situation there are many possible options—not just two. A person who presents an either-or argument has a closed mind, seeing no possibilities other than the two extremes he or she presents. Whenever you are faced with a problem to solve, it is good practice to try to list as many solutions as is possible.

Exercise 10

Identify the fallacy in each of the following arguments.

Faulty premise	Attacking the person, not the issue
Begging the question	Either-or fallacy

1. Senator X is asking us to vote for his amendment on the defense appropriations bill. But how can we take this amendment seriously when it is a matter of public record that Senator X has not attended twelve out of the last eighteen defense committee meetings?

2. Some redheaded people have bad tempers. Craig has red hair, so he must be bad-tempered.

3. Either the federal government relaxes its air pollution standards, or most of the nation's factories will have to close.

4. The United States must continue its economic aid to developing nations because those nations are in need of aid.

5. If we cannot stop the robberies and assaults in this neighborhood, we must level the neighborhood completely and move its residents elsewhere.

Exercise 11

Look for an example of a fallacy in conversations you have or in newspaper editorials, magazine articles, television talk shows, and advertisements. Write a brief report of the example. Identify the fallacy if you can and tell how you would rewrite the argument to eliminate the fallacy.

Exercise 12

On a sheet of paper, write an argument to support one of the following conclusions. Notice that for each conclusion, you have a choice of an affirmative or a negative wording. Give at least three reasons—more if you can—to support the conclusion. Proofread your argument to make sure that it includes none of the fallacies you have studied.

1. The federal government should (should not) institute wage and price controls to curb inflation.

2. Imports of foreign cars should (should not) be severely limited.

3. If a draft system is instituted, women should (should not) be as eligible for the draft as men.

4. The legal age for drinking should (should not) be raised to twenty-one.

5. Laws that strictly control the purchase and use of handguns should (should not) be passed in this state.

6. Gasoline should (should not) be rationed.

7. More nuclear power plants should (should not) be built.

8. Smoking should (should not) be banned in public places.

9. Gambling should (should not) be legalized in all states.

10. The federal government should (should not) provide a national health insurance plan for all persons.

7 Persuasive Writing

The Purpose of Persuasion

Persuasion—whether in the form of a toothpaste ad, a Presidential candidate's speech, or an editorial about smoking in public places—attempts to persuade you to change the way you think or behave.

In this chapter you will study some of the basic techniques of persuasive writing, and you will learn to plan and write a persuasive essay.

The Emotional Power of Language

One of the basic principles of persuasion is that language has the power to affect the way people feel. Most English words have two kinds of meaning: *denotative* and *connotative*.

The *denotative* meaning of a word is the meaning given by a dictionary.

The *connotative* meaning of a word is the feeling or tone associated with it.

A word may have either positive (good) or negative (bad) connotations, or it may arouse a whole range of feeling associations. Connotative meanings may vary with individual experiences. *Kitten*, for example, arouses positive feelings in most people who enjoy the playful softness of young cats. For someone who is deathly afraid of cats, however, or who has severe allergies to them, the word *kitten* may stir negative feelings.

Many words, such as *ten*, *cause*, and *however*, are neutral, having neither positive nor negative connotations. The formal language of scientific reports, textbooks, and documents is usually without emotion, made up of words that are emotionally neutral. On the other hand, the language of advertising, poetry, drama, and political speeches relies heavily on the connotative meanings of words. You should recognize that some kinds of language are deliberately filled with emotion-charged words calculated to have an effect on the reader or listener. There is nothing inherently wrong in using language in this way, but you need to be aware of how such use of language affects your feelings and behavior, so that you are not manipulated into making decisions on the basis of your emotions alone.

Consider the following list of words, all of which have approximately the same denotative meaning.

Slim	Skinny	Underweight
Thin	Bony	Gaunt

Which of these words would you consider complimentary, if applied to you? Which would you be insulted by? Which, if any, are neutral?

Slim and *thin* have positive connotations and are often used in advertisements for health spas, reducing aids, and exercise equipment. *Skinny*, *bony*, and *gaunt* are less complimentary words with negative connotations. Who wants to look like a skeleton—undernourished and underfed? Of all the words, *underweight* is probably the only neutral one.

You should be aware that persuaders—people who use language to try to change your thinking or behavior—can trigger emotional reactions by using words with powerful positive connotations. Most people would like to have possessions that are *elegant* and *luxurious*. Most would like to be associated with political candidates who are *fair*, *honest*, and *sincere*, who want every citizen to achieve *the American Dream*. Watch carefully for such powerful persuading words; they are appealing not to your reason but to your emotions.

Exercise 1

Each of the following terms has a negative connotation. On a sheet of paper, write a word or phrase that has the same denotative meaning but that has a neutral or positive connotation.

Example

a. Strange (negative connotation)
a. Unfamiliar (neutral)

1. Messy	6. Long-winded explanation
2. Argument	7. Timid
3. Gossip	8. Goody-goody
4. Broken home	9. Loner
5. Pushy	10. Deceptive advertisement

Exercise 2

The following words are often found in ads for food products. Choose several words from this list and write a short advertisement for an imaginary food. Give your product a name. Your purpose is to create a positive feeling so that readers will go out and buy your product.

Appetizing	Free	Mouthwatering	Rich
Crisp	Fresh	Natural	Satisfying
Delectable	Guaranteed	Nutritious	Savor
Delicate	Healthy	Old-fashioned	Spicy
Delicious	Homemade	Pure	Super
Elegant	Luscious	Refreshing	Tasty

Emotional Appeals in Advertising

Advertisers often use words and photographs to associate their product in your mind with the fulfillment of certain basic human needs. Everyone needs food, shelter, and warmth, but there are emotional needs that are almost as important as the physical needs: the need to be loved, the need to be respected, the need to feel attractive, the need to enjoy life, and the need to be free of anxiety. Who can resist buying a soap if the advertisement practically guarantees that someone attractive will love you if you use it? Other basic needs that ads appeal to are the desire to feel financially secure, the desire to feel successful, and the desire to remain youthful-looking.

Emotional appeals are not necessarily bad. Writers of public service advertisements, for example, frequently use emotional appeals to convince Americans to support such causes as conserving energy, preserving endangered species of animals, supporting medical research, and reducing pollution. It is important, however, to recognize when emotional appeals are being used and to know why they are being used.

Exercise 3

From a source such as a magazine or newspaper ad or a radio or television commercial, find an example of an appeal to emotion. Then write a summary of the ad, describing the emotional appeal that is being made. Conclude your summary by evaluating the emotional appeal. Is the appeal an acceptable one, or do you feel that it is in some way dishonest or deceptive?

Exercise 4

Choose three advertisements from magazines or newspapers. (Be sure to choose ads that have photographs or drawings as well as text.) Judge the effectiveness of each ad by answering the following questions.

1. What words in the text appeal to the emotions?
2. What words in the text appeal to satisfying basic human needs, such as the need for self-esteem, love, or respect?
3. What does the ad want the reader to do or to believe? Are you persuaded by the ad?
4. How would you rate the effectiveness of the photograph or artwork? Does the photograph or art arouse feelings or appeal to the need for satisfying basic human needs? How?
5. How could the ad be made more effective?

Appeals to Emotions

The following techniques are often used by advertisers to appeal in a negative or dishonest way to audiences. These techniques appeal to emotional fears—fears that one might not be loved, happy, successful, or well-liked. It is important to learn to recognize these techniques and to avoid them in your own writing.

Glittering Generality

A *glittering generality* is a word or phrase with a powerful positive connotation that is used to persuade. Usually glittering generalities appeal to patriotic feelings or family and group loyalties. When they are used without clarification, they are vague yet powerful appeals to emotion, as the following examples show.

> If elected, I will work to make the American Dream a reality for every one of our citizens in America.

> We [ethnic group] must stick together, for if we don't take care of our own people, what will become of us? Who can we depend on if not ourselves?

The Bandwagon

Have you ever been persuaded to go somewhere because "everyone else" was going? That is *the bandwagon* appeal.

> Two hundred and sixty condominiums sold; only six left!

> More people buy Sudsy Shampoo than any other brand.

The bandwagon appeal may be disguised by the use of statistics:

> Eighty-five per cent of all doctors surveyed use this brand of aspirin for their own families.

How accurate are such statistics? You would have to know more about the survey and the sampling before you could verify the reliability of such figures.

Plain Folks

The *plain folks* approach appeals to the tendency people have to like and trust others who are "just like" themselves. For example, an ad for a soft drink might show ordinary-looking people dressed in everyday clothes enjoying the kinds of activities that are within reach of most people—nothing fancy. When a political candidate wears work clothes, kisses babies, and eats ethnic food, he or she is trying to be one of the plain folks. Read the following candidate's approach.

> You and I—we all share the same concerns and face the same problems: how to pay the bills, how to keep our jobs, how to get the best for our children and keep our marriages going, and how to care for the old folks. And we share the same concerns for this country and its future. When you vote for me, you'll

know that there's someone you can trust in office—someone who thinks and feels the way you do.

The candidate does not mention that he or she is a millionaire with two vacation homes and a private jet. Before you fall for this plain folks appeal, you might want to find out more about the candidate's views on various issues.

Snob Appeal

Snob appeal is the opposite of the plain folks appeal. Ads that show women in evening gowns wearing expensive jewelry and men in tuxedos driving luxury cars appeal to a desire to be like wealthy, carefree people.

> People who care about quality and luxury turn to Centennial Federal for their personal banking needs.
>
> Jordan watches are for the privileged few.
>
> Women who wear Tigress perfume stand out from the crowd.

Slogans like these appeal to a desire to be superior to most people, to achieve the highest possible status.

Transfer

Both plain folks and snob appeal use another emotional device—*transfer*. Elegantly dressed people may be advertising a certain product—an antiperspirant, for example—and the readers or viewers then transfer their feelings about the people to the product itself. If a testimonial by a movie star convinces people to buy a brand of dog food, the buyers are transferring their feelings of admiration for, and approval of, the movie star to the product that the star recommends.

Exercise 5

Describe the appeals used in each of the following advertisements.

1. As part of this introductory offer, there's no charge for the initial install-ment of your cable TV. You'll save almost a hundred dollars. But hurry—the offer only lasts three more days. Don't be the only person in your neighborhood not to have cable TV. Don't miss all the special movies, concerts, and sporting events available only to those privileged audiences who select cable TV.

2. A farm couple in Iowa stand next to their mailbox, holding a letter informing them that they have just won a prize in a large sweepstakes. "I didn't believe it was possible to win," says the farmer, "but I do now."

3. An advertisement for a make of automobile shows the car parked in front of an imposing house with stately columns. A man and woman dressed in elegant evening clothes are about to enter the car, the door being held open by a uniformed chauffeur.

4. A professional football player explains the merits of a carpet company, encouraging viewers to buy carpet from this particular company.

5. A group of employees stands outside a business. Two of the employees are busy raising the American flag; a third speaks to the camera: "What this country needs is more flag raising. Let's join in supporting America." The name of the company is clearly visible in the background.

Exercise 6

For several days keep a log of advertisements that you see on television or that you read in newspapers and magazines. Try to enter in your log at least one example of an advertisement that uses each of the methods discussed in this chapter. Record the name of the product, the date and place you heard or saw the ad, and a brief description of the ad, including the appeals used.

Appeals to Reason

Appeals to reason are based on a logical presentation of ideas. A persuader using an appeal to reason presents *sound reasons* why a person should change his or her actions or beliefs. (*Sound reasons* are those that can be supported with evidence.)

An *argument* is a logical presentation of ideas.

To make your arguments convincing, review the techniques of inductive and deductive reasoning. Avoid hasty generalizations, stereotypes, and other logical fallacies. Try to eliminate from your argument devices for manipulating emotion.

In the remaining sections of this chapter, you will learn how to write a persuasive essay, in which you present and develop a logical argument.

Writing the Persuasive Essay

Choosing a Topic

A persuasive essay should be about a current issue. For example, the future budget for America's space exploration program is an acceptable topic for a persuasive essay, but an essay about the fifth woman doctor in America or about the Aztec civilization is not. These last two are topics suitable for exposition, the kind of writing that explains. Remember that persuasive writing aims to convince the reader to take an action and must therefore deal with an issue that is as yet unsettled.

Besides being current, the topic should also be controversial. More than one opinion or position should be defensible. The need for world peace is not a good topic for a persuasive essay because almost everyone agrees to that need. However, whether or not there should be national health insurance is a suitable topic because it is a much-debated issue with many arguments marshaled to support both yes and no positions.

As in any essay, it is important to limit the topic of a persuasive essay so that it can be adequately covered in an essay—not in a book. One way to make sure that your topic is restricted enough is to outline your argument briefly. If you can support your opinion well with three or four reasons, chances are you have chosen a limited topic.

Defining Your Views

If you are uncertain about your opinion on a topic, a good approach is to do some research to become familiar with the issue. Even if you know what your position is, you will need to gather evidence to support it. If your topic is indeed current and controversial, you should be able to find many articles listed in the *Readers' Guide to Periodical Literature.* Take notes as you read, for you will want to use some of the facts you uncover in your essay and perhaps quote from some of the authorities. You will find it helpful also to read what others—even those who are not authorities—think about the issue. Outline their arguments, paying special attention to the reasons that they advance.

You may also find it helpful to discuss the issue with people that you know. Ask relatives, teachers, and friends what they think and why. You will soon discover that people disagree about controversial issues and give different reasons to support their opinions. Perhaps you can find an authority—someone who works in the field or is involved in some way with the issue—who is willing to discuss the issue with you. Listen, too, to radio and television shows on which the issue is debated, discussed, or explained. At the end of your research period, you should be able to formulate the pros and cons of the issue and have a clearer idea of your own opinions about it.

Exercise 7

For this assignment select an issue that is both current and controversial. If you are not certain of your opinion on the issue, spend time reading articles of general interest on the topic and discussing it with friends. Then take a position—either pro or con—on the issue you have chosen. Finally, state your position clearly in a sentence or two.

You might want to consider using one of the following issues as the basis for this assignment.

1. Drafting women
2. Instituting wage and price controls as a means to curb inflation
3. Banning smoking in public places
4. Limiting foreign car imports
5. Rationing gasoline as a means to reduce consumption
6. Paddling students as a means of punishment
7. Limiting Presidents to a single six-year term
8. Instituting a required one-year public service period for men and women at age eighteen

9. Censoring television by prohibiting the showing of acts of violence

10. Removing from school property all machines that sell junk food

---

Developing a Proposition

The thesis statement of a persuasive essay is called a *proposition*.

In formal persuasion a proposition is worded as a positive statement of opinion:

> Smoking should be banned in public places.
>
> Paddling should be prohibited as punishment in public schools.
>
> Women should be drafted.

If you have adopted a negative position on an issue (for example, that junk food should not be sold in public schools), reword your opinion so that it is a positive statement.

> The sale of junk food should be prohibited in public schools.

In your reading you will often encounter examples of persuasive writing, such as letters-to-the-editor, editorials, or persuasive essays, in which the proposition is implied rather than directly stated. However, beginning a persuasive essay with a clearly worded proposition is a good way to ensure that your essay is focused.

Exercise 8

Write a proposition for a persuasive essay. If you have completed Exercise 7, you may wish to rewrite your opinion as a proposition.

Supporting the Proposition

The proposition of a persuasive paper should be *supported* by reasons that explain the writer's opinion.

Before beginning your persuasive essay, be certain that you have enough reasons to support your opinion. Few readers would be convinced, for example, that a vegetarian diet is the ideal diet if the only reason you give for your opinion is that vegetables are generally lower in calories than most kinds of meats.

Each reason that supports the argument should be developed with supporting details and evidence. The evidence may include facts and figures, examples, personal experience, and statements by authorities. For example, suppose that the writer of a persuasive essay advocating vegetarianism gives as one reason for his or her opinion the following statement.

> A vegetarian diet is healthier than a diet that includes meat.

The writer could then support this reason with evidence, such as the following items.

1. A study showing a relationship between the consumption of meat and heart disease

2. Statistics that demonstrate the harm from chemicals inserted by the meat industry

3. Statements by leading nutritionists on the benefits of a low-cholesterol vegetarian diet.

Supporting details and evidence can be gathered by reading magazine and newspaper articles and, if possible, by interviewing authorities.

Exercise 9

For this exercise use either a proposition you have already written or a new one. First, list at least three reasons to support your proposition. Then, for each reason list at least three pieces of supporting evidence. When you finish, you will have a rough outline to guide the writing of your persuasive essay.

Making Meaning Clear

A poet deliberately uses words to suggest many meanings. For example, in the three lines that begin "The Waking," the American poet Theodore Roethke does not try to pin down a single, exact meaning for the reader:

> I wake to sleep, and take my waking slow.
> I feel my fate in what I cannot fear.
> I learn by going where I have to go.[1]

Even though the words are simple, it is difficult to say precisely what each line means. Taken all together—or even separately—the lines are puzzling and tantalizing. Many meanings suggest themselves, which is what the poet intends.

The language of a persuasive essay is just the opposite. Meanings must be clear in order for the writer to be certain that the reader understands the argument. In a persuasive essay that proposes the creation of a citizens' advisory panel in each election district, the following statement appears.

Each person must be responsible for the welfare of the community.

The writer goes on to clarify this statement, which is both vague and abstract, by defining the terms *community* and *responsible*.

A community consists of a defined group of streets, businesses, dwellings, and people who live in those dwellings. For the purpose of this paper, a community in this city will be defined as a single election district as drawn by the Board of Elections.

Each person in the community is expected to obey the laws of the community and report to the police any instances of lawbreaking. Each person has

---

[1]"The Waking" copyright 1953 by Theodore Roethke from the book *The Collected Poems of Theodore Roethke*. Reprinted by permission of Doubleday & Company, Inc. and Faber and Faber Ltd.

an obligation to pay taxes to provide services that benefit the community as a whole, such as police protection, fire fighting, schools, and a library. Each person is obligated to make the community a clean and pleasant place to live. Each person is expected to aid people facing a serious crisis, such as lack of food, shelter, or water, or a life-threatening danger, such as a robbery or fire. If a person cannot help his or her neighbor directly, the person has an obligation to contact the proper authorities immediately. Each person also has the obligation to express his or her opinions by voting in all elections. Finally, each person must work to improve the quality of life within the community.

Vagueness has no place in a persuasive essay, for the writer's purpose is to communicate ideas as clearly as possible. Reasons, facts, and opinions should be expressed in such a way that the reader never has to ask, "What does that mean?" Abstract words (such as *loyalty, patriotism, happiness,* and *success*) are especially important to define, since they mean different things to different people.

In your writing always say what you mean as simply as possible. Do not try to use technical terms or abstract language in order to sound impressive. It is much better, for example, to talk of "rewards and punishments" than of "behavior modification reinforcement techniques."

Another obstacle to the communication of ideas is ambiguity. A word or phrase is *ambiguous* when it has several different denotative meanings, and the intended meaning is not clear from the context:

Hi-Fli Aircraft takes a nose dive.

The preceding statement is ambiguous because it does not make clear whether an actual airplane crashed or whether the stock of the Hi-Fli Aircraft Company has dropped in price.

Ms. Nina Reardon refused to accept the suit offered by Davidson and Company.

Did Ms. Reardon refuse a lawsuit or a jacket, skirt, and slacks? The word *suit* is ambiguous in the example sentence.

Exercise 10

Each of the following terms is abstract and vague. Choose one of the terms and define it as exactly as you can. You may define the term by giving a list of examples, characteristics, or specific instances. Make your definition so complete that a reader knows exactly what you mean and can judge whether a specific person or thing is an example of the term defined—for example, whether Marcia is a good friend or whether one nation has committed an aggressive act against another. Eliminate all vague and ambiguous language from your writing.

1. Right to privacy
2. A good friend
3. Personal freedom
4. A patriotic citizen

5. The responsibilities of parents to their children

6. The responsibilities of children to their parents

7. An aggressive act by one nation toward another

8. "The American Dream"

9. A good athlete

10. A mentally healthy person

11. A successful person

12. A happy family

13. An evil act

14. For the good of the community

15. In the national interest

Knowing Your Audience

Your *audience* affects both what you say—the arguments you offer—and how you say it.

A good example of a speaker adjusting persuasion to an audience is Mark Antony's famous speech to the Romans at Caesar's funeral. (Antony loved Caesar and opposed Brutus.) Mark Antony knows that most Romans admire Brutus, who has murdered Caesar, and that they would not be sympathetic to Antony's condemning Brutus. Therefore, throughout his speech Antony repeats that "Brutus is an honorable man." At the same time, however, Antony reminds his audience of Caesar's accomplishments. As you read the speech, look for the ways Antony manages to show that Caesar was actually the honorable one.

Interrèd means "buried."

Friends, Romans, countrymen, lend me your ears.
I come to bury Caesar, not to praise him.
The evil that men do lives after them,
The good is oft interrèd with their bones.
So let it be with Caesar. The noble Brutus
Hath told you Caesar was ambitious.
If it were so, it was a grievous fault;
And grievously hath Caesar answered it.
Here, under leave of Brutus and the rest—
For Brutus is an honorable man;
So are they all, all honorable men—
Come I to speak in Caesar's funeral.
He was my friend, faithful and just to me.
But Brutus says he was ambitious;
And Brutus is an honorable man.

The *general coffers* are the public treasury.

He hath brought many captives home to Rome,
Whose ransoms did the general coffers fill.
Did this in Caesar seem ambitious?

When that the poor have cried, Caesar hath wept;
Ambition should be made of sterner stuff.
Yet Brutus says he was ambitious;
And Brutus is an honorable man.
You all did see that on the Lupercal
I thrice presented him a kingly crown,
Which he did thrice refuse. Was this ambition?
Yet Brutus says he was ambitious;
And, sure, he is an honorable man.
I speak not to disprove what Brutus spoke,
But here I am to speak what I do know.
You all did love him once, not without cause.

Mark Antony's speech illustrates an important point about persuasion: get the audience on your side. For example, suppose you write an editorial for your student-teacher-parent organization's newsletter objecting to a shortened lunch period at your school. Beginning the editorial with a sentence such as "The administration of this school has no right to shorten our lunch period" would not help you in winning over the parents, faculty, and administrators in your audience. A better approach might be to begin with a sentence such as the following one.

Developing a schedule that will accommodate 2,000 hungry students is not an easy task, and we appreciate the efforts of our administrators to do so. However, we feel there are several valid reasons why a means other than shortened lunch periods should be used to solve the problem.

To a large extent the kind of language you use can also help you succeed in your attempt at persuasion. Decide beforehand the level of usage that is most appropriate for your audience. For example, in formal persuasive writing, such as a letter to the editor of *The New York Times*, your audience would probably be offended by use of slang and constructions that are not a part of Edited Standard English. In the sample persuasive essay on pages 145–147, the writer uses such informal constructions as *guys* and *teens*. Because that essay was written for *Seventeen* magazine, however, such informal language is acceptable. The readers of this magazine are teenagers, an audience that probably would not consider such casual language offensive.

The tone of the essay—how it "sounds" to the reader—should be factual, objective, and emotionally neutral. By avoiding highly emotional language, you enable the reader to concentrate on the soundness of your argument and on the evidence you offer to support your position. The more reasonable and calm your argument sounds, the more likely it is to be convincing.

Exercise 11

The following paragraphs are the beginning of Robert Ebel's essay on standardized testing, which appeared in *The New York Times*. First, read the excerpt carefully, using a dictionary if you need help with vocabulary. Then write a paragraph in which you discuss whether or not you think the excerpt would be appropriate for a student audience, such as the readers of your school newspaper. Support your opinion with specific words and phrases from the passage.[1]

Are standardized tests headed for extinction? To judge from news reports, magazine articles and some popular books the answer might seem to be yes. A variety of charges have been laid against them, and there is substance to some. But the effects are neither so overpowering nor so harmful as the critics imply. On balance the case for standardized tests is persuasive.

A common accusation is that some pupils have, and others lack, a special talent for taking tests and that tests end up measuring this ability rather than academic achievement. Only on a carelessly or ineptly constructed test, though, can a pupil inflate his score by special test savvy. Most widely used standardized tests have been constructed carefully by experts. Unfamiliarity with the item types or response modes employed in a standardized test can indeed handicap a naïve examinee. But that kind of naïveté can be removed quite easily by careful instructions and practice exercises.

Bear in mind that the test score reports only the level of knowledge the pupil possesses, not how frequently or how effectively he makes use of it. It reports what the pupil can do, not what he typically does. What a pupil does, and how well he does it, depends not on his knowledge alone. It depends also on his energy, ambition, determination, adroitness, likableness and luck, among other things. A pupil's knowledge as measured by a standardized or any other test is one ingredient—but only one—of his potential success in life.

For Your Journal

Use your journal as a place to respond to attempts at persuasion. Perhaps you are especially moved by an emotional appeal, or perhaps you think that a letter-to-the-editor of your local or school newspaper is especially well-written. Describe the advertisement, letter, speech, or essay in your journal, telling how you feel about it and why.

Reading a Persuasive Essay

The following essay, "Staying Well" by Eve Scott, was first published in *Seventeen* magazine. As you read, look for the reasons the writer uses to develop her argument that teenagers should use seat belts.[2]

Following this selection is a For Discussion activity.

A driver-education teacher I know keeps a record of students' excuses for not wearing seat belts. Her collection includes such familiar standbys as: "It's my right not to wear one." "We're only driving a couple of blocks." "It'll wrinkle my dress." "What if I broke my arm in an accident and couldn't get the buckle open?"

---

[1]"Are Standardized Tests Headed for Extinction?" by Robert L. Ebel in *The New York Times*, May 1, 1977. © 1977 by The New York Times Company. Reprinted by permission.
[2]Excerpt from "Staying Well" by Eve Scott in *Seventeen* Magazine, May 1980. Copyright © 1980 by Triangle Communications Inc. Reprinted by permission of Triangle Communications Inc. and Elaine Markson Literary Agency, Inc. All rights reserved.

Chances are, you've heard all these excuses before. You may even use them yourself. What you may not know is that such rationalizations may cause hundreds of teens to die each year: In fact, they're among the reasons why motor vehicle accidents are far and away the biggest killers of teens. Consider these facts:

More females die in automobile accidents between the ages of fourteen and nineteen than at any other age. In 1977, the latest year for which full statistics are available, 2,184 young women in this age group were killed in car crashes in the United States.

For each of those deaths, ten teen-age girls were injured severely enough to warrant a hospital visit.

For guys, the statistics are even grimmer. Their rate of death and injury is three times that for females, probably because males drive more often and under more risky conditions—for example, late at night after drinking at parties.

Though auto accidents cause the greatest number of vehicle injuries and deaths, motorcycle accidents claim the lives of about 500 riders of all ages each year. A recent trend among states to repeal mandatory helmet laws is disheartening: In the twenty-six states where it's now legal to ride without a helmet, helmet use has dropped 50 percent, and the number of cycle deaths has *increased* 30 percent. A study by Princeton University researchers estimates that the death rate for unprotected cyclists is 60 percent higher than for those who wear helmets.

For both cyclists and drivers, "taking unnecessary chances" plays a major role in injury and fatality rates, according to the Insurance Institute for Highway Safety and the U.S. Department of Transportation. Of the more than 750,000 auto deaths recorded since the 55-mile-an-hour-maximum-speed law went into effect, most were due to drivers' "gambles" that didn't pay off.

"Not wearing seat belts or shoulder harnesses is one of those gambles," says Dr. Susan Baker, of Johns Hopkins University, in Baltimore, who studies patterns and causes of accidents. "It simply makes no sense." Results of a study in Sweden by a well-known automaker back her up. The study showed that *no one* in that country has ever been killed—even traveling at 50 or 60 miles per hour—while wearing a shoulder harness. And no one wearing a lap belt has been killed traveling at speeds under 35 miles per hour.

The nagging question for safety experts, then, is why teens won't use belts, harnesses, and helmets. Two possible explanations are that teens view safety precautions as "uncool" and that they see not taking precautions as a matter of freedom of choice. "If we want to take a chance, it's our business," the argument goes. "After all, we'll be the only losers."

Teens killed in vehicle accidents *aren't* the only losers, of course. They leave behind families and friends who may never recover from their grief. And teens who sustain severe injuries may require public aid for the rest of their lives.

"Frankly, we're at a loss," says Ben Kelley, senior vice-president of the Insurance Institute for Highway Safety. "Education campaigns don't seem to convince teens. I think the threat of death or injury seems too remote to young, healthy, vigorous people. They believe accidents only happen to other people, never to them, despite the gory statistics."

Mr. Kelley has asked SEVENTEEN readers to try an experiment: "Envision what happens in a car or on a motorcycle that crashes," he says. "Sit in a parked car, and feel how hard the steering wheel and dashboard are. Then imagine what would happen if you were thrown against them at a speed of forty or fifty miles per hour." He also asks you to consider that in addition to the thousands of teens who die each year in high-impact crashes, a great number are injured and scarred while traveling at speeds as low as 15 miles per hour.

"Using belts, harnesses, and helmets is simply a matter of enlightened selfishness," Mr. Kelley says. "When I see a person who doesn't wear them, I can only conclude that he or she places little value on life. Taking proper precautions reflects a positive self-image."

Automakers, government regulators, and other safety experts are currently working to develop such passive restraints as air bags that inflate automatically, windows that don't blow out on impact, and doors that stay shut in a crash. But, for now at least, the burden still falls on drivers and passengers to protect themselves.

For Discussion

1. Is there a clearly stated proposition in the preceding essay, or is it implied? In your own words state the proposition.

2. Summarize briefly all the reasons the writer uses to support her position.

3. Name the authorities the writer cites. How do they support her position?

4. What use does the writer make of statistics? What are the sources of the statistics?

5. Is the writer's appeal to reason, to emotions, or to both? Support your answer by citing specific examples from the essay.

Writing the Introduction

The opening paragraphs of your persuasive essay should accomplish several things. First, you should capture your readers' interest. Depending on your audience's familiarity with the topic, the opening paragraphs may also provide background information to make the readers aware of how and why the topic is important to them.

The second purpose of the *introduction* is to state your point of view. Usually this is accomplished in a single sentence (the proposition) that states what you will prove in your essay. In the following introductory paragraph the proposition is in *italics.*

Unless there is a draft, millions of young Americans may go throughout their lives with little thought to serving their country. *I believe that all eighteen-year-olds, both men and women, should be required to spend one year in some kind of local, state, or national service.* Such service could be working with children in urban areas, aiding the elderly who live alone, or maintaining our national parks and forests.

For a single year of their lives, American young people could take part in a kind of national Peace Corps, aimed at improving the quality of lives of the citizens of this country.

Writing Practice 1

Using the following guidelines, write an introduction for a persuasive essay.

1. Include a proposition that is clearly worded and straightforward. Avoid vague and abstract language; say it simply. You may want to try several different wordings until you come up with one that satisfies you.

2. Imagine that your audience knows nothing about the issue you are discussing. What information do you need to include in the introduction so that they can follow your argument? Give the needed background information.

3. Think about how to make the readers want to read your essay. Why is the topic relevant to their lives? Perhaps you can use an anecdote or a question to involve the reader immediately.

Writing the Body of the Paper

The reasons and supporting details that make up the *body* of the paper are called the *argument*.

As you try to persuade your reader to your point of view, make sure that you follow the principles of logical reasoning discussed in Chapter 6. Avoid logical fallacies and deceptive appeals to the emotion. Try to convince your reader by means of a tightly constructed argument of reasons and evidence.

If you have developed an outline of reasons and supporting details, go over the outline carefully. This time think about how to order the reasons most effectively. You may decide to present your reasons in the order of their importance, with the most important ones first and the least important last. Another approach would be to choose the two strongest arguments to use first and last, and to sandwich the weaker arguments between.

Before you begin to write, think carefully about what to keep and what to discard. Do not try to include everything that you know about the topic. Remember that your goal is to produce a strong, tight, and convincing argument. You will want to avoid wordiness and digressions, eliminating reasons or evidence that will weaken your argument.

One approach to paragraphing is to make each of your reasons the topic sentence of a paragraph. Each paragraph would then be developed with examples and details that support the topic sentence. (See pages 47–60 for a review of paragraph development.) Use the facts, statistics, and quotations you have gathered during your research as support for your reasons.

As part of your argument, you will probably want to consider and refute opposing points of view. The writer of "Staying Well," for example, chose to present two common arguments against wearing seat belts: that wearing them is thought "uncool" and that the one who chooses not to wear them would be the only loser in the event of an accident. The writer refutes the second argument by pointing out that families, friends, and possibly even the government would be involved in the event of an accident.

In your essay state the opposition's arguments clearly and tell why you think each reason is not valid or justified. Some writers choose to refute opposing reasons one by one as they develop their own argument. If you prefer, you may save a discussion of the opposing point of view until you have finished your own argument. A serious consideration of the opposing viewpoint will give your reader the impression that you are fair and knowledgeable. If you do not bring up the opposing point of view, your reader may not be persuaded without first considering the opposition's arguments.

Writing Practice 2

Before you begin to write the body of your paper, you might want to do a detailed outline of the entire essay in which you decide how many reasons you will give and the order in which you will present them. If you do, sort through your notes to determine the reasons and evidence that will make the most effective argument. Then consider which of the opposition's reasons you will discuss, how best to refute each reason, and where in the paper you will refute the opposition's view. Then write the body of the paper.

Writing the Conclusion

The *concluding paragraphs* of any essay should leave the reader with a sense of completeness. In writing a persuasive argument this can be accomplished in several ways.

If the essay is a long one, a summary of the argument to remind the reader of important points can be an effective conclusion. Another possibility is to end the essay with a call to action, telling readers what they can do if they agree with your viewpoint. Perhaps you will suggest that the readers write to their elected officials or volunteer their time for a community project.

Yet another way to end a persuasive essay is to consider possible solutions to a problem. However, remember that once you have stated your argument and refuted the opposition's views, your paper is almost complete. Avoid the temptation to ramble; instead, keep your conclusion brief and to the point.

Warning readers what will happen if they do not support your opinion can also be a good approach. For example, Representative Bud Shuster from Pennsylvania argued against mandatory seat belt laws in an essay for *Motor Trend* magazine. He concluded the essay with a warning of what would happen if Congress passed such a law:

> In this election year, we are hearing much about the evils of big government and regulation from Washington of our daily lives. It's well to remember that big government will continue to exert ever-greater influence on us as long as we relinquish to it our responsibility for our own health and safety. For this reason, I say we should let every individual make the wise choice to wear a safety belt.

Writing Practice 3

Using one of the methods discussed in the previous section or one of your choosing, write a conclusion for your persuasive essay. Do not weaken your

---

[1]Excerpt from "Should seat belt usage be mandated by law?" by Bud Shuster reprinted by permission from *Motor Trend* Magazine, August 1976.

paper with a rambling, vague ending. Keep the conclusion specific—and short.

Revising the Persuasive Essay

Use the Checklist for Proofreading on page 17 to check your paper for features that are not a part of Edited Standard English.

Once you have written a rough draft, use the points in the following checklist as a guide for *revision*. (Your teacher may want to read your rough draft before you begin revising.) Write revisions of words, phrases, and sentences between the lines of your essay. If you need to rearrange paragraphs, you can do so by cutting the paragraphs apart and taping them in the proper order on another sheet of paper. When you have finished, recopy the essay as your teacher directs.

Checklist for Revising a Persuasive Essay

1. Emotional appeals, if any, are used for a positive purpose; they are not an appeal to emotional fears.
2. Fallacies in logic, such as hasty generalizations, are avoided.
3. The topic of the essay is both current and controversial.
4. The essay has a clearly stated, positively worded proposition.
5. The proposition is sufficiently supported with reasons to be convincing to the reader.
6. Each reason is developed with supporting details and evidence.
7. The language is neither vague nor ambiguous.
8. The content of the essay is designed to appeal to the audience; the language is appropriate for the audience.
9. The opening paragraphs of the essay capture the reader's interest and provide necessary background information.
10. The introductory paragraph contains the proposition.
11. Each paragraph in the essay is developed with details and examples that support the topic sentence.
12. The opposition's main arguments are stated and refuted.
13. The essay has a concluding paragraph.

8 Writing for Business

Writing Business Letters

Business letters differ from social and personal letters in purpose, content, and appearance.

Before you begin to write a business letter, think about the answers to the following questions.

1. What is the purpose of the letter?

Business letters are written primarily to get something done: to order a product, subscribe to a service, apply for a job, ask for a certain response, or to achieve a similar purpose. Since a business letter often asks the reader to respond in a certain way, it must be clear, direct, and complete in stating the purpose and desired response.

2. What is the content of a business letter?

A business letter should be about one subject only. It is not appropriate for a writer to tell about his or her personal life, nor to carry on a conversation about everyday events. If the purpose of the letter is to order a product, all the necessary information to fill the order promptly and accurately should be included. If the letter is meant to compliment or criticize a public official, the writer's point of view should be stated clearly, in firm but polite language.

3. How should a business letter look?

The correct form for a business letter is shown on page 152.

Social letters may differ in appearance, but a business letter follows a definite form. By observing certain standard forms in business writing, writers help readers find information quickly and leave readers with a positive impression of the writer.

The writer of the business letter on page 152 observes good writing practices. As you read the letter, note how the writer states the purpose clearly, gives accurate information, and makes a positive impression through the appearance of the letter.

The writer has directly stated the purpose of her letter: She has lost a backpack at the terminal and wants it returned if it has been found. She has provided the reader enough information to identify the particular backpack by describing its contents and make. Also, she has written a clear, direct business letter that leaves a good impression with the addressee and tells him how to respond.

```
                                    5051 South 102nd Street
                                    Greenfield, WI 53228
                                    November 27, 1984


Richard Saunders, Manager
Airport Operations
General Mitchell Field
5300 South Howell Ave.
Milwaukee, WI 53209


Dear Mr. Saunders:

    On November 21, 1984, I left a small backpack in the Republic
Airlines terminal.  It is a blue canvas haversack with a black
shoulder strap.  In it are a change of clothing, including a
pair of jeans, size 10, a gray sweatshirt with a hood (the draw-
string is missing), and a pair of size 6 blue tennis shoes, and
a copy of the January issue of Omni magazine.

    If you have found such a backpack, please send it to me
at my home address:  5051 South 102nd Street, Greenfield, WI
53228.  I will be happy to pay the cost of shipment.  Or you
may call me at 529-1160 any weekday after 4:00 P.M. or on week-
ends, and I will make arrangements to have the backpack picked
up at the terminal.

    Thank you for your consideration.


                              Sincerely,

                              Carol Szyplik

                              Carol Szyplik
```

**Business
Letter Form**

A business letter should be written on plain white paper, usually 8½ by 11 inches. Typewritten letters are preferable because they are easier to read. However, if you do not have a typewriter or do not type well, write in ink in your most legible handwriting. To keep your handwriting in even lines, place a piece of lined composition paper underneath the plain white paper.

The appearance of your letter makes a positive or negative statement about you. A good business letter should not show smudges or cross-outs, and it should have no spelling, usage, or punctuation errors. That means you must edit your letter carefully so that it will make the best possible impression upon your reader.

Other conventions to observe when you write a business letter follow.

1. The pages of a business letter should be framed in white by margins around the letter.

    First, you will have to judge how long your letter will be so you can leave enough room for margins. A good practice is to write a rough draft first and then rewrite it for a better appearance. Top and bottom margins should be about the same; left- and right-hand margins should also be about the same. The left-hand margin should be absolutely straight; try to keep the right-hand margin as straight as possible. Do not write on the back of the first sheet of a business letter. If you have to write a second page, begin it at the same level as the body of your letter on the first page. A second page should have at least three lines of the body of the letter.

2. The *heading* of a business letter is the three-line part that appears in the upper right-hand section of the first page.

    The first line of the heading contains your street address and apartment number, if there is one, or your rural route. The second line contains your city, state, and ZIP code number. The third line contains the date. In the sample letter on page 152, notice how punctuation is used to separate city, state, day of the month, and year. There is no comma between the state and the ZIP code or at the end of lines in the heading.

A list of two-letter state abbreviations approved by the U.S. Post Office is on page 159.

3. The *inside address* gives the name of the person or company you are writing to, the street address, the city, state, and ZIP code.

    If you write to a particular person whose title is short, include that person's title on the first line:

    Ms. Mary Grimaldi, Vice President

    If the title is a long one, however, write it on the second line:

    Dr. Frank Unamuno
    Supervisor of Outpatient Care

    If you do not know the person who will respond to your letter, address it to a title (such as *Personnel Director* or *Manager of Customer Relations*) or to a department (such as *Admissions Office* or *Credit Department*). Always try to specify the department in a company or organization to which you are writing. Avoid using *To Whom It May Concern*.

4. The *salutation* contains the name of the person or office to which you are writing.

Skip a line of space below the inside address and then write the salutation. In a business letter the salutation begins with the word *Dear* followed by the name of the person to whom you are writing and is punctuated with a colon:

Dear Ms. Carruthers: Dear Personnel Department Manager:
Dear Dr. Stumpf: Dear Sir or Ms:

5. The *body* of a business letter begins two lines of space below the salutation and is single-spaced with a line of space between paragraphs.

If you use the semiblock style, as in the example on page 152, the first line of each paragraph is indented a few spaces (usually five spaces on the typewriter). In the block styles, however, no paragraphs are indented.

As in any kind of writing, each paragraph of the business letter contains one topic. Many business letters, such as an order letter, contain only a single paragraph; others may contain several paragraphs.

6. The *closing* appears two lines of space after the body and is appropriate for a business letter.

Yours truly,   Sincerely,   Very truly yours,

7. The *signature* appears directly below the closing.

If you type your letter, skip four lines below the closing and type your name. Sign your name in ink in the space between the closing and your typewritten name.

Yours truly,   Sincerely,   Very truly yours,

George Truman   *Cecilia Tauhy*   *Kim Wang*

George Truman   Cecilia Tauhy   Kim Wang

If you write your letter in script, simply sign your name below the closing.

Yours truly,   Sincerely,   Very truly yours,

George Truman   *Cecilia Tauhy*   *Kim Wang*

Semiblock, Block, and Full Block Forms

You can choose from three basic business letter forms—*semiblock*, *block*, and *full block*—when you type or write a letter by hand, although the full block is most often used for typed letters. The forms vary in indentation and alignment of letter parts.

1. *Semiblock Form*

The model letter on page 152 is written in semiblock form. The first line of each paragraph in the letter is indented five spaces. The heading, closing, and signature are aligned slightly to the right of the center of the page. All the other parts of the letter are aligned with the left-hand margin.

2. *Block Form*

In the block form, paragraphs in the body of the letter are not indented. However, the heading, closing, and signature are aligned with each other slightly to the right of the center of the page.

3. *Full Block Form*

In the full block style every line, whether typed or written by hand, begins at the left-hand margin. Paragraphs in the body of the letter are not indented. This form saves time typing because nothing has to be indented.

A diagram of the three business letter forms is shown below.

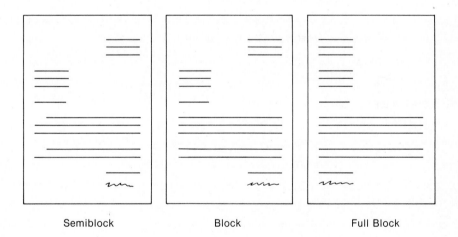

Semiblock   Block   Full Block

Writing Practice 1

On a sheet of paper, set up forms for two of the following business letters. Draw lines to indicate the body of the letter and write all of the other parts according to the information provided. Use today's date or a future date. Select a different form for each of the two letters.

1. César Perez, of 209 Brush Creek Boulevard, Apartment 51, Kansas City, Missouri 64112, is writing to Mrs. Helen Goff, Manager of Consumer Affairs, Gayle Enterprises, whose mailing address is Box 504, Fairleigh Station, Saint Joseph, Missouri 64506.

2. Joanna Vandermere, who lives at 2291 E. Fifty-Fifth Street in Cleveland, Ohio 44103, is writing to the Admissions Officer of Rider College at 2083 Lawrenceville Road, Trenton, New Jersey 08602.

3. Ms. Sarah Chung, who lives on Rural Route 10, Taos, New Mexico 87571, is writing to the Air Force Recruitment Office, United States Air Force, Kirtland Air Force Base, Albuquerque, New Mexico 87117.

4. Dr. Victoria St. John, of 226 W. Fourth Street in Davenport, Iowa 52801, is writing to Dr. B. R. Gasco, Head of Pediatrics at Children's Hospital, 226 N. Kuakini, Honolulu, Hawaii 96817.

Folding the Letter

There are two acceptable ways to fold a business letter, depending on the size of stationery and the size of the envelope. If possible, it is best to write or type a business letter on 8½ × 11 inch plain, unlined paper and to send it in a business-size envelope, 4¼ × 9½ inches.

1. If you use a long envelope for a letter on 8½ × 11 inch paper, use the following directions:
    a. Fold the bottom third of the paper toward the top of the page and make a crease.
    b. Fold the top third of the paper down and make a second crease.
    c. Insert the letter with the open end at the top into the envelope.
2. If you use a smaller envelope, fold your letter in the following way:
    a. Fold the letter in half, bringing the bottom half up. Make a crease.

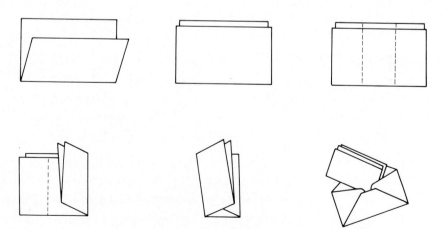

b. Fold the right third of the letter toward the left side and make a crease.

c. Fold the left third of the letter over the right third and make a crease.

d. Insert the letter with the open end at the top into the envelope.

Addressing the Envelope

Always mail a business letter in a plain, white business envelope. The name and address of the person or company to whom you are writing should be typed or written exactly as it appears on the inside address of the letter. Begin writing the address slightly below and to the left of the envelope's center. Your name and address goes in the upper left-hand corner as the return address.

See page 159 for a list of state abbreviations accepted by the post office. Always be sure to include the ZIP code in your return address and in the receiver's address, since letters sent without one may be delayed. If you do not know the ZIP code of the recipient, you can look it up in the ZIP code directory found in every post office and in many libraries.

```
Thomas Butterfield, Jr.
Washington Carver Village, No. 10
3530 Colony Forest Dr.
Columbia, SC 29203




                         Superintendent of Documents
                         Government Printing Office
                         Washington, D.C. 20402
```

Writing Practice 2

On a sheet of paper, draw outlines for three envelopes. Then use the following addresses, with your name and home address for the return address. Address the envelopes.

1. You are writing to Pacific Woodstove Distributors, P.O. Box 1148, Dept. 4J, Santa Cruz, CA 95060.

2. You are writing to Ms. Connie Navarro, Customer Relations Department, the Calligraphy Studio, 240 Kings Hwy., Orangeburg, NY 10962.

3. You are writing to Sun Designs Studio, 36802 Genesee Lake Rd., Oconomowoc, WI 53066.

Writing an Effective Letter   Business letters are effective if they accomplish their purpose. As you read the following letter, decide why it is not effective.

                                                1175 Piedmont Avenue
                                                Augusta, GA 30902
                                                January 4, 1984

Mr. Paul N. Peterson
Executive Vice President
Geological Society of America
121 Ave. of the Americas
New York, NY 10020

Dear Mr. Peterson:

I sent your organization an order for two gift subscriptions
to Geological Guide, the monthly magazine. But the two
friends who were to receive the gift subscriptions have not
seen their magazines yet. I even filled out a form, and they
dont't know about these gifts yet.

                            An angry customer,

                            Frank Alitorro

                            Frank Alitorro

Abbreviations   In the following list are two-letter abbreviations that the United States Post Office has approved for use with ZIP codes.

Alabama AL	Missouri MO	Wisconsin WI
Alaska AK	Montana MT	Wyoming WY
Arizona AZ	Nebraska NE	Canal Zone CZ
Arkansas AR	Nevada NV	District of Columbia DC
California CA	New Hampshire NH	
Colorado CO	New Jersey NJ	Guam GU
Connecticut CT	New Mexico NM	Puerto Rico PR
Delaware DE	New York NY	Virgin Islands VI
Florida FL	North Carolina NC	Alberta AB
Georgia GA	North Dakota ND	British Columbia BC
Hawaii HI	Ohio OH	Manitoba MB
Idaho ID	Oklahoma OK	New Brunswick NB
Illinois IL	Oregon OR	Newfoundland NF
Indiana IN	Pennsylvania PA	Northwest Territories NT
Iowa IA	Rhode Island RI	Nova Scotia NS
Kansas KS	South Carolina SC	Ontario ON
Kentucky KY	South Dakota SD	Prince Edward Island PE
Louisiana LA	Tennessee TN	
Maine ME	Texas TX	Quebec PQ
Maryland MD	Utah UT	Saskatchewan SK
Massachusetts MA	Vermont VT	Yukon Territory YT
Michigan MI	Virginia VA	Labrador LB
Minnesota MN	Washington WA	
Mississippi MS	West Virginia WV	

Writing Practice 3

Rewrite the letter to the Executive Vice President of the Geological Society of America. Provide all of the missing information, making up any details that you need. (You may want to write more than one paragraph in your letter.) Write a more polite closing that will not offend the addressee.

Kinds of Business Letters

You can write a business letter to cover any situation by following the guidelines discussed in this chapter. In the following sections you will gain additional practice with five common types of business letters.

Letters of Request

A sample letter of request is on page 161.

In a *letter of request* you ask for something—information, maps, or an appointment, for example.

Occasionally you may want to write a letter asking someone to do a favor, such as speak to a class or club. A letter of request must be clear about what you want. It should be especially courteous because you are asking someone to give of his or her time. If you are asking for information, include a stamped, self-addressed envelope with your request.

If you are thinking about going to college or professional school, you will want to write several letters of request for catalogues and interview appointments.

Writing Practice 4

A checklist for proofreading business letters is on pages 166–167.

Write one of the following letters of request, using your own address as the return address on both the letter and the envelope. If you prefer, write your own letter of request.

1. Write to the Public Relations Office of the Tennessee Valley Authority, Knoxville, TN 37902, for their brochures on careers with the TVA, especially in industrial hygiene and health physics.

2. Write a letter to Technical Information Center, Department of Energy, Box 62, Oak Ridge, TN 37830, requesting information about these areas: home energy savings, chemical *do's* and *don'ts*, and driving hazards. You are responding to an advertisement in the most recent *National Geographic* magazine.

3. Write a letter to Federal Laboratories, P.O. Box 6799, Philadelphia, PA 19101, for thirty-five free reprints of their "Forum for Action" series on economics. You want to use the copies in a talk on free markets in your economics class in six weeks.

4. Write a letter to the head of the reference section of a nearby library (public or university) asking that person to speak to your English class in the near future. Your class is especially interested in learning how to use the reference section effectively and in finding out what services the reference librarians offer to help students research subjects.

4500 Royal Gorge Rd.
Canon City, CO 81246
April 30, 1984

Director of Admissions
Detroit Business Institute
19100 Fort
Riverview, MI 48192

Dear Sir or Ms.:

I am a senior in high school and will graduate next winter. I am
interested in attending business school to get training as a
medical clerical specialist. My counselor has told me that the
Detroit Business Institute has an excellent program in medical
administration.

Will you please send me your current catalogue for the Institute
as well as any additional information you may have about courses
of study or special programs related to training for medical
clerical specialist. I would also like information about financial
aid for students.

Thank you very much.

Sincerely,

Troy Monroe

Troy Monroe

Order Letters

An *order letter* contains a request for a company to send you merchandise.

In an order letter you should describe the merchandise completely and exactly. Write the size, model number, color, price, and any special features of the product you are ordering. It might help to mention when and where you saw the merchandise advertised.

A sample order letter is on page 162.

Be sure to say in the letter how you are paying for the order. Usually either a check or a money order is enclosed with an order letter. Do not send cash through the mail; it may be lost, and you then have no proof that payment was sent. Study the sample order letter on page 162.

```
                                    3228 Plainview Road
                                    Washington, D.C. 20580
                                    February 2, 1984

       Grice's Scientific Company
       Department 242   K218
       Nescorp Building
       Tulsa, OK 74106

       Dear Sir or Ms.:

       Please send me one Solar Calculator (No. 51CZ). I saw your
       advertisement for the Solar Calculator in the October issue of
       Today's Computers magazine.

       I am including a money order payable to Grice's Scientific
       Company for $28.38.  This amount includes the price of the
       Solar Calculator ($25.88) plus the $2.50 charge for
       guaranteed delivery.

       Please also include the instruction book that tells how to use
       the calculator.

       Thank you.

                                    Yours truly,

                                    John P. Davis

                                    John P. Davis
```

Writing Practice 5

A checklist for proofreading business letters is on pages 166–167.

Using your own name and address and today's date, write one of the following order letters.

1. Musich Electronic Supply, 304 El Capitan Ave. N., Denver, CO 80231, has available a catalogue of low-cost, high-quality electronic equipment. The cost of the catalogue is $3.00. Order the catalogue. (You saw it advertised in the September issue of *Scientific Equipment* magazine.)

2. Order from SHIRTS, Box 2116, Anderson, IN 46011, one sweat shirt for $16 or two for $26 in light gray, size S, M, L, XL. Ask for one of the following imprints: Alice in Wonderland, Bach, Einstein, Joan of Arc,

Scrooge, or St. Nick. The shipping charge is seventy-five cents per shirt. The order must be paid in advance.

3. Write to Government Information Services, Department GM-11, Box 99249, San Francisco, CA 94109, and order their comprehensive directory of government surplus items and places to buy them in your area. The directory costs $2.00.

Letters of Adjustment

A *letter of adjustment* is written to convince a company to replace damaged merchandise, refund money, or correct an error in billing.

A sample letter of adjustment is on page 164.

In order to correct the mistake, the recipient will have to know all necessary information. In your letter state the problem and then present evidence as clearly and logically as you can. You may want to describe the problem step by step, in chronological order but remember to include only the necessary details. Be clear and brief.

After you have stated and described your problem, tell the company or individual what it is you want done. If you do not know the best method of making the adjustment, say so. Indicate whether you want a refund or your account credited for the cost of the merchandise or the faulty products repaired or replaced.

Letters of adjustment should be courteous in tone. Assume that the company or individual is reliable and that you will get the adjustment you seek. If you do not hear from the recipient within a few weeks, send a follow-up letter, citing the date of your first letter and restating the problem.

Writing Practice 6

A checklist for proofreading business letters is on pages 166–167.

Write one of the following letters of adjustment. Use your own name and address and the current date. Make up any details you need in order to write an effective letter of adjustment.

1. You sent $8.50 for a one-year subscription to *Computers Today*, a new quarterly magazine about computer technology. However, it has been six months, and you have not yet received your first copy. Write to *Computers Today* Subscription Department, P.O. Box 201, Martinsville, NJ 08836, asking it either to cancel your subscription and return your money or to send you the two back issues you are missing.

2. You ordered an army surplus fatigue jacket from the Recycling Store, 330 Lee Street B, Des Plaines, IL 60016. You had saved your money to buy this jacket at $17.50 plus $2.25 shipping and handling cost and were disappointed to find that, when it arrived, the buttons were missing. You want the company to replace the jacket with one that has no defects.

3. You bought a new shampoo that claimed it would leave hair that was damaged from permanents or tinting "like new, soft and shining—with no split and broken ends," or the company would refund your money. After one application the shampoo left your hair in worse condition than

7555 Caldwell Ave.
Chicago, IL 60648
January 22, 1984

Order Department
Cahill & Company
145 Palisade Street
Dobbs Ferry, NY 10522

Dear Order Department:

On October 20 I ordered a boxed set of <u>A Space Trilogy</u> by Madeleine L'Engle, Item No. 921 priced at $5.25 for the paperbound set. At the same time I ordered a C.S. Lewis Calendar, Item No. 005 at $3.95. A package from you arrived today, but it contained items other than the ones I ordered. You sent me a Great Cathedrals Calendar and a boxed set of <u>The Chronicles of Narnia</u> by C.S. Lewis.

I am returning both the Great Cathedrals Calendar and the set of <u>The Chronicles of Narnia</u> by mail today. Please send me as soon as possible the two items I originally ordered. For your convenience, I am repeating that order:

    1 boxed set of <u>A Space Trilogy</u> by Madeleine L'Engle, No. 921, $5.25

    1 C. S. Lewis Calendar, No.005, $3.95

I sent you a money order for $11.15 with my original order to cover the cost of the books and calendar as well as the $1.95 shipping charge.

Thank you very much.

                              Sincerely,

                              Elena Dimarata

                              Elena Dimarata

before. Tell the company that you are returning the label from the bottle of shampoo and ask them to refund your money. The shampoo is made by Universal Hair Care Products, 2321 Greenway Road, Montgomery, AL 36108.

Letters of Appreciation

A *letter of appreciation* is the business version of a thank-you note.

Because people in business and public life often get critical letters and complaints, they especially appreciate a letter of praise or thanks for work well done. When you write a letter of appreciation, be sure to identify yourself,

```
                                    17 Tufts Avenue, E.
                                    Chicago, IL  60648
                                    September 23, 1984

          Public Broadcasting System
          Channel 11, WTTW
          5400 N. St. Louis
          Chicago, IL  60625

          Dear Channel 11:

          I want to express my appreciation for the fine new series
          Cosmos that Channel 11 broadcasts on Sunday evenings in my
          area.  Cosmos fits my criteria for a good program; it explains
          scientific phenomena clearly, teaches facts about our universe,
          and is visually interesting and entertaining.

          My friends and I usually watch the program together on Sunday
          evenings.  Afterwards we talk about the ideas Dr. Sagan presented
          that evening, and we sometimes use the information we learned
          from the show in our science class at school.  For instance, we
          didn't really understand the concept of "black holes" until it
          was graphically explained on a recent showing of Cosmos. Now that
          we have seen the concept explained, the textbook explanation
          makes better sense.

          I hope that the Public Broadcasting System will continue to show
          editions of Cosmos and other scientific, informative programs
          like it.  I have gained much from watching the show, and my
          interest in science has increased.

          Thank you again for producing such an excellent program.

                                    Sincerely,

                                    Maria Solares

                                    Maria Solares
```

usually at the beginning of the letter. Explain why you are writing the letter and express your thanks briefly and courteously.

Writing Practice 7

Write a letter of appreciation to some person or organization that you think is doing a good job. You may choose from among the following suggestions or use one of your own.

1. An elected public official in your town, county, or state government
2. Your senator or representative in Congress
3. An organization that worked for legislation that benefited your community
4. A newspaper or magazine that published an educational story or series
5. An entertainer who has helped raise funds for an organization or cause to aid people in need
6. A community or church leader
7. A radio or television station that broadcasts a program you enjoy
8. A company that has given you especially good service
9. A newspaper columnist who wrote a column you especially admired
10. A teacher or school official who did a special favor for you

Proofreading a Business Letter

Because you want a business letter to make a good impression, proofread it carefully to make sure that it is complete, follows standard form, and is free from errors. Use the following checklist as a guide in proofreading your business letters.

Checklist for Proofreading a Business Letter

FORM AND APPEARANCE

1. The letter is neatly written in ink or typed, with no smudges or obvious corrections.
2. The letter is centered on the page, with each part having the correct amount of spacing above and below.
3. The left-hand margins are exactly even: the left-hand margin of the heading aligns with the left-hand margin of the closing and signature; the left-hand margin of the inside address aligns with the left-hand margin of the salutation.
4. The right-hand margin of the body of the letter is fairly even.
5. Your signature is legible and written in ink.

PUNCTUATION

1. In the heading and inside address, a comma comes between the city and state. There should be no comma between the state and ZIP code.

2. A comma comes between the day of the month and the year in the heading.

3. A colon follows the salutation.

4. A comma follows the closing.

CAPITALIZATION

1. Capitalize the names of streets, cities, and states in the heading and inside address.

2. Capitalize the month in the heading.

3. Capitalize the title of the person you are writing to and the names of the department and company listed in the inside address.

4. Capitalize the word *Dear* and all nouns in the salutation.

5. Capitalize only the first word of the closing.

Letters of Application

A sample letter of application is on pages 168–169.

A *letter of application* is written to apply for a job.

When you want to apply for a job you have heard about or seen advertised, plan a letter of application that will impress the prospective employer enough to contact you for an interview. The letter should give the impression that you are neat and responsible, as well as qualified for the job. Because employers receive many letters for a single job, they often discard those that do not make a good impression because of messy appearance or errors in spelling and grammar.

A letter of application should contain at least the following information.

1. *The source of information about the job.* Identify the job you are applying for and tell when and how you learned about it.

2. *Personal data.* Include your age, grade in school, grade average, health, and any other information that might be pertinent to the job.

3. *Your qualifications.* Include your previous experience, special training, and interest in the field. If the job for which you are applying is in a field that might become part of your long-range career plans, mention those plans briefly.

   If you do not have any direct experience in the kind of job for which you are applying, think of experiences you have had that are in some way related to the job. Also, be sure to include personal characteristics such as reliability, promptness, and a willingness to work.

4. *Your references.* Give the names and addresses of two or three adults who can attest to your character and ability. Do not list relatives as your references; instead, choose an adult who knows you well, such as a teacher, rabbi, priest, minister, former employer, or neighbor. Before you give a person's name as a reference, be sure to ask him or her for permission.

2663 Fergus
Santa Barbara, CA 93104
May 6, 1984

Personnel Director
Home Picture Technical Labs, Inc.
2500 LaArcada
Santa Barbara, CA 93104

Dear Personnel Director:

I wish to apply for the full-time opening you described in the <u>Santa Barbara Post</u> last Sunday for a film lab worker during summer vacation, June 10 through September 14. I have experience working with photographic equipment, and I am now helping a professional photographer in a part-time job after school.

I am a seventeen-year-old junior at Granada High School. My grade point average is 3.0, or "B." Although I am preparing for college or trade school, I have taken two photography courses in high school and have attended classes given by a local camera shop in order to learn more about professional photography. If I can become more skilled in working with cameras and film production, I hope to be able to support myself while I attend college.

On weekends, during school vacations, and on two evenings a week, I work at Frank's Cameras, Unlimited. My duties include accepting and sending film for development, managing the 16-mm educational film rental service, checking stock on hand, ordering supplies, and assisting the store night manager by waiting on customers. I am frequently asked to suggest filming techniques or to explain the proper use of complicated camera equipment to customers who need help taking or developing better photos. In addition to my job, I have a well-stocked darkroom at home where I can experiment with developing techniques to improve my own photography.

The following people can tell you more about my interest in and qualifications for the job at Home Picture Technical Labs, Inc.:

5. *A request for an interview.* Ask for an interview to be held at the employer's convenience and be sure to tell when and where you can be reached by telephone to make an appointment.

It is a good idea to write a first draft of your letter in pencil. Then revise the letter to make it sound as positive as you can. Carefully proofread the revised letter for errors in spelling, punctuation, and usage. Finally write the letter neatly in ink or type it. If necessary, rewrite your letter until you think it presents you in the most favorable light. Do not mail your letter of application until it is completely free of errors.

```
Personnel Director
Page Two
May 6, 1984

        Ms. Jennifer Carswell, Head Counselor, Granada High School,
            1148 Tulsa Avenue, Santa Barbara, CA 93104

        Mr. Antonio Barrego, Fine Arts Department, Granada High
            School, 1148 Tulsa Avenue, Santa Barbara, CA 93104

        Mr. Martin S. Frank, Frank's Cameras, Unlimited, 2020 S.
            Babcock Ave., Isla Vista, CA 93107

        For further references about my personal qualifications
    and characteristics, please call or write the following people:

        Rev. Mary E. Easterwood, St. Martin's-on-the-Hill,
            735 Montecito, Santa Barbara, CA 93101

        Dr. Li Min-Ray, Osteopathic Clinic No. 4, PO Box 4001,
            Milpas Station, Santa Barbara, CA 93103

        At your convenience I would be happy to come to your office
    for an interview.  You can reach me at home after school and on
    Monday, Wednesday, and Friday evenings.  My telephone number is
    491-1929.

                                    Sincerely yours,

                                    Penny Pilipuf

                                    Penny Pilipuf
```

Writing Practice 8

A checklist for proofreading business letters is on pages 166–167.

Think about a part-time or summer job you would like to have and for which you feel qualified. Use the classified pages of a telephone directory or look in the classified advertisement section of a newspaper to find the name of a company that might have this kind of job. Then write a letter of application to the personnel director, being certain to include all the information listed on pages 167–168. Proofread your letter carefully, following the correct form for business letters.

```
                                            15 Front Street
                                            Dallas, TX 75218
                                            April 14, 1984


    Florence Boucher, Manager
    Sinbad Travel, Inc.
    8 Wright Street
    Empire Bank Building
    Dallas, TX 75207

    Dear Ms. Boucher:

    Mr. Ted Cosby, work experience coordinator at my school, has
    informed me that you have an opening for a part-time assistant
    at Sinbad Travel, Inc.  He suggested that I write to you to
    present a résumé of my qualifications and experience.

    I have always been interested in working with people.  My ability
    to speak several languages makes it possible for me to help those
    who need information but do not understand English.  I can assist
    both travel agents and clients in translating English into four
    languages--Spanish, Tagalog, Japanese, and French--so that travel
    arrangements can be made accurately.

    My school schedule permits me to have afternoons and evenings
    free for extracurricular activities and part-time employment.  I
    can also work on Saturdays and during school holidays.

    Please contact me at my home any afternoon or evening, or ask
    Mr. Cosby to arrange an interview for us at your convenience.
    You may phone Mr. Cosby at 732-8824 between 8:00 A.M. and 3:00 P.M.

    Thank you very much.


                                        Sincerely,

                                        Marian Quingyuan

                                        Marian Quingyuan
```

Writing a Résumé

As an alternative to the long letter of application, you may choose to outline your background and experience in a personal résumé, such as the one on page 171. Written in outline form to make it easier for an employer to read and find the necessary information quickly, a résumé also gives a neat and businesslike appearance.

The purpose of a résumé is to interest the prospective employer in you. You do not have to include every bit of information about your life, but you should include information that has a direct bearing on your qualifications for the job. You can use a well-written résumé when applying for several jobs.

```
                        Marian L. Quingyuan

         Address:      15 Front Street
                       Dallas, Texas 75218

         Telephone:    482-3387

         Personal:     Born September 9, 1967 in Brownsville, TX
                       Health:  Excellent
                       Social Security number:  043-66-4439

         Education:    Junior, Dallas Academy
                       Major studies:  College preparatory courses with
                          concentration in foreign languages and history
                       Grade point average:  3.2  (B)
                       Other schooling:  Attended grades 8-10 in Manila,
                          Republic of the Philippines

         Summer and
         Part-Time
         Work
         Experience:   Summer 1983        Clerk-typist and receptionist
                                          YWCA Summer Camp Office,
                                          Dallas, TX
                       Oct.-Feb., 1984    Tutored Japanese and Tagalog-
                                          speaking preschool children
                                          in English, American Language
                                          School, Manila

                       Current            Part-time assistant translator in
                                          Spanish, Legal Aid Society, Dallas

         Skills:       Can speak and translate Tagalog, Spanish, and English
                          fluently
                       Can type 50 words per minute
                       Can research information in reference works accurately
                       Can conduct telephone interviews as well as personal
                          interviews.

         Special
         Interests:    Swimming, photography,
                       skating

         References:   Mrs. Margret Mendoza, Special Services Director,
                       American Language School, Manila, The Republic
                       of the Philippines

                       Mr. Jackson P. Emerson, Head, Summer Programs, YWCA
                       3811 N. Switzer Ave., Dallas, TX 75216

                       Ms. Genevra Bowen, Attorney-at-Law, Legal Aid Society,
                       Randolph Towers, 601 Commerce, Dallas, TX 75202

                       Mr. Grant Hammersly, Principal, Dallas Academy,
                       Box 13501 Hall Station, Dallas, TX 75202
```

Tagalog is the official language of the Philippines.

A sample cover letter is on page 170.

When you use a résumé to apply for a job, you also need to write a short cover letter. The cover letter should not repeat the information given in the résumé; instead, it should begin by identifying the job for which you are applying and by telling how you heard about it. You can then add some interesting or useful piece of information that is not included in the résumé but that you think will help your chances of getting the job with that particular business. State in your cover letter that you are enclosing a résumé of your qualifications and references. Since the purpose of your cover letter is to secure an interview, end your letter with a request for an interview and indicate when you can be reached to set up an appointment.

Writing Practice 9

Choose a summer job in which you are interested or find a newspaper ad for a job you might like. Then write a personal résumé and cover letter you might send to the prospective employer.

Filling Out Forms

Business and government offices use forms to obtain and store information. You will be filling out forms of one kind or another most of your life. The following sections will give you practice and instruction on how to fill out forms accurately and efficiently.

The following guidelines apply to all types of forms—long or short, simple or complicated.

1. Always use blue or black ink or a typewriter. Never use a pencil unless the form expressly directs you to do so.

2. Print—do not write—the information requested on the form. Make sure that any numbers you write are clear and legible. If there are boxes or lines on which to write, stay within the boundaries given.

3. Always read the directions carefully and completely before filling out a form. Although directions often come at the beginning of a form, they sometimes appear at the end or on the reverse side. If the form is a complicated one, such as a credit application or an income tax return, there may be an accompanying booklet telling you how to fill the form out.

4. Read the fine print carefully.

5. Most forms require a signature at the end. Sign your name as you usually write it for legal and business purposes.

Voter Registration Form

The example on page 173 shows the kind of government form that you will be asked to fill out when you register to vote for the first time. This particular voter registration form is written both in English and in Spanish because the county from which it comes has so many Spanish-speaking residents that it has officially become a bilingual county.

When you fill out a government form, a clerk is usually nearby to answer any questions you may have. Be especially careful not to write in the areas

DO NOT WRITE ABOVE THIS LINE - NO ESCRIBA SOBRE ESTA LINEA		PRECINCT NO	REGISTRATION NO		

LAST NAME - APELLIDO	FIRST - NOMBRE	MIDDLE - SEGUNDO	PARTY - PARTIDO	SEX - SEXO	RACE - RAZA

RESIDENT ADDRESS - DIRECCION RESIDENCIAL	APT - APTO	CITY - CIUDAD	ZIP - ZONA POSTAL	MUN. CODE

MAILING ADDRESS - DIRECCION POSTAL	CITY - CIUDAD	ZIP - ZONA POSTAL	HOME TEL /TEL CASA	OFFICE TEL /TEL OFICINA

DATE OF BIRTH FECHA DE NACIMIENTO	PLACE OF BIRTH LUGAR DE NACIMIENTO	IF FOREIGN BORN, ARE YOU A NATURALIZED U.S CITIZEN? YES ☐ NO ☐ IF NO, EXPLAIN BELOW SI NACIO EN EL EXTRANJERO. ¿ES CIUDADANO NATURALIZADO DE EE UU ? SI ☐ NO ☐ ¡SI NO EXPLIQUE!

SOCIAL SECURITY NO. (OPTIONAL) SEGURO SOCIAL NO. (OPCIONAL)	REGISTRATION DATE FECHA DE INSCRIPCION	FELONY CONVICTION? / ¿DELITO GRAVE?	REQUIRES ASSISTANCE / NECESITA AYUDA
		IF YES. ATTACH AFFIDAVIT	PHYSICALLY DISABLED INCAPACITADO ☐ BLIND CIEGO ☐ ILLITERATE ANALFABETA ☐

Oath: I do solemnly swear (or affirm) that I will protect and defend the Constitution of the United States and the Constitution of the State of Florida, and that I am qualified to register as an elector under the Constitution and laws of the State of Florida, and that I am a citizen of the United States and a legal resident of Dade County, Florida. That I have ☐ never previously registered to vote in any other jurisdiction ☐ been registered under the name of _____ at _____ and request that my prior registration be cancelled, and that all of the information on this form is true.

Juramento: Juro (o afirmo) solemnemente que protegeré y defenderé la Constitución de Estados Unidos y la Constitución del Estado de la Florida, y que estoy habilitado para inscribirme como elector según la Constitución y las leyes del Estado de la Florida, y que soy ciudadano de los Estados Unidos y residente legal del Condado de Dade, en el Estado de la Florida. Que nunca ☐ he estado inscripto anteriormente para votar en otra jurisdicción ☐ que he estado inscripto con el nombre de _____ en _____ y, solicito que sea cancelada mi inscripción previa, y que toda la información en este formulario es verdadera.

DEPUTY SUPERVISOR OF ELECTIONS / SUPERVISOR ADJUNTO DE ELECCIONES 105.05-10 *METROPOLITAN DADE COUNTY, FLORIDA*	SIGNATURE OF VOTER / FIRMA DEL ELECTOR	LETTER OF PARTY AFILIACION DE PARTIDO

designated for office use. Notice, for example, that the first line of the voter registration form says, "Do not write above this line."

On the voter registration form you are asked to write your Social Security number. However, that information is optional. If you already have a Social Security number, make sure you bring it with you whenever you plan to fill out a form of any kind. If you do not yet have a Social Security number, apply for one from your local office of the Social Security Administration. You will use this identifying number for the rest of your life.

One of the essentials in filling out forms correctly is to put the information in the correct place in the order requested. For example, at the bottom of the voter registration form is an oath that requires you to swear to uphold the Constitution and to swear that the information given on the form is true. You might be tempted to write your signature underneath the oath in English; it looks as if there is space for it there. If you look carefully, however, you will see that the signature belongs in the bottom right-hand corner.

In what order does the sample voter registration form ask you to write your name? Incorrect order is one of the most common mistakes that people make in filling out forms. Many forms ask for your last name first. Others request that you write your first name first. Be sure to see which order is required before you write your name.

Dade County voter registration form. Reprinted by permission of James J. Kohanek, Assistant Supervisor of Elections, Dade County, Florida.

Financial Aid Form To see an example of the kind of longer, more complicated forms that you may be asked to complete, look at the ACT Student Data form on this page. This is a request for financial aid to be completed by students who are plan-

R  **ACT STUDENT DATA FORM (SDF) 1982-83**

Students: Complete this form and mail to ACT with your FFS. If you are requesting only one ACT code in item 2, you may send this completed form directly to the institution. Information on this form won't affect ACT's analysis, but institutions can use it when they consider you for aid.

Please print, using black ink.

STUDENT INFORMATION

1. Did you give ACT permission to send information from your FFS to the Department of Education? (See question 74 of the FFS.) ☐ Yes ☐ No

2. In the boxes to the right, copy the same ACT codes in the same order as your answer to question 76 of your FFS. ACT will send copies of this form **only** to the schools whose ACT code numbers are listed to the right.

1st Code | 2nd Code | 3rd Code | 4th Code

3. NAME _____ last _____ first _____ middle

4. PERMANENT MAILING ADDRESS _____ number _____ street _____ apt no _____ city _____ state _____ zip code

5. PHONE (_____) _____

6. SOCIAL SECURITY NUMBER (optional) _____

7. SEX (optional) ☐ Male ☐ Female

8. STATUS DURING 1982-83 SCHOOL YEAR
☐ Full-time student ☐ Half-time student ☐ Less than half-time student

9. CLASSIFICATION DURING 1982-83 SCHOOL YEAR
☐ Beginning freshman ☐ Continuing/returning ☐ Transfer student

10. MAJOR AREA OF STUDY _____

11. WHERE WILL YOU LIVE DURING THE 1982-83 SCHOOL YEAR?
☐ On campus ☐ With parents ☐ Off campus

If you are sending reports to more than one school, and your living plans will be different for each school, explain in item 19 below.

12. INDICATE FINANCIAL AID PREFERENCE (enter 1 for first choice, 2 for second choice, etc.)
___ Grant
___ Long-term loan
___ Part-time work
___ Academic scholarship
___ Activity scholarship (name activity) _____
___ Other (specify) _____

13. DATES FINANCIAL AID DESIRED DURING 1982-83 SCHOOL YEAR
from _____ month/year to _____ month/year

PARENT INFORMATION

14. FATHER/ STEPFATHER/ LEGAL GUARDIAN _____ name _____ address _____ city _____ state _____ zip code

OCCUPATION _____

EMPLOYER _____ NO. OF YRS. WITH _____

15. MOTHER/ STEPMOTHER/ LEGAL GUARDIAN _____ name _____ address _____ city _____ state _____ zip code

OCCUPATION _____

EMPLOYER _____ NO. OF YRS. WITH _____

16. NAMES AND AGES OF PARENTS' DEPENDENTS

1. Name _____ Age _____
2. Name _____ Age _____
3. Name _____ Age _____
4. Name _____ Age _____
5. Name _____ Age _____
6. Name _____ Age _____

17. STUDENT'S ESTIMATED RESOURCES

INCOME AVAILABLE TO MEET EXPENSES DURING TERM(S) FINANCIAL AID IS DESIRED

Personal savings	$
Total summer earnings $ _____ amount saved for school	$
Earnings while in school (exclude College Work-Study)	$
Parental support	$
Spouse's income	$
Social Security benefits	$
Veterans benefits/War Orphans benefits	$
Welfare benefits	$
Alimony	$
Scholarship received (name source)	$
Private loans	$
Other income (name source)	$
TOTAL INCOME	$

18. MARRIED STUDENTS (OR SINGLE WITH DEPENDENTS)

NUMBER OF DEPENDENTS _____ AGES _____

SPOUSE'S NAME _____

SOCIAL SECURITY NO. (optional) _____ AGE _____

SPOUSE'S OCCUPATION _____

SPOUSE'S EMPLOYER _____

SPOUSE'S GROSS EARNINGS FROM JULY 1, 1982 TO JUNE 30, 1983 $ _____

WILL YOUR SPOUSE BE A STUDENT DURING 1982-83? ☐ Yes ☐ No

IF YES, AT WHICH SCHOOL OR COLLEGE? _____

WILL YOUR SPOUSE APPLY FOR FINANCIAL AID FOR 1982-83? ☐ Yes ☐ No

19. If there are any unusual circumstances that seriously affect your family's financial situation, explain here. For more space, use the back.

ACT's 1982–83 Student Data Form. Copyright 1981 by The American College Testing Program. All rights reserved. Reproduced with permission.

ning to attend college and who want to apply for financial aid. This form has an accompanying booklet to help guide the student in providing the necessary information.

Writing Practice 10

You may never apply for financial aid for college, but it is good practice for you to try to work your way through a form like the ACT Student Data form (page 174). On a separate sheet of paper, write what you would put in each of the blanks on this form. Before you begin, make sure that you understand the meaning of the following terms: *grant, dependent, spouse, alimony,* and *gross earnings.* In the section titled "Colleges, Schools, or Agencies to Receive This Form," leave the ACT code numbers blank. Write the names of at least two colleges, schools, or agencies you might attend.

Writing Practice 11

Try to obtain one of the following forms and complete it as fully as you can. Follow the guidelines given on page 172.

1. A job application
2. An income-tax form
3. An application to a college or vocational school
4. A drivers license application
5. A credit card application

9 Imaginative Writing

Learning About Imaginative Writing

All writing relies in some way on the imagination. In general, though, only writing that is based primarily on the imagination is called *imaginative writing.*

Imaginative writing includes stories, novels, plays, and poems.

One purpose of imaginative writing is to make a creation of the mind—invented characters, places, and situations—that readers can share. In addition, many fiction writers, playwrights, and poets write to make their readers aware of the richness and beauty of the language that people use in everyday life. Another purpose of imaginative writing, then, is to explore language for its own sake.

In this chapter you will learn about imaginative fiction and poetry. You will also learn how to explore your own imagination and to express it in writing.

Elements of the Short Story

The word *story* is related to the Latin word for "history." Like history, a fictional story tells the reader about events; unlike history, most of the characters and events in fiction are invented rather than taken directly from life.

Four basic elements are needed to compose a short story: *characters, setting, plot,* and *conflict.* Two other considerations in short story composition are *point of view* and *style.*

A story's *point of view* is the way its information is given to the reader. Information may be related by one of the characters in the story or by an *omniscient*, or all-knowing, *narrator*.

Style refers to choices the writer makes. The use of words, ideas, and feelings all combine to create a writer's individual style.

Learning About Characters

One way in which writers introduce their *characters* is by telling the reader about them directly.

The paragraph that follows is the opening paragraph of a short story by John Cheever titled "The Enormous Radio." This paragraph introduces the two main characters by describing their physical appearance and telling about their personalities. As you read, notice the descriptive details that Cheever uses to make these characters come alive.[1]

> Jim and Irene Westcott were the kind of people who seem to strike that satisfactory average of income, endeavor, and respectability that is reached by the statistical reports in college alumni bulletins. They were the parents of two young children, they had been married nine years, they lived on the twelfth floor of an apartment house near Sutton Place, they went to the theatre on an average of 10.3 times a year, and they hoped someday to live in Westchester. Irene Westcott was a pleasant, rather plain girl with soft brown hair and a wide, fine forehead upon which nothing at all had been written, and in the cold weather she wore a coat of fitch skins dyed to resemble mink. You could not say that Jim Westcott looked younger than he was, but you could at least say of him that he seemed to feel younger. He wore his graying hair cut very short, he dressed in the kind of clothes his class had worn at Andover, and his manner was earnest, vehement, and intentionally naïve. The Westcotts differed from their friends, their classmates, and their neighbors only in an interest they shared in serious music. They went to a great many concerts—although they seldom mentioned this to anyone—and they spent a good deal of time listening to music on the radio.

What John Cheever tells about the physical appearance of his characters helps the reader to understand their personalities. For example, the description of Irene Westcott's "wide, fine forehead upon which nothing at all had been written" not only tells that her face is unlined but also that she has been untouched by her experiences in life. Her husband is the same way. Cheever describes him as still wearing the same kind of clothes he wore in school and states that he is "intentionally naïve." These details help the reader visualize the characters and understand them. What other details does Cheever use to present his characters? What do these details tell you about the personalities of the characters?

---

[1]Excerpt from "The Enormous Radio" from *The Stories of John Cheever*, by John Cheever, 1947. Originally appeared in *The New Yorker*. Reprinted by permission of Alfred A. Knopf, Inc.

Writing Practice 1

Imagine that you are preparing to write a short story based on two main characters. Your first paragraph will describe them directly: what they look like, what they are like inside, what their relationship is to one another, and how they feel about one another. Select one of the following pairs of characters or substitute your own and write one paragraph describing them.

1. A girl and boy, standing in the school corridor, making a date to meet after school

2. Best friends, worried about a test, walking to school

3. Enemy aliens meeting on a space station after not seeing one another for a light year

4. A teacher and student, after class, discussing the student's grade

5. A worker at a restaurant dealing with a dissatisfied or impatient customer

Learning About Setting

The following paragraphs begin the short story "Sophistication" by Sherwood Anderson. They describe the general setting of the story, which takes place in a small town called Winesburg, Ohio, in the early part of this century. As you read, notice the descriptive details that Anderson uses to tell you about the sights and sounds you would encounter in this setting.[1]

> It was early evening of a day in the late fall and the Winesburg County Fair had brought crowds of country people into town. The day had been clear and the night came on warm and pleasant. On the Trunion Pike, where the road after it left town stretched away between berry fields now covered with dry brown leaves, the dust from passing wagons arose in clouds. Children, curled into little balls, slept on the straw scattered on wagon beds. Their hair was full of dust and their fingers black and sticky. The dust rolled away over the fields and the departing sun set it ablaze with colors.
>
> In the main street of Winesburg crowds filled the stores and the sidewalks. Night came on, horses whinnied, the clerks in the stores ran madly about, children became lost and cried lustily, an American town worked terribly at the task of amusing itself.

The preceding scene takes place in late fall on a warm and pleasant evening. Descriptive details of the field "covered with dry brown leaves" and of the clouds of dust rising from the wagons of the country people coming into town help the reader visualize the scene. What other sights does Sherwood Anderson show the reader? What details help you hear the sounds that are part of the scene?

Sherwood Anderson sets a scene by presenting realistic sights and sounds to the reader. Writers also help the reader visualize and experience physical surroundings by showing them through the minds of the characters.

---

[1]Excerpt from "Sophistication" from *Winesburg, Ohio* by Sherwood Anderson. Copyright 1919 by B. W. Huebsch. Copyright 1947 by Eleanor Copenhaver Anderson. Reprinted by permission of Viking Penguin Inc.

The following paragraph from "The Jilting of Granny Weatherall," by Katherine Anne Porter, is seen through the eyes of Granny Weatherall, who is sick and on her deathbed. Lying here, she notices the picture of her dead husband John and the blue lampshades made by her daughter Cornelia. As you read, be aware of what else she sees in the room.[1]

> Her eyes opened very wide and the room stood out like a picture she had seen somewhere. Dark colors with the shadows rising towards the ceiling in long angles. The tall black dresser gleamed with nothing on it but John's picture, enlarged from a litte one, with John's eyes very black when they should have been blue. You never saw him, so how do you know how he looked? But the man insisted the copy was perfect, it was very rich and handsome. For a picture, yes, but it's not my husband. The table by the bed had a linen cover and a candle and a crucifix. The light was blue from Cornelia's silk lampshades. No sort of light at all, just frippery. You had to live forty years with kerosene lamps to appreciate honest electricity. She felt very strong and she saw Doctor Harry with a rosy nimbus around him.

A nimbus is a halo.

In the preceding paragaph you learn about the scene through the eyes of Granny Weatherall. What specific details does she notice about the room? When she sees the room in "dark colors," what does this tell you about her? How does Granny Weatherall feel about what she is seeing?

Writing Practice 2

Imagine that you are writing a short story and that your opening paragraph or paragraphs will describe the setting of the story. First, decide if you are going to describe the scene from a general point of view, as in the example by Sherwood Anderson, or from a character's point of view, as in the example by Katherine Anne Porter. Next, read the following questions to help imagine your setting. Use the questions to help picture your setting in detail and write these details on a piece of scratch paper. Then write a one- or two-paragraph description of the setting, selecting the details that seem most important.

1. Where does the story take place: in a city, small town, rural setting, or perhaps in another country or on another planet? Is it night, afternoon, or morning?

2. What colors, sounds, or motions can be noticed? Are the leaves turning color? Is a dog barking somewhere? If there are people in this scene, what are they doing?

3. Imagine yourself in the middle of the setting you want to describe: What do you smell and feel? Do you smell flowers, bread baking, diesel fumes? Has rain begun to fall, or is the sun shining?

4. If you are describing this scene from a general point of view, what is the most important sight or sound that you want your readers to notice?

5. If you are describing this scene from a character's point of view, what is the character thinking and feeling while observing the scene?

---

[1]Excerpt from "The Jilting of Granny Weatherall" from *The Flowering Judas and Other Stories* by Katherine Anne Porter. Reprinted by permission of Harcourt Brace Jovanovich, Inc. and Jonathan Cape Ltd.

For Your Journal

After reading the descriptions of settings in the preceding section, consider writing about the places that are a part of your world in your journal. Using descriptive details, record your impressions of sounds, tastes, smells, and textures, as well as sights.

You might also practice writing about a scene from different viewpoints. How, for example, might a man dressed in faded jeans and stained work hat observe the scene at the bus stop? A tired young woman with two active children? A teenager with a large portable radio and a tennis racket?

Learning About Plot and Conflict

A *plot* is a plan of action that involves conflict and that is brought to a resolution.

A plot is more than an event or a series of connected events. Imagine, for example, that you read a story about a teenage girl who wakes up, goes to school, eats lunch, goes to swimming practice, and then returns home. This is a series of related events, but not a plot.

A plot requires *conflict:* the struggle between opposing forces.

There are several different types of conflict. Conflict often occurs between characters. For example, the preceding events could be turned into a plot by adding conflict between the girl and her swimming coach, who does not think the girl is good enough to be on the team.

Conflict is often resolved by one of the characters winning or by both deciding to put aside their differences. It can also happen that, although the conflict continues, the characters reach an understanding of it. In the preceding example, the girl could triumph over her coach's expectations and beat a school record during practice, or she and her coach could have an argument and then agree to treat each other with more respect in the future. It could also happen that the girl learns that the coach really believes in her, but thinks she is lazy and treats her strictly so that she will live up to her potential.

Sometimes, conflict is represented as one character's inner battle. This battle can center on a personal issue or on indecision about how to treat a particular person or situation. In the preceding example the conflict could be in the mind of the girl herself, who has doubts about her abilities.

Conflict can also refer to the circumstances in which the characters find themselves and that test them in some way. In the preceding example the conflict could occur when the team's best swimmer becomes ill, and circumstances force the main character to take the best swimmer's place on the team.

Conflict is central to any plot. As you read the following plot summary of the short story "Everyday Use" by Alice Walker, decide where the conflict lies.

A successful daughter returns with her boyfriend to visit her mother and sister who have remained on the farm where they grew up. The daughter, Dee (her new name is Wangero), now admires all the country things she used to hate. She asks her mother for some handmade quilts which had been promised to her sister Maggie. The mother doesn't know what to do. Maggie says that Dee can have them, but the mother refuses. They fight. Dee goes away, leaving the mother and Maggie sitting contentedly in their yard.

The conflict between Dee and Maggie is central to the plot. In the opening paragraphs of "Everyday Use," the mother is speaking. As you read, notice how Alice Walker introduces the conflict at the very beginning.[1]

I will wait for her in the yard that Maggie and I made so clean and wavy yesterday afternoon. A yard like this is more comfortable than most people know. It is not just a yard. It is like an extended living room. When the hard clay is swept clean as a floor and the fine sand around the edges lined with tiny, irregular grooves anyone can come and sit and look up into the elm tree and wait for the breezes that never come inside the house.

Maggie will be nervous until after her sister goes: she will stand hopelessly in corners homely and ashamed of the burn scars down her arms and legs, eyeing her sister with a mixture of envy and awe. She thinks her sister has held life always in the palm of one hand, that "no" is a word the world never learned to say to her.

The preceding paragraphs give important information about the plot: You learn that the speaker is waiting for her daughter to visit and that her other daughter is nervous about seeing her sister. You also learn why Maggie is nervous: She envies and admires her sister and is ashamed of herself because she is homely. She feels inferior to her sister. What other information do you learn about the plot and characters in the preceding paragraphs?

Writing Practice 3

The suggestions that follow are for conflicts between two characters in a short story, conflict within a character, or conflict between characters and their environment. Select one of these conflicts or substitute one of your own and write the opening paragraph of a short story that sets forth this conflict.

1. The characters are two male friends. One knows that the other likes a girl in their class but is shy and has not asked her out yet. The friend decides he likes the girl, too, and asks her out himself. The conflict arises when he tells his friend about the date.

2. The characters are a girl and her parents. The parents are going away on a short trip and want a relative to come and stay with the daughter when they are away. The girl feels that she is being treated like a child. She is a junior in high school and knows she can take care of herself. The conflict comes out during dinner one evening when her parents make their plans.

---

[1]Copyright © 1973 by Alice Walker. Excerpted and reprinted from "Everyday Use" in her volume *In Love and Trouble* by permission of Harcourt Brace Jovanovich, Inc. and Julian Bach Literary Agency, Inc.

3. The character is a boy who has been drafted into the Union Army during the Civil War. He is a pacifist, but he also feels a moral obligation to support the Union and not to shirk duty. He wonders if he might be, in part, a coward and how he will react when he has to fight in a battle.

4. The characters are a boyfriend and girlfriend. They have been going out together for a year. The conflict is that the boy is more possessive and tends to be jealous; the girl likes him very much but cannot stand being told what to do. The conflict comes when he accuses her of paying too much attention to a friend of his at a party.

5. The characters are a party of people whose plane has crashed on a remote island. The conflict arises from their attitudes on how to handle the situation: to stay with the downed aircraft or to try to find help.

Learning About Point of View

There are several methods of telling a story.

In *first-person point of view*, the story is told by one speaker.

A first-person speaker, an invented character, uses the pronoun *I* to relate what is happening. All the information you learn in a first-person story comes from this one character.

In the following paragraph by Walker Percy, the first-person narrator, a broker who lives outside New Orleans, tells about himself.[1]

> In the evenings I usually watch television or go to the movies. Week-ends I often spend on the Gulf Coast. Our neighborhood theater in Gentilly has permanent lettering on the front of the marquee reading: Where Happiness Costs So Little. The fact is I am quite happy in a movie, even a bad movie. Other people, so I have read, treasure memorable moments in their lives: the time one climbed the Parthenon at sunrise, the summer night one met a lonely girl in Central Park and achieved with her a sweet and natural relationship, as they say in books. I too once met a girl in Central Park, but it is not much to remember. What I remember is the time John Wayne killed three men with a carbine as he was falling to the dusty street in *Stagecoach*, and the time the kitten found Orson Welles in the doorway in *The Third Man*.

In the preceding paragraph the narrator tells you about his life. What important memories does this person have? How does he compare them with other people's memories? In your own opinion what sort of person do you think the narrator is?

A story can also be told from a *character's point of view*.

In this second method the character is not the narrator of the story—that is, the character does not relate the story in the first person. Instead, you learn about what happens from the vantage point of that character. For example, in the following excerpt from "We're the Only Colored People Here" by Gwendolyn Brooks, you learn about the scene from the point of view of

---

[1] Excerpt from *The Moviegoer* by Walker Percy. Reprinted by permission of Alfred A. Knopf, Inc. and McIntosh and Otis, Inc., and Martin Secker & Warburg Limited.

the character Maud Martha. As you read, notice what she observes and how she feels.[1]

> Maud Martha laughed happily to herself. It was pleasant out, and tonight she and Paul were very close to each other.
>
> He held the door open for her—instead of going on round to the driving side, getting in, and leaving her to get in at her side as best she might. When he took this way of calling her "lady" and informing her of his love she felt precious, protected, delicious. She gave him an excited look of gratitude. He smiled indulgently.
>
> "Want it to be the Owl again?"
>
> "Oh, no, no, Paul. Let's not go there tonight. I feel too good inside for that. Let's go downtown?"

What is Maud Martha's mood in the preceding paragraph? What are some of the descriptive words the writer uses to tell you how she feels?

In the first-person method and the character method of telling a story, information is presented through a single point of view. The reader can know only what the speaker knows and experiences.

A greater range in point of view can be gained by using an *omniscient*, or *all-knowing, narrator.*

With the omniscient point of view, the story is told by an unseen observer who can relate information about the activities, thoughts, and feelings of all the characters, as well as describing the setting.

The following excerpt from "A Worn Path," by Eudora Welty, describes one of the characters in the story, Phoenix Jackson. As you read, notice what details the writer selects to introduce the character.[2]

> It was December—a bright frozen day in the early morning. Far out in the country there was an old Negro woman with her head tied in a red rag, coming along a path through the pinewoods. Her name was Phoenix Jackson. She was very old and small and she walked slowly in the dark pine shadows, moving a little from side to side in her steps, with the balanced heaviness and lightness of a pendulum in a grandfather clock. She carried a thin, small cane made from an umbrella, and with this she kept tapping the frozen earth in front of her. This made a grave and persistent noise in the still air, that seemed meditative like the chirping of a solitary little bird.
>
> She wore a dark striped dress reaching down to her shoe tops, and an equally long apron of bleached sugar sacks, with a full pocket: all neat and tidy, but every time she took a step she might have fallen over her shoelaces, which dragged from her unlaced shoes. She looked straight ahead. Her eyes were blue with age. Her skin had a pattern all its own of numberless branching wrinkles and as though a whole little tree stood in the middle of her forehead, but a golden color ran underneath, and the two knobs of her cheeks were illumined

[1]Specified excerpt from "we're the only colored people here" from *The World of Gwendolyn Brooks* by Gwendolyn Brooks. Copyright 1951 by The Curtis Publishing Company. Copyright 1953 by Gwendolyn Brooks Blakely. Reprinted by permission of Harper & Row, Publishers, Inc.

[2]Copyright 1941, 1969 by Eudora Welty. Excerpted and reprinted from "A Worn Path" in her volume *A Curtain of Green and Other Stories* by permission of Harcourt Brace Jovanovich, Inc. and Russell & Volkening, Inc.

by a yellow burning under the dark. Under the red rag her hair came down on her neck in the frailest of ringlets, still black, and with an odor like copper.

An omniscient narrator gives you the sense of looking at a character from the outside in. What words tell you how Phoenix Jackson looks as she walks through the woods? What words describe the setting of the story?

Writing Practice 4

Write at least one paragraph about a character, using one of the following scenes and points of view or substitute a scene of your choice and indicate the point of view you will use. Remember to include descriptive details.

FIRST-PERSON OR "I" POINT OF VIEW

1. A boy is upset about not being invited to a party and thinks about it as he sits on his porch on Saturday night.

2. A girl lies awake thinking about the track meet in which she will compete the next day.

CHARACTER-AS-SPEAKER POINT OF VIEW

1. During an argument with one of her students, Ms. Gomez remembers her own student days.

2. John, who has just transferred to a new school, walks to school alone.

OMNISCIENT (ALL-KNOWING) POINT OF VIEW

1. It is a cold Saturday morning in the fall, and a football game between rival schools is about to take place.

2. The year is 2000, and the lost continent of Atlantis emerges from the sea.

Learning About Dialogue

Dialogue is conversation between characters.

Dialogue has many uses in imaginative writing. First, dialogue can reveal the personality of characters and how they relate to one another. As a reader you notice not only what characters say about themselves but also how they say it and what kind of a mood they are in when they speak.

In the following example from the short story "Wunderkind" by Carson McCullers, a music teacher is speaking to a pupil once thought to be a wunderkind but whose talent has failed to develop. As you read, think about each character: What sort of a person is the teacher? What is his pupil feeling?[1]

Wunderkind means "wonder child," or "precocious child."

Quotation marks indicate when lines of dialogue begin and end.

Adagio means "in slow time."

> Arrestingly his hand rose up from the score. "Wait! Think a minute what you're playing. How is this beginning marked?"
> "An-*andante*."
> "All right. Don't drag it into an *adagio* then. And play deeply into the keys. Don't snatch it off shallowly that way. A graceful, deep-toned *andante*—"

---

[1]From "Wunderkind," in *Ballad of the Sad Cafe and Collected Short Stories* by Carson McCullers. Copyright 1936, 1941, 1942, 1950, 1951, 1955 by Carson McCullers. Reprinted by permission of Houghton Mifflin Company and the Estate of Carson McCullers, Floria Lasky, Executrix.

She tried again. Her hands seemed separate from the music that was in her.

"Listen," he interrupted. "Which of these variations dominates the whole?"

"The dirge," she answered.

Andante means "in moderately slow time."
Dolce means "smooth."

"Then prepare for that. This is an *andante*—but it's not salon stuff as you just played it. Start out softly, *piano*, and make it swell out just before the arpeggio. Make it warm and dramatic. And down here—where it's marked *dolce* make the counter melody sing out. You know all that. We've gone over all that side of it before. Now play it. Feel it as Beethoven wrote it down. Feel that tragedy and restraint."

She could not stop looking at his hands. They seemed to rest tentatively on the music, ready to fly up as a stop signal as soon as she would begin, the gleaming flash of his ring calling her to halt. "Mister Bilderbach—maybe if I— if you let me play on through the first variation without stopping I could do better."

When the student says haltingly, *"An-andante,"* you can tell that she is upset or nervous about her playing. When the teacher interrupts her playing and says, "You know all that. We've gone over all that side of it before," what tone of voice do you suppose he is using? Why?

Dialogue is also a way of giving background information about a story to the reader. As you read the following excerpt from "Land of Our Enemies" by Jesse Stuart, notice what the characters say that locates this story in a specific time and place. In this story a boy and his father have just come to be present at the grandfather's funeral. Their relatives have come to meet them at the train.[1]

"Air ye a-goin' to Cousin Mick Powderjay's funeral?" one of the men asked Pa soon as we had stepped off the train.

"That's where we're a-goin'," Pa said. "Is he akin to you?"

"We're brother's children," the man said. "I'm Zack Powderjay. And this is my brother, Dave Powderjay! We're Zack Powderjay's boys."

"I'm Mick Powderjay," Pa told them. "Pap's eleventh child by his first wife!"

"We've heard of ye," Zack Powderjay said. "See, we had to leave the Big Sandy a long time ago."

"When did you leave?" Pa asked.

"In President Hayes's administration," Dave Powderjay said.

"I left in Grover Cleveland's second administration," Pa said.

"Why did you leave?" Dave Powderjay asked Pa.

"Trouble with the Hornbuckles," he said.

"Trouble with th' Hornbuckles and Dangerfields caused us to leave," Dave said.

"Did Cousin Mick die a natural death?" Zack Powderjay asked Pa.

"I ain't heard yet but I know Pap didn't die a natural death," Pa said. "He had more enemies than he had ailments of the body."

You can tell from the preceding dialogue, since the characters talk about Presidents Hayes and Cleveland, that the story takes place around the turn

---

[1]Excerpt from "Land of Our Enemies" by Jesse Stuart. Reprinted by permission of The Jesse Stuart Foundation, Inc.

of the century. What clues does the dialogue give you about where the story takes place? What conflict do you learn about from the dialogue?

A third use of dialogue is to advance the action of the plot. By listening to characters talk, the reader learns what they think, how they act, and what they intend to do. Dialogue is one way of showing conflict developing between characters.

In the following dialogue from the short story "With All Flags Flying" by Anne Tyler, the conflict between Mr. Carpenter and his daughter Clara is made apparent. Mr. Carpenter has just come to his daughter's house because he realizes he is too weak to live alone anymore. As you read, notice what the characters think and how they act toward one another.[1]

> "Now . . ." he said, starting toward the house. He was thinking of the best way to put it. "I came to a decision. I won't be living alone any more. I want to go to an old folks' home. That's what I *want*," he said, stopping on the grass so she would be sure to get it clear. "I don't want to live with you—I want an old folks' home." Then he was afraid he had worded it too strongly. "It's nice *visiting* you, of course," he said.
>
> "Why, Daddy, you know we always asked you to come and live with us."
>
> "I know that, but I decided on an old folks' home."
>
> "We couldn't do that. We won't even talk about it."
>
> "Clara, my mind is made up."
>
> Then in the doorway a new thought hit her, and she suddenly turned around. "Are you sick?" she said. "You always said you would live alone as long as health allowed."
>
> "I'm not up to that anymore," he said.
>
> "What is it? Are you having some kind of pain?"
>
> "I just decided, that's all," he said. "What I *will* rely on you for is the arrangements with the home. I know it's a trouble."
>
> "We'll talk about that later," Clara said. And she firmed the corners of her mouth exactly the way her mother used to do when she hadn't won an argument but wasn't planning to lose it yet either.

The preceding dialogue tells you that the conflict between Mr. Carpenter and his daughter is going to continue. When Mr. Carpenter first talks to his daughter, he chooses his words very carefully. What does this tell you about his relationship with his daughter and how he expects her to react?

Writing Practice 5

Write a brief dialogue between two characters, using one of the following situations or a situation of your choice. The purpose of the dialogue is to let your readers find out about the characters, to show them in conflict, or to move forward the action of the story.

1. A father and son discuss the son's need for more spending money.

2. Two friends who will be leaving each other, one for college, the other for military service, talk about their futures.

---

[1]Excerpt from "With All Flags Flying" by Anne Tyler. Reprinted by permission of Russell & Volkening, Inc. as agents for the author. Copyright © 1977 by Anne Tyler.

3. A grandmother reminisces on her girlhood as an immigrant from Europe, while her grandchild asks questions.

4. The murdered body of a wealthy industrialist is discovered. Two of his associates talk about his questionable business practices and the enemies he made.

5. Explorers talk about preparations for a dangerous trip into the interior of New Guinea.

For Your Journal

As a way of learning about dialogue, consider asking a friend or relative to allow you to interview him or her. Using a list of questions you have prepared beforehand, capture your subject's responses on tape or in writing. Then use your journal as a place to record the interview, transcribing the dialogue as closely as possible to the way it was actually spoken. Possible topics for questions include your subject's family history, childhood, school experiences, and occupation.

To prepare for the interview, you might want to read some of the interviews in the *Foxfire* series, in *American Mosaic*, or in books by Studs Terkel, such as *Working*.

Writing Practice 6

Using the elements of character, setting, plot, and conflict, write a short story. Decide on the point of view of your story and give some thought to style before you begin writing. If you wish, you may incorporate one of the paragraphs describing character, setting, or conflict from previous writing practices in this section. You can base your story on a realistic experience, or you may make it a fantasy or science fiction story.

Use the photographs on pages 188 and 189 to help generate ideas for your story if you do not know what to write about. As you look at each photograph, decide what the people are doing and what sort of people they are and try to imagine the conflict that could be involved in their situation.

Learning About Poetry

Poetry relates to other imaginative writing, such as short stories, in that it sometimes has characters, setting, plot, conflict, and dialogue, as stories do. However, poetry does not always have these elements; instead, some poetry concentrates on creating an image or impression in the reader's mind through a special combination of sounds and meaning.

The language of poetry is in general more rhythmic and musical than everyday language or the language of fiction. One way to begin understanding

poetry is to look at some of the elements that help to give poetry this sense of sound: the elements of rhyme, meter, and verse patterns.

Understanding Rhyme

Sound patterns make poetry closely related to music: the repeating sounds and rhythms create effects similar to those of repeated musical notes and phrases.

In poetry the patterns of repeating sounds are called *rhyme* and *alliteration*, the pattern of repeating rhythm is called *meter*, and the patterns of repeating lines are called *stanzas*.

Words *rhyme* when they share the same sound.

When a poem has a rhyme pattern, the rhyming words occur as the final words in each line and follow a specific order. Although there are many varieties of rhyme, the most common is called *exact*, or *perfect*, *rhyme*. The following poem by Philip Dacey uses exact rhyme in a simple pattern: The final word in each line rhymes with the others.

Small Dark Song[1]

The cherry-tree is down, and dead, that was so high,
And Wind, that did this thing, roams careless while you cry,
For Wind's been everywhere today, and has an alibi.

—Philip Dacey

"Small Dark Song" uses the words *high, cry,* and *alibi* as exact rhymes. The repeating sound of these rhymes enhances the musical quality of the poem, which is linked by its title to a "song."

Not all rhymes sound exactly alike. When words share repeated vowel sounds in a poem, the rhyme is called *assonance*; the rhyming pairs of words

---

[1]"Small Dark Song" from *How I Escaped from the Labyrinth* by Philip Dacey. Copyright © 1977 by Carnegie-Mellon University Press. Reprinted by permission of Carnegie-Mellon University Press.

right/sigh and *moan/low* are examples of assonance. When words share repeated consonant sounds, the rhyme is called *consonance*. In consonance the rhyme is based on the repeated consonants at the ends of words: *late/white* and *cool/pale*. Notice that in consonance the vowel sounds do not rhyme.

The following love poem by Louise Glück uses exact rhyme, assonance, and consonance for musical effect. After you read the poem, identify each set of rhyming words.

Early December in Croton-on-Hudson[1]

Hudson refers to the Hudson River.

> Spiked sun. The Hudson's
> Whittled down by ice.
> I hear the bone dice
> Of blown gravel clicking. Bone-
> pale, the recent snow
> Fastens like fur to the river.
> Standstill. We were leaving to deliver
> Christmas presents when the tire blew
> Last year. Above the dead valves pines pared
> Down by a storm stood, limbs bared . . .
> I want you.

> *—Louise Glück*

The first exact rhyme in the preceding poem is *ice/dice;* the first example of consonance is *Hudson's/Bone;* the first example of assonance is *Bone/snow.* Name the other sets of rhyming words in the poem.

Alliteration is another sound pattern commonly used in poetry. When words begin with the same sound, the effect is called *alliteration.* Like rhyme, alliteration is used to create a sense of music and to emphasize the meaning of the words. In the following lines by Wallace Stevens from "On the Manner of Addressing Clouds," alliteration is used for comic emphasis.[2]

> **G**loomy **g**rammarians in **g**olden **g**owns,
> **M**eekly you keep the **m**ortal rendezvous, . . .

In the following lines from "Sunday Morning," however, the subject is serious, and Stevens uses alliteration to highlight the important words. As you read, look for the alliterated words and also for rhyming words.[3]

> Deer walk upon our mountains, and the quail
> Whistle about us their spontaneous cries;
> Sweet berries ripen in the wilderness;

---

[1]"Early December in Croton-on-Hudson" from *Firstborn*, to be reissued by The Ecco Press in 1982. Reprinted by permission.

[2]Excerpt from "On the Manner of Addressing Clouds" from *The Collected Poems of Wallace Stevens*, by Wallace Stevens, 1957. Reprinted by permission of Alfred A. Knopf, Inc.

[3]Excerpt from "Sunday Morning" from *The Collected Poems of Wallace Stevens*, by Wallace Stevens, 1957. Reprinted by permission of Alfred A. Knopf, Inc.

And, in the isolation of the sky,
At evening, casual flocks of pigeons make
Ambiguous undulations as they sink,
Downward to darkness, on extended wings.

Undulations are wavy motions.

The alliteration of "Downward to darkness" makes this phrase stand out in the poem. Why is the darkness important? For what purpose do you think Stevens emphasizes the phrase?

Words that alliterate can occur in a random pattern throughout a poem. Rhyming words occurring randomly rather than in a set pattern at the ends of lines are called *internal rhyme.* In the preceding lines from "Sunday Morning," internal rhyme helps link one line to the next and gives a harmonious musical quality to the passage. For example, *cries* rhymes with the end word *sky,* but it also rhymes with *ripen* and *isolation.* Another sound that is repeated through the poem is the *s* sound: The line "Whistle about us their spontaneous cries" shows this effect. Look for other phrases that echo the *s* sound. What feeling does the *s* repetition convey to you?

Writing Practice 7

Use the Discovering Ideas for Writing section that follows to help you write your poem.

Write a poem of at least four lines, using the musical effects of rhyme and alliteration. You may choose exact rhyme, assonance, consonance, or a mixture of these. Do not use the same end rhyme throughout. Alternate sets of rhymes or rhyme the first two lines and the third and fourth lines.

Discovering Ideas for Writing

Many poems, such as the one by Louise Glück on page 190, recapture a strong memory. In that poem the poet is driving along the Hudson River in early December. She recalls an experience of going to deliver Christmas presents with her boyfriend and noticing the sight of tree limbs stripped by a winter storm above their heads. This moment stays clearly etched in her memory.

To begin thinking about your own poem, take time to remember a place that made a special impression on you for some reason. It can be an ordinary place that you pass every day or a place that you visited only once. Often a strange place leaves a stronger and more colorful impression on your memory than one with which you are familiar. This place could be a landscape, a city scene, a scene by the ocean, or any other that comes to your mind.

Once you have this place in your imagination, write down the words that seem associated with it. For example, if you remember the time your family visited Chicago, your list of words might include *skyscrapers, lake, crowd of shoppers, traffic, bright yellow street lights, hurry, rushing, white Water Tower, dirt, sirens, glass elevator,* and *heels clicking on the sidewalk.*

Look over the list when you finish and decide what detail stands out most in your mind. You can use this detail to begin your poem. For example, suppose that what you remember most is your first sight of the skyscrapers along the lakefront. Your poem could begin the following way:

> Skyscrapers rim the lake.

Now that you have your first line, you know that the word *lake* will be one of the rhyming words in the poem. You might want to jot down any rhyming words for *lake* that come into your mind.

The next impression that stands out in your memory might be the crowds of people rushing along. You recall that you were walking slowly, admiring the buildings and other sights, but almost against your will you felt caught up in the rush. You think, "We were trying to take our time." The word *take*, you notice, creates a rhyme for *lake*. Your poem might continue:

> Skyscrapers rim the lake.
> Masses of people throng
> The wide streets. We take
> Our time . . .

Finally, you need to find a rhyming word for *throng* that completes the idea of the poem. To do this, stop for a moment and think about the line, "We take/our time." You recall feeling hurried and the hurry makes you think of a ticking clock. This thought helps you finish the poem:

> Skyscrapers rim the lake.
> Masses of people throng
> The wide streets. We take
> Our time but it ticks us along.

The alliteration in the words *take*, *time*, and *ticks* emphasizes the idea of hurrying in the poem; it sounds like a clock ticking.

Some writers prefer to begin with a title for their poems; some wait until they have finished to decide on a title. Choose whichever way you prefer, but always include a title for the poems you write.

Understanding Meter

Meter is the pattern of repeating rhythm in a poem.

You can hear the meter of a poem by listening to the pattern of accented and unaccented syllables in each line. In most words it is easy to hear which syllable is accented. For example, the word *meter* is pronounced with the accent on the first syllable (me´·ter).

Much formal poetry has a regular pattern of accented and unaccented syllables. The following line is from the poem "Aunt Jennifer's Tigers" by Adrienne Rich. Read the line aloud or listen to it read so that you can hear the regular pattern of an unaccented syllable followed by an accented one: "Thĕy dó nŏt feár thĕ mén bĕneáth thĕ tŕee."

Some of the other lines in "Aunt Jennifer's Tigers" have the same pattern of unaccented/accented syllables. Some are variations on that pattern. Read the poem all the way through, or listen to someone read it aloud, so that you can hear the basic pattern of unaccented and accented syllables. This is the rhythmic pattern, or meter, of the poem.

Aunt Jennifer's Tigers[1]

Denizens are
inihabitants.
Chivalric means
"noble."

Aunt Jénnifer's tígers pránce acróss a scréen,
Bríght tópaz dénizens of a wórld of gréen.
They dó not feár the mén beneáth the trée;
They páce in sléek chiválric cértainty.

Aunt Jennifer's fingers fluttering through her wool
Find even the ivory needle hard to pull.
The massive weight of Uncle's wedding band
Sits heavily upon Aunt Jennifer's hand.

When Aunt is dead, her terrified hands will lie
Still ringed with ordeals she was mastered by.
The tigers in the panel that she made
Will go on striding, proud and unafraid.

—Adrienne Rich

The preceding poem tells about the character of Aunt Jennifer by describing her in the act of making a panel embroidered with tigers. The poet contrasts Aunt Jennifer and her life with the "proud and unafraid" tigers on the screen. In the poem the regular meter gives the reader a sense of the regular, ordered world that Aunt Jennifer lives in. The meter is there to enhance the meaning of the poem.

Writing Practice 8

Write a short poem, using a regular meter in each line. Decide before you begin to write how many stresses you will use for your line. (It may be helpful to reread Adrienne Rich's poem on this page. The following ideas can be used as suggestions for your poem.

1. In "Aunt Jennifer's Tigers" Adrienne Rich writes about a woman in conflict with herself. Aunt Jennifer has a secret desire to be like her proud tigers, but in real life she is meek, dominated by her fears. Write a poem about a character in conflict with himself or herself. You may begin by thinking of a secret wish of your own. How is it in conflict with the reality of your life? Begin the poem, as Adrienne Rich does, by describing the secret wish.

2. "Aunt Jennifer's Tigers" also presents a special object, the embroidery panel, which the poet connects with her aunt. Write a poem about an object or a place that you connect with another person. Why does this object or place remind you of the person? Begin the poem by describing the object with vivid details.

3. Write a poem about an experience involving your senses. Tell of something you saw, heard, felt, smelled, or tasted. Perhaps this experience

---

[1]"Aunt Jennifer's Tigers" reprinted from *Poems, Selected and New,* 1950–1974 by Adrienne Rich, by permission of W. W. Norton & Company, Inc. Copyright © 1975, 1973, 1971, 1969, 1966 by W. W. Norton & Company, Inc. Copyright © 1951 by Adrienne Rich.

was a surprise, perhaps it was a pleasant or harsh experience. For example, imagine the shock of cold water on your feet as you cross a mountain stream in the heat of summer. Tell your reader the concrete details of your experience in the poem.

Figurative Language in Poetry

Figurative language goes beyond the literal meaning of words to create a new image, or a fresh impression, in the mind of the reader.

The two most widely used types of figurative language are *simile* and *metaphor.*

Similes and metaphors make comparisons to bring out hidden likenesses between things that are not apparently similar. Find the comparison in the following lines from "Black Money" by Tess Gallagher. The poet describes her father returning from work at the pulp mill, where the sulphur fumes turn everything black.

[From] Black Money[1]

His lungs heaving all day in a sulphur mist,
then dusk, the lunch pail torn from him
before he reaches the house, his children
a cloud of swallows about him.

—*Tess Gallagher*

When the children are compared with "a cloud of swallows," what picture does this give of them? In what ways are children like a flock of birds?

A *simile* is a figure of speech stating a comparison with words such as *like, as, than,* and sometimes *seems* or *appears.*

In the concluding stanzas from "Black Money," the first simile compares the sun to a whip. This comparison tells you that the sun is not welcome: It wakes the tired people as if it were a whiplash. Look for the other similes in the poem as you read.

[From] Black Money[1]

The mill burns on, now a burst of cinders,
now whistles screaming down the bay, saws jagged
in half light. Then like a whip
the sun across the bed, windows high with mountains
and the sleepers fallen to pillows
as gulls fall, tilting
against their shadows on the log booms.
Again the trucks shudder the wood framed houses
passing to the mill. My father

---

[1]"Black Money" by Tess Gallagher is reprinted from *Instructions to the Double* (Graywolf Press, 1976), © 1976 Tess Gallagher.

snorts, splashes in the bathroom,
throws open our doors to cowboy music
on the radio, hearts are cheating,
somebody is alone, there's blood in Tulsa.
Out the back yard the night-shift men rattle
the gravel in the alley going home.
My father fits goggles to his head.

From his pocket he takes anything metal,
the pearl-handled jack knife, a ring of keys,
and for us, black money shoveled
from the sulphur pyramids heaped in the distance
like yellow gold. Coffee bottle tucked in his armpit
he swaggers past the chicken coop,
a pack of cards at his breast.
In a fan of light beyond him
the Kino Maru pulls out for Seattle,
some black star climbing
the deep globe of his eye.

The Kino Maru is a train.

—Tess Gallagher

The second simile uses *as:* "the sleepers fallen to pillows/as gulls fall, . . ." What image of the sleepers does this comparison convey to you? How do gulls look when they fall toward the water?

The final simile compares the sulphur to "yellow gold." Sulphur is the color of gold in the sunlight, but why else does the poet make this comparison? What is the significance of the sulphur seeming like gold in the poem?

A *metaphor* is also a special type of comparison.

Like a simile, a metaphor makes a connection between two different types of items; unlike a simile, however, the metaphor does not have linking words such as *like, seems,* or *appears.* In a metaphor the comparison is implied rather than directly stated. For example, while the comparison "the sun was sinking like a ship" is a simile, the comparison "the sun was a sinking ship" is a metaphor.

The following poem, "At Zero" by Charles Wright, uses metaphor to give impressions of a day when the temperature is at zero degrees. The metaphor in the first line compares heaven to a cold kitchen. Look for other metaphors in the poem as you read:

At Zero[1]

In the cold kitchen of heaven,
Daylight spoons out its cream-of-wheat.

Beside the sidewalk, the shrubs
Hunch down, deep in their bibs.

---

[1]"At Zero" by Charles Wright. Copyright © 1975 by Charles Wright. Reprinted from *China Trace.* By permission of Wesleyan University Press. This poem first appeared in *The Ohio Review.*

The wind harps its same song
Through the steel tines of the trees.

The river lies still, the jeweled drill in its teeth.

I am glint on its fingernails.
I am ground grains on its wheel.

—Charles Wright

"At Zero" also uses a special kind of metaphor called *personification*. *Personification* attributes human appearance, emotion, or other qualities to nonhuman subjects.

In the second line, Wright personifies daylight as a human spooning out cereal. How does he personify the shrubs in stanza 2? How does he personify the wind and the river?

Writing Practice 9

Write a poem based on simile, metaphor, or personification. Some of the following suggestions may be helpful in writing your poem:

1. "Black Money" on pages 194–195 is a poem that describes a person. Tess Gallagher writes about her father as he goes through typical daily situations. She uses details of his appearance, sounds that she hears after waking up in the morning, and her memory of watching him walk off to work as key elements in the poem. Write a poem about a relative or close friend, situating the person in a typical daily situation. Describe the person's appearance and behavior and your own reactions. What comparisons does the person or situation suggest to you? Incorporate these comparisons into your poem.

2. "Black Money" uses a simile to describe the sun falling "like a whip" across faces. Imagine yourself waking up in the morning or falling asleep. What does the sun filtering into your room, or the darkness, or the moonlight remind you of? Use these comparisons as the basis of your poem.

3. "At Zero" on pages 195–196 describes an intense physical and emotional experience. Write a poem about a time you were highly aware of how you felt physically: a time of extreme coldness, heat, pain, excitement, or exhaustion. What comparisons express how you felt? What comparisons express your emotional reactions? Use the comparisons you think of as the basis of your poem.

4. "At Zero" personifies the sky, the wind, and the river. Write a poem that personifies a natural force, such as rain, snow, night, sunrise, dew, or waves. If this force were like a person, how would it move and what would it look like? If it spoke, what would it say? Use the personification as the basis of your poem.

2 Resources for Writing

10 Library Resources

Contents of the Library

If you want to find out how to make stuffed grape leaves, you can find what you are looking for in a library. You can also find science fiction, adventure novels and mysteries, poems, and plays. Great ideas are stored in libraries and stories of the lives of exceptional women and men. Fantasies and facts—they're all yours for the borrowing.

Most libraries contain the following sections.

1. The card catalogue
2. Fiction books
3. Nonfiction books
4. The *Readers' Guide to Periodical Literature*
5. Magazines and newspapers
6. Specialized reference books, such as biographical dictionaries and books of quotations
7. The vertical file or information file
8. Reserved books
9. New books
10. Rare books or special collections, such as local history and regional writers
11. Records, tapes, films, microfilms

In this chapter you will learn how to locate and to use the material in the preceding list. Such skills are important whether you are using the library for a research assignment or for your own pleasure.

The Card Catalogue

A key to using the library efficiently is understanding how to use the *card catalogue*.

The *card catalogue* is a file of cards listing books and other reference materials in alphabetical order.

Each fiction book in the library has two cards, one for its title and one for its author or editor.

To locate a work of fiction in the library, you must know the author's name, since books of fiction are grouped separately and arranged in alphabetical order on the shelves according to the author's last name. If there are several books by a single author, they are arranged alphabetically according to the first *main* word of their titles. (The articles *a*, *an*, and *the* are not considered main words. The pronoun *I*, however, is considered a main word.)

Collections of short stories are often grouped at the end of the fiction section, arranged in alphabetical order according to the name of the author or editor.

See the sample title, author, and subject cards on page 200.

The card catalogue holds three cards for each nonfiction work: one for title, one for author or editor, and one for subject. Unlike fiction, nonfiction books are not arranged alphabetically in the library. Each of the three catalogue cards and the book itself bear a *call number*.

The call number helps you to locate the book by its classification in the Dewey decimal system.

The Dewey Decimal System

Nonfiction books are classified and placed in the library according to the *Dewey decimal system*, a system developed by American librarian Melvil Dewey. Dewey's system divides nonfiction works into the following ten general categories.

000–099 General Works:	Includes encyclopedias, periodicals, book lists, and other reference books.
100–199 Philosophy:	Includes the fields of psychology, conduct, and personality.
200–299 Religion:	Includes Bibles and other religious texts; theology books, and mythology.
300–399 Social Sciences:	Includes economics, education, etiquette, fairy tales, folklore, legends, government, and law.
400–499 Language:	Includes grammars and dictionaries of different languages, including English.
500–599 Science:	Includes animals, astronomy, biology, botany, chemistry, geology, general science, mathematics, anthropology, and physics.

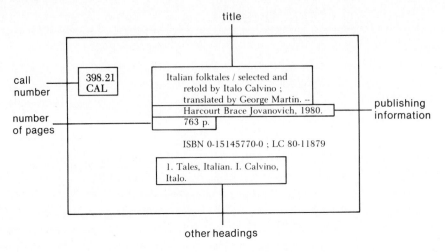

title

call number

398.21 CAL

Italian folktales / selected and retold by Italo Calvino ; translated by George Martin. -- Harcourt Brace Jovanovich, 1980. 763 p.

number of pages

publishing information

ISBN 0-15145770-0 ; LC 80-11879

1. Tales, Italian. I. Calvino, Italo.

other headings

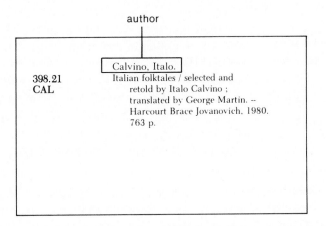

author

398.21 CAL

Calvino, Italo.
Italian folktales / selected and retold by Italo Calvino ; translated by George Martin. -- Harcourt Brace Jovanovich, 1980. 763 p.

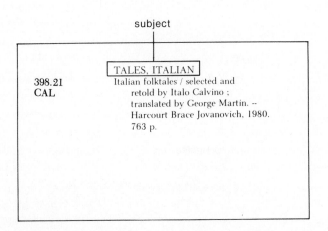

subject

398.21 CAL

TALES, ITALIAN
Italian folktales / selected and retold by Italo Calvino ; translated by George Martin. -- Harcourt Brace Jovanovich, 1980. 763 p.

600–699 Technology:	Includes agriculture, aviation, business, engineering, health, home economics, manual training, and television.
700–799 Fine Arts:	Includes movies, painting, photography, sculpture, recreation, and sports.
800–899 Literature:	Includes poetry, drama, essays, criticism, and history of literature.
900–999 History:	Includes geography, travel, history, and collective biography.

Within these ten general divisions are many subdivisions of the subject, each with its own number. The following is a small sampling of some of the divisions under the heading *Fine Arts*.

700—FINE ARTS
709—History of Art
710—Landscaping
720—Architecture
730—Sculpture
738—Pottery
739—Metalworking
740—Drawing and Lettering
744—Technical Drawing

By using numbers and decimal points, the Library of Congress and other cataloguing agencies can fit any nonfiction book into the system and assign it its own number.

Using the Call Number

When you have found the *call number* of a nonfiction book in the card catalogue, you can easily find the book itself. All nonfiction books are together on the shelves, arranged in numerical order. The spine of the book is stamped with its call number so that it can be quickly located.

Exercise 1

Using the general Dewey decimal system classifications on pages 199 and 201, tell in what general category and under what number books on the following specific subjects would be found.

Examples

a. Dentistry

a. Dentistry—Technology, 600–699

b. Poems of Elizabeth Barrett Browning

b. Poems of Elizabeth Barrett Browning—Literature, 800–899

1. Encyclopedia
2. African history
3. Amphibians
4. Child psychology
5. History of musical comedy
6. Irish mythology
7. Electrical circuits
8. A French dictionary
9. The rules for chess
10. Your state government
11. Women's rights
12. Christian Science
13. A biography of Harriet Tubman
14. The Vietnam War
15. A collection of humorous essays
16. Subatomic physics
17. Data processing
18. Crime prevention
19. Modern philosophies
20. Shakespeare's plays

Exercise 2

Use the card catalogue to see if your library has a book on each of the following. If so, write down the title, author, and call number of the book.

1. A novel by N. Scott Momaday
2. A biography of Eleanor Roosevelt
3. Bacteriology
4. Opera
5. South American history
6. Folklore
7. English grammar
8. Library science or use of the library
9. Heredity
10. Ancient philosophy

Exercise 3

Use the card catalogue to find out if your library has any of the following. If so, write the answers to the questions about the book.

1. How many books by Carl Sagan does your library own? Give the titles and call numbers.

2. Give the title, author, publisher, and publication date of a book about English literature.

3. Does your library contain a book by Jane Austen? Give the title, publisher, and publication date.

4. Does your library contain a biography of Sarah Bernhardt? Who is its author, and what is its title?

5. Does your library contain a collection of poems by George Gordon, Lord Byron? If so, who is the editor, and what is the book's title? What is its call number?

6. Does your library have a book on first aid? List its author, title, and call number.

7. Does your library have a book on automotive repairs? List the author, title, and call number.

8. How many novels by W. Somerset Maugham does your library contain? What are their titles? How many collections of his short stories? What are their titles? How many nonfiction books by Maugham? What are their titles?

9. Give the title, author, call number, and publisher of a book on holidays or on a specific holiday.

10. Does your library contain books on solar energy? If so, give the author, title, publisher, publication date, and call number of at least one.

More Uses for the Card Catalogue

The card catalogue gives more information than just where to find a book. The following information can also be found on the cards.

1. Facts about the author or editors: the author's full name, joint authors, and illustrator, if any

2. Facts of publication: the publisher's name and the publication date

3. Facts about the book: whether it has diagrams, maps, illustrations, and how many pages it has

Information on the cards can help you decide whether or not a source would be useful to you. For example, a book's publication date may indicate if you need bother to consult it. If you are writing about recent developments in rocketry, you may not need to consult *The Latest Facts About Rockets*, published in 1898.

Abbreviations in the Card Catalogue

The following abbreviations may be used on author, title, and subject cards as a way of saving space.

anon.	anonymous, author unknown
c.	copyright
cf.	compare
cm.	centimeter (The size of the book is indicated in centimeters on the catalogue card.)
diagrs.	diagrams
ed.	editor or editors; *also* edition
et al.	and others (used to indicate several editors and authors)
illus.	illustrated, *or* illustrations; *also* illustrator
mounted pl.	full-page illustrations inserted
pseud.	pseudonym, pen name
rev.	revised (material has been updated)
tr.	translated, translator
v., vol., vols.	volume, volumes

Parts of the Book and Terms About Books

A knowledge of the following specialized terms can be useful in locating the books you need.

appendix:
(*Plural:* appendices) Supplementary material at a book's end; presents information that is related but not essential to the book, such as statistics, historical background, other data

bibliography:
Lists the books and other references the writer has used, or books and articles the reader may wish to consult for further information

copyright:
Indicated on the back of the book's title page; tells when the book was copyrighted and by whom (If there are several copyright dates, the latest indicates when the book was last revised.)

gazetteer:
A list of geographical places, their names and descriptions

glossary:
A list of key terms used in the book, with their definitions

index:
An alphabetized list of names, places, and subjects treated in the book, along with the page or pages on which they are discussed

introduction, foreword, preface:
Refers to introductory material to the book, whether by the author or someone else

text:
The main body of the book

title page:
The page near the book's front stating title, author, publisher, place of publication; may also state original publication date

Exercise 4

Find the title card for the following books. For some questions you will need to find the book as well. Then answer the following questions.

1. Find a book by Miguel de Cervantes. What is its title? Who is its translator? Does it have illustrations?

2. Find a book by Carl Sagan. What is its title and copyight date? Does it have a bibliography? An index?

3. Find a novel by George Eliot. ("George Eliot" is a pseudonym.) What is the author's real name? What is the title of the book? Does it have an introduction, and if so, by whom?

4. Find a collection of poems by Edna St. Vincent Millay. What is its title? Is there an editor, and if so, who? What is the date of publication, the publisher, and place of publication?

5. Find a book on electrical repairs or electricity. When was it copyrighted? Are there diagrams and illustrations? Is there an index?

"See" and "See Also" Cards
When searching for information on a subject, be aware that you may have to check out several subject headings. If you are seeking facts about modern slang, you might consult the card catalogue only to find no listing for *slang*. You would then check under other appropriate subject headings, such as

language or *English usage.* Some card catalogues use *cross-referencing* to help you locate information. A *"see" card* refers you to another subject heading.

> Slang
>> See Language, Usage

Another kind of cross-reference you may encounter is the *"See Also" card.* The "See Also" reference means there is information under the heading you have found, but there may be additional helpful information under another heading.

> Railroads
>> See also Freight Transport
>> See also Transportation

Biography:
An Exception

A biography is an account of a person's life, written by another; an autobiography is a writer's own account of his or her life.

The only nonfiction books that do not conform to the numerical ordering of the Dewey decimal system are *biographies* and *autobiographies.*

Biographies and autobiographies are usually classified under the number *921* and then arranged alphabetically according to the *subject's* last name. By this method all the biographies of one person, such as Booker T. Washington, will be found together. Some libraries label their biographies with a large capital *B* and then put the first letter of the subject's last name beneath the *B.* Thus, all biographies of Emily Dickinson would be labeled *D.* Practices may differ slightly from one library to another.

Books containing several biographies, called *collective biographies,* are usually classified under the number *920* and then arranged alphabetically according to the writer's or editor's last name. Dee Brown's book, *The Gentle Tamers,* for instance, contains the biographies of several memorable women in the American West. It might be catalogued as $\frac{920}{B}$ (the *920* indicating a collection of biographies, the *B* indicating the author's name).

Reference
Books in the
Card Catalogue

Most libraries have special *reference sections* where encyclopedias, atlases, and other books that are collections of special information are kept. If you look up a book in the card catalogue and find the letter *R* or the abbreviation *Ref.* above its call number, the book has been shelved in the reference section, not among its fellow volumes in the general nonfiction section.

The books collected in the reference section are arranged according to their original Dewey decimal numbers. Thus, encyclopedias, numbered *030,* would be in the first section of the reference area, and atlases and maps, with their *912* numbers, would be among the last volumes in the section. Books in the reference section usually cannot be checked out; they must be used in the library.

The *Readers' Guide to Periodical Literature*

Much of the reference work done in high school concerns current events.

Research on current events demands current facts; therefore, such information will more often be found in newspapers and periodicals than in books.

A basic research tool for finding recent facts and events is the *Readers' Guide to Periodical Literature*. The *Readers' Guide* is an index of stories and articles from almost 200 magazines. It is published twice a month from September through January, and from March through June, and once a month in February, July, and August. Thus, an issue of the *Readers' Guide* appears twice monthly for nine months of each year, listing a great quantity of the most recent material on a multitude of subjects. There are also cumulative *Readers' Guides*, or collections of past indexes, gathered into one volume. The most recent cumulative issues summarize the indexes of recent months. At the end of the year, all indexes are compiled into one volume for quick reference; at the end of two years, a two-year index is compiled.

Using the Readers' Guide

All issues of the *Readers' Guide* index authors and subjects alphabetically; under each subject heading is a list of relevant articles and the magazine in which each article is found. A sample column from the *Readers' Guide* is on page 207.

As you can see, the *Readers' Guide* uses many abbreviations. Each issue of the publication contains, before the index begins, a complete explanation of the abbreviations used. With this explanation the entries are relatively easy to read. For example, consider the following entry.

TECHNOLOGY
Needed: conviction to match our science. L. M. Branscomb, Science 209:641
Ag 8 '80

The preceding entry, under the subject "Technology," is for an article titled "Needed: Conviction to Match Our Science." (Notice that the *Readers' Guide* style is to capitalize only the first word of the title.) Written by L. M. Branscomb, the article appears on page 641 of the August 8, 1980 (Volume 209) issue of *Science* magazine.

The *Readers' Guide*, like the catalogue cards, contains "See" and "See Also" references. These references serve the same purpose as they do on catalogue cards: to indicate when a subject is listed under a different heading and to direct users to headings where more information can be found on the subject.

Past and current issues of the *Readers' Guide* are usually kept together in the reference section of the library. Your library may also have a posted list indicating which magazines it has available. Use this list to save time; there is no need to copy down articles in magazines that are not available.

TAUB, Eric
    Videodance. il Dance Mag 54:48-50 Ag '80   *entry by author*
TAUB, Jack R.
    Hard times for The Source. il por Bus W p 112 + S 15 ;80 *
TAVRIS, Carol
    Sexual jealousy: how it can wreck your happy home. il Redbook
      155:15 + Ag '80
TAX credits
    New crop of tax shelters in energy. il Bus W p80-2 S 1 '80
TAX evasion
    Sin subsidy: triple divorcees lose tax fight [A. and D. Boyter] pors
      Time 116:60 Ag 18 '80
TAX laws and regulations. See Taxation
TAX planning
    Finding shelter from the storm. il Time 116:43 S 1 '80   *entry by title*
    Hitting a tax gusher [royalty trust spinoffs] R. Phalon. Forbes
      126:72 Ag 4 '80
    New crop of tax shelters in energy. il Bus W p80-2 S 1 '80
    Railroad tax shelter in search of a partner [Central Jersey Indus-
      tries] D. G. Santry. Bus W p85 Ag 25 '80
    Siamese shares [paired sharing of stapled stocks] il Forbes 126:59-
      60 + S 1 '80
    Texas-size tax dodges [trust schemes] il Time 116:61 S 15 '80
    Why the rich are renting out rigs [limited-partnership tax shelters]
      A. L. Morner. il Fortune 102:91-3 Ag 25 '80
TAXATION   *subject heading*
    See also
    Social security—Taxation
    Urban Jobs and Enterprise Zone Act (proposed)

                     Canada
      See also
    Income tax—Canada
            New Brunswick (province)   *secondary subject heading*
    Tax credits by the tankful [law exempting storage tankks of Irving
      Oil from taxation] D. Folster. il Macleans 93:18-19 Ag 4 '80
TAXATION, State
    Honey pot [taxing oil companies] W. Baldwin. il Forbes 126:31-2   *title, issue, and date*
      Ag 4 '80   *of magazine*
TAXATION of works of art
    Professional page. B. Chamberlain. Am Artist 44:10 + Ag '80
TAXICABS
                     Fares
    Crime on four wheels [overcharging by drivers in New York City]
      L. O'Toole. il Macleans 93:25 Ag 18 '80
TAYLOR, Billy
    Billy Taylor updates and clarifies his story. Down Beat 47:12 Ag '80
TAYLOR, James Edward
    War correspondent: 1864. O. Jensen. il Am Heritage 31:48-64 Ag/
      S '80 *
TAYLOR, Marc Scott
    Among forensic pathologists, Quincy's a social crusader. M. Gros-
      swirth. il Sci Digest 88:64-7 S '80 *   *page numbers of article*
TAYLOR, Paul
    Graham's Frescoes, Taylor's Sacre. J. Maskey. il Hi Fi 30:MA15
      Ag '80 *
    Taylor's domain: the Paul Taylor Dance Company, New York City
      Center. April 15-May 4, 1980. T. Tobias. il Dance Mag 54:60-1
      Ag '80 *
TEA (beverage)
    Iced tea tips. Bet Hom & Gard 58:62 Ag '80
    Summer cooler: iced tea. Good H 191:157 Ag '80
TEA tax (American colonies)
    See also
    Boston Tea Party, 1773   *"see" cross reference*
TEACHER shortage. See Teachers—Supply and demand
TEACHERS
                   Awards
    17-second interview [Teacher of the Year] B. J. Bimes. Seventeen
      39:67 Ag '80

            Supply and demand
    Wanted: a few good teachers. G. Sewall and G. Hackett. Newsweek
      96:102 S 15 '80
TEACHERS and students
    Class clod: six questions not to ask the teacher. A. E. Schraff. il
      Seventeen 39:66 Ag '80

Either the list or your librarian should tell you whether back issues of the library's magazines are kept. *Back issues* are magazines from previous months and years. Large libraries may have extensive collections of back issues; smaller libraries may not have the storage room. Some libraries, to save space, have back issues on microfilm reels, which can be read on a microfilm machine in the library.

Exercise 5

Answer each of the following questions.

1. Where is the *Readers' Guide* located in your library? Is there a list of magazines to which your library subscribes? Where are current magazines kept? Does your library keep back issues, and if so, where?

2. Does your library contain a microfilm machine? Are any periodicals kept on microfilm? How do you check out microfilm? How do you find the article you want on microfilm?

3. Which of the following magazines does your library subscribe to: *Newsweek*, *Time*, the *Congressional Digest*, *U.S. News and World Report*, *The New Yorker*, *Harper's*, *Atlantic Monthly*, *Smithsonian?* Does the library keep back issues of any of these magazines? If so, how far back do these issues go?

4. Look in the *Readers' Guide* at the "Abbreviations of Periodicals Indexed" in the front of the index. For what magazines do the following abbreviations stand: *Sci Am, Yale R, For Affairs, Bsns W, Bull Atom Sci, M Labor R?* How many of these magazines does your library subscribe to?

5. Using the *Readers' Guide* "Abbreviations of Periodicals Indexed" and its "Key to Abbreviations," answer the following questions about the sample column from the *Readers' Guide* on page 207.

    a. Who is the author of an article on tax planning titled "Siamese Shares"?
    b. Under what heading would you look to find an article on teacher shortages?
    c. What is the title of an article about taxation in a province of Canada?
    d. From the two articles about Paul Taylor, what is his occupation?
    e. In what issue of what magazine could you find an interview with the teacher of the year?

Reference Books

Suppose that you want to find the answer to a specific question, such as "Who invented toothpaste?" or "What is the tallest building on earth?" You can find answers to any factual question in reference books, which summarize, alphabetize, and make accessible all factual knowledge. In the following sections, you will learn about encyclopedias, almanacs, atlases, books of quotations, and other specialized reference books.

Encyclopedias   The word *encyclopedia* is derived from a Greek word meaning "circle of knowledge." An encyclopedia is designed to present a well-rounded collection of information in all branches of learning. The first encyclopedia was written over 2,000 years ago in Greece, and only a few fragments of it survive. Modern students may think of an encyclopedia as a set of many books, but smaller one- and two-volume encyclopedias also exist.

Encyclopedias are a valuable tool to use at the *beginning* of your research.

Encyclopedias are valuable for two reasons: first, they provide a general discussion of the subject; and second, they may provide a bibliography, a list of other books you can consult for further information. In addition, the encyclopedia will probably have cross-references to other pertinent articles on your subject or an index that will direct you to such articles.

Because events and scientific knowledge advance so swiftly, encyclopedias must be kept up-to-date to be useful. Minor revisions may be made each time an encyclopedia is reprinted. In addition, many encyclopedias publish a yearly supplement that supplies updated information and new developments. Finally, the entire encyclopedia is revised thoroughly from time to time and a completely new edition brought out.

The following encyclopedias are used in many libraries.

Collier's Encyclopedia. A work in twenty-four volumes, this encyclopedia is noted for its readable style and fine bibliography. The bibliography is in the twenty-fourth volume. An annual yearbook supplies new information.

Compton's Encyclopedia and Fact Index. This twenty-six volume set was designed for school use by younger students—but may be helpful to adults as well. The fact index lists all articles that may be relevant to a certain subject. A yearbook is also published.

Encyclopedia Americana. In thirty volumes, with the index in volume thirty, the *Encyclopedia Americana* is noted for its excellent treatment of science and technology, its historical summaries, and its biographies. A yearbook, *Americana Annual*, is published.

Encyclopaedia Britannica. The thirty-volume set presents a new idea in arranging material. The first volume, *Guide to the Britannica*, is introductory and lists divisions of human knowledge, indicating where relevant articles on specific topics can be found in the other volumes. The next ten volumes, called the *Micropaedia*, present short articles and in the case of complex subjects give cross-references to articles in the next section. The next and last section is the *Macropaedia*, containing thorough articles on all subjects treated. The *Macropaedia* also provides bibliographies for further study on a subject. The *Encyclopaedia Britannica* is one of the most comprehensive and scholarly works of its kind; it is noted especially for its treatment of historical subjects.

World Book Encyclopedia. Twenty-one volumes comprise this work, with a research guide and index in Volume Twenty-Two. Although designed for young people, adults can also profit from it. Noted for its colorfulness and many illustrations, the *World Book* is useful in its presentation of a subject's highlights.

One- and Two-Volume Encyclopedias

One- and two-volume encyclopedias, sometimes called *desk encyclopedias*, can be helpful as a short, general introduction to a subject.

Three of the most useful desk encyclopedias are the following ones.

The Columbia Encyclopedia. This one-volume encyclopedia contains brief, concise articles on a surprising multitude of subjects. It also supplies bibliographies but has no illustrations.

The Columbia-Viking Desk Encyclopedia. This is a one-volume abridgment of the *Columbia Encyclopedia.* It contains no bibliographies but does have illustrations and charts.

The Lincoln Library of Essential Information. This single-volume work arranges information under twelve subject areas and has an index. It provides a general introduction to much information but contains no bibliographies.

Exercise 6

Locate your school library's encyclopedias and then answer the following questions:

1. Does your library contain any one- or two-volume encyclopedias? If so, write down their names.

2. How many multivolume sets of encyclopedias does your library have? Write down the names of at least two sets.

3. Flip through one or two volumes of a set of encyclopedias until you locate an interesting subject. Then look at the end of the article to see if a bibliography is listed. Write down the subject heading and the names of the books listed for further reference.

4. Look at two or more sets of encyclopedias to see if an index is a part of the set. If so, look up a subject of interest to you in the index. Write down subject headings you could look under to find more information about that subject.

5. Look at two or more sets of encyclopedias to see if a yearbook is a part of the set. If so, skim through the yearbook to get a general idea of the kinds of subjects that are brought up-to-date. Then write down five subjects that are included in the yearbook.

Using the Dictionary

The reference book you will probably have the most occasion to use is the *dictionary.*

The sample dictionary entry on page 212, from *Webster's New World Dictionary,* and the key on page 211 provide a review of the basic information found in most dictionaries.

A Guide to Using the Dictionary

These numbered items explain each number on page 212.

1. Guide words are printed at the top of the page to show the first and last words on that page.

2. Word entries are printed in **boldface** type. Words are in alphabetical order.

3. Other forms of the word are also given. These forms may include plurals, principal parts of verbs, and comparative forms of adjectives and adverbs.

4. Syllables are indicated in word entries with a raised dot between syllables. These syllable markers show where words may be divided at the end of a line of writing.

5. Pronunciation is shown with diacritical marks and simplified spellings. These follow the word entry and are in parentheses.

6. Usage markers show whether a word is slang, colloquial, or archaic. Words that are part of Standard English are not marked. Meanings of abbreviations for usage labels can usually be found in the front of the dictionary.

7. The part of speech is shown by an abbreviation. The meanings of part-of-speech abbreviations are also listed in the front of the dictionary.

8. Word origins are shown in brackets after the part-of-speech abbreviation. Look in the front of the dictionary for help reading the history of a word.

9. A new word entry is given for each word. When one entry has exactly the same spelling as the one that follows it, the two are distinguished by raised numbers.

10. In *Webster's New World Dictionary*, definitions of the words are numbered with Arabic numbers, with the oldest meanings having the lowest numbers. When a word has many definitions, the definitions are grouped according to the part of speech.

11. Phrases and compound words appear as entries.

12. Synonyms (words that mean nearly the same) often appear after definitions. *See* means "see the dictionary entry for the word."

13. Information about people, places, and events is often given.

14. A pronunciation key is often found at the bottom of every other page. A more complete key can be found in the front of the dictionary.

Unabridged Dictionaries

An *unabridged dictionary* is a larger and more extensive version of the standard dictionary found in most classrooms.

Unabridged dictionaries give more extensive information on word histories, usage, foreign words, new words, and idiomatic expressions. In addi-

gribble   615   **grin**

grib·ble (grib'l) *n.* [prob. dim. < base of GRUB] a small marine crustacean (order Isopoda) that bores into wooden objects under water and destroys them

grid (grid) *n.* [short for GRIDIRON] 1. a framework of parallel bars; gridiron; grating 2. a network of evenly spaced horizontal and vertical bars or lines, esp. one for locating points when placed over a map, chart, building plan, etc. 3. *Elec.* a metallic plate in a storage cell for conducting the electric current and supporting the active material 4. *Electronics* an electrode, usually a wire spiral or mesh, having one or more openings for controlling the passage of electrons or ions in an electronic tube —*adj.* [Slang] of football

grid bias the direct-current voltage applied to the control grid of an electron tube to make it negative with respect to the cathode

grid current the flow of electrons between a grid and the cathode of an electron tube

☆**grid·der** (grid'ər) *n.* [< GRID, *adj.* & GRIDIRON] [Slang] a football player

grid·dle (grid'l) *n.* [ME. *gredil* < Anglo-Fr. *gridil* < OFr. *gredil*, var. of *grail* < L. *craticula*, small gridiron < *cratis*, *wickerwork*: see CRATE] a heavy, flat, metal plate or pan for cooking pancakes, etc. —*vt.* **-dled, -dling** to cook on a griddle

grid·dle·cake (-kāk') *n.* a thin, flat batter cake cooked on a griddle; pancake

gride (grid) *vt., vi.* **grid'ed, grid'ing** [metathesis of ME. *girden*, to pierce (see GIRD), adopted (< Lydgate) & popularized by Spenser] 1. to scrape or grate with a rasping sound 2. [Obs.] to pierce or wound —*n.* a harsh, rasping sound made by scraping or grating

grid·i·ron (grid'i'ərn) *n.* [ME. *gredirne*, folk etym. on *irne* (see IRON) < *gredel*, var. of *gredil*: see GRIDDLE] 1. a framework of metal bars or wires on which to broil meat or fish; grill 2. any framework or network resembling a gridiron ☆3. a football field

grief (grēf) *n.* [ME. < OFr., sorrow, grief < *grever*: see GRIEVE] 1. intense emotional suffering caused by loss, disaster, misfortune, etc.; acute sorrow; deep sadness 2. a cause or the subject of such suffering 3. [Obs.] *a)* hardship, suffering, or pain *b)* a cause of any of these —SYN. see SORROW —**come to grief** to fail or be ruined

grief-strick·en (·strik'n) *adj.* stricken with grief; keenly distressed; sorrowful

Grieg (grēg; *Norw.* grig), **Ed·vard** (**Hagerup**) (ed'värd; *Norw.* ed'värt) 1843–1907; Norw. composer

griev·ance (grē'vəns) *n.* [ME. *grevaunce* < OFr. *grevance* < *grever*: see ff.] 1. a circumstance thought to be unjust or injurious and ground for complaint or resentment 2. complaint or resentment, or a statement expressing this, against a real or imagined wrong 3. [Obs.] *a)* the inflicting of injury or hardship *b)* a cause of injury or hardship —SYN. see INJUSTICE

grieve (grēv) *vt.* **grieved, griev'ing** [ME. *greven* < OFr. *grever* < L. *gravare*, to burden, grieve < *gravis*, heavy, grievous: see GRAVE²] 1. to cause to feel grief; afflict with deep, acute sorrow or distress 2. [Archaic] to harm; injure —*vi.* to feel deep, acute sorrow or distress; mourn; lament —**griev'er** *n.*

griev·ous (grē'vəs) *adj.* [ME. *grevous* < OFr. *grever*: see prec.] 1. causing grief 2. showing or characterized by grief [a *grievous* cry] 3. causing suffering; hard to bear; severe [*grievous* pain] 4. deplorable; atrocious; heinous [a *grievous* crime] —**griev'ous·ly** *adv.* —**griev'ous·ness** *n.*

griffe (grif) *n.* [Fr., lit., a claw < OFr. *grif* < Frank. **grif*, akin to OHG. *grif*: see GRIPE] *Archit.* a clawlike ornament extending from the base of a column

grif·fin (grif'ən) *n.* [ME. *griffon* < OFr. *grifoun* < OHG. or It. *grifo*, both < L. *gryphus* < Gr. *gryps*, griffin < *grypos*, hooked, curved (prob. so called from its hooked beak) < IE. base **ger-*, whence CROOK] a mythical animal with the body and hind legs of a lion and the head and wings of an eagle

Grif·fith (grif'ith) [W. *Gruffydd* < I., L. *Rufus*: see RUFUS] 1. a masculine name 2. **D(avid) W(ark)** (Lewelyn) (–), 1875–1948; U.S. motion-picture producer & director

GRIFFIN

grif·fon (grif'ən) *n.* [Fr., lit., a griffin] 1. *same as* GRIFFIN 2. any of a Belgian breed of very small dog with a flat face 3. any of a Dutch breed of medium-sized dog with a wiry coat

☆**grift·er** (grif'tər) *n.* [prob. altered < GRAFTER] [Slang] a petty swindler, as one who operates a dishonest gambling device at a carnival; confidence man —**grift** *vi., vt., n.*

grig (grig) *n.* [ME. *grege*, anything diminutive, dwarf, prob. < Scand., as in Norw. *krek*, Sw. dial. *krik*, little animal] 1. a lively, animated person 2. [Obs. or Dial.] a small eel 3. [Obs. or Dial.] a grasshopper or cricket

Gri·gnard reagent (grē nyärd') [after F. A. V. Grignard (1871–1935), Fr. chemist] any of a class of reagents with the general formula RMgX, in which R is an alkyl or aryl radical and X is a halide: these reagents have a great variety of compounds and are used in the synthesis of organic compounds

☆**gri·gri** (grē'grē) *n. same as* GRIS-GRIS

grill¹ (gril) *n.* [Fr. *gril* < OFr. *grail*: see GRIDDLE] 1. a framework of metal bars or wires on which to broil meat or fish; gridiron 2. a large griddle 3. grilled food ☆4. *short for* GRILLROOM —*vt.* [Fr. *griller* < the *n.*] 1. to cook on a grill; broil 2. to torture by applying heat ☆3. to question relentlessly; cross-examine searchingly —*vi.* to be subjected to grilling

grill² (gril) *n. same as* GRILLE

grill·age (-ij) *n.* [Fr., wirework, grating, frame < *grille*: see ff.] a system of beams laid crosswise to form a foundation for a building in soft soil

grille (gril) *n.* [Fr. < OFr. *graille* < L. *craticula*: see GRIDDLE] 1. an open grating of wrought iron, bronze, wood, etc., forming a screen to a door, window, or other opening, or used as a divider 2. *Court Tennis* a square opening high on the back wall of the court on the hazard side

grilled (grild) *adj.* 1. having a grille 2. cooked on a grill or gridiron; broiled

Grill·par·zer (gril'pär'tsər), **Franz** (fränts) 1791–1872; Austrian dramatist

grill·room (gril'room') *n.* a restaurant, club, or dining room that makes a specialty of grilled foods

grill·work (-wurk') *n.* a grille, or something worked into the form of a grille

grilse (grils) *n., pl.* **grilse, grils'es:** see PLURAL, II, D, 2 [ME. *grills* < ? OFr. *grisle*, dim. < *gris*, gray] a young salmon on its first return from the sea to fresh water

grim (grim) *adj.* **grim'mer, grim'mest** [ME. < OE. *grimm*, akin to G. *grimm* < IE. base **ghrem-*, to make a loud sound, roar angrily, whence Russ. *grom*, thunder & GRUMBLE] 1. fierce; cruel; savage 2. hard and unyielding; relentless; stern; resolute [*grim* courage] 3. appearing stern, forbidding, harsh, etc. [a *grim* face] 4. repellent; uninviting [a *grim* task] 5. dealing with unpleasant subjects; frightful; ghastly [*grim* humor] —SYN. see GHASTLY —**grim'ly** *adv.* —**grim'ness** *n.*

gri·mace (gri mās', grim'əs) *n.* [Fr., altered (with pejorative suffix) < OFr. *grimuche*, prob. < Frank. **grima*, a mask, akin to OE. *grima* < IE. base **ghrei-*, to smear, rub over, whence Gr. *chrisma*, ointment & GRISLY] a twisting or distortion of the face, as in expressing pain, contempt, disgust, etc., or a wry look, as in seeking to amuse —*vi.* **-maced', -mac'ing** to make grimaces —**gri·mac'er** *n.*

Gri·mal·di man (gri mal'dē, -môl'-) [from the remains found near *Grimaldi*, village in Italy] an Aurignacian man, similar to the Cro-Magnon

gri·mal·kin (gri mal'kin, -môl'-) *n.* [earlier *gray malkin*] 1. a cat; esp., an old female cat 2. a malicious old woman

grime (grim) *n.* [Early ModE., prob. < Fl. *grijm:* for IE. base see GRIMACE] dirt, esp. sooty dirt, rubbed into or covering a surface, as of the skin —*vt.* **grimed, grim'ing** to make sorry or distress —*vi.* to make grimaces —**gri·mac'er** *n.*

☆**Grimes (Golden)** (grimz) [short for *Grimes Golden Pippin,* variety grown (c. 1790) by T. P. *Grimes,* W.Va. fruit grower] a yellow autumn eating apple

Grimm (grim), **Ja·kob (Ludwig Karl)** & **Wil·helm (Karl)** (vil'helm) 1786–1859; Ger. brother philologists & collaborators in the collection of fairy tales

Grimm's law (grimz) [after formulation (1822) by Jakob GRIMM of parallels noticed by R. K. Rask & himself] a systematic statement of a series of prehistoric changes of Indo-European reconstructed consonants to proto-Germanic consonants: these assumed prehistoric sound shifts are reflected by consonant correspondences between Germanic words and their cognates in non-Germanic Indo-European languages: (1) IE. voiceless stops (p, t, k) = Gmc. voiceless fricatives (f, th, h); hence, L. *pater* (cf. PATERNAL) = E. *father,* L. *tenuis* (cf. TENUOUS) = E. *thin,* Gr. *kardia* (cf. CARDIAC) = E. *heart* (2) IE. voiced aspirated stops (bh, dh, gh) = Gmc. voiced fricatives or stops (b, d, g); hence, Sans. *bhrātar* (cf. FRATERNAL) = E. *brother,* Sans. *mădhu,* honey (Gr. *mēthy,* wine: cf. METHYL) = E. *mead,* L. *hostis* (IE. **ghostis:* cf. HOSTILE) = E. *guest* (3) IE. voiced stops (b, d, g) = Gmc. voiceless stops (p, t, k); hence, L. *bucca* (cf. BUCCAL) = OE. *pohha,* a sack, L. *decem* (cf. DECIMAL) = E. *ten,* L. *genu* (cf. GENUFLECT) = E. *knee* These correspondences show the kinship, stressed in the etymologies of this dictionary, between various native English words and the English words borrowed from the Classical or Romance languages

Grims·by (grimz'bē) seaport in Lincolnshire, NE England, at the mouth of the Humber estuary; pop. 95,000

grim·y (grī'mē) *adj.* **grim'i·er, grim'i·est** covered with or full of grime; very dirty —SYN. see DIRTY —**grim'i·ly** *adv.* —**grim'i·ness** *n.*

grin (grin) *vi.* **grinned, grin'ning** [ME. *grennen* < OE. *grennian,* to gnash or bare the teeth, akin to OHG. *grennan,*

fat, āpe, cär; ten, ēven; is, bīte; gō, hôrn, tōōl, look; oil, out; up, fur; get; joy; yet; chin; she; thin, *then;* zh, leisure; ŋ, ring; ə for *a* in *ago, e* in *agent, i* in *sanity, o* in *comply, u* in *focus;* ' as in *able* (ā'b'l); Fr. bāl; ë, Fr. coeur; ö, Fr. feu; Fr. mon; ô, Fr. coq; ü, Fr. duc; r, Fr. cri; H, G. ich; kh, G. doch. See inside front cover. ☆ Americanism; ‡foreign; *hypothetical; < derived from

tion, unabridged dictionaries usually explain in greater detail differences between words with similar meanings and give more examples of words being used in context.

Since unabridged dictionaries are so large, libraries usually display them on a table or dictionary stand for easy use. The unabridged dictionaries your library is most likely to have are the *Webster's Third New International Dictionary*; the *Random House Dictionary of the English Language, Unabridged Edition*; and *Funk & Wagnalls New Standard Dictionary of the English Language.*

Yearbooks and Almanacs

Yearbooks and *almanacs*, published annually, contain lists, statistics, and facts on topics subject to change, such as population, nations and governments, elections, current events, and awards. Everything from current postal rates to state mottos can be found in these works. An almanac or yearbook presents information about the preceding year; that is, if you want statistics on the election of 1980, you would look in the 1981 almanac. Yearbooks and almanacs commonly available are as follows:

Information Please Almanac
New York Times Encyclopedic Almanac
The Official Associated Press Almanac
Statesman's Yearbook
Statistical Abstracts of the United States
World Almanac and Book of Facts

Atlases

Topography is the science of representing surface features of a region on a map.

An *atlas* is a book of maps; it may also include tables and diagrams. The maps may supply far more information than the locations of a country's cities and boundaries. They can also show topography, climate, political and religious distributions, and much more. When using an atlas, check its copyright date. The political and religious turmoil of the past forty years, as well as the changes in world economy, has kept countries—and thus their maps—in change. Atlases commonly available are as follows:

The Encyclopaedia Britannica World Atlas International
National Geographic Atlas of the World
New York Times Atlas of the World
Rand McNally New Cosmopolitan World Atlas

Historical Atlases

Historical atlases provide maps illustrating the world's past. A good historic map is more than a collection of outdated maps; it gives information on explorations, ethnic and religious groups and movements, transportation, trade routes, and agriculture. Two excellent general historic atlases are Lord's *Historical Atlas of the United States* and Shepherd's *Historical Atlas*. Many specialized historical atlases exist as well, covering many areas and topics, ranging from biblical maps to maps of battles and wars.

General Biographical Reference Works

Your library's reference area probably contains a section devoted to collections of brief biographies of people both living and dead.

Biographical References to Living People

Current Biography is a monthly publication devoted to people in the news, containing biographies from one to two pages in length. At the year's end the monthly issues are collected, with a comprehensive index, into one volume.

International Who's Who is a biographical dictionary published yearly; it gives brief biographies of internationally prominent people in government, arts, and science.

Who's Who, also published annually, contains biographies of prominent British subjects, including those living in British commonwealths, such as Canada. The biographies are brief, with facts such as birthdate, birthplace, education, and achievements.

Who's Who in America, another annual publication, is the counterpart of the British *Who's Who*, giving concise biographical information on over 50,000 living Americans.

Biographical Reference to People Both Living and Deceased

Biographical Index, published four times a year, is an index of biographical material appearing in both books and magazines.

Webster's Biographical Dictionary gives brief biographical sketches of prominent people, both living and dead.

Biographical References to Deceased People

Dictionary of American Biography is a multivolume set with an index and supplements. It treats its subjects, people who have distinguished themselves in America's past, in greater depth and detail than do many other reference works.

Dictionary of National Biography is another multivolume set with an index and supplements. It deals with prominent British people, and many of its biographies are lengthy and thorough.

Who Was Who, published at intervals, contains biographies of people originally listed in *Who's Who* but who are no longer living.

Who Was Who in America is the American counterpart of *Who Was Who*; it includes deceased people formerly listed in *Who's Who in America*.

Reference Works on Literature and Languages

Your work in English probably requires that you do some research on literature and perhaps on language. The following sources can be valuable aids.

Books About Writers

The following biographical references are devoted to authors.

American Authors, 1600–1900 contains about 1,300 entries.

British Authors Before 1800 contains about 650 entries.

British Authors of the Twentieth Century contains about 1,000 entries.

Twentieth Century Authors contains about 1,850 authors. It was published in 1942 and has supplements with biographies of authors who have appeared since the original publication.

Cyclopedia of World Authors treats approximately 750 important writers in some depth.

The Writers Directory, pubished every two years, contains short biographies on almost 20,000 contemporary writers.

Indexes to Short Works and Plays

Locating a single poem, short story, or one-act play can be difficult unless you know how to use special reference works. Similarly, full-length plays are sometimes hard to find since they are published more frequently in collections of plays than under their own titles. The following indexes are designed to help you track down such works.

Granger's Index to Poetry
Index to One-Act Plays
Index to Plays
Short Story Index

Finding Quotations

When writing an essay, speech, or article, you may wish to make use of quotations. The four books that follow are excellent sources.

Bartlett's Familiar Quotations is a collection of quotations, arranged by authors and listed chronologically. There is an extensive index of both authors and subjects to help you locate needed material.

Peter's Quotations; Ideas for Our Time by Laurence J. Peter collects pithy and often amusing quotations according to subject. Subjects are arranged in alphabetical order.

Stevenson's *Home Book of Quotations* and *Home Book of Proverbs, Maxims, and Familiar Phrases* also group quotations according to subject matter.

General Reference Works on Literature and Language

The following references on literature are also valuable sources of information.

American Authors and Books
Book Review Digest
Bulfinch's Mythology
The New Century Classical Handbook
Oxford Companion to American Literature
Oxford Companion to Classical Literature
Oxford Companion to English Literature

For questions about grammar, usage, or style, consult any of the following sources.

A Dictionary of Contemporary American Usage by Bergen and Cornelia Evans
The Elements of Style by E. B. White and William Strunk
American Usage and Style: The Consensus by Roy H. Copperud
Writer's Guide and Index to English by Porter G. Perrin

Exercise 7

Name the reference work you would use to find the following information.

1. A map of medieval Europe
2. The population of Guatemala in 1982
3. A brief biography of the United Kingdom's Princess Anne
4. A brief biography of American politician Hubert Humphrey
5. A climate map of Africa
6. The location of Shirley Jackson's short story "The Lottery"
7. Information about the Roman goddess Diana
8. The location of Langston Hughes' poem "A Dream Deferred"
9. A thorough article about the endocrine system
10. Biographies of several American Puritan writers

Other Special Sources Your Library May Provide

The Vertical File

Because pamphlets, photographs, and newspaper clippings cannot be kept on the library's shelves, they are usually stored in a special filing cabinet called the "Vertical File" or the "Information File." If you are researching a current topic, you may find helpful information in this file. Governments, businesses, colleges and universities, and other organizations publish pamphlets on a variety of subjects.

Reserved Books

When a teacher wishes to have a book remain in the library so that a number of students can consult it, he or she places the book *on reserve*. Reserve books are usually kept at the librarian's desk and are checked out for use in the library. Sometimes, a student is allowed to take a reserve book home overnight if he or she can return it at the time the library reopens in the morning.

New Books

Recently purchased books are often placed in a special section of the library so that users will know that new material is at their disposal.

Rare Books and Special Collections

Some libraries are fortunate enough to have rare books that are kept separately from the main collection; such books may generally be used only by permission and may not be taken from the library.

Many libraries have "special collections." Your library may keep its books on local and state history in a special section, and frequently books by writers from your state or area are shelved together as special collections.

Records, Tapes, Films, Microfilm

Books are a product of the technology of print; new technologies have brought new resources to the library. Many libraries have record albums that can be checked out: music, plays, and authors reading from their works. More and more libraries are turning to microfilm to store information. Microfilm allows the library to house an enormous amount of material in a small space. Easy-to-use microfilm viewers are available in such libraries.

11 Developing Your Vocabulary

Using Context Clues

You can sometimes decide the meaning of a word by examining the *context* in which it occurs.

The *context* of a word is the words, phrases, sentences, and paragraphs that surround it.

Consider the following sentence.

Cheryle has several yards of *madras* that she is going to make into a sundress.

The words *yards*, *make*, and *sundress* in the preceding sentence are clues that *madras* is some kind of cloth.

A word may have different meanings in different contexts.

Lois learned Spanish in six weeks; she has a *preternatural* ability for languages.

In the preceding sentence Lois has accomplished an amazing feat—learning Spanish in such a short time. In that sentence *preternatural* means "unusual" or "beyond the ordinary."

We don't know what makes the moaning noise in our attic when there is a full moon; I hope it's nothing *preternatural*.

In the preceding sentence the phrases *moaning noise* and *full moon* suggest a different meaning for *preternatural*. In this case *preternatural* means "supernatural; outside the limits of our human reality."

Exercise 1

On a sheet of paper, copy the *italicized* words in each of the following sentences. Then write a sentence or two about each word in which you give a definition for it and explain what context clues in the sentences led you to that definition.

Example

a. His *parsimonious* nature was such that he even refused to buy a newspaper; instead, he walked two miles to read the library's copy.

a. parsimonious—*The words "even refused to buy" suggest that the word means "stingy."*

1.   Although we had high hopes for the plan, it proved *unviable*.

2.   Malcolm mistook his sister's *quiescence* for agreement; actually she was thinking of something else altogether.

3.   Marcia thought the comic was funny, but Juanita thought he was merely *fatuous*.

4.   My cousin cries at every little thing that is the slightest bit sad; she is the most *lachrymose* person I've ever met.

5.   Some people will not eat catfish because catfish themselves eat *offal*.

6.   Terry claimed to be sick, but Coach Washington suspected it was a bad case of *malingering*.

7.   It was a long Sunday afternoon, and we all became droopy-eyed in the atmosphere of general *lassitude*.

8.   Pat decided not to study for the test, and her decision proved to be *injudicious*.

9.   John Carradine was a tall, *cadaverous* actor with sunken cheeks and bony hands who frequently starred in horror movies.

10.   There is much debate about whether capital punishment is truly a *deterrent* to the crime of murder.

Exercise 2

On a sheet of paper, write down the *italicized* words in each of the following quotations. After each word give a brief definition of it from the context. If you cannot deduce the word's meaning from context, look it up and supply the dictionary definition that best fits the word's context.

1.   As for life, it is a battle and a *sojourning* in a strange land; but the fame that comes after is *oblivion*.   —Marcus Aurelius Antoninus

2.   Early impressions are hard to *eradicate* from the mind. When once wool has been dyed purple, who can restore it to its previous whiteness?
                                                                     —St. Jerome

3.   What more *felicity* can fall to creature,
     Than to enjoy delight with liberty.   —Edmund Spenser

4.   Literature is my *Utopia*. Here I am not *disfranchised*. No barrier of the senses shuts me out from the sweet, gracious *discourse* of my book friends.   —Helen Keller

5.   At the close of the services, the people hurried out with *indecorous* confusion—eager to communicate their pent-up amazement, and conscious of lighter spirits the moment they lost sight of the black veil.

Some gathered in little circles, huddled closely together, with their mouths all whispering in the center; some talked loudly and profaned the Sabbath day with *ostentatious* laughter. —Nathaniel Hawthorne

6. The most alarming of all man's assaults upon the environment is the contamination of air, earth, rivers, and sea . . . this pollution is for the most part *irrecoverable.* —Rachel Carson

7. Society in its full sense . . . is never an *entity* separable from the individuals who compose it. No individual can arrive even at the threshold of his *potentialities* without a culture in which he participates.[1]
  —Ruth Benedict

8. Indian people have managed to maintain a *viable* and *cohesive* social order in spite of everything the non-Indian society has thrown at them in an effort to break the tribal structure. —Vine DeLoria, Jr.

9. Granny made it *imperative,* however, that I attend certain all-night ritualistic prayer meetings. She was the oldest member of her church and it would have been unseemly if the only grandchild in her home could not be brought to these important services; she felt that if I were completely *remiss* in religious conformity it would cast doubt upon the *staunchness* of her faith, her capacity to convince and persuade, or merely upon her ability to apply the rod to my backside.[2]
  —Richard Wright

10. Hazel Morse was a large, fair woman of the type that incites some men when they use the word "blonde" to click their tongues and wag their heads *roguishly.* —Dorothy Parker

The Structure of Words

Word Roots A *root* is a core of meaning that cannot be further analyzed.

Roots cannot be divided into smaller units of meaning. Some roots, such as *foot, join, calm, wear,* and *view,* are also words. Other roots are words only when they combine with other roots or with elements of meaning called *affixes.*

An *affix* consists of a syllable (or sometimes word) that carries meaning when joined to a root or to a word.

Roots that are independent words are called *free roots;* those that cannot stand alone are called *bound roots.*

In the English language are many words formed from bound roots that came into English from Greek. Because these roots usually carry specific

---

[1] Excerpt from *Patterns of Culture* by Ruth Benedict, 1934. Reprinted by permission of Houghton Mifflin Company.

[2] From *Black Boy* by Richard Wright. Copyright 1937, 1942, 1944, 1945 by Richard Wright. Reprinted by permission of Harper & Row, Publishers, Inc. and Jonathan Cape Ltd. on behalf of Mrs. Ellen Wright.

meanings, a knowledge of the roots and those meanings can help you in determining the definition of a word. For example, the Greek root -*crypt*- has the meaning "secret, hidden"; in English -*crypt*- combines with the affix -*ic* to form the word *cryptic*, meaning "having a secret meaning."

Many English words consist of two Greek roots bound together: *microcosm* from -*micro*- ("small") and -*cosm*- ("world"); *anthropology* from -*anthrop*- ("man, mankind") and -*log*- ("study of"); *autograph* from -*auto*- ("self") and -*graph*- ("write, writing"). Analyzing the meaning of compound roots such as these can sometimes help you to decipher the word's meaning.

In the following list are some of the most common roots that have come into the language from Greek, their meanings, and examples of English words composed of those roots. (Notice that a root is written in the following way: -*aud*-. Roots are written in this manner to show that affixes may be added to either the front or the end of the root.)

These roots are derived from Greek.

ROOT	DEFINITION	ENGLISH DERIVATIVES
-anthro-	man, mankind	anthropology, anthropomorphic
-astron-	star	astronaut, astronomical
-auto-	self	automatic, autocratic
-biblio-	book	Bible, bibliography
-bio-	life	biography, bionic
-bot-	plant	botany, botanical
-chrom-	color	monochrome, chromatic
-chron-	time	chronology, chronic
-dem-	people	democrat, demagogue
-derm-	skin	epidermis, dermatology
-geo-	earth	geology, geophysical
-gram-	write	telegram, grammar
-graph-	write	photograph, graphology
-log-	word, study	logic, logo
-micr-	little	microbe, microcosm
-neur-	nerve	neuron, neurotic
-ortho-	straight	orthodox, orthodontist
-neo-	new	neoclassic, neophyte
-phil-	like, love	philosophy, Philadelphia
-poly-	many	polygraph, polymorphous
-psych-	mental	psychology, psychiatry
-soph-	wisdom, knowledge	philosopher, sophist
-therm-	heat	thermal, thermometer
-zoo-	life, animal	zoo, zoology

Exercise 3

On a sheet of paper numbered 1–10, write down each of the following words and the Greek root from which each is derived. Using the list of roots and their meanings in the previous section, supply a definition for the word. Look in your dictionary to check and, if need be, revise your definition.

1. anthropoid
2. orthopedics
3. thermoplastic
4. logos
5. philanthropy
6. sophisticated
7. polyandry
8. psyche
9. zoologist
10. biopsy

Exercise 4

Using your dictionary or drawing on your own vocabulary, list and define two words in which each of the following roots appears. Do not give words previously used as examples in this chapter.

1. -therm-
2. -neo-
3. -bio-
4. -graph-
5. -neur-
6. -chron-
7. -micr-
8. -auto-
9. -chrom-
10. -derm-

The English language borrows more words from Latin than from any other language. It is natural, then, that many English words have Latin roots. In the following list are some of the most common Latin words, their meanings, and examples of words containing the roots.

These roots are derived from Latin.

ROOT	DEFINITION	ENGLISH DERIVATIVES
-am-, -amis-	friend, love	amiable, amorous
-aud-, -audi-	hear	audio, auditory
-ben-, -bene-	good	benefit, beneficial
-cent-	hundred	centennial, century
-cogn-	know	recognize, cognizant
-duc-, -duct-	draw, lead	conduct, deduct
-fid-	faithful	fidelity, infidel
-fin-	end	final, infinity
-gen-	kind, birth	generation, congenital
-jud-	judge	judge, injudicious
-junct-	join	junction, conjunction
-loc-	place	locate, locale
-magn-	large	magnify, magnificent
-man-	hand	manual, manicure
-mor-, -mort-	death	mortician, immortal
-omni-	all	omnipresent, omnivorous
-port-	carry	portable, import
-prim-	early	primitive, primeval
-sci-	know, knowledge	science, conscience
-spir-	breath	inspire, expire
-tract-	pull	tractor, traction
-uni-	one	universe, unite
-vid-, -vis-	see	video, vision
-vit-	life	vital, vitality

Exercise 5

On a sheet of paper numbered 1–10, write down the following words and the Latin root from which each is derived. Using your knowledge of the root, supply a definition for the word. Look in your dictionary to check and, if need be, revise your definition.

1.	beneficiary	6.	ductile
2.	prescience	7.	judiciary
3.	omnipresent	8.	retraction
4.	detract	9.	agitate
5.	locality	10.	vitamin

Exercise 6

Using your dictionary or drawing on your own vocabulary, list and define two words containing each of the following roots. Do not give words previously used as examples in this chapter.

1.	-aud-	6.	-fid-
2.	-gen-	7.	-jud-
3.	-omni-	8.	-magn-
4.	-prim-	9.	-mor-, -mort-
5.	-spir-	10.	-port-

Prefixes   A *prefix* is a syllable (or sometimes two) that is attached to the beginning of a root or word and that modifies its meaning.

Any one prefix usually combines in numerous ways to expand the vocabulary of a language. The following is a list of common prefixes, their meanings, and examples of words formed with them. Note that some prefixes have more than one spelling.

PREFIX	MEANING	EXAMPLE
ab-	from, away	absent, abscond
ante-	previous	antechamber, antebellum
anti-	against	antiwar, antibiotic
auto-	self	automotive, autosuggestion
bi-	two, twice	biweekly, bisect
con-, com-	with	contact, compare
contra-	against, opposing	contradict, contraband
de-	down, from	debase, dejection
dis-	out	disdain, distaste
e-, ex-	from, out of	egress, expel
fore-	before, previous	foretell, forewarn
hyper-	excessive	hyperactive, hypertension

PREFIX	MEANING	EXAMPLE
hypo-	under, below	hypodermic, hypothalamus
in-, im-	not, against	intangible, impossible
inter-	between, among	interchangeable, interstate
mis-	wrong, not	mistake, misspell
post-	after	postwar, postpone
pre-	before	precede, preview
pro-	for, forward	progress, promote
re-	back, again	reject, revive
semi-	half	semiconscious, semiprecious
sub-	under, beneath	subconscious, submarine
sym-	together, with	symbiosis, sympathetic
trans-	across	transfer, transport
un-	not	unhappy, unsafe

Exercise 7

On a sheet of paper numbered 1–10, write down the following words and underline the prefix each contains. Then use each word correctly in a sentence, checking with your dictionary if necessary.

1. abdicate
2. unmitigated
3. transcend
4. symmetry
5. projectile

6. prevail
7. automaton
8. bilingual
9. misconstrue
10. immutable

Suffixes   A *suffix* is a syllable (or sometimes two) that is attached to the end of a root or word.

Some suffixes, such as *-ed*, *-ing*, and *-s*, change only the tense or number of the word to which they are attached.

walk	walk**ed**
glow	glow**ing**
choice	choice**s**

Other suffixes can be added to a root to create new words. Sometimes, a suffix transforms the root from one part of speech into another.

terror—noun	serve—verb
terr**ify**—verb	serv**ant**—noun
terror**ist**—noun	serv**ile**—adjective
terr**ific**—adjective	serv**itude**—noun

Since suffixes can determine a word's part of speech, the following common suffixes are arranged according to what part of speech they form.

NOUN-FORMING SUFFIXES

SUFFIX	MEANING	EXAMPLE
-age	rank, process, state	mileage, foliage
-ance	being, condition of	utterance, ambulance
-ation	action, state of	starvation, donation
-dom	state, rank, condition	kingdom, stardom
-hood	state, rank, condition	sisterhood, neighborhood
-ism	act, manner, doctrine	atheism, baptism
-ist	doer, believer	capitalist, artist
-ment	means, result, action	predicament, movement
-ness	quality, state	evenness, fairness
-tude	quality, state, result	quietude, pulchritude

ADJECTIVE-FORMING SUFFIXES

-able	able to	lovable, capable
-en	made of	wooden, golden
-ful	having qualities of	forceful, frightful
-ish	suggesting	greenish, selfish
-less	without	thoughtless, colorless
-like	similar	childlike, deathlike
-some	apt to, showing	wholesome, winsome
-ward	in the direction of	forward, backward

VERB-FORMING SUFFIXES

-en	cause to be	darken, heighten
-ate	become, form, treat	dictate, meditate
-esce	become, continue	coalesce
-fy	make, cause to have	signify, glorify
-ize	make, cause to be	customize, organize

Exercise 8

Write out each of the following words and underline the suffix. Write a definition of the word and then use it correctly in a sentence.

Example

a. pacifism

a. pacif*ism*: *belief in peaceful rather than forceful answers to disputes Many people advocated pacifism during the Vietnam War.*

1. culpable
2. fulsome
3. untoward
4. chasten
5. magnitude

6. deify
7. thralldom
8. mediate
9. pulchritude
10. ineffable

Analyzing Meaning Through Structure

Sometimes, you can determine the meaning of a word by examining its parts: the root and any prefixes or suffixes the word may have. Consider, for example, the word *transcription*. By breaking it into its major parts, you would see it is formed in the following way.

PREFIX	ROOT	SUFFIX
tran-	-scrip-	-tion
("over, across")	("to write")	("something created")

In its most common usage, *transcription* means "a copy": something written over, reproduced. A knowledge of roots and *affixes* (prefixes and suffixes) will help you to deduce the meaning of many unfamiliar words, as well as understand the construction and original meaning of more common words.

Exercise 9

Divide the following words into affixes and roots. Be prepared to explain the meaning of each part of the word. Then use the word correctly in a sentence, consulting your dictionary if necessary.

Example

a. subscript

a. *subscript: sub- a prefix meaning "under, beneath"; -script-, a root meaning "write"; subscript—"a figure or letter written to the side and below another one"*
The chemical formula for water consists of an H with a subscript 2 plus an O.

1. bicentennial
2. cognizant
3. graphology
4. conspirator
5. intractable
6. hypothermia
7. misanthropist
8. dislocate
9. mortify
10. neolithic

Review Exercise A

The following sentences contain words whose meaning you should be able to deduce either by context clues or by your knowledge of word roots and affixes. On a sheet of paper numbered 1–25, supply a definition for each *italicized* word.

Example

a. The volunteer fire department was prepared to deal with local problems but not with one of such *magnitude* as the burning railroad tank cars.

a. *magnitude: great size or importance*

1. Marilu is not very sociable, but she is no *misanthropist*; she likes a number of people.

2. Someone donated a thousand dollars to the building fund, but no one knows who is the author of the *beneficent* act.

3. The doctor *proscribed* everything I like—no more desserts or fattening foods for me.

4. Mrs. Washington works for many *philanthropic* causes, including the Red Cross, the library committee, and rehabilitation of prisons.

5. There were several *anachronisms* in the movie, such as a flag with fifty stars flying over the frontier fort.

6. The members of the team *synchronized* their watches; actions had to be performed at precisely the right second.

7. My grandmother is almost *omniscient*; she seems to know everything we're up to.

8. The doctor could find no physical source for the patient's backache; she concluded it must be *psychosomatic*.

9. Some African tribes are *polytheistic*, for they believe in several gods and goddesses.

10. Many people think the band director is *hypercritical*; he finds fault in everything.

11. The Ramirez family is noted for its *conviviality*; they are always having pleasant parties and gatherings.

12. Kim was very sick, but now she is *convalescing*.

13. I don't want a book containing just a few of Gwendolyn Brooks' poems; I'd like an *omnibus* edition.

14. We had a party after we lost the game, but all we did was *commiserate*.

15. Although none of the singers was spectacular alone, together they were wonderful; it was a classic example of *synergy*.

16. To make sure the commercials at the TV station will be of the correct length, the technicians use several sorts of *chronographs*.

17. Scientists are investigating the power of some animals to *regenerate* limbs; young frogs, for instance, can often grow a new leg in place of one surgically removed.

18. The music you hear over your car radio is *monaural*, unless, of course, you install a system that has more than one sound source.

19. The school authorities issued a new *edict* on parking rules; it was announced over the intercom systems all through lunch hour.

20. Before you are accepted as an FBI agent, your patriotism and loyalty will be investigated because the agency will accept no one with a history of *subversive* activities.

21. Bill has an enormous collection of books and says he wants to be known as a *bibliophile*.

22. In case a student has a *protracted* illness and is absent two or more weeks, the school system will supply a tutor and make-up assignments.

23. Gold is an extremely *ductile* metal; it can be hammered into thin plates of gold leaf or drawn into fine wires.

24. The book has a section on each country's *demography*, with statistics on size, distribution, and density of population.

25. Our poinsettia is beginning to wither and droop; I fear it is *senescent*.

Active and Passive Vocabulary

You have two vocabularies: an *active vocabulary*, composed of the words you use in speaking and writing, and a *passive vocabulary*, comprised of words you recognize and to an extent understand but that you do not use.

One way to expand your active vocabulary and make your speaking and writing more precise is to learn to use the words in your passive vocabulary, to put them into action rather than simply reacting to them. There are several ways to do this. First, look up the word in a dictionary to check on its meaning and also its pronunciation. Say the word softly to yourself several times, so that you are certain of its pronunciation and do not hesitate to use it because you may mispronounce it. Next, use the word; make up several sentences employing it.

A word unused is much like a muscle unused: It will remain weak and ineffectual. By exercising your vocabulary, you build and strengthen it.

Exercise 10

Look up each of the *italicized* words in the following sentences and be prepared to define them as well as pronounce them. Then write two original sentences of your own in which you make it clear from the context that you understand the meaning of the word.

Example

a. Mort is the most *amiable* dog I know, but consequently he's not much of a watchdog.

a. *We had expected her to be rude, but the clerk was quite amiable when we returned the gift for the third time.*
The coach was almost amiable to us after we won the game; he actually smiled.

1. We had better realize that this town has a *burgeoning* political problem.

2. My sister is always *deriding* TV commercials.

3. Never let him get you cornered at a party; he's the most *garrulous* person you'll ever meet.

4. The road took an *aberrant* course through the woods.

5. The house was gaunt and old, the yard weedy, and several broken statues guarded the gates. I've never seen a more *sepulchral* place.

6. The play was meant to be tragic, but it became mere *pathos*.

7. We pleaded, we argued, we reasoned, but Mr. Chin ignored us; he was absolutely *insensate*.

8. Maria is very serious about her career and made it clear to the men in the office that she had no time for or interest in *dalliance*.

9. The hyena may look frightening, but it is actually quite *pusillanimous*.

10. I don't lack *temerity*; that's why my character gets killed each time we play Dungeons and Dragons.

A Word List As an aid to your vocabulary study, the following *word list* has been compiled. The words on the list are among those appearing most often in the reading that you are likely to do and that therefore may be of greatest use to you. The most effective way to use the list is to set a goal for yourself, such as mastering ten words a week. Some words may seem familiar, but look them up and investigate any second and third meanings they may have.

To make a word your own, check its meaning or meanings in a reliable dictionary (small pocket-sized dictionaries are adequate for emergencies and crossword puzzles, but they frequently skimp on definitions). Pronounce the word until you can say it correctly and with confidence. Notice its structure, for its root and affixes may help you understand words you encounter later.

You will master a word more easily if you write it down, jot a brief definition, and list several synonyms for it. You may wish to do this in a special notebook; such a notebook will be handy for reference, and you can also watch your vocabulary grow as you add new words. Writing down one or two sentences using a new word in an appropriate context will be an invaluable aid and help engrave the word more firmly in your memory.

A	bigoted	coherent	decrepit
abort	botulism	commitment	defiant
accentuate	bourgeois	commodity	defunct
ad lib	brevity	compatible	deign
advocate	bureaucrat	compensate	deplete
affluent		competency	depreciate
alleviate	C	concise	diarrhea
ambidextrous	cadaver	connotation	dilemma
annotation	callous	conscientious	disclose
antiquity	candidly	consensus	discretion
astute	canvass	continuity	divergent
atheist	catalyst	convene	double-entendre
	censure	coordinate	
B	centaur	criteria	E
bedlam	chivalrous		effigy
belligerent	chronology	D	elapse
benevolent	cite	debris	elite
benign	clemency	debutante	eminent
bias	coalition	decapitate	entice

enumerate
enunciate
erroneous
etymology
excerpt
explicit

F
fallible
farce
feasible
fidelity
filial
foliage
forefront
franchise
frustrate

G
generality
gerontology
gnarled
gridiron
grievous
grotesque
gullible

H
habeas corpus
halitosis
hemorrhage
herbivorous
heretic
heterogeneous
hierarchy
hindrance
hombre
hors d'oeuvre
humility
hypothetical

I
ideology
idiom
immaculate
impartial
impediment
impregnable

impromptu
inadvertent
inalienable
incentive
incoherent
incumbent
infallible
inference
initiative
intangible
intermittent
itinerary

J
judicious

K
kindred

L
laudable
legacy
leniency
liquidate

M
malevolent
malicious
malignancy
marquee
martyr
masochism
meager
mediocre
merger
metabolism
microcosm
mime
mnemonic
momentum
mortality

N
naive
nautical
negotiable
nonconformist
notoriety
novice

O
obesity
oblivious
onomatopoeia
opportune
ornithology

P
pagan
paraphernalia
parody
penitent
perpetual
pertinent
plausible
plebeian
posthumous
precarious
precedent
prerequisite
prestige
prevalent
prodigy
protocol
provocative

Q
quadruplicate
query

R
rapport
ravenous
recipient
reconciliation
referendum
reimburse
relevance
reliant
reminisce
reprieve
restraint
revoke

S
self-esteem
serene
skepticism
solicit

staccato
status quo
strategic
subsequent
synchronize

T
tactical
tangible
terminate
therapeutic
thesaurus
threshold
transcribe
trilogy
trivial

U
ulterior
ultimatum
unconventional
understate
unorthodox
unwarranted

V
vacuous
vagrancy
valedictorian
valor
vehemence
verbatim
verbiage
verbose
versatile
violate
vivacious
vulnerable

W
waive
wan
winsome
writhe
wry

Y
yeoman

Z
zealous

3 Reading

12 Reading Social Studies Materials

Levels of Comprehension

Successful reading of social studies materials requires that you be able to read at three different *levels of comprehension*.

First, you must be able to read and answer questions at the *literal level* of comprehension.

When you read at the literal level of comprehension, you are reading to identify or remember explicitly stated information. You read, for example, for details of *who? what? where? when? why? how?* or *to what degree?* where the author has directly stated this information in the passage. You also read for the main ideas and views presented directly by the author. Reading at the literal level requires both understanding and remembering as you process information explicitly stated in the essay.

Second, you must be able to read and answer questions at the *interpretive level* of comprehension.

When you read at the interpretive level of comprehension, you must first obtain the explicitly stated information and then interpret or figure out what it means. To do this you use your intuition, personal experiences, and previous knowledge. For example, when you read a newspaper article about a new law passed by your state government and you figure out how that law will affect your local community, you are reading at an interpretive level. The article does not specifically state how the law will affect local communities, but you can determine this by using the information presented and your previous knowledge. When you have to figure out *who? what? where? when? why? how?* or *to what degree?* from information presented, you are reading at the interpretive level. Often, the main idea is not directly stated in a topic sentence, and you must interpret it from the details given.

Third, you must be able to read and answer questions at the *applied level* of comprehension.

When you read at the applied level of comprehension, you go beyond the information presented and your interpretation of what it means. At this level you make judgments or evaluations. You make judgments about whether or not the information presented is *accurate, complete, colored by unidentified bias* (in other words fair or not in its presentation to the parties or events involved), or *significant*.

The applied level of comprehension requires you to read critically. Many books call this type of reading *critical reading*, and it is extremely important for you to use your applied, or critical, reading skills as you study about the events, ideas, people, and forces discussed in social studies materials. For example, you may be presented information from two different points of view and have to judge the merits of the two views in order to make up your mind about what you believe. You may have to determine that there is not one best answer to a problem and that different judgments are possible. The importance of *informed reasoning*—identifying facts, interpreting them, and using them to support judgments—will become more and more obvious to you as you read about the impact of people's judgments on the history of human beings and nations.

Patterns of Writing

There are many different *patterns of writing*, or ways of organizing and presenting material. In social studies materials four major patterns are *explication, sequential, comparison-contrast*, and *cause-effect*. More than one pattern may be used in the same passage.

The Explication Pattern

The *explication pattern* is often used to present background data or to inform generally.

The explication pattern involves presentation of a main idea and supporting details or the definition and explanation of a concept or term.

Examples are often used in the explication pattern of writing. The reader of a passage using explication can improve his or her study of the passage as follows:

1. *Survey the passage.*

   Note the title or heading. Skim or look through the material very quickly to determine the general idea. If the passage does not have a title, this skimming will help you determine the general idea.

2. *Note presentation of points.*

Are they enumerated or numbered. If so, are they listed in order of importance? Are examples used? If so, are they identified? Are definitions included?

3. *Read the material for relationships.*

Observe relationships among the details and the main idea. Note the different types of details given.

The following newspaper account is an example of a passage that uses the explication pattern. Newspapers and magazines are an important source of information about current events and, as such, are important social studies materials. In news stories the main idea usually appears in the headline, and the article attempts to present facts objectively and correctly. No attempt is made by the writers of news stories to explain what the events mean, although they may quote sources who express their views about the events.

Activity 1

Read the following news story from the *Tallahassee Democrat* and answer the questions that follow. (Remember that you are reading to be informed, to be given a main idea about a topic and the details.)[1]

House Sanctions Protecting Press from Searches

WASHINGTON (AP)—The House, voting in effect to overturn a controversial 1978 U.S. Supreme Court ruling, Monday passed a bill to protect newsrooms from surprise police searches.

The bill, passed by voice vote, would sharply restrict police seizure of "documentary material" belonging to reporters, authors, filmmakers, photographers, academics and free-lance writers if they are not suspected of a crime.

Supporters of the legislation described it as Congress' response to a 1971 police search of the Stanford (Calif.) Daily's files for photographs of a campus demonstration.

That search led to a 1978 landmark Supreme Court case that upheld the police search as justified under a standard of "reasonableness." The court also ruled that newspapers had no special protection from such searches.

The ruling prompted widespread criticism from journalistic associations and civil liberties groups that saw it as a threat to the freedom of the press.

The House bill now goes to the Senate, where similar legislation was approved in August. The House bill is the result of a request President Carter sent to the Justice Department following the Supreme Court decision to recommend guidelines for search warrants involving First Amendment privileges.

Rep. Robert W. Kastenmeier, D-Wis., a principal sponsor, said the legislation represented Congress' "historic obligation" to protect First Amendment rights.

---

[1] AP report from Washington, "House sanctions protecting press from searches," September 23, 1980, *Tallahassee Democrat*, Tallahassee, Florida. Reprinted by permission.

However, Rep. George E. Danielson, D-Calif., argued that the bill's protections were too broad and would "diminish to some extent" the availability of search warrants to police for legitimate law enforcement purposes.

The bill bars local and federal law enforcement officials from using search warrants to obtain documentary materials in the possession of those engaged in "First Amendment activities," except in five circumstances.

The exceptions are:

✔ If there is probable cause to believe that the person in possession of the materials has committed the offense for which the materials are sought.

✔ If there is reason to believe that immediate seizure of the materials is necessary to prevent death or serious bodily injury.

✔ If there is reason to believe that obtaining a subpoena would result in the destruction or concealment of the material.

✔ If the subpoena has been obtained and failed to produce the material.

✔ If the material consists of contraband or the fruits or instruments of a crime.

1. What is the headline?
2. What does *sanction* mean?
3. Who is *the House?*
4. Where is the House meeting?
5. What did the House do?
6. When was the bill passed?
7. Why did the House vote on the bill?
8. How was the bill passed?
9. Did everyone in the House favor the bill?
10. Journalistic associations and civil rights groups felt that the 1978 Supreme Court ruling had threatened what freedom?
11. What happens to the bill now?
12. Whose request to the Justice Department resulted in the bill?
13. List three types of people protected by the bill.
14. Are there any exceptions to the protections of the bill?
15. If so, how are they presented?

The Sequential Pattern

The *sequential pattern* of writing uses time relationships to organize information.

Chronological order is a very important pattern in relating history to the reader. When reading sequential passages, the reader's major purpose is to follow the order and determine the relationships among the events recounted or told. Four types of clues can help the reader follow sequential material.

Time words are important clues for following the order of events.

Important time words and phrases include the following: *meanwhile, after, finally, during, next, until, before, later, previously, now, at the same time, first, simultaneously,* and *prior.*

Another type of clue to the order of events is the use of dates or other words that indicate time.

Clues to time can include references to certain customs, wearing apparel, methods of transportation, or popular words. These time clues can also be definite or indefinite. The sentences "Germany declared war on Russia on August 1, 1914" and "The Archduke Francis Ferdinand and his wife had been killed by a Serbian assassin on June 28, 1914" use specific dates. The sentences "The neutrality of Belgium had been guaranteed by the great powers in 1839" and "The nations that marched to war in the summer of 1914 thought that the conflict would be brief and decisive" use specific years. "Since the late 1800s Germany's foreign policy had been very daring" is even less specific. An indefinite time clue occurs in the sentence "They had come to America many years before."

Verb tenses can be important in following the sequence of events.

In the sentences "The Russo-Japanese War had shown Russia's weakness. World War I exposed it still further," the verbs *had shown* and *exposed* tell the reader that the Russo-Japanese War occurred before World War I.

A final clue is whether the order makes sense.

Certain things cannot logically happen before certain other things. You may not always be able to use common sense alone in explaining events, but usually it can help you in ordering them.

Activity 2

The following passage about the Panama Canal, from the textbook *Men and Nations: A World History*, relates how the United States came to be involved in building the canal. Read the passage for the sequence of events, remembering to use the four types of clues as you read.[1]

> In addition to governing its new and far-flung areas, the United States was also obliged to defend them. The major problem of defense came to light during the Spanish-American War.
>
> Before the war the American battleship *Oregon* had been stationed on the Pacific coast. When war became likely, this ship was needed to strengthen American forces in the Caribbean Sea. It had to go at high speed all the way around South America, a distance of over 11,000 miles. The United States realized that it would either have to build two complete navies to protect its empire or find some easier and quicker way to move warships between the Atlantic and Pacific oceans.
>
> A canal across the Isthmus of Panama had long been talked about. The same French company that built the Suez Canal had also tried unsuccessfully to build a canal across Panama. The United States government now began negotiating for permission and a right of way to build a canal.

---

[1] From *Men and Nations*, Third Edition, by Anatole G. Mazour and John M. Peoples, copyright © 1975 by Harcourt Brace Jovanovich, Inc. Reprinted by permission of the publisher.

First, the United States arranged with the British to be released from an earlier treaty which pledged that any canal should be built jointly by Great Britain and the United States. Next, Americans bought the rights of the French company. Then they began to negotiate with Colombia for a lease to a strip of land across the isthmus in Panama, at that time a province of Colombia (see map, page 575).

In these latter negotiations, the United States struck a snag. After a treaty had been negotiated, the Colombian senate adjourned without ratifying it. There was great indignation in the United States. People felt that Colombia was trying to bargain for more money. The United States government investigated a possible canal route through Nicaragua.

There was also indignation in the province of Panama. The people of the province were eager to have the canal built there because it promised them great benefits. When negotiations between the United States and Colombia seemed to break down, the people of Panama began a revolution to gain independence from Colombia.

American warships stationed at Panama prevented Colombian troops from moving in to suppress the revolt, and the revolution succeeded. The United States then quickly recognized the independence of Panama. In 1903 a treaty between the two governments was drawn up and speedily ratified, giving the United States all the rights necessary to build a canal across Panama.

On a sheet of paper, answer the following questions about the preceding passage and the way in which it is written.

1. When did the United States discover the need to move men and ships more quickly between the Pacific and the Caribbean Sea?

2. Skim the passage and list as many clue words as you can find. Which paragraph has the easiest-to-follow order?

3. Without looking back at the passage, list the following events in order:

   a. The Colombian senate adjourned without ratifying the treaty to lease lands to the U.S. for a canal.
   b. The United States arranged with the British to be released from a treaty concerning a joint U.S.-British canal.
   c. The people of the Colombian province of Panama revolted against Colombia.
   d. The idea of a canal across the Isthmus of Panama was conceived.
   e. America bought the French company's rights to build a canal across the Isthmus of Panama.
   f. A French company tried to build a canal across Panama.
   g. The United States fought the Spanish-American War.
   h. The United States began to negotiate with Colombia for a lease to a strip of land across the Isthmus of Panama.
   i. American warships stationed at Panama prevented Colombian troops from suppressing the Panamanian revolt.
   j. The United States recognized Panama as a country and signed a treaty giving the U.S. the rights to build a canal across Panama.

4. You probably noticed that the sentences you have just ordered are written somewhat differently from the original passage. What is missing?

5. Besides simply remembering what you read in the passage, what type of clue did you have to rely on in sequencing the events in Question 3?

    a. Dates
    b. Verb tenses
    c. Time clue words
    d. Sense

Now that you have completed the activity, go back and check your sequencing. You probably had more difficulty sequencing the sentences given in the activity than you would have had in sequencing the actual sentences from the passage. That is because the clue words were largely missing. As they read, good readers take advantage of all the clues authors provide.

Time Lines and Time Charts

Many authors of social studies materials assist their readers in following the sequence of events and seeing the relationships among them by including adjunct, or study, aids in their works. Two important aids in following sequence are the *time line* and the *events chart*. Where authors do not provide these, readers are wise to develop their own.

A *time line* is simply either a vertical or horizontal line with demarcations or marks showing the occurrence of events.

Time lines have one advantage over *events charts* (chronologies), which are simply lists of important events during a given time period. The advantage of time lines is that they allow readers to see how close together or far apart events take place. Both types of aids can be general (giving only a general time reference) or specific (giving the actual dates when events occurred).

Time lines and events charts are often placed at the beginning of the chapter as a preview of the contents or at the end of a chapter as a review. You can make your reading more efficient and complete by surveying these aids carefully before and after you read a chapter.

Activity 3

Study the three time lines that follow. On a sheet of paper, answer the questions about the time lines.

A.

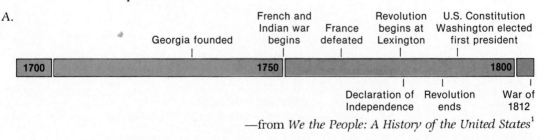

—from *We the People: A History of the United States*[1]

---

[1] Excerpt from *We the People: A History of the United States* by Bidna, Greenberg, Spitz. Reprinted by permission of D. C. Heath.

B.

The Chapter in Outline

1. Open war between the British and the colonists.

2. The colonists' decision to declare their independence.

3. Waging the Revolutionary War in the early years.

4. Victory of the American Patriots over the British.

5. A favorable treaty of peace for the victorious Americans.

| 1450 | 1750 | 1800 | 1850 | 1900 | 1950 | 1980's |

—from *Rise of the American Nation*[1]

C.

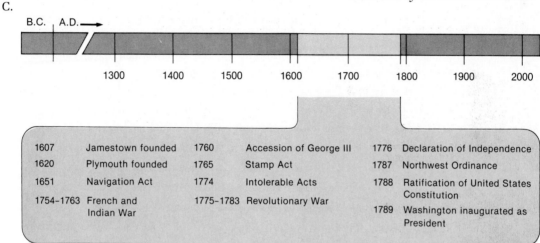

B.C. A.D. →

| 1300 | 1400 | 1500 | 1600 | 1700 | 1800 | 1900 | 2000 |

1607	Jamestown founded	1760	Accession of George III	1776	Declaration of Independence
1620	Plymouth founded	1765	Stamp Act	1787	Northwest Ordinance
1651	Navigation Act	1774	Intolerable Acts	1788	Ratification of United States Constitution
1754–1763	French and Indian War	1775–1783	Revolutionary War	1789	Washington inaugurated as President

—from *Men and Nations: A World History*[2]

1. Which time line is marked off by centuries?

2. Which two time lines are marked off by half-centuries?

3. Time lines *B* and *C* have breaks in them. What do these breaks mean?

4. Which time line has the earliest beginning point?

5. The time lines relate to important events in what country?

6. Which time line has as its purpose simply to identify the general time period of the chapter in American history?

7. Which time line gives the order of events in the chapter?

8. Which time line gives specific dates (years) for events?

9. Which time line contains an events chart?

[1]From *Rise of the American Nation*, Heritage Edition by Lewis Paul Todd and Merle Curti, copyright © 1977 by Harcourt Brace Jovanovich, Inc. Excerpted and reprinted by permission of the publisher.

[2]Adapted from *Men and Nations*, Third Edition, by Anatole G. Mazour and John M. Peoples, copyright © 1975 by Harcourt Brace Jovanovich, Inc. Reprinted by permission of the publisher.

10. From which of the following chapters does each time line come?
   a. "The Search for Independence"
   b. "The American Revolution Created a New Nation in North America (1607–1789)"
   c. "Winning a War for Independence (1775–1788)"

Activity 4

Using the time lines in Activity 4, answer the following questions on a sheet of paper. Beside your answers indicate which time line you used. (You may use more than one time line.)

1. Which came first—the French and Indian War or the American Revolutionary War?
2. Did Washington become President before or after the end of the Revolutionary War?
3. Was Washington inaugurated before or after the Constitution was ratified?
4. Was the Declaration of Independence signed before or after the events at Lexington?
5. Was Georgia founded in the 1600s or 1700s?
6. Who was the King of England when the Stamp Act was passed?
7. In what year was the U.S. Constitution ratified?
8. The American Revolutionary War covered a period of how many years?
9. Did the French win or lose the French and Indian War?
10. Was the War of 1812 before or after the American Revolutionary War?

The Comparison/ Contrast Pattern

Comparison/contrast is still another pattern of writing used extensively in social studies materials. The *comparison/contrast* pattern indicates how ideas and information are *similar* with (comparison) or *different* from other ideas and information.

Comparison/contrast is a useful pattern because it allows the author to make a point, present a concept, or explain the nature of something by making use of what the reader knows.

Activity 5

Read the following passage and, on a sheet of paper, list the points of comparison/contrast the writer uses to inform the reader of what a visitor from outer space looks like.

> The alien visitor looked strange. He stood upright on two legs like a human being, and he had a neck and head, too. The neck looked like it might have belonged to a giraffe. That was okay—I could accept a long, skinny neck, but the alien's head was something else. It looked like it belonged on a giant bird,

maybe an eagle. There was a sharp beak, and the eyes were large and bright like spotlights. But the hair certainly wasn't like ours or like an eagle's feathers either, for that matter. There wasn't much hair, no more than twenty strands, and each strand was thick like a section of clothesline. On the end of each strand of hair was some kind of sensing device that reminded me of the round ball on the top of a microphone.

Clue Words in Comparison/Contrast Patterns

Clue words are important in reading the comparison/contrast pattern of writing.

You probably noticed the two clue words used in the paragraph in Activity 5: *like* to indicate similarity or comparison and *but* to indicate differences or contrasts. Other comparison words include *similarly, also, likewise, and, as well as;* other contrast words include *in contrast, rather, conversely, however, on the other hand, although, to the contrary.* These clue words can be very important in helping you to follow the two types of comparison/contrast passages.

The two types of comparison/contrast development are also discussed on pages 56–57.

One type of comparison/contrast development is called *block comparison.* In this type of passage, two or more things are compared, but each is described completely before the next is introduced. The second type is called *point by point.* In this type of comparison/contrast passage, certain points are identified and then compared or contrasted in turn. The reader has to keep up with the shifts between the two items being compared as each point is introduced. Many clue words are used in point-by-point comparisons and being able to follow them is vital in understanding the material presented.

Activity 6

Read the following paragraph from the textbook *Men and Nations: A World History* and answer the questions on a sheet of paper.[1]

> Another important group of Indians was the Toltecs. Originally from the Pacific coast of North America, the Toltecs had established themselves as rulers of part of central Mexico by about 700 A.D. Their capital was at Tula. They were pyramid builders, too, but their art was inferior to that of the Mayas. They were probably responsible, however, for introducing the use of metals into Central America.

1. What two groups of Indians are being discussed?
2. In what way were they alike?
3. What comparison clue word is used to show this similarity?
4. The art of the two groups is contrasted. What was the difference in their art?
5. What clue word is used to show this difference?
6. The contrast word *however* in the last sentence suggests that the Toltecs were superior to the Mayas in at least one way. How were they superior?

---

[1] From *Men and Nations*, Third Edition, by Anatole G. Mazour and John M. Peoples, copyright © 1975 by Harcourt Brace Jovanovich, Inc. Reprinted by permission of the publisher.

The Cause/ Effect Pattern

Perhaps the phrase *cause/effect relationship* sounds like something both sophisticated and complicated. Regardless of how the phrase may sound, the cause/effect relationship pattern, in general, is fairly simple. It is nothing more than an attempt to find out why something happened (*Why did the rowboat sink?*) or why a condition exists (*Why is there an oil shortage?*). In daily life people look for cause/effect relationships whenever they try to solve a problem.

Activity 7

In the first column that follows are listed some effects; listed in the second are some possible causes. Using your background knowledge, select what might be the best cause for each effect. There may be more than just one possible, and sensible, cause for an effect. If that is the case, list both answers on your answer sheet.

EFFECTS

1. The car stopped running.
2. The football team lost the game.
3. The cow jumped over the moon.
4. Little Miss Muffet ran away.
5. The elevator stopped between the third and fourth floors.
6. The elevator stopped at the fourth floor.
7. Dinosaurs are extinct.
8. The American colonists threw a shipload of tea into Boston Harbor.
9. An astronaut walked on the moon.
10. The corn harvest is poor.

CAUSES

a. A spider sat down beside her.
b. An electrical generating plant broke down.
c. *The Old Man and the Sea* is a good book.
d. The running backs kept fumbling.
e. There was a severe drought.
f. The U.S. and the Soviet Union were in a space race.
g. A high tax had been placed on tea.
h. A new cold age began.
i. The cow got excited.
j. Steaks are expensive.
k. It ran out of gas.
l. Poor coaching caused it.

m. Walking is good exercise.

n. They wanted to make a point about taxation without representation.

o. High jumping is fun.

p. The driver turned off the ignition.

q. She hates insects.

r. A passenger lived on the fourth floor.

Clue Words in Cause/Effect Relationships

Sometimes, the reader's task of recognizing cause/effect relationships is made easier by clue words that announce such a relationship. Some clue words to indicate this type of relationship are *because, consequently, since, therefore,* and *thus.* Sometimes, the cause/effect relationships are indicated by phrases such as *as a result, for this reason, in consequence,* and *so that.*

Activity 8

Read the following paragraph and identify the clue words announcing cause/effect relationships. Remember that you are reading to find out why something has happened or why a situation exists. Write these words on a sheet of paper.

> The town of Dumbville was broke. In consequence, the Chamber of Commerce decided to make money by promoting tourism. As a result of this decision, a committee was formed to find a means for attracting tourists to Dumbville. Months passed but the committee came up with no suggestions because, as it turned out, the Chamber of Commerce had failed to identify the people appointed to the special committee. Since the committee members didn't know they were on the committee, they never showed up for the meetings. The membership list was published in the town's newspaper, *The Dumbville Crier,* and for this reason, the next committee meeting was well attended. Thus, the committee finally got to work, and, therefore, the Chamber of Commerce was confident a solution to the town's empty treasury would soon be found.
>
> The committee met every week for three months, and all the members racked their brains for something to lure tourists to Dumbville. Consequently, an answer to their question was found; unfortunately, however, the answer wasn't very good. The committee proposed the town sponsor an annual seashell festival featuring a seashell-finding contest. The Chamber of Commerce liked the idea and sponsored the festival so that the town could make money from the tourists who would come from all around to enjoy the beautiful seashells found in Dumbville. What nobody realized was that there were not many seashells in Dumbville because Dumbville was located 3,000 miles from the nearest sea coast.

Activity 9

Read the following passage, from a history textbook by John Garraty, about the effects (or problems) caused by adding California to the United States as a state. On a sheet of paper, list the effects. Notice that you can read to find effects for causes just as you can read to find causes for effects.

Adding California to the Union caused new problems. In the past the movement of white settlers into new lands had forced most of the native Indian population to retreat westward. But the California Indians had their backs to the ocean. As a result those who had not been forced to labor on the great California ranches were practically wiped out by the invading white settlers.

In earlier times most new territories had been added to the United States before many settlers had entered them. But California already had a well-established Spanish population. Then the gold rush, as we have just seen, greatly increased the population. Everyone realized that California did not need to go through the territorial stage of development. Like Texas it would enter the Union directly as a state. But should California be a free state or a slave state?

Always in the past, northern territory had become free, southern slave. The Northwest Ordinance of 1787 had declared that the land north of the Ohio River and east of the Mississippi should be free. Kentucky and the rest of the territory south of the Ohio became slave states.

In 1820 a sharp conflict had developed over the admission of Missouri as a state. Missouri, which was part of the Louisiana Purchase, extended far north of any of the slave states. But its white citizens wanted slavery. The Missouri Compromise of 1820 allowed Missouri to become a slave state. Congress "balanced" this decision by creating a new free state, Maine, which had previously been part of Massachusetts.

The Missouri Compromise also divided the rest of the Louisiana Purchase into free and slave territory. The land south of Missouri's southern border was opened to slavery. The land west and north of Missouri was to be free.

After the Treaty of Guadalupe Hidalgo some people favored extending this line dividing free territory from slave all the way to the Pacific. But that would have split California in two. And the people who were living in California did not want any of it to become a slave state. The Spanish in California had no wish to restore slavery. The gold miners were opposed to slavery because they were afraid that big mining companies would bring in large numbers of blacks to compete with individual prospectors.

Yet if California became a free state, the eastern slave states would expect something in return. What about slavery in the rest of the territory obtained from Mexico? The problem led to a great debate in Congress and throughout the country.[1]

Facts and Opinions

A major consideration in reading social studies materials involves facts and opinions. Remember that *facts* are pieces of information that can be proved or verified.

Facts

The very same facts or pieces of information may be interpreted in two or more very different ways.

Consider the following piece of verifiable information and possible interpretations of it.

---

[1]From *American History* by John Garraty, copyright © 1982 by Harcourt Brace Jovanovich, Inc. Reprinted by permission of the publisher.

Weather Forecaster:	"During the night eight inches of snow fell in Asheville and the surrounding area."
Skier:	"That's great news. The ski season can now begin."
Police Officer:	"That's bad news. We'll have dangerous driving conditions for quite a while."
School Child:	"That's good news. No school today."
Business Person:	"That's bad news. We'll lose customers."

Another important consideration about facts is that reports or accounts may involve "selected" facts, so that the whole story is not told.

There are so many events, names, and dates in history, for example, that it would be impossible to present them all in one book.

A third important consideration about so-called facts in social studies materials is that material presented as factual may not always be accurate.

Sometimes, the collected information simply contains inaccuracies. Other times, information (perhaps about events that took place many, many years ago) that has been accepted as fact is disproved as the study of people and their past continues. It is important, then, in reading social studies materials to be able to identify information presented as factual, to know how to verify information, to realize that presentation of facts may be selective, and to understand how facts are interpreted.

Activity 10

A list of sources for finding information is in the chapter "Library Resources," pages 198–217.

Read the following sentences in which information is stated as though it were indeed factual. Number a sheet of paper 1–10. Beside each number write *yes* if the sentence states a "true" (actual, verifiable) fact. Then list a way you think you can verify or prove your answer. Be prepared to discuss your answers. (Your sources of verification might include history books, dictionaries, newspapers, library books, and almanacs.) Be sure you can trust your source. Write *no* if the sentence is incorrect.

1. Richard Nixon resigned from office (President of the U.S.A.) in 1974.
2. Tennessee has two senators in the U.S. Senate.
3. The United States is bordered on the north by Mexico.
4. President Eisenhower's first name was John.
5. The capital of Nebraska is Omaha.
6. South Carolina was the eighth state admitted to the Union.
7. *Geography* is the study of the surface of the earth and how it is divided into continents. It also deals with the climates, plants, animals, and minerals of the earth.
8. Albert Einstein was born in Germany in 1879.
9. Harry Truman coined the expression "The buck stops here."
10. The head of the West German government is called *Chancellor*.

In many cases you may not have had firsthand knowledge of the accuracy of the preceding statements. You can see, then, that it is important to find reliable sources to help you in determining the accuracy of information presented.

Opinions

An *opinion* is not a fact; it is a belief, view, judgment, or appraisal that may be based on an interpretation of facts.

An opinion may be held with confidence, but it cannot be proved absolutely, and people can have different opinions about the same facts.

Fact:	The United States signed a treaty returning possession of the Panama Canal to Panama.
Opinion:	This treaty was a good move.
Opinion:	This treaty was a bad move.
Fact:	History is a branch of knowledge that records and explains past events.
Opinion:	Studying history is exciting.
Opinion:	Studying history is boring.

Opinions are very important. People are elected to public office, hired for positions, respected or not, based upon their opinions. Your best interpretive and critical thinking skills should be used in developing your own opinions and in evaluating the opinions of others.

Activity 11

Number a sheet of paper 1–10 and then read each of the following statements. If the statement is a fact, write *fact*. If the statement is a belief or opinion, write *opinion*. Be prepared to discuss your answers.

1. America is the greatest country in the world.
2. Gasoline taxes should be increased to reduce gasoline consumption.
3. Eighteen-year-olds should not have the right to vote.
4. The all-volunteer army has failed. The draft should be reinstituted.
5. The United States is a member of NATO.
6. The Roman Empire fell because of lead poisoning.
7. Power corrupts.
8. American space exploration led to medical and technological breakthroughs.
9. Pasteur developed a rabies vaccination.
10. The United States made a mistake in acknowledging the Ayatollah Khomeini's government in Iran.

4 Sentence Combining

13 Joining Sentences

Combining Sentences Skillfully

Good writers not only share worthwhile ideas with their readers but also express those ideas in the best possible way. Skillful writers understand that sentences are pliable: They can be rearranged, combined, or tightened to improve expression. For example, while the following writing contains good details, they are not presented in an interesting or economical way. Far too many short, choppy sentences that follow the same pattern are used.

> The students pour out of the doors. The doors are glass. They are at the front of the school. The arms of the students are weighted with books. The students are laughing. The students fill the sidewalks with color and confusion. This happens every day at 3 o'clock.

Using some of the sentence-combining techniques in this chapter, the writer might state the same information in one of the following ways.

> Every day at 3 o'clock laughing students, whose arms are weighted with books, pour out of the glass doors at the front of the school, filling the sidewalks with color and confusion.

> Every day at 3 o'clock the sidewalks fill with color and confusion as laughing students, their arms weighted down with books, pour out of the glass doors at the front of the school.

The sentence-combining techniques in this chapter will increase your options as a writer by helping you to shape your sentences in interesting, varied ways. You will learn how to avoid short, choppy sentences by combining sentences, how to avoid unnecessary repetition, and how to achieve economy and variety by inserting one sentence into another.

Using Connectors

You can eliminate short, choppy sentences and show relationships more clearly by using *connectors* to link statements of equal importance. Each of the following connectors indicates a specific relationship between two statements.

Connectors, also called *coordinating conjunctions*, are discussed on page 406 in Using Grammar.

CONNECTOR	RELATIONSHIP
and	similarity
but	opposition or contrast
yet	opposition or contrast
or	choice
nor	negation
so	cause and effect
for	an explanation

In each of the following examples, connectors are used to combine two sentences. The word in parentheses, indicating which connector to use, is called a *signal*. Notice that a comma precedes the connector unless the sentences are very brief and closely related.

Sentences:	Maria carefully cleaned the inside of the smoke detector with a cotton swab. She purchased a new battery at the grocery store. (AND)
Combined:	Maria carefully cleaned the inside of the smoke detector with a cotton swab, *and* she purchased a new battery at the grocery store.
Sentences:	I love classical music. My sister does not. (BUT)
Combined:	I love classical music *but* my sister does not. [Because the sentences are brief, a comma is not essential.]
Sentences:	That plant does not look like horseradish. It does not have the pungent odor typical of horseradish. (NOR)
Combined:	That plant does not look like horseradish, *nor* does it have the pungent odor typical of horseradish.

Nor follows the same pattern as the other connectors but also causes a change in word order. Also, since *nor* already indicates a negative, the word *not* is removed from the second sentence.

Exercise 1

The following sentences can be combined with one of the sentence connectors you have studied. In the first five sentences the signal in parentheses tells you which connector to use; for the last five sentences choose the connector you think works best. Study the examples first and then write each combined sentence on a sheet of paper.

Examples

a. The magazine contained only six articles.
   They were all about politics or sports. (AND)

a. *The magazine contained only six articles, and they were all about politics or sports.*

b. The trainer rewarded the dog generously.
Still the animal did not respond. (BUT)

b. *The trainer rewarded the dog generously, but still the animal did not respond.*

1. The meat spoiled by the time I returned home.
I had forgotten to put it in the refrigerator when I left. (FOR)

2. Most new cars are now equipped with radial tires.
The chances for common blowouts are reduced. (SO)

3. Carlotta won the tennis match easily.
She continued to make careless errors. (YET)

4. This book on Georgia O'Keeffe has no color illustrations of her work.
It does not discuss her early training. (NOR)

5. Eudora Welty's short stories usually intrigue me.
I enjoy the unusual characters she creates. (FOR)

6. Julio's dad was offered a better job in California.
He and his family will be moving in January.

7. Warm wind whispered through the willows.
The evening sun lingered on the water.

8. The family can stay with Grandmother tonight.
They can drive home.

9. Noburu is admired by his fellow eleventh-graders.
He speaks both Japanese and English fluently.

10. It was not raining when we began the hike.
There were no signs of an approaching storm.

Using Paired Connectors

Paired connectors are especially helpful in clarifying the relationship between two sentences of equal importance. The connectors *either . . . or* indicate a choice between alternatives; *not only . . . but also* indicate an additional idea in the second sentence. A comma precedes the second connector in sentences combined with paired connectors.

Paired connectors, also called correlative conjunctions, are discussed on page 406 of Using Grammar.

Sentences:	We can strip off the old paint.
	We can disguise these flaws by antiquing the trunk. (EITHER . . . OR)
Combined:	*Either* we can strip off the old paint, *or* we can disguise these flaws by antiquing the trunk.
Sentences:	Vandalism destroyed the attractive appearance of the small city park.
	The costly repairs used up funds the city had budgeted for new playground equipment. (NOT ONLY . . . BUT ALSO)

Combined: *Not only* did vandalism destroy the attractive appearance of the small city park, *but* the costly repairs *also* used up funds the city had budgeted for new playground equipment.

Sometimes, you may want to change words or word order when you use paired connectors. In the preceding example *destroyed* was changed to *did destroy* and *also* was added immediately before the verb.

Exercise 2

After studying the example, combine the following sets of sentences, using paired connectors. Write each new, combined sentence on a sheet of paper. (Remember to insert a comma before the second sentence.)

Example

a. This goulash is less expensive than roast beef.
   It has a more interesting flavor. (NOT ONLY . . . BUT ALSO)
a. *Not only is this goulash less expensive than roast beef, but it also has a more interesting flavor.*

1. The pianist was not familiar with that request.
   He did not want to play rock-and-roll. (EITHER . . . OR)

2. The senior citizens did produce an excellent musical.
   They donated all the proceeds to the local hospital. (NOT ONLY . . . BUT ALSO)

3. Wilma Rudolph won only one gold medal in the 1960 Olympics.
   The information in this sports almanac is incorrect. (EITHER . . . OR)

4. A bill must be passed by both houses of Congress.
   It must be approved by the President. (NOT ONLY . . . BUT ALSO)

5. The earliest American postcards contained no picture at all.
   They had only a small picture on half the card. (EITHER . . . OR)

The Semicolon as Connector

The *semicolon* can be used to combine two sentences of equal importance when the sentences are closely related in thought. In the following examples the signal (;) indicates that two related sentences can be combined in this way.

For more information on the semicolon, see pages 512–513.

Sentences: Saturday morning Bill shopped for groceries.
Saturday afternoon he prepared the food for the party. (;)

Combined: Saturday morning Bill shopped for groceries; Saturday afternoon he prepared the food for the party.

Sentences: The county board debates and votes on all proposals for new land developments.
It meets every two weeks on Monday evenings. (;)

Combined: The county board debates and votes on all proposals for new land developments; it meets every two weeks on Monday evenings.

Exercise 3

Combine each of the following sets of sentences into a single sentence. Since the sentences lack signals, decide whether to use a connector and comma or a semicolon. Some sentences can be combined in more than one way. Study the example before you write your new sentences on a sheet of paper.

Example

a. We've only had the puppy for a month.
   It is still shy with strangers.

a. We've only had the puppy for a month, so it is still shy with strangers.

or

We've only had the puppy for a month; it is still shy with strangers.

1. I'll save these pine cones for Mr. Ortega.
   He wires them together in large wreaths.

2. Carlotta wants to visit the Art Museum soon.
   She's anxious to see the exhibit on Georgia O'Keeffe.

3. Please lend me that magazine you were reading yesterday.
   The article on women in government sounded interesting.

4. The weather turned very cold.
   We did not have the concert outdoors.

5. The first American postcards appeared in 1873.
   These early cards contained no pictures.

6. Pewter is an alloy of tin and copper.
   It is not a form of silver.

7. In 1880 Maria Longworth Nichols began the Rookwood Pottery in a converted schoolhouse.
   By 1930 the enterprise was the foremost producer of art pottery in the United States.

8. Cowhide hinges were used in the first houses built in America.
   Homemade iron strap hinges appeared only later.

9. Katherine Dunham gained recognition for introducing African folk dances to American audiences.
   She is also the author of *Touch of Innocence*.

10. Farmers in colonial America cut wood in January.
    They believed timbers cut under the old January moon would be straight and true.

Connecting Sentences of Unequal Importance

Connecting words called *subordinators* can be used to join two statements of *unequal importance*. Subordinators like those in the following list attach a subordinate statement, one of lesser importance, to a major statement by indicating the relationship between the two.

after	before	until
although	even though	when
as if	just as	whenever
as long as	just when	where
as soon as	since	wherever
as though	so that	whether
because	unless	while

For more information about subordinate clauses, see pages 468–484.

When a subordinator is placed in front of a statement, a new structure, called a *subordinate clause* is created.

The clause (a subordinator + statement) cannot stand alone but is dependent on the major statement. For example, when the subordinator *because* is added to the statement *Her eyesight is impaired*, the resulting clause (*because her eyesight is impaired*) is no longer independent and cannot function as a separate sentence.

Sentences: Mrs. Romero records all her business transactions on tapes.
             Her eyesight is impaired. (BECAUSE)
Combined: Mrs. Romero records all her business transactions on tapes, *because* her eyesight is impaired.

In the previous example the subordinate clause was attached at the end of the major statement, but subordinate clauses can also appear at the beginning of the combined sentence. As the following example shows, a comma usually follows a subordinate clause at the beginning of a sentence, separating the clause from the rest of the sentence. A subordinate clause at the end of a sentence usually does not require a comma.

Sentences: We tried to find seats with our friends.
             The grandstand was already crowded with alumni waiting to see the homecoming game. (EVEN THOUGH)
Combined: We tried to find seats with our friends *even though* the grandstand was already crowded with alumni waiting to see the homecoming game.

or

Even though the grandstand was already crowded with alumni waiting to see the homecoming game, we tried to find seats with our friends.

Exercise 4

On a sheet of paper, combine the following pairs of sentences by using subordinators. In the examples notice that the signal appears immediately after the sentence that will become the subordinate clause. However, when the sentences are combined, the subordinator appears at the beginning of the clause. When no signal is given, choose the subordinator you think is appropriate, remembering that the combined sentence can be written in more than one way.

Examples
a. A warm campfire was blazing steadily.
    The weary hikers arrived. (WHEN)

a. *A warm campfire was blazing steadily when the weary hikers arrived.*

or

When the weary hikers arrived, a warm campfire was blazing steadily.

b. The heavy rains swamped the diamond.
    The girls' softball championship game was postponed.

b. *After the heavy rains swamped the diamond, the girls' softball championship game was postponed.*

or

The girls' softball championship game was postponed, because the heavy rains swamped the diamond.

1. The class reads John Steinbeck's "The Chrysanthemums." (AFTER)
    They will discuss the author's purpose for writing the short story.

2. We approached the river and looked down from the ridge. (AS SOON AS)
    We could see large sections of "white water."

3. I visited my neighborhood after being away twenty years. (WHEN)
    I was overcome with nostalgia.

4. She finished the test. (AS SOON AS)
    She left.

5. Be sure to wear dark glasses.
    You wish to avoid the sharp glare of the snow. (IF)

6. The lights flashed in the lobby.
    The patrons knew that the intermission was ending.

7. The chord will sound discordant.
    The guitar is properly tuned.

8. Marian Anderson sang at the Lincoln Memorial on Easter Sunday in 1939.
    A crowd of 75,000 people gathered to hear her concert.

9. Asparagus is grown primarily as a food.
    It also has some medicinal value.

10. We visited the homes of Louisa May Alcott, the novelist, and Ralph Waldo Emerson.
    We were in Concord, Massachusetts.

Review Exercise A

This exercise is a paragraph practice covering the combining signals you have studied. Follow the signals and combine the sentences in the order they appear. Study the example before you begin and then write out your sentences as a complete paragraph.

Examples

a. Anita was eighteen years old.
She had never had a summer job. (BUT)

a. Anita was eighteen years old, but she had never had a summer job.

b. She enjoyed being outside. (BECAUSE)
She answered an advertisement asking for a handyman-gardener.

b. Because she enjoyed being outside, she answered an advertisement asking for a handyman-gardener.

c. Her new employer showed her where the tools were kept and explained Anita's responsibilities. (AFTER)
The young girl set to work cleaning dead leaves out of the gutters.

c. After her new employer showed her where the tools were kept and explained Anita's responsibilities, the young girl set to work cleaning dead leaves out of the gutters.

d. She made several mistakes in the first week. (ALTHOUGH)
She was conscientious and worked hard at every task she was assigned.

d. Although she made several mistakes in the first week, she was conscientious and worked hard at every task she was assigned.

e. Anita tended the vegetable garden and roses competently all summer.
She mowed the lawn and repaired the mower. (NOT ONLY . . . BUT ALSO)

e. Not only did Anita tend the vegetable garden and roses competently all summer, but she also mowed the lawn and repaired the mower.

f. In September her pleased employer asked her to continue working on Saturdays or after school.
Smiling with satisfaction, Anita agreed. (;)

f. In September her pleased employer asked her to continue working on Saturdays or after school; smiling with satisfaction, Anita agreed.

PARAGRAPH FORM

Anita was eighteen years old, but she had never had a summer job. Because she enjoyed being outside, she answered an advertisement asking for a handyman-gardener. After her new employer showed her where the tools were kept and explained Anita's responsibilities, the young girl set to work cleaning dead leaves out of the gutters. Although she made several mistakes in the first week, she was conscientious and worked hard at every task she was assigned. Not only did Anita tend the vegetable garden and roses competently all summer, but she also mowed the lawn and repaired the mower. In September her pleased employer asked her to continue working on Saturdays or after school; smiling with satisfaction, Anita agreed.

1. Housing can shape a society.
Climate and terrain can influence a culture. (JUST AS)

2. The Hopi Indians of New Mexico are also termed western Pueblos.
They lived in communities called pueblos. (BECAUSE)

3. The Hopi pueblo was a single flat-roofed structure.
   It had several stories laid out in tiers. (YET)

4. A large pueblo could cover up to twelve acres.
   It was composed of hundreds of rooms in connecting rows. (SINCE)

5. The pueblo was often located on top of a steep-sided mesa.
   This offered the peaceful Hopi further protection from attack. (FOR)

6. Later pueblos were often made of adobe, a mixture of clay and straw.
   The earliest pueblos were built of stone masonry. (WHILE)

7. Women were responsible for building the pueblo.
   Men governed the community and farmed the land. (EVEN THOUGH)

8. Most ground floor rooms had no doorways.
   One entered by ladder through an opening in the roof. (SO)

9. A secret ceremonial chamber called a *kiva* was located at the center of the pueblo.
   It was used for religious ceremonies and meetings of the governing councils. (;)

10. The connected homes of the Hopi Pueblo created a close-knit community. (NOT ONLY . . . BUT ALSO)
    They fostered a society in which the group had greater importance than the individual.

Review Exercise B

The following sets of sentences contain no signals. Using a variety of the connectors you have learned, combine each set into one sentence. Remember that some sets can be combined in more than one way. On a separate sheet of paper, write your combined sentences in paragraph form.

Hint: Try a paired connector such as (NOT ONLY . . . BUT ALSO).

1. In 1957 and 1958 Althea Gibson won the women's tennis title at Wimbledon, England.
   She captured the Women's National Singles Championship at Forest Hills, New York.

2. Few spectators understood the obstacles Althea had overcome as a teenager to reach this peak in her career.
   They understood her powerful overhand smash.
   They understood her quick serve.

3. She was already a tough, streetwise high school dropout.
   A playground leader in her impoverished Harlem neighborhood introduced her to tennis.

4. He got her a secondhand racket.
   She could play a few matches with some of his friends.

5. Her playing was so good that players on the other courts stopped to watch her.
   She was still inexperienced.
   She had had only the simplest training.

6. Gaining professional training seemed an impossibility.
   Althea had a natural talent for tennis.
   She beat other amateur players soundly.

7. Althea could get only menial jobs that paid very little.
   She did not have a high school diploma.

8. However, some generous members paid her membership fee at an exclusive private tennis club.
   She could take lessons from a talented professional.

9. With training Althea's natural ability blossomed.
   She won national titles in several tournaments both in 1944 and 1945.
   Racial barriers still kept her from competing in the major tennis tournaments.

10. Her progress again seemed hopeless.
    Two physicians decided to invest in her future.

11. They hoped to get her a college scholarship.
    They had no luck.
    Her high school grades were disastrous.

12. One of the doctors offered to take in Althea as a member of his own family.
    She could return to high school.
    She could earn her diploma.

13. Althea returned to high school for three years.
    She was several years older than the other students.
    She finished tenth in her graduating class.

14. Her hard work paid off in 1949.
    Florida A&M University offered her an athletic scholarship.

15. In the next few years she completed a college degree in physical education.
    She made great strides as a tennis player.
    Breaking down racial barriers, she participated in the U.S. Nationals at Forest Hills in 1950.
    She played at Wimbledon in 1951.

Writing Exercise A

Every year the United States Post Office issues small numbers of special stamps called *commemoratives*. A *commemorative* usually pictures an individual, a group, an anniversary, or an event that has local or national importance. For example, a commemorative stamp was issued to recognize James Naismith's invention of basketball. In 1979 special stamps honored seeing eye dogs and the fiftieth anniversary of talking motion pictures. Stamps recognizing everything from newspaper carriers to blood donors have been designed; in 1972 a stamp even honored the famous literary character Tom Sawyer. Think about someone or something you believe has had local or national significance and write a well-organized proposal suggesting a commemorative stamp be created to recognize your nominee. Support your proposal with good reasons. You may want to suggest what design or picture would be appropriate on the stamp.

As you write your proposal, remember to use some of the sentence-combining techniques you have studied.

Writing Exercise B

Many tasks seem difficult when you do them for the first time, but as you repeat them, you work automatically, almost without thinking. Only later, perhaps when you try to explain the task to someone else, do you realize how complicated it was at the beginning. Think of some activity you have mastered and write a clear step-by-step explanation of it that a beginner could understand and follow. You might explain how to change the oil in a car, how to iron a shirt, or how to parallel park a car. Perhaps you could explain a sports skill or a skill related to some hobby such as framing a drawing or repotting a plant. Whatever you choose as your topic, remember to explain each step in the process clearly.

As you write, concentrate on using some of the sentence-combining skills you have studied.

14 Inserting Sentences

Inserting Modifiers

Sometimes, rather than joining sentences together, writers use one sentence as a *base sentence* and expand it by inserting *modifiers* from the second sentence.

Adjectives, adverbs, prepositional phrases, and other words whose purpose is to describe another word are called *modifiers*.

As the following example illustrates, several modifiers can be added to the base sentence as long as each is clearly attached to the word it describes.

Base Sentence:	The senator's speech never directly addressed the state's need for a better program.
Insert:	The senator's speech was long.
Insert:	It was a program of land conservation.
Combined:	The senator's *long* speech never directly addressed the state's need for a better program *of land conservation.*

Notice that only modifiers describing a word in the base sentence are inserted in the combined sentence. Since *long* modifies (or describes) the same speech mentioned in the base sentence, and *of land conservation* describes *program*, these modifiers can be inserted without altering the writer's meaning. The combined sentence, however, is a more interesting, economical version of the original sentences.

When two modifiers describe the same word, they can often be interchanged. In the following example, notice that the modifiers *brutal* and *realistic* can be reversed.

Base Sentence:	Walt Whitman's poems recreate images of war's devastation.
Insert:	The poems are about the Civil War.
Insert:	They vividly recreate images.

Insert:	The images are brutal.
Insert:	The images are realistic.
Combined:	Walt Whitman's *Civil War* poems *vividly* recreate *brutal, realistic* images of war's devastation.

or

Walt Whitman's poems *about the Civil War vividly* recreate *realistic, brutal* images of war's devastation.

When modifiers are inserted into a base sentence, it may be necessary to add punctuation or the word *and*. Watch for the signals (,) or (AND) or (, AND) at the end of insert sentences. Place the comma, the word *and*, or the comma with *and* before the inserted modifier in the combined sentence. In the following examples two signals are used.

Base Sentence:	Like discontented ghosts, the cornstalks rustled as I walked across the field.
Insert:	The cornstalks were dry.
Insert:	The cornstalks were brittle. (,)
Insert:	They rustled wearily.
Insert:	They rustled ominously. (AND)
Combined:	Like discontented ghosts, the *dry, brittle* cornstalks rustled *wearily and ominously* as I walked across the field.

Modifiers can be inserted at different places in the base sentence, but they must be clearly attached to the words they modify so that readers do not misunderstand the writer's meaning. The following examples show how modifiers can be correctly inserted in different places and also illustrate how misplaced modifiers change meaning.

Base Sentence:	The old photograph looked stunning.
Insert:	The photograph was in its antique gold frame.
Insert:	It looked stunning against the dark green walls.
Insert:	The walls were in her office.
Combined:	*In its antique gold frame*, the old photograph looked stunning *against the dark green walls in her office*.

or

Against the dark green walls in her office, the old photograph *in its antique gold frame* looked stunning.

Base Sentence:	Mrs. Ortega asked to see the hotel manager, but the clerk insisted that the manager was unavailable.
Insert:	Mrs. Ortega asked at that moment.
Insert:	The clerk was impolite.
Insert:	The clerk insisted persistently.
Combined:	*At that moment* Mrs. Ortega asked to see the hotel manager, but the *impolite* clerk *persistently* insisted that the manager was unavailable.

but not

Persistently, Mrs. Ortega asked to see the hotel manager, but the impolite clerk insisted that the manager was unavailable at that moment.

In the previous example *persistently* cannot be moved to the beginning of the sentence because this modifier describes how the clerk insisted. Also, the phrase modifier *at that moment* cannot be inserted at the end of the sentence since these words tell when Mrs. Ortega asked for the manager.

Exercise 1

Combine the following sets of sentences by inserting modifiers, considering the first sentence the base sentence. Follow the signals given in parentheses. When there are no signals, use your own judgment about how to combine the sentences for the last five, unsignaled sets. Study the examples before you write out your combined sentences on a sheet of paper.

Examples

a. While serving as the consul, James Weldon Johnson wrote "O Black and Unknown Bards," a tribute to the creators of spirituals.
    The consul was American.
    Johnson was the consul to Venezuela.
    The tribute was moving.
    The tribute was poetic. (,)
    The creators were anonymous.

a. *While serving as the American consul to Venezuela, James Weldon Johnson wrote "O Black and Unknown Bards," a moving, poetic tribute to the anonymous creators of spirituals.*

b. The cellar invited the children's exploration.
    The cellar was dim.
    The cellar was dusty.
    The cellar was under the old barn.
    The children were curious.
    The exploration was cautious.

b. *The dim, dusty cellar under the old barn invited the curious children's cautious exploration.*

1. The museum was established.
    It was established by descendants.
    They were descendants of the Mesa Verde Indians.
    It was established near the original site.
    This was the site of the cliff dwellings.

2. The woman finally found the exact artifact she had been seeking.
    The woman was serious.
    The woman was dignified. (,)
    She found the artifact under a pile of tapestries.
    The tapestries were on an old table.
    The table was in the back of the antique shop.

3. The thoroughbred chafed under the bit, longing for the release of its energies at the crack of the starter's gun.
    The thoroughbred was sleek.

The bit was steel.
The release was instant.
The crack was sudden.

4. The book was an edition signed by the author.
The book was priceless.
It was a book with ornate decorations.
The decorations were on the cover.
The cover was leather.
The edition was the first.

5. The ground stroke artist drilled a winner past his opponent to win the match.
The artist was impassive.
The artist was calm. (,)
He drilled aggressively.
The winner was two-fisted.
The winner was cross-court. (,)
His opponent was outstretched.
The match was a marathon.

6. Without fear the lifeguard swam.
The fear was of the riptides.
The riptides were severe.
She swam into the swollen surf.
She swam during the sudden storm.

7. The ice skater traced an arc across the ice as the audience watched.
The ice skater was tall.
The ice skater was graceful.
The arc was perfect.
The ice was silver.
The audience watched silently.
The audience watched in amazement.

8. The moon, imparting a strangeness to objects, gave an appearance to the yard.
The moon was opaque.
The strangeness was beautiful.
The objects were familiar.
The appearance was mysterious.
The yard was ordinary.

9. The streets lay before him, the lights extinguished in all the houses.
The streets were strange.
The streets were desolate.
The houses were worn.
These were houses of the small town.

10. The architecture of the houses, some of whose roofs were broken into peaks, while others ascended into a point, is typical of this neighborhood.

The architecture was irregular.
The architecture was often quaint.
The roofs were tiled.
The peaks were numerous.
They ascended steeply.
They ascended narrowly.
The point was single.

Inserting Participial Phrases as Modifiers

For information on participial phrases, see page 455.

The present participle of a verb ends in -*ing*. The past participle is the form used with *has* or *have*.

Inserting *participial phrases as modifiers* is another way to make your writing more concise and sophisticated. Although they function as adjectives, *participial phrases* begin with a present participle or a past participle. In the following example a portion of the insert sentence is added to the base sentence as a participial phrase describing *teens*.

Base Sentence: The young teens contributed 500 hours of volunteer work at the nursing home.
Insert: The teens were *working after school and on Saturdays.*
Combined: *Working after school and on Saturdays*, the young teens contributed 500 hours of volunteer work at the nursing home.

When they are inserted as descriptive phrases, some verbs must be changed to the -*ing* form. In the next example the signal (ING) indicates that the verb must be changed to this form. The words in *italics* show what part of the insert sentence will be inserted in the base sentence.

Base Sentence: They realized they would need warmer clothes.
Insert: They *glanced at the other hikers.* (ING)
Insert: They *noticed the parkas and heavy sweaters.* (ING)
Combined: *Glancing at the other hikers, noticing the parkas and heavy sweaters*, they realized they would need warmer clothes.

As the next example shows, participial phrases may be inserted at the beginning, in the middle, or at the end of the sentence, but to avoid confusing or nonsensical statements, phrases should be closely attached to the word or words they describe.

Base Sentence: The small child played contentedly on the lawn beside the mother.
Insert: The child was *wearing only a diaper.*
Combined: *Wearing only a diaper*, the small child played contentedly on the lawn beside the mother.

or

The small child, *wearing only a diaper*, played contentedly on the lawn beside the mother.

but not

The small child played contentedly on the lawn beside the mother *wearing only a diaper.*

Participial phrases inserted at the beginning of a sentence are usually followed by a comma. Those appearing at the end or in the middle of the sentence are set off by a comma or paired commas only when they provide information not essential to understanding the sentence's meaning.

Base Sentence:	The painting is a rare watercolor by Mary Cassatt.
Insert:	The painting is *hanging directly above the walnut dresser*.
Combined:	The painting *hanging directly above the walnut dresser* is a rare watercolor by Mary Cassatt.
	[Because the phrase provides essential information about which painting is a rare watercolor, no commas are used.]

Base Sentence:	Paula completed her work on the essay.
Insert:	She *revised the final paragraph*. (ING)
Insert:	She *checked for careless spelling errors*. (ING) (AND)
Combined:	*Revising the final paragraph and checking for careless spelling errors*, Paula completed her work on the essay.

or

Paula completed her work on the essay, *revising the final paragraph and checking for careless spelling errors.*
[A comma sets off the inserted phrases because they are not essential.]

In the preceding example notice how two participial phrases joined by the connector *and* are inserted into the base sentence.

Exercise 2

Combine each of the following sentence sets by inserting the *italicized* participial phrases into the base sentence. Insert the phrases wherever they make the most sense and add commas when they are necessary. After studying the examples, write out each combined sentence on a sheet of paper.

Examples

a. Todd stepped into fresh asphalt.
   He walked hurriedly. (ING) (BUT)
   He didn't watch where he was going. (ING)
   He ruined his shoes. (ING)

a. *Walking hurriedly but not watching where he was going, Todd stepped into fresh asphalt, ruining his shoes.*

b. The audience demanded an encore from the pianist.
   They were pleased with her performance.

b. *Pleased with her performance, the audience demanded an encore from the pianist.*

1. Marvin was ready for the costume party.
   He *changed into the gorilla suit*. (ING)

2. The archeologist found the prehistoric burial ground.
   She *searched for several years*. (ING)
   She *never gave up hope*. (ING) (AND)

3. Sylvia is especially reliable.
   She *consistently arrives on time.* (ING)
   She is *always willing to do more than her share.* (ING) (AND)

4. The apprentice carpenter still managed to fix the stoop.
   She was *hampered by a lack of equipment.*

5. The hunters waited patiently for first light.
   They were *camouflaged perfectly behind the blind.*
   They *listened for the beat of wings.* (ING)

6. The amazing escape artist earned the crowd's admiration.
   He *broke out of the locked safe.* (ING)
   He *returned to the surface of the pool.* (ING)
   He *threw the loosened straightjacket into the air.* (ING) (AND)

7. The ball carrier raced down the field.
   He *scampered around right end.* (ING)
   He *cut sharply up the field.* (ING)
   He *zig-zagged through tacklers to the end zone.* (ING) (AND)

8. Ms. Nelson asked her neighbors to be more quiet.
   She was *disturbed by the loud music next door.*
   She was *exhausted after a long day.* (AND)

9. Zora Neale Hurston's novel, *Their Eyes Were Watching God*, is also based on a biblical motif.
   The novel *incorporates Afro-American folklore and dialect.* (ING)

10. Mary McLeod Bethune developed a school for the children of impoverished railroad workers in Daytona.
    She *started in a run-down shack near the ocean.* (ING)

Exercise 3

On a sheet of paper, combine each of the following unsignaled sentence sets by inserting participial phrases. Sometimes, the base sentence will be the first sentence in the set, but in other sets the second or third sentence may work more effectively as the base. Remember that you may need to change a verb to the *-ing* form or add commas when you insert a phrase. Study the examples before you write the combined sentences on a sheet of paper.

Examples

   a. The playful kitten landed on our startled old terrier Max.
      The kitten leaped from the chair like a lion.

   a. *Leaping from the chair like a lion, the playful kitten landed on our startled old terrier Max.*

   b. They were securing the safety of this year's skiers.
      They were haunted by the memory of last year's avalanche.
      The ski patrol loosened the newly fallen snow.

   b. *Securing the safety of this year's skiers but haunted by the memory of last year's avalanche, the ski patrol loosened the newly fallen snow.*

or

Haunted by the memory of last year's avalanche, the ski patrol loosened the newly fallen snow, securing the safety of this year's skiers.

1. She hoped she would be able to reach to the ledge above.
   She judged the distance carefully.
   Anita dropped the rope down to her friend.

2. Juan decided to hike around the lake.
   He distrusted the rowboat's seaworthiness.
   He traded time and convenience for safety.

3. It was suspended on the thinnest ledge.
   The mountain goat warily proceeded along the mountain's face.
   It perched itself on yet another precarious rock.

4. We found the escaped puppy sleeping under the porch swing.
   He was given up for lost.
   He was exhausted from the adventure.

5. They crashed the funny red car into one barrier.
   They careened into another wall.
   The young sisters were ecstatic about their first bumper car ride.

6. Dr. Alice Hamilton opened a children's clinic at Hull House.
   Dr. Hamilton was influenced strongly by Jane Addams' goals and determination.

7. San Benito is proud of its Indian and Mexican heritage.
   San Benito was settled before the territory became a state.

8. Katherine Dunham later wrote several books about her experiences.
   She traveled throughout the West Indies to study the survival and transformation of African dance.

9. Paul Robeson gave up both these activities to launch a career in theater.
   He played professional football on weekends.
   He attended Columbia Law School during the week.

10. Marian Anderson became an alternate delegate to the United Nations in 1958.
    She made a twelve-nation goodwill tour of the Far East in 1957.
    She traveled everywhere with enthusiasm.

Inserting Adjective Clauses

For more information about adjective clauses, see pages 472–473.

Specific information can also be added to a base sentence by inserting an *adjective clause*. While an *adjective clause* contains a subject and verb, it cannot stand alone as a sentence. Instead, the clause is dependent on the noun or pronoun it describes in the base sentence.

Frequently the clause begins with a relative pronoun, adjective, or adverb that replaces a word in the insert sentence. In the following example a clause containing further information about Alice Walker is inserted into the base sentence. The words *Alice Walker* are removed from the insert sentence and replaced by the relative pronoun *who*. In the combined sentence *who* attaches the clause to the noun it modifies: *Alice Walker*.

Base Sentence:	Alice Walker published her first book of poetry in 1973.
Insert:	Alice Walker grew up in a small Georgia town. (WHO)
Combined:	Alice Walker, *who grew up in a small Georgia town*, published her first book of poetry in 1973.

Adjective clauses often begin with one of the following words.

who, whom, that	relate to people
whose	relates to possessives (its, her, his, their, our)
which, that	relate to things
where	relates to a place
when	relates to a time
why	relates to a reason

In sentences combined with adjective clauses, the signal replaces a noun or pronoun in the insert sentence and helps relate the inserted clause to the base sentence. In the following examples, notice that the signal introducing the clause is clearly attached to the noun or pronoun it modifies in the base sentence.

Base Sentence:	Alfredo explained how to reach the auditorium.
Insert:	He will give his organ recital at the auditorium. (WHERE)
Combined:	Alfredo explained how to reach the auditorium *where he will give his organ recital.*
Base Sentence:	Ms. Wong is now working for the Environmental Protection Agency.
Insert:	Ms. Wong has a degree in conservation. (WHO)
Combined:	Ms. Wong, *who has a degree in conservation*, is now working for the Environmental Protection Agency.

For more information about punctuating essential and nonessential clauses, see page 508.

When a clause is essential to a sentence's meaning, it is not set off by commas. However, when a clause is not essential and can be omitted without changing the sentence's meaning, it is separated from the rest of the sentence by a comma or by paired commas.

Base Sentence:	Those residents of southern California don't find it necessary to build a swimming pool.
Insert:	They have the Pacific Ocean in their own back yards. (WHO)
Combined:	Those residents of southern California *who have the Pacific Ocean in their own back yards* don't find it necessary to build swimming pools. [Because the clause identifies the specific group of residents—those who have the Pacific Ocean in their back yards—it is *essential*. No commas are needed.]
Base Sentence:	*His Eye Is on the Sparrow* describes the poverty and hardship Ethel Waters faced as a child.
Insert:	The book is a touching autobiography. (WHICH)

Combined: *His Eye Is on the Sparrow, which is a touching autobiography,*
describes the poverty and hardships Ethel Waters faced as
a child.
[Because the clause provides nonessential information, it is
set off by commas.]

Exercise 4

Using the signals at the end of the insert sentences, combine each of the
following sentence groups by adding adjective clauses to the base sentence
(the first sentence in each set). Remember to use commas when the inserted
clauses contain nonessential information.

Examples

a. Yesterday Bismarck had the lowest temperature in the nation.
Bismarck is the capital of North Dakota. (WHICH)

a. *Yesterday Bismarck, which is the capital of North Dakota, had the*
lowest temperature in the nation.

b. Drivers could suffer severe injuries because of their carelessness.
The drivers don't bother to fasten their seat belts. (WHO)

b. *Drivers who don't bother to fasten their seat belts could suffer severe*
injuries because of their carelessness.

1. Because the convention center was so large, Ms. Ortez was unable to
locate the exhibit.
She had agreed to meet her assistant at the exhibit. (WHERE)

2. At the end of an elephant's trunk are small, fingerlike extremities used
for picking up small objects.
An elephant's trunk is really an elongated, muscular nose. (WHICH)

3. The Embargo Act failed to keep American ships from traveling to foreign ports.
The act was signed by Thomas Jefferson in 1807. (WHICH)

4. Linda is anxious about her family's move to Texas.
Linda has always lived in a large city. (WHO)
In Texas they will live in a small town. (WHERE)

5. The center fielder failed to make the catch.
Her eyes were blinded by the bright sun. (WHOSE)

6. We tried to contact Buddy.
He is never home. (WHO)
He never returns our calls. (WHO) (AND)

7. In her televised speech the senator spoke of several reasons.
For those reasons voters should oppose a cut in government services.
(WHY)

8. The retired gentleman is an active volunteer at the city historical
museum.
I introduced you to him at dinner. (WHOM)

9. A collector is called a *numismatist*.
   The field of the collector is limited to rare coins, medals, and paper money. (WHOSE)

10. This picture frame will complement the pen and ink drawing very nicely.
    I salvaged the frame from the attic. (WHICH)

Inserting Appositives

For more information about appositives, see pages 458–459 and 508.

Inserting an *appositive* is another way to add information to a base sentence.

An *appositive* or *appositive phrase* is used as a noun and placed beside another word to further explain it.

In the following example the appositive phrase *prehistoric inhabitants of southern Arizona* renames and further identifies the noun *Hohokam Indians*.

Base Sentence:	The Hohokam Indians decorated shells by etching them with acid from cactus fruit.
Insert:	The Hohokam Indians were *prehistoric inhabitants of southern Arizona.*
Combined:	The Hohokam Indians, *prehistoric inhabitants of southern Arizona,* decorated shells by etching them with acid from cactus fruit.

In this lesson *italics* serve as a signal identifying the word or phrase to be inserted in the base sentence.

For variety an appositive can sometimes be placed at the beginning of the combined sentence, preceding the word it explains or identifies.

Base Sentence:	The ivory-billed woodpecker is nearly extinct today.
Insert:	The bird was *once a common inhabitant of primeval swamp forests in the southeastern United States.*
Combined:	The ivory-billed woodpecker, *once a common inhabitant of primeval swamp forests in the southeastern United States,* is nearly extinct today.

or

Once a common inhabitant of primeval swamp forests in the southeastern United States, the ivory-billed woodpecker is nearly extinct today.

Because they provide additional information not essential to understanding a sentence's meaning, appositives are usually set off by commas.

Exercise 5

Combine each of the following sets of sentences by inserting appositives or appositive phrases into the base sentence. The first five sets use *italics* as a signal; the last five sets are unsignaled. Remember that some appositives can be shifted to the beginning of the sentence for variety. After studying the examples, write out each combined sentence on a sheet of paper.

Examples

a. The teacher efficiently marshaled the class out of the room when the fire alarm sounded.

The teacher was *an experienced educator.*

a. *The teacher, an experienced educator, efficiently marshaled the class out of the room when the fire alarm sounded.*

b. "Bartleby the Scrivener" may be a metaphor for the author's experience as a writer.

"Bartleby the Scrivener" is *an unusual story by Herman Melville.*

b. *An unusual story by Herman Melville, "Bartleby the Scrivener" may be a metaphor for the author's experience as a writer.*

1. Johann Pachelbel composed the lyrical Canon in D Major.
He was *a seventeenth-century German composer.*

2. The sun is 93 million miles from our planet.
It is *the star closest to earth.*

3. The flowers line the narrow stone walkway to the back of the house.
They are *graceful lilies of the Nile.*

4. Among the guests were Jennifer, Mr. Garcia, and Ms. Johnson.
Jennifer is *my cousin from Albany.*
Mr. Garcia is *our neighbor.*
Ms. Johnson is *my mother's boss.*

5. Marvin won the waltz contest Saturday.
He was *an accomplished dancer.*
Saturday was *the day he turned twenty-one.*

6. We saw a duck decoy carved 2,000 years ago by a waterfowl hunter.
The hunter was a member of the Desert Culture living in west central Nevada.

7. The cheetah was once trained to hunt the plains deer.
The cheetah is perhaps the fastest living mammal.
The plains deer is an agile but easily exhausted relative of the antelope.

8. Near the Sawangi we located the overgrown footpath.
The Sawangi is a wide, muddy river.
The footpath was a trail used years ago by the Indians.

9. The piece of ancient pottery was broken when its owner died and was buried in the owner's grave.
The pottery was a bowl fashioned by a member of the Mimbre Indian tribe.

10. Babe Ruth is best known for batting 714 home runs during his career.
He was also a talented pitcher.

Review Exercise A

Although the following sentences lack signals, you can write each set as a single sentence by using the combining techniques you have studied. Combine each set and write the finished sentences in paragraph form on a sheet of paper.

1. Families could order merchandise from the catalogue.
   This was in 1900.
   The families lived hundreds of miles from a major American city.
   The merchandise was necessary.
   The catalogue was ever popular.
   The catalogue was mail-order.

2. A farmer could purchase an Acme Steel windmill.
   The windmill could be purchased for sixteen dollars.

3. This windmill was not one of those affairs.
   It was according to the catalogue.
   The affairs were cheap.
   The affairs were flimsy.
   The affairs blew to pieces.
   They did this in the first storm.

4. Children longed instead for the Blue Hill kite.
   They cared little about farm equipment.
   The kite was invented by H. H. Clayton.
   It was used for weather experiments.
   The weather experiments were at the Blue Hill Observatory.

5. The catalogue stated that anybody could fly the Blue Hill.
   It went straight up.
   It went up from the hand.
   It went up like a bird.

6. Young men were fascinated by the Peerless Talking Machine.
   They longed for an interesting career.
   The Peerless Talking Machine was an early phonograph.
   The phonograph both recorded and played back sound.

7. The Peerless could also launch a young man in an exhibition business.
   The Peerless was advertised as the highest class of home entertainment.
   The business was pleasant.
   The business was profitable.

8. The machine recorded on metal cylinders.
   The cylinders could be erased.
   This could be done in less than a minute.
   Cylinders were erased with the Liqui-Para process.

9. The Peerless came with advertising posters and 1,000 admission tickets.
   The Peerless was housed in its own oak carrying case.
   The Peerless was "a most wonderful little machine."
   There were 500 advertising posters.

10. Family members could order a medicine case.
    They ordered from another section of the catalogue.

The case was equipped with cures.
The cures were twelve.
The cures were homeopathic.
The cures were of their choice.

11. These tablets were cures for everything from toothaches to pimples.
The tablets were called handy pocket remedies.
The tablets were small.
The tablets were inexpensive.
The cures were guaranteed.

12. A gentleman could purchase a toupee by mail.
The gentleman suffered from baldness.
The toupee was custom-made.

13. The gentleman, of course, had to enclose a lock and a piece of paper.
The lock was from his hair.
The paper had been cut in the size and shape of his bald spot.

14. Customers might try Princess Hair Restorer.
The customers could not afford a toupee.
Princess Hair Restorer was a secret formula.
The formula promoted growth.
The growth was thick.
The growth was luxuriant.
It was growth of the hair.

15. The mail-order catalogue was the rural family's department store in print.
It provided everything from iceboxes to velocipedes.
The velocipedes were steel-rimmed.

Writing Exercise A

The phrase "generation gap" was coined in the sixties to describe the differences between teens and adults and the communication problems that resulted from them. Although this term is still used frequently by speakers and writers of the eighties, it is often used carelessly or imprecisely with little attention to defining its exact meaning. Using the following questions, write a well-organized paragraph that redefines "generation gap" or some aspect of the generation gap for the eighties.

Use the following questions and ideas to decide how you will treat this subject.

1. What does the term "generation gap" mean to you? Can you give examples or incidents you have experienced to explain the term?

2. What specific differences in dress, language, interests, or attitudes between teens and adults create a generation gap? How do these differences hamper communication?

3. Is the term "generation gap" outdated? How effective is communication between generations today? You may want to argue that communication in the eighties has improved.

4. If a generation gap still exists, what can teens do to lessen it and to build better relationships with adults? In what way can adults improve their relationships with teens? Can you think of individuals who have found successful ways to communicate with members of a different generation?

As you write, use the sentence-combining techniques in this chapter to create economical, varied sentences.

Inserting Absolute Phrases

An *absolute phrase* consists of a noun or pronoun modified by a participle.

Inserting *absolute phrases* into your sentences allows you to vary sentence structure and add information in an interesting way. While an *absolute phrase* is related in meaning to the sentence in which it is inserted, it does not modify any specific word in the sentence. In the next example notice that the helping verbs are omitted when the absolute phrases are added to the base sentences.

Base Sentence:	She raced toward her teammate.
Insert:	*The baton* was *grasped tightly in her hand.*
Insert:	*Her legs and arms* were *pumping like a machine.*
Combined:	She raced toward her teammate, *the baton grasped tightly in her hand, her arms and legs pumping like a machine.*

To create sentence variety, absolute phrases can be inserted at the beginning of the sentence:

Base Sentence:	Mr. Rodriguez frantically searched his pockets for the house key.
Insert:	*A bag of groceries* was *in one hand.*
	His briefcase was *under his arm.*
Combined:	*A bag of groceries in one hand and his briefcase under his arm*, Mr. Rodriguez frantically searched his pockets for the house key.

Absolute phrases are always separated from the rest of the sentence by a comma or paired commas.

Exercise 6

After studying the examples combine each of the following sets of sentences by inserting absolute phrases. The first five sentence groups have *italicized* signals; the last five are unsignaled. Remember that absolute phrases can be inserted at the beginning of the sentence for variety and that they are set off by commas. Write each of the combined sentences on a sheet of paper.

Examples
a. The parts of the old machine worked smoothly.
   Each gear was *carefully cleaned and greased.*
a. *Each gear carefully cleaned and greased, the parts of the old machine worked smoothly.*
b. The textbook already showed signs of abuse.
   Its cover was *torn.*

Its pages were *dog-eared*. (AND)

b. *The textbook, its cover torn and its pages dog-eared, already showed signs of abuse.*

1. Ms. Santos shared some details with the reporter about her campaign for a seat in the state legislature.
   Her guard was *relaxed.*

2. Juanita turned out the lights and locked the door of the pet shop.
   The streets were *already silent.*

3. Tom and Tiña fed the dinner plates through the restaurant dishwasher.
   Towels were *wrapped around their waists.*
   Their faces were *obscured by steam.* (AND)

4. Joan worked late registering voters for the upcoming election.
   Her desk was *littered with stacks of applications.*

5. Maria kept the ten-year-old car scrupulously clean.
   The body was *polished to a high gloss.*
   The engine was *free of grease spots and dirt.* (AND)

6. Luis felt confident as he entered the personnel office.
   His shoes were polished.
   His shirt was carefully pressed.

7. The school custodian pushed a large dust mop up and down the basketball court.
   The game was over.
   The gym was empty.

8. John completed his homework without interruption.
   The groceries were put away.
   The garbage was carried to the curb.

9. She leaned forward over the pool, listening for the starter's gun.
   Her goggles were on tight.
   The nose clamp was in place.

10. The house painters carried the aluminum ladders out to the truck.
    The cans were resealed.
    The brushes were clean.

Inserting Noun Clauses

Noun clauses are discussed on page 476 of Using Grammar.

Changing a sentence to a *noun clause* and inserting it into a base sentence is another sentence-combining technique. A *noun clause* contains a subject and verb but cannot stand alone as a sentence. Instead, the clause functions as a noun in the combined sentence. In this lesson the base sentence contains the signal SOMETHING or SOMEONE, which is replaced by a noun clause composed of all or part of the insert sentence.

Base Sentence:	Mrs. Wong believed SOMETHING.
Insert:	Her training as a keypunch operator was excellent.
Combined:	Mrs. Wong believed *her training as a keypunch operator was excellent.*

The signals (WHO), (WHAT), (WHEN), (WHERE), (WHY), and (HOW) are frequently used to attach the noun clause to the base sentence. The next examples show how these signals work.

Base Sentence:	A landscape architect can tell you SOMETHING.
Insert:	You can plant trees and shrubs to cut heating costs. (WHERE)
Combined:	A landscape architect can tell you *where you can plant trees and shrubs to cut heating costs.*
Base Sentence:	SOMETHING is still a national problem of major importance.
Insert:	Chemical wastes can safely be disposed of. (HOW)
Combined:	*How chemical wastes can safely be disposed of* is still a national problem of major importance.
Base Sentence:	The local fire fighters could not determine SOMETHING or SOMETHING.
Insert:	The fire started somewhere. (WHERE)
Insert:	Something caused it. (WHAT)
Combined:	The local fire fighters could not determine *where the fire started or what caused it.*
Base Sentence:	Do you know SOMEONE?
Insert:	Someone wrote the book *Up from Slavery.* (WHO)
Combined:	Do you know *who wrote the book* Up from Slavery?

In the following examples other signals such as (IT . . . THAT), (THE FACT THAT . . .), (HOW LONG), or (HOW FAR) are used to insert noun clauses. Notice that the word order of a sentence sometimes changes when it is inserted as a noun clause.

Base Sentence:	SOMETHING was obvious.
Insert:	All the plants had been watered earlier that morning. (IT . . . THAT)
Combined:	*It* was obvious *that all the plants had been watered earlier that morning.*
Base Sentence:	SOMETHING never dawned on Jerry as he struggled with the jigsaw puzzle.
Insert:	His mischievous friends might have removed some of the pieces. (THE FACT THAT . . .)
Combined:	*The fact that his mischievous friends might have removed some of the pieces* never dawned on Jerry as he struggled with the jigsaw puzzle.
Base Sentence:	None of the meteorologists seemed to know SOMETHING.
Insert:	The cold snap destroying the fruit crops would last. (HOW LONG)
Combined:	None of the meteorologists seemed to know *how long the cold snap destroying the fruit crops would last.*

Exercise 7

Combine the following sets of sentences by inserting noun clauses into the base sentence (the first one in each set). The first five sentences contain signals; the last five sentences have no signals, and you must decide how to combine the sentences using a noun clause. Study the examples before you write your combined sentences on a sheet of paper.

Examples

a. You should dress neatly for the job interview, but SOMETHING is not necessary.
You wear a suit and tie. (IT . . . THAT)

a. *You should dress neatly for the job interview, but it is not necessary that you wear a suit and tie.*

b. Mr. Sanchez showed the crafts class SOMETHING.
A small table loom is threaded.

b. *Mr. Sanchez showed the crafts class how a small table loom is threaded.*

1. The new owners did not know SOMETHING.
The old wiring would need repair. (HOW MUCH)

2. The veterinarian explained SOMETHING and SOMETHING to her new employee.
The animals should be fed. (WHEN)
The kennels should be cleaned. (HOW)

3. Luis hoped SOMETHING.
One more hour of guitar practice a day would pay off. (THAT)

4. Since drivers cannot make change, SOMETHING is essential.
You have the exact fare ready when you board the bus. (THAT)

5. SOMETHING suggests she works hard to reach her goals.
Mrs. Watson spent six years in night classes to earn a college degree. (THE FACT THAT . . .)

6. SOMETHING is almost impossible to believe.
The figurine we saw at the museum was carved by a Hopewell Indian around 700 B.C.

7. I'd like to know SOMETHING.
The Barnum and Bailey circus chose to spend the winter months in Wisconsin rather than in a warmer climate.

8. In anthropology class we learned SOMETHING.
Shards of pottery found in Indian burial mounds can be used to date the site.

9. Mrs. Noburo, a retired photographer, advised me about SOMETHING and SOMETHING.
A camera would suit my needs.
I should purchase it somewhere.

10. Until my great grandfather told me, I didn't know SOMETHING.
He worked as an Army nurse during World War I.

Inserting Gerunds

Sometimes, the part of one sentence that can be inserted into another sentence is a *gerund*. When the *-ing* form of a verb is used as a noun, it is called a gerund.

In the following example the verb *canoes* is changed to the gerund *canoeing* in the combined sentence, replacing the noun SOMETHING in the base sentence.

For more information about gerunds, see page 456.

Base Sentence:	According to my grandfather, SOMETHING is the best way to see the seasons change.
Insert:	He canoes on the river. (ING)
Combined:	According to my grandfather, *canoeing on the river* is the best way to see the seasons change.
Base Sentence:	The development of the balloon-frame in the 1830s cut the cost of SOMETHING by half.
Insert:	Workers were building a house. (ING)
Combined:	The development of the balloon-frame in the 1830s cut the cost of *building a house* by half.

In the previous examples the subject of the insert sentence is not included in the combined sentence. However, in many cases the subject is changed to a possessive and inserted directly in front of the gerund. The *possessive* form of a noun, used to show ownership, is made by adding an apostrophe (') or apostrophe and the letter *s* ('*s*) to the end of the noun. The signal (POS) indicates that the subject should be made possessive. Both possessives (POS) and gerunds (ING) are used in the following sentence combinations.

Base Sentence:	SOMETHING did not bother his roommate, who slept soundly.
Insert:	Ricardo was typing late at night. (POS)
Combined:	*Ricardo's typing late at night* did not bother his roommate, who slept soundly.
Base Sentence:	Energy, imagination, and a distinctive tone were characteristics of SOMETHING.
Insert:	Louis Armstrong played the trumpet. (POS) + (ING)
Combined:	Energy, imagination, and a distinctive tone were characteristics of *Louis Armstrong's trumpet playing*.
Base Sentence:	SOMETHING seemed to please the young performers immensely.
Insert:	We clapped at the end of each musical number. (POS) + (ING)
Combined:	*Our clapping at the end of each musical number* seemed to please the young performers immensely.

In the previous example the personal pronoun *we* was changed to the possessive *our*. The following list shows the possessive form of other personal pronouns.

PRONOUN	POSSESSIVE PRONOUN
I	my
she	her
he	his
they	their
it	its
you	your
we	our

Notice how possessive pronouns are used in these examples.

Base Sentence:	SOMETHING and SOMETHING made work much easier for the other members of Ms. Taguchi's committee.
Insert:	She organized. (POS) + (ING)
Insert:	She planned before every meeting. (POS) + (ING) + (AND)
Combined:	*Her organizing and her planning before every meeting* made work much easier for the other members of Ms. Taguchi's committee.
Base Sentence:	SOMETHING will make SOMETHING easier and more enjoyable.
Insert:	You wear the right shoes. (ING)
Insert:	You jog in the park every day. (POS) + (ING)
Combined:	*Wearing the right shoes* will make *your jogging in the park every day* easier and more enjoyable.

Exercise 8

On a separate sheet of paper, combine each of the following sets of sentences into one sentence. Signals for inserting possessives and gerunds are given in the first five sentences; the last five sentences lack signals but can also be combined with possessives and gerunds. Study the examples before you begin.

Examples

a. Dr. Percy Julian developed an important cure for inflammatory arthritis by SOMETHING.
He extracted sterols from soybeans. (ING)

a. *Dr. Percy Julian developed an important cure for inflammatory arthritis by extracting sterols from soybeans.*

b. SOMETHING helped Angela meet many of her expenses at the University of Minnesota.
She won an athletic scholarship. (POS) + (ING)

b. *Her winning an athletic scholarship helped Angela meet many of her expenses at the University of Minnesota.*

1. Some early American doctors told their patients that SOMETHING would cure baldness.
They could rub fresh peach leaves on their heads. (POS) + (ING)

2. SOMETHING has improved SOMETHING enormously.
Dan coached. (POS) + (ING)
The children sing. (POS) + (ING)

3. SOMETHING paid off when Tina took first place in the city track meet.
   She jogged six miles every day. (POS) + (ING)

4. According to her counselor, SOMETHING will help her get into a pre-med program.
   Anna trained as a nurse's aide. (POS) + (ING)

5. After SOMETHING, the cast met in the wings to decide on costumes and makeup for the musical.
   They blocked the first two acts onstage. (POS) + (ING)

6. SOMETHING and SOMETHING are two of Ms. Santos' responsibilities as an accountant.
   She audits a company's books.
   She prepares their tax returns.

7. Laurel and Hardy successfully moved from silent to sound motion pictures by SOMETHING.
   They adopted voices suitable to their comic characters.

8. Nineteenth-century farmers used the scythe for SOMETHING and SOMETHING.
   They mowed grass.
   They cut large fields of oats.

9. One farm chore my grandmother disliked was SOMETHING.
   She collected eggs from the hens' nests in the barn.

10. Arthur Mitchell, a noted American legislator, began his college education by SOMETHING.
    He walked sixty-five miles to serve as Booker T. Washington's office boy.

Inserting Infinitives

For more information about infinitive phrases, see pages 457–458.

In this lesson you will learn to insert one sentence into another by forming an *infinitive phrase*, a phrase generally used as a noun but composed of the word *to* plus a verb. As the following examples show, the (TO + VERB) combination replaces the word SOMETHING in the base sentence.

Base Sentence:	Ellen needs SOMETHING before the track meet.
Insert:	Ellen washes her gym clothes. (TO + VERB)
Combined:	Ellen needs *to wash her gym clothes* before the track meet.
Base Sentence:	To do SOMETHING one must have courage as well as a great deal of stamina.
Insert:	One chops onions successfully. (TO + VERB)
Combined:	*To chop onions successfully* one must have courage as well as a great deal of stamina.
Base Sentence:	During her first year of retirement my neighbor wants SOMETHING and SOMETHING.
Insert:	She will go backpacking in the mountains. (TO + VERB)
Insert:	She will write a book about her teaching experiences. (TO + VERB)

Combined:	During her first year of retirement my neighbor wants *to go backpacking in the mountains* and *to write a book about her teaching experiences.*

Sometimes, the verb will change form when it is inserted into the base sentence as an infinitive phrase. In the next examples *discusses* becomes *to discuss*, *writes* becomes *to write*, and *is* becomes *to be*. Remember that *is, are, was,* and *were* are forms of the verb *be* and that *has* and *had* are forms of the verb *have*.

Base Sentence:	The instructions directed the student SOMETHING or SOMETHING.
Insert:	He discusses the short story in a small group. (TO + VERB)
Insert:	He writes a paragraph about the main character's motivations. (TO + VERB) (OR)
Combined:	The instructions directed the student *to discuss the short story in a small group or to write a paragraph about the main character's motivations.*
Base Sentence:	Any student who wants SOMETHING must request a private audition.
Insert:	One is a member of the Chicago Youth Symphony. (TO + VERB)
Combined:	Any student who wants *to be a member of the Chicago Youth Symphony* must request a private audition.

Exercise 9

Combine each of the following sentence sets into a single sentence by following the (TO + VERB) signal. In the first five sentences the signals are included; in the last five sentences no signals are given, and you must decide how to combine each sentence by inserting infinitive phrases. Write your sentences out on a sheet of paper after you study the examples.

Examples

a. If Roy wants SOMETHING, he should try out for the debate team. He improves his logic. (TO + VERB)

a. *If Roy wants to improve his logic, he should try out for the debate team.*

Note: (*To do*) appears in the base sentence to keep the sense of the sentence. Drop this construction in the combined sentence.

b. In order (to do) SOMETHING, many citizens read magazines and newspapers for information about the candidates and their policies. They cast their votes wisely.

b. *In order to cast their votes wisely, many citizens read magazines and newspapers for information about the candidates and their policies.*

1. Mrs. Clark likes (to do) SOMETHING with an old push mower because it is quieter than the power mower.
    She mows her lawn. (TO + VERB)

2. The committee wanted volunteers (to do) SOMETHING.
    They represent the school at the district convention. (TO + VERB)

3. Initially Western homesteaders used barbed wire (to do) SOMETHING. The wire protected their fields from marauding cattle. (TO + VERB)

4. Special greeting cards (to do) SOMETHING were not developed until the 1830s, and comic valentines did not appear until the 1870s. The cards celebrated Valentine's Day. (TO + VERB)

5. Our neighbors tried (to do) SOMETHING but now must cut it down (to do) SOMETHING. They save the old elm tree. (TO + VERB) They prevent the Dutch elm disease from spreading to other trees on the block. (TO + VERB)

6. Adélie penguins use the sun (to do) SOMETHING. They orient themselves during their migration across 200 miles of snow and ice.

7. The flipperlike wings of the penguin and its paddle feet allow the bird (to do) SOMETHING with great success. It captures fast-moving fish.

8. Do you prefer SOMETHING or SOMETHING on weekends? You stay in the city. You travel to your aunt's farm.

9. SOMETHING is what my grandfather likes to do. He canoes down the river (to do) SOMETHING. He fishes near the dam at Yorkville.

10. (To do) SOMETHING you will need (to do) SOMETHING. You reach the museum on public transportation. You transfer at the Jefferson Park bus terminal.

Using the Colon, Dash, and Parentheses

The chapter "Punctuation" provides more information about the colon, dash, and parentheses.

The *colon, dash,* and *parentheses* can also be used to insert information from one sentence into another. However, writers must be careful to use each of these punctuation marks correctly and must avoid relying too heavily on them. The new signals for these combinations are (COLON), (DASH), (PAIRED DASHES), and (PARENS).

The *colon* (:) appears at the end of the base sentence and introduces a specific listing that further identifies or explains something mentioned in the base sentence. In the next example the word *equipment* is further explained by the words *softballs, bats, gloves, and batter's helmets* in the list following the colon.

Base Sentence:	Each team in the conference tournament must bring its own equipment.
Insert:	The equipment is softballs, bats, gloves, and batter's helmets. (COLON)
Combined:	Each team in the conference tournament must bring its own equipment: *softballs, bats, gloves, and batter's helmets.*

Base Sentence:	The dusty old trunk we found in the attic contained interesting relics of Aunt Millie's past.
Insert:	The trunk contained a tarnished silver thimble, a packet of yellowed letters, and two long silk dresses. (COLON)
Combined:	The dusty old trunk we found in the attic contained interesting relics of Aunt Millie's past*: a tarnished silver thimble, a packet of yellowed letters, and two long silk dresses.*

A *dash* (—) follows a specific list of items that *precedes* the base sentence.

Base Sentence:	The very best gymnasts possess all these abilities.
Insert:	The abilities are timing, coordination, and finesse. (DASH)
Combined:	*Timing, coordination, and finesse* — the very best gymnasts possess all these abilities.

A *dash* or *paired dashes* can also be used to insert information indicating a sudden change of thought into the base sentence.

The punctuation separates the interruption from the rest of the sentence.

Base Sentence:	Last year we spent our vacation camping in Colorado and Montana.
Insert:	No, it was two years ago. (PAIRED DASHES)
Combined:	Last year — *no, it was two years ago* — we spent our vacation camping in Colorado and Montana.

Notice that the inserted sentence is not capitalized.

or

Last year—*no, two years ago*—we spent our vacation camping in Colorado and Montana.

Parentheses are used to insert additional information when the writer does not want to draw attention away from the base sentence.

Base Sentence:	Anita will help us develop these photographs in her darkroom.
Insert:	She's my older sister. (PARENS)
Combined:	Anita (*she's my older sister*) will help us develop these photographs in her darkroom.

or

Anita (*my older sister*) will help us develop these photographs in her darkroom.

Exercise 10

On a separate sheet of paper, combine each of the following sentence sets, using the signals to add a colon, dash, paired dashes, or parentheses. Study the example before you write your sentences.

Example

a. After twenty years of safe driving, Mother still believes in the same principles.

These principles are always keep a long interval, drive defensively, and keep the car properly serviced. (COLON)

> a. *After twenty years of safe driving, Mother still believes in the same principles: always keep a long interval, drive defensively, and keep the car properly serviced.*

1. These were the types of wrenches the mechanic wanted most.
   The mechanic wanted socket wrenches, open-end wrenches, box wrenches, and adjustable wrenches. (COLON)

2. While in Washington, five diplomats dined at the Café Parisian.
   Four of the diplomats were born in France. (PAIRED DASHES)

3. When engineers met to discuss the new design with the plant owner, they expected his honest criticism.
   The owner was a stickler for detail. (PAIRED DASHES)

4. The vast majority of representatives came from only three southern states.
   The states were Alabama, Georgia, and Florida. (COLON)

5. Instructions for the test are to be followed exactly.
   Test instructions are on the second page. (PARENS)

6. Our local poll revealed that the candidate was leading in the primaries.
   A nationwide survey showed the same results. (PAIRED DASHES)

7. The golfer hit a four wood to the green.
   No, maybe it was a three wood. (PAIRED DASHES)

8. These items are asked for on a rental application.
   The items are present job and income, last place of residence, and personal references. (COLON)

9. The vast majority of students passed the achievement test.
   Eighty-four percent passed the test. (PARENS)

10. Karen paid for our lunch, and then we left for the matinee.
    Karen paid about six dollars plus the tip. (PARENS)

Review Exercise B

In the following paragraph practice, absolutes, noun clauses, gerunds, infinitives, and special punctuation marks are used to combine each group of sentences into a single sentence. Follow the signals, combining the sentences in the order they appear. On a separate sheet of paper, write out the combined sentences as a complete paragraph. *Italics* indicate words to be included in the combined sentence.

1. Commercial rodeo's popularity really began with SOMETHING.
   Cheyenne, Wyoming celebrated Frontier Days in 1897. (POS) + (ING)

2. *Wyoming, the first state allowing women the right* (to do) SOMETHING, *was also the first state* (to do) SOMETHING.
   Women voted. (TO + VERB)
   The state admitted them to the rodeo. (TO + VERB)

3. Bertha Kaepernick, the first female rodeo participant, launched her career at Cheyenne.
    The crowd was *watching with interest.*

4. She entered two demanding events.
    The events were bronco-busting and wild horse riding. (COLON)

5. These were the only articles of equipment permitted a bronco-buster. The articles were a plain halter, one rein, and a regulation saddle. (DASH)

6. Strict rules for bronco-busting state SOMETHING and SOMETHING.
    The rider must remain on the bronco for ten seconds. (THAT)
    The rider must keep one hand off the reins. (THAT)

7. Bertha rode her bronco to a dramatic finish in front of the grandstand.
    The full ten seconds were *ticking off the clock.*
    The crowd was *wild with enthusiasm.* (AND)

8. SOMETHING encouraged other rodeos (to do) SOMETHING.
    Women contestants were attracting large crowds at Cheyenne. (THE FACT THAT . . .)
    Other rodeos initiated a variety of events for women. (TO + VERB)

9. Lucille Mulhall's skills with the lariat demonstrated SOMETHING.
    Buffalo Bill Cody called her the greatest cowgirl on earth. (WHY)
    She handled a rope better than most men. (PAIRED DASHES)

10. SOMETHING amazed audiences at rodeos throughout the West.
    She roped eight horses with a single throw of the lariat. (POS) + (ING)

11. Teddy Roosevelt was dumbfounded by SOMETHING.
    He was a guest at the Mulhall ranch. (PARENS)
    Lucille easily roped a racing coyote from horseback. (HOW)

12. SOMETHING was the event in which Tillie Baldwin, another early rodeo competitor, excelled.
    She wrestled steers. (ING)

13. SOMETHING depended on SOMETHING.
    One succeeded at bulldogging or steer wrestling. (POS) + (ING)
    It took the rider some time (to do) SOMETHING and SOMETHING. (HOW LONG)
    The rider jumped from horseback. (TO + VERB)
    The rider wrestled the steer to the ground. (TO + VERB)

14. SOMETHING never occurred to these women.
    They were breaking down centuries-old sexual stereotypes. (IT . . . THAT)

15. These were survival skills most women in the West had mastered to some degree.
    The survival skills were SOMETHING, SOMETHING, and SOMETHING.
    They rode. (ING)
    They roped. (ING)
    They handled cattle. (ING)

PART

5 Language

15 Language and Meaning

Language as a System of Symbols

Historically, language was spoken for centuries before writing systems were developed, and some languages never crossed the gap from spoken to written language. The Incas, who established a vast empire high in the Andean mountains of South America, spoke their own language, *Quechua,* but as far as anyone knows, they never invented a way of writing it. There is, however, no known instance of a written language that was never spoken.

All written languages are made up of marks called *symbols.*

In most languages today these symbols are letters that stand for individual sounds. In much earlier languages, however, pictures of objects were used to tell a story or to give a message. Although this form of communication, called *picture writing,* was extremely useful, it had several limitations. The pictures, called *pictographs,* which were usually quite simple, were limited to what could be seen, such as people and objects in nature. One obvious limitation was that the pictures could be drawn quite differently by individual writers and thus be interpreted differently. Another limitation was that one pictograph might symbolize several ideas. A picture of a sun, for instance, might have stood for *sun, day, light, heat,* or even a *sun god.* Picture writing of this kind was widely used by the native Americans of North and South America and is illustrated by the hieroglyphics of the early Egyptians.

Because of the limitations of picture writing, a system of writing called *ideography* developed. In this system *ideograms,* which are much more abstract symbols, were formed by combining the earlier pictographs. The Chinese, for example, constructed an ideogram for the concept "east" by combining the pictographs for "sun" and "tree." (East is where the sun rises through the trees.) The great advantages of ideography were that abstract ideas and concepts could be expressed and that the meaning remained the same from one writer to another. The modern writing systems of both Chinese and Japanese are partly based on ideograms.

Most other modern written languages use characters called *letters*, and each letter or combination of letters symbolizes a sound. When combined, these letters represent the sound of a word.

The total system of letters that a language uses for writing is called an *alphabet.*

Since there are over 3,000 written languages, there are probably nearly as many alphabets whose sounds and symbols vary greatly. The letters that make up the alphabet of a language are so important to the use of the language that special means have been found to make the alphabet accessible to those with sight or hearing impairments.

Language and Culture

If you study any language, you will see in it reflection of the people who speak it—their surroundings and their history. For instance, the Arabic language has many different words for "camel." This is because the life of the Arabs has always been closely connected to this animal. They eat its meat, drink its milk, and use it for transportation and as an article of trade. English, however, has only one word for camel; the Arabic language has twelve. Similarly, the Eskimos of Baffin Island have twenty-one distinct names for snow, but since they live in the Arctic well above the tree line, they have no words for trees. In contrast, the inhabitants of the tropical forests of the Ivory Coast, where more than 500 varieties of trees flourish, make little or no distinction between varieties of ice and snow.

As a *culture* grows and changes, so does its *language.*

Explorations into space, for example, have made it necessary to develop a new vocabulary to name the equipment used, the people involved, and the discoveries made. Many of the technical words that were developed, such as *exosphere* and *astronaut*, were coined from Greek and Latin roots. Others reflected a new meaning for words already in the language, such as *bird* for *rocket*, *brain* for *guidance system*, and *scrub* for *cancellation of a mission.*

Languages also die.

When civilizations break up as nations are conquered, people often adopt the language of the conquering nation. Classical Greek and Latin, once major European languages, are now very limited in use for this reason. Not one culture speaks or writes in either language.

Language Activity 1

Make a list of all the words you know in our language that mean *automobile*, including brand names and slang. Then write a paragraph explaining what this list of words reflects about the automobile's position in our culture.

Euphemisms

A *euphemism* is the substitution of a more agreeable term for one that might be considered offensive.

The notion that certain words are forbidden (taboo) in polite society is a widespread one. In many South Sea islands, for example, the names of the dead cannot be mentioned, nor can words these people were accustomed to saying. Among certain Japanese the word for *four (shi)* is avoided because another word, with a similar pronunciation, means "death."

Sometimes, euphemisms are used to avoid hurting people's feelings. An overweight person may be called *large-boned* rather than *fat*; a person with a history of emotional problems is called *emotionally disturbed* rather than *crazy*. You should understand the nature of euphemisms, however, because frequently they are used to control how you think, feel, or behave. For instance, a salesperson who wants you to buy on credit may offer you *convenient terms*. If you looked into these *convenient terms*, however, you might find that they consist of an interest rate exceeding 20 per cent. A city official who wants to play down the problem of inadequate housing in the inner city may refer to *substandard housing* rather than to *slums*.

As you read the following list of commonly used euphemisms, think of situations where you might have heard the terms.

EUPHEMISM	MEANING
Memorial park	Cemetery
Mortician	Undertaker
Slumber room	Place where body is displayed
Passing away	Dying
Janitor	Custodian
Sanitary engineer	Garbage collector
Mobile home	Trailer
Senior citizen	Old person
Motion discomfort	Airsickness
Disadvantaged	Poor
Dentures	False teeth
Previously owned car	Used car
Recycled	Used
Waste water	Sewage
Flow augmentation	Dilution of sewage
House of detention	Prison
For your convenience please see that a sales clerk has removed the inventory tag before you leave the store.	If you try to steal this garment, the tag will cause a buzzer to sound as you leave the store.

Language Activity 2

With your teacher and classmates compile a dictionary of euphemisms, consisting of those you encounter in your everyday lives.

Gobbledygook

Gobbledygook, like euphemisms, may confuse and misrepresent the meaning of words.

Gobbledygook, also known as *bafflegab, Pentagonese,* and *officialese,* is the excessive use of needlessly complicated or technical words.

Gobbledygook may sound impressive, sophisticated, and official, but when it is "translated," you find that many of the words have little or no meaning. For example, the following excerpt is the beginning of a common fairy tale written in gobbledygook by Russell Baker. In the first sentence the words *a point in time* are needlessly used to mean *time.* What are other examples of longer words or too many words replacing common words that make the writing difficult to understand?[1]

> Once upon a point in time, a small person named Little Red Riding Hood initiated plans for the preparation, delivery, and transportation of foodstuffs to her grandmother, a senior citizen residing at a place of residence in a forest of indeterminate dimension.
>
> In the process of implementing this program, her incursion into the forest was in mid-transportation process when it attained interface with an alleged perpetrator. This individual, a wolf, made inquiry as to the whereabouts of Little Red Riding Hood's goal as well as inferring that he was desirous of ascertaining the contents of Little Red Riding Hood's foodstuffs basket, and all that.
>
> "It would be inappropriate to lie to me," the wolf said, displaying his huge jaw capability. Sensing that he was a mass of repressed hostility intertwined with acute alienation, she indicated.
>
> "I see you indicating," the wolf said, "but what I don't see is whatever it is you're indicating at, you dig?"
>
> Little Red Riding Hood indicated more fully, making one thing perfectly clear—to wit, that it was to her grandmother's residence and with a consignment of foodstuffs that her mission consisted of taking her to and with.

Language Activity 3

Unscramble the following gobbledygook proverbs and write them as they are commonly said. Use your dictionary for help with word meanings.

1. It requires an entirety of species to fabricate a cosmos.
2. A copiousness of culinary facilitators impair the steaming succulence.
3. Precipitousness occasions depletion.
4. The sum total of matter which scintillates is not necessarily bullion.
5. Veracity engenders unparalleled expedience.

Nonsexist Language

The use of *nonsexist language* is an attempt to control the way women are perceived; it is also a good example of how language changes to meet the needs of the people who use it. When women assumed new roles during the

---

[1]Excerpt from "Little Red Riding Hood Revisited" by Russell Baker. © 1980 by The New York Times Company. Reprinted by permission.

second half of this century, they found that many of the words that were formerly used to describe these positions were limited to men only. Since words are used to assign meaning, the need to change language arose.

Some of the changes were in words referring to occupations that could be either female or male.

WORD	ALTERNATIVE
Businessman	Businessperson
Fireman	Fire fighter
Mailman	Mail carrier
Steward, stewardess	Flight attendant
Policeman, policewoman	Police officer
Chairman	Chairperson

Rather than concealing or confusing reality, as euphemisms and gobbledygook do, nonsexist language hopes to reveal the change in society. For this reason the use of the word *man* to represent all human beings is being questioned. Possible alternatives include the following.

WORD	ALTERNATIVE
Mankind	Humanity, human beings, people
Man's achievements	Human achievements
The best man for the job	The best person for the job
The common man	The average person, ordinary people
Manmade	Synthetic, manufactured, crafted, machine-made

Because people control language, the move to nonsexist language will continue only if users agree that it will. If only some people use these new nonsexist words, our language will reflect that not everyone sees the need to change. However, if the majority of people use these new terms, the words will become a part of our language. People change, needs change, language changes.

Language Activity 4

The following words were previously used to name occupations. Next to each word write an appropriate nonsexist equivalent.

Assemblyman	Draftsman	Ticket girl
Bellboy	Foreman	House mother
Brakeman	Repairman	Girl Friday
Cameraman	Salesman	Script girl

Language Activity 5

Do you see any other parts of our society changing? Is it possible that some part of our society will change in the future? Choose an aspect of society that you see changing or that you think will change in the future and describe what effects this change will have on our language.

16 History of the English Language

The Indo-European Language Family

The English language, with which you are familiar, is just one member of a very large family of languages called *Indo-European*, a family network of relationships that is illustrated by the chart on page 292. Linguists believe that the languages of the Indo-European family have all come from one common, ancient "mother" language spoken in central Europe around 4000 B.C.

By examining the appearance of words used in different languages, linguists have been able to group together languages that show similarities in structure and sound. According to the chart on page 292, the languages grouped together in the small boxes in the right-hand column show the closest relationships. English, because it is a descendant of the Germanic (or Teutonic) branch, shares very close relationships to other members of the group, such as Dutch, German, Swedish, and Danish. The similarities among several commonly used words in each of these languages helps to demonstrate this close relationship.

ENGLISH	GERMAN	DUTCH	SWEDISH	DANISH
one	ein	een	en	een
two	zwei	twee	tva	to
three	drei	drie	tre	tre
four	vier	vier	fyra	fire
father	vater	vader	fader	fader
mother	mutter	moeder	moder	moder
brother	bruder	broeder	broder	broder
sister	schwester	zuster	syster	søster

The Indo-European Language Family[1]

INDO-EUROPEAN				
GERMANIC or TEUTONIC		WESTERN GERMANIC	ENGLISH FRISIAN (N. Sea) DUTCH AFRIKAANS (S. Afr.) FLEMISH (Belg.) GERMAN YIDDISH PA. DUTCH (USA)	
		NORTHERN GERMANIC	SWEDISH DANISH NORWEGIAN ICELANDIC	
GREEK	BALTO-SLAVIC	NORTHERN SLAVIC	LETTISH (Latvia) LITHUANIAN	
		EASTERN SLAVIC	RUSSIAN UKRAINIAN WHITE RUSSIAN	
		NORTHWEST SLAVIC	POLISH CZECH SLOVAK	
		SOUTHERN SLAVIC	SERBIAN CROATIAN (Yug.) SLOVENIAN BULGARIAN	
ARMENIAN				
ALBANIAN GHEG (North) TOSK (South)		ROMANCE	PORTUGUESE SPANISH CATALAN FRENCH PROVENCAL SARDINIAN ROMANSH (Swit.) ITALIAN RUMANIAN	
LATIN				
CELTIC		GOIDELIC	IRISH (Erse) SCOTS GAELIC MANX	
		BRYTHONIC	WELSH BRETON CORNISH	
INDO-IRANIAN	SANSKRIT	PALI PRAKRIT		FARSI (Persian) PASHTO GUJARATHI MARATHI PUNJABI RAJASTHANI ORIYA BENGALI BIHARI
			HINDUSTANI	HINDI URDU PAKISTANI SINGHALESE (Ceylon)

---

[1]From *Young Students Encyclopedia*, Volume 11, with permission of Xerox Educational Publishers.

Notice also the similarity in the pattern of verbs in each language:

ENGLISH	GERMAN	DUTCH	SWEDISH	DANISH
sing	singen	zingen	sjunga	synge
sang	sang	zong	sjöng	sang
sung	gesungen	gezongen	sjungit	sungen
fish	fishchen	visschen	fiska	fiske
fished	fischte	vischte	fiskade	fiskede
fished	gefischt	gevischt	fiskat	fisket

A similar comparison can be seen between English (a Germanic descendant) and other Indo-European groups, such as Latin, Greek, and French (a descendant of Latin):

ENGLISH	LATIN	FRENCH	GREEK
one	unus	un	oinē
two	duo	deux	duo
three	tres	trois	treis
father	pater	père	pater
mother	mater	mère	meter
brother	frater	frère	phrater

The similarities across groups are not as close as within groups, but still they are close enough to make a large number of languages common members of one language family, the Indo-European language.

Language Activity 1

Each of the following Modern English words can be traced back to an Indo-European base. Look up each word in a dictionary and then on a sheet of paper write the Indo-European base and its meaning. For help in reading word origins, consult the front of your dictionary under "Etymology."

Example

a. heart

a. Indo-European base: †*kerd—means "heart"*

The dagger (†) in word origins indicates that scholars cannot be certain about the form of the Indo-European base word.

1.	three	6.	bear
2.	seven	7.	corn
3.	cup	8.	weave
4.	head	9.	sew
5.	crank	10.	night

The History of the English Language

Language changes when people and their way of living change.

The causes of some changes in language are quite noticeable, as when one country invades and overpowers another, eventually causing the two languages to intermix. Most changes in language, however, take place so slowly that they are difficult to notice. Only by tracing back the history of a language can such subtle changes be recognized.

The English you speak today has taken centuries to develop. The history of English is generally divided into three periods:

Old English (O.E.):	450–1100
Middle English (M.E.):	1100–1500
Modern English (Mod. E.):	1500 to the present

These periods overlap or blend from one to another. Obviously, speakers did not use Old English one day and then Middle English the next; the evolution of language is always gradual. In the following sections you will learn about the changes that took place during the three periods of the English language: changes in vocabulary, sounds, and syntax.

Old English

English is not the original language of the country known today as England. Early in the history of that part of the world, a form of the Celtic language was spoken by the ancient Britons who populated the country. During the Roman occupation of Britain (A.D. 43–A.D. 410) Latin must also have been widely used.

It was not until the fifth century, when the Teutonic tribes—the Angles, Saxons, and Jutes—began to conquer the Britons and to impose their speech on the country, that the history of the English language began. Each of these tribes settled in a separate area of Britain and remained separated from each other. In spite of the relative isolation, however, each group managed to influence the language of the others. The language that emerged, a mixing of the three dialects, was called *Anglo-Saxon*, or *Old English*.

Old English Vocabulary

The Old English vocabulary was very small by today's standards and consisted mainly of Teutonic, or Germanic, words. A few Celtic words and many Latin words were kept, mostly military and commercial ones used by the Romans during their long occupation of the country. Many of the Latin words later absorbed into Old English were religious terms used by the missionaries who brought Christianity to England. Many of these Latin words, such as *abbot, angel, candle, disciple, martyr, mass,* and *psalm,* are still used in Modern English. Below is an Old English version of the Lord's Prayer. If you find many of the Old English words familiar, it is because so many Latin religious terms have remained in the language.

> Fæder ure, θu θe eart on heofonum, si θin nama gehalgod. Tobecume θin rice. Gewurθe ðin willa on eor ðan swa swa on heofonum. Urne gedæghwamlican hlaf syle us to dæg. And forgyf us ure gyltas, swa swa we forgyfað urum gyltendum. And ne gelæd θu us on costnunge, ac alys us of yfele. Soθlice.

The Sounds of Old English

The Old English sound system shows many differences from that of Modern English. For example, although the short vowels of Old English are similar to Modern English, the use of long vowels is quite different, as the following illustration shows.

O.E. Vowel	O.E. Words	Mod. E. Words
ā	hām, bān, āc, stān	home, bone, oak, stone
a	man(n), lamb	man, lamb
ǣ	dǣd, sǣd	deed, seed
æ	æt, glæd	at, glad
ē	wē, fēt	we, feet
e	settan, wel	set, well
ī	mīn, tīd	mine, tide
i	sittan, hit	sit, it
ō	gōd, sōna	good, soon
o	God	God
ū	hūs, ūt, cū, mūs	house, out, cow, mouse
u	ful, lufu	full, love
ȳ	hȳdan, mȳs	hide, mice
y	pytt, synn	pit, sin

The Syntax of Old English

One of the main differences in *syntax*, or word order, in Old English from Modern English was the tendency to place the verb at the end of the sentence, as in the following examples.

se cyning frið nam   *him ða aðs sworon*
the king peace made   to him oaths they swore

For variety sentences sometimes began with verbs:

com ða to rec ede rinc siðian
came then to the hall the warrior march

Language Activity 2

Read the following paragraph from *Beowulf*, written in Old English, and the word-for-word translation printed between the lines. Then rewrite the para-agraph using Modern English syntax and vocabulary. Use your dictionary for help with meanings.

Hwæt, we Gar-dena in geardagum
Lo! we of the Spear-Danes in former days
Þeodcyninga þrym gefrunon,
Of the kings of the people the glory heard,
Hu ða æþelingas ellen fremedon!
How the heroes valour performed.
Oft Scyld Scefing sceaþena þreatum,
Often Scyld, son of Sceaf, from the enemies' troops

Monegum mægþum meodosetla ofteah,
[From] *many tribes* [*their*] *mead-benches took away,*

Egsode eorlas, syððan ærest wearð
Terrified the warriors, since first [*he*] *was*

Feasceaft funden.
Abandoned found.

Middle English

In 1066 William, duke of Normandy (*Normandy* was a province of northwest France), defeated King Harold of England, bringing a period of French rule to England.

For over 200 years the French language of the Normans influenced the development of *Middle English*, particularly in new vocabulary. Since French was based on Latin, however, most Middle English words had Latin origins. Also, since Latin itself had borrowed many words from Greek, English by this time had traces of the Celtic, Germanic, Latin, Greek, and French languages. Because of the Viking invasions into the island in the latter years of the eighth century, some Scandinavian influence was also felt.

Although French remained the language of the ruling classes in England for several hundred years, the great majority of the English people making up the poorer classes continued to use English. Beginning in 1337, England and France began a long conflict known as the Hundred Years' War. By the time the war ended, English was once again established as the language of government and schools.

Middle English Vocabulary

Scandinavian and French had the greatest impact on the Middle English vocabulary. Many words with *sk (sc)* (as in *scant, skill, skin, score,* and *bask*) are of Scandinavian origin. The pronouns *they, their,* and *them,* as well as many place-names ending in *-by,* the Scandinavian word for *town,* were also contributed by the Scandinavians. French words that were added to the English vocabulary fall into the following groups.

MILITARY TERMS		POLITICAL AND LEGAL TERMS	
army	prison	defendant	parliament
battle	siege	innocent	plaintiff
defeat	soldier	judge	sentence
hostage	victory	jury	verdict
navy	war		

ART TERMS		ABSTRACT TERMS	
artist	literature	avarice	liberty
ballad	music	charity	purity
color	poetry	courage	religion
comedy	tragedy	equality	vice
dance	verse	faith	virtue
letters		fraternity	

The Sounds of Middle English

Many of the spelling changes from Old English to Middle English did not change the sound of words.

For example, when the spelling of the Old English word for "house" changed from *h-u-s* to *h-o-u-s*, the pronunciation did not change. The vowel sounds in both forms of the word were pronounced like the *ou* sound in *through* and *group*.

O.E.	M.E.	MOD. E. EQUIVALENT SOUND
hus	hous	through, group

Other spelling changes did indicate a difference in pronunciation, a difference that was one step closer to Modern English.

O.E.	M.E.	MOD. E.
ham	hoom	home
ban	boon	bone
ac	ook	oak
stan (*a* pronounced as *a* in *father*)	stoon (pronounced *hawm, bawn, awk, stawn*)	stone

For example, the Old English word for "home," *ham*, was pronounced with the *a* sound in *father*. When the Middle English spelling changed to *h-o-o-m*, the vowel sound changed also.

The Syntax of Middle English

Two interesting changes occurred in Middle English that still affect Modern English. Both changes developed because many of the *inflectional endings*, endings that signal how a word is to be used in a sentence, were dropped. In Old English the inflectional ending *-es* on a word showed possession, as in *eorles helm*, "the warrior's helmet." The influence of the French word *de*, meaning "of," added a new way to show possession in Middle English. Using *of* changes the word order and makes many expressions clearer: instead of "the wall's side," speakers could say "the side of the wall."

Inflectional endings for nouns in Middle English were used to show singular and plural. Earlier endings that were used to show whether a noun was used as a subject or an object were dropped, causing a change in word order and helping the language to become more standardized.

Language Activity 3

Read the following selection, "The Prioress," from the *Prologue to the Canterbury Tales*, written in Middle English by Geoffrey Chaucer. As you read, look for words that resemble Modern English words. Then write out your own translation of this description of the passage in Modern English.

THE PRIORESS

From the *Prologue to the Canterbury Tales*

Ther was also a Nonne, a Prioresse,
That of hir smyling was ful simple and coy;

Hir gretteste ooth was but by sëynt Loy;
And she was cleped madame Eglentyne.
Ful wel she song the service divyne,
Entuned in hir nose ful semely;
And Frensh she spak ful faire and fetisly,
After the scole of Stratford atte Bowe,
For Frensh of Paris was to hir unknowe.
At mete wel y-taught was she with-alle;
She leet no morsel from hir lippes falle,
Ne wette hir fyngres in hir sauce depe.
Wel coude she carie a morsel, and wel kepe,
That no drope ne fille up-on hir brest.
In curteisye was set ful muche hir lest.
Hir over lippe wyped she so clene,
That in hir coppe was no ferthing sene
Of grece, whan she dronken hadde hir draughte.
Ful semely after hir mete she raughte,

Modern English

Two events helped to bring about the change in language from Middle English to *Modern English*. One was the introduction of the printing press into England in 1476 by William Caxton. (The influence of printing was slow to take effect; it became important only when the gradual spread of education increased the number of people who could read.) Another important event in the early Modern English period was the Renaissance, an influence that introduced a large number of Latin *loanwords* into English (*loanwords* are words borrowed from another language).

The Vocabulary of Modern English

The greatest period of expansion in the English vocabulary has been during the Modern English period. Borrowing increased when Renaissance scholars and writers revived an interest in Greek and Latin classical literature. Also, as new lands were explored and new discoveries were made, words from other languages were customarily borrowed to describe these findings. The borrowed words that were used most frequently still remain in the English language today.

Many of the Greek and Latin words borrowed are found in the sciences: *geology, geography, philology, psychology, ideology, phenomenon.* The French words borrowed during this period reflect a French pronunciation rather than English speech habits: *machine, picturesque, fiancé, chic, lingerie, ensemble.*

Most German words were borrowed during the nineteenth century and contribute to our scientific and philosophical vocabulary: *zinc, cobalt, aesthetic, transcendentalism, complex, introvert, chromosome, dynamo, relativity.*

The Dutch contributed a number of words that are used in shipping and art: *boom, sloop, cruise, landscape, sketch.*

The Italian words borrowed are particularly important to the arts, especially music: *soprano, contralto, piano, violin, viola, sonata, prima donna, maestro, fresco, studio.*

More words have been borrowed from the Scandinavian languages during the Modern English periods: *ski, fiord, geyser, viking, smorgasbord.*

From Russia were borrowed *czar, vodka, soviet,* and *sputnik.*

Spanish words that have been borrowed include *matador, toreador, bolero, junta, desperado, renegade, comrade, siesta, cigar, cork,* and *sherry.*

The Sounds of Modern English

The transition from Middle English to Modern English is marked by two important changes in sound: the loss of final vowels and the "great vowel-shift."

In Old English every letter in a word, including the final vowel, was pronounced. In Middle English, word endings were reduced but still pronounced. In Modern English many of the final vowel endings remain in spelling, but they are not pronounced.

O.E.	M.E.	MOD. E.
ce*pan*	kep*ee*	keep
heor*te*	her*te*	heart
nam*a*	nam*e*	name

The great vowel-shift basically consists of a series of changes that affected the long vowels of Middle English and gradually transformed them into quite different sounds in Modern English. This shift, which affected the pronunciation of all Modern English words, is still more noticeable in sound than in spelling. In fact, during the transition from Middle English to Modern English, many consonant endings and combinations were no longer pronounced. The final *b* in *comb* and *lamb* was no longer pronounced; the *k, g,* and *w* were no longer pronounced in *know, gnaw,* and *wrong;* and the *gh* in *right* and *night* lost its sound, while in other words it changed its sound to *f,* as in *cough* and *laugh.*

The Syntax of Modern English

The verb form called *progressive,* consisting of a form of *to be* plus an *-ing* verb, was not widely used until the Modern English period. Until this time sentences such as "I'm studying English," were not constructed.

In the early part of the Modern English period, the double negative and double comparative and superlative were still widely heard. Gradually, however, they were used less and less by educated speakers, a change that is particularly noticeable when comparing Shakespeare's language of the seventeenth century with that of today.

Shakespeare: "I will *not* budge for *no* man's pleasure, I." *(Romeo and Juliet)*

Today:	I will not budge for *any* man's pleasure.
Shakespeare:	"This was the *most* unkind*est* cut of all." (*Julius Caesar*)
Today:	This was the *most* unkind cut of all.

Perhaps the greatest change during the Modern English period was one of attitude. Before the eighteenth century educated speakers and writers were not greatly concerned with "rules" of usage. Such a respected writer as Shakespeare, for example, in the *Merchant of Venice* wrote, "All debts are cleerd between you and I." Similarly Shakespeare and other acknowledged masters of the language did not bother themselves with such distinctions as those between *who/whom* and *shall/will* or with double negatives or other niceties that students in most English classes today must observe.

The idea that there were "right" and "wrong" usages originated in the eighteenth century with the belief in the divine origin of language and the concept of universal grammar. According to holders of the "divine origin" theory, language was divinely inspired and as such was perfect in its beginnings but since then has been in constant danger of being changed by less than perfect speakers and users. The "universal grammar" theory held that there was a "pure" grammar (Latin), whose rules could be applied to all languages. For this reason the first English grammars were based on Latin grammars.

Language Activity 4

The following words have either widened or narrowed their meanings in Modern English. Look up each word in a dictionary and trace its meaning. On a sheet of paper, write the form of the word and its meaning in the language from which it comes and then its meaning in Modern English.

Example

a. deer
a. *Old English form* deor *meaning "wild animal"; Modern English meaning "any of a family of hoofed, cud-chewing animals"*

1.	picture	6.	guy
2.	chagrin	7.	lyric
3.	ballad	8.	cafeteria
4.	fond	9.	humor
5.	miscreant	10.	silly

The Growth of American English

American English and British English are variations, or *dialects*, of the same language. Although the earliest settlers brought their British English with them, once they were isolated from Britain in a strange new environment, this language began to change.

How American English developed is closely tied to the nation's history. The earliest *loanwords* came from early settlers' contact with the native Americans. Confronted with unfamiliar plants and animals, settlers found it easy to adopt Indian words, such as *squash, pemmican, coyote, succotash, hickory,* and *skunk.* As the country expanded, Indian names were used to identify existing places *(Mississippi, Chicago),* and the names of tribes or leaders were assigned to new settlements: *Miami, Cheyenne,* and *Pontiac.* The language grew to include familiar terms associated with Indian life: *squaw, moccasin, powwow,* and *wigwam.*

After the Louisiana Purchase, when settlers' contact with French traders increased along the country's northwest borders, many French loanwords were added to the language: *portage, crevasse, prairie, sashay,* and *cache.* Westward expansion led to contact with the ranching culture of the Southwest and the addition of Spanish loanwords for clothing *(poncho, sombrero),* ranching terms *(ranch, lariat, rodeo, corral),* and new plants and animals *(alfalfa, bronco, mustang).*

Large waves of immigrants in the late 1800s improved travel, and increasing communication allowed American English to grow even richer. Borrowing from the German language, Americans sent their children to *kindergarten* and ordered *frankfurters* at the local *delicatessen.* Italians added *spaghetti* and *ravioli* to the American menu, while *boss, sleigh,* and *spook* were borrowed from the Dutch. From the Japanese came *soybean* and *tycoon,* while the Chinese loanwords allowed people to have a *yen* for *chop suey.* Loanwords from Africa allowed Americans to enjoy *jazz* and prepare a *gumbo* of *okra* and other vegetables. From Yiddish came such words as *schlep* ("to carry"), *schmaltzy* ("sentimental"), and *schmoose* ("to talk").

Language Activity 5

All of the following loanwords have become part of the American language. On a separate sheet of paper, write each word, its definition, and the language from which it is borrowed. Before you begin, check the front of your dictionary to be certain it provides information about etymology (the origin of words).

Example

a. canoe

a. canoe—*a narrow light boat with sides that meet sharply at each end; from Spanish*

1. charivari
2. mackinaw
3. chinook
4. depot
5. plaza

6. goober
7. bureau
8. patio
9. cruller
10. bonanza

Regional Dialects

While all Americans share in a rich heritage of borrowed words, all Americans do not share exactly the same language. Just as the language of an American teenager differs from that of a London teenager, so the English spoken in a rural Georgia classroom differs from that heard in a New Hampshire school because American English includes many *regional dialects*.

A *regional dialect* is a variation of a language shared by people living in a particular area.

Regional differences developed in complex ways. Originally colonists from different parts of England with slightly different dialects settled in widely separated parts of the colonies. The lack of communication and difficulty of traveling isolated some communities such as those in the Ozarks, where speech patterns today are similar in many respects to those of Elizabethan English. Waves of new immigrants altered the speech patterns in other communities; for example, an influx of Scottish-Irish, who settled farther to the west and pronounced their *r*'s clearly, may explain why the *r* in par*k* is sounded in the North Midland region but not in the eastern New England area.

While an individual's dialect may suggest where he or she lives or what kind of work the person does, no one dialect is superior to another. Each regional dialect is an equally acceptable mixture of variations in pronunciation, vocabulary, and grammar. For example, Midwesterners are often intrigued by the way New Englanders pronounce the *r* in *cart* and *farm*—as if it were an *h* (ca*h*t and fa*h*m), but they rarely hear the *r* many of their neighbors include in *wash* (*warsh*). While Bostonians find *warsh* unfamiliar, they often fail to notice their own pronunciation of *Cuber* and *Asiar* for *Cuba* and *Asia*. Finally, speakers of Black English, a dialect shared by many black people living in the United States, might vary the *r* in another way, by pronouncing *sure* as *show*.

Speakers of different regional dialects also have differences in vocabulary. In southern Wisconsin a carbonated drink is a *soda*; in northern Illinois, only fifty miles away, the same beverage is *pop*, while in New England it is *tonic*. A New Englander may use a *spider* to cook the fish caught in a *brook* with *night crawlers*, but someone farther south might use a *skillet* to cook the fish caught in a *branch* with *redworms* as bait.

Differences in grammar also give a flavor and character to regional dialect. Depending on the speaker's dialect, he or she may be *to home* or *at home*. A Southerner might ask if *you-all are at home*, while a Northerner will wonder if *you are at home*.

Language Activity 6

Prepare a list of the words, expressions, pronunciations, and word order that you think characterize your regional dialect. Compare your list with those of other students in your class.

Choosing Language Levels

Just as individuals dress one way to clean the basement and another way to attend a banquet, so they *choose a level of language* appropriate to their audience and the occasion.

When you are talking with close friends or relatives or writing a personal letter or a note to yourself, you probably use *informal English.* Informal English is casual and conversational; often it contains slang, dialect words, contractions, and conversational tags such as *well* or *you know.* Incomplete sentences or ungrammatical expressions such as "It's me" are even found in spoken informal English.

On the other hand, when you are interviewing for a job, presenting a group report, or writing to a public official, you are addressing a general public audience or someone you have never met. On these occasions you want to use language in a considerate and more formal manner. Polite *formal English* is serious, objective, and observes the guidelines for accurate punctuation, spelling, and grammar found in Edited Standard English.

In most cases formal English does not include slang, contractions, incomplete sentences, or conversational tags. The use of formal English in appropriate situations suggests that you are knowledgeable about choosing language appropriate for different situations.

Language Activity 7

On a sheet of paper numbered 1–5, identify each of the following statements as formal or informal English. Your teacher may ask you to explain how you made your decision.

1. Creative minds always have been known to survive any kind of bad training.
   —*Anna Freud*

2. My best friend is the man who'll get me a book I ain't read.
   —*Abraham Lincoln*

3. Idealists foolish enough to throw caution to the winds have advanced mankind and have enriched the world.
   —*Emma Goldman*

4. Fame creates its own standards. A guy who twitches his lips is just another guy with a lip twitch—unless he's Humphrey Bogart.
   —*Sammy Davis, Jr.*

5. Science may have found a cure for most evils, but it has found no remedy for the worst of them all—the apathy of human beings.
   —*Helen Keller*

Standardizing Language

The campaign to establish a standard for American English dates back to the early years of American history. Only a short time after the American Revolution, John Adams proposed that Congress set up an academy to correct, improve, and preserve the English language. Ben Franklin was also concerned about preserving the integrity of the language. In a 1789 letter to Noah Webster, author of the first American dictionary, Franklin made the following comment:

> I cannot but applaud your zeal for preserving the purity of our language, both in its expressions and pronunciation, and in correcting the popular errors several of our States are continually falling into with respect to both. Give me leave to mention some of them, though possibly they may have already occurred to you. I wish, however, in some future publication of yours, you would set a discountenancing mark upon them. The first I remember is the word *improved*. When I left New England, in the year 1723, this word had never been used among us, as far as I know, but in the sense of *ameliorated* or *made better*, except once in a very old book of Dr. Mather's, entitled *Remarkable Providences*. As that eminent man wrote a very obscure hand, I remember that when I read that word in his book, used instead of the word *imployed*, I conjectured it was an error of the printer, who had mistaken a too short *l* in the writing for an *r*, and a *y* with too short a tail for a *v*; whereby *imployed* was converted into *improved*.
>
> But when I returned to Boston, in 1733, I found this change had obtained favor, and was then become common; for I met with it often in perusing the newspapers, where it frequently made an appearance rather ridiculous. Such, for instance, as the advertisement of a country-house to be sold, which had been many years *improved* as a tavern; and, in the character of a deceased country gentleman, that he had been for more than thirty years *improved* as a justice of the peace. This use of the word *improved* is peculiar to New England, and not to be met with among any other speakers of English, either on this or the other side of the water.

Noah Webster's own efforts to set language standards extended as far as advocating that Congress pass laws to fix the language and keep it pure.

Although no academy or national laws were ever created for the preservation of the American language, an unofficial standard dialect did develop in the United States as schools and businesses gradually adopted similar guidelines for acceptable communication. Today this dialect, called Standard English, is commonly found in newspaper and magazine articles. It is also the dialect used by most radio and television announcers.

The term *Edited Standard English* (ESE) refers to the written form of Standard English.

The "Using Grammar" and "Mechanics" parts of this textbook will help you to learn the features of Edited Standard English.

Although it is important to learn Standard English and to use it in appropriate situations—job interviews, essays, business correspondence—it would be wrong to assume this is the only correct form of language. It is, however, the dialect preferred by many businesses and cultural and educational leaders and represents their efforts to use language as clearly and effectively as possible.

PART

6 Using Grammar

17 The Parts of Speech

The Eight Classes of Words

In the study of grammar it is customary to divide words into eight classes called *parts of speech*.

The parts of speech are *nouns, pronouns, verbs, adjectives, adverbs, prepositions, conjunctions,* and *interjections*.

Words are usually classified as one of the eight parts of speech depending on how they function in a sentence. For example, words that name are classified as *nouns*; words that modify nouns and pronouns are classified as *adjectives*. However, many words can function as more than one part of speech as their use in a sentence changes. In the sentence, "Put the mower in the garage," *garage* is a noun, but in the sentence, "The garage roof needs repairing," *garage* is used as an adjective to modify the noun *roof*. In your study of grammar, you will encounter many such instances.

In this chapter you will find two types of sections about each part of speech: *Understanding* and *Using*. In the Understanding sections you will learn how to identify the part of speech; in the Using sections you will learn how to use that part of speech in your writing. As you work through a Using section, refer back to the Understanding section for any help that you may need in recognizing the part of speech and the way it functions in a sentence.

Understanding Nouns

Nouns are naming words. Your own name is a noun, and so are the names of all the people, animals, plants, places, and things in the world. The names of ideas—like *fairness* and *love* and *fear*—are also nouns. In the sections that follow you will learn three different ways to recognize nouns: by definition, by types of nouns and their characteristics, and by features that distinguish nouns from other parts of speech.

Defining a Noun

A *noun* is usually defined as a word that names a person, place, thing, or idea.

Bernice designs and hand-screens fabrics.	[name of person]
Russia sold *Alaska* to the *United States*.	[names of places]
Don't use a *hammer* for that job.	[name of thing]
What do you think constitutes *success?*	[name of idea]

Exercise 1

Write out the following sentences and underline all the nouns. Above each noun write whether it names a person, place, thing, or an idea.

Example
a. Veronica has a fear of high places.

    person   *idea*   *thing*
a. <u>Veronica</u> has a <u>fear</u> of high <u>places</u>.

1. The organization called NOW works for the political and economic equality of women and men.

2. *The Garlic Times* is the title of the newsletter published by an organization called The Lovers of the Stinking Rose.

3. Jay Green and his daughter Lisa juggle professionally in fairs and on television.

4. Sugar not only causes decay of teeth but also is associated with obesity and diabetes.

5. When Sigmund Freud was a boy, his father said, "That boy will never amount to anything."

6. Angel Falls in eastern Venezuela, the highest waterfall in the world, is more than twice as high as the Empire State Building.

7. Sally had a swarm of bees in her closet, seeping through the keyhole and under the door.

8. *Apocalypse Now*, a movie about the war in Vietnam, is loosely based on a novel about Africa called *The Heart of Darkness* by Joseph Conrad.

9. Sara Bonovich moved from the town of Why, Arizona, to the city of Whynot, Mississippi.

10. The responsibilities of adults include paying taxes and bills; providing their own food, shelter, and clothing; and caring for dependents.

Classifying Nouns

In the large category *nouns*, there are several smaller classes.

Nouns are either common or proper.

A *proper noun* names a specific person, place, thing, or idea. All other nouns are called *common nouns*.

PROPER NOUNS	COMMON NOUNS	
Jo Jo Starbuck	skater	[person]
New Orleans	city	[place]
Idaho	state	[place]
Ordinary People	novel	[thing]
King Kong	gorilla	[thing]

Proper nouns always begin with capital letters, but common nouns are not capitalized.

The *school* offers a six-week course.	[common noun]
The College of Comedy offers a six-week course.	[proper noun]
The *judge* mysteriously disappeared.	[common noun]
Judge Joseph Crater mysteriously disappeared.	[proper noun]

Nouns may be classified as either concrete or abstract.

A *concrete noun* names something you can see or touch, such as *elephants* or *butterflies*. An *abstract noun* names an idea or a quality, such as *beauty* or *skill*.

concrete   abstract
Dr. *Martin Luther King, Jr.*, led the fight for *civil rights*.
concrete   abstract
Coretta Scott King continued his *work* after his death.

All nouns may be classified as either common or proper, concrete or abstract. *Jane Austen*, for example, is a proper noun and a concrete noun. *Family* is a common noun and an abstract noun.

Some nouns are called *collective nouns* because they stand for a whole group of people or things.

Words like *committee*, *team*, *herd*, and *group* are collective nouns.

A *pride* of lions lived in the Animal Preserve.	[collective noun]
The *jury* could not agree on a verdict.	[collective noun]

Compound nouns are made up of two or more words that are joined together to name one person, place, or thing.

Many proper nouns are compound, such as *Los Angeles Rams*, *Appalachian Trail*, and *Future Farmers of America*.

When common nouns are compound, they may be spelled as one word, two separate words, or a hyphenated word. If you are writing a compound noun, be sure to use a dictionary to see how it is spelled.

One Word:	lighthouse, weekend, campground, jetport, grandparent
Two Words:	ice cream, forest fire, high school, windshield wiper
Hyphenated Word:	merry-go-round, brother-in-law, secretary-general

Exercise 2

Write out the following sentences, and underline each noun. Write *C* above each common noun and *P* above each proper noun. (Be sure to underline the entire noun if it is compound.) Draw a circle around every concrete noun and leave the abstract nouns uncircled.

Examples

a. Mr. Sandu, the piano tuner, worked for an hour to tune the piano.

P   C   C   C

a. (Mr. Sandu,) the (piano tuner,) worked for an hour to tune the (piano.)

b. Cree is a language spoken by Indians who live in Ontario, Saskatchewan, and Manitoba.

P   C   P   P

b. Cree is a language spoken by (Indians) who live in Ontario, Sas-

P   P

katchewan, and Manitoba.

1. Every winter a flock of turkey vultures roost atop the Dade County Courthouse.

2. Mu Lan, an ancient Chinese heroine, disguised in armor as a man, fought bravely for her country.

3. Mrs. Kumble rented a pressure cleaner from Uleta Rentals.

4. How many Americans have won the Nobel Prize for Literature?

5. Our neighbor, Henry Paczak, who is a retired railroad engineer, has a huge collection of license plates from every state in the United States.

6. This time last year Victor Etayo and his cousin were visiting his sister-in-law in Oklahoma City.

7. After they finish their training, Maria Pacheco and Isabel Thomas are planning to open a day-care center in a shopping center.

8. In an emergency the shoots of young cattails, which grow abundantly along lakes and rivers, are edible.

9. In a last effort to save their lives, the Jews of the ghetto in Warsaw, Poland, fought bravely for a month against the overwhelming power of the Nazis.

10. The New York Mets beat the Atlanta Braves in three straight games in the playoffs to win the National League East Championship.

Finding a Noun by Its Features

Learning the four characteristics that distinguish nouns from other parts of speech will help you to identify nouns. Most nouns have at least one of these features.

1. Nouns often follow *determiners.*

Determiners are words such as *my, his, her, your, this, that, these, one, some,* and *many.* The three most common determiners—*a, an,* and *the*—are called *articles*. Determiners signal that a noun will follow, although one or more words may separate the determiner and the noun.

N	N
some patience	*four* green and white flags
N	N
the Gottliebs	*many* new students
N	N
an early show	*these* dusty, old trunks

2.   Nouns are *singular* or *plural*.

One of the features of nouns is that they show number. Most nouns have different forms to show singular (one) or plural (more than one) number. Some nouns keep the same form for both singular and plural. The rules for forming the plurals of nouns are on pages 312–317.

SINGULAR	PLURAL
one *watchdog*	two *watchdogs*
a *woman*	several *women*
one *journey*	many *journeys*
the *knife*	six *knives*
one *sheep*	twenty-nine *sheep*

3.   Nouns may change form to show ownership or relationship.

Nouns change form to show possession by adding an apostrophe (') and an *-s* or an apostrophe alone. The possessive form of a noun usually shows that one noun possesses another.

> *Ira's* saxophone   *Melinda's* jokes

The possessive form may also indicate the relationship of one noun to another.

> the *committee's* recommendations   the *siren's* wail

See pages 318–320 for rules about forming the possessive of nouns.

4.   Nouns may be formed with a *noun suffix*, such as *-ation*, *-ism*, *-ment*, *-ness*, and *-ance*.

When one of these suffixes is added to another word, the resulting word is always a noun. You can learn to recognize nouns by learning noun suffixes.

prepare + *-ation*	=	preparation
tour + *-ism*	=	tourism
measure + *-ment*	=	measurement
silly + *-ness*	=	silliness
utter + *-ance*	=	utterance

Exercise 3

Many of the nouns in the following paragraphs are preceded by a determiner. Write out the paragraphs and draw a circle around each determiner and underline the noun that follows it.

Example

a. Betsy Kregenow, a ninth-grader in my homeroom, has found a job she likes.

a. *Betsy Kregenow,* $\underline{a}$ *ninth-grader in* $\overparen{my}$ *homeroom, has found* $\underline{a}$ *job she likes.*

For three months she has been working as a wrapper in The Unicorn. This gift shop on Sunset and Red Road is a special favorite with many young people. During Christmas vacation the store was so crowded that a line of customers waited outside for their turn to get in.

Betsy got her job by walking into The Unicorn one day and asking the manager for part-time work. She works every Saturday and three afternoons after school. Even though she isn't yet sixteen, Betsy is earning more than thirty dollars each week, more than she ever made as a baby-sitter. Because she has always been talented in art, Betsy makes an excellent wrapper. She uses her imagination to create new wrappings with the materials available in the store. "Each wrapping is a challenge," Betsy says proudly. "I love my work, and I love earning money."

Review Exercise A

Identify the nouns in the following paragraph from Doris Lessing's "Through the Tunnel." To determine whether a word is a noun, ask whether it names, whether it belongs to one of the noun classes, or whether it has any of the features of nouns. Write out the paragraph and underline each noun. You should find thirty nouns.[1]

He put on his goggles, fitted them tight, tested the vacuum. His hands were shaking. Then he chose the biggest stone he could carry and slipped over the edge of the rock until half of him was in the cool, enclosing water and half in the hot sun. He looked up once at the empty sky, filled his lungs once, twice, and then sank fast to the bottom with the stone. He let it go and began to count. He took the edges of the hole in his hands and drew himself into it, wriggling his shoulders in sidewise as he remembered he must, kicking himself along with his feet.

Soon he was clear inside. He was in a small rockbound hole filled with yellowish-gray water. The water was pushing him up against the roof. The roof was sharp and pained his back. He pulled himself along with his hands—fast, fast—and used his legs as levers. His head knocked against something; a sharp pain dizzied him.

Mastery Exercise A

Read the following paragraphs, written by a woman who in 1963 underwent serious brain surgery. Using any of the ways you have learned to identify nouns, you should be able to list at least fifty nouns on a sheet of paper. Be prepared to say how you identified each noun.

---

[1]Specified excerpt from "Through the Tunnel" in *The Habit of Loving* by Doris Lessing. Originally published in *The New Yorker*. Copyright © 1955 by Doris Lessing. Reprinted by permission of Harper & Row, Publishers, Inc. and Curtis Brown, Ltd. on behalf of Doris Lessing.

I was handicapped cosmetically, my face was changed, and the voice I heard when I talked was not familiar. I walked with a stagger. I just knew I would never be accepted by society like this, and I kept thinking, "Why did this have to happen to me?"

For recreation, my family persuaded me to accompany them to shopping centers, out to lunch, or to concerts. They were gentle and considerate and guided me over curbstones, up and down escalators, across streets, and through crowds of people who eyed me curiously. They urged me to stand on my own two feet and face the world alone. I tried walking around my block, but I simply could not stand the mocking laughter of children nor the giggles of some neighbors. When I walked to the shops alone, clerks gave me disdainful glances and occasionally would toss my purchases at me. Once in a while some crank would telephone me and taunt me. How did I react to the jeers and sarcastic remarks? Usually I cried, and sometimes even enjoyed my suffering. For months, I became a recluse.

One day this thought occurred to me, "Why are you wasting your energy in feeling sorry for yourself—you don't have time for that. You cannot help the way that people perceive you to be—an ugly derelict." So I forgave myself for looking like I did, I began to feel sorry for everyone who could not empathize with another person's problem. I watched for quiet, sad-looking people on the street, in the stores, on the bus. I spoke to them, we shared a lovely day, a bird's song, a shower—whatever. Suddenly, each day was brighter. I was smiling again—just like the doctor said I would be able to do. I found another way to smile. I practiced putting enthusiasm into my voice. I even developed a pretty good sense of humor.[1]

Mastery Exercise B

Choose two paragraphs from a magazine, newspaper, or book you have read. Then use the various ways you have learned for recognizing nouns to identify all of the nouns in the paragraphs. Finally make a list of the nouns on a sheet of paper and be prepared to explain how you identified each one.

Using Nouns

In the following sections you will practice forming the regular and irregular plurals of nouns, including compound nouns, and the possessives of nouns. The writing exercise will help you to use concrete nouns and proper nouns to add specific details to your writing.

Forming the Regular Plurals of Nouns

Most nouns form their plural with -s or -es added to the singular form. These are called *regular plurals.*

Add the suffix -s to form the regular plural of most nouns.

---

[1] Reprinted from *Shyness* by Philip G. Zimbardo, Copyright © 1977, by permission of Addison-Wesley Publishing Co., Reading, MA.

SINGULAR	PLURAL
one *yacht*	two *yachts*
one *message*	several *messages*
one *Skylab*	three *Skylabs*

Add the suffix *-es* to form the regular plural of nouns ending in *s*, *sh*, *ch*, *x*, or *z*.

SINGULAR	PLURAL
one *pass*	four *passes*
one *push*	many *pushes*
a *watch*	two *watches*
one *fox*	several *foxes*
one *waltz*	endless *waltzes*

Add the suffix *-s* to form the plural of nouns ending in *o* preceded by a vowel. Nouns that end in *o* and have to do with music also form their plurals by adding the suffix *-s*.

SINGULAR	PLURAL
one *rodeo*	many *rodeos*
one *studio*	two *studios*
one *soprano*	a dozen *sopranos*
one *trio*	several *trios*

Add the suffix *-es* to form the plural of some nouns ending in *o* preceded by a consonant.

SINGULAR	PLURAL
one *tomato*	three *tomatoes*
a *potato*	several *potatoes*
an *embargo*	both *embargoes*

However, many nouns ending in *o* preceded by a consonant may be spelled either with an *-s* or *-es*. If you are not sure how to spell the plural of a noun ending in *o*, it is a good idea to use a dictionary. The following entries tell you that both spellings are acceptable for *mosquito*, *halo*, and *volcano*.

mos·qui·to *n., pl.* -toes, -tos
ha·lo *n., pl.* -los, -loes
vol·ca·no *n., pl.* -noes, -nos

Add the suffix *-s* or *-es* to a proper name to form the plural.

Alan McCrary's family are the *McCrarys*.
Amelia Esteves' family are the *Esteveses*.
Harriet Orloff's family are the *Orloffs*.
Barry Thomas' family are the *Thomases*.
Jenny Jones' family are the *Joneses*.

Exercise 1

Write out the following sentences and change each *italicized* noun to its plural form by adding either *-s* or *-es*. Underline the nouns you make plural.

Example

a. Gas drove the *miner* from the *tunnel*.

a. *Gases* drove the *miners* from the *tunnels*.

1. When the *stitch* ripped, the *seam* of the *shirt* opened.

2. Suzanna waited for the *phone call* from her *boyfriend*, who had won the first *prize* at the *rodeo*.

3. Contrary to folk *belief* the white *spot* on your *fingernail* came from mild damage to the *nail*.

4. The *hero* and *heroine* in native American mythology often trick their *opponent* to achieve their *goal*.

5. The VIP *pass* admitted the *soprano* to the *concert* by the visiting *orchestra*.

6. "Did you hear that!" the *princess* exclaimed. "The loud *noise* came from the *closet* in the queen's *chamber*."

7. Hungarian composer Franz Liszt could play the difficult piano *composition* while balancing the *glass* of water on the *back* of his *hand*.

8. During the Colonial period the New England mill *owner* used the *movement* of the *tide* to power their *waterwheel*, which in turn moved the *grindstone*.

9. The *student* in Mrs. Beckwith's *class* interviewed the elderly *resident* of the *ghetto* to ask for the *recommendation* for improving the community.

10. In Carl Sandburg's poem about *war*, *grass* covered the *battlefield* and the dead *soldier*.

Forming the Irregular Plurals of Nouns

Nouns that are not made plural with *-s* or *-es* added to the singular form have irregular plurals.

For most nouns that end in *y*, change the *y* to an *i* before adding the suffix *-es*.

SINGULAR	PLURAL
one *party*	many *parties*
one *bureaucracy*	several *bureaucracies*
one *battery*	two *batteries*

For nouns that end in *y* preceded by a vowel, simply add the suffix *-s* to the singular form.

SINGULAR	PLURAL
one *monkey*	three *monkeys*
one *Saturday*	several *Saturdays*

Some of the most common irregular plurals are formed by changing an internal vowel sound.

SINGULAR	PLURAL	SINGULAR	PLURAL
tooth	te**e**th	man	m**e**n
foot	f**ee**t	goose	g**ee**se
woman	wom**e**n	mouse	m**i**ce

Most nouns ending in *f* or *fe* simply add *s* to form the regular plural.

SINGULAR	PLURAL	SINGULAR	PLURAL
roof	roof**s**	safe	safe**s**
belief	belief**s**	puff	puff**s**
handkerchief	handkerchief**s**	sheriff	sheriff**s**

For many nouns ending in *fe* or *f*, change the *f* to a *v* before adding the suffix *-es*.

SINGULAR	PLURAL	SINGULAR	PLURAL
calf	cal**ves**	self	sel**ves**
elf	el**ves**	sheaf	shea**ves**
half	hal**ves**	shelf	shel**ves**
knife	kni**ves**	thief	thie**ves**
leaf	lea**ves**	wife	wi**ves**
life	li**ves**	wolf	wol**ves**
loaf	loa**ves**		

Some nouns have the same form for the singular and plural.

Many of these nouns name fish or other animals. The following words use the same form for both singular and plural.

bass	deer	moose	sheep
carp	fish	pike	trout
cattle	grouse	salmon	

Nick caught one rainbow *trout*.	[singular]
Nick caught three rainbow *trout*.	[plural]

Nouns that name people who live in certain countries also use the same form for both singular and plural.

Chinese	Japanese	Portuguese	Swiss

A *Japanese* painted this scroll ninety years ago.	[singular]
Four *Japanese* painted these scrolls ninety years ago.	[plural]

Some nouns form their plurals by a change of spelling.

SINGULAR	PLURAL	SINGULAR	PLURAL
alumnus	alumni	hypothesis	hypotheses
basis	bases	index	indexes *or* indices
child	children	ox	oxen
crisis	crises	phenomenon	phonomena
datum	data	radius	radii *or* radiuses

Be sure to check a dictionary if you are in doubt about the plural form of any noun.

Exercise 2

Some of the *italicized* nouns in the following sentences have irregular plurals. Write out each sentence and change each *italicized* noun to its proper plural form. Underline the nouns you change.

Example

a. The *mouse* plundered the *grocery* on the *shelf* of the storeroom.

a. The <u>mice</u> plundered the <u>groceries</u> on the <u>shelves</u> of the storeroom.

1. Do you know the *basis* for their *hypothesis* about the causes of the death of *pike*, *bass*, and other *fish* in the canals?

2. The *goose* hissed furiously at the fox and didn't budge from the safety of the barnyard *roof.*

3. The *wife* of the *man* on the football team suffered through the *crisis* of each season.

4. In the *story* the *elf* stole the *loaf* of immortal bread that the *chef* of the *dwarf* had baked.

5. Can you think of any way to gather *datum* to test the *theory* that the *woman* in all cultures can soothe crying *baby* better than the *man?*

6. The *child* kept careful track of how much money the tooth *fairy* left for their old *tooth.*

7. On *Sunday* jugglers, clowns, trained *monkey*, and tame *deer* entertained the *family* at the hospital.

8. The howls of the *wolf* in the night warned the *herdsman* of the danger to the *sheep.*

9. On the *journey* through the *valley* and rain forests, the *donkey* are reliably surefooted.

10. *Potato* that baked in piles of burning *leaf*, eaten steaming hot with salt, were called *Mickey*, one of the *delicacy* of fall.

Forming the Plurals of Compound Nouns

When compound nouns are written as one word, the plural is formed by making the last word of the compound plural.

SINGULAR	PLURAL
one *tablespoonful*	four *tablespoonfuls*
one *butterfly*	many *butterflies*
one *Dutchman*	a crowd of *Dutchmen*
one *playwright*	several *playwrights*
one *teenager*	three *teenagers*
one *teakettle*	some *teakettles*

The one exception to this rule is *passer-by*, whose plural is *passers-by*.

When compound nouns are written as separate words or as hyphenated words, the plural is formed by making the most important word in the compound plural.

SINGULAR	PLURAL
one *player piano*	two *player pianos*
one *fox terrier*	sixteen *fox terriers*
one *sister-in-law*	all of the *sisters-in-law*
one *man-at-arms*	two *men-at-arms*

Sometimes, it is difficult to know which is the main word in a compound noun, as with *sixteen-year-olds* and *merry-go-rounds*. When in doubt, check your dictionary for the spelling of plural forms of compound nouns.

Exercise 3

Each of the following sentences contains one or more compound nouns in its singular form, as well as other nouns with irregular plurals. Rewrite the sentence and change each *italicized* noun to its plural form. Underline the compound nouns you make plural.

Example
a. Who found the *rain check* for the *playoff*?
a. Who found the <u>rain checks</u> for the *playoffs*?

1. The *congresswoman* announced the *press conference* to be held during the *weekend*.

2. On sunny days *two-year-old*, *senior citizen*, and all ages in between enjoy the antique *merry-go-round* near the zoo.

3. The *passer-by* dialed 911, and two *policeman* arrived within five minutes after the *pickup* had crashed.

4. Whenever the *town meeting* became unruly, the *sergeant-at-arms* would bang the gavels and call for quiet.

5. The *teenager* carved *nutcracker* in the shapes of rugged *woodsman* and laughing *housewife*.

6. To relieve the stings of *Portuguese man-of-war* and other *jellyfish*, the *lifeguard* recommended applying unseasoned meat tenderizer immediately.

7. According to the *cookbook* several *tablespoon* of raisins and two *teaspoon* of shredded coconut may be added to *bowlful* of steamed rice.

8. At which *university* did the *attorney-general* meet to discuss gun control and other *crisis* in law enforcement?

9. Nadia's *sister-in-law* worked on the *assembly line* at several different automobile manufacturing *company*.

10. The *beekeeper* gathered the *cupful* of honey produced by the *honeybee* from *wildflower*.

Forming the Possessives of Nouns

The *possessive* form of a noun shows ownership or possession.

> Elaine wrote a report on *George Washington Carver's* work.
> Have you seen *Theo's* new roller skates?

The possessive form of a noun may also show relationship or origin.

> Two veterinary students attended the *calf's* birth.
>
> Some of *Thomas Jefferson's* ideas were dropped from the Declaration of Independence.

Form the possessive of a singular noun by adding an apostrophe (') and an -*s*.

SINGULAR NOUN	POSSESSIVE FORM
the coat of the *collie*	the *collie's* coat
the front tire of the *bus*	the *bus's* front tire
a novel by *James Baldwin*	*James Baldwin's* novel

When a singular noun that ends in *s* has more than one syllable, the possessive may also be formed by adding only the apostrophe.

the *compass'* needle	*Jesus'* words
for *completeness'* sake	*Douglas'* illness

Form the possessive of a plural noun ending in *s* by adding an apostrophe only.

the signals of the *referees*	the *referees'* signals
the armies of the *nations*	the *nations'* armies

Form the possessive of a plural noun that does not end in -*s* by adding an apostrophe and an -*s*.

You will recognize the nouns whose plurals do not end in -*s* as irregular plurals. (See pages 314–316.) Fortunately there are not many of them. Remember that it is necessary to add both an apostrophe and an -*s* to form the possessive of an irregular plural.

the rights of *women*	*women's* rights
the drawings of the *children*	the *children's* drawings
the feathers of the *geese*	the *geese's* feathers

Exercise 4

Write out the following sentences and supply the possessive form of each noun given in parentheses. Check whether the noun is singular or plural before you form its possessive. Underline the possessive nouns you form.

Examples

a. _____ brakes must be inspected regularly for safety. (cars)

a. Cars' brakes must be inspected regularly for safety.

b. The _____ crying didn't disturb the _____ calm. (babies, nurses)

b. *The babies' crying didn't disturb the nurses' calm.*

1. The _____ recommendations were made immediately after reading each _____ paper. (committee, student)

2. Each _____ representatives met to discuss the _____ food crisis. (country, world)

3. The _____ locker room is on the opposite side of the gym from the _____ locker room. (boys, girls)

4. Seven _____ work is shown in the _____ annual exhibit of young artists. (artists, museum)

5. _____ _____ birthdays are all in the month of February. (Phyllis, children)

6. Have you seen Mrs. _____ prize-winning roses? (Montoya)

7. Where is the sale of _____ shirts and _____ blouses? (men, ladies)

8. The executive committee of the _____ union voted to improve _____ hospitalization benefits. (carpenters, members)

9. The _____ responsibilities include serving on juries, listening carefully to _____ speeches, voting in elections, and becoming aware of the _____ problems. (citizens, candidates, community)

10. Jenny _____ goal is to visit each of the _____ national parks. (Michelmas, United States)

When two or more persons possess something in common, only the last person mentioned is in the possessive form.

> We visited *Sean* and *Moira's* grandparents.
> The *dog* and *cats'* owner left without feeding the animals.

Only the last noun is made possessive in names of companies and organizations and in hyphenated nouns.

> *Petry and Goldfarb's* catalogue lists kits for making leather moccasins.

> The *National Organization of Women's* platform calls for the equality of women and men.

> During the noisy meeting the *sergeant-at-arms'* gavel broke.

When two or more persons possess something separately, each noun is in the possessive form.

> Did you see the inaugural gowns of *Washington's*, *Lincoln's*, and *Eisenhower's* wives?

> The *candidates'* and the *moderator's* speeches were brief and to the point.

In the following expressions of time and amount, the possessive form of the noun is used.

AMOUNT	TIME
twenty *cents'* worth	six *minutes'* pause
a *dime's* worth	two *hours'* delay
two *dollars'* value	a *day's* work
three *weeks'* vacation	a *month's* absence

Exercise 5

Write out the following sentences, adding possessive forms of nouns where necessary. Underline the possessive forms.

Examples

a. Jeff and Sheila mother works in the president office.
a. Jeff and Sheila's mother works in the president's office.

b. Milan and Company new offices are in the Leader Building.
b. Milan and Company's new offices are in the Leader Building.

1. There will be two hours delay before the plane can take off.

2. Many of Welloff, Ramirez, and Company clients speak only Spanish.

3. Bob and Gwen sailboat sank when it crashed against the rocks.

4. At the end of every season, the students and faculty basketball teams play against each other.

5. Russian Jews have many years wait for immigration visas to Israel.

6. The orchestra and choir performance of Handel's *Messiah* was an outstanding achievement for high school musicians.

7. In the first half of the game, the players and cheerleaders uniforms were completely soaked.

8. Amy and David parents have been separated for more than a year.

9. "I remember when a nickel worth of candy was a big bagful," Grandpa sighed.

10. Labor and management representatives met separately to discuss the terms of the new contract.

Writing with Nouns

You can make your writing more interesting by using nouns that add specific details. Instead of using vague and abstract nouns such as *things* or *stuff*, use concrete nouns. For example, suppose that you were writing about an overnight backpack trip.

Vague: For the trip I packed *a lot of food.*
Improved: For the trip I packed *dehydrated macaroni and cheese, a large thermos of water, two peanut butter sandwiches, trail mix, and several oranges.*

Proper nouns will also make your writing more specific and informative.

> Vague: *Several composers* wrote *musical pieces* before they were ten.
> Improved: *Wolfgang Amadeus Mozart* and *Franz Schubert* wrote *symphonies* before they were ten.

Writing Exercise A

Rewrite each of the following sentences, making the writing more specific by using concrete nouns or proper nouns to replace the *italicized* words.

1. Last night I watched *some good television shows.*
2. In Washington, D.C., we visited *a lot of points of interest.*
3. *My relatives* usually get together on *holidays.*
4. I like listening to *some rock groups* better than *others.*
5. For changing a flat tire, you need to have *some special stuff.*
6. On the morning of her sixteenth birthday, Ilene found a huge bouquet of *flowers* on her doorstep.
7. I enjoyed reading *those books.*
8. When I took a walk in the woods, I saw *a lot of things.*
9. The children applauded the *animals* in the circus parade.
10. *Many black Americans* have made important contributions to American history.

Review Exercise A

Write out the following sentences, making each of the *italicized* nouns plural. Underline the plurals that you write.

Example

a. The *foot* of the *child* should not be muddy.
a. *The feet of the children should not be muddy.*

1. She trims the *bush* and the *hedge* about once a month.
2. Did you look at all of the *datum* in the experiments with motherless *monkey?*
3. *Prince* and *princess, count* and *countess* attended the coronation *ceremony.*
4. Proudly the *parent* bragged of the *accomplishment* and *personality* of the *baby.*
5. The private *life* of *congressman* and *congresswoman* are of interest to the public.
6. Julie's *sister-in-law* and *brother-in-law* are working for advanced *degree* at *university* in southern California.
7. In the dry season it is easier to spot *alligator* and *deer* in the Everglades.
8. The police *detective* photographed the *body* in the *hallway.*

9. Do you know the *basis* for the *change* in the zoning laws?

10. *Salmon, trout,* and other *fish* are delicious when poached.

11. The *moose* lifted their heads, stared a moment, and disappeared.

12. "*Teenager* can be as difficult to live with as *two-year-old*," Mac's mother complained.

13. The *neighbor* who hired a painter to paint a dozen *roof* each saved a hundred dollars.

14. Sam and Linda built inexpensive *bookshelf* from *board* and *cement block*.

15. The *wife* of the *boxer* watched the fights nervously, fearing *knockout* and other *injury*.

16. The *attorney* filed the *brief* for the information of the court.

17. The *valley* and *gulch* are hazardous because they are filled with dry *grass*.

18. During the typhoon the *fisherman's family* waited anxiously for news of the missing *man*.

19. In order to pass her oral exam, the researcher had to defend her *hypothesis* and *method* before a committee of university *scholar*.

20. Owen threw the *loaf* of bread to the *elk*.

Review Exercise B

Rewrite each of the following sentences, putting the *italicized* nouns into their possessive form. Underline the possessive forms of the nouns.

Examples

a. Neighbors finally complained about the *dogs* barking.
a. *Neighbors finally complained about the <u>dogs'</u> barking.*

b. Do you read your horoscope in each *day* newspaper?
b. *Do you read your horoscope in each <u>day's</u> newspaper?*

1. During the two *hours* turbulence, the *stewardesses* smiles seemed strained.

2. *Charles* friend works as a sign painter in her *mother* store.

3. *Mrs. Wong* picture is in the early edition of this *morning* paper.

4. To paint the house took almost ninety *dollars* worth of paint and a *week* labor.

5. The *children* librarian showed a film about emperor *penguins* daily life in the Antarctic.

6. In China until fairly recently, all *girls* feet were bound so that adult women were small-footed and could hardly walk, characteristics thought to be a symbol of the *family* wealth.

7. Shirley MacLaine, who is *Warren Beatty* sister, set out to have a *dancer* career.

8. Who are the current world record holders for the *men* and *women* 200-meter dash?

9. Muriel and *Ricky grandfather* stamp collection contains one of the *country* most complete collections of Latin American stamps.

10. *Mr. Solomon* job is to interpret *students* scores on nationally standardized exams.

11. *Carmen* sudden appearance from Bolivia was this *week* biggest and best surprise.

12. High winds and a ten-inch snow closed *O'Hare Airport* runways and paralyzed *Chicago* streets.

13. After each of the *birds* tricks, the audience applauded the *cockatoos* and *macaws* performances.

14. We were startled to hear that the *lawyer* fee would be seventy-five dollars for each *hour* work.

15. The *actress* three daughters wrote books about their *mother* private life.

16. When the *cattle* weight kept dropping instead of increasing, *Doris* husband fired the *ranch* manager.

17. The *plumber* work on the *sinks* drains will take more than an hour.

18. *Joan mother-in-law* birthday is the same day as *Bob*.

19. *Elephants* tusks, once a popular African souvenir, are now protected by law from the ivory *hunters* greed.

20. In the *play* third act, the villain tried to marry the *boss* daughter, but she refused and went off to her job as a *printer* apprentice.

Writing Exercise B

Write at least a paragraph on one of the following suggested topics. Be as specific as possible by your careful choice of proper nouns and concrete nouns.

1. You have volunteered for one month's duty as a forest ranger atop an isolated mountain in Alaska. You will be living completely alone and will not have any visitors. There are no television or radio stations within reach. Describe what you will take along with you for your month's stay. (The cabin is already well-stocked with food and drink.)

2. As the grand prize winner on a television quiz show, you have just won the vacation of your dreams. You can choose any country in the world to visit for one week, all expenses paid. Tell where you would go and what you would expect to do and see on your vacation.

3. In your job as a newspaper reporter, you have just been assigned to write a story about someone important in your community. Write the story, telling why the person you are writing about is important and what he or she has done for the community.

4. After studying the photographs on pages 324–325, write a comparison of the two people, comparing not only the physical characteristics, but

also what you think might be the personalities of the two characters. What differences and likenesses might there be in their attitudes toward school, friends, and life in general? Is one likely to be more outgoing? Is one likely to prefer being alone? When you have finished, underline the nouns that you have used.

Understanding Pronouns

Pronouns, words that take the place of nouns, are an important part of speech because of the effect they can have on a writer's style. Without pronouns William Faulkner's famous Nobel Prize Acceptance Speech would have read in the following way.

> William Faulkner believes that man will not merely endure: man will prevail. Man is immortal, not because man alone among creatures has an inexhaustible voice, but because man has a soul, a spirit capable of compassion and sacrifice and endurance.

Instead, the use of pronouns gives the speech an eloquence it might otherwise not have had:

> I believe that man will not merely endure: he will prevail. He is immortal, not because he alone among creatures has an inexhaustible voice, but because he has a soul, a spirit capable of compassion and sacrifice and endurance.

In the following sections you will learn to identify pronouns as a first step toward using them in your own writing.

Defining Pronouns

A *pronoun* is usually defined as a word that takes the place of a noun.

The noun that the pronoun replaces and refers to is called the *antecedent* of the pronoun.

In the following examples an arrow indicates the pronouns' antecedents.

She tore a tendon in *his* knee.

Mrs. Reardon owned the *houseboat that* sank.

Wendy's parents are the *people who* complained.

A single noun may be the antecedent of several pronouns.

Donna lost *her* diving mask when *she* sat down to take off *her* flippers.

The antecedent of a pronoun may also appear in the preceding sentence.

Juan recovered the fumble and scored a *touchdown. It* was the second touchdown of the game.

Sometimes, a pronoun may take the place of another pronoun.

Both of the windows are broken again. *They* were fixed only last week.

Exercise 1

Underline the pronouns in the following sentences. Then draw an arrow from each pronoun to its antecedent. (Some sentences have more than one pronoun.)

Examples

a. The bank was crowded because its computers were broken.

a. The bank was crowded because its computers were broken.

b. Cindy was the student who wrote the editorial.

b. Cindy was the student who wrote the editorial.

1. When the racetrack closed, it was made into a park.

2. Every person who signs up for the canoeing trip must be able to swim.

3. The book that Maria thought she had lost had fallen behind her bed.

4. A reception will be given for students and their families.

5. Before she signed the forms that the bank teller gave her, Elizabeth read them carefully and found two mistakes.

6. During the school year Lee Ann volunteers twice a week at the Veterans Hospital, talking to patients and writing letters for them.

7. The project to develop the atomic bomb had a code name. It was called the Manhattan Project.

8. Craig listened to the haunting song of the Corn Festival. He never forgot it.

9. The Museum of Science is looking for volunteers for its soon-to-be-opened minitheater.

10. The poems in the literary magazine were written by students. Several are about the pains and pleasures of being in love.

Classifying Pronouns

Pronouns can be divided into the following classes: *personal, relative, interrogative, demonstrative,* and *indefinite.* In the following sections you will learn how to identify each of these kinds of pronouns.

1. *Personal Pronouns*

Personal pronouns are used to refer to one or more persons or things. Except for the pronoun *you,* personal pronouns have entirely different singular and plural forms.

	SINGULAR	PLURAL
First Person:	I, me, my, mine	we, us, our, ours
Second Person:	you, your, yours	you, your, yours
Third Person:	he, him, she, her, it, his, her, hers, its	they, them, their, theirs

The person of a pronoun tells the relationship of the pronoun to the speaker. First-person pronouns *(I, me, we, us)* refer to the speaker or to a group to which the speaker belongs.

I [the speaker] am sleepy.
We [the speaker and others] are hungry.

The second-person pronoun *you* refers to the person being spoken to. Notice that *you* is both the singular and plural form.

You [one person] are my best friend.
You [two or more persons] are my best friends.

The third-person pronouns are used to refer to persons other than the speaker who are spoken about but not addressed directly.

She is studying ballet.
They skated on the frozen pond.
It is too big for this room.

Personal pronouns have reflexive forms that are made up of the pronoun plus the word *self* or *selves.*

SINGULAR	PLURAL
myself	ourselves
yourself	yourselves
himself	
herself	themselves
itself	
oneself	

Note: The words *hisself* and *theirselves* are not acceptable in Edited Standard English.

The reflexive forms of personal pronouns may be used in two ways. They may be used reflexively to refer to the person or thing named in the subject.

On cold winter mornings Paul drags *himself* out of bed.

The baby looked at *herself* in the mirror and laughed.

The reflexive form of personal pronouns may also be used intensively to show emphasis.

The governor *herself* greeted the guests.

Albert Einstein *himself* tutored his young neighbor in math.

Exercise 2

In the order they appear, list the personal pronouns in the following paragraphs from Caroline Bird's essay on queuing (standing in line). Remember that in contractions such as *I'd* and *you're*, list only the pronoun.[1]

People and things can be lined up by the speed at which they move so that fast movers are not slowed to the pace of slow movers ahead of them. High-speed lanes for cars, toll lines reserved for those with exact change, and express checkout counters in supermarkets line up or queue the fast movers.

People react strongly, and variously to being queued. Russians line themselves up without being told. Moscow theater audiences file out, last row first like school children marching out of assemblies. In America, on the contrary, theatrical performances break up like the Arctic ice in springtime. Commuters and the constitutionally impatient gather themselves for a dash up the aisle, while the rest of the audience is still applauding. Fidgeters and people who can't bear having anyone ahead of them sidle across rows to emergency exits, while placid souls who seem to enjoy the presence of others drift happily up the aisle with the crowd. In Moscow, the theater is emptied faster. In New York, you can get out fast if you're willing to work at it.

Even on a first-come, first-served basis, Americans don't like queues. Rather than put some people in front of other people, we prefer to row them up horizontally on the starting line and let the best man win, the way they did when they shot off a gun to open the Oklahoma land rush. West Indians like queuing even less. There were so many bus-boarding accidents in Bridgetown that the British-bred Barbados Assembly passed a law requiring passengers to form a line of not more than two abreast whenever six or more persons were waiting for a bus.

---

[1] Excerpt from "Queue" from *The Crowding Syndrome* by Caroline Bird. Copyright © 1972 by Caroline Bird. Reprinted by permission of Caroline Bird. Reprinted by permission of Alfred A. Knopf, Inc.; McIntosh and Otis, Inc.; and Martin Secker & Warburg Limited.

2. *Relative Pronouns*

A *relative pronoun* is used to introduce a subordinate clause. The relative pronoun connects the clause to some other word in the sentence.

Peter's taco casserole, *which* won first prize, is delicious.
The newspaper *that* we found in the attic is dated 1798.

When the following words are used to introduce subordinate clauses, they function as relative pronouns.

which	who	whose
that	whom	

See pages 469–477 for a full discussion of subordinate clauses.

3. *Interrogative Pronouns*

An *interrogative pronoun* is used to ask a question.

Who is the prime minister of Canada?
For *whom* is the telegram?
Which is Yolanda's boyfriend?
What is the capital of Nevada?

The following words function as interrogative pronouns when they stand alone to introduce a question.

who	whose	what
whom	which	

When one of these words modifies a noun, however, it is not an interrogative pronoun but a modifier.

What is the answer?	[interrogative pronoun]
What answer did you give?	[modifier]
Which is your apartment?	[interrogative pronoun]
Which apartment is yours?	[modifier]

4. *Demonstrative Pronouns*

A *demonstrative pronoun* is used to point out a specific person, place, thing, or idea.

This is my first painting.
That is Beethoven's second symphony.
These are bromeliads, or air plants.
Those are the highest mountains in Peru.

There are only four demonstrative pronouns:

this	that	these	those

When one of these words is used before a noun, it is an adjective, not a demonstrative pronoun.

These are my most comfortable shoes. [demonstrative pronoun]

These shoes are extremely comfortable. [adjective]

Have you seen *this*? [demonstrative pronoun]

Have you seen *this* movie? [adjective]

5. *Indefinite Pronouns*

An *indefinite pronoun* does not refer to a specific person or thing. Indefinite pronouns may take the place of a noun in a sentence but often do not have antecedents.

No one knew what time the party was supposed to start.
Few of the tomatoes were ripe.
During the storm the lifeguard told *everyone* to get out of the pool.

Most indefinite pronouns have either singular or plural meanings.

SINGULAR INDEFINITE PRONOUNS

anybody	everyone	no one
anyone	much	one
each	neither	somebody
either	nobody	someone
everybody		

PLURAL INDEFINITE PRONOUNS

both	few	many	others	several

A few indefinite pronouns, however, can be either singular or plural, depending on how they are used in a sentence.

all	any	most	none	some

All the money was stolen. [singular]
All the windows are open. [plural]
None of the seeds have sprouted. [plural]
None of the mail has arrived. [singular]

Exercise 3

Write out the following sentences. Underline each pronoun and identify the class to which it belongs.

Example

a. What is the deadline for filing your income tax?

a. *What is the deadline for filing your income tax.*

What—interrogative pronoun; your—personal pronoun

1. Someone started to laugh, and before long everyone was laughing.

2. Your grandfather is married to Alice's aunt's sister, who is my Aunt Sadie.

3. Which is the fire station closest to our house?

4. All of the applicants who were accepted have two weeks to notify the college of their decision.

5. "Whose are these?" she asked, holding up a tattered, grimy pair of sneakers.

6. The Gallarzos use their car only for their business, which is delivering home-cooked meals to families who subscribe to their service.

7. Much of the fair was devoted to a flea market that seemed to have something for everybody.

8. This is the fish that Mike himself caught and filleted for us.

9. "Don't put your babies to bed with a bottle," the dentist warned, "or the sugar in the milk will rot their teeth."

10. No one that I know can play the oboe.

Finding a Pronoun by Its Features

Pronouns have three features that distinguish them from other parts of speech. Personal pronouns have all three of these features; most other kinds of pronouns have at least one.

1. A pronoun may be *singular* or *plural*.

Personal, reflexive, demonstrative, and indefinite pronouns have singular or plural meanings.

SINGULAR	PLURAL
I	we
he, she, it	them
myself	ourselves
himself, herself, itself	themselves
this, that	these, those
each, neither, everybody	both, many, several
anybody, no one, one	few, others

Pronoun-verb agreement is discussed on pages 362–363.

Pronouns with singular meanings take the singular form of the verb, while pronouns with plural meanings take the plural form of the verb.

Each of the representatives *is* here.   [singular]
Many of the representatives *are* here.   [plural]

Relative pronouns and interrogative pronouns do not show number. The same forms are used with both singular and plural antecedents.

2. Pronouns may *change form* to show their function in a sentence.

Only personal pronouns have this characteristic. Personal pronouns have both subject forms and object forms.

SUBJECT FORMS	OBJECT FORMS
I, we	me, us
you	you
he, she, it, they	him, her, it, them

The subject form of the pronoun is used when the pronoun functions as the subject of the sentence or as a complement.

Subject: *She* bought a pair of tan leather boots.

Complement: The winners of the contest were Jeff and *I.*

The object form of the personal pronoun is used when the pronoun functions as a direct object, an indirect object, or the object of a preposition.

Direct Object: Please call *me* tonight.

Indirect Object: The letter carrier handed *me* a tiny package.

Object of Preposition: The package wasn't for *me.*

3. Pronouns may show *gender*.

Personal and reflexive pronouns may be masculine, feminine, or neuter.

Masculine: he, him, his, himself

Feminine: she, her, hers, herself

Neuter: it, its, itself

Words like *I*, *me*, and *myself* can be either masculine or feminine, depending on the speaker. Words like *they*, *them*, *we*, and *us* may refer either to groups of men or of women or to mixed groups of both sexes, depending on the context.

Exercise 4

Write out the following sentences, underlining all pronouns. Beneath each sentence identify the class to which each pronoun belongs.

Example

a. None of the women at the court of French queen Catherine de Medici could have her waistline larger than thirteen inches.

a. *None of the women at the court of French queen Catherine de Medici could have her waistline larger than thirteen inches.*
none—indefinite; her—personal

1. What is the work of Mother Teresa of Calcutta, who won the Nobel Peace Prize in 1979?

2. Raoul says that his favorite record is a collection of gospel songs and hymns by Marian Anderson.

3. Benjamin Franklin, who believed fasting benefits everyone, wrote in his *Poor Richard's Almanack*, "Eat few suppers and you'll need few medicines."

4. Do you know the original names of Johnny Appleseed, Pancho Villa, and the Sundance Kid?

5. The daily calorie intake of people who live in the United States is almost twice that of those who live in Haiti and Algeria.

6. To purify water let it settle for twenty-four hours and then boil it for three to five minutes.

7. Frank Sinatra, Dick Cavett, and Eleanor Roosevelt have something in common; they are only children.

8. In 1969 a Kansas insurance salesman vowed he would eat a frog if the Jets beat the Colts in the Super Bowl, and they did.

9. The Russian empress Catherine the Great kept her hairdresser in an iron cage in her room for three years so no one would find out that she wore a wig.

10. About 50,000 persons who live in the southeastern section of East Germany speak Sorbian, which has two distinct dialects—one resembling Polish and the other resembling Czech.

11. Before she took up flying, Amelia Earhart was a truck driver, a pre-med student, and a social worker.

12. All of the 3,500 members of The Bald-Headed Men of America believe "bald is beautiful."

13. Few of the ghosts that have been reported by excited observers have ever been sighted by others.

14. Anybody who smokes more than two packs of cigarettes a day can expect to lose eight years from his or her life.

15. Euphemia Allen, a sixteen-year-old British girl, wrote "Chopsticks" in 1877 and published it under a male pseudonym.

16. *I Heard the Owl Call My Name* by Margaret Craven is about a young vicar who works with the Tsawataineuk tribe in Kingcome Village, British Columbia.

17. Someone at General Motors has designed a robot named Sophisticated Sam, who bleeds and bruises like us and is used to test auto safety.

18. Fritz Perls, the late Gestalt therapist, told his patients and all who would listen to him to live in the "here and now."

19. On a windy day in November 1955, with a temperature of zero degrees F., only one person paid to see Washington State play its opponent, San Jose State. That was the worst paid attendance on record.

20. When he produced his first automobile, Henry Ford overlooked something important. He forgot to put a reverse gear in it.

Mastery Exercise A

Using what you have learned about pronouns, identify the thirty pronouns in the following paragraphs from Daniel Cohen's *Supermonsters*. List the pronouns on a sheet of paper in the order they appear; beside each pronoun write the class to which it belongs.[1]

> At one time practically everybody believed in magic. In magic, if something looks like something else, then in a way it becomes like that other thing. To people who believed in magic, when someone put on a wolf skin, then in a sense he became like a wolf.

---

[1] Reprinted by permission of Dodd, Mead & Company, Inc., Daniel Cohen, Henry Morrison, Inc. from pages 80–81 of *Supermonsters* by Daniel Cohen. Copyright © 1977 by Daniel Cohen.

There was another reason for putting on animal skins. If you wore an animal disguise, no one knew who you were. You could do things without being recognized. Twenty years ago there was a series of brutal murders in Africa. Victims were attacked at night and when they were alone. Their bodies were often badly slashed. It looked as if they had been killed by a wild animal.

Investigators found out that animals were not responsible. The killers were a group of hired murderers called "leopard men." They were paid to kill certain people. Before they went out they put on leopard skins. Their costumes were also armed with sharp steel claws.

These costumes terrified people. Many thought that the killings were being done by leopards. While a "leopard man" was in his costume, no one knew who he was. The "leopard men" also spread the rumor that they really could turn into animals. They hoped to frighten people into keeping quiet about them.

The police finally broke up the gang. Many "leopard men" were imprisoned or executed. But gangs like this in the past could have led to a belief in were-wolves or other were-animals.

Using Pronouns

In the next sections you will learn the features of pronoun usage that are a part of Edited Standard English. You will also practice using pronouns in your own writing.

Agreement in Number and Gender

A pronoun must *agree* with its antecedent in number.

When an *antecedent* is singular, the pronoun used to refer to it must be singular.

Even if the antecedent is followed by a prepositional phrase containing a plural noun, the antecedent remains singular, and a singular pronoun is used.

Everyone on the girls' swim team has *her* lifesaving certificate.

Each of my brothers has *his* own key.

When the antecedent is plural, a plural pronoun is used to refer to it.

Several of the boys have finished *their* reports.

Many of the women have improved *their* bowling averages.

A list of singular and plural indefinite pronouns is on page 330.

The pronouns *all*, *any*, *some*, and *none* may be either singular or plural in meaning, depending on their use in a sentence.

Some of the snakes have shed *their* skins.　　　　　[plural meaning]

Some of the lawn is full of weeds, but the rest of *it* is fine.　　　　　[singular meaning]

When two or more singular antecedents are joined by *and*, a plural pronoun is used to refer to them.

Lin and Kiyuku always do *their* share of the cooking and cleaning.

Noah and his family were glad when *their* ark hit dry land.

When two or more singular antecedents are joined by *or* or *nor*, a singular pronoun is used to refer to them.

Either Gregg or Pablo will bring *his* thermos.

Neither Kate nor Annemarie has finished *her* speech.

A pronoun must agree with its antecedent in gender.

When a singular antecedent is clearly masculine, the pronouns *he, him,* or *his* are used. *She, her,* or *hers* are used to refer to singular feminine antecedents; *it* and *its* are used when the antecedent is neuter.

One of the Burpee sisters is getting *her* master's degree in chemistry.

The boy in the yellow jacket left *his* book on the counter.

The class watched as the moth emerged from *its* pupa.

In the past, students have been taught to use a singular masculine pronoun *(he, him, his)* when the antecedent is a singular indefinite pronoun.

Everyone should bring *his* lunch on Saturday.

Critics have pointed out that such use of language is not fair to women, since the indefinite pronoun usually refers to a mixed group of women and men. In such sentences it would be better to use the expression *his or her* or to reword the sentence so that the antecedent is plural.

Everyone should bring *his or her* lunch.

All of the students should bring *their* lunches.

Students should bring *their* lunches.

Exercise 1

Additional exercises are on pages 423–424.

Write out the following sentences and choose the pronoun in parentheses that agrees with its antecedents. Underline the pronoun you have chosen.

Examples

a. Neither Barbara nor Ellie knows (her, their) Social Security number.

a. *Neither Barbara nor Ellie knows her Social Security number.*

b. Each of the puppies wagged (their, its) tail.

b. *Each of the puppies wagged its tail.*

1. Each of the women has (her, their) own savings account.

2. Someone must have dropped (his, his or her) car keys.

3. Neither Carmelita nor her mother could find (her, their) watch.

4. In the past, several of the carpenters have volunteered (his or her, their) services for the auction.

5.   None of the teachers have used up all of (his or her, their) sick days.

6.   All of the committee members have worked hard to get (his, their) neighbors to attend the block meeting.

7.   Either Tamar or her mother will have (her, their) hair cut before the holidays.

8.   Both Sonia and her sister are famous for (her, their) baking.

9.   Either Frank or Rudolfo will give (his, their) acceptance speech when the election results are announced.

10.   The precinct captains called all of the registered voters to see if (he, they) had voted.

Using Subject Pronouns

The *subject form* of the personal pronoun (sometimes called the *nominative case*) includes the following pronouns.

SINGULAR	PLURAL
I, you, he, she, it	we, you, they

Subject and object forms of personal pronouns cannot be used interchangeably. Each form performs certain specific functions in a sentence.

1.   Use a *subject form* of the personal pronoun when the pronoun is the subject of a sentence.

The androids and *they* met on the football field.
Juanita and *he* are engaged.

Predicate pronouns are discussed on pages 436–437.

2.   Use a *subject pronoun* when the pronoun follows a form of the verb *be* and renames or identifies the subject of the sentence.

The last person to arrive was *he.*
My closest friends are Dave and *she.*

The expression "It's me" is acceptable in informal speaking. However, in formal situations and in Edited Standard English, the subject form of the pronoun is required in sentences such as the following ones.

When the caller asked for Kathleen, she said, "This is *she.*"
It's *they* who are causing all of the trouble.

Most mistakes in pronoun usage occur when the pronoun is part of a compound subject or complement. Which pronoun is correct in the following sentence?

Rudy and (I, me) went for a walk to Lorenzo's.

Try each pronoun alone as the subject of the sentence to see which form sounds right.

As asterisk (*) indicates a sentence with a feature that is not part of Edited Standard English (ESE).

*Me went for a walk to Lorenzo's.
I went for a walk to Lorenzo's.
Rudy and *I* went for a walk to Lorenzo's.

Try this method to find the correct pronoun in the following sentence.

Have you and (her, she) been to the Sunshine Skateway?

*Has her been to the Sunshine Skateway?
Has *she* been to the Sunshine Skateway?
Have you and *she* been to the Sunshine Skateway?

Exercise 2
Write out the following sentences. Choose the pronoun that correctly completes each sentence and underline the pronoun.

Examples
a. Cheryl and (she, her) were late for choir rehearsal.
a. *Cheryl and she were late for choir rehearsal.*
b. Armando and (I, me) have the same birthday.
b. *Armando and I have the same birthday.*

1. Either Peggy or (him, he) will give the nominating speech.
2. The people who scored highest on the test were Benjamin, Evelyn, and (me, I).
3. Commissioner Menendez and (she, her) talked for an hour about how to improve the community's relations with the police.
4. The likeliest suspects in the mystery novel were the doctor and (her, she).
5. Will you and (her, she) come to the grievance committee meeting?
6. Last year's winners of the Citizenship Awards were Rosa and (she, her).
7. (Him and me, He and I) made twenty dollars on Saturday washing cars.
8. Have Larry and (them, they) had their gamma globulin shots yet?
9. (Them and us, They and we) are entering the Golden Games.
10. Did you know that you and (me, I) are second cousins once removed?

Using Object Pronouns

The *object form* of the personal pronoun is sometimes called the *objective case.*

SINGULAR	PLURAL
me, you, him, her, it	us, you, them

1. Use an *object form* of the personal pronoun when the pronoun is the *direct object.*

Duane sent Louise and *me* to Topeka.
Karim and her dad found *us* on the pier.

2. Use an *object form* of the personal pronoun when the pronoun is the *indirect object*.

Jennie sent Lynn and *me* alpaca sweaters from Ecuador.
The officer gave *us* several reasons why we couldn't park there.

3. Use an *object form* of the personal pronoun when the pronoun is the *object of a preposition*.

Just between you and *me*, I think this painting is ridiculous.
Did you ask for Mrs. Wing or for *her?*

4. Use an *object form* of the personal pronoun when the pronoun is the *subject*, *object*, or *predicate pronoun* of an infinitive.

The infinitive form of the verb begins with the word *to: to dance, to weep, to sing*. Infinitive phrases have subjects, objects, and complements just as sentences do.

The committee wants *her* to run for governor.
[*Her* is the subject of the infinitive *to run*.]

I asked the doctor to call *me*.
[*Me* is the object of the infinitive *to call*.]

Mom and Dad want the winner to be *me*.
[*Me* is the predicate pronoun following the infinitive *to be*; it renames the subject *winner*.]

Infinitive phrases are discussed on pages 457–458.

Confusion over which form of the pronoun to use is most likely to occur when the pronoun is part of a compound construction. Try the pronoun alone to see which form sounds better.

Did you see Tiija and (she, her) at the football game?
*Did you see she at the football game?
Did you see *her* at the football game?
Did you see Tiija and *her* at the football game?

An asterisk (*) indicates a sentence with a feature that is not part of Edited Standard English (ESE).

Exercise 3

Write out the following sentences. Choose the pronoun that correctly completes each sentence and underline the pronoun.

Examples

a. Dr. Greenfield sent Tom and (she, her) tickets to the opera.
a. Dr. Greenfield sent Tom and her tickets to the opera.

b. Please give these apples to Dottie or (he, him).
b. Please give these apples to Dottie or him.

1. Wendy hugged Frank, Jeff, and (I, me) and then boarded the train.
2. When you fill out this form, ask Ms. White or (she, her) for help.

3. Before handing out the diplomas, the principal congratulated all of the parents and (us, we).

4. I'd like to ask Owen and (her, she) to come to my party.

5. Please tell Mercedes and (he, him) the story of your broken leg.

6. Mom has promised to build Jeff and (me, I) new bookcases.

7. At the Beethoven Fest we sat in the row behind Barry and (her, she).

8. The ghosts in the church steeple turned out to be Mac and (he, him).

9. Can you give Susie or (me, I) the petitions when they're signed?

10. Without the actors and (we, us), the show wouldn't go on.

Using Pronouns Correctly

Whenever you must decide between the subject or object form of a pronoun, the following general rules apply.

1. First, decide how the pronoun *functions* in the sentence.

2. If the pronoun is used in a *subject function* (subject, predicate pronoun), use the *subject form*.

3. If the pronoun is used in an *object function* (direct object, indirect object, object of the preposition), use the *object form*.

Who/Whom

The pronouns *who* and *whom* follow these same principles. Use *who* when the pronoun is used in a subject function; use *whom* when the pronoun is used in an object function.

Who and *whom* are interrogative pronouns when they introduce a question. Although *whom* is not often used in informal conversation, it is still required in formal speech and Edited Standard English.

Subject Function:	*Who* called the fire department? [*Who* is the subject of the sentence.]
	The winner was *who?* [*Who* is the predicate pronoun.]
Object Function:	*Whom* did you see at the beach? [*Whom* is the direct object of the verb *did see*.]
	To *whom* was Marconi's first message sent? [*Whom* is the object of the preposition *to*.]

Subordinate clauses are discussed on pages 469–477.

Who and *whom* are relative pronouns when they introduce a subordinate clause. To decide which pronoun to use, first determine the pronoun's function within the clause.

Subject Function:	Wanda is the skater *who won the bronze medal.* [*Who* is the subject of the *italicized* subordinate clause.]

| Object Function: | The Sandorffs are the couple *whom my grandparents met in Mesa Verde National Park.* |
| | [*Whom* is the direct object of the verb *met* in the *italicized* subordinate clause.] |

We/Us

When *we* or *us* is followed by a plural noun, use *we* if the noun has a subject function. Use *us* if the noun has an object function.

Subject Function:	*We* gardeners like to read seed catalogues.
	The first ones here were *we* bicyclists.
Object Function:	Mrs. Pilar gave *us* students a personality test.
	Please wake *us* sleepyheads at 7 o'clock.

Pronouns as Appositives

When a pronoun is an appositive, its form is determined by the function of the noun with which it is in apposition.

An *appositive* renames or explains a noun that immediately precedes it. If the noun is in a subject position, use the subject form of the pronoun. If the noun is in an object position, use the object form of the pronoun.

Subject Function:	The candidates—Roy, Judy, and *I*—waited for the results.
	[The pronoun *I* is an appositive for the noun *candidates*, which functions as the subject of the sentence.]
Object Function:	The line drive narrowly missed the people in the third row—the Rotkowitzes and *us*.
	[*Us* is an appositive for the noun *people*, which functions as the direct object in the sentence.]

Possessive Pronoun Before a Gerund

Use the possessive form of the personal pronoun before a gerund—a noun ending in -*ing*.

Participles are discussed on page 455, gerunds on page 456.

Two kinds of words formed from verbs end in -*ing*: participles and gerunds. Gerunds are nouns; participles are modifiers. The possessive form of the personal pronoun is always used when the pronoun precedes a gerund.

Glinda objects to *my* calling after 10 o'clock.
What do you think of *our* going to Quebec for vacation?

Exercise 4

Rewrite the following sentences to correct all pronoun errors. Underline the pronouns you correct.

Examples

a. For who are you waiting?
a. *For* <u>whom</u> *are you waiting?*

b. The telephone keeps interrupting him studying.
b. *The telephone keeps interrupting* <u>his</u> *studying.*

1. The puppeteers, Juliette and him, have been rehearsing for weeks.
2. Who did the committee nominate for vice president?
3. Without the help of we volunteers, the carnival would never make a profit.
4. The neighbors objected to them practicing their songs outdoors.
5. Hank is the driver who the police officer gave the ticket to.
6. The audience cheered the soloists, Paula and she.
7. That pleasant young man was once the child who no one could handle.
8. Me winning first prize in the art contest really surprised us all.
9. Josh addressed his letter "To who it may concern."
10. Us having dinner ready when Mom comes home from work is a tremendous help, she says.

Writing with Pronouns

To communicate effectively writers and speakers must make certain that their pronouns clearly reveal who or what they are talking about. They avoid three kinds of unclear pronoun reference: ambiguous, general, and indefinite.

Reword sentences in which the antecedent of the pronoun is ambiguous.

When something is ambiguous, it has two or more possible meanings. Ambiguous pronoun references can usually be corrected by rewording the sentence or by replacing the pronoun with a noun.

Ambiguous:	Charlie and Phil will play tennis after he finishes his homework. [Who has to do the homework—Charlie or Phil?]
Clear:	Charlie and Phil will play tennis after Charlie finishes his homework.
Ambiguous:	Rita told Lois that her new boyfriend was wonderful.
Clear:	Rita told Lois, "My new boyfriend is wonderful."

Reword sentences in which the pronouns *which*, *this*, *that*, or *it* refer to ideas that are vaguely expressed.

The antecedent of a pronoun may be a whole series of ideas. When it is not clear what the pronoun refers to, the sentence should be rephrased.

General:	The hayride was scheduled to start at 10, but the weather was bad, and the horses were delayed, and almost no one came. *That* was clearly the fault of the entertainment committee.
Clear:	The hayride was scheduled to start at 10, but the weather was bad and the horses were delayed. The fact that almost no one came was clearly the fault of the entertainment committee.
General:	The baby wailed, the dog barked furiously, the television blared, and the vacuum was going full blast. The visitor left because of *it*.
Clear:	The visitor left because the baby was wailing, the dog was barking furiously, the television was blaring, and the vacuum was going full blast.

Reword sentences in which the pronouns *it, they,* and *you* do not have a clear antecedent.

People often use the expression "They say . . ." or "It says . . ." to refer to some indefinite authority. Avoid such indefinite pronoun reference by naming specifically who or what is the source of the information.

Indefinite:	*They* say that *The Great Gatsby* is F. Scott Fitzgerald's greatest novel.
Better:	Professor Hawkins thinks that *The Great Gatsby* is F. Scott Fitzgerald's greatest novel.
Indefinite:	What did *it* say about tomorrow's weather on television?
Better:	What did the television weather forecaster say about tomorrow's weather?
Indefinite:	For two dollars *you* can launch *your* boat at the Dinner Key Marina.
Better:	For two dollars boaters can launch their boats at the Dinner Key Marina.

Writing Exercise A

Rewrite the following sentences to avoid ambiguous, indefinite, and overly general pronoun antecedents.

Examples

a. When we finally reached the stadium, they told us that the concert was sold out.

a. *When we finally reached the stadium, the ticket seller in the box office told us that the concert was sold out.*

b. When Melanie and Pam arrive, will you please tell her that I want to see her immediately?

b. *When Melanie and Pam arrive, will you please tell Melanie that I want to see her immediately?*

1. Jerry opened the pack of cigarettes, and it said that cigarette smoking is dangerous to your health.

2. Outside Las Vegas, Nevada, they have turquoise mines and other great places for rock hunters.

3. Toby and Whit left his baseball mitt on the beach when they went for a swim.

4. In Temple Israel they have a reproduction of Marc Chagall's stained-glass windows.

5. The police roped off the street and set up barricades, and crowds gathered around the United Nations, which made traffic come to a standstill.

6. May showed her aunt the quilt she had made when her daughter was born.

7. On some holidays the stores and banks are closed, but the mail is delivered. On other holidays the stores and post office are open, but the banks are closed, which is confusing.

8. They say that you should change the oil and oil filter in a car every five or six thousand miles.

9. On television it said that you should do some form of vigorous exercise at least three or four times a week.

10. In 1938 Orson Welles' *Mercury Radio Theatre of the Air* presented an adaptation of H. G. Wells' *The War of the Worlds*, in which a small town in New Jersey was invaded by Martians, which panicked listeners all over America, who thought the drama was a real news broadcast.

Review Exercise A

Rewrite each of the following sentences, correcting any errors in pronoun usage.

1. Thelma and her mother forgot where her car was parked.

2. Some of the students turned in his lab books before the semester ended.

3. Many of the workers do not know the full extent of his or her employee benefits.

4. Before the race each of the cyclists adjusted their helmet.

5. Everyone who is a boxer knows the risks they face each time they fight.

6. All of the employees are entitled to take his or her birthdays off as a holiday.

7. Some of the tourists are careless about the time he spends in the sun.

8. When everybody opened his paycheck, he was pleased at his raise.

9. Do you know any of the people who left his or her jackets in the gym?

10. None of the students have had his graduation pictures taken yet.

11. Anyone who raises a family knows that he has both responsibilities and pleasures.

12. When the lieutenant asked for volunteers, no one raised their hand.

13. Neither Ed nor Cal has finished their answers to the essay question.

14. Both Carmel and Gwynn have her cars here.

15. Either the captain or the coach will appeal the ruling as soon as they can.

16. When football players have knee injuries, they can do wonders for a torn ligament or tendon.

17. They say that people may harm their bodies when they take overdoses of certain vitamins.

18. In the almanac it says that Gracie Allen's real name was Grace Ethel Cecile Rosalie Allen.

19. Older people who are inactive feel useless and unwanted and can make themselves weak with lack of exercise and a poor diet. This is a serious problem.

20. When she was twenty, Kate decided to quit school, move to Alaska, break up with her boyfriend, and become an actress, which surprised her parents.

Review Exercise B

Choose the correct pronoun from those given in parentheses. Write out the sentences and underline the pronoun you have chosen.

1. Please give Adrian Fong and (she, her) my telephone number.
2. Jessica, Tamar, and (I, me) are ushers at the opera.
3. The guard asked Cal and (he, him) for their drivers licenses.
4. The contestants on the game show were Bill Cosby, Glenda Radnor, and (she, her).
5. Missie's parents and (them, they) are taking fencing lessons.
6. Jenny, Harvey, and (I, me) are going to see the exhibit of Black artists at the Cleveland Institute of Art.
7. Mr. Wing, the librarian, asked Pete and (I, me) if we had watched the Summer Olympics.
8. Gary told (she and I, her and me) that ears were originally pierced to let the demons out of one's head.
9. Between you and (I, me) hospitals are a great place to stay out of.
10. The frightened campers—Lee, Winn, and (him, he)—told of a gigantic animal that wrecked their tent during the night.
11. Anyone planning to hike into the swamp must notify one of the naturalists—either Mrs. O'Rourke or (I, me)—before setting out.
12. (Who, Whom) are you visiting in Kankakee?
13. One person (who, whom) I really trust is Susie Guber.
14. When we arrived, the first person (who, whom) we saw was Jodi.
15. Raymond is a young man (who, whom) everyone respects for graduating at the top of his class despite his blindness.
16. (Who, Whom) is going to help Grandma with her shopping when she comes home from her trip?
17. Gloria Steinem's grandmother was an activist (who, whom) was president of the Ohio Women's Suffrage Association from 1908 to 1911.
18. At (who, whom) are you directing that angry look?
19. In Sophocles' *Antigone* the heroine stands up to her Uncle Creon, ruler of Thebes, (who, whom) everyone fears.
20. (Us, We) patients have been waiting impatiently for two hours.

Writing Exercise B

Choose one of the following assignments and write a short paper as directed. When you have finished your first draft, check the pronoun usage carefully.

Have you used the subject and object forms correctly? Are the antecedents of all pronouns clear?

1. You and your two best friends are spending a rainy afternoon listening to records, eating your favorite foods, and talking about dating. Describe what you and your friends would do and say. Write part of your conversation.

2. Write a play-by-play description of one of the following activities: part of an inning of a baseball game, a game of tennis, or a ping-pong game; plays leading up to a goal in hockey or in soccer or to a touchdown in football. Make up names for the players, being certain that the antecedent of each pronoun is clear.

3. Tell who you think would make the best candidate for the next President of the United States. Write a short nominating speech, telling about that person's accomplishments and qualifications. Tell as specifically as you can why you think he or she would make a good President.

4. Make up an explanation for the origin of one of the following customs. Use your imagination. Your explanation can be in the form of a story or a serious explanation.

> Shaking hands
> Blowing out birthday candles
> Knocking on wood
> Touching glasses as a toast before you drink

Understanding Verbs

In the next sections you will learn to identify verbs through their definition, the classes into which they can be divided, and the features that distinguish them from other parts of speech.

Defining a Verb   A *verb* is usually defined as a word that expresses action (physical or mental) or a state of being.

For the Year of the Monkey, Mr. Hsueh *drew* three monkeys.	[physical action]
Paolo *thought* for a long time about his sister's present.	[mental action]
Every day after school Marcia *is* in the gym.	[state of being]
Terry *is* optimistic about his grades this term.	[state of being]

A *state of being verb* describes the location, existence, or state of a person, place, or thing. *Is, am, are, was,* and *were*—forms of the verb *be*—are the most frequently used verbs that express a state of being.

Exercise 1

Write out the following sentences, underlining each verb. (Some sentences may have more than one verb.)

Examples

a. Steve Poborski had the best time in the downhill trial runs.

a. Steve Poborski <u>had</u> the best time in the downhill trial runs.

b. Janie laughed and cried as she hugged her brother.

b. Janie <u>laughed</u> and <u>cried</u> as she <u>hugged</u> her brother.

1. Frédéric Bartholdi, a French sculptor, used his mother as the model for the Statue of Liberty's face.

2. Her colleagues call Chien-Shiung Wu, who disproved one of nature's laws, "the queen of nuclear physics."

3. Few people know that John Hanson, not George Washington, was the first President of the United States.

4. Pink grapefruit contains vitamins A and C, but white grapefruit has only vitamin C.

5. Sarah Caldwell, founder of the Opera Company of Boston, conducted the New York Philharmonic in a concert of works by female composers.

6. Henry J. Heinz, who sold homegrown vegetables to Pittsburgh grocers when he was sixteen, chose the slogan "Heinz 57 Varieties" because he liked the sound of the number 57.

7. Sarah Winnemucca, a Paiute Indian, pressured government officials for the return of her people to their homeland in Oregon.

8. Soldiers during World War I used the first facial tissues as filters for their gas masks.

9. In 1892 Dr. Washington Wentworth Sheffield invented what became an essential part of every American household: the toothpaste tube.

10. The writer Gertrude Stein's last words were, "What is the answer?" and when no one replied, she asked, "In that case, what is the question?"

Classifying Verbs

Verbs can be classified as either action or linking verbs and as either main or helping verbs.

1. *Action Verbs*

   An *action verb* shows either a physical or mental action.

Most action verbs express some kind of physical movement, but some express a mental action that cannot be seen by others.

José *leaped* for the ball.	[physical action]
She *squeezed* through the crowd.	[physical action]
Tanya *wants* an end to world hunger.	[mental action]
Mother always *hopes* for the best.	[mental action]

2. *Linking Verbs*

Predicate nominatives and predicate adjectives are discussed on pages 436–438.

A *linking verb* links the subject of the sentence with a noun or an adjective that comes after the verb.

Linda Fratiane *is* a champion skater.
[*Is* is a linking verb because *skater* is a predicate noun that renames the subject, *Linda Fratiane.*]

Sari's homemade ravioli *tastes* delicious.
[*Tastes* is a linking verb because *delicious* is a predicate adjective that describes the subject, *ravioli.*]

The most commonly used linking verbs are forms of the verb *be: am, are, is, was, were, been,* and *being.* Other verbs may also be used as linking verbs:

appear	look	sound
become	remain	stay
feel	seem	taste
grow	smell	turn

Many of the verbs in the preceding list may be either action verbs or linking verbs.

The pickles *tasted* too sour.
[*Tasted* is a linking verb because *sour* is an adjective describing the subject, *pickles.*]

In Wonderland Alice *tasted* the tiny cake.
[*Tasted* is an action verb because *cake* does not rename or describe the subject, *Alice.*]

Everyone *kept* calm.
[*Kept* is a linking verb because *calm* describes the subject, *everyone.*]

Gina *kept* her corsage in the refrigerator.
[*Kept* is an action verb because *corsage* does not rename or describe the subject, *Gina.*]

3. *Main Verbs and Helping Verbs*

A verb may be either a single verb or a verb phrase. A *verb phrase* consists of two or more verbs that act as a single verb. The last verb in a verb phrase is called the *main verb.* The other verbs in the verb phrase are called *helping verbs,* or *auxiliary verbs.*

We *had slept* for only four hours.
The physical therapist *should have been* here before noon.
The McGuire twins *will be graduating* in June.

The following list contains common helping verbs.

is	been	will	has
are	do	shall	had
was	does	should	may
were	did	would	might
am	can	have	must
be	could		

Sometimes, a main verb is separated from a helping verb by other words in the sentence. *Always, usually, never, not,* and other modifiers are not part of the verb phrase.

Do you *like* blintzes and sour cream?
That clock *has* always *been standing* in the hallway.
Todi and Alvin *have* probably *been married* for twenty years.
Mr. and Mrs. Kitajima *have* never *visited* Japan.

In some sentences the helping verb is part of a contraction.

Sheila *won't be coming* to the meeting.
[The verb phrase in this sentence is *will be coming* because *won't* is a contraction of *will not.*]

I'll be home by 5 o'clock.
[The verb phrase is *will be* because *I'll* is a contraction of *I will.*]

Exercise 2
Write out the following sentences. Beneath each sentence write the verb phrase.

Example
a. Julie doesn't like her uncle's chili.
a. Julie doesn't like her uncle's chili.
   does like

1. Paul won't change his mind.
2. My parents have always been proud of me.
3. What is making that strange sound?
4. How long has Avi's family lived in Charleston?
5. Before taking X-rays, the dentist has been putting a lead shield on his patients.
6. Doesn't anyone have change for a dollar?
7. Admiral Robert E. Peary would never have reached the North Pole in 1909 without his friend and companion, Matthew Henson.
8. Ricky's younger brother has been raised much more strictly than she.

9. The Herrera family has been planning a grand reunion for the holidays.

10. A farmer in Mexico can grow gigantic vegetables in regular soil and without fertilizers.

Finding a Verb by Its Features

Knowing the three features of verbs will not only help you to identify verbs but also to use them correctly.

1. Verbs have *tense*.

Verbs are the only part of speech that express time through changes in form. Every verb has three forms, called its *principal parts*. These three principal parts are the *present*, the *past*, and the *past participle*.

PRESENT	PAST	PAST PARTICIPLE
love	loved	(had) loved
bring	brought	(had) brought
sing	sang	(had) sung

These three principal parts are used together with helping verbs to form all of the different tenses of English verbs.

The *-ing* form of the verb, sometimes called the *present participle*, is made up of the present form of the verb plus *-ing*.

love + ing = loving   bring + ing = bringing   sing + ing = singing

The *-ing* form of the verb together with the helping verb *be* is used in the progressive form of the various tenses.

is helping   was wishing   had been painting

2. Verbs may *change form* to agree in number with the subject.

In the present tense every verb has two different forms. The singular form of the verb, which ends in *s* or *es*, is used with a singular noun as subject and with the pronouns *he*, *she*, and *it*.

SINGULAR FORM
The quarterback *passes* the football.
She *steps* on a thumbtack.
The cat *licks* its paws.

The plural form of the verb is the present form of the principal parts. The plural form is used with plural nouns as subjects and with the pronouns *I*, *you*, *we*, and *they*.

PLURAL FORM
The players *pass* the football.
They *step* on thumbtacks.
The cats *lick* their paws.

3. Verbs have *mood*.

Verbs have three moods: *indicative, imperative*, and *subjunctive*.

The *indicative mood* expresses something factual that has happened, is happening, or will happen. Almost all of the verbs you use in speaking and in writing are in the indicative mood.

INDICATIVE MOOD
Bob *eats* too quickly.
Ira *sprained* his shoulder.
Jo Ann *will arrive* tomorrow.

The *imperative mood* is used for commands or requests.

IMPERATIVE MOOD
Please *stop* at the next gas station.
Lock the door behind you.

The *subjunctive mood* expresses a wish or a statement that is contrary to fact.

SUBJUNCTIVE MOOD
If he *were* more understanding, the fight would not have started.
If I *were* you, I would look for another job.
She wishes that he *were* coming home today.

Exercise 3

Using what you have learned about the definition, classes, and features of verbs, identify the verbs and verb phrases in the following paragraphs from T. H. White's story of the legend of King Arthur, *The Once and Future King*. List the verb and verb phrases on a sheet of paper in the order they appear.[1]

Note: *Rounding* is a verb form used as an adjective, called a *participle*.

Example

a. "What?" cried Sir Kay, suddenly rounding upon him. "Did you just say this sword was stuck in a stone?". . .

a. cried, did say, was stuck

Sir Kay stared at him for several seconds in amazement, opened his mouth, shut it again, licked his lips, then turned his back and plunged through the crowd. He was looking for Sir Ector, and the Wart followed after him.

"Father," cried Sir Kay, "come here a moment."

"Yes, my boy," said Sir Ector. "Splendid falls these professional chaps do manage. Why, what's the matter, Kay? You look as white as a sheet."

"Do you remember that sword which the King of England would pull out?"

"Yes."

"Well, here it is. I have it. It is in my hand. I pulled it out."

Sir Ector did not say anything silly. He looked at Kay and he looked at the Wart. Then he stared at Kay again, long and lovingly, and said, "We will go back to the church."

---

[1]Excerpt from *The Once and Future King* by T. H. White. Copyright 1939, 1940 by T. H. White, © 1958 by T. H. White. Reprinted by permission of G. P. Putnam's Sons and David Higham Associates Limited.

"Now then, Kay," he said, when they were at the church door. He looked at his firstborn kindly, but straight between the eyes. "Here is the stone, and you have the sword. It will make you the King of England. You are my son, that I am proud of, and always will be, whatever you do. Will you promise me that you took it out by your own might?"

Kay looked at his father. He also looked at the Wart and at the sword. Then he handed the sword to the Wart quite quietly.

He said, "I am a liar. Wart pulled it out."

Review Exercise A

Write out the following sentences, underlining each verb or verb phrase. (Some sentences have more than one verb.)

1. Leotards are the invention of a nineteenth-century French acrobat, Jules Léotard.

2. Scott Joplin, king of the ragtime composers, wrote *Treemonisha*, an opera about a black woman who freed her people.

3. During his lifetime Thomas A. Edison received 1,300 American and foreign patents.

4. At the age of eighty-four, Agatha Christie was still writing mysteries.

5. In mountainous Bird Village in Turkey, the villagers' whistle language can be heard for miles.

6. The words *voodoo*, *jazz*, and *banjo* have come from African languages.

7. The Earth is twenty-six miles wider in diameter at the equator than it is from pole to pole.

8. After Annie Oakley outshot marksman Frank Butler, they fell in love and married.

9. Bessie Hillman founded the Amalgamated Clothing Workers of America and was, for many years, the only woman union leader in the clothing industry.

10. Julia Ward Howe wrote "The Battle Hymn of the Republic" after she had visited a soldiers' camp during the Civil War.

11. Legendary spy and lover Mata Hari was executed for her work for the Germans during World War I.

12. Some scientists theorize that the sun will eventually lose its brightness, but this won't happen for at least 5 billion years.

13. At the age of twelve, Charles Dickens really did wash and label bottles like the hero in his *Oliver Twist*.

14. Before he died in 1980, Joseph B. Rhine had been experimenting with extrasensory perception (ESP) for nearly fifty years.

15. The small town of Rugby, North Dakota, has been declared the geographical center of North America.

16. In six months' time Bobbie, a mongrel dog, traveled 3,000 miles from Indiana to Oregon and found his way home again.

17. When a male elephant flirts with a female elephant, he will offer her food or squirt water over her back.

18. Ruth told her mother-in-law, "Whither thou goest, I will go; and where thou lodgest, I will lodge."

19. After a series of strokes that nearly killed her, actress Patricia Neal fought her way back to recovery and resumed her acting career.

20. Labor leader Marry Harris ("Mother") Jones advised women, "No matter what your fight, don't be ladylike."

Mastery Exercise A

Using what you have learned about identifying verbs, locate each verb and verb phrase in the following passage from Joan Didion's *The White Album*. Do not include infinitives, participles, or gerunds, which are given in brackets (see pages 455–457). List at least thirty verbs or verb phrases on a sheet of paper in the order they appear.[1]

> On the evidence of her work and what she has said about it, Georgia O'Keeffe is neither "crusty" nor eccentric. She is simply hard, a straight shooter, a woman clean of [received] wisdom and open to what she sees. This is a woman who could early on dismiss most of her contemporaries as "dreamy," and would later single out one she liked as "a very poor painter." (And then add, apparently by way of [softening] the judgment: "I guess he wasn't a painter at all. He had no courage and I believe that [to create] one's own world in any of the arts takes courage.") This is a woman who in 1939 could advise her admirers that they were missing her point, that their appreciation of her famous flowers was merely sentimental. "When I paint a red hill," she observed coolly in the catalogue for an exhibition that year, "you say it is too bad that I don't always paint flowers. A flower touches almost everyone's heart. A red hill doesn't touch everyone's heart." This is a woman who could describe the genesis of one of her most well-known paintings—the "Cow's Skull: Red, White and Blue" [owned] by the Metropolitan—as an act of quite deliberate and derisive orneriness. "I thought of the city men I had been seeing in the East," she wrote. "They talked so often of [writing] the Great American Novel—the Great American Play—the Great American Poetry. . . . So as I was painting my cow's head on blue I thought to myself, I'll make it an American painting. They will not think it great with the red stripes down the sides—Red, White, and Blue—but they will notice it."

Mastery Exercise B

From a magazine, newspaper, or textbook, select several paragraphs about the length of the selection in Mastery Exercise A. Then identify the verbs or verb phrases and list them in the order they appear, on a sheet of paper. Beside each verb or verb phrase indicate whether it is action or linking by writing the letter *A* or *L*.

---

[1]Excerpt from *The White Album* by Joan Didion. Copyright © 1979 by Joan Didion. Reprinted by permission of Simon & Schuster, a Division of Gulf & Western Corporation and Wallace & Sheil.

Using Verbs

In the following sections you will study and practice the features of verb usage that are a part of Edited Standard English. These features include forming verb tenses, using the three moods of verbs, making verbs agree with subjects, and choosing between frequently confused pairs of verbs.

Forming Verb Tenses

Verbs show *tense*—or time—through their three principal parts: present form, past form, and past participle form.

The marchers *carry* colorful banners.	[present form]
The fire fighter *carried* the child.	[past form]
Sam has never *carried* much money.	[past participle form]

All verbs may be classified as either regular or irregular, depending on how their principal parts are formed. *Regular verbs* form their past and past participle with *-ed* or *-d* added to the present form.

PRESENT	PAST	PAST PARTICIPLE
annoy	annoyed	(had) annoyed
admire	admired	(had) admired
shop	shopped	(had) shopped
occupy	occupied	(had) occupied

Notice that certain verbs (such as *shop* and *occupy*) have spelling changes when *-ed* is added to the present form. (See pages 541–543 for rules about these spelling changes.) All verbs that are not regular verbs are irregular verbs. *Irregular verbs* do not form their past and past participle according to any rules. The following list gives the principal parts of the most common irregular verbs.

More exercises on irregular verbs appear on pages 416–421.

PRESENT	PAST	PAST PARTICIPLE *(has, have, or had)*
become	became	become
begin	began	begun
break	broke	broken
bring	brought	brought
build	built	built
burst	burst	burst
buy	bought	bought
catch	caught	caught
choose	chose	chosen
come	came	come
cost	cost	cost
dive	dove or dived	dived
do	did	done
draw	drew	drawn
drink	drank	drunk
drive	drove	driven

PRESENT	PAST	PAST PARTICIPLE (*has, have,* or *had*)
eat	ate	eaten
fall	fell	fallen
fly	flew	flown
forget	forgot	forgotten
freeze	froze	frozen
give	gave	given
go	went	gone
grow	grew	grown
hit	hit	hit
keep	kept	kept
know	knew	known
lay	laid	laid
lie	lay	lain
ride	rode	ridden
ring	rang	rung
rise	rose	risen
run	ran	run
see	saw	seen
shake	shook	shaken
shrink	shrank	shrunk
sing	sang	sung
sink	sank	sunk
slay	slew	slain
speak	spoke	spoken
spend	spent	spent
spring	sprang	sprung
steal	stole	stolen
strive	strove	striven
swear	swore	sworn
swim	swam	swum
take	took	taken
teach	taught	taught
think	thought	thought
throw	threw	thrown
wear	wore	worn
write	wrote	written

If you are not sure of the principal parts of a verb, check your dictionary, which uses the present form as the entry form for all verbs.

> **unwrap** v., **-wrapped, -wrap·ping**
> **clarify** v., **-fied, -fy·ing**

For all irregular verbs dictionaries list the past and past participle forms in the same order that they are listed in the chart on page 353–354. If only one form is listed, as for *fight*, that means the past and past participle forms are the same.

> **fight** v., **fought, fight·ing**

When two forms are listed, the first is the past form and the second is the past participle.

eat v., **ate, eat·en, eat·ing**

Occasionally a dictionary will list alternate past or past participle forms. Both are acceptable, but the one listed first is preferred.

forbid v., **-bade** or **-bad, -bid·den** or **-bid, -bid·ding**

Remember that the -*ing* form of any verb—either regular or irregular—is formed by adding -*ing* to the present tense: *annoying, fighting, eating, forbidding.*

Exercise 1

Additional exercises on irregular verbs are on pages 416–421.

Each of the following sentences contains an irregular verb. Write out the sentences. In the blank write the appropriate principal part of the verb in parentheses. (Remember that the past participle form is always used with the helping verb *has*, *have*, or *had*.) Underline the verb or verb phrase.

Examples

a. Cindy has _____ all her old books to the Veterans Hospital. (take)
a. *Cindy has taken all her old books to the Veterans Hospital.*

b. When she was sick, she _____ a quart of chicken soup. (drink)
b. *When she was sick, she drank a quart of chicken soup.*

1. Joe Tigertail has _____ the toughest broncos in the rodeo. (ride)
2. What have you _____ about the overdue notice? (do)
3. We had almost _____ about Mal's birthday party. (forget)
4. Clem leaped up and _____ the line drive to right field. (catch)
5. Lynn has _____ to go to the University of Denver. (choose)
6. The Miller brothers had _____ an expensive chess set to the match. (bring)
7. I _____ you would cooperate with the investigators. (know)
8. After the bell_____ , the audience returned to their seats. (ring)
9. Have you ever _____ in an icy mountain lake? (swim)
10. Dario has _____ to visit his father in Nantucket. (go)

Using Verb Tenses

Simple Tenses

The three *simple tenses* are the present tense, past tense, and future tense.

1. *Present Tense*

Verbs in the *present tense* express action happening at the present moment or action that happens habitually.

Heidi *trips* over the last hurdle. [present action]
A strange noise *comes* from the closet. [present action]
Hanni *goes* to Memphis every summer. [habitual action]
Elaine and Jim *bite* their nails. [habitual action]

The *present progressive form* of the verb also shows action happening in the present or continuing action.

We *are winning* by twenty-one points.
She *is trying* to paint a self-portrait.

2. *Past Tense*

Verbs in the *past tense* express action or a state of being that has been completed in the past.

The applicants *waited* for more than four hours.
The prime minister *signed* the peace treaty.

The *past progressive form* of the verb expresses a continuing past action.

Laura *was having* a difficult time making a decision.
Yolanda *was feeling* upset about her argument with Raoul.

3. *Future Tense*

The *future tense* is formed with the helping verb *will* or *shall* and the present form. Verbs in the future tense express an action that will take place sometime in the future.

Future tense verbs may also make a prediction or give an order.

The Mets *will play* a double-header on Sunday.
Luanne *will* surely *win* the election.
Will you please *say* what you really mean?

The *future progressive form* also indicates future action.

I'*ll be* seeing you.
Leander *will be arriving* at midnight.

Perfect Tenses

The three *perfect tenses* are the present perfect tense, the past perfect tense, and the future perfect tense.

4. *Present Perfect Tense*

The *present perfect tense* is formed by using *has* or *have* with the past participle of a verb. Verbs in the present perfect tense are used to describe an action that began in the past and continues to the present.

Ginger *has had* a lot of trouble with her knee.
We *have waited* a month for this appointment.

The present perfect tense may also be used to express an action that has been completed at some indefinite past time.

We *have visited* every museum in Boston.
Professor Alpiner *has arrived* for her lecture.

The *progressive form* of the present perfect tense indicates past action that continues to the present.

I *have been hoping* you would call.
Julio *has been baby-sitting* for his nephew.

5. *Past Perfect Tense*

The *past perfect tense* is formed by using the helping verb *had* with the past participle. Verbs in the past perfect tense express an action that was completed in the past at some time before another action took place.

Before she graduated, Marcia *had worked* as a day-care assistant.
I *had* already *returned* by the time he started out to look for me.

The *progressive form* of the past perfect tense uses *had been* plus the *-ing* form of the verb.

Teig *had been sneezing* a lot until the first frost.
Until a week ago we *had been expecting* to move to Nebraska.

6. *Future Perfect Tense*

The *future perfect tense* uses *will have* or *shall have* plus the past participle form of a verb. Verbs in the future perfect tense express a future action that will be completed before another future action.

In August they *will have known* each other a year.

According to her Social Security earnings report, she *will have earned* almost $200,000 by 1990.

The *progressive form* of the future perfect tense consists of *shall* or *will have been* plus the *-ing* form of the verb.

In another five minutes we *will have been driving* for eight hours.

Exercise 2

Write out each of the following sentences, supplying the tense of the verb shown in parentheses. Underline the verb or verb phrase.

Examples

a. Octavio's grandmother _____ ninety-two years old this spring.
   (*be*—future tense)
a. *Octavio's grandmother will be ninety-two years old this spring.*
b. Mr. and Mrs. Lange _____ to adopt a child.
   (*try*—progressive form of present tense)
b. *Mr. and Mrs. Lange are trying to adopt a child.*

1. Six of the cups _____ when he opened the cupboard door. (*break*—past tense)

2. _____ you please _____ a sample of your handwriting to Madame Olenka? (*send*—future tense)

3. Until you called, I _____ to hear from your brother Saul. (*expect*—progressive form of past tense)

4. Runar _____ three inches in the past six months. (*grow*—present perfect tense)

5. We could see that Nancy _____ before she opened the door. (*cry*—progressive form of past perfect tense)

6. Jeanette _____ a jar of almond-stuffed olives. (*bring*—past tense)

7. _____ you _____ your report by next Monday? (*finish*—future perfect tense)

8. On his first two trips Jack _____ successfully from the person-eating giant. (*escape*—past perfect)

9. Mirianne and Gregg _____ all morning for the stolen bicycle. (*look*—progressive form of present perfect tense)

10. Toby Bletter _____ Mandarin Chinese for his master's degree. (*study*—progressive form of present tense)

Using the Different Moods of Verbs

The word *mood* in grammar refers to the speaker's attitude toward what is being expressed—whether something is a fact or contrary to fact, a wish, or a command. In English all verbs are in one of three moods: indicative mood, imperative mood, or subjunctive mood. Native speakers of English have no trouble using the indicative and imperative moods, nor do they even have to think about how or when to use these moods. The subjunctive mood, however, may cause some problems.

Indicative Mood

The *indicative mood* is used to express facts—something that has actually happened, is happening, or will happen.

Almost all of the verbs that you use in speaking and in writing are in the indicative mood.

> Gloria *is* quiet.
> Marvin *wastes* a lot of time.

Imperative Mood

The *imperative mood* is used to express commands.

Even when the command is softened by the word *please*, the verb is still in the imperative mood.

> Please *be* quiet.
> Don't *waste* so much time.

Subjunctive Mood

The *subjunctive mood* is used to express wishes, possibilities, or statements that are contrary to fact.

The subjunctive mood almost always involves the verb *be* after an expression such as *if* or *as though*.

In the present tense subjunctive the word *be* is used for both singular and plural subjects.

> PRESENT TENSE
> If this *be* reality, I'd rather be dreaming.

In the past tense subjunctive, *were* is used for both singular and plural subjects.

> PAST TENSE
> If I *were* you, I'd find a new boyfriend.   [contrary to fact]
> Wouldn't it be great if today *were* a holiday!   [contrary to fact]
> Lorenzo wishes he *were* six inches taller.   [wish]
> I wish that I *were* president of General Motors.   [wish]

Exercise 3

Write out the following sentences. In the blank write the appropriate form of the verb called for in parentheses. Then underline the verb that you have written in the blank.

> **Examples**
> a. If this _____ the year 2500, how do you think you'd be dressed? (*be*—subjunctive)
> a. *If this were the year 2500, how do you think you'd be dressed?*
>
> b. Please _____ my valentine. (*be*—imperative)
> b. *Please be my valentine.*
>
> c. I _____ tired of being criticized all the time. (*be*—indicative)
> c. *I am tired of being criticized all the time.*

1. With all that makeup Lola looks as if she _____ forty. (*be*—subjunctive)

2. Please _____ careful when you wash the good dishes. (*be*—imperative)

3. Unless I _____ mistaken, today is Anna's birthday. (*be*—indicative)

4. "If you _____ only older, you'd understand," sighed Grandpa. (*be*—subjunctive)

5. When you pick me up on Wednesday, please _____ on time. (*be*—imperative)

6. If Gloria _____ only fifteen pounds lighter, she'd be much more attractive. (*be*—subjunctive)

7. I wouldn't let you talk to me like that if I _____ your mother. (*be*—subjunctive)

8. Harriet _____ a psychiatric social worker in New York City. (*be*—indicative)

9. I wish that you _____ more sympathetic to others' problems. (*be*—subjunctive)

10. "Would that I _____ one of the simple folk," said King Arthur. (*be*—subjunctive)

Making Verbs Agree with Subjects

A verb must *agree* with its subject in number.

Agreement between subject and verb is a problem only when the main verb or helping verb is in the present tense. Past and future tense verbs use the same form of the verb for both singular and plural subjects. In the present tense, however, *-s* or *-es* is added to the third-person singular form of the verb.

SINGULAR FORM OF THE VERB		PLURAL FORM OF THE VERB	
she, he, it	has does jumps invites	I, you, we, they	have do jump invite

Note: The verb *be* is an exception to this rule since it has two singular present tense forms—*is* and *am*—and two past tense forms—*was* and *were*. See page 367 for a special discussion of the unusual verb *be*.

A singular subject takes the singular form of the verb; a plural subject takes the plural form of the verb.

SINGULAR
Jerry *cuts* the firewood.
Dionne *invites* us to her party.

PLURAL
Jerry and I *cut* the firewood.
Dionne and Wendy *invite* us to their party.

Exceptions: The personal pronouns *you* and *I*, even when they refer to only one person, take the plural form of the verb.

You *cut* the firewood.
I *invite* you to my party.

When one or more nouns come between the subject and the verb, you must find the true subject of the sentence so that you can choose a verb that agrees with the subject.

Remember that the subject of a sentence is never found in a prepositional phrase.

The *box* of slides *is* on the table.
[*Box* is the subject of the sentence.]

The *bag* that was on the steps *weighs* five pounds.
[*Bag* is the subject of the sentence.]

Mrs. Saito, as well as her neighbors, *has signed* the petition.
[*Mrs. Saito* is the subject of the sentence.]

In a question the subject follows the verb. Be sure to find the subject of the sentence so that you can choose the verb that agrees with it.

Where is the carton of old clothes?

Who is the representative of the cutters?

The subject also follows the verb in sentences that begin with *here* or *there*. Neither *here* nor *there* is ever the subject of a sentence.

Here are the bills that you asked for.

There is much displeasure with the new building laws.

There are too many citizens who are not registered voters.

Exercise 4

Write out the following sentences, choosing the form of the verb in parentheses that agrees with the subject. Then underline the subject once and the verb twice.

Examples

a. A singular subject (take, takes) a singular verb.
a. A singular subject takes a singular verb.

b. In many of the sentences, the subject (is, are) plural.
b. In many of the sentences, the subject is plural.

c. There (is, are) two exceptions to the rule.
c. There are two exceptions to the rule.

1. Every weekend Delia's parents (catch, catches) enough fish for several meals.

2. This dish of cracked wheat, cabbage, and sausage (is, are) delicious.

3. If you (want, wants) me, I'll be working in the library.

4. I (like, likes) to make stir-fried vegetables.

5. The belt for my jeans (is, are) missing again.

6. The pianist in the Beaux Arts Trio (use, uses) his whole body when he (play, plays).

7. Where (is, are) that album of Josh's pictures of Sara?

8. Here (is, are) the last slices of the oatmeal-raisin bread.

9. There (go, goes) the students in Mrs. Johnson's anthropology class.

10. The carton of eggs (slip, slips) off the table, and broken eggs (splatter, splatters) all over the floor.

Subject-Verb Agreement with Indefinite Pronouns

When an *indefinite pronoun* is the subject of a sentence, the verb must agree with the pronoun in number.

The following indefinite pronouns are always singular and take the singular form of the verb.

anybody	everybody	no one
anyone	everyone	one
each	neither	somebody
either	nobody	someone

Everybody who signed up for the trip is here.

One of the crown jewels is missing.

Someone in the grandstands has a trombone.

Only five indefinite pronouns are always plural and take the plural form of the verb.

both	many	several
few	others	

Several of the paintings are of mothers and children.

Others have their own problems.

Many of the books have disappeared.

Five indefinite pronouns may be either singular or plural, depending on their meaning in a sentence.

all	most	some
any	none	

For the five indefinite pronouns in the preceding list, a noun coming between the subject and verb is helpful in determining the correct verb form. When *all, any, most, none,* and *some* refer to a plural noun, they take the plural form of the verb. When they refer to a singular noun, they take the singular form of the verb.

All of the snow has melted.	[singular]
All of the boxes are packed.	[plural]
Most of my work is finished.	[singular]
Most of the workers want more pay.	[plural]
None of the money has been returned.	[singular]
None of his records please her.	[plural]

Exercise 5

Write each of the following sentences, choosing the correct form of the verb in parentheses. Then underline the subject once and the verb or verb phrase in each sentence twice.

Examples

a. Each of the gold boxes (is, are) decorated with rubies.
a. *Each of the gold boxes is decorated with rubies.*

b. Both of the sisters (is, are) left-handed.
b. *Both of the sisters are left-handed.*

1. All the students (know, knows) Mollie Hatchet.

2. Everyone eligible for Merit scholarships (has, have) a chance to win financial aid regardless of need.

3. Some of the information in the stories (is, are) inaccurate.

4. Others in the class (has, have) chosen to write an original ballad instead of a research paper.

5. Neither of the mechanics (know, knows) what is causing the leak.

6. Anyone who takes Mr. Bizet's courses in chemistry or physics (is, are) going to learn a lot.

7. Several of the students (was, were) alarmed when Mitchell fainted.

8. None of the sales clerks (seem, seems) to be busy at the moment.

9. Some of the apples in the bowl on the kitchen table (is, are) already spoiled.

10. Neither of the sailboats (has, have) an auxiliary motor.

Subject-Verb Agreement with Compound Subjects

When two or more subjects are joined by the word *and*, they always take the plural form of the verb.

Kiyo and Hiromi are black-belt karate experts.

Both students and faculty members have made suggestions.

When two or more singular subjects are joined by *or* or *nor*, the singular form of the verb is used.

Although two or more names are mentioned, only one of the subjects performs the actions.

Petula, JoAnna, or Steve is the new president of the junior class.

Neither Rodina nor her brother knows how to ski.

Either Louis or Howie picks up their brother from nursery school.

When two or more plural subjects are joined by *or* or *nor*, the plural form of the verb is used.

Either movies or plays are her favorite form of entertainment.

Neither parents nor children are always right.

When one part of a compound subject is plural and one part is singular, the verb agrees with the subject that is closer to the verb.

Neither the coach nor the players expect to win.

Neither the players nor the coach expects to win.

Either you or Marianela has the soccer ball.

Either Marianela or you have the soccer ball.

Exercise 6

Each of the following sentences contains a compound subject. Write out the sentences and choose the verb form in parentheses that agrees with the subject. Then underline the subject once and the verb or verb phrase twice.

Examples

a. Both the roof and the shingles (need, needs) repair.

a. Both the roof and the shingles need repair.

b. Neither Lois nor her sisters (has, have) ever baby-sat.

b. Neither Lois nor her sisters have ever baby-sat.

c. Every evening Gary or his brother (walk, walks) his dog.

c. Every evening Gary or his brother walks his dog.

1. An alto recorder or a soprano recorder (is, are) easy to play.

2. Neither the Boy Scouts nor the Girl Scouts (has, have) meetings at Floral Park Elementary School.

3. A necklace or earrings (is, are) what she wants for her birthday.

4. Either stray cats or dogs (is, are) pawing through the garbage cans.

5. An opossum and her family (live, lives) under the neighbors' house.

6. Either solar energy or wind energy (is, are) being seriously considered by more and more homeowners.

7. On Sundays George Avilar or his father (bake, bakes) enough bread to last all week.

8. Two elephants, three white horses, and a giraffe (lead, leads) the circus parade.

9. The avocado plant or the ferns probably (needs, need) more sunlight or less watering.

10. Neither she nor I (know, knows) John Oliphant's address or phone number.

Some Common Problems in Subject-Verb Agreement

1. *Collective Nouns*

Words like *committee, group, family, jury, herd,* and *team* are called *collective nouns* because they name a group of persons or things. Collective nouns may be either singular or plural in meaning.

When a collective noun is thought of as acting together as a unit, the noun has a singular meaning and takes the singular form of the verb.

Most nights our <u>family</u> <u><u>eats</u></u> at 6 o'clock.

The <u>committee</u> <u><u>recommends</u></u> the new candidates.

However, when the individual members of the group are thought of separately, the collective noun has a plural meaning and takes the plural form of the verb.

My mother's <u>family</u> <u><u>are</u></u> scattered all over the country.

The <u>committee</u> <u><u>disagree</u></u> on how to implement the new by-laws.

2. *Nouns That Are Plural in Form*

Use the singular form of the verb for nouns that are plural in form but have a singular meaning.

athletics	genetics	news
civics	mathematics	physics
economics	mumps	politics

<u>Genetics</u> <u><u>is</u></u> the study of hereditary influences on living things.

<u>Economics</u> <u><u>is</u></u> Jackie's favorite subject.

3. *Nouns That Have No Singular Form*

Use a plural form of the verb with nouns that have no singular form.

jeans	pliers	shears	suspenders
pants	scissors	slacks	trousers

These <u>jeans</u> <u><u>are</u></u> four years old.

However, if the word *pair* precedes one of these nouns, use a singular form of the verb.

A <u>pair</u> of scissors <u><u>is</u></u> on my desk.

4. *Titles and Names of Countries*

Use the singular form of the verb for titles of works of art or for the names of countries.

Shakespeare's <u>Complete Works</u> <u><u>is</u></u> more than a thousand pages.

The <u>United States</u> <u><u>is</u></u> a permanent member of the Security Council.

<u>The Night-Watch</u> <u><u>is</u></u> one of Rembrandt's most famous paintings.

5. *Amounts*

Use a singular form of the verb for words and phrases that express time and amounts (money, fractions, weight, volume).

<u>Thirty meters</u> <u><u>is</u></u> equal to almost one hundred feet.

<u>Two thirds</u> of the class <u><u>has</u></u> paid for the yearbooks.

<u>Twenty dollars</u> <u><u>doesn't</u></u> <u><u>fill</u></u> the gas tank anymore.

When such amounts are thought of individually and not as a unit, the plural form of the verb may be used.

These dollar <u>bills</u> <u>have</u> just been printed.

The <u>years</u> <u>seem</u> to whiz by.

6. *Predicate Nominatives*

When the subject and the predicate nominative are different in number, use a verb that agrees in number with the subject.

My worst <u>problem</u> <u>is</u> my younger brother and sister.

Honest, concerned <u>officials</u> <u>are</u> the responsibility of the voters.

7. Every *and* Many a

Use the singular form of the verb when the words *every* or *many a* precede the subject.

Every man, woman, and child *has* needs that must be met.
Many a student *leaves* an assignment until the last possible moment.
Every bush and tree *needs* water, light, and soil.

8. Doesn't *and* Don't

Use *doesn't* with singular nouns and the pronouns *he, she,* and *it.* Use *don't* with plural nouns and the pronouns *I, you, we,* and *they.*

Doesn't is a contraction of the singular verb *does* plus *not*; *don't* is a contraction of the plural verb *do* plus *not.* Avoid using *don't* with *he, she,* and *it.*

Exercise 7

Write the following sentences, choosing the form of the verb in parentheses that agrees with the subject. Underline the word you have chosen.

Examples

a. The aerobic exercise group (meet, meets) every Thursday at nine.
a. The aerobic exercise group <u>meets</u> every Thursday at nine.

b. The Netherlands (has, have) a population of more than 12 million.
b. The Netherlands <u>has</u> a population of more than 12 million.

c. Where (is, are) the pair of pliers we lent you?
c. Where <u>is</u> the pair of pliers we lent you?

1. Applied mathematics (provide, provides) excellent career opportunities into the 1980s.

2. During the season the football team (practice, practices) every day for three hours.

3. The jury (listen, listens) to the evidence and then (decide, decides) whether the defendant is guilty or not guilty.

4. Two thirds of the voters (is, are) a sizable majority.

5. She (don't, doesn't) have her key to the mailbox.

6. Every employee, even the president, (wear, wears) an identification badge.

7. Many an aspiring writer (is, are) unable to make a living without a second job.

8. Politics (appeal, appeals) to people who (like, likes) power.

9. *Seven Famous Greek Plays* (contain, contains) plays by Aeschylus, Sophocles, Euripides, and Aristophanes.

10. Four hours (is, are) a long time to wait.

The Verb *Be*

Be is the most irregular of all English verbs because it has three present tense forms and two past tense forms. Since *be* is also the most commonly used verb, it is important that you learn to use its forms correctly.

PRESENT TENSE

SINGULAR	PLURAL
I *am*	We *are*
You *are*	You *are*
He/She/It *is*	They *are*

Notice that the word *be* is not listed as a present tense form. Although it may be used in spoken dialects, this use of *be* is not part of Edited Standard English.

An asterisk (*) indicates a sentence with a feature that is not a part of Edited Standard English.

*I be really tired tonight.
I *am* really tired tonight.

*He be glad to be home.
He *is* glad to be home.

PAST TENSE

SINGULAR	PLURAL
I *was*	We *were*
You *were*	You *were*
He/She/It *was*	They *were*

Avoid using *was* with *you*, *we*, and *they*.

*We was hoping to win that last game.
We *were* hoping to win that last game.

*They was disappointed when you wasn't home.
They *were* disappointed when you *weren't* home.

The past participle of *be* is *been*, which is always used with a helping verb.

*I been so busy I haven't eaten yet.
I *have* (or *I've*) been so busy I haven't eaten yet.

Exercise 8

Write out the following sentences, choosing the form of the verb in parentheses used in Edited Standard English. Underline the word you chose.

Example

a. (Was, Were) you there when the fire broke out?

a. *Were you there when the fire broke out?*

1. We (was, were) in the space museum when it rained.

2. They (was, were) up at 5 o'clock every morning.

3. Dr. Bialko always (been, has been) a good person to talk to when you have a problem.

4. "You (is, are) lucky to be alive," Marc told Debbie after the accident.

5. The boys (is, are) planning a surprise for the girls.

6. The strawberries look good, but they (be, is, are) too expensive.

7. I (be, is, am) worried about Jerry's strange behavior.

8. The pencil sharpener (been, has been) broken for two months.

9. This year Peg and Sue (isn't, aren't) on the bowling team.

10. Grandma (be, is, am) happy to talk with her neighbors' children.

Verbs Often Confused

Three pairs of verbs are often confused because they sound alike and have somewhat similar meanings. These verbs are not interchangeable, however. To write Edited Standard English you need to know the principal parts of these verbs and their meanings.

lie and *lay*

Lie and *lay* are probably the most confusing pair because they not only have similar meanings but also share a common form.

PRESENT	PAST	PAST PARTICIPLE
lie	lay	(had) lain
lay	laid	(had) laid

Notice that the word *lay* is the present form of the verb *lay* and also the past form of the verb *lie.*

Lie means "to recline" or "to be in a horizontal position."

Lay means "to place something" or "to put something down."

When you use the verb *lay*, tell what object is being put down or placed somewhere.

In order to decide whether to use a form of *lie* or *lay*, you must first decide which verb fits the meaning of the sentence. If you can substitute the word *put* in the sentence, use the verb *lay.*

Lay: Mrs. Holloway gently *laid* the kitten next to its mother.
Kevin *laid* the new tiles in the bathroom.

Lie: The records warped when they *lay* in the sun.
Some people like to *lie* in bed till noon.

sit and *set*

In some dialects the word *set* is used to mean "sit down." In Edited Standard English, however, *sit* and *set* have distinctly different meanings.

Sit means "to occupy a seat" or "to rest."

Set means "to put or place something."

When you use *set* in a sentence, you must always tell what object is being placed or put somewhere.

The principal parts of *sit* and *set* are not difficult to memorize.

PRESENT	PAST	PAST PARTICIPLE
sit	sat	(had) sat
set	set	(had) set

Sit:	Won't you please *sit* next to the President?
	We have often *sat* at the end of the pier.
Set:	Please *set* the pitcher of milk on the kitchen table.
	We *set* four places for dinner.

rise and *raise*

Rise means "to go up" or "to get up."

Raise means "to move something upward."

Sentences containing the verb *raise* must always mention the object that is being moved upward.

Raised is a regular verb, but *rise* is an irregular verb.

PRESENT	PAST	PAST PARTICIPLE
rise	rose	(had) risen
raise	raised	(had) raised

Rise:	The consumer price index *rose* again last week.
	Will you please *rise* and state your name and address.
Raise:	Odette has *raised* an important question.
	Please *raise* the window shade a little.

Exercise 9

Choose the correct verb in parentheses to complete each sentence. Write the sentences and underline the word you have chosen from parentheses.

Examples

Additional exercises with these verb forms are on pages 421–422.

a. Joyce Eng (rose, raised) her hand.

a. *Joyce Eng raised her hand.*

b. He has been (lying, laying) the shingles for the new roof.

b. *He has been laying the shingles for the new roof.*

c. (Sit, Set) down and rest awhile.

c. *Sit down and rest awhile.*

1. Why are you (laying, lying) on the picnic table?

2. The jackets have (lain, laid) outside on the porch all night.

3. The passengers (lay, laid) stretched out on the sun deck.

4. Please (lay, lie) the packages on the table.

5. Hank's grandfather (lay, laid) down after dinner for a nap.

6. We must have (set, sat) and waited for an hour.

7. Please (set, sit) the telephone on the metal cabinet in the bedroom.

8. The doctors have (risen, raised) their prices again.

9. In her sleep Celia (raised, rose) and opened the refrigerator.

10. The editorial (raises, rises) issues that must be investigated.

Review Exercise A

In the following paragraph from *The Iliad, Book I,* fourteen verbs or verb phrases have been underlined. On a sheet of paper numbered 1–14, identify the tense and mood of each of the underlined verbs or verb phrases.[1]

Example

a. He uttered winged words and addressed her: "Why have you come O Child of Zeus of the Aegis, once more?"

a. *uttered—past tense, indicative; addressed—past tense, indicative; have come—present perfect tense, indicative*

Then in answer the goddess gray-eyed Athene spoke to him: "I have come down to stay your anger—but will you obey me?—from the sky; and the goddess of the white arms Hera sent me, who loves both of you equally in her heart and cares for you. Come then, do not take your sword in your hand, keep clear of fighting, though indeed with words you may abuse him, and it will be that way. And this also will I tell you and it will be a thing accomplished. Some day three times over such shining gifts shall be given you by reason of this outrage. Hold your hand then and obey us."

Review Exercise B

Write out the following sentences, providing the correct form of the verb in parentheses. Underline all of the verbs or verb phrases in each sentence.

Example

a. Neither the country nor the city (be) completely free of crime.

a. *Neither the country nor the city is completely free of crime.*

1. Eric Heiden has (break) another Olympic speed-skating record.

2. Since her mother's remarriage, Shelley has (become) much happier.

3. We must have (ride) at least twenty miles today.

4. Last weekend Katie Crenshaw (fly) her first solo flight.

---

[1]Excerpt from *The Iliad of Homer* by Richard Lattimore, © 1961. Reprinted by permission of The University of Chicago Press.

5. The pond has (freeze) only once since winter (begin).

6. How many cabins have your father and uncle (build)?

7. News stories of crime and corruption have (shake) my belief in the basic decency of people.

8. I had (know) Bo for a year before we started dating.

9. For the third time someone has (steal) all the hubcaps off the Cochrans' new car.

10. Mrs. Barrateau, who is seventy, has (swim) a mile every day ever since she moved to California.

11. When Professor Olson asked for an interpretation of the poem, no one (speak).

12. Have you ever (eat) crepes filled with ratatouille?

13. No one was home when the pipes (burst).

14. If I could have (choose) my family, I would've (choose) a different brother.

15. A Coast Guard buoy tender (sink) after colliding with a freighter in Tampa Bay.

16. Everyone has (go) to the clogging contest down at Tennessee Bob's.

17. Have you already (write) to the Varosela family in Athens?

18. Sidney's tuba practice has (drive) us all from the house.

19. How could they have (keep) their engagement a secret?

20. In the face of great difficulties, she has always (strive) to do her best.

21. Dolores Fitzwilliam (spend) her prize money on a new car.

22. "I've really (fall) in love again," Bluebeard sighed.

23. Have Earl and Fay (bring) their guitars?

24. Ever since the church was (build), the bells in the carillon have (ring) each day at noon.

25. Marcie thinks she (catch) her cold from the lady she (sit) next to at the opera.

Review Exercise C

Read the following passage from *Great Expectations* by Charles Dickens. Then, on a sheet of paper, write the correct past or past perfect form of the verb given in parentheses. Some of the verbs are regular verbs, and some are irregular.

Example

a. Business had (take) Herbert on a journey to Marseilles.

a. (1) taken

I (be) alone, and (have) a dull sense of being alone. I sadly (miss) the cheerful face and ready response of my friend. It (be) wretched weather; stormy and wet, stormy and wet; mud, mud, mud, deep in all the streets. We (live) at the top of the last house, and the wind rushing up the river (shake) the house that night, like discharges of cannon or breakings of a sea. I (see) that the lamps in the court (be) blown out, and that the lamps on the bridges and the shore (be) shuddering, and that the coal fires in barges on the river (be) being carried away before the wind like red-hot splashes in the rain.

I (read) with my watch upon the table, purposing to close my book at eleven o'clock. As I (shut) it, all the church clocks in the city (strike) that hour. The sound (be) curiously flawed by the wind; and I (be) listening, when I (hear) a footstep on the stair.

What nervous folly (make) me start, and awfully connect it with the footstep of my dead sister, matters not. It was past in a moment, and I (listen) again, and (hear) the footstep stumble in coming on. Remembering then that the staircase lights (be) blown out, I (take) up my reading lamp and (go) out to the stairhead. Whatever (be) below had (stop) on seeing my lamp, for all (be) quiet.

Review Exercise D

Write out the following sentences, choosing the form of the verb in parentheses that agrees with the subject. Underline the word you have chosen.

Examples

a. Six dollars (is, are) not a lot to pay for a shirt.

a. *Six dollars is not a lot to pay for a shirt.*

b. Janice (doesn't, don't) remember her father, who died when she was three.

b. *Janice doesn't remember her father, who died when she was three.*

c. Seven years (is, are) a long time to wait.

c. *Seven years is a long time to wait.*

1. Both Rog and Dianne (get, gets) up early enough to jog before work.
2. Marie usually (doesn't, don't) like to ask for help.
3. The dark-haired man with the glasses (play, plays) the viola.
4. At the peak of the harvest, everyone (help, helps) pick potatoes.
5. The plate of sandwiches (has, have) mysteriously disappeared.
6. Where (is, are) the manicure scissors?
7. There (is, are) a crowd of reporters waiting outside.
8. If you (is, are) going shopping, here (is, are) the coupons.
9. The contestant who seemed most talented (was, were) either Miss Ohio or Miss Delaware.
10. Everyone in Mrs. Garzziano's classes (was, were) excited about the play.
11. Few of the faculty (has, have) doctorate degrees.
12. All of the snow (has, have) melted, alas.

13. Some of the stolen money (has, have) been recovered.

14. Several of the sheep (has, have) strayed from the flock.

15. Today none of the fish (look, looks) freshly caught.

16. Either Murray or Carlos (is, are) in charge of student loans.

17. Neither the clerks nor I (has, have) the authority to approve this purchase.

18. Laura, Bennett, and Sam (has, have) lived in Pawtucket all their lives.

19. Each month the debate team (elect, elects) a new captain.

20. Physics, which (deal, deals) with matter and energy, (has, have) been of prime importance in Space Age technology.

21. Dad's colorful suspenders (was, were) hand-woven in Guatemala.

22. *Ghosts* (is, are) a powerful drama by the Norwegian playwright Henrik Ibsen.

23. One half (does, do) not make a majority.

24. We (was, were) hoping you'd visit us soon.

25. They (was, were) concerned about Leona, who (been, has been) depressed for the past few days.

Writing Exercise A

Choose one of the following assignments and write a brief paper. Check your first draft to make sure that you have used the verb forms correctly.

1. Describe a process with which you are familiar. Imagine that you are writing your directions for someone who knows absolutely nothing about the process you are describing. Tell what must be done, step by step, in the order that each step must be accomplished. The following processes are some suggestions.

Tying a shoelace	Catching a fish
Building a fire	Changing a flat tire
Hooking a rug	Writing a poem
Making a sand painting	Washing a dog

2. Imagine what you would see if you looked down from the top of one of the following structures.

A skyscraper in a big city	The roof of an apartment building
A mountain	A flagpole
A tall pine tree in a forest	An anthill

   Describe what you would see during a five-minute period, telling in as much detail as you can what the people or animals would be doing.

3. You are representing your school in a statewide competition. Tell how you feel before, during, or as you cross the finish line in one of the following races.

220-yard dash   5-mile bicycle race
500-meter speed-skating   10-mile marathon
giant slalom   20-mile cross-country running or skiing

4. Observe two people in animated discussion. Examine their faces closely and then write one or two paragraphs explaining what you think they could be discussing and why. Support your explanation by referring to specific details that you have observed.

Understanding Adjectives

Without *adjectives*, descriptions would be so limited that you could never talk about colors, tastes, sizes, or shapes. Consider the descriptions in the following two sentences.

The woman rode the horse into the forest.

The young, brown-haired woman rode the sleek white and gray horse into the foreboding forest.

Adjectives in the second sentence give details that make the scene easier to picture.

In the following sections you will learn how to identify adjectives and how they differ from other parts of speech.

Defining Adjectives

An *adjective* is usually defined as a word used to modify a noun or a pronoun. Adjectives limit or qualify nouns or pronouns by telling *what kind, which one, how many*, or *how much*.

What kind: a *friendly* kitten, a *tall* tree, an *elderly* woman

Which one: *this* morning, *these* pancakes, *that* exit, *those* sneakers

How many: *one* ticket, *six* eggs, *several* points, *few* applicants

How much: *less* noise, *more* hugging, a *scarce* supply

Exercise 1

Write out the following sentences and underline all the adjectives. (*A, an*, and *the* are always adjectives.) Do not count possessive pronouns, such as *our, my*, and *your*; these are considered pronouns, not adjectives.

Examples

a. Few jurors had read about the double murder.
a. Few jurors had read about the double murder.

b. The oldest member of our family is Grandpa Max, who is ninety.
b. The oldest member of our family is Grandpa Max, who is ninety.

1. Many boatloads of refugees land each week.

2. This key opens the secret drawer in the old, wooden desk.

3. Joel is intelligent, imaginative, and irresponsible.

4. In emergencies, such as blackouts and blizzards, people who live in large cities become friendlier.

5. Elaine has had a sore throat and high fever for two days.

6. Sheila wants to meet a young man who likes hiking, bicycling, and classical music.

7. At one time or another, all teenagers must make important decisions.

8. There is not much room for three people in the back seat of that car.

9. Jana found a tattered, black wallet containing fifty dollars.

10. She can be angry and argumentative one moment and pleasant the next minute.

Grouping Adjectives by Classes

Although many common adjectives cannot be grouped into any special class, other adjectives may fit into one or more of the categories discussed in this section.

1. The most common adjectives are the articles *a, an,* and *the.*

A and *an* are called *indefinite articles* because they do not point out a definite person, place, or thing. *The,* which points out a specific thing or person, is called a *definite article.*

Indefinite Article:	Please bring me *a* book.
Definite Article:	Please bring me *the* book.
Indefinite Article:	*A* state senator will speak on nuclear power.
Definite Article:	*The* state senator will speak on nuclear power.

A is used before words that begin with a consonant sound, *an* before words beginning with a vowel sound.

a horrible accident	*an* herb
a difficult decision	*an* open mind
a hysterical student	*an* honest answer

2. Adjectives formed from proper nouns are called *proper adjectives.*

A proper adjective always begins with a capital letter.

*D*anish pastry   *D*emocratic party
Central American trade   *S*hakespearean sonnet
*F*rench bread   *Polish-American* club

3. Adjectives usually come before the noun they modify.

    Buttons is a *furry, noisy* mutt.

    Some adjectives, however, are separated from the word they modify.
    An adjective that follows a linking verb and modifies the subject of the sentence is called a *predicate adjective.*

    Toby is extremely *confident.*
    The fire fighters were both *courteous* and *helpful.*
    I feel *upset* and *angry.*

4. Many words that are sometimes pronouns may also be adjectives, depending on how they are used in a sentence.

    The following words are adjectives when they modify a noun or pronoun. When they stand alone, they are considered pronouns.

all	few	one	this
another	many	other	those
any	more	several	what
both	most	some	which
each	much	that	
either	neither	these	

Pronoun:	*This* is her third try.
Adjective:	She will succeed on *this* try.
Pronoun:	*Many* of the records are missing.
Adjective:	*Many* records are missing.
Pronoun:	The clerk left *several* of the samples.
Adjective:	We looked at *several* samples.

5. A noun that modifies another noun is considered an adjective.

    Such nouns used as adjectives always come directly before the noun they modify.

    We ordered three *turkey* sandwiches.
    Luisa plays in a *softball* game every *Saturday* morning.
    Yuri sells *magazine* subscriptions by telephone.

Exercise 2

Write out the following sentences, underlining all adjectives. If the adjective falls into one of the special classes—article, proper adjective, predicate adjective, pronoun used as adjective, or noun used as adjective—write the adjective and its label beneath the sentence. Do not count possessive pronouns (words such as *my, your,* and *ours*) as adjectives.

Example

a. In 1902 Theodore Roosevelt became the first American President to ride in an automobile.

a. *In 1902 Theodore Roosevelt became the first American President to ride in an automobile.*

the—*article*; American—*proper adjective*; an—*article*

1. Seventy percent of the people in the world do not have radio, television, or newspapers.

2. In Hunza, a Pakistani mountain valley, most men and women live to be one hundred years of age.

3. The highest wave ever ridden by a Hawaiian surfer was fifty feet high.

4. The North American duck hawk, the fastest animal on earth, can dive at speeds up to 175 miles per hour.

5. A thirty-foot whale swam next to a man for almost thirteen hours during his twenty-two mile swim from Catalina Island to San Pedro, California.

6. The Buddhist saying, "Hurt not others in ways that you yourself would find hurtful," has the same message as the Golden Rule of Christianity and Judaism.

7. In 1924 a Scandinavian lumberjack claimed that he was kidnaped for a week by a family of giant human-like creatures that are known today as Sasquatches.

8. According to a Navaho creation myth, the first world was populated only by insects and insect-like people.

9. Gambler's Anonymous, a self-help fellowship, aims to help compulsive gamblers stop their gambling.

10. The last words of the American poet and novelist Edgar Allan Poe were, "Lord help my poor soul."

Finding an Adjective by Its Features

You can identify adjectives by learning the features that distinguish them from other parts of speech.

1. Adjectives may change form to show degrees of comparison. Many—but not all—adjectives can show degrees of comparison.

   There are three degrees: *positive, comparative,* and *superlative.* The *positive degree* describes a quality or characteristic; it is the "plain form" of the adjective. The *comparative degree* of an adjective is used to compare two persons or things. The *superlative* degree is used to compare three or more persons or things.

Positive:	Lee is *considerate.*
Comparative:	Lee is *more considerate* than his brother.
Superlative:	Lee is the *most considerate* person in his family.

Positive:	This chili is *hot*.
Comparative:	This chili is *hotter* than the Won Ton soup.
Superlative:	This is the *hottest* chili I've ever eaten.

See pages 380–381 for information about using the comparative and superlative degrees.

The comparative and superlative forms of adjectives are formed in two different ways.

All adjectives of one syllable and a few of two syllables have *-er* added to form the comparative degree and *-est* to form the superlative degree.

POSITIVE	COMPARATIVE	SUPERLATIVE
cool	cooler	coolest
thin	thinner	thinnest
cruel	crueler	cruelest
fancy	fancier	fanciest

Most adjectives of two syllables and all adjectives of more than two syllables form the comparative degree with the word *more* and the superlative degree with the word *most*.

POSITIVE	COMPARATIVE	SUPERLATIVE
helpful	more helpful	most helpful
delicious	more delicious	most delicious
important	more important	most important

The words *less* and *least* are used before all adjectives to indicate less of a quality.

POSITIVE	COMPARATIVE	SUPERLATIVE
odd	less odd	least odd
expensive	less expensive	least expensive
unpleasant	less unpleasant	least unpleasant

A few common adjectives form their comparative and superlative degrees irregularly. (See pages 381–382.)

2. Adjectives may follow intensifiers.

Words like *very*, *quite*, *extremely*, and *rather* are called *intensifiers*. (See page 387.) They qualify the word that follows by telling "to what extent." Both adjectives and adverbs may follow intensifiers.

Beatrice is very *logical*.

I feel extremely *lucky* to have been born in America.

We were rather *upset* after the near-accident.

3. Adjectives may be formed with suffixes.

Certain suffixes, such as *-able*, *-en*, *-ful*, *-ish*, *-less*, *-like*, and *-ous*, are used to form adjectives. These suffixes signal that the word ending in the suffix is an adjective.

mysterious	changeable	careful
lovable	cautious	childish
wooden	careless	childlike

Exercise 3

Write out the following paragraphs and underline each adjective. To determine whether a word is an adjective, ask yourself whether it modifies a noun or a pronoun or whether it has any of the features of adjectives. Be sure to classify as adjectives nouns or pronouns that modify nouns. You should find twenty-six adjectives.

Example

a. One of the hardest things to deal with is peer pressure.
a. One of the hardest things to deal with is peer pressure.

It is difficult to be different; everyone wants to be popular. Many teenagers start smoking, for example, because "everybody is doing it." Even though medical and scientific evidence continues to show that cigarette smoking causes cancer and other lung diseases, the number of teenage smokers continues to increase. To young smokers death and disease seem impossible.

Listen to Martha tell why she doesn't smoke: "I watched my favorite aunt die from lung cancer last year. It was a horrible, painful death. She always used to smoke two packs of cigarettes a day. She tried to quit several times, but she was really addicted, I guess. I feel sorry for the kids who have been smoking since they were fourteen. Nobody will ever get me to wreck my health—not with drugs or cigarettes or alcohol. Life's too great!"

Mastery Exercise A

Use your knowledge of the definition, classes, and features of adjectives to identify the adjectives in the following paragraphs from a short story called "Music When Soft Voices Die" by Frank O'Connor. List the adjectives on a sheet of paper in the order they occur.[1]

They were nice girls, though. Joan, who was nineteen, was my favorite. She was masterful and warmhearted; she would take my part when I got into trouble, and whenever she saw me with the sign of tears, she would say, "Look, Larry—*you* tell Mr. Scally if he says *another* word to you, I'll tear his *eyes* out." She talked like that, all in italics. I liked Nora, too, but not so much. Sometimes she was very sweet and sometimes she didn't see you, and you never knew which it would be. Marie I didn't really like at all in those days. She was the prettiest of the three—thin, tall, and nunlike, with a queer stiff way of holding herself and an ironic intonation in her beautiful voice. Marie usually just didn't see you. I thought she was an old snob.

The three girls had fellows, and I knew these, too, mostly from seeing them hang about the office in the evening. Joan was going with a long-haired medical student called Mick Shea, with no hat and no religion, and she was always making novenas for his conversion. Nora went with a dressy fellow in Montenotte, the classy quarter of Cork, but she had a sort of underground understanding with a good-looking postman called Paddy Lacy, who used to stop me in the street and give me gallant messages for her. She never walked out with him that I knew of, but he was certain she loved him, and it shocked me that a superior fellow like a postman would not have more sense. Marie was going

---

[1]Excerpt from "Music When Soft Voices Die" from *A Set Of Variations* by Frank O'Connor. Story first appeared in *The New Yorker Magazine*. Reprinted by permission of Joan Daves.

strong with a chap called Jim Holbrook, a rather snobbish intellectual type, who lived up my way.

Thirty years has turned the girls and myself into old friends. Only Nora is still at the office. Joan owns a private hotel, and Marie is the harassed mother of two wild children. She is still beautiful, sedate, and caustic. Not one word of their conversation ever seemed to register in my memory, which was full of valuable information about American states and Indian nations, wigwams, colts, derringers, and coyotes; yet now that I cannot remember anything of what I read, it seems to me that I can hear the girls as though they were in the same room with me, like the voices of Shelley's poems, trembling on the edge of pure music.

Caustic means "cutting or sarcastic."

Writing Exercise A

Choose someone you know well—a friend or relative or even yourself. Then make a list of twenty different adjectives that you think describe the person you have chosen. Your adjectives can describe the person's physical appearance as well as his or her personality. (Make sure that all the words on your list are adjectives.) Using the words on your list, write a short paper describing that person. When you have finished, underline each adjective.

Mastery Exercise B

Choose three paragraphs from a novel or short story. Use the features of adjectives, the definition, and the classes of adjectives to identify all the adjectives in the paragraphs. List each adjective on a sheet of paper and be prepared to explain how you identified each one.

Using Adjectives

In the following sections you will practice using both regular and irregular forms of degrees of comparison. You will also practice writing with adjectives that provide exact descriptions and sense details.

Using Comparative and Superlative Degrees

The following guidelines will help you to use adjectives in a way that conforms to Edited Standard English.

1. The comparative degree is used to compare two things.

    Comparative: Julie's horse is *faster* than her father's horse.
    This popcorn is *better* than the popcorn we had yesterday.

    The superlative degree is used to compare three or more things.

    Superlative: Julie's horse is the *fastest* filly in the country.
    This is the *best* pistachio ice cream I have ever eaten.

2. Use the words *other* or *else* when comparing a person or thing with the rest of a group to which it belongs.

    *Octavio is brighter than anyone in his class.
    Octavio is brighter than anyone *else* in his class.

    *Cactus survives better than any desert plant.
    Cactus survives better than any *other* desert plant.

3. Avoid double comparisons. Do not use the *-er* or *-est* form together with the word *more* or *most*.

    *That is the most scariest movie I ever saw.
    That is the *scariest* movie I ever saw.

    *Your eyes are more bluer than your brother's.
    Your eyes are *bluer* than your brother's.

Exercise 1

Some of the following sentences contain errors in the use of adjectives. If a sentence is incorrect, rewrite it correctly. If a sentence is correct, write *C*.

Examples

a. Of all four of my grandparents, Grandma Jennie is the more interesting.
a. *Of all four of my grandparents, Grandma Jennie is the most interesting.*

b. Ira is older than anyone else in his class.
b. *C*

1. Hortie seems more cheerfuler today.
2. The Russian village where my grandfather was born is smaller than any village in Russia.
3. Eleanor's mother's bowling average is the most highest in the league.
4. Of the two sisters Winoa is the nicest.
5. Myra Ling is the best speaker in her class.
6. Of the ten finalists Tom was judged the more talented sculptor.
7. Which of Noah's three sons was the more reliable?
8. Sheila's pottery is more beautifuler than the pottery in the China Barn.
9. Of the two cars the larger car has the least efficient engine.
10. What is the most tallest mountain in South America?

Using Irregular Adjectives

The comparative and superlative degrees of most adjectives are formed with either the suffixes *-er* and *-est* or the words *more* and *most*.

A few commonly used adjectives form their degrees of comparison *irregularly*.

POSITIVE	COMPARATIVE	SUPERLATIVE
bad, ill	worse	worst
good	better	best
little	less or lesser	least
many	more	most
much	more	most
well	better	best

Craig felt *ill* on Sunday and *worse* on Monday.
More students are taking psychology this year.

Exercise 2

Write out the following sentences, using either the comparative or the superlative degree of the adjective in parentheses. Underline the adjective.

Example

a. Yuri seems to have the (bad) luck of anyone in his family.
a. Yuri seems to have the worst luck of anyone in his family.

1. Are you feeling (well) than yesterday?
2. Sean always takes the (little) amount of dessert possible.
3. In every culture (many) people speak at least one language.
4. Tonsillitis was the (bad) disease Aunt Cele had ever experienced.
5. Lorin is a (good) driver than her brother Alec.
6. Gary feels (bad) about the lie than he does about the accident.
7. (Much) of the arguments in our family are caused by money than by anything else.
8. Of all the tacos I have ever eaten, these are the (good).
9. When the sailboat anchored in the harbor, Donna felt (ill) than she had at sea.
10. She has (little) difficulty seeing at a distance than she does up close.

Writing with Adjectives

Specific nouns and verbs help to communicate exact pictures to a reader. In the same way adjectives can add specific details and sense details to make your descriptions more interesting. Suppose, for example, you wanted to describe a pizza fresh from the oven:

The *golden-brown* crust enclosed a *bubbly*, *steamy* sea of *liquid* mozzarella, *tomato* sauce, *spicy* sausages, and *tender* mushrooms.

Notice how the *italicized* adjectives add details that appeal to the senses of taste and sight. What specific adjectives could you use to describe the *smell* of a freshly baked pizza?

Suppose you wanted to describe a sunset. Exact adjectives help make the description more vivid:

Crimson streamers slashed the *gold-rimmed* clouds, slowly fading into *night-blue* sky.

Too many adjectives—one of the dangers of student writing—can be just as boring as none at all. Use adjectives for special, vivid effects. As a rule, avoid long strings of adjectives.

Another adjective trap to avoid is using overworked adjectives. Words like *nice*, *pretty*, and *terrific* are so vague and overused that they no longer communicate much. Try to use exact adjectives to say what you mean.

Writing Exercise A

Rewrite the following sentences, adding details that make the description more specific. Try to avoid using overworked adjectives, but do use adjectives that evoke sensory details. Underline each adjective that you use.

Example
a. Clouds filled the sky.

a. *Gigantic, snowy clouds filled the bright sky.*

1. A girl approached the house.
2. The dog lay on the rug next to the chair.
3. The man on the bicycle passed the car.
4. Katie picked the vegetables in the garden.
5. Roy liked to imagine the car he would buy someday.
6. Mother brought the food to the dinner table.
7. Snow covered the ground.
8. Two women fed the pigeons.
9. The bird sang from the top of the tree.
10. After the storm everything looked nice.

Review Exercise A

Some of the following sentences contain errors in the use of adjectives. If a sentence is incorrect, rewrite it correctly. If a sentence is correct, write *C*.

Example
a. Sally has the most beautifulest handwriting in the class.

a. *Sally has the most beautiful handwriting in the class.*

1. Of the four boys Barry is the more reliable.
2. Marianne is a better gymnast than anyone in her class.
3. I want to buy the most cheapest three-speed bicycle I can find.
4. Carla has the truest soprano of all the singers in the chorus.
5. I hope that you are feeling more better today.
6. Mr. Pugliese, Ralph's father, is much iller than when I saw him last.
7. I am least optimistic than she is.

8. What is the most funniest movie you have ever seen?

9. Betty Joe is the more successful of all six motorcycle salespersons in the showroom.

10. Your room is a much bigger mess than mine.

11. Paula's attendance record is worser this month than last.

12. Lately the two brothers have had much littler conflict.

13. Paolo and Kim are the more skillful of all the carpenters in town.

14. Stop looking for the absolutely better solution and just decide something.

15. Most residents in the building complain that the rent is too high.

16. That was the most bad scandal in the history of this county.

17. Which do you think is the least satisfactory of your two choices?

18. Marriage is the most difficult and demanding contract that most people ever enter into.

19. After the concert Mrs. O'Connelly felt so much more ill that we rushed her to the hospital.

20. Without your help, we would have been less ready for the exam.

Writing Exercise B

Choose one of the following situations and write several paragraphs of description, using exact adjectives to make your writing specific. When you have finished, underline each adjective.

1. You accidentally stray into a time warp and find yourself alone on another planet, light-years from earth. Describe what you see as you explore the planet on your first day there.

2. You meet someone of the opposite sex, whom you think is ideal. You would like to know that person better and spend time with him or her. Describe that person and tell why you are attracted to him or her. If you wish, write part of the conversation the two of you might have.

3. You have just won a sweepstakes that allows you to spend $1,000 on anything you want in your favorite department store. In as much detail as possible, describe the things you would choose to buy with the money.

4. The photograph on page 385 evokes different moods in different people. Making use of adjectives, describe the mood the photo creates for you and explain what it is about the scene that makes you feel that way. Underline the adjectives you include.

Writing Exercise C

Find a paper you have written some time within the past year. Underline every adjective and check to see if you have used the adjectives correctly. Have you used overworked adjectives? Do you see sentences that would be improved

by adding specific adjectives or adjectives that evoke sense details? If so, rewrite those sentences.

Understanding Adverbs

English has two parts of speech that serve as modifiers—adjectives and adverbs. You have seen that adjectives modify nouns or pronouns. In the following sections you will learn how to identify *adverbs* by their function in a sentence and by their features. You will also learn to identify the different kinds of adverbs.

Defining Adverbs   An *adverb* is usually defined as a word that modifies a verb, an adjective, or another adverb.

Modifies a Verb: The mockingbird sings *loudly*.
Modifies an Adjective: Lloyd feels *extremely* happy.
Modifies an Adverb: She plays chess *quite* well.

Adverbs answer the questions *how? how often? when? where?* or *to what extent?*

How: James Baldwin writes *well*.
How Often: James Baldwin's books appear *frequently*.
When: James Baldwin lives in Paris *now*.
Where: He has lived *there* for many years.
To What Extent: He has been *extremely* candid about his experiences as a black man in America.

Exercise 1

Write out the following sentences, underlining all adverbs. Beneath each sentence identify the questions answered by each adverb.

Example

a. Yesterday I volunteered to count turtle nests along the beach.

a. *Yesterday I volunteered to count turtle nests along the beach.*
yesterday—When?

1. The two friends seldom write to each other, but their friendship remains.
2. Sandy and Lou moved here in 1980.
3. On opening night a crowd of devoted fans waited outside.
4. If you had told me earlier, I would have called her.
5. Joyfully the child hugged her father.
6. When Mrs. Eisenberg speaks, everybody listens attentively.
7. Cockatoos can be trained to perform extremely complex tricks.
8. Shaheen always knew he wanted to be a physicist.
9. Dara says that Paul's parents give him too much freedom.
10. Ray Youngbear is now studying electrical engineering.

Grouping Adverbs by Classes   Most adverbs are like *sometimes, suddenly, eagerly,* and *painfully*. They fall into no special class or group. There are, however, four special kinds of adverbs. Knowing these classes of adverbs will help you to identify adverbs in general.

Interrogative Adverbs

The adverbs *how, when, where,* and *why* are called *interrogative adverbs* when they begin a sentence that asks a question.

> *How* well do you know Mercedes?
> *Where* are you going after school today?
> *Why* didn't you call me back?
> *When* are you going roller-skating?

Negative Adverbs

Not (and its contraction *n't*), *never, seldom, scarcely, barely,* and *hardly* are called *negative adverbs*. They deny the truth of the statement being made.

Positive:	I wash windows well.
Negative:	I do*n't* wash windows well.
Negative:	I *never* wash windows well.
Positive:	She is honest.
Negative:	She is *seldom* honest.
Negative:	She is*n't* honest.

Intensifiers

Intensifiers are adverbs that answer the question *to what extent?* They come immediately before the word they modify, which may be either an adjective or an adverb. The following adverbs are common intensifiers.

completely	quite	too
exceptionally	rather	totally
extremely	really	unusually
fairly	so	very

Modifies Adjectives:	Deer are *extremely* shy.
	The gas tank is *almost* empty.
Modifies Adverbs:	Ria finished the test *rather* quickly.
	Manuela sanded the desk *very* thoroughly.

In your writing try to avoid the tendency to overuse *very*. Choose other intensifiers from the preceding list to vary your writing.

Nouns Used as Adverbs

Just as nouns are sometimes used as adjectives, so some nouns are used as adverbs. Nouns that answer the questions *when? where? how much?* or *to what extent?* should be classified as adverbs.

> The wounded cat dragged itself *home*.
> This rain will last all *day*.
> *Yesterday* Nina and Jerry broke up.

Exercise 2

Write out the following sentences and underline each adverb. If the adverb belongs to a special class, write the adverb beneath the sentence and indicate its type. (Some sentences have more than one adverb.)

Example

a. Where are my sunglasses?

a. *Where are my sunglasses?*
   where—interrogative

1. Some people think she won the award rather unfairly.
2. How will Justin get to work now?
3. Mike was extremely disappointed when he didn't hear from Margie.
4. Baked goods from the Darling Bakery are seldom delicious.
5. Mary Jane D'Leon is eagerly and nervously waiting to hear if she can qualify for a mortgage.
6. Daisy seems to be an unusually serious person.
7. My parents seldom go out to dinner because it is too expensive.
8. Lila is so thin that she is trying to gain some weight.
9. Mrs. Bessie Johnson, Benny's grandmother, has won several prizes for her extremely beautiful roses.
10. Why didn't you finish the race when you were so close to winning?

Finding an Adverb by Its Features

Adverbs and adjectives, both modifiers, share the same three features. In order to distinguish an adverb from an adjective, you must determine what word it modifies in the sentence. Remember that adverbs modify verbs, adjectives, and other adverbs. Adjectives can only modify nouns or pronouns.

1. Adverbs may change form to show degrees of comparison.

Some—but not all—adverbs may show degrees of comparison. Adverbs that end in -*ly* form their comparative and superlative degrees with the words *more* and *most*.

POSITIVE	COMPARATIVE	SUPERLATIVE
slowly	more slowly	most slowly
cautiously	more cautiously	most cautiously
mysteriously	more mysteriously	most mysteriously

Most one-syllable adverbs form their degrees of comparison with -*er* and -*est* added to the positive degree. Most such adverbs may also function as adjectives.

POSITIVE	COMPARATIVE	SUPERLATIVE
fast	faster	fastest
hard	harder	hardest
late	later	latest
long	longer	longest
slow	slower	slowest
quick	quicker	quickest

2. Adverbs may be used with intensifiers.

Intensifiers are a special class of adverbs that answer the question *to what extent?* (A list of intensifiers is on page 387.) Intensifiers can be thought of as modifier signals because an adjective or an adverb always comes right after the intensifier.

> Luisa can speak Mandarin Chinese *extremely* fluently.
> Lorenzo plays the flute *very* well.
> Georgina was *unusually* quiet tonight.
> We were *quite* upset at the news.

3. Adverbs may be formed with suffixes.

The most common adverb suffix is *-ly*, which means "in a certain manner or at a certain time."

> annually   completely   wickedly

Not all words that end in *-ly* are adverbs, however. *Friendly, lonely, lovely,* and *only* are all adjectives.

Other adverb-forming suffixes include *-ward (upward, downward), -ways (sideways, endways)* and *-wise (lengthwise, slantwise).*

Exercise 3

Write out the following sentences, underlining all adverbs. If the adverb ends in a suffix, circle the suffix. (Some sentences may have more than one adverb.)

Example

a. The word *porcupine*, which comes from medieval France, means literally "thorny pig."

a. *The word* porcupine, *which comes from medieval France, means literal(ly) "thorny pig."*

1. The Oregon Trail stretched northward and westward from Independence, Missouri.

2. During its new moon phase the moon is completely dark when seen from earth.

3. The poet John Keats says that the nightingale, of all birds, sings most beautifully.

4. The vinegarroon is a rather large whip scorpion that emits a fluid that smells like vinegar.

5. The shamrock, a fairly common cloverlike plant, is the national emblem of Ireland.

6. The Everglades kite is one of the animals most recently placed on the endangered species list.

7. Because "the hand moves more quickly than the eye," prestidigitation and legerdemain are successful.

8. When measured lengthwise, the bald eagle is 2½ feet, but its wing-spread ranges up to 7½ feet.

9. According to the Beaufort wind scale, the wind blows more strongly during a hurricane (over 65 knots) than in a storm (56–65 knots).

10. Peanuts, which are the fruit of the peanut plant, grow totally underground.

Review Exercise A

Identify fifteen of the adverbs in the following paragraphs, using your knowledge of the definition of an adverb, its classes, and its features to identify them. (Remember that in order to distinguish an adverb from an adjective, you must determine what word it modifies in the sentence.) Write out the paragraphs, underlining each adverb and drawing an arrow to the word it modifies.

Example

a. An ancient Greek myth tells of a teenager who almost destroyed the earth.

a. *An ancient Greek myth tells of a teenager who <u>almost</u> destroyed the earth.*

Phaethon never knew who his father was. One day his mother told him that he was the son of Helios, the sun god. Phaethon was extremely curious about his father and very eager to meet him. He made the dangerously long journey to the Palace of the Sun God in the east. Phaethon stood bravely before his father's dazzling throne. "Am I really your son?" he asked. "If I am, grant me a very special favor."

Unthinkingly, Helios agreed. But Phaethon foolishly chose to drive the sun god's chariot across the sky. Four fiery horses pulled the chariot across the sky daily with Helios at the reins. This, the Greeks believed, explained the rising of the sun in the East and its setting in the West.

Phaethon could not be dissuaded from his request. Unfortunately, he couldn't control his father's horses, who soon realized their master was not driving. The chariots swooped too close to earth, setting crops and trees on fire. Finally, Zeus himself, king of the gods, ended Phaethon's dangerous journey by striking the terrified boy with a thunderbolt. Phaethon died, the ancient Greeks firmly believed, because he dared to do what only gods can do.

Mastery Exercise A

List fifteen of the adverbs in the following paragraph from Katherine Anne Porter's short story "The Jilting of Granny Weatherall" on a sheet of paper.[1]

In her day she had kept a better house and had got more work done. She wasn't too old yet for Lydia to be driving eighty miles for advice when one of the children jumped the track, and Jimmy still dropped in and talked things

---

[1] Excerpt from "The Jilting of Granny Weatherall" from *The Flowering Judas and Other Stories* by Katherine Anne Porter. Reprinted by permission of Harcourt Brace Jovanovich, Inc. and Jonathan Cape Ltd.

over: "Now, Mammy, you've a good business head, I want to know what you think of this? . . ." Old. Cornelia couldn't change the furniture around without asking. Little things, little things! They had been so sweet when they were little. Granny wished the old days were back again with the children young and everything to be done over. It had been a hard pull, but not too much for her. When she thought of all the food she had cooked, and all the clothes she had cut and sewed, and all the gardens she had made—well, the children showed it. There they were, made out of her, and they couldn't get away from that. Sometimes she wanted to see John again and point to them and say, Well, I didn't do so badly, did I? But that would have to wait. That was for tomorrow.

Mastery Exercise B

From a newspaper or magazine article or from a story you have read recently, select several paragraphs. Using what you have learned in this section about identifying adverbs, find the adverbs in the passage and list them on a sheet of paper.

Using Adverbs

In the following sections you will practice using the comparative and superlative forms of *adverbs*—both regular and irregular. You will learn to distinguish between some adjective and adverb word pairs that are often confused, and you will learn why it is necessary to avoid double negatives.

Using Comparative and Superlative Forms of Adverbs

The rules for using the *comparative* and *superlative degrees* are the same for adverbs as they are for adjectives.

When two or more items are being compared, the comparative degree of the adverb is used.

> Ginger works *harder* than I do.
> Ella eats *more quickly* than Cal.

When three or more items are being compared, use the superlative degree of the adverb.

> Ginger works *hardest* of all the people in this class.
> Of all the people in our family, Ella eats *most quickly*.

Exercise 1

Write out the following sentences, using either the comparative or superlative degree of the adverb in parentheses. Underline the adverb you have used.

Examples

a. Nancy threw the ball (far) than Pat.
a. *Nancy threw the ball <u>farther</u> than Pat.*

b. Of all the students in our class, Alice writes (neatly).

b. *Of all the students in our class, Alice writes <u>most neatly</u>.*

1. Ramiro lives (dangerously) than his brother.

2. Don ran the mile (speedily) than Sean.

3. I stayed (late) than Rich did.

4. Of the three boys Ryan waits (patiently).

5. I hope this package arrives (soon) than the last one.

6. According to my grandmother, when my father was young, of all his brothers and sisters he acted (foolishly).

7. I have three very good friends, but of them all, Livvy listens (sympathetically) to my problems.

8. Dogs whose owners reward them with praise and affection obey orders (willingly) than dogs whose owners give no rewards.

9. Isabel smiles much (readily) now that her braces are off.

10. On the day of the blizzard, we stayed at the library (long) than we had intended.

Using Irregular Forms of Adverbs

Adverbs that end in *-ly* use the words *more* and *most* to form their degrees of comparison, while one-syllable adverbs use *-er* or *-est*.

A few commonly used adverbs form their comparative and superlative degrees irregularly.

POSITIVE	COMPARATIVE	SUPERLATIVE
badly	worse	worst
far	farther	farthest
little	less	least
much	more	most
well	better	best

You may recognize that some of the words in the preceding list may also be used as adjectives. Remember that they are adverbs only when they modify a verb, an adjective, or another adverb.

His broken finger hurts *less* than it did yesterday.

I work *best* when I feel happy.

Exercise 2

Write out the following sentences, using the comparative or superlative degree of the adverb in parentheses. Underline each adverb and draw an arrow to the word it modifies.

Examples

a. Of all the sprinters, Jack can run (far) in two minutes.

a. *Of all the sprinters, Jack can run <u>farthest</u> in two minutes.*

    b. Right now, that is the (little) important thing to worry about.

    b. *Right now, that is the least important thing to worry about.*

1. June plays the recorder (badly) than I do.

2. This time we measured the window (much) carefully than last time.

3. Raoul paints (well) than he sings.

4. She is (little) interested in making money than she is in establishing her reputation.

5. Which of the six cars drove (far) on ten gallons of gas?

6. Who do you think dances (well)—Gene Kelly or Fred Astaire?

7. Which of the three sisters do you know (well)?

8. Although Brad has been dieting for two weeks, he weighs (much) now than when he started.

9. Of all the people I know, I am the (little) likely to have my ears pierced.

10. The choir sings (badly) this year than last.

Choosing Between Adjectives and Adverbs

In writing and speaking you will often have to choose between *an adjective* and *an adverb*. If you are unsure which modifier should be used, check to see what word is being modified.

Use an adverb to modify a verb, an adjective, or another adverb. Use an adjective to modify a noun or a pronoun.

> Howard stared (silent, silently) at the ghostly figure.
> The mysterious shape was also (silent, silently).

You probably had no trouble choosing *silently* in the first sentence and *silent* in the second. Problems arise, however, when the adjective or adverb is so often misused that the wrong choice begins to sound right. Three such adjective-adverb pairs are discussed in the following paragraphs.

bad/badly

Bad is an adjective that modifies a noun or a pronoun. *Bad* is often used after linking verbs, such as *feel*, *look*, or *taste*.

> I felt *bad* after Leo stopped calling me.
> Thea's fruit salad tastes *bad*.

Badly is an adverb that tells how an action is performed.

> Katie plays Scrabble *badly* but still enjoys it.

good/well

Good is an adjective; it should never be used as an adverb.

> That is *good* news.
> The custard tastes *good*.

Well is a troublesome modifier because it can either be an adjective or an adverb. *Well* is an adjective when it is used to mean "healthy, attractive, or satisfactory."

Meg didn't feel *well* after dinner.

You look *well* in blue.

"Twelve o'clock, and all is *well!*"

Well is an adverb that tells how an action is performed.

Luis plays the French horn *well.*

slow/slowly

Slow is an adjective that means the opposite of *fast.*

Sales are *slow* during the summer months.

Slow has become accepted as an adverb because of its use on highway signs.

Drive *slow.*   Go *slow.*

However, the adverb *slowly* should be used after all other action verbs.

Walk *slowly* down the hall and look at the ceiling.

She spoke *slowly*, searching for the right words.

Exercise 3

Write out the following sentences, choosing the correct modifier from the pair in parentheses. Underline the modifier you have chosen.

Examples

a. Kirstin looks (well, good) in her cap and gown.

a. Kirstin looks well in her cap and gown.

b. We opened the door (slow, slowly) and peered inside.

b. We opened the door slowly and peered inside.

1. After the argument Jim felt (bad, badly) about what he had said.
2. Mischa and his brother work (good, well) together.
3. The flute player also plays the trumpet (good, well).
4. George has not been feeling (good, well) for several days.
5. "All's (good, well) that ends (good, well)," she sighed.
6. Don't you think the horseradish smells (bad, badly)?
7. He writes so (bad, badly) that it is hard to read his letters.
8. "Remember to drive (slow, slowly)," she cautioned.
9. Harriet opened the package (slow, slowly) and carefully.
10. The ketchup flowed (slow, slowly) until it all came out with a plop.

**Using
Negatives
Correctly**

An asterisk (*)
denotes a sentence
with a feature that is
not a part of Edited
Standard English.

When two negative words appear in the same sentence, the construction is called a *double negative.*

Avoid using double negatives in speaking and in writing.

> *I didn't say nothing.
> I didn't say anything.
> I said nothing.

> *I don't have no umbrella.
> I don't have an umbrella.
> I have no umbrella.

Remember that the adverbs *barely, scarcely,* and *hardly* are negative words and should not be used with other negatives.

> *Jana couldn't hardly stay awake till midnight.
> Jana could hardly stay awake till midnight.
> Jana couldn't stay awake till midnight.

The words *but* and *only* also have negative meanings in the expressions *haven't but, can't help but,* and *haven't only.* Avoid using these double negative expressions in writing Edited Standard English.

> *Glynnis hasn't but twenty cents in her pocket.
> Glynnis has but twenty cents in her pocket.

> *I can't help but wonder what happened to Clark.
> I can't help wondering what happened to Clark.

Exercise 4

Rewrite each of the following sentences in Edited Standard English, removing the double negative.

> **Examples**
> a. Frederico can't hardly carry a tune.
> *a. Frederico can hardly carry a tune.*
> b. The parakeet can't say but one word.
> *b. The parakeet can say but one word.*

1. Ed's parents haven't said nothing to him yet about his grades.
2. Patti hasn't hardly been to work this week.
3. Nobody never asks Charlie for his advice.
4. Mrs. Chin couldn't barely speak a word of English when she started kindergarten.
5. Tonio says he can't help but bite his fingernails.
6. Mr. Washington hasn't told us nothing about the final exam.
7. Howie's grandfather hasn't only one grandson.

8. When Shana is reading, she doesn't hardly hear nothing that goes on around her.

9. Davie hasn't never learned to ride a bicycle.

10. Beverly didn't hardly say a word to nobody all during dinner.

Writing with Adverbs

Just as adjectives help the reader to visualize a person, place, or thing, so adverbs help the reader visualize an action. Consider the action described in the following sentences. Can you see the power of each adverb?

> She smiled *warmly.*
> She smiled *nervously.*
> She smiled *wanly.*

Use exact adverbs to help the reader visualize an action.

Writing Exercise A

Improve each of the following sentences by using one or more adverbs to describe the action precisely. You may also add phrases and specific nouns, verbs, and adjectives to make the sentences more interesting.

Example

a. The band marched across the field.

a. *After an hour of drill, the band straggled wearily across the blazingly hot field.*

1. The two-year-old cried when he fell.

2. Each day she waits for the letter carrier.

3. The shortstop hit the ball.

4. Wendy stood on the high-diving board.

5. The hunter walked through the woods.

6. When her name was called, Madeline went up to the stage.

7. The father looked at his newborn daughter.

8. After the crash the pilot got out of the plane.

9. The telephone rang at 3 A.M.

10. "Go away!" he shouted through the door.

Review Exercise A

Write out the following sentences, choosing the correct modifier from the pair in parentheses. Underline the word you have chosen.

1. Of all the students in the class, Abbie draws the (worse, worst).

2. Which do you like (better, best)—apricot or raspberry yogurt?

3. Todd speaks (more, most) effectively than the other candidate.

4. The people-mover system will be finished (more, most) quickly than the transit system.

5. Yolanda (can, can't) hardly reach the ninth-floor button in the elevator.

6. Perry (had, hadn't) never seen an opera before.

7. Before she started jogging, Margo (could, couldn't) hardly walk two miles.

8. Nathan Hale said, "I (have, haven't) but one life to give for my country."

9. Dr. Evans graduated (recent, recently) from Bethune Cookman College.

10. Honey feels (bad, badly) about her parents' separation.

11. Since she gained a few pounds and had her hair cut, Betty Lou really looks (good, well).

12. I can't understand unless you speak more (slow, slowly).

13. "This roast tastes (bad, badly)," said Rosemary.

14. Of the four candidates Jordan compaigned the (harder, hardest).

15. Willie and Sue really dance (good, well) together.

16. He may be a good songwriter, but he sings (bad, badly).

17. The chairman said he (had, hadn't) only one suggestion to make.

18. I play tennis (littler, less) often than my parents.

19. Rosa and her mother are getting along (bad, badly) again.

20. "Spread the butterfly's wings (careful, carefully)," Mrs. Avila said.

21. Whom do you like (better, best)—Frances or Craig?

22. The wind was so strong we (could, couldn't) hardly walk.

23. Kramer swims the breast stroke (worser, worse) than I do.

24. He always acts (friendlier, more friendlier) on Saturdays.

25. They (have, haven't) only three more miles to go.

Writing Exercise B

Write one or more paragraphs of step-by-step directions for one of the following actions, telling someone how to perform the action. Be as precise as you can. When you have finished writing, underline each adverb you have used.

1. Tying a shoelace

2. Tying a necktie

3. Loading a camera with film

4. Looking up a word in a dictionary

5. Flying a kite

6. Making toast

7. Threading a needle

8. Starting a bonfire when you are camping
9. Putting up a tent
10. Skating backward on roller skates or ice skates

Understanding Prepositions

Prepositions are one of the parts of speech that help words work together in groups. A change in prepositions can make a big difference in the meaning of a sentence.

Lois saw a mouse *behind* the refrigerator.
Lois saw a mouse *beside* the refrigerator.
Lois saw a mouse *inside* the refrigerator.

In the next sections you will learn how to identify prepositions.

Defining a Preposition A *preposition* is usually defined as a word that shows the relationship of a noun or pronoun to some other word in the sentence.

The girl stood hesitantly *before* the two closed doors.

In the preceding sentence the preposition *before* shows the relationship of the noun *doors* to the verb *stood*. The preposition *before* tells where the girl stood in relation to the doors.

A preposition always introduces a prepositional phrase, which contains two essential parts: a preposition *(P)* and the object of the preposition *(OP)*.

A prepositional phrase may also contain one or more modifiers.

P OP   P   OP
Gregorio is waiting (*for* you) (*at* the bus stop).
P   OP   P   OP
(*After* an hour) (*in* the windy cold), we felt frozen.

A single preposition may also have a compound object.

P   OP   OP
The orientation meeting is intended (*for* all students and their parents).
P OP   OP   OP
She wore a striped sundress (*of* red, green, and purple).

The preposition usually comes before the object of the preposition. In fact, for many years students were taught that it is incorrect to end a sentence with a preposition. Some writers still believe that in formal writing sentences should never end with prepositions. However, in questions and in spoken English, it often seems natural to end a sentence with a preposition.

Where did this package come *from?*
What are you talking *about?*
What day will the tournament be held *on?*
Pete wants to know whom the letter is *for.*

The object of a preposition is usually a single word, but it may also be a group of words.

$$\overset{OP}{\overbrace{}}$$

These tickets are (*for* whoever wants to come).

$$\overset{OP}{\overbrace{}} \qquad\qquad\qquad \overset{OP}{}$$

(*Before* accepting the job), Lorenzo talked (*to* several employees).

In the following list are some commonly used prepositions.

about	beyond	over
above	but (meaning	past
across	*except)*	since
after	by	through
against	concerning	throughout
along	down	to
among	during	toward
around	except	under
at	for	underneath
before	from	until
behind	in	unto
below	into	up
beneath	like	upon
beside	of	with
besides	off	within
between	on	without

Besides these one-word prepositions, there are several *compound prepositions* that are made up of more than one word. Each of the following terms is considered a single preposition.

according to	because of	out of
along with	by means of	owing to
aside from	in front of	subsequent to
as to	in spite of	together with

Across, down, behind, below, in, under, up, and other prepositions may also function as adverbs. Remember that a preposition always introduces a prepositional phrase. If you can find no object of the preposition, the word is being used as an adverb.

Adverb: Please come *in.*

Preposition: Your lunch is *in* the kitchen.
                             P   OP

Adverb: She put the package *down* and hurried to the door.
                                    P   OP

Preposition: The ring fell *down* the drain.

Adverb: "Go *below!*" the captain shouted.
                                              P   OP

Preposition: The pencils are on the shelf *below* the radio.

The infinitive is   Do not confuse the infinitive *to* with the preposition *to*. The infinitive is
discussed on pages   the form of the verb that begins with the word *to*.
457–458.

Infinitive: Martha's goal is *to succeed* in television.
                                              P   OP

Preposition: Lenora and Juan are going *to* the movies tonight.

Exercise 1

Write out each of the following sentences. Put parentheses around each prepositional phrase and underline the preposition once and the object of the preposition twice. (Some sentences contain more than one phrase.)

Examples

a. According to Mrs. D'Leone juniors are invited to attend College Night.

a. *(According to Mrs. D'Leone) juniors are invited to attend College Night.*

b. When she sat down, her jeans tore across the left knee.

b. *When she sat down, her jeans tore (across the left knee).*

1. You will find your life preserver underneath your seat.

2. Everyone but Maria can come to the beach on Saturday.

3. The surveyor walked slowly around the perimeter of the lot.

4. Owen raced from the steamy sauna into the icy pool.

5. Important changes are often made out of necessity.

6. Just between you and me, he is the least confident person in our class.

7. I'll meet you in front of the school after 3 o'clock.

8. Gloria and Chloe, together with several other students in the county, are among the top scorers in the National Math Contest.

9. For whom is the electric typewriter on the kitchen table?

10. After he read the college handbook, nothing could stop Prentice from applying to all of the Big Ten schools.

Mastery Exercise A

Write out the following paragraphs from Eudora Welty's "A Visit of Charity." Put parentheses around twenty-five prepositional phrases and underline each preposition.

It was midmorning—a very cold, bright day. Holding a potted plant before her, a girl of fourteen jumped off the bus in front of the Old Ladies' Home, on the outskirts of town. She wore a red coat, and her straight yellow hair was hanging down loose from the pointed white cap all the little girls were wearing that year. She stopped for a moment beside one of the prickly dark shrubs with which the city had beautified the Home, and then proceeded slowly toward the building, which was of whitewashed brick and reflected the winter sunlight like a block of ice. As she walked vaguely up the steps she shifted the small pot from hand to hand; then she had to set it down and remove her mittens before she could open the heavy door.

"I'm a Campfire Girl. . . . I have to pay a visit to some old lady," she told the nurse at the desk. This was a woman in a white uniform who looked as if she were cold; she had close-cut hair which stood up on the very top of her head exactly like a sea wave. Marian, the little girl, did not tell her that this visit would give her a minimum of only three points in her score.

"Acquainted with any of our residents?" asked the nurse. She lifted one eyebrow and spoke like a man.

"With any old ladies? No—but—that is, any of them will do," Marian stammered. With her free hand she pushed her hair behind her ears, as she did when it was time to study Science.[1]

Mastery Exercise B

Select several paragraphs from your state drivers handbook or from another practical source, such as the maintenance guide for a car. Using what you have learned about identifying prepositions, find the prepositional phrases in the paragraphs and list them on a sheet of paper. Underline the prepositions once and the objects twice.

Using Prepositions

In this section you will study several prepositions that are often used incorrectly. Learn to avoid these errors in preposition usage.

beside/besides

Beside means "by the side of." *Besides* means "in addition to, moreover, or except."

We stood *beside* the lake and watched the white ibises.
Besides taking chemistry this year, Renee is also taking physics.
No one *besides* Jeff brought aluminum cans for recycling.

between/among

Between refers only to two persons or things, while *among* is used to refer to three or more persons or things.

---

[1]Excerpt from "A Visit of Charity" from *A Curtain of Green and Other Stories* by Eudora Welty. Copyright 1941, 1969 by Eudora Welty. Reprinted by permission of Harcourt Brace Jovanovich, Inc. and Russell & Volkening, Inc.

We have forty dollars *between* the two of us.
The treasure was divided *among* the four divers.

Between is sometimes used to compare the items within a group when each is considered individually.

What is the difference *between* Renaissance, Baroque, and Romantic music?

different from

Use the preposition *from* after the adjective *different*. *Different than* is considered incorrect in Edited Standard English.

Franz is very different *from* his brother.
Kerri's shoes are quite different *from* yours.

except/accept

Except is a preposition that means "excluding." *Accept* is a verb meaning "to take or receive." Never use *accept* as a preposition.

We took pictures of everyone *except* Lillya.
She will *accept* the job as a systems analyst.

in/into

In means "inside of or within." *Into* shows a movement from the outside to the inside of something.

She is standing *in* the courtroom.
She walked *into* the courtroom.

Kiyo is swimming *in* the pool.
Kiyo jumped *into* the pool.

Exercise 1

Write out the following sentences, choosing the correct word in parentheses. Underline the word you have chosen.

Example
a. Your chess set is different (than, from) mine.
a. *Your chess set is different from mine.*

1. How many students can speak a language (beside, besides) English?
2. Bicycles have been stolen from the bike rack (beside, besides) the movie theater.
3. Rumors of an impeachment spread (between, among) the student council members.
4. Responsibilities for the talent show were shared equally (between, among) Rafael and Georgette.
5. What are the differences (among, between) the cattle egret and the snowy egret?

6. Do you see any substantial differences (between, among) the six candidates for President?

7. In person Mrs. Bethune looked very different (than, from) her photographs.

8. Jed's plan is different (from, than) the one proposed by the committee.

9. After the game the players rushed triumphantly (in, into) the locker room.

10. All of the boxes (accept, except) this one belong in the truck.

Writing Exercise A

Using one of the following suggested topics, write at least a paragraph. As you write, concentrate on using prepositions that conform to Edited Standard English usage.

1. Imagine that you are watching a sports event or recall an event that you have seen either in person or on television. Describe an especially exciting minute of that event so that readers can share it with you.

2. "The things that are wrong with the country today are the sum total of all the things that are wrong with us as individuals."

    —*Charles Towne*

    Charles Towne implies in the preceding quotation that individuals could solve some of the nation's problems by improving themselves. Decide if you agree or disagree and then write about the role each citizen can play in solving national problems. For example, what can one person do to conserve energy? To end pollution or littering?

3. "What a wonderful life I've had. I only wish I'd realized it sooner."

    —*Colette*

    This author's comment suggests that she experienced many happy moments but did not realize her happiness at the time. Think back to a day, a week, or a year when you were happy but did not fully appreciate the experience. Describe your happiness and, if you can, explain why you appreciate it more now than you did then.

4. The photograph on page 404 shows high school athletes in a moment of tension and great effort. Some educators and parents feel high school sports are becoming too competitive and that too much emphasis is placed on winning rather than on enjoyment. A few schools have done away with the more competitive team sports such as football and basketball and are emphasizing golf, tennis, and jogging instead. State your ideas on competitive team sports and the pressures put on young athletes or, if you wish, write about one of the characters in the photograph and what he is feeling and thinking.

Understanding Conjunctions

Conjunctions, like prepositions, help join the parts of a sentence. In the sections that follow, you will learn to recognize the three different kinds of conjunctions and the work they do.

Defining a Conjunction

A *conjunction* is usually defined as a word that connects other words or groups of words.

Some of the smallest and most common words in the English language are conjunctions. Words like *and*, *but*, *or*, *for*, and *yet* may join either single words or groups of words.

> Juana *and* Bettie work for the Growers Association.
> Juana is a secretary, *and* Bettie is a bookkeeper.
>
> Mr. Louis is forceful *yet* tactful.
> His employees respect him, *yet* they also like him.

Conjunctions like *either . . . or*, *neither . . . nor*, *both . . . and*, and *not only . . . but also* work together as a pair.

> *Neither* Mr. Castellow *nor* his son saw the intruder enter the house.
> *Either* Mamie *or* her sister will change the oil.
> He was *not only* angry *but also* obnoxious.

Conjunctions such as *after*, *because*, *before*, *since*, *when*, and *where* join whole groups of words to the rest of the sentence.

> Wayne felt awkward *when* he introduced his girlfriend to his parents.
> *Before* the phone rang, I had just been thinking of you.
> Ruth can't buy the bike yet *because* she hasn't enough money.

Exercise 1

Write out the following sentences, underlining the conjunctions. Be certain to look for conjunctions that work in pairs, such as *either . . . or* and *neither . . . nor*.

Example

a. Both Penny and her husband prefer snorkeling or fishing to sailing.
a. *Both Penny and her husband prefer snorkeling or fishing to sailing.*

1. When Mark Antony heard of Cleopatra's rumored suicide, he fell on his sword.

2. Before the Battle of Little Bighorn, Sitting Bull told his people, "Warriors, we have everything to fight for, and if we are defeated, we shall have nothing to live for."

3. Both Walt Whitman and John Greenleaf Whittier were poets and Quakers.

4. In 1977 Dr. Rosalyn Yalow became the second woman ever to win the Nobel Prize for Medicine and the eighth woman ever to win a Nobel Prize.

5. Green, a sacred color to the Muslims, was the symbol of victory to the Moors and ancient Greeks.

6. Mahatma Gandhi was married when he and his bride were twelve years old.

7. Hundreds of people spent St. Patrick's Day of 1842 in boats off the shore of Europe because Dr. John Dee predicted the end of Europe on that day.

8. On February 21, 1965, as he was about to speak in a Manhattan ballroom, Malcolm X was assassinated.

9. Deborah Sampson fought as a soldier during the Revolutionary War, for she had disguised herself as a man.

10. In her will Janis Joplin left $2,500 for an all-night party for 200 friends after she died.

Classifying Conjunctions

There are three different types of conjunctions: *coordinating conjunctions, correlative conjunctions,* and *subordinating conjunctions.*

1. *Coordinating Conjunctions*

    And, but, or, yet, and *for* are *coordinating conjunctions.*

    Coordinating conjunctions join single words, phrases, or clauses. When two or more sentence parts are joined by a coordinating conjunction, the parts are of equal importance.

    They were excited *yet* reluctant.
    We found a discarded snakeskin *but* not the snake.
    You will find Dara in the pool *or* in the locker room.
    We had better find some shelter, *for* the storm is approaching fast.
    I have not changed my mind, *nor* do I expect to.

2. *Correlative Conjunctions*

    Correlative conjunctions are used only in pairs.

    both . . . and   not only . . . but also
    either . . . or   whether . . . or
    neither . . . nor

    Both Winston *and* his sister have the measles.
    Either Garrity will make the speech *or* Sheldon will.
    Do you care *whether* Louise baby-sits *or* Fred does?

3. *Subordinating Conjunctions*

Adverb clauses are
discussed on pages
474–475.

Subordinating conjunctions are used to introduce adverb clauses.

A subordinating conjunction expresses the relationship of the subordinate clause to the main clause by showing time, place, cause, purpose, limitation, or special condition. The following list is of the most commonly used subordinating conjunctions.

after	how	so that	when
although	if	than	whenever
as	inasmuch as	that	where
as much as	in order that	though	wherever
as soon as	provided	unless	whether
because	since	until	while
before			

Nicky tries to get to work at 8 *whenever* he can.

The thief entered easily *although* the doors were locked.

Because Mr. and Mrs. Wing are celebrating their fiftieth anniversary, their picture was in the paper.

Unless the rain stops, the hayride will be postponed.

Review Exercise A

Write out the following sentences, underlining all conjunctions and indicating the class to which each belongs. Use the following abbreviations.

Coor.—Coordinating conjunction
Cor.—Correlative conjunction
Sub.—Subordinating conjunction

Some sentences have more than one conjunction.

Examples

a. Neither Pete nor Rubin knows Penn's telephone number.
       Cor.   *Cor.*

a. *Neither Pete nor Rubin knows Penn's telephone number.*

b. Please be ready to leave at 8 o'clock so that we can find a parking space near City Hall.
                                               Sub.

b. *Please be ready to leave at 8 o'clock so that we can find a parking space near City Hall.*

c. Do you know the address of the gallery, or shall we look it up in the phone book?
                                          Coor.

c. *Do you know the address of the gallery, or shall we look it up in the phone book?*

1. We waited for more than an hour, but no one came.

2. Either Shari or Shizuo will design the cover for the yearbook.

3. She has to get a duplicate drivers license because her wallet was stolen.

4. I have tried calling the office of the district superintendent, yet no one seems able to answer my question.

5. Until Ramon moved next door, I had never eaten tacos, tortillas, or refried beans.

6. Both Mrs. Levine and her husband jog two miles every morning.

7. June not only finished her model city on time but also won a prize for the best model submitted.

8. Frederico will quit his job next week, for he leaves for the University of Denver in August.

9. Whenever I try to work late, I feel sorry for myself because everyone else in the house is asleep.

10. Grandpa Margot built this log cabin at the lake where he had fished when he was a boy.

11. Sometimes he seems cool and indifferent, but at other times he seems both loving and caring.

12. After he graduates, Marc plans to join the Peace Corps and work in either Central or South America.

13. There was so much unrest that tourists were advised not only to avoid traveling alone after dark but also to remain in their hotels.

14. "He still has a high fever," said Dr. Kim, "but I'm sure he'll be all right by morning."

15. When the school bus was two hours late, most of the students decided to walk, but some went home.

16. Although he is only five feet tall, Bernie's father is a powerful tennis player.

17. Have you ever seen the sun rise or slept outdoors?

18. Karim broke her left wrist when she fell after her bicycle hit a parking meter.

19. Mrs. Dubin wept when she saw the damage to her apartment.

20. Exhausted but triumphant, two nine-year-olds crossed the finish line of the ten-kilometer run.

Mastery Exercise A

Write out the following paragraphs from Ursula Le Guin's *The Farthest Shore*. Underline each conjunction and above it write the class to which it belongs. Use the following abbreviations:

Coor.—Coordinating conjunction
Cor.—Correlative conjunction
Sub.—Subordinating conjunction

Example

Coor.

The boat rounded a short promontory, <u>and</u> he saw on the shore what he took for a moment to be a ruined fortress.

It was a dragon. One black wing was bent under it and the other stretched out vast across the sand and into the water, so that the come and go of waves moved it a little to and fro in a mockery of flight. The long snake-body lay full length on the rock and sand. One foreleg was missing, the armor and flesh were torn from the great arch of the ribs, and the belly was torn open, so that the sand for yards about was blackened with the poisoned dragon-blood. Yet the creature still lived. So great a life is in dragons that only an equal power of wizardry can kill them swiftly. The green-gold eyes were open, and as the boat sailed by, the lean, huge head moved a little, and with a rattling hiss steam mixed with bloody spray shot from the nostrils.[1]

Mastery Exercise B

Choose two or three paragraphs from a novel, short story, or piece of non-fiction that you have read recently. Using what you have learned about identifying conjunctions, find all the conjunctions in the passage. List them on a sheet of paper and beside each one write its type: coordinating, correlative, or subordinating. If you prefer, choose one of your own compositions as the basis for this assignment.

Using Conjunctions

Conjunctions can improve your writing when you use them to connect related words, ideas, and sentences. In the next two sections you will practice combining sentences with conjunctions and practice punctuating those sentences correctly.

Writing with Conjunctions

You can avoid having a series of choppy sentences by using conjunctions to combine them. The type of conjunction you choose depends on the meaning you wish to convey.

In the following sentences, coordinating conjunctions are used to combine ideas of equal importance.

We heard an eerie scream. No one was in sight.
We heard an eerie scream, *yet* no one was in sight.

The child pointed to dark shapes in the tree. We could not see what they were.
The child pointed to dark shapes in the tree, *but* we could not see what they were.

---

[1]Excerpt from *The Farthest Shore* by Ursula K. Le Guin. Copyright © 1972 by Atheneum Publishers. Reprinted with the permission of Atheneum Publishers.

Subordinating conjunctions express the specific relationship of the subordinate clause to the main clause.

RELATIONSHIP	SUBORDINATING CONJUNCTIONS
Cause:	as, because, for, since, so
Purpose:	in order that, so that
Limitation:	although, in spite of, the fact that, though
Time:	after, as, as soon as, before, since, until, when, while
Place:	where, wherever

In the following sentences subordinating conjunctions are used to combine two short sentences. What relationship does each subordinating conjunction express?

Maria has never had an art lesson. Her paintings and drawings are exceptional.
Although Maria has never had an art lesson, her paintings and drawings are exceptional.

David speaks fluent Hebrew. He spent a year in Israel.
David speaks fluent Hebrew *because* he spent a year in Israel.

School ends. We are leaving for a week in Vermont.
As soon as school ends, we are leaving for a week in Vermont.

Exercise 1

Combine the following short sentences, using an appropriate conjunction. Underline the conjunction you use.

Examples

a. Pat has a dentist appointment. She doesn't want to go.
a. *Pat has a dentist appointment, but she doesn't want to go.*

b. George's friends call him Tiny. He weighs 200 pounds.
b. *George's friends call him Tiny because he weighs 200 pounds.*

1. In Arizona we camped at Montezuma Castle. We camped at Petrified Forest. We camped at Canyon de Chelly.

2. Tonia and her sister are saving for a trip to Florence, Italy. Their father was born in Florence.

3. Eight species of whales are on the endangered species list. Three species of bats are on the endangered species list.

4. Please bring in the sleeping bags. The storm drenches them.

5. Things haven't been the same. A major league baseball team came to town.

6. Everything will be all right. You follow directions precisely.

7. The Great Smoky Mountains are in North Carolina. The Great Smoky Mountains are in Tennessee.

8. The state flower of Missouri is the hawthorn. The bluebird is its state bird.

9. Norm appears to be organized. His desk and room are a mess.

10. Gasoline prices keep going up. We try to drive less. We try to walk more.

Punctuating with Conjunctions In a series of words, phrases, or clauses, commas are used to take the place of the conjunction that is omitted. A comma also precedes the conjunction at the end of the series.

> Please pass the onions, relish, and ketchup.
> Either Jamie, Brian, or Marsha will announce the winner.

However, no commas are necessary if the conjunctions are not omitted. (This type of construction is not used often.)

> Please pass the onions and relish and ketchup.
> Either Jamie or Brian or Marsha will announce the winner.

A comma separates the subordinate clause from the main clause when the subordinate clause begins the sentence.

> Because the potatoes aren't done yet, dinner will be late.
> Whenever Marilyn started to sing, everyone cheered.

When the subordinate clause comes at the end of a sentence, a comma is usually not necessary.

> Dinner will be late because the potatoes aren't done yet.
> Everyone cheered whenever Marilyn started to sing.

Exercise 2

Write out the following sentences, adding commas wherever necessary. If a sentence is correctly punctuated, write *C*. Circle the commas that you insert.

1. If everyone in the school votes this year we will have the largest voter turnout in the school's history.
2. Although all four of her grandparents are living Claudia rarely gets to see them.
3. Tina chased a lizard under the bed behind the dresser and into the bathroom.
4. The smoke alarm usually goes off whenever we are broiling chicken.
5. This year Caroline is taking English Spanish physics and European history.
6. Unless they get summer jobs soon Paul and Barry will have to give up their plans for their trip at the end of August.
7. Mom says that cleaning the refrigerator dusting the furniture and putting away groceries are the household jobs she dislikes most.
8. Before you buy a new appliance it's a good idea to check the consumers' magazines in the public library.
9. Ted kicked off his shoes dropped his books and collapsed on his bed.
10. As soon as my homework is done I'm going swimming.

Review Exercise A

Combine the following sentences by using a coordinating conjunction or a subordinating conjunction. In some sentences you may need to use more than one kind of conjunction. Check to see that your sentences are properly punctuated.

1. Lock the door. Turn off the lights. Shut the windows.

2. His mother remarried. Leslie Lynch King, Jr., changed his name to Gerald R. Ford, Jr.

3. The planet Neptune has two moons. It is 17.3 times the size of the earth.

4. The Belgian Congo became independent in 1960. It became the nation of Zaire.

5. As a child Charles Darwin was a poor student. He was lazy. He was an avid collector of coins. He also collected bugs and shells.

6. Esperanto is an artificial language. Volapuk and Interlingua are also artificial languages.

7. A music editor nicknamed Louis Armstrong "Satchelmouth." It soon became "Satchmo." He had such a large mouth.

8. Levi Hutchins was twenty-six years old in 1787. He invented the alarm clock. He could wake up at 4 A.M.

9. Five grams equals one teaspoon. Fifteen grams equals one tablespoon.

10. Autophobia is the fear of being alone. Astraphobia is the fear of lightning. Ombrophobia is the fear of rain.

Writing Exercise A

Using one of the following suggestions, write at least a paragraph. When you have finished, underline the conjunctions you have used, checking to be certain that you have used the correct punctuation.

1. You have just discovered the diary of a teenager written 300 years ago. In the diary the teenager tells about a dangerous journey across your state under very difficult circumstances. Write part of the diary.

2. Interview your oldest relative, friend, or neighbor. Ask him or her to describe what it was like to grow up "in the good old days." Write down some of the interesting things you learn, being certain to tell when and where the person you are interviewing grew up.

3. Write a dialogue between the following two characters: a student who is convinced he or she has observed a UFO (unidentified flying object) and a police officer who is skeptical about the report.

4. The photograph on page 413 shows people in the middle of an argument. Imagine what each person is like and what the argument is about. Describe the scene and the action.

Understanding Interjections

An *interjection* is usually defined as a word that shows strong or sudden feeling, such as sorrow, joy, or pain.

Unlike other parts of speech, interjections have no grammatical relationship to the rest of the sentence. They stand apart—as exclamations or expressions of feeling.

> *"No way!"* she said. "I'll never go out with Ryan."
> *Ouch!* You're standing on my foot.

Some interjections express milder feelings, such as surprise.

> *My goodness*, will you look at that!
> *Oh*, are these yours?
> *Well*, it's about time you showed up.

The following is a partial list of some words that are commonly used as interjections.

ah	goodness	never
aha	great	nonsense
alas	help	phew
congratulations	hey	ugh
dear me	hooray	whew
gee	hurrah	wow
golly	my	yippee

Notice that some of the words in the preceding list may also be used as other parts of speech.

Can you *help* us unpack the cartons?	[verb]
Help! The boat is sinking!	[interjection]
"Have you seen *my* other sneaker?" she asked.	[pronoun]
My, how you've fixed up your room.	[interjection]

More than many other parts of speech, interjections go in and out of fashion. Your grandparents probably said "Pshaw!" or "Shucks!" just as later generations said "No way!" or "Hey, man!"

Exercise 1

Write out the following sentences and underline each interjection.

Example

a. Wow, am I glad that's over!

a. <u>*Wow*</u>, *am I glad that's over!*

1. Ugh! Do we really have to eat that?

2. Phew! These garbage cans need to be cleaned.

3. Huge tears rolled down her cheeks as she murmured, "Alas! I am sorry I ever met him, for my heart is broken."

4. After staring at the puzzle for several minutes, she cried, "Aha! I have it!" but she didn't.

5. When the final bell rang on the last day of school, the students yelled "Hooray!" and fled.

6. "Never! Never! Never!" he vowed, and his promise lasted all through one day.

7. Oh, did you hear the news about Barbara Yang's art scholarship to Cooper Union in New York City?

8. Well, you certainly can't fool me again.

9. Oh no! I just locked the keys in the car!

10. "Nonsense!" he objected. "We can raise the money."

Using Interjections

Interjections may be followed either by a comma or by an exclamation point. These two punctuation marks convey the level of feeling in the sentence. An exclamation point indicates strong feeling, while a comma indicates a milder emotion.

> *Aha!* We've got you trapped this time, you thief!
> [indicates strong feeling]

> *Oh,* were you talking to me?
> [indicates milder emotion]

Notice that the word following the exclamation point is capitalized because it is the first word in a new sentence. When a comma is used after an interjection, however, the next word is part of the same sentence and does not begin with a capital letter.

In a direct quotation use either a comma or an exclamation point—not both.

> "*Wow!*" she said. "I've never seen a statue like that before."
> "*Oh,*" Mr. Ramirez replied, "I guess they're not coming after all."

Exercise 1

Write out the following sentences and underline each interjection. Place an exclamation point after an interjection that shows strong or sudden feeling. Use a comma after an interjection that expresses a milder emotion. (Remember to capitalize the first word following an exclamation point.) Circle the punctuation marks you insert.

Example

a. Good grief someone has just picked my pocket!
a. *Good grief! Someone has just picked my pocket!*

1. Oh do you know what time it is?

2. Wow what a terrific touchdown pass that was!

3. Dear me the movie has already started.

4. Help Janet's hand is caught in the car door!

5. Hey who was that handsome guy I saw you with last night?

6. "Whew" he murmured. "It sure is hot today."

7. My goodness the bus is late again.

8. "Gee" he said "when is it going to be my turn?"

9. "Oh my goodness" she sighed "I forgot to turn on the light in the hallway."

10. Hurrah we've won the championship!

Writing Exercise A

Select one of the following characters and situations and write a dialogue based on it, making use of appropriate interjections to help the dialogue seem realistic. Use care in punctuating and in capitalizing sentences that have interjections.

1. A teacher and student are having a discussion after school. The teacher feels that the student is bright but not working up to potential and wants to know why. The student is not being cooperative.

2. At a party two adults, friends for years, are discussing life in America. One is a Democrat, one is Republican (or your choice of parties), and the discussion becomes very lively. The two friends are discussing current problems and politics.

3. Two friends are walking home from school. One feels rejected by the other, who has a new set of friends he or she is spending time with instead of with old friends. The other is irritated but does not want to hurt his or her old friend's feelings.

4. Two aliens from planet Alpha X are discussing their recent observations of the planet earth. They speak in English, but their interjections can be in English or in Alpha X language. They are astonished by what they have seen and heard.

More Practice Using the Parts of Speech

Using Irregular Verbs

Exercise 1

Study the present, past, and past participle forms of the following *irregular verbs*.

PRESENT	PAST	PAST PARTICIPLE
become	became	(had) become
begin	began	(had) begun
break	broke	(had) broken
bring	brought	(had) brought
build	built	(had) built

Write out the following sentences, supplying the correct form of the verb in parentheses. Underline the word you write in the blank.

Example

a. The concert had already _____ when we arrived. (begin)
a. *The concert had already begun when we arrived.*

1. The lamp _____ when it fell. (break)

2. After many years of study, Hal _____ a minister. (become)

3. We have _____ many sand castles better than this one. (build)

4. The snow _____ at 6 o'clock last night. (begin)

5. The pages of the photograph album have _____ torn and worn. (became)

6. Sharri has _____ the state record for the 110-meter dash. (break)

7. Were you here when Roger _____ his cabin in the canyon? (build)

8. Who _____ the French bread and the cheese? (bring)

9. Despite the storm the wedding _____ promptly at 10 o'clock. (begin)

10. Kim _____ her best records to the party. (bring)

Exercise 2

Review the forms of the irregular verbs *buy*, *catch*, *choose*, *come*, and *dive* on page 353. Then choose the word in parentheses that completes each sentence. Write out the sentences, underlining your choices.

Example

a. Did Barney (buy, bought) his graduation pictures?
a. Did Barney buy his graduation pictures?

1. Uncle Ed (catched, caught) a five-pound snapper.

2. Have they (chose, chosen) the baby's name yet?

3. He has (came, come) to Grand Lake every summer for sixteen years.

4. Jeff (caught, catched) a bad cold over the weekend.

5. If I could have (chosen, chose) dessert, I would have picked fresh pine-apple.

6. The kitten leaped off the chair and (doved, dived) behind the couch.

7. When he crossed the bridge, the knight (come, came) to an enchanted tree.

8. Have you (buyed, bought) everything you need for the trip?

9. Lorna has (dived, dove) from the high board since she was six.

10. José (bought, buyed) Maria a pair of earrings for her birthday.

Exercise 3

Review the forms of the irregular verbs *do*, *draw*, *drink*, *drive*, and *eat* on pages 353–354. Then write the correct form of the verb to complete each sentence. Write out the sentences and underline the correct form.

Example

a. Tom and Huck _____ a lot of work. (do)
a. Tom and Huck did a lot of work.

1. Have you _____ all of your homework? (do)
2. Juliette _____ a map of downtown Boston in the 1850s. (draw)
3. How many glasses of apple juice have you _____ ? (drink)
4. Alan has _____ all night without stopping. (drive)
5. Cory had _____ the last piece of cold chicken. (eat)
6. Anya has _____ four self-portraits in charcoal and pastels. (draw)
7. They _____ the tea from blue and white Japanese cups. (drink)
8. She asked what she had _____ to make him so angry. (do)
9. Have you ever _____ fresh papaya? (eat)
10. Before she went to college, Patti _____ a laundry truck. (drive)

Exercise 4

Review the forms of the irregular verbs *fall, fly, forget, freeze, give,* and *go* on page 354. Then choose the word in parentheses that completes each sentence. Write out the sentences, underlining your choices.

Example

a. Francesca has (gave, given) blood three times.
a. Francesca has given blood three times.

1. All of the leaves have (fallen, fell) from the maple tree.
2. Have you ever (flew, flown) over mountains?
3. Marty has (forgot, forgotten) his lunch again.
4. The lettuce has (froze, frozen) because the refrigerator is too cold.
5. Gerry's brother has (went, gone) to work in a fishery in Alaska.
6. Madeline must have (gave, given) us the wrong phone number.
7. The hummingbird (flew, flown) to the feeder and remained in one place.
8. She (forgot, forget) to enclose the check when she paid the bill.
9. Yesterday we (went, go) to the Exploratorium for the day.
10. When Justine went skating, her feet (froze, freezed).

Exercise 5

A list of irregular verb forms is on pages 353–354.

Some of the following sentences contain errors in verb usage. Rewrite the sentences, using the correct form of the verb. If the sentence is correct, write *C.* Underline any corrections you make.

Examples

a. Katie's tomato plant has growed several inches this week.
a. Katie's tomato plant has grown several inches this week.

b. The cat hit the kitten on the head.
b. C

1. Josh keeped his skis under his bed.

2. I have never knowed anyone as caring as you are.

3. The messenger has ridden all day without stopping to rest.

4. When you finally made up your mind, I knowed you could do it.

5. In his garden Mr. Wang growed lettuce, peppers, tomatoes, and onions.

6. Doris has hitted three balls over the left-field fence.

7. Catherine has kept your secret for twenty years.

8. We have rode our bicycles to the lake every morning before sunrise.

9. Sam and Rose knew each other in junior high school.

10. I keeped trying to call you, but your line was busy.

Exercise 6

Review the forms of the irregular verbs *ring, run, see, shake,* and *shrink* on page 354. Then choose the correct form of the verb in parentheses to complete each sentence. Write out the sentences, underlining the correct forms.

Example

a. Where were you when the doorbell _____ ? (ring)
a. Where were you when the doorbell rang?

1. Jill _____ a bookstore before the twins were born. (run)

2. After the company left, we _____ out the tablecloth outside. (shake)

3. The cotton sweater _____ when he washed it in hot water. (shrink)

4. The telephone had _____ just before the doorbell _____ . (ring)

5. I _____ a movie about Helen Keller and her teacher. (see)

6. Have you _____ a black and white collie puppy? (see)

7. As she stood before the firing squad, her knees _____ . (shake)

8. Gary has _____ two miles every night for a month. (run)

9. The roast _____ when it was cooked. (shrink)

10. Libby _____ a brown rat in the basement. (see)

Exercise 7

Review the forms of the irregular verbs *sing, sink, slay, speak,* and *spend* on page 354. Choose the word in parentheses that correctly completes each sentence. Write out the sentences and underline your choices.

Example

a. The freighter (sank, sunk) two miles off the coast of Georgia.
a. The freighter sank two miles off the coast of Georgia.

1. She (sang, sung) an aria from *La Bohème* by Puccini.

2. Whenever he (spoke, speaked) about art, his eyes sparkled.

3. Cain (slew, slain) Abel.

4. How much money have you (spend, spent) on groceries this week?

5. For more than a minute no one on stage (speak, spoke).

6. Have you ever (sang, sung) all of the verses to "America"?

7. Few people have ever (speaked, spoken) to Merlin.

8. When the battle was over, sixty-five knights had been (slayed, slain).

9. The old rowboat had (sank, sunk) during the last storm.

10. Her heart (sank, sunk) as she looked at the work that needed to be done in the kitchen.

Exercise 8

Review the forms of the irregular verbs *spring, steal, strive, swear,* and *swim* on page 354. Some of the following sentences contain errors in verb usage. Rewrite the sentences, using the correct form of the verb. If the sentence is correct, write *C*. Underline any corrections you make.

Examples

a. William has strove to keep his grades up this semester.
a. William has <u>striven</u> *to keep his grades up this semester.*

b. Someone has stolen Adrienne's tennis racket.
b. C

1. The cat sprung from the roof to the tree limb.

2. Who has stole the television section of the Sunday newspaper?

3. He swore never again to eat chili peppers.

4. Sarah swum twice across the lake and back.

5. Have you ever swum in a glacial lake?

6. The judge swore to uphold the Constitution and perform her duties.

7. "I have always strived to do my best," she said, "even though I have made many mistakes."

8. Paula's brother has already swam fifty laps and is still going strong.

9. A staghorn fern worth several hundred dollars has been stole from the library.

10. Mushrooms sprung up on the lawn after the heavy rains.

Exercise 9

Review the forms of the irregular verbs *take, teach, think, throw, wear,* and *write* on page 354. Then write out the following sentences, supplying the correct form of the verb in parentheses. Underline the word you supply.

Example

a. Have you _____ all of your thank-you notes? (write)
a. Have you <u>written</u> *all of your thank-you notes?*

1. Greta has _____ several courses on child development. (take)
2. Marlowe has never _____ the tie we gave him. (wear)
3. I have always _____ that you are a talented artist. (think)
4. Hal has _____ science and math for twenty years. (teach)
5. She _____ the puddle jumper from the upper deck of the house. (throw)
6. He had _____ three straight balls. (throw)
7. Who _____ you how to drive a car? (teach)
8. Yesterday she _____ her sandals on the wrong feet. (wear)
9. "You have _____ too little," Uncle Max said, as he heaped the salad on her plate. (take)
10. He has _____ all of his term paper except for the bibliography. (write)

Using Verbs Often Confused

Exercise 10

Review the forms of the verbs *lie* and *lay* on page 368. Remember that *lie* means "to recline" and that *lay* means "to place something" or "put something down." Complete the following sentences by choosing the correct verb in parentheses. Write out the sentences and underline the word you select.

Example
a. Andy carefully (lay, laid) the stencil on the board.
a. Andy carefully <u>laid</u> the stencil on the board.

1. Have you been (laying, lying) the tile in the bathroom?
2. The book has (laid, lain) on the kitchen table for a week.
3. "Someone has been (laying, lying) on my bed," said the little bear.
4. Just (lay, lie) the suitcase on the bench.
5. Teresita (lay, laid) six places at the table.
6. Roosevelt gently (lay, laid) the sleeping baby in the crib.
7. The prisoners (lay, laid) their plans for an escape.
8. When Jessie feels sick, she (lays, lies) on the couch all day.
9. Bonnie (lay, laid) the carton of eggs on the front seat.
10. We have been (laying, lying) on the beach since 7 o'clock.

Exercise 11

Review the forms of the verbs *sit* and *set* on page 369. Remember that *sit* means "to occupy a seat" or "to rest" and that *set* means "to put or place something." Complete the following sentences by choosing the correct verb in parentheses. Write out the sentences and underline the word you select.

Example

a. The fly (sat, set) on the edge of the plate.
a. The fly <u>sat</u> *on the edge of the plate.*

1. Did you ever (sit, set) in a field of wildflowers?
2. Someone has (sat, set) a wet glass on the wooden table.
3. Won't you come in and (set, sit) awhile?
4. Please (set, sit) the timer for two hours.
5. How long have you been (sitting, setting) here in the dark?
6. Maureen (sat, set) on the top railing of the corral.
7. The children are (sitting, setting) on the fire escape watching the parade go by.
8. "(Sit, Set) your feet on this hassock," she commanded.
9. Victor Beauchamp claims he (set, sat) the money on the desk.
10. I have been (setting, sitting) and waiting for forty minutes.

Exercise 12

Review the forms of the verbs *rise* and *raise* on page 370. Remember that *rise* means "to go up." *Raise* means "to cause something to move upward" and always takes a direct object. Complete the following sentences by choosing the correct verb in parentheses. Write out the sentences and underline the word you select.

Example

a. The price of gasoline has (risen, raised) sixty cents in the past year.
a. The price of gasoline has <u>risen sixty</u> *cents in the past year.*

1. Meg (rose, raised) the issue of students' rights at the school board meeting.
2. The bearded young man (rose, raised) and stated his name and address.
3. Please (rise, raise) the window shade in the bedroom.
4. As she began to speak about how she felt, her voice (raised, rose).
5. The sun will (rise, raise) at 6:10 A.M.
6. When the vote was called, the delegate (rose, raised) and left the room.
7. Hiromi (rose, raised) her hand to ask the lecturer a question.
8. After her child had burned his mouth on the dishwashing detergent, Mrs. Bartosz (rose, raised) the box of cleaning supplies to a high shelf.
9. How can we (rise, raise) the water pressure in this community?
10. Allen has (raised, risen) an important issue that must be considered carefully before the election.

**Making
Pronouns
Agree with
Antecedents**

Exercise 13

Review the list of singular and plural indefinite pronouns on page 330. Choose the pronoun that correctly completes each of the following sentences. Write out the sentences and underline the pronoun you select.

> **Example**
> a. Everyone is supposed to bring (their, his or her) camera.
> *a. Everyone is supposed to bring his or her camera.*

1. Each of the women has (their, her) degree in biochemistry.
2. Only one of the boys knew (his, their) Social Security number.
3. Neither of the girls had ever had (their, her) fortune told before.
4. Everyone on the men's track team has set (his, their) own goals for the week's training period.
5. Several of the young men have already completed (his, their) requirements to enter the School of Business.
6. Do you know anyone who will lend me (their, his or her) calculator?
7. Some of the flowers had lost (their, its) petals.
8. Only a few of the students remembered to bring (his or her, their) notebooks on the field trip.
9. Everybody wants (his or her, their) own way.
10. Many of my friends have already written (their, his or her) research papers.

Exercise 14

Remember that when two or more singular antecedents are joined by *and*, a plural pronoun is used to refer to them. When two or more singular antecedents are joined by *or* or *nor*, a singular pronoun is used to refer to them. Complete the following sentences by choosing the correct pronoun in parentheses. Write out the sentences, underlining the pronoun you select.

> **Examples**
> a. Katie and Mary have had (her, their) ceramics accepted in a crafts show.
> *a. Katie and Mary have had their ceramics accepted in a crafts show.*
> b. Either Owen or Patrick will bring (his, their) guitar.
> *b. Either Owen or Patrick will bring his guitar.*

1. The boy and his father spread (his, their) sleeping bags in the sun to dry.
2. Neither the soprano nor the alto learned (her, their) part completely.
3. Both Lynn and her cousin returned (her, their) overdue books.
4. The Margates and Mrs. Ewing have painted (her, their) mailboxes red.

5. Either the coach or the assistant has left (his, their) cap on the bench.

6. Dr. Mingo and his research assistants have planned (his, their) experiments for the fall.

7. Neither Jed nor his brother can find (his, their) key to the savings bank.

8. The announcer and the newsroom staff turned in (his or her, their) weekly time sheets.

9. Either Rhea or Fran will deliver (her, their) speech before the student assembly this Friday afternoon.

10. Mr. and Mrs. Horin and their daughter Sheila plan to leave on (her, their) vacation next week.

18 The Sentence

Understanding Sentences

In any language the rules by which words are combined to make *sentences* are learned by children in their first few years—and never forgotten. You would never say, for example, "Coat my where is." When you were very young, you learned that the proper order for those words in English is, "Where is my coat?" Also, because that is a question, you learned to raise your voice at the end of the sentence.

In the section that follows, you will concentrate on the sentence. Even though you have no trouble speaking sentences, understanding their parts and how they work will help you to write effective sentences.

Defining a Sentence

A *sentence* is usually defined as a group of words that expresses a complete thought.

Incomplete:	The girl on the flying trapeze. [What did the girl do? What happened to her?]
Complete:	The girl on the flying trapeze landed on her partner's shoulders.
Incomplete:	Without locking all the doors. [what? who?]
Complete:	Never park your car without locking all the doors.
Incomplete:	Stayed up until 3 A.M. [who?]
Complete:	In order to finish her research paper, Sara stayed up and worked until 3 A.M.

The groups of words that convey incomplete thoughts leave you with unanswered questions, such as *who? did what? what about it? what happened?* Whenever you have such questions, the group of words you have been reading does not convey a complete thought and is therefore not a sentence.

Exercise 1

Decide whether each of the following items expresses a complete thought. Then on a sheet of paper, write *S* for sentences and *NS* for groups of words that are not sentences. For the words that are not sentences, add whatever words you need to make a complete thought.

Examples

a. Maya Angelou's autobiography is *I Know Why the Caged Bird Sings*.
a. S

b. Because the banks weren't open.
b. NS—Julie couldn't cash her paycheck because the banks weren't open.

1. The end of a rainbow emerging from the clouds.
2. Emily Dickinson lived as a recluse.
3. Because of a misunderstanding about where we would meet.
4. She proudly displayed the Zebra butterfly in her Riker mount.
5. An equalizer heightens different instruments or voices.
6. For the past six weeks, there has been no rain.
7. Collecting autographs of movie stars.
8. Six seeds sprouted overnight.
9. When you catch a barracuda, it gives off a terrible smell.
10. After bicycling for fifteen miles.

Identifying Kinds of Sentences

Sentences may be classified in two ways—according to their *purpose* and their *structure*. A speaker or writer may have four different purposes in joining words together to form a sentence.

1. A *declarative sentence* makes a statement.

   Declarative statements always end with a period.

   Nat Turner led a slave revolt in Southampton, Virginia, in 1831.
   The giant squid reaches a length of fifty feet.

2. An *interrogative sentence* asks a question.

   An interrogative sentence always ends with a question mark.

   Have you seen Stanley Kubrick's *2001: A Space Odyssey*?

   What is the average life span of an elephant?

3. An *imperative sentence* gives a command or makes a request.

An imperative sentence may be followed either by a period or an exclamation mark. The subject of an imperative sentence is always *you*, the person or persons being addressed. Even when *you* does not appear in the sentence, the subject *you* is understood.

> (You) Please buy a quart of milk and a loaf of bread.
> (You) Hurry up!

4. An *exclamatory sentence* expresses strong feeling. It is usually followed by an exclamation mark.

> How lucky we were to have missed the accident!
> What an extraordinary day it has been!

Exercise 2

Write out the following sentences, placing the appropriate end punctuation after each one. Beneath each sentence write the label that identifies its purpose: declarative, interrogative, imperative, or exclamatory.

Example

> a. Have you ever heard Dylan Thomas reading his poetry
> a. *Have you ever heard Dylan Thomas reading his poetry?*
>   *Interrogative*

1. Tea, coffee, and cola drinks contain caffeine
2. What is the largest city in Utah
3. What a narrow escape that was
4. Don't forget to keep track of the amount of each check
5. Where is the nearest public shelter
6. How awful it must have been waiting to be rescued
7. Kyoto, an early capital of Japan, has many ancient shrines
8. Who was the first person to run the mile in less than four minutes
9. Turn in your exams, please
10. For much of her life, the American painter Mary Cassatt lived and worked in Paris

Understanding the Parts of a Sentence

Every sentence has two essential parts: the *subject* and the *predicate*.

The *subject* is usually defined as that part of the sentence about which something is being said. The subject is often a person or a thing.

The *predicate* is usually defined as that part of the sentence that says something about the subject.

Subject   *Predicate*
Sixteen inches of rain | fell in a single day.

Subject   *Predicate*
All plants | need water.

Subject   *Predicate*
Some people | cannot talk to telephone-answering machines.

In most English sentences the subject comes before the predicate. In some sentences, however, the subject follows all or part of the predicate.

Predicate   *Subject*
Before the fireplace lay | the old collie.

Predicate   *Subject*
On the top shelf in the linen closet are | the beach towels.

Exercise 3

Identify the subject and the predicate in the following sentences. Write out each sentence and draw a line separating the subject and the predicate. Then label each part.

Examples

a. Mr. Korzybski began to cook at the age of fifty-two.
    Subject   *Predicate*
a. *Mr. Korzybski | began to cook at the age of fifty-two.*

b. At the bottom of the fire escape is a broken ladder.
        Predicate   *Subject*
b. *At the bottom of the fire escape is | a broken ladder.*

1. Koreen and Jaffa showed us their photographs of Tel Aviv and Jerusalem.

2. I live in the building on the corner of McGregor Street and First.

3. José and his mother will visit their family in Mexico this year.

4. The electricity went off at exactly 6 o'clock during the thunderstorm.

5. All third-period physical education classes have been canceled.

6. The accounting department sent apologies for the mistake in the June statement.

7. Holly's grandparents are attending an Elder Hostel at the University of Massachusetts this summer.

8. Twenty-six people, including a ten-year-old girl, applied for the position of poet laureate of Florida.

9. Playing the soprano recorder is easy.

10. In the top right-hand drawer are paper clips and staples.

The Complete Subject and the Simple Subject

The *complete subject* tells who or what the sentence is about.

In the following sentences the complete subject is in italics.

> *Gary's sculpture in the shape of a torch* is an ashtray.
> *One of our next-door neighbors* fixed the broken step.
> *The hibiscus in our yard* has huge red flowers.

The *simple subject* is the main word or words in the complete subject.

The simple subject is never part of a prepositional phrase, nor does it ever include modifiers. In the following sentences the simple subject is *italicized*.

> Gary's *sculpture* in the shape of a torch is an ashtray.
> *One* of our next-door neighbors fixed the broken step.
> The *hibiscus* in our yard has huge red flowers.

When the simple subject is a proper name, it may be more than one word.

> The *Milky Way* is about 12 billion years old.
> *Hyman L. Lipman* invented the pencil with an eraser in 1858.

In discussing the parts of the sentence, the word *subject* is usually used to refer to the simple subject, not the complete subject.

Exercise 4

Write out the following sentences, underlining the complete subject once and the simple subject twice.

Examples

a. LouAnn, not her sister, is borrowing the car tonight.
a. *LouAnn, not her sister, is borrowing the car tonight.*

b. None of the books has a biography of Benjamin Banneker.
b. *None of the books has a biography of Benjamin Banneker.*

1. A sixty-five-year-old woman from Bozeman, Montana, ran one kilometer in five minutes, four seconds.

2. Terry's new Honda has twelve-inch tires.

3. Ellen's cast on her left arm will be coming off tomorrow.

4. A liter of gasoline equals 1.05 liquid quarts.

5. Mr. Renzo carved the initials on this apple tree more than sixty years ago.

6. Painting with acrylics is in some ways more difficult than painting with oils.

7. The blonde girl in the red T-shirt is Vache's cousin Anya.

8. The stepsisters failed to fit Cinderella's slipper on their feet.

9. The sound of the telephone awakened me at 1:40 A.M.

10. David's parents have been seeing a marriage counselor for several months.

Complete Predicate and Simple Predicate

The *predicate* is the part of the sentence that tells something about the subject. The *complete predicate* is made up of the verb and all of its modifiers.

> Mrs. Marguez *spoke for more than an hour to the education committee.*
> Mitchell and Adam *have been composing songs.*
> Gail *slammed a triple into right field.*

The *simple predicate* is the verb or verb phrase. It is the main word or words in the complete predicate.

> Mrs. Marguez *spoke* for more than an hour to the education committee.
> Mitchell and Adam *have been composing* songs.
> Gail *slammed* a triple into right field.

In discussing the parts of a sentence, the word *verb* is used more often than the term *simple predicate*.

Exercise 5

Write out the following sentences, underlining the complete predicate once and the simple predicate (verb) twice. Be sure to look for verb phrases.

Examples

a. Silica is used in glass and paint.
a. *Silica is used in glass and paint.*

b. Owls can see better in partial darkness than in daylight.
b. *Owls can see better in partial darkness than in daylight.*

1. Galileo Galilei built the first telescope in 1609.

2. The heart normally beats about seventy-two times a minute.

3. Eskimos prefer the name Innuit, "the people."

4. Thomas Jefferson bathed his feet in cold water every day to prevent colds.

5. The sun's surface temperature is approximately 11,000 degrees F.

6. The element francium was discovered by Marguerite Perey of France.

7. Duke Paoa Kahanamoku, a Hawaiian swimmer, held every international swimming record up to the half mile between 1912 and 1928.

8. Richard Kim has written a fascinating book about his Korean ancestry.

9. Sojourner Truth was one of the first people to work for the emancipation of slaves and the rights of women.

10. Orville Wright and Wilbur Wright, inventors of the airplane, did not graduate from high school.

Finding the True Subject

In the usual pattern of English sentences, the subject appears before the verb.

The <u>bucket</u> with the mangrove seedling <u>is</u> full of tadpoles.

In some sentences, however, all or part of the verb appears before the subject. Being able to identify the true subject of a sentence is essential when choosing verbs that agree in number with the subject.

1. The verb may precede the subject in a question.

Where <u>is</u> my yellow and purple <u>shirt</u>?
<u>Have</u> <u>you</u> <u>seen</u> Paolo's sister?
Why <u>is</u> <u>she</u> <u>going</u> to the principal's office?
<u>Did</u> <u>they</u> <u>follow</u> my directions?

2. For variety some sentences are inverted. That is, they are purposely written so that the subject follows the verb.

Behind the piano <u>lay</u> the lost <u>python</u>.
In a secret compartment of the old desk <u>was</u> a yellowed <u>diary</u>.

3. In sentences that begin with *there* and *here*, the subject follows the verb.

Here <u>is</u> the <u>home</u> of Emilio Sanchez.
There <u>is</u> the <u>entrance</u> to the Wax Museum.

There and *here* are introductory words called *expletives*. Sometimes, the word *it* is also an expletive.

It <u>is</u> difficult <u>to find your way in a labyrinth</u>.

To find the true subject of a sentence, first find the verb. Then ask *who?* or *what?*

Another way of locating the subject of a sentence is to change a question or inverted sentence into a statement with the subject preceding the verb.

<u>You</u> <u>have seen</u> Paolo's sister.
<u>They</u> <u>did follow</u> my direction.
The lost <u>python</u> <u>lay</u> behind the piano.
The <u>home</u> of Emilio Sanchez <u>is</u> here.

The subject of an imperative sentence is always the word *you*, the person or persons being addressed. When the word *you* does not appear in the sentence, it is understood as the subject.

(You) Sign these papers and mail them promptly.
(You) Please return my call when you have a chance.

One last obstacle to locating the true subject of a sentence is the prepositional phrase. When a prepositional phrase modifies the subject, the object of the preposition may seem to be the subject. However, remember that the subject never appears in a prepositional phrase.

$$\overset{\text{P}}{}\qquad\overset{\text{OP}}{}$$
A huge pile (of dirty laundry) lay on the bathroom floor.

$$\overset{\text{P}}{}\qquad\overset{\text{OP}}{}$$
The closest (of all Leona's friends) is Katrina.

Exercise 6

Write out the following sentences, underlining the simple subject once and the verb or verb phrase twice. If the subject is understood, write *(You)* in parentheses after the sentence.

Examples

a. When was the deadline for the loan application?
a. *When was the deadline for the loan application?*

b. From far across the fields came the sound of a howling dog.
b. *From far across the fields came the sound of a howling dog.*

1. There are at least three species of butterflies in this meadow.
2. Through the doors rushed thousands of eager bargain hunters.
3. The easiest of all the questions on the essay exam was the last.
4. Here in the valley are the finest of the cherry orchards.
5. Who are the members of the nominating committee this year?
6. Please return these overdue books to the library.
7. There is the gold-covered dome of the state capitol.
8. Around the track jogged all of the members of Overeaters Anonymous.
9. A herd of cattle and sheep peacefully grazed on the hillside.
10. How much money did you earn last summer?

Compound Subjects and Verbs

Compound means "having two or more parts." Like any other part of a sentence, subjects and predicates may be compound.

A *compound subject* consists of two or more simple subjects joined by a conjunction. The parts of a compound subject have the same verb.

Sun, wind, and water are clean sources of energy.

The Greek-Americans on the South Side and the Hungarian-Americans from Mulberry Street are planning a community fair.

A *compound verb* consists of two or more verbs that are joined by a conjunction. The parts of the compound verb have the same subject.

The motor coughed, spit, and died.

The mayors of six cities in the county have suggested several reforms but have so far failed in their efforts.

A sentence may contain both a compound subject and a compound verb.

Nina and her sister organized the campaign and collected all the signatures necessary for the petition.

Mr. O'Neill, the adviser, and the newspaper editors met after each issue and discussed the paper's merits and flaws.

Exercise 7

Write out the following sentences, underlining the simple subject once and the verb twice. Remember to look for compound subjects and verbs.

Example

a. Urie plays the piano well and is studying the flute.

a. Urie plays the piano well and is studying the flute.

1. Debbie, Genie, or Pat will baby-sit for the Olins tonight.
2. Houseflies do not bite but spread disease picked up from decaying matter and filth.
3. Dolphins and whales are aquatic mammals.
4. Fiorello La Guardia was mayor of New York City for many terms and then became the director of the United Nations Relief and Rehabilitation Administration.
5. Newfoundland dogs are known for their skill as swimmers and have saved many people from drowning.
6. The thirty-ton brontosaurus and the more slender diplodocus were plant-eating dinosaurs.
7. Diego Rivera, José Clemente Orozco, and David Alfaro Siqueiros are Mexican artists famous for their murals.
8. Insecticides, tobacco, and snuff contain nicotine.
9. Contact with poison ivy and poison oak irritates most people's skin and causes blisters, itching, and redness.
10. The Italian, or Petrarchan, sonnet has fourteen lines and is composed of an octave and a sestet.

Review Exercise A

Write out the following sentences, underlining the simple subject once and the verb or verb phrase twice. Be certain to watch for compound subjects and verbs.

Example

a. Elizabeth Foster Goose lived in Boston from 1665 to 1757 and is supposedly the real Mother Goose.

a. *Elizabeth Foster Goose* <u>lived</u> *in Boston from 1665 to 1757 and* <u>is</u> *supposedly the real Mother Goose.*

1. The first meeting of the United Nations was held in San Francisco in 1945.

2. One pound of butter equals less than half a kilogram.

3. Pine nuts are also called pignolias and Indian nuts.

4. Babe Zaharias set several track and field records in the 1932 Olympics and then became a world champion golfer.

5. Henry Kissinger won the 1973 Nobel Peace Prize for his work in negotiating a cease-fire agreement in Vietnam.

6. The author of Pericles' famous funeral oration was probably a woman, Aspasia of Miletus.

7. Soybeans provide twice the protein of meat or cheese and have ten times the protein of milk.

8. What is your great-aunt's recipe for guacamole?

9. More than a thousand members of the International Wizard of Oz Club sponsor annual conventions for Munchkins.

10. Traditionally, garlic has been used as a protection against vampires.

11. Have you heard of the 20,000-year-old Lascaux Cave paintings in France?

12. In a test of her ESP, a New York woman correctly guessed 1,850 Zener cards, almost 1,500 more than mere chance.

13. Next Tuesday at Parkway Hospital there is a course in CPR.

14. A large reward is being offered for the return of Salvador Dali's painting of four floating chairs.

15. Which do you think is larger—the Pacific Ocean or all of the land masses on earth?

16. Herds of elephants are ruled by females and led by the oldest female in the herd.

17. Lewis and Clark with their Corps of Discovery started from East Alton, Illinois, in 1804 and journeyed overland to Oregon.

18. *Cotton, coffee, algebra,* and *zero* are a few of the English words that come from Arabic.

19. Osceola, a young Seminole leader, was captured by American troops during a white-flag truce talk.

20. According to legend many Incas escaped from white explorers by descending into the inner earth through a secret tunnel.

Understanding Sentence Patterns

Sentence Pattern: S–V   All English sentences can be classified according to a few basic *sentence patterns*. The simplest pattern is *S–V*, in which *S* is for *subject*, and *V* is for *verb*. In this pattern the verb is always an action verb.

> S V
> Everyone laughed.

Modifiers do not affect the sentence pattern. Even though both the subject and the verb may have modifiers, the basic sentence pattern remains unchanged.

> S V
> Everyone in the class laughed uproariously.

The preceding sentence may be expanded still further without changing the *S–V* pattern.

> S V
> Everyone in Mrs. Anselmo's sixth-period biology class laughed uproariously (when the mouse shot out of the beaker).

The word group in parentheses is a clause (see pages 468–484), which does not affect the sentence pattern.

A verb phrase counts as a single *V*.

> S V
> Maria Tallchief was dancing in *The Firebird* ballet.
> S V
> Gregg's sister will be married in September.

In any sentence pattern one or more of the elements may be compound.

> S S V V
> Scott and Elaine arrived early and set up the tables.
> S V V
> Wendy Sue slipped and fell on the ice.

The *S–V* pattern remains unchanged even though the verb may appear before the subject, as in a question or an inverted sentence.

> V S
> Where are the binoculars?
> V S
> On the counter of my desk is a five-dollar bill.

Complements   Sentences express complete thoughts by means of the subject (the part of the sentence that tells whom or what the sentence is about) and the predicate (the part that tells something about the subject). Some sentences express a complete thought with only a subject and a verb.

$$S \quad V$$
The girl works.

Many English sentences, however, contain a third important sentence part—a *complement*.

A *complement* is usually defined as a word or group of words that completes the meaning of the verb and the subject.

Incomplete:	The third baseman hit. [Hit what?]
	$S \quad V \quad Comp.$
Complete:	The third baseman hit a line drive.
Incomplete:	Miss Tobias is. [Is what?]
	$S \quad V \quad Comp.$
Complete:	Miss Tobias is a physical therapist.

Complements, like subjects, are never found within a prepositional phrase.

$$S \quad V$$
Julie is in the army. [*In the army* is a prepositional phrase.]
$$S \quad V \quad Comp.$$
Julie is a lieutenant in the army.

In the next sections you will learn to identify several different kinds of complements and the sentence patterns associated with them.

The Predicate Nominative

A list of linking verbs is on page 347.

One type of complement is the *predicate nominative*, which is sometimes called a *predicate noun* or *predicate pronoun*.

A *predicate nominative* is usually defined as a noun or pronoun that follows a linking verb and renames or identifies the subject of the sentence.

Jenny's cousin has become a television *announcer*.
Are you the *author* of the letter to the editor?
The winners of the dance contest are *Jeff* and *she*.

Predicate nominatives only occur after linking verbs, such as *be* and *became*. A predicate nominative never follows an action verb.

Sentence Pattern: S–LV–PN

A sentence containing a predicate nominative has the following pattern: *S–LV–PN*.

$$S \quad LV \quad PN \quad PN$$
My favorite relatives are *Aunt Sue* and *you*.

Adding modifiers does not change the basic sentence pattern.

                S   *LV*   *PN*

Henry James' "The Turn of the Screw" *is* a scary *story*.

         S   *V*   *PN*

The person with the highest academic standing is the *valedictorian*.

Exercise 8

Write out the following sentences, labeling each part of the sentence according to its sentence pattern. (Not all sentences contain predicate nominatives.) Underline the words you label.

Examples

   a. Earline is an excellent shortstop.

        S *LV*   *PN*

 a. *Earline is an excellent shortstop.*

   b. Mom's bowling scores have improved tremendously.

                    S   *V*

 b. *Mom's bowling scores have improved tremendously.*

1. Terry is the short young man with the dark beard.
2. She is the only experienced diver in our family.
3. In 1824 Texas was a province of Mexico.
4. Nauru is located 1,300 miles northeast of Australia.
5. Teddy Roosevelt became the twentieth-sixth President of the United States.
6. Francesco A. Lentini's three legs were the star attraction of the circus.
7. In the 1820s the first Greek immigrants to America were young male university students.
8. Writers Mary McCarthy and Flannery O'Connor are Irish-Americans.
9. In 1862 Captain Nathaniel Gordon became the last American pirate to be hanged.
10. Rita Moreno was one of the stars of the first production of *West Side Story*.

Predicate Adjectives   *Predicate adjectives*, like predicate nominatives, are complements that follow linking verbs. The difference between them is that the predicate adjective is always an adjective; the predicate nominative is always a noun or pronoun.

She became *seasick* after an hour.

During the summer Phoenix is extremely *hot* and *dry*.

These potato knishes do not taste *spicy* enough.

Occasionally, but not often, a predicate adjective may precede the verb in an inverted sentence or an exclamation.

How *kind* you are!
Exhausted were the members of the rescue team.

Sentence Pattern: S–LV–PA

Sentences containing a predicate adjective have the following pattern: *S–LV–PA*.

Remember that a predicate adjective may only follow a linking verb, not an action verb.

      S   *LV* *PA*
Owen Glendower is *angry* about his stolen car.
      S   *LV*   *PA*
The streets were completely *empty*.
      S   *LV*   *PA*
Dee Cheng seems *happier* than ever with her new job.

Exercise 9

Write out the following sentences, labeling each part of the sentence according to its pattern. (Not all sentences contain predicate adjectives.) Underline the words you label.

Examples

  a. Leonora is usually, but not always, extremely tactful.
       S *LV*   *PA*
  a. Leonora is usually, but not always, extremely tactful.
  b. Jorge is waiting impatiently for his final grades.
       S   *V*
  b. Jorge is waiting impatiently for his final grades.

1. One of her feet is longer than the other.
2. In the Sonoran desert some cactuses are fifty feet tall.
3. Mrs. Klinger is confident about her abilities.
4. The empty field behind the school has become a junkyard.
5. After several hours the crowd outside the embassy became noisy and unpleasant.
6. Fear of the dark is common among young children.
7. Does this flounder look fresh to you?
8. The incense in the room smelled overpoweringly sweet.
9. Skiing and surfing can be dangerous.
10. Kyle's favorite pastime is reading.

Direct Objects   Verbs may be classified as either action or linking. Two kinds of complements, predicate nominatives and predicate adjectives, may follow linking verbs. Three kinds of complements may follow action verbs. The first of these is the *direct object*.

A *direct object* is usually defined as a word or group of words that receives the action of the verb.

A direct object follows an action verb and answers the question *what?* or *whom?*

The knave of hearts stole some *tarts*.
[What did the knave steal?]

The detective questioned the *witness*.
[Whom did the detective question?]

The spy destroyed all her secret *papers*.
[What did the spy destroy?]

Direct objects may be nouns, pronouns, phrases, or clauses.

DO Laurie divided the *fruit* among the six of us.	[noun]
DO We met *him* in front of the fountain.	[pronoun]
DO Keith denied *sending the anonymous letter*.	[phrase]
DO She wants desperately *to finish her assignment*.	[phrase]
DO I hope *that they will arrive before dark*.	[clause]
DO Do you know *what you will do this summer*?	[clause]

Action verbs may be classified as either *transitive* or *intransitive*.

An *intransitive verb* is an action verb that does not have a direct object. *Transitive verbs* are action verbs that are followed by a direct object.

Most English verbs may be either transitive or intransitive, depending on how they are used in a sentence.

	DO
Transitive:	Rusty *called* his girlfriend.
Intransitive:	He *called* from a phone booth.
	DO
Transitive:	Helene *will finish* her thesis next month.
Intransitive:	The roofer *will finish* tomorrow.
	DO
Transitive:	Roy *asked* a good question about censorship.
Intransitive:	She *asked* about your plans for Saturday.

Sentence Pattern: S–V–DO

When a sentence contains a direct object, its sentence pattern is *S–V–DO*.

All verbs in this sentence pattern are transitive verbs because they have a direct object.

>   *S*   *V*   *DO*
> The ball *hit* the umpire on his right arm.
>   *S*   *V*   *DO*
> (You) Please *finish* your chores before dinner.

Exercise 10

Write out the following sentences, labeling each part of the sentence according to its pattern. (Not all sentences have direct objects.) Underline the words you label.

Examples

a. Bonnie Siefert asked us to dinner on Saturday.
>   *S*   *V* *DO*
> *a.* *Bonnie Siefert* *asked* *us* to dinner on Saturday.

b. Many children watch too much television.
>   *S*   *V*   *DO*
> *b.* *Many children* *watch* too much *television.*

c. She works best early in the morning.
>   *S*   *V*
> *c.* *She works* best early in the morning.

1. During the dance Esther Lopez lost her wallet.
2. Each month the bank charges two dollars for the checking account.
3. Howard and his mother waited at the hospital for news.
4. Dwane Elmore owns an art gallery on Sixth Avenue.
5. I bought some carbon paper at the bookstore.
6. Cynthia caught a bad case of the measles.
7. Next month she plans to vacation in San Francisco.
8. Alfredo is taking a course in native American history.
9. Yesterday afternoon Mrs. Gasthalter's dog bit the letter carrier.
10. Kuma Akita is selling his prize-winning landscape.

Indirect Objects

A sentence containing a direct object may also have an *indirect object*.

An *indirect object* is usually defined as a word that tells to whom or for whom the action of the verb is done. The indirect object always comes immediately before the direct object.

IO DO
Fran gave her *brother* her collection of Indian-head pennies.

       IO   DO
The University of Texas awarded *Craig* a baseball scholarship.

IO   DO
She gave *him* her phone number.

Indirect objects, like other kinds of complements, are never found in a prepositional phrase. When the word *to* or *for* is used, the noun or pronoun that follows is the object of a preposition, *not* an indirect object.

     IO   DO
Betsy Kahn sent the *President* a *telegram*.

      DO   OP
Betsy Kahn sent a telegram to the President.

      IO   DO
Grandma Anna knit *me* a long-sleeved sweater.

       DO   OP
Grandma Anna knit a long-sleeved sweater for me.

Sentence Pattern: S–V–IO–DO

A sentence must contain a direct object in order to have an indirect object. No sentence may have an indirect object alone. Not all sentences with direct objects, however, have indirect objects also.

Sentences containing an indirect object have the pattern *S–V–IO–DO*.

    S V IO   DO
Noel's parents made *him* a surprise birthday party.

    S   V   IO   DO
The representative handed her *secretary* a draft of the bill.

Exercise 11

Write out the following sentences, underlining the indirect object, if there is one, and labeling each sentence part. (Not every sentence contains an indirect object.)

Examples

a. Sue Ann bought her poodle a sweater.
   S   V   IO DO
a. *Sue Ann bought her poodle a sweater.*

b. We gave the kitchen ceiling a second coat of paint.
  S V   IO   DO
b. *We gave the kitchen ceiling a second coat of paint.*

1. No one tells me anything.

2. Did you send the bill to her?

3. The calico cat gave me a steady, loving look.

4. Theo and Rolf have sent us their new address.

5. The judge returned the shrimp boats to their owners.

6. Mrs. Lockley offered us tea and cookies.

7. The police officer gave Carlos a ticket for speeding.

8. Dylan asked me about Mildred's upcoming party.

9. Will Mr. Lipton give you a chance to make up the math final?

10. Mom told us the story of her getting lost in the Rockies.

Objective Complements

An additional complement following a direct object is called an *objective complement* because it refers to the object.

An *objective complement* is usually defined as a noun or an adjective that completes the meaning of the verb and refers to the direct object.

Objective complements follow only a few action verbs:

appoint	consider	make
choose	elect	name

The poodle considered all children a *menace*.
[The noun *menace* is an objective complement. It modifies the direct object *children* and tells what the children were considered.]

The junior class elected Jeremiah *president*.
[The noun *president* is an objective complement. It modifies the direct object *Jeremiah* and tells what Jeremiah was elected.]

Sentence Pattern: S–V–DO–OC

In order to have an objective complement, a sentence must also contain a direct object. The sentence pattern for a sentence with an objective complement is *S–V–DO–OC*.

$$\begin{array}{ccccc} S & V & DO & OC & OC \end{array}$$
The ancient Greeks considered Athena *wise* and *just*.

$$\begin{array}{cccc} S & V & DO & OC \end{array}$$
The committee will appoint Susan *chairperson*.

Exercise 12

Write out the following sentences, labeling each part of the sentence according to its pattern. (Not all sentences contain objective complements.) Underline the words you label.

Examples

a. Uncle Larry considers Georgia peaches the best.
$$\begin{array}{cccc} S & V & DO & OC \end{array}$$

a. *Uncle Larry considers Georgia peaches the best.*

b. Mr. and Mrs. Osaka have made their business successful.
      S   *V*   *DO*   *OC*

b. *Mr. and Mrs. Osaka have made their business successful.*

1. A majority of the voters elected him President.
2. Shel considers Peru the most beautiful country in South America.
3. What is the state flower of Arkansas?
4. For thirty-five years the Mercers have made Kentucky their home.
5. Cleve's brother and sister-in-law named their baby Melissa.
6. Do you consider Ramiro handsome?
7. The senior class elected Paula chairperson of Senior Day.
8. Karl and Bill named their dog Rothschild.
9. The President named him ambassador to Egypt.
10. After a year as assistant editor, Sue Ling has been appointed editor-in-chief of the school paper.

Active and Passive Voice

Transitive verbs (those that take direct objects) may be either active or passive.

When the subject of the verb performs an action, the verb is said to be in the *active voice*. When the action is performed upon the subject of the verb, the verb is in the *passive voice*.

In the following sentences the object of the verb in the active voice becomes the subject of the sentence in the passive voice.

                          S   *V*

Active: Ginnie's father prepared Cantonese chicken.

[The subject *father* performs the action.]

                         S   *V*

Passive: Cantonese chicken was prepared by Ginnie's father.

[The action is performed upon the subject.]

                        S   *V*

Active: The young soloist played a Chopin nocturne.

                        S   *V*

Passive: A Chopin nocturne was played by the young soloist.

                             S   *V*

Active: During the riot stray bullets wounded several bystanders.

                             S   *V*

Passive: During the riot several bystanders were wounded by stray bullets.

Notice that verbs in the passive voice are made up of a form of the verb *be* and the past participle of the verb.

Exercise 13

Rewrite each of the following sentences. If the verb is in the active voice, change it to the passive. If the verb is in the passive voice, change it to the active.

Examples

a. *The Indian Heritage of America* was written by Alvin Josephy, Jr.

a. *Alvin Josephy, Jr., wrote* The Indian Heritage of America.

b. Dr. Hannah Thompson gave the Environment Club a slide show about coral reefs.

b. *A slide show about coral reefs was given the Environment Club by Dr. Hannah Thompson.*

1. The President awarded her the Medal of Honor.
2. The record for staying awake was broken by the disc jockey.
3. Gilbert and Sullivan's operetta *Utopia Limited* was performed by the D'Oyly Carte Opera Company.
4. The hockey players broke a bottle of ammonia in the locker room.
5. During the five-mile hike Jerry drank two quarts of water.
6. Pilar was nominated for class president by Antony.
7. A band of masked men was seen by the stagecoach driver.
8. Madeline received two invitations to the senior prom.
9. The roll of film was accidentally exposed by Ted.
10. Dad gave Mom a calculator for her birthday.

Mastery Exercise A

Write each of the following sentences, underlining the simple subject once and the verb twice. Then label each part of the sentence according to its pattern.

Examples

a. Pancho Segura uses a two-handed forehand.

    S   *V*   *DO*

a. *Pancho Segura uses a two-handed forehand.*

b. According to Ann Landers people must keep their commitments.

                        S   *V*   *DO*

b. *According to Ann Landers people must keep their commitments.*

c. Mayor Ghribaldi appointed Juan Fernandez chairman of the committee.

        S   *V*   *DO*   *OC*

c. *Mayor Ghribaldi appointed Juan Fernandez chairman of the committee.*

1. The real Norma Rae is Crystal Lee Sutton, a textile-union organizer.
2. More than a billion Elvis Presley records have been sold.
3. Ananda Chkrabarty received a United States patent for creating an oil-eating Superbug.
4. So far this week there have been two homicides resulting from arguments over parking places.
5. Frank Palmer has built and has flown his own motorized glider.
6. Internal reviews of the police department are monitored by the Office of Professional Compliance.
7. Defensive tackle Bill Barnett is the Dolphins' number three draft choice.
8. Nancy Lopez-Melton bogeyed the sixth hole yesterday.
9. A commission is studying the proposal about tripling the annual quota of immigrants.
10. A bilingual French and English version of "O Canada" is the new Canadian national anthem.
11. Nine people died of heatstroke during the 113-degree heat wave in Texas.
12. Have you seen the new laser show at the Planetarium?
13. Fire fighters from five states are battling an 8,000-acre forest fire in Colorado.
14. Nitrites in cured meats prevent the growth of botulism.
15. The security guard asked us for our ID cards.
16. The Coast Guard is investigating the causes of the mysterious fish-kill.
17. Researchers at the Mayo Clinic have sent the press their study on the effects of laetrile on cancer patients.
18. According to legend sea beans and sea hearts will keep you from getting lost.
19. There are more than 150 women's soccer teams in the area in and around the city of Seattle.
20. The Nuclear Regulatory Commission has approved the venting of radioactive krypton gas from the Three Mile Island nuclear plant.

Writing Effective Sentences

Good writing style means more than grammatically correct sentences. To be effective your writing should express what you have to say both clearly and smoothly. In the following sections you will learn ways to improve your writing style.

**Avoiding
Run-On
Sentences**

A *run-on sentence* occurs when two sentences are joined together into one sentence, either separated by a comma or run together with no punctuation at all. Always avoid using run-on sentences in your writing.

You can correct run-on sentences in several ways.

First, you may separate the two sentences with a period, writing them as two complete sentences.

Run-On:	Dolphins have a complex communication system some scientists compare it to human language.
Correct:	Dolphins have a complex communication system. Some scientists compare it to human language.

Second, you may separate the two sentences with a semicolon when they are closely related in meaning.

Run-On:	Sequoya was a Cherokee scholar he is famous for developing a written alphabet for his language.
Correct:	Sequoya was a Cherokee scholar; he is famous for developing a written alphabet for his language.

Third, you may use a semicolon plus a conjunctive adverb to join the two sentences.

A conjunctive adverb, which shows the relationship between the sentences, is always followed by a comma.

Run-On:	During the first film the class was noisy and unresponsive, nonetheless, the teacher decided to show the second film.
Correct:	During the first film the class was noisy and unresponsive; nonetheless, the teacher decided to show the second film.

Coordinating conjunctions are discussed on page 406.

Fourth, you may combine two sentences with a comma followed by a coordinating conjunction.

Run-On:	Today Scott Joplin is enormously popular as a ragtime composer his ragtime ballet and opera scores were not successful in his lifetime.
Correct:	Today Scott Joplin is enormously popular as a ragtime composer, but his ragtime ballet and opera scores were not successful in his lifetime.

Subordinate clauses are discussed on pages 469–477.

A fifth way to correct run-on sentences is to change one of the sentences into a subordinate clause.

Run-On:	Isadora Duncan is famous as an innovator in modern dance she rebelled against the formal choreography of ballet.
Correct:	Isadora Duncan, who is famous as an innovator in modern dance, rebelled against the formal choreography of ballet.

Writing Exercise A

On a separate sheet of paper, write out corrections for each of the following run-on sentences. Make the corrections in whatever way seems most appropriate to you.

Example

a. In 1969 the *Apollo 11* spacecraft landed on the moon the landing site is known as the Sea of Tranquillity.

a. In 1969 the Apollo 11 *spacecraft landed on the moon. The landing site is known as the Sea of Tranquillity.*

1. The cooperative commune Brook Farm was established in 1841 one of its members was the writer Nathaniel Hawthorne.

2. William Jennings Bryan urged radical political reforms such as suffrage for women and the popular election of senators his skills as an orator made him famous.

3. When the Constitution was written the United States had no standing army therefore the Constitution guaranteed the right of its citizens to bear arms.

4. Lord Byron gained immediate fame with the publication of *Childe Harold's Pilgrimage* the poem was so popular that Byron earned a fortune in royalty payments from its sales.

5. Many people do not remember their dreams research shows that humans have an intense physical need to dream.

6. In 1923 blues singer Bessie Smith made her first recording the song "Down Hearted Blues" was a great success.

7. For centuries garlic has been valued for its medicinal properties it is a member of the plant family that contains the onion.

8. Stonehenge is a massive stone monument in England one theory as to its purpose suggests that it was constructed as an astronomical observatory and calendar.

9. Dame Agatha Christie's mystery novels have sold over 300 million copies worldwide she is the most widely translated English author, next to Shakespeare.

10. Chinese is the oldest living language the oldest known written language is Sumerian, which dates back to 3500 B.C.

Avoiding Sentence Fragments

A *sentence fragment* is a group of words written incorrectly as a complete sentence.

A complete sentence meets all three of the following requirements.

1. A sentence expresses a complete thought.

2. A sentence has a subject.

3. A sentence has a verb.

The following examples are fragments because they do not meet all the requirements for a complete sentence.

Fragment (Incomplete Thought):	Because he wanted the apartment to be immaculate for the party
Complete Sentence:	Because he wanted the apartment to be immaculate for the party, Dan spent Saturday cleaning and polishing.
Fragment (No Subject):	Scurried across the fresh blanket of snow
Complete Sentence:	The small gray rabbit scurried across the fresh blanket of snow.
*Fragment (No Verb):	The senior citizens building a large wooden jungle gym and fort for the neighborhood day-care center
Complete Sentence:	The senior citizens are building a large wooden jungle gym and fort for the neighborhood day-care center.

Participles are discussed on page 455.

*The example indicated by the asterisk contains a participle, a verb form usually ending in *-ing* or *-ed*. Because it is used as an adjective, a participle cannot be considered the verb in a sentence.

PARTICIPLE	VERB PHRASE
located	is located
sitting	will have been sitting

Phrases as Fragments

Some sentence fragments are created because a *prepositional phrase, infinitive phrase, gerund phrase,* or *participial phrase* is written as a complete sentence. Because a phrase does not express a complete thought, it should not be punctuated as a complete sentence, as the following examples show. These fragments often need to be attached to the complete sentences preceding or following them.

See pages 452–467 for more information about phrases.

Fragment:	Waiting patiently inside the store's main entrance. Anita watched the holiday shoppers hurry up and down the busy street.
Sentence:	Waiting patiently inside the store's main entrance, Anita watched the holiday shoppers hurry up and down the busy street.
Fragment:	She used an old toothbrush dipped in varnish remover. To loosen the finish in the small, narrow grooves of the old chest.
Sentence:	She used an old toothbrush dipped in varnish remover to loosen the finish in the small, narrow grooves of the old chest.
Fragment:	An interesting assortment of pottery and antique baskets lined the top shelf. Of the walnut bookcase in the far corner of the living room.
Sentence:	An interesting assortment of pottery and antique baskets lined the top shelf of the walnut bookcase in the far corner of the living room.

Clauses as Fragments

A *subordinate clause* contains both a subject and a verb but does not express a complete thought. Subordinate clauses must be attached to an independent clause; they cannot stand alone. In the following examples notice how the sentence fragment is eliminated when the subordinate clause is attached to a related independent clause.

A discussion of subordinate clauses begins on page 469.

Fragment:	Although she worked as a pharmacist for several years. Ann Petry later became famous for her short stories and novels.
Sentence:	Although she worked as a pharmacist for several years, Ann Petry later became famous for her short stories and novels.
Fragment:	I bought a copy of Maya Angelou's book last week. Because I enjoyed the excerpt we read in English class.
Sentence:	I bought a copy of Maya Angelou's book last week because I enjoyed the excerpt we read in English class.

Appositive Phrases as Fragments

An *appositive phrase* is a group of words placed beside a noun or pronoun to explain or identify it. Although an appositive phrase always contains a noun or pronoun, it cannot be punctuated as a sentence because it does not express a complete thought nor does it include a verb. In the following examples the fragments are corrected by attaching each appositive phrase to the noun or pronoun it describes.

Appositive phrases are discussed on pages 458–459.

Fragment:	Luis learned chess from his grandmother. A former chess champion.
Sentence:	Luis learned chess from his grandmother, a former chess champion.
Fragment:	The only bottlenose dolphin in the zoo. Skipper loved the adoring attention he received from the crowds of visitors.
Sentence:	The only bottlenose dolphin in the zoo, Skipper loved the adoring attention he received from the crowds of visitors.

Writing Exercise B

Rewrite each of the following sentences, correcting all sentence fragments.

Example

a. Beckwourth Pass in the Sierra Nevada Mountains was discovered by James Beckwourth. A former slave and Crow chief.

a. *Beckwourth Pass in the Sierra Nevada Mountains was discovered by James Beckwourth, a former slave and Crow chief.*

1. Her husband was born in West Allis. A city located to the west of Milwaukee, Wisconsin.

2. Working hard from dawn until dusk. The student council members transformed the cafeteria for the last dance.

3. After earning her degree from the Massachusetts Institute of Technology. Anna Ramirez accepted a position as an industrial engineer in New Mexico.

4. Although it is probably not valuable. She loves the old willow basket because her grandmother made it.

5. The white frame house stood on the crest of the hill. To the left of the large weather-beaten barn and the black iron windmill.

6. A quiet man who greeted everyone with warmth. Mr. Alberts will be missed by everyone in the neighborhood.

7. Masterfully carved from dark wood and polished to a high gloss. The African mask is the most stunning piece in Karim's art collection.

8. The newspaper states that the children might have been saved from the fire. If smoke alarms had been installed near their bedroom.

9. Mr. O'Rourke still works full time as a free-lance artist. Even though he must undergo kidney dialysis once a week.

10. A spectacular member of the banana family. The blue and orange bird-of-paradise grows in humid tropical climates.

Review Exercise A

On a separate sheet of paper, write out each of the following sentences, correcting sentences that are fragments or run-ons.

Example

a. The beat generation refers to a group of American writers and artists. Popular during the 1950s.

a. *The beat generation refers to a group of American writers and artists who were popular during the 1950s.*

1. The caffeine in coffee acts as a stimulant, it is mildly habit-forming.

2. Minority rights groups have made significant gains in the United States much still remains to be done in the areas of integrated housing and employment opportunities.

3. The highest peak in Australia. Mt. Kosciusko is part of the Australian Alps.

4. Tarot cards are used for fortunetelling gypsies are thought to have introduced tarot cards into Europe during the fifteenth century.

5. The first English professional female writer was Aphra Behan. A playwright and novelist born in 1640.

6. The Berlin wall is a fortified barrier separating East and West Berlin. Which was erected during 1961.

7. Tecumseh was chief of the Shawnee and a great leader his efforts to unite widespread tribes into an Indian military movement failed.

8. Most basketball players bounce the ball once or twice. When preparing for a free throw.

9. The sinking of the *Titanic* cost more than 1,500 lives, the disaster helped bring about improved safety measures at sea.

10. The Toltec were an ancient people of Mexico. Whose name in the Nahuatl language means "master builders."

11. The purpose of John Brown's raid on Harpers Ferry was to establish a republic of fugitive and freed slaves, the raid was supported with funds from Canadian and New England abolitionists.

12. The tachistoscope is a film projector that flashes messages so quickly that the viewer isn't aware of seeing them nevertheless the viewer's behavior is supposed to be affected by the repeating message.

13. Druid priests were a powerful political force among the Celts, they organized rebellions against the Roman invasion at the time of Julius Caesar.

14. Sarah Bernhardt gained fame as one of the greatest actors of the theater her first three performances were panned by critics, and she almost left the stage.

15. Modern scientists believe the outer core of the earth is solid due to the great internal heat, the inner core is molten.

16. Mahatma Gandhi, George Bernard Shaw, and Count Tolstoy all had one thing in common they were vegetarians.

17. People should do five to ten minutes of warm-up exercises. Before engaging in strenuous sports such as jogging.

18. The Black Death was a form of bubonic plague between 1347 and 1351 it killed over 75 million people.

19. In 1986 Halley's comet will travel close enough to the earth to be seen. Which was last visible in 1910.

20. Many explorers claim to have seen evidence of the Yeti. Also known as the Abominable Snowman.

19 The Phrase

Understanding Phrases

Phrases (multiword modifiers) can add a great deal of information to a sentence, as the following example shows.

> The man gave her directions.

> The man *working in the office of information at the Parks Department* gave her directions *on how to get to the new zoo.*

In the following sections you will learn to identify the various kinds of phrases and to understand how they function in a sentence.

Defining a Phrase

A *phrase* is usually defined as a group of words that functions as a single part of speech and that does not contain both a subject and a verb.

A phrase may function in a sentence as a noun, a verb, an adjective, or an adverb.

Noun phrases are usually defined as a noun and its modifiers.

> *The entire swimming team* is ill with *intestinal flu.*
> *Old science fiction movies* are *Joan's favorite pastime.*

Verb phrases are made up of a main verb plus one or more helping verbs.

> You *could have asked* for some advice.
> Tobin's parents *are celebrating* their twentieth anniversary.

In the following sections you will study three kinds of phrases: prepositional phrases, verbal phrases, and appositive phrases. These may function as nouns, adjectives, and adverbs.

Noun:	Her main goal is *to see all of the national parks.*
Adjective:	*Stretching its neck*, the baby gazelle nibbled the leaves.
Adverb:	The last gas station is a mile ahead *on the left.*

Prepositional Phrases

A *prepositional phrase* is made up of a preposition, its object, and any modifiers the object may have. The *object of a preposition* is the noun or pronoun (or group of words that function as a noun) that ends the prepositional phrase.

In the following examples the prepositional phrase is in parentheses and the object of the preposition is *italicized*.

Ira has moved (to an *apartment*) (across the *street*) (from his old *one*).
A bright, flashing red and yellow light moved slowly (toward *them*).
Carole dozed (between *periods*) (of *studying*) (for her comprehensive *exams*).

Before you proceed further, turn to page 399 for a review of the most commonly used prepositions. Remember that some prepositions, such as *in spite of* and *on account of,* are made up of more than one word.

Prepositional phrases cannot stand on their own. They are modifiers, functioning as either adjectives or adverbs.

Adjective Phrases

An *adjective phrase* modifies a noun or a pronoun. Like single-word adjectives, an adjective phrase tells *what kind, which one,* or *how many.*

Modifies Noun:	The representative *from Arkansas* voted no. [The phrase *from Arkansas* answers the question *which one?*]
Modifies Noun:	A dozen *of her photos* have been accepted. [The phrase *of her photos* answers the question *what kind?*]
Modifies Pronoun:	One *of his boots* is missing. [The phrase *of his boots* answers the question *what kind?*]

In a series of prepositional phrases, an adjective phrase may modify the object of a preposition in the preceding phrase.

We bought the jeans (at *one*) (of the *booths*) (at the *flea market*).

Adverb Phrases

Like single-word adverbs, *adverb phrases* can modify three different parts of speech: a verb, an adjective, or another adverb.

Adverb phrases answer the questions *where? when? how?* and *how much?*

Modifies Verb:	Galileo dropped a feather *from the tower.*
	[The phrase *from the tower* answers the question *where?*]
	She left *in a hurry.*
	[The phrase *in a hurry* answers the question *how?*]
Modifies Adverb:	Paul last wrote early *in March.*
	[The phrase *in March* answers the question *when?*]

Two or more adverb phrases may be used in succession to modify the same word.

Suddenly Mike's cap blew (from his head) (into the river).
[Both phrases modify the verb *blew.*]

Exercise 1

Write out the following sentences, underlining each prepositional phrase and labeling it as either an adjective phrase (*Adj.*) or an adverb phrase (*Adv.*).

Examples

a. Can you meet me at 6 o'clock at O'Connell's?

               Adv.   *Adv.*

a. *Can you meet me <u>at 6 o'clock</u> <u>at O'Connell's</u>?*

b. David's cousin is the violinist in the third row.

                                  Adj.

b. *David's cousin is the violinist <u>in the third row</u>.*

1. Since June we have seen Dr. Greenfield at least twice.
2. No one in the pool heard Katya's call for help.
3. The first exit after the toll is Coral Ridge Road.
4. Six ships steamed past Fowry's Light and turned into the channel.
5. Although some people on the street object, the neighborhood council is planning a block party sometime later in the month.
6. The players from East End Avenue scrambled over the fence into the locked basketball court.
7. By the side of the swollen canal, we watched the slowly receding waters.
8. Together with Pearl, Rosie has met all of the requirements for her lifesaving certificate.
9. A dense cloud of smog hung over the valley for a week.
10. The child hid the box of frogs under the pile of boots.

Verbal Phrases   There are three different kinds of verbals: *participles, gerunds*, and *infinitives*. A verbal is formed from a verb but does not function as a verb in a sentence. A participle is an adjective; a gerund is always a noun; and an infinitive may be a noun, an adjective, or an adverb.

When a verbal has a complement or a modifier, it becomes part of a *verbal phrase.* In the following sections you will learn to identify the three types of verbal phrases: participial phrases, gerund phrases, and infinitive phrases.

Participial Phrases

A *participle* is a form of the verb that is used as an adjective. Participles have present, past, and perfect forms.

Present:	*Squawking* noisily, the jay defended its nest.
Past:	He built a tree house *hidden* completely by the branches.
Perfect:	*Having lost* ten pounds, Mrs. Korsakoff considered the diet successful.

A *participial phrase* is introduced by a participle and followed by one or more modifiers and complements. A participial phrase always functions as an adjective, modifying a noun or a pronoun.

Notice that both the complement and modifier may be phrases and clauses, as well as single words.

Having finally decided to cut her hair, she studied her face in the mirror.
[*Finally* is an adverb modifying the participle *having decided. To cut her hair* is the direct object of the participle. The entire participial phrase modifies the pronoun *she.*]

The Fourth of July fireworks, *exploding into rainbow-colored puffballs,* lit up the sky.
[*Into rainbow-colored puffballs* is a prepositional phrase modifying the participle *exploding.* The entire participial phrase modifies the noun *fireworks.*]

Exercise 2

Write out the following sentences, underlining the participial phrases and drawing an arrow to the word each phrase modifies.

Examples

a. Barking furiously, the dog lunged at the locked gate.

a. *Barking furiously, the dog lunged at the locked gate.*

b. Who are the three elderly ladies watching the tryouts?

b. *Who are the three elderly ladies watching the tryouts?*

1. Justine handed round the watermelon, cut into huge wedges.

2. Surprised by the call from his old friend, Thomas could hardly speak.

3. Having made sure that no one was at home, the exterminators began to cover the house with a tent.

4. Showing his favorite photographs of marine animals and plants, Douglas Faulkner spoke to a standing-room-only crowd.

5. *Robinson Crusoe*, published in 1719 by Daniel Defoe, remains one of the best adventure stories ever written.

6. The hikers hurried onward, hoping to reach the lodge before the storm hit.

7. Irritated by Jan's slowness, the rest of us decided to leave without her.

8. Renee, shocked by the news of her friend's death, needed someone to talk to.

9. Having completed the first round of the tournament, Gina felt relieved.

10. Mr. Giacommo replanted his garden, destroyed by a late spring frost.

Gerund Phrases

A *gerund* is a form of the verb that is used as a noun. Gerunds may be used in any way that nouns are used in sentences—as subjects, objects, and predicate nominatives.

> S
> *Painting* is her favorite pastime.

> OP
> Dwight has won six trophies for his *diving*.

See page 340 for a discussion of the use of a possessive pronoun before a gerund.

A *gerund phrase* is made up of a gerund and its complements and modifiers.

In a gerund phrase the modifiers may be single words, phrases, or clauses.

Last year he mailed his income tax without *signing it*.
[*It* is the object of the gerund *signing*. The gerund phrase *signing it* functions as the object of the preposition *without*.]

We loved *seeing your baby pictures*.
[*Your baby pictures* is the object of the gerund *seeing*. The gerund phrase *seeing your baby pictures* functions as the direct object in the sentence.]

Sampling many different kinds of foods is their idea of a perfect meal.
[The gerund phrase functions as the subject of the sentence. Within the gerund phrase *kinds* is the direct object; *many*, *different* and *of foods* modify the word *kinds*.]

You will not confuse gerund phrases and participial phrases if you remember to look to see how the phrase functions in a sentence.

1. A participial phrase always functions as an adjective.

2. A gerund phrase always functions as a noun.

Exercise 3

Write out the following sentences and underline the gerund phrases. (Some sentences may have more than one.) Then write the function each phrase performs.

Examples

a. Seeing in the dark is difficult for humans.

a. *Seeing in the dark is difficult for humans.—subject*

b. What is the purpose of buying ten pounds of bananas?

b. *What is the purpose of buying ten pounds of bananas?—object of preposition*

1. Ken hates having to stand on the train.
2. Trying to assemble a bicycle challenges one's abilities and patience.
3. Whose job is washing the dishes?
4. Bill and his sister earn extra money by mowing the neighbors' lawns.
5. Upon removing your shoes, you may enter the temple.
6. Mrs. Petraske's ambition is writing a children's book.
7. Anita suffers from worrying too much about everything.
8. Whistling tunes on key is difficult for me.
9. Flying too high in the sky is my idea of nothing to do.
10. The least effective way of solving a problem is ignoring it completely.

Infinitive Phrases

The *infinitive* is a form of the verb preceded by the word *to*. Infinitives may be used as nouns, adjectives, or adverbs.

Roy wants *to sleep.*	[noun]
Today is a day *to remember.*	[adjective]
This pen is too hard *to use.*	[adverb]

An *infinitive phrase* is made up of an infinitive, its modifiers, complements, and subject.

An infinitive phrase may serve as the subject of a sentence, the direct object, the predicate nominative, or as an adjective or adverb.

To sing professionally is Powell's ambition.	[subject]
Ava's father wants *to invite us to dinner.*	[object]
Her approach is *to be completely honest about her feelings.*	[predicate nominative]
Moira finally has a job *to challenge her abilities.*	[adjective]
The living room is too big *to paint in half a day.*	[adverb]

Unlike other verbal phrases, the infinitive phrase may also have a subject, which is part of the infinitive phrase. The subject of an infinitive phrase comes after the main verb and immediately before the infinitive.

We asked *them to be here before 10.*
Dora wants *us to meet her twin brother.*
Alonzo's friends persuaded *him to enter the contest.*

The subject of an infinitive only follows action verbs such as *urge, order, persuade, invite,* and *ask.*

Notice that the pronouns that function as subjects or objects in an infinitive phrase are always in the object form (*me, him, her, us, them*).

Subject of Infinitive:	He asked *us to come back later.*
Direct Object of Infinitive:	Mr. Carlozzi wants *to see them right away.*
Indirect Object of Infinitive:	George tried *to give her some advice.*

Exercise 4

Write out the following sentences and underline the infinitive phrases. Be sure to include subjects of the infinitive phrase.

Examples

a. Sheila and Ed volunteered to sell ads for the newspaper.
a. *Sheila and Ed volunteered to sell ads for the newspaper.*

b. The guard told us to wait here.
b. *The guard told us to wait here.*

1. Albert's parents like to try new dances.
2. Mrs. Ronke prefers to drink hot tea, while her husband likes his iced.
3. This book is too good to put down.
4. With a little care it is possible to keep a friendship going for a lifetime.
5. This is the way to enter the orchestra pit.
6. She had hoped to find *Kiss Me, Kate* on sale at the record store.
7. To cash a check without having an account is practically impossible.
8. Mrs. Lindstrom wants Todd to remove the old wallpaper from the bedroom.
9. Did you remember to notify the post office to hold our mail?
10. They wanted us to know that they had been here.

Appositive Phrases

An *appositive* is a noun or pronoun that identifies or explains a nearby noun or pronoun.

The Sierra Club, *a wilderness group,* is having a three-day sail to the Dry Tortugas.

Craig Mendenhall, *Bennett's cousin,* is a National Merit Finalist.

An *appositive phrase* is made up of an appositive and its modifiers, which may be single-word modifiers, phrases, or clauses.

> Laura wants to enroll in Coleman Institute, *a vocational college.*

> Julio Daddonna, *the dancer that I introduced you to,* is having a recital next Friday.

> Nick, *the tall young man wearing the red shirt,* is Sally's boyfriend.

Exercise 5

Write out the following sentences and underline the appositive phrases.

Examples

a. Leora Daeton, a research chemist, is an expert witness in the trial.

a. Leora Daeton, <u>a research chemist</u>, is an expert witness in the trial.

b. The Everglades kite, one of several endangered species, feeds exclusively on apple snails.

b. The Everglades kite, <u>one of several endangered species</u>, feeds exclusively on apple snails.

1. The Natural I, a co-op on Center Street, sells organic vegetables and fruits.

2. Jalil and Armond, participants in a student exchange program, are spending their senior year in Helena, Montana.

3. Mom was appalled to find that her favorite plant, the spider plant in the kitchen, had developed scale.

4. The Mexican government once put up for sale Popocatépetl, a dormant volcano southeast of Mexico City, but no one offered to buy it.

5. William John Hartack, a Slovakian-American, rode five Kentucky Derby winners.

6. Next week the Rotary Club will honor Antony Figueroa, director of the Youth Service Training Association.

7. The Galápagos Islands, an Ecuadorian archipelago in the Pacific, were named for their resident 500-pound land tortoises.

8. Antonio Vivaldi, a Venetian composer who lived from 1675 to 1741, wrote such memorable music as *The Four Seasons.*

9. July Fourth and Memorial Day, national holidays for most workers, are the occasions each year for many traffic deaths.

10. *The People's Almanac* by David Wallechinsky and Irving Wallace, son and father, is a fascinating collection of little-known facts.

Review Exercise A

Identify the different kinds of verbals and verbal phrases in the following paragraphs. Underline each phrase and, above it, use the following labels.

Prep.	(prepositional phrase)
Part.	(participial phrase or participle)
Ger.	(gerund phrase or gerund)
Inf.	(infinitive phrase or infinitive)
App.	(appositive phrase or appositive)

If a phrase is part of a larger phrase, enclose it in parentheses. Be sure to distinguish infinitive phrases from prepositional phrases beginning with the preposition *to*.

Example

a. The 1920s saw a flowering of black writing, art, music, and thought that came to be known as the Harlem Renaissance.

          Ger.   *Prep.*

a. *The 1920s saw <u>a flowering</u> (<u>of black writing, art, music, and thought</u>)*

          Inf.   *Prep.*

  that came <u>to be known</u> (<u>as the Harlem Renaissance</u>.)

The entry of the United States into World War I had created a boom in American industry, and as a result many blacks moved from the South to take jobs in Northern industrial plants. Blacks remained in large Northern cities, notably Chicago and New York. Harlem, a section of New York, became the cosmopolitan center of black life in America. Among the writers living in Harlem were the poets Claude McKay, Jean Toomer, Langston Hughes, and Countee Cullen.

Claude McKay (1890–1948) was the oldest of the Harlem Renaissance writers and the first to publish. He was born in Sunny Ville, Jamaica, in the West Indies. When he was fourteen, he moved to Kingston, where he later became a police officer. In Kingston he began to write poems in the Jamaican dialect. When he was twenty-two, he published two collections of poems and won a medal and an award of money from the Institute of Arts and Letters. The money enabled him to emigrate to the United States, where he attended Tuskegee Institute and Kansas State College. For some years he lived in Harlem, supporting himself with odd jobs, and in 1922 he published his most important collection of poems, *Harlem Shadows*. In addition to poems, McKay wrote several novels, including *Home to Harlem* (1928). Both his poetry and his fiction are marked by strong protest against the injustices done to blacks.[1]

Mastery Exercise A

Write out each phrase in the following paragraphs from a *Miami Herald* article. Identify each phrase by using the following abbreviations.

Prep.	(prepositional phrase)	Inf.	(infinitive phrase)
Part.	(participial phrase)	App.	(appositive phrase)
Ger.	(gerund phrase)		

---

[1]Excerpt from "The Harlem Renaissance" from *Adventures in American Literature*, Heritage Edition. Copyright © by Harcourt Brace Jovanovich, Inc. Reprinted by permission of the publisher.

If a phrase is part of a larger phrase, enclose it in parentheses and label it.[1]

Example

a. The benefits of being married to a professional athlete are obvious.

Ger.   Prep.

a. being married (to a professional athlete)

Money. Fame. The opportunity to meet glamorous people in glamorous places.

But wives work as hard as their husbands for those benefits. And they do so without the recognition and acclaim given their spouses.

If marriage is a partnership, the wife of an athlete is the senior partner. She must do almost all the unglamorous work necessary to raise a family and make a marriage work. And she must do much of it alone.

Life as an athlete's wife means:

• Acting as a nurse for her husband's physical injuries and as a shrink for blows to the psyche.

• Living with a permanent feeling of impermanence, knowing he can suffer a career-ending injury, or if he plays a team sport, he can be traded, released or sent down. A wife must always be ready to pull up stakes and move, with all the major, often traumatic decisions and adjustments that entails.

• Coming to grips with an identity crisis straight out of a psychology textbook. Unless she develops a deep sense of self worth, she can disappear completely in her husband's shadow.

• Establishing upside-down living schedules to accommodate her husband's upside-down playing schedule. Lunch at four, dinner at midnight, kids to bed at 1 a.m. and hopefully not up until 10.

• Being thrown together with other athletes' wives and expected to get along, though the women usually come from completely different backgrounds. Frequently she must survive competition, jealousy and cliquishness that Sally John, wife of Yankee pitcher Tommy, calls, "ridiculous and childish . . . real garbage."

• Living alone. Separations are a central fact of life for athletes' wives.

Separations mean overcoming fear and loneliness.

Separations mean fixing the clogged sink, finding the new apartment, selecting the furniture, getting the sick child to the hospital and sleeping by yourself.

Separations mean playing mother and father.

Mastery Exercise B

From a magazine, newspaper, textbook, or recent paper you have written, select a passage about the length of that in Mastery Exercise A. Using what you have learned about identifying phrases, find the phrases in your selection and list them on a sheet of paper in the order they appear. Beside each phrase identify its type.

---

[1]Excerpt from *The Miami Herald*, July 6, 1980. Reprinted by permission of The Miami Herald.

Using Phrases

You can use *phrases* of all kinds to combine related ideas in a single sentence, thus avoiding a series of short, choppy sentences.

> The air was full of dust. The dust was blown from the dry hills. The hills were east of the mountains.

> The air was full of dust *blown from the dry hills east of the mountains.*

In the next sections you will learn how to punctuate phrases correctly—avoiding phrase fragments and using commas where necessary. You will also practice placing phrases so that they communicate their meaning clearly. Also, you will see how using phrases can give variety to your sentences.

Punctuating Phrases

A phrase cannot be a sentence because it has no subject or verb and does not communicate a complete thought. A phrase cannot be punctuated as a sentence.

Avoid phrase fragments in your writing.

A phrase must be attached to the sentence that comes before or after it, where it logically belongs.

Fragment:	Clapping and shouting "Bravo." The audience demanded an encore.
Sentence:	Clapping and shouting "Bravo," the audience demanded an encore.
Fragment:	Warren is afraid. To move to a city where he knows no one.
Sentence:	Warren is afraid to move to a city where he knows no one.

In the following situations commas are used to set off phrases from the rest of the sentence.

1. Appositives are set off by commas except when the appositive is a single word and closely related to the noun it follows.

   > Bruce's sister *Ellen* is a counselor at Walking Tree Camp.

   > Oxygen and silicon, *the two most common elements in the earth's crust,* occur in quartz.

2. When two or more prepositional phrases or a long prepositional phrase comes at the beginning of a sentence, it is usually set off by a comma.

   > *At the end of the first quarter,* Dallas led 7–0.
   > *In spite of her broken arm,* she managed to type her thesis.

3. An introductory participial phrase is set off by a comma.

   > *Buried for nearly a century,* the metal box was covered with rust.
   > *Reading from his speech,* the Senator accidentally skipped a page.

4. Participial phrases are set off by commas when they are not essential to the meaning of the sentence.

Phrases that are not essential are called *nonrestrictive phrases*. Commas are not used when the phrase is *restrictive* and essential to the meaning of the sentence.

Restrictive:	The boy *carrying the trombone* is Michael.
Nonrestrictive:	Michael, *carrying his trombone*, tripped and fell.
Restrictive:	The fire fighter *knocked unconscious by a falling beam* remains in critical condition.
Nonrestrictive:	Wayne Nejewski, *knocked unconscious by a falling beam*, remains in critical condition.

Exercise 1

Write out the following sentences, correcting any phrase fragments and any errors in punctuation. If a sentence is correctly written, write C.

Examples

a. At high tide at certain times of the month the water covers the road.
a. *At high tide at certain times of the month, the water covers the road.*

b. Gasping for air, the diver rose to the surface.
b. *C*

c. The troposphere is the layer of air. Lying closest to the earth.
c. *The troposphere is the layer of air lying closest to the earth.*

1. The young man, stretched out in the hammock, is Arthur.
2. Wallace's dog a Labrador retriever named Tom Mix is blind in one eye.
3. After having spent three years painting the Sistine Chapel Michelangelo was nicknamed "the Divine One."
4. Broccoli, a dark green vegetable in the United States, is the British name for cauliflower.
5. Established in 1914 as a national holiday Mother's Day was the result of Anna Jarvis' persistent lobbying of legislators, clergy, and the press.
6. In the first few minutes of their lives newborns will usually breathe by themselves.
7. For siding with the British during the Revolutionary War Benjamin Franklin's son was tried as a traitor.
8. The word *robot*, coined by the Czech playwright Karel Čapek, refers to a humanlike machine or a machinelike human.
9. The rope bridge of San Luis Rey in Peru built about 1350 is the focus of a novel by Thornton Wilder.
10. Believing in the dignity of all human beings Woody Guthrie wanted to sing songs that would make people take pride in themselves and in their work.

Misplaced and Dangling Modifiers

When phrases are used as modifiers, they must come as close as possible to the word they modify. Otherwise, the meaning may not be clear. Two kinds of problems occur in using phrases as modifiers: *misplaced modifiers* and *dangling modifiers*.

Occasionally a modifier is placed so that it seems to modify a noun or pronoun other than the one it was intended to modify. Comic results may occur.

Misplaced:	Sally washed the sow wearing her oldest jeans.
	[Who was wearing the oldest jeans—Sally or the sow?]
Corrected:	Wearing her oldest jeans, Sally washed the sow.
Corrected:	Sally, wearing her oldest jeans, washed the sow.

In your writing place a modifier as near as possible to the word it is meant to modify.

Misplaced:	John discovered bunches of dried wildflowers cleaning the attic.
Corrected:	Cleaning the attic, John discovered bunches of dried wild-flowers.
Misplaced:	The teller recognized the bank robber looking through police photos.
Corrected:	Looking through police photos, the teller recognized the bank robber.

When a sentence does not contain a word or words for a phrase to modify, the phrase is said to be *dangling*.

Dangling:	Having badly sunburned legs, it was difficult to sit down.
	[The phrase does not modify any word in the sentence. Who has badly sunburned legs?]
Corrected:	Having badly sunburned legs, Adam had difficulty sitting down.

In your writing make sure that a phrase clearly modifies a word or words in the sentence.

Dangling:	Jerking the wheel to the right, the car skidded into the bus bench.
Corrected:	Jerking the wheel to the right, the driver could not prevent the car from skidding into the bus bench.
Dangling:	Hoping for good news, the telegram was opened.
Corrected:	Hoping for good news, she opened the telegram.

Exercise 2

Correct the following sentences by placing the modifiers next to the word they modify.

Example

a. Frightened by the thunder, we could not find Emma.
a. Frightened by the thunder, Emma hid in the closet.

1. Attempting to provide information for students, a college fair was held with representatives from seventy-two colleges.

2. Roger was talking to a woman with a snow blower named Smathers.

3. The police officer found the stolen jewelry in a garbage can on duty outside the theater.

4. Promised by her owners when she was six weeks old, Shirley delivered the puppy to the Stanfords.

5. Completely surrounded by an electric fence, the palace guard stopped all visitors.

6. Expecting to win the tournament easily, the final score was 6–1, 4–6, 7–6.

7. Attending the reception for the winners, a photograph appeared in the Sunday paper.

8. Searching through the pile of old records, three great bargains were found.

9. The tree behind the house was cut into logs by Ben Chin blown over by the hurricane.

10. Without reading the directions carefully, the seeds were planted too deep.

Writing with Phrases

Using phrases enables you to combine closely related ideas into a single sentence.

> Helen Kester and Irving Millimet saw each other for the first time. They met at the orchid booth at the plant show.

> Helen Kester and Irving Millimet saw each other for the first time at the orchid booth at the plant show.

Phrases can also enrich your sentences by adding details. Consider, for example, the following sentence.

> The streets were crowded.

Although it communicates an idea clearly, such a bare sentence leaves the reader with questions: *Which streets? Why were they crowded? When?* Notice how the *italicized* phrases expand the idea in the original sentence:

> *On clear, warm nights* the streets *surrounding the plaza* were crowded *with strumming guitarists, noisy vendors, and laughing groups of young people.*

The expanded sentence not only adds details that make the sentence more specific but also adds details that appeal to the senses.

Phrases can also be used for sentence variety. When every sentence follows the same pattern, beginning with a subject and followed by a verb, the writing becomes dull and monotonous. Using an occasional introductory phrase can help break up the monotony and add variety to the paragraph. Notice how Eudora Welty adds interest to the following passage from her story "A Worn Path" by using a series of phrases at the end of a sentence.[1]

> Then she went on, *parting her way from side to side with the cane, through the whispering field. At last* she came *to the end, to a wagon track* where the silver grass blew *between the red ruts.* The quail were walking around *like pullets, seeming all dainty and unseen.*
>
> "Walk pretty," she said. "This the easy place. This the easy going."
>
> She followed the track, *swaying through the quiet bare fields, through the little strings of trees silver in their dead leaves, past cabins silver from weather, with the doors and windows boarded shut, all like old women under a spell sitting there.* "I walked *in their sleep,*" she said, *nodding her head vigorously.*
>
> *In a ravine* she went where a spring was silently flowing *through a hollow log.* Old Phoenix bent and drank. "Sweet gum makes the water sweet," she said, and drank more. "Nobody knows who made this well, for it was here when I was born." [italics added]

Writing Exercise A

Expand the following sentences with phrases to make the paragraph more interesting. Write a rough draft first, making sure that you have punctuated the phrases correctly. Then write your final draft. Make up any details that you need.

1. Sounds came through the closed windows. The girl found it difficult to concentrate. She went to the window. She saw two cars. A police car and an ambulance had already arrived. The ambulance attendants were bending over a figure. She recognized her crumpled bike. She rushed out of the apartment to the street.

2. The man stopped working. He stared at the horizon. Something was approaching. He heard a low humming. He saw a dark cloud. The noise increased. The afternoon darkened. The man turned and ran toward his house. Behind him the dark cloud blotted out the sun.

Writing Exercise B

Choose one of the following assignments and write as many paragraphs as you need to complete what you have to say. Write a rough draft first. Then go over what you have written, paying particular attention to how you can use phrases to improve your writing. Can some of the sentences be combined? Can you add details by using phrases? Have you used phrases effectively to give variety to your sentences? Write your final draft with these corrections in mind.

1. You are a television writer planning a new soap opera for television. Describe the main characters and write a summary of a single episode.

---

2. You are a scientist transported accidentally to the interior of the earth. You are astonished to find there strange life forms organized into an efficient culture. Write a journal of your experiences.

3. You are an aide to a state senator. For three weeks you have been listening to the complaints, requests, and opinions of the people who live in the senator's district. Write a report to the senator telling him or her what you think about the issues that concern the people in his or her district.

4. You are the coach of a (basketball, baseball, football, or soccer) team. Write a letter you will hand out to each of your players before the championship game.

20 The Clause

Understanding Clauses

In the following section you will learn to identify *clauses* by studying their definition and the classes into which they can be divided. Selections from literature will help you to see how professional writers use clauses to add variety to their writing.

Defining a Clause

A *clause* is usually defined as a group of words containing a subject and a predicate; it functions as part of a sentence.

You can see that the definition of a clause resembles the definition of a sentence. A clause has two of the characteristics of a sentence—a subject and a verb. The only way in which a sentence differs from a clause is that a sentence must also express a complete thought; a clause does not necessarily express a complete thought.

All of the following are clauses.

$$S \qquad V$$
that the forecaster predicted

$$S \quad V$$
whenever Louis feels unhappy

$$S \qquad V$$
Alvaro introduced us.

S V
Myra is extremely sensitive to cold.

There are two kinds of clauses: independent clauses and subordinate clauses.

Independent Clauses

A clause that can stand on its own as a sentence is called an *independent*, or *main, clause*.

Every sentence contains at least one independent clause, which includes the subject, verb, single-word modifiers, and phrase modifiers.

Ruthanna's sister teaches biochemistry at Cal Tech.

Have you seen Merle's bicycle pump?

A sentence may contain two or more independent clauses connected by a conjunction or a semicolon.

Wilma is left-handed, but everyone else in her family is right-handed.

Seas are running three feet with a moderate chop; small-craft warnings are in effect.

A sentence may also contain an independent clause and a subordinate clause. In the following sentences the subordinate clauses are *italicized*.

Mrs. Hendel has been depressed *since her husband died.*

Whenever it rains, the streets flood.

Subordinate Clauses

The word *subordinate* means "of lower rank." A subordinate clause is of lower rank than an independent clause because it cannot stand alone as a sentence. It must be attached to—and be dependent upon—an independent clause.

A *subordinate clause* is usually defined as a clause that cannot stand on its own as a sentence.

Subordinate Clause:	*Unless Tom joins the Air Force*
Sentence:	Tom and Janie will marry in June *unless Tom joins the Air Force.*
Subordinate Clause:	*who came to the party* [not a question]
Sentence:	Everyone *who came to the party* wore a costume.
Subordinate Clause:	*that she sent to her grandfather*
Sentence:	Mae Wing made the birthday card *that she sent to her grandfather.*

Exercise 1

Write out the following sentences. Beside each sentence write *S* if the *italicized* group of words is a subordinate clause; write *I* if it is an independent clause.

Example

a. *How old was your mother* when you were born?

a. *How old was your mother when you were born?—I*

1. *Dottie was delighted to get the job.*
2. I eat whole-grain breads *whenever I have a choice.*
3. When the concert ended, *we went to Gerry's house.*
4. What was in the box *that Aunt Sadie sent you?*
5. Although he had several close friends, *he often felt lonely.*
6. *Since I last spoke to you,* I have talked to Ned and Rita twice.
7. Soo Mee enjoys writing letters to everyone *whom she has ever met.*
8. *The candidate* who seems most likely to win *is Gary Braden.*
9. *Where were you* when I needed you?
10. Because the transit workers are on strike again, *she has been bicycling to work all week.*

Exercise 2

Each of the following items is a subordinate clause. Add an independent clause to make each one a complete sentence.

Example

a. that Paula brought

a. *No one can find the portable radio that Paula brought.*

1. if the rumor is true
2. until the prince kissed her
3. whenever she comes to visit
4. because it was raining too hard
5. who sits behind me in algebra
6. unless my parents object
7. where we won't be disturbed
8. before it is too late
9. that you should know
10. so that everyone has a fair chance

Classifying Sentences by Structure

Sentences may be classified according to the number of independent and subordinate clauses they contain. There are four types of sentences: *simple, compound, complex,* and *compound-complex.*

1. A *simple sentence* is made up of one independent clause with no subordinate clauses.

Someone pounded on the door.
The postal clerk asked me to put the ZIP code on the package.

A simple sentence may have a compound subject, a compound predicate, or both.

Popeye and Olive Oyl often fight yet always reconcile.
The electric bill and the water bill are overdue.

2. A *compound sentence* is made up of two or more independent clauses with no subordinate clauses.

Freddy rowed, and Wes bailed water from the leaky boat.

We had expected a small crowd, but more than a hundred people came.

Sari's mother and my mother are best friends; our fathers cannot stand each other.

3. A *complex sentence* is made up of one independent clause and one or more subordinate clauses.

In the following sentences the subordinate clauses are *italicized.*

When he flew too near the sun, Icarus fell into the sea.

The dawn horse, *which is the ancestor of our modern horse,* was about the size of a rabbit.

Emiliano Zapata, leader of the Mexican Revolution, was assassinated in 1919, *when he met with Colonel Guajardo, who was acting for the federal government.*

4. A *compound-complex sentence* is made up of two or more independent clauses and one or more subordinate clauses.

A special delivery package arrived Sunday night, but *since no one was home,* it was returned to the post office.

When W. C. Handy was a boy, his father, a Methodist minister, objected to his studying music, but Handy persisted and became "the father of the blues."

Exercise 3

Write out the following sentences. Beside each sentence write the label that indicates its structure. Use the following abbreviations.

S	(simple)	*Cx*	(complex)
Cd	(compound)	*Cd-Cx*	(compound-complex)

Example

a. The bird that you saw yesterday is a black skimmer.
a. *The bird that you saw yesterday is a black skimmer. Cx*

1. At Shark Valley part of the fifteen-mile bike path was once a road that led to an oil-drilling operation.

2. Three of the people who were invited called to say that they could not come, but everyone else is coming.

3. Under hypnosis the novelist Taylor Caldwell remembered eleven past lives, but she still was not convinced that reincarnation occurs.

4. Phrenologists believed that a person's character could be read from the shapes and bumps in the skull.

5. Hives look like a rash, and they are usually a reaction to some food, drug, pollen, or stress.

6. Cheryl has sent me two postcards from Monkey's Eyebrow, Kentucky, and Tightwad, Missouri.

7. The image that appears on the retina is upside-down, but the brain corrects the image so that you "see" objects right-side up.

8. Castor oil, which is derived from castor plant beans, is a heavy, oily liquid still used as a laxative.

9. In 1905 an educator named Mary Lyon became the first woman in the Hall of Fame for Great Americans.

10. Clogged pores can lead to acne, boils, and blackheads; sunlight, mild soap, and fresh air can help prevent these conditions.

Adjective Clauses

An *adjective clause* is a subordinate clause that modifies a noun or a pronoun. In the following sentences the adjective clauses are *italicized*.

This is the house *where I was born.*

She is the person *whom you must see about a visitor's pass.*

High tea, *which is usually eaten in the late afternoon or early evening,* is a meal of meat, salad, fruit, tea, and cake.

Everyone *whose last name begins with A through K* must register on Thursday.

An adjective clause is usually introduced by a relative pronoun.

who   whom   whose   which   that

Relative pronouns refer to the noun or pronoun in the sentence that the adjective clause modifies. Within the clause the relative pronoun may function as the subject of the clause it introduces.

$$S \quad V$$
High blood pressure is a condition *that affects many people.*

$$S \quad V$$
Honey is the person *who ordered the six-foot submarine sandwich.*

Relative pronouns may also serve as the object of the clause or as the object of a preposition within the clause.

$$Obj. \quad S \quad V$$
Ted, *whom you met at the picnic last week,* can speak six languages, including Swahili.

OP   S   V
Lynn has always been someone *in whom I can confide.*

Where and *when* (which are relative adverbs) also serve to introduce adjective clauses.

Is this the spot *where you lost your keys?*

The 1960s were a time *when there was a great deal of unrest and protest, especially among young people.*

Sometimes, a relative pronoun is omitted when the clause has a subject and verb and the meaning of the sentence is quite clear. For example, in the following sentences, the relative pronoun has been dropped.

The animal *I wanted you to see* is the pangolin.
[The relative pronoun *that* has been dropped from the clause.]

Sondra, the person *we stayed with in Denver*, has a huge vegetable garden.
[The relative pronoun *whom* has been dropped from the subordinate clause.]

Exercise 4

After writing out the following sentences, underline the adjective clause in each and draw an arrow to the word the clause modifies. Remember that a relative pronoun may be omitted.

Example

a. My brother Gianni, who is trying to grow a beard, works for a car-leasing company.

a. *My brother Gianni, who is trying to grow a beard, works for a car-leasing company.*

1. Marianela is a person whom everyone trusts.
2. This is the last quarter that I have.
3. Diane and her husband, who are both doctors, share an office and a beeper.
4. All nine of the Gain sisters, whom you know, have Lynn as part of their first names.
5. Of all the photographers I know, Dorothea Lange is the best.
6. Few people buy houses at a time when mortgage rates are high.
7. The car Randy Williams borrowed from his neighbor had a flat tire on the turnpike.
8. Len's car uses diesel fuel, which is less expensive than regular gasoline.
9. Mrs. Guillermo, whose son teaches first grade, has just earned her master's degree in psychology despite having multiple sclerosis.
10. Ken Martin, to whom the package is addressed, has never lived here.

Adverb Clauses

An *adverb clause* modifies a verb, an adjective, or an adverb.

Like adverbs and adverb phrases, an adverb clause may answer various questions such as *why? where? when? how? to what extent?* or *under what conditions?*

MODIFYING A VERB

Check your tires *before you begin a long bicycle trip.*
[The clause tells *when.*]

If Renata stops by, tell her to wait.
[The clause tells *under what conditions.*]

MODIFYING AN ADJECTIVE

Jenny was afraid *that everyone would laugh at her.*
[The clause modifies the adjective *afraid* and tells *why.*]

I am glad *that you are feeling better.*
[The clause modifies the adjective *glad* and tells *why.*]

MODIFYING AN ADVERB

Nancy can climb higher *than her little brother can.*
[The clause modifies the adverb *higher* and tells *to what extent.*]

Warren has been practicing much harder *than any of the other pitchers.*
[The clause modifies the adverb *harder* and tells *to what extent.*]

An adverb clause always begins with a subordinating conjunction.

after	as though	since	when
although	because	so that	whenever
as	before	than	where
as if	if	though	wherever
as long as	in order that	unless	while
as soon as	provided that	until	that

You may recognize many of the words in the preceding list as other parts of speech. For example, *as, before, since,* and *until,* can also be prepositions; *after* and *before* can be adverbs. In order to be classified as a subordinating conjunction, these words must introduce an adverb clause. Unlike a relative pronoun, a subordinating conjunction never functions as a subject or object within the clause.

The subordinating conjunction is important because it expresses the relationship of the idea in the subordinate clause to the idea in the main clause. Notice how changing the subordinate clause changes the meaning of a sentence:

Unless she has a fever, she will go to school.
Although she has a fever, she will go to school.
Because she has a fever, she will go to school.
Whenever she has a fever, she will go to school.

When two ideas are combined into a single sentence, either one may be subordinated to the other—depending upon which idea the writer thinks is more important. Notice that the meaning of the combined sentences is somewhat different.

Harry is a good father. He listens to his children.
Because Harry is a good father, he listens to his children.
Harry is a good father *because he listens to his children.*

Adverb clauses may be elliptical. An *elliptical clause* is one in which a word or words have been omitted.

The omitted words are understood by both the speaker and the listener or the writer and the reader. Notice that the omitted words, shown in brackets, may be the subject of the clause or the verb, or both:

Elliptical Clause: *While [she was] snorkeling*, she saw two gigantic crabs.

While [he was] going to college, Uncle Ron worked as a waiter.

I am several years older *than he [is]*.

Be sure to see the Japanese Tea Garden *when [you are] in San Francisco.*

Exercise 5

Write out the following sentences, underlining the adverb clauses and circling the subordinating conjunctions. If the clause is elliptical, write the words that have been omitted in parentheses beneath the sentence.

Example

a. When studying for her finals, Rona is always irritable.

a. (When) *studying for her finals, Rona is always irritable.*
    (she is)

1. Although the Jetstreams had ten hits, the Wondergirls won the game 6–3.

2. We are leaving for Mexico early Friday provided that Dad can fix the car before then.

3. Paul's mother weighs thirty pounds less than her twin sister.

4. Ben Ogilvie hit a double when he came to bat in the second inning of the All-Star Game.

5. When marigolds are planted among vegetables, their odor keeps away many insect pests.

6. A centipede is not an insect because insects have only six legs.

7. Although everyone knew her as Calamity Jane, her real name was Martha Jane Burke.

8. Mr. O'Donnell is using a plumb rule so that the door jamb will be perpendicular.

9. The lignum vitae tree, which has extremely heavy wood, means literally "tree of life" because it was once used as a medicine.

10. When cruising international waters west of Cuba, the *Blue Fire* was seized by the crew of the Coast Guard cutter *Diligence*.

Noun Clauses

A *noun clause* is a subordinate clause used as a noun.

A noun clause may be the subject of an independent clause, the direct object, the indirect object, the predicate nominative, the object of a preposition, or an appositive. In short, a noun clause may serve any function that a noun does.

Whatever you decide is all right with me.	[subject]
Did you know *that Ralph won first prize?*	[direct object]
He gave *whoever was in line* tickets to the exhibition game.	[indirect object]
The committee adopted her suggestion *that everyone share the cost.*	[appositive]
My main concern is *that someone will be hurt.*	[predicate nominative]
Please give this to *whoever is in charge.*	[object of preposition]

Adjective clauses usually begin with relative pronouns, and subordinating conjunctions always introduce adverb clauses. Some of these same words introduce noun clauses, but they are not considered relative pronouns or subordinating conjunctions. When any of the following words begin a noun clause, they are considered introductory words.

that	whatever	where	whoever
what	when	who	whomever

In noun clauses, as in adjective clauses, the introductory word is sometimes omitted.

Exercise 6

Write out the following sentences, underlining the noun clauses. (Some sentences contain more than one noun clause.) Beside or beneath each sentence, indicate how each clause is used.

Example

a. I suspect that the butler did it.

a. I suspect *that the butler did it.*—direct object

1. A complaint is handled by whoever opens the letter.

2. Whatever the researchers conclude from the data will be reported next month.

3. Mrs. Fejardo probably knows when the committee meeting will be held.
4. I certainly hope that she is well enough to go on the trip.
5. The course is open to whoever registers for it.
6. What nobody knows yet is that the principal has been reassigned.
7. That he forgot one of his sneakers is a good reason to come back.
8. Who was at fault has not yet been determined.
9. I think I know whose dog this is.
10. Until noon Nancy Anne gives whoever calls a cheery greeting.

Review Exercise A

On a sheet of paper, list each of the subordinate clauses in the following passage from N. Scott Momaday's *The Way to Rainy Mountain.* Then indicate how the clause is classified: noun, adjective, or adverb clause.[1]

> Once there was a lot of sound in my grandmother's house, a lot of coming and going, feasting and talk. The summers there were full of excitement and reunion. The Kiowas are a summer people; they abide the cold and keep to themselves, but when the season turns and the land becomes warm and vital they cannot hold still; an old love of going returns upon them. The aged visitors who came to my grandmother's house when I was a child were made of lean and leather, and they bore themselves upright. They wore great black hats and bright ample shirts that shook in the wind. They rubbed fat upon their hair and wound their braids with strips of colored cloth. Some of them painted their faces and carried the scars of old and cherished enmities. They were an old council of warlords, come to remind and be reminded of who they were. Their wives and daughters served them well. The women might indulge themselves; gossip was at once the mark and compensation of their servitude. They made loud and elaborate talk among themselves, full of jest and gesture, fright and false alarm. They went abroad in fringed and flowered shawls, bright beadwork and German silver. They were at home in the kitchen, and they prepared meals that were banquets.
>
> There were frequent prayer meetings and great nocturnal feasts. When I was a child I played with my cousins outside, where the lamplight fell upon the ground and the singing of the old people rose up around us and carried away into the darkness. There were a lot of good things to eat, a lot of laughter and surprise. And afterwards, when the quiet returned, I lay down with my grandmother and could hear the frogs away by the river and feel the motion of the air.

Mastery Exercise A

Using what you have learned about identifying clauses, find the subordinate clauses in each of the two following passages. Then list them on a sheet of paper in the order they appear, indicating whether they are classified as noun, adjective, or adverb clauses.

---

[1] Excerpt from *The Way to Rainy Mountain* by N. Scott Momaday. Copyright © 1969 by University of New Mexico Press. Reprinted by permission of the University of New Mexico Press.

A.

Evenings were spent mainly on the back porches where screen doors slammed in the darkness with those really very special summertime sounds. And, sometimes, when Chicago nights got too steamy, the whole family got into the car and went to the park and slept out in the open on blankets. Those were, of course, the best times of all because the grownups were invariably reminded of having been children in the South and told the best stories then. And it was also cool and sweet to be on the grass, and there was usually the scent of freshly cut lemons or melons in the air. Daddy would lie on his back, as fathers must, and explain about how men thought the stars about us came to be and how far away they were.

I never did learn to believe that anything could be as far away as *that.* . . .[1]

—From Lorraine Hansberry, *To Be Young,*
Gifted and Black

B.

None of them knew the color of the sky. Their eyes glanced level, and were fastened upon the waves that swept toward them. These waves were of the hue of slate, save for the tops, which were of foaming white, and all of the men knew the colors of the sea. The horizon narrowed and widened, and dipped and rose, and at all times its edge was jagged with waves that seemed thrust up in points like rocks.

Many a man ought to have a bathtub larger than the boat which here rode upon the sea. These waves were most wrongfully and barbarously abrupt and tall, and each froth top was a problem in small-boat navigation.

The cook squatted in the bottom, and looked with both eyes at the six inches of gunwale which separated him from the ocean. His sleeves were rolled over his fat forearms, and the two flaps of his unbuttoned vest dangled as he bent to bail out the boat. Often he said, "Gawd! that was a narrow clip." As he remarked it, he invariably gazed eastward over the broken sea.

—From Stephen Crane, "The Open Boat"

A *gunwale* is the upper edge of the side of a boat.

Using Clauses

In the next few sections you will practice using what you know about *clauses* to improve your writing. Punctuating clauses correctly, knowing when to use *who* and *whom*, and combining sentences by using subordinate clauses are skills that you will put to use in your writing.

Punctuating Clauses Correctly

An introductory adverb clause is set off from the rest of the sentence by a comma.

Since our birthdays are on the same day**,** let's celebrate together.
When the electricity went off**,** everything in the freezer melted.

---

[1] Excerpt from the book, *To Be Young, Gifted and Black* adapted by Robert Nemiroff.© 1969 by Robert Nemiroff and Robert Nemiroff as Executor of the Estate of Lorraine Hansberry. Published by Prentice-Hall, Inc., Englewood Cliffs, NJ 07632.

No comma is usually necessary, however, when an adverb clause comes at the end of a sentence.

> Let's celebrate if we both pass the exam.
> Everything in the freezer melted when the electricity went off.

An adjective clause that is essential to the meaning of the sentence is called a *restrictive clause*. A restrictive clause points out the particular noun it modifies. The sentence is about that particular noun—and none other.

Do *not* use commas to set off restrictive clauses.

> Restrictive: The pictures *that you took* came out blurry.
> [Not all of the pictures were blurry—only the ones *that you took.*]
>
> The grasshopper *that Elaine caught* won the Superbug award.
> [Not just any grasshopper, but the one *that Elaine caught,* won the award.]

A *nonrestrictive clause* is one that adds information to the sentence but is not essential. The sentence would make perfectly good sense if the clause were dropped.

Commas are used to set off nonrestrictive clauses from the rest of the sentence.

> Nonrestrictive: That librarian is Mrs. Jones, *who is Wendy's mother.*
> Yogurt, *which is easy to make at home,* is a nutritious and inexpensive food.

Avoid punctuating subordinate clauses as sentences.

Remember that a subordinate clause must be attached to an independent clause. It cannot stand alone as a sentence.

> Fragment: Because the price is so high
> Sentence: Because the price is so high, we have stopped buying cantaloupes very often.
>
> Fragment: Although he seemed interested
> Sentence: He never called again although he seemed interested.

Exercise 1

Rewrite the following sentences, adding commas where necessary. If a sentence is punctuated correctly, write *C*.

Examples

a. Roberta is the person to whom you should talk.

a. C

b. Rocky Mountain National Park which is in Colorado is one of the most beautiful national parks.

b. Rocky Mountain National Park, which is in Colorado, is one of the most beautiful national parks.

1. When Muhammad Ali fought Leon Spinks on February 15, 1978 he lost his heavyweight title in a split decision.

2. Cleveland's major league baseball club changed its name from the Cleveland Spiders which was its original name to the Cleveland Indians because of Louis Sockalexis, its star Indian player.

3. New Orleans kicker Tom Dempsey who was born with only half a right foot holds the NFL record for the longest field goal.

4. Dick Gregory who fasted for more than a year as a protest against the Vietnam War lost more than fifty pounds.

5. When Henry Ford created his first automobile he forgot to put a reverse gear in it.

6. Although he was blind from birth and could not read or write Tom Wiggins could play any musical piece he heard once.

7. You use seventy-two different muscles when you speak a single word.

8. Clairvoyance which is the ability to see something by other than sensory means has been extensively tested by Dr. J. B. Rhine and his wife Dr. Louisa Rhine.

9. One of the two known survivors of the Mount Pelée eruption in 1902 was a young man who was locked in an underground dungeon.

10. After his ship was torpedoed during World War II a Chinese seaman named Poon Lim survived alone on a raft for 133 days.

Using *Who* and *Whom* in Clauses

Who and *whom* are interrogatory pronouns when they begin a question.

Who is knocking at the door?
Whom do you wish to see?

The use of *who* and *whom* as interrogative pronouns is discussed on page 329.

Who and *whom* are also used to introduce adjective clauses and noun clauses. Whenever they appear, they may cause problems. Some writers think that *whom* "sounds" more educated; others prefer to ignore *whom* completely and stick to *who.* There are, however, distinct rules that govern the usage of *who* and *whom* in Edited Standard English. In order to decide which of these two words to use in a sentence, you must first determine the function of *who* or *whom* within the subordinate clause.

Who is used when it is the subject of the clause. *Whom* is used when it functions in the clause as the direct object or the object of the preposition.

Alice is the one *who cares the most about the hamsters.*
[*Who* is the subject of the adjective clause.]

Carl is the neighbor *whom I met at the concert.*
[*Whom* is the direct object of the adjective clause.]

Mrs. Corin is a teacher *to whom the class is indebted.*
[*Whom* is the object of the preposition in the adjective clause.]

Who attends the meetings is on the public record.
[*Who* is the subject of the noun clause.]

Whom the voters choose as mayor will greatly affect the city.
[*Whom* is the direct object of the noun clause.]

Notice that you must determine the function of *who* or *whom* within the clause—not within the sentence.

The words *whoever* and *whomever* follow the same rules. *Whoever* is the subject form, and *whomever* is the object form.

Use *whoever* as the subject of the clause. Use *whomever* as a direct object or the object of the preposition.

Whoever was in charge of the picnic did an excellent job.
[*Whoever* is the subject of the noun clause.]

Please give this message to *whoever answers the phone.*
[*Whoever* is the subject of the noun clause that serves as the object of the preposition.]

The trophy is given to *whomever the committee selects.*
[*Whomever* is the direct object of the noun clause that serves as the object of the preposition.]

Exercise 2

Write out the following sentences, choosing and underlining the correct word from the pair in parentheses. Remember that you must first determine how the word is used within the clause in order to decide which word to choose.

Examples

a. Janie is the second girl (who, whom) Ted has asked to the dance.
a. *Janie is the second girl <u>whom</u> Ted has asked to the dance.*

b. (Whoever, Whomever) wins a prize must claim it promptly.
b. *<u>Whoever</u> wins a prize must claim it promptly.*

1. Aunt Aggie is the relative (who, whom) I most admire.

2. Write to (whoever, whomever) is in charge of the survey.

3. Loretta, (who, whom) you met last night, writes her own songs.

4. Mozart, (who, whom) was only eight when he composed his Symphony Number 4, was certainly a genius.

5. (Whoever, Whomever) arrives first should start the fire.

6. Grandma Greenwood, (who, whom) is ninety years old, hikes the Appalachian Trail.

7. Mr. Firenze is the adviser (who, whom) everyone likes best.

8. (Whoever, Whomever) asks three people for advice is likely to find three different opinions.

9. Free maps are available for (whoever, whomever) requests them.

10. Mel is the student (who, whom) sold the most ads for the newspaper.

Review Exercise A

Write out the following sentences, correcting any errors in punctuation or word choice. If a sentence is correct, write *C*.

1. Because we had only three days we could not stop to climb Mount Whitney.
2. Dr. Hovland who is a civil engineer is a specialist in soil movement.
3. The person, whom you should contact, is Mariko Amalya.
4. Whomever painted the mural knows a lot about the city's history.
5. Though Corky's is always crowded the food is expensive and mediocre.
6. The Olins' home which is in Berkeley is on the San Andreas Fault.
7. Where is the recipe that Maribelle sent.
8. When the roofers had finished removing the old roof a ten-inch rain began.
9. Everybody who entered the poster contest received a certificate.
10. Lynn saved the young bluebird from Shamus who delights in hunting birds.
11. The letter, that he sent, made her cry.
12. Toby's grandparents who are in their eighties walk three miles each day.
13. Dan handed in his lab report which was a week late.
14. The invocation was read by Rabbi Cohen who founded the Youth Counseling Service.
15. Although she has a degree in biochemistry she works as a public relations director.
16. Whomever receives a summons must testify before the committee.
17. Rhea lost her watch which was a present from her boyfriend.
18. Mrs. Gallagher is a person who everyone respects.
19. Barry is being billed for a book that he never ordered.
20. The zucchini bread, that Sandy brought to the picnic, was delicious.

Writing Exercise A

Using a mixture of noun, adjective, and adverb clauses, write a brief paper on one of the following suggested topics. Use care in punctuating the clauses and in choosing between *who* and *whom*, and *whoever* and *whomever*.

1. In some states a commission of educators and other experts advises the governor about issues and problems relating to young adults. Suppose a member of such a commission asked you to write a short letter about the concerns and major problems facing teens in your state. Considering how your state could best serve the needs of its young people, write the clearly organized, one-page letter you would send to the member of this commission.

2. America has changed dramatically in the past fifty years. With this in mind, write about the impact one development has had on the American way of life. For example, how have fast-food chains or shopping centers changed our country? What benefits have resulted from this development? Has this change hurt society in any way? Has it influenced people's habits or thinking? Has it led to other changes?

3. When John Lennon was killed in 1980, many fans of this former Beatle felt they had lost a spokesman for their generation, someone who had represented the ideals of the 1960s youth. Write about a person who, in your opinion, reflects the values of young people growing up in the 1980s. What are the qualities of this person that make him or her a reflection of your generation?

4. Imagine that you have agreed to explore the deserted house in the photograph on page 483 with a friend. Describe the sights and sounds of the house, as well as your own thoughts and feelings when you investigate.

7 Mechanics

21 Capitalization

Capitalization in Edited Standard English

You have probably noticed that the use of capital letters is not always the same; a certain leeway is allowed for style. For example, the poet e. e. cummings did not capitalize his name or the first word of each line of poetry. For your purposes now, however, you should let the rules of Edited Standard English guide your use of capitals. In this chapter you will learn and practice the rules of capitalization for Edited Standard English.

Capitals That Set Off Groups of Words

1. Capitalize the first word of a sentence.

   A capital letter signals a new sentence, separating it from the preceding sentence.

   > **A** drop in barometric pressure usually signals bad weather. **A**ccording to the weather report, the barometer was rising.

2. Capitalize the first word of a direct quotation.

   Capitalize the first word of a direct quotation even if the quotation is a fragment. If a quotation is interrupted, capitalize only the first word of the quotation. Do not capitalize the word that begins the second part of the quotation.

"**S**chools will be closed on Martin Luther King Day," Manuela said.

"**S**chool will be closed on Monday," Manuela said. She explained, "**F**or Martin Luther King Day."

"**W**ill schools be closed on Monday," asked Manuela, "in celebration of Martin Luther King Day?"

Exercise 1

Write out each of the following sentences, using capital letters where necessary to conform to Edited Standard English. Underline the words you capitalize.

Example

a. "you may not have a cold," Nina explained. "just allergies," she added.

a. "*You may not have a cold,*" *Nina explained.* "*Just allergies,*" *she added.*

1. "acrylic sweaters are less expensive," the salesperson argued, "but wool sweaters are warmer."

2. turn your television off when you're not watching it. this will save electricity.

3. karla remembered some cold weather advice she'd heard. you'll stay warmer if you dress in layers.

4. "the state building code now requires that you insulate all new homes," the builder advised. "insulation helps retain heat," he added, "so you'll stay warmer."

5. wood stoves cut down electric bills. the stoves are dangerous, however, if they're not properly installed.

6. marta read, "wear a down jacket this winter. it's warm. it's lightweight." then she added, "and expensive. i'll wait for a sale."

7. "because they are water repellent, plastic and rubber are good materials for rain boots," Jack said. "but they trap heat," he noted, "so your feet may perspire."

8. having grown up in the South, Carolyn never thought about being too cold. she laughed, "in the South we worried about staying cool."

9. "scientists predict another Ice Age," Raoul said, "though it may not be a major one. are ice floes moving down from the Arctic?"

10. "my biggest problem in the cold is starting my car," David said. "it's temperamental and never starts," he added, "if the temperature is below freezing."

3. Capitalize the first word in a complete line of poetry.

(Although the capitalization of poetry may vary with a poet's style, the first word of a line is usually capitalized.)

> **S**hall I compare thee to a summer's day?
> **T**hou art more lovely and more temperate.
> **R**ough winds do shake the darling buds of May,
> **A**nd summer's lease hath all too short a date.
> —*William Shakespeare*

4. Capitalize the first word, the last word, and all other important words in the title of any work of art.

This rule applies to the titles of books, chapters, stories, magazines, poems, plays, movies, newspapers, musical works, works of art, historical documents, and so on. Prepositions and conjunctions that have fewer than five letters are not capitalized within a title. However, if the words *a*, *an*, or *the* are the first word of a title, you should capitalize them.

How does the ***D**eclaration of **I**ndependence* begin?

***F**rom **H**ere to **E**ternity* has been a book, a movie, and a television series.

Ambrose Bierce's story "**P**arker **A**nderson" was one of the short stories televised on *The **A**merican **S**hort **S**tory*, a series of shows on PBS.

Exercise 2

Write out each of the following sentences, using capital letters where necessary to conform to Edited Standard English. Underline the words you capitalize and be prepared to explain why you capitalized the words you did.

Example

a. Which poet wrote, "something there is that doesn't love a wall"?
a. Which poet wrote, "<u>Something</u> there is that doesn't love a wall"?[1]

1. The television series *the name of the game* was not a quiz show; it was a dramatic series about a publisher.

2. The television series *alice* is based on the movie *alice doesn't live here anymore.*

3. The play *ain't misbehavin'* celebrates the music of Fats Waller, who wrote songs such as "honeysuckle rose" and "lonesome me."

4. A book entitled *between the waters: great poets of england* must contain works by Tennyson. Please see if it has any excerpts from *idylls of the king.*

5. Rachel Carson's book *the sea around us* was one of the sources Elana used for her report, "the preservation of the earth is the responsibility of us all."

---

[1]From "Mending Wall" from *The Poetry of Robert Frost* edited by Edward Connery Lathem. Copyright 1930, 1939, © 1969 by Holt, Rinehart and Winston. Copyright © 1958 by Robert Frost. Copyright © 1967 by Lesley Frost Ballantine. Reprinted by permission of Holt, Rinehart and Winston, Publishers; Jonathan Cape Ltd.; and the Estate of Robert Frost.

6. Isn't the song "raindrops keep fallin' on my head" from *butch cassidy and the sundance kid?*

7. A recent newspaper article in *the new york times*, "rent control is the right of the people," infuriated landlords; they replied in an article "rent control: a dinosaur in modern times."

8. Duchamp's painting, "nude descending a staircase," was one of the famous works mentioned in an article, "a brief history of cubism," which appeared in *art news*.

9. The movie *all the president's men* was based on the investigative reporting of two reporters for the *washington post*.

10. One of my favorite lines of poetry is from T. S. Eliot's poem, "the love song of j. alfred prufrock."

Capitals That Set Off Proper Nouns and Adjectives

The following are rules for capitalizing proper nouns and adjectives.

1. Capitalize the names of specific people.

   Mark **N**orth's friend **A**line caught a ball hit by **R**eggie **J**ackson.
   Paula **R**ichards and **M**ax **C**onnell are cousins.

Note: Sometimes, capitals occur within a surname, such as *Mac**H**enry* and *Mac**D**onald*. The spelling of such names, however, varies.

2. Capitalize a title that precedes a person's name or a title that replaces a person's name, as in direct address.

   General Patton was one of the most colorful generals in history.
   "Tell me, **G**overnor, if the city will get state funds," **M**ayor Marks said.
   Did the mayor know **J**udge Crater?

Note: Capitalize the words *president* and *vice president* only when they precede a person's name or refer to the highest government offices.

   Will the senator run for **P**resident?
   President Grant was once a general.
   Who is the company's vice president?

3. Capitalize the abbreviation for a person's name or title.

   Please call **D**r. **T**hos. Manuelos for an appointment.
   Ask **M**s. Kramer if Jay Wallace, **J**r., is a doctor, too.

4. Capitalize words that show family relationships when they precede a person's name or when they are used in place of a person's name.

   Never ask **U**ncle Hank about his dog.

   Don't forget the tickets, **M**other, because David's mother said we can't get in without them.

Note: These words are normally not capitalized when they are preceded by a possessive noun or pronoun.

5.   Capitalize the names of specific places and proper adjectives formed from the names of specific places.

> Archaeologists scour the floor of the **A**egean **S**ea near **C**rete looking for ruins.
>
> The **C**aribbean islands of **T**rinidad and **T**obago are near **V**enezuela.
>
> One of the longest streets in the **U**nited **S**tates is **S**unset **B**oulevard in **L**os **A**ngeles.

Note: Capitalize the names of compass directions only if they refer to a specific region or are part of an address.

> New York's main avenues, such as Fifth Avenue and Park Avenue, run north and south.
>
> Is Janesville, Wisconsin, north of Chicago? I'm unfamiliar with the **M**idwest.
>
> Atlanta is a fast-growing city in the **S**outh.

Exercise 3

Write out each of the following sentences, using capital letters where necessary to conform to Edited Standard English. Underline the words you capitalize and be prepared to explain why you capitalized the words you did.

Example

a.   aunt mary, who is Aline's favorite aunt, lives in a small suburb east of phoenix.

a.   *Aunt Mary, who is Aline's favorite aunt, lives in a small suburb east of <u>Phoenix</u>.*

1.   The education committee elected ms. juanita bartlett, president; mark snaders, jr., vice president; and dr. lee morton, treasurer; they all will attend mayor morton's seminar next week.

2.   Maggie macklin's son paul became a father yesterday; his son's name is paul macklin, jr.

3.   Grits are a southern specialty. professor henrietta riggs, who grew up in tacoma, washington, has never eaten them; but her sister julia moved to charleston, south carolina, and eats grits once a week.

4.   The spanish and portuguese governments subsidize hotels; dr. geo. kaplan, whose brother lives near madrid, recommends staying at these government inns.

5.   Winds and air currents usually move from west to east; snow in chicago on Thursday might mean a storm in boston by Saturday.

6.   If you follow these directions, grandfather, you won't get lost: go north on larabee boulevard, turn right onto tumbleweed terrace, and go two blocks; gen. smith's house is on the corner.

7. Haven't african countries changed recently? Is rhodesia called rhodesia, zimbabwe, or zimbabwe-rhodesia?

8. At camp david, president carter negotiated the meetings between anwar sadat of egypt and israel's prime minister begin.

9. Listen, mother, and I'll explain how I know. My friend marge hutton's older sister rita used to date nicholas sliver; his sister married josé perez, who is a doctor in beverly hills, and one of his patients is barbra streisand's cousin.

10. The dallas–ft. worth airport, which is bigger than manhattan island, was jammed with passengers arriving from south dakota and south america.

6. Capitalize the names of buildings, institutions, monuments, businesses, and organizations.

> Most visitors to Washington, D.C., see the **W**ashington **M**onument, the **J**efferson **M**emorial, the **L**incoln **M**emorial, the **C**apitol, and the **W**hite **H**ouse.

> Report poor business practices to the **B**etter **B**usiness **B**ureau, which has an office in the **S**quibb **B**uilding.

> The **L**eague of **W**omen **V**oters sponsored a lecture at the **D**elmonico **H**otel.

7. Capitalize the names of nationalities, religions, races, and languages. Proper adjectives formed from these nouns are also capitalized.

> **F**rench food and **I**talian food are two popular cuisines.
> According to **J**ewish tradition, holidays begin and end at sunset.
> The **H**opi are the oldest continuous inhabitants of the United States.

8. Capitalize the abbreviations A.D., B.C., A.M., and P.M.

Note: Abbreviations for some measurements *(kg, oz., cm, sec.)* are not capitalized.

> Julio's party begins at 8:30 **P.M.**
> Julius Caesar was assassinated in 44 **B.C.**

9. Capitalize the names of stars, planets, and other heavenly bodies.

> The **B**ig **D**ipper and the **L**ittle **D**ipper are easy to find in the night sky.
> Is there another planet beyond **P**luto?

Note: The words *sun, moon,* and *earth* are not usually capitalized. Never capitalize them when they follow the word *the.*

Exercise 4
Write out the following sentences, using capital letters where necessary to conform to Edited Standard English. Underline the words you capitalize and be prepared to explain why you capitalized the words you did.

Example

a. The french are proud of their monuments: the louvre, notre dame, and versailles.

a. The *French* are proud of their monuments: the <u>Louvre</u>, <u>Notre Dame</u>, and <u>Versailles</u>.

1. Marissa works at paradox records, inc., which is on the second floor of the empire state building.

2. On Thursday at 6:00 p.m., there will be a service at st. basil's cathedral to celebrate the russian Orthodox Easter.

3. Photos from space clearly show the rings around saturn and moons around jupiter.

4. Peking's imperial palace was built during the Ming Dynasty a.d. 1368–1644; the dynasty was founded by a buddhist peasant.

5. The world travel organization is a swiss-based group open to canadian, british, french, and spanish students.

6. The photography show at the museum of modern art was funded by grants from corporations, including mobil corporation, xerox, and western electric.

7. In order to protect its monuments, the mexican government has imposed strict regulations on visitors to the ancient aztec, toltec, and mayan ruins; some of these ruins date from about 1100 b.c.

8. The american cancer society, the heart association, and the kidney foundation will sponsor a benefit at 8:00 p.m., Friday, at the plaza hotel.

9. Gasoline prices soar when OPEC (organization of petroleum exporting countries) raises its wholesale prices; companies such as exxon and standard oil raise their retail prices, and americans pay more for gasoline.

10. Two jamaican musicians have opened a reggae club—the kingston corner—near the clark state university campus; on weekends the club is open from 8:00 p.m. until 3:00 a.m.

Review Exercise A

Write out each of the following sentences, using capitals where necessary to conform to Edited Standard English. Underline the words you capitalize.

Example

a. every year many tourists climb japan's beautiful mount fuji, located southwest of tokyo.

a. *Every year many tourists climb* <u>Japan's</u> *beautiful* <u>Mount Fuji</u>, *located southwest of* <u>Tokyo</u>.

1. yesterday, mother, we saw a horror movie at the sherman theater. it was an english film (supposedly set in transylvania) called *dracula has risen from the grave*.

2. "did you know," asked peter, "that professor marinez, who teaches spanish art at ramapo college in mahwah, new jersey, is married to kendra's brother?"

3. much of today's popular music evolved when Black music merged with american and european folk music.

4. dr. durea's article, "borrowing from our neighbor to the south" appeared in last month's *english language journal.* she pointed out spanish and mexican words such as *taco, donkey, corral,* and *patio,* which have been incorporated into english.

5. "last night uncle jack, rita, and I heard paul read his poetry at the amateur poets' society," nick moaned. "when he began, 'glistening, sparkling, windswept snow,' I knew we were in for trouble."

6. james baldwin describes life in new york's harlem in works such as *notes of a native son* and *go tell it on the mountain.*

7. in 1980 southern california and phoenix, arizona, had some of the heaviest rain ever to hit the american southwest. in fact, katie morano's aunt and uncle (dr. and mrs. morano) had to evacuate their home in laurel canyon.

8. does the hayden planetarium have a show on sunday at one p.m.? the planetarium, which is part of the american museum of natural history, is on west eighty-first street at central park.

9. sgt. morgan's son michael owns a record shop—disc discounts—in the blue star shopping center on rte. 22 in north plainfield, new jersey.

10. many catholics, as well as protestants and jews, turned out to see pope john-paul II when he visited america and spoke in new york, boston, chicago, and washington.

11. i read, senator, that you will meet with the president and vice president. according to an article in the *st. louis post–dispatch,* the president will talk with state officials about federal funding to cities in missouri, kansas, nebraska, and in other parts of the midwest.

12. professor parnard explained, "the annual flooding of the nile river always provided the ancient egyptians with fertile soil for farming; however, since the building of the aswan high dam and the creation of lake nasser, the river no longer floods."

13. "do you realize," aunt claire asked, "that we had not traveled from the earth into space until a.d. 1957?" then she added, "amazing! since then we have landed on the moon."

14. the relatively young teton mountains have jagged peaks; the appalachian mountains in the east are older, and their peaks are rounder and smoother from time.

15. aunt mary and uncle richard vacationed in cozumel, an island in the gulf of mexico, just off the east coast of mexico's yucatán peninsula. they stayed at the beachcomber inn.

16. barbara montez, president of montez electronic company, will teach a course at howard university. she has just written a book, *how to begin your own business*, which will be published by success press of chicago, illinois.

17. my cousin pablo cavazos, jr., studied dance with twyla tharp, merce cunningham, bob fosse, and louis falco. he will dance next month at the kennedy center for the performing arts in washington, d.c.

18. in order to aid vietnamese refugees, the cleveland symphony orchestra and the metropolitan opera company of new york will perform at the hollywood bowl at 3 p.m. Sunday afternoon. if you drive north on the hollywood freeway, you'll see the signs.

19. on Sunday rev. h. g. argus, jr., of the unitarian church will give a sermon entitled "without hope, what is life's meaning?" the church is at 423 west oak drive in north adams.

20. the parker williamson gallery in galveston, texas, has the largest collection of french art west of the mississippi. the gallery has just acquired a painting by paul cézanne called "young woman with apples."

10. Capitalize the names or words referring to a supreme being. Capitalize the word *Bible* and holy books of all religions.

> Rev. Graham proclaimed, "**G**od remembers all who worship **H**im."
> Ellen said that her faith in the **L**ord gave her courage.
> The **T**almud, a sacred Jewish work, is a collection of ancient writings.

Note: Do not capitalize the word *god* when it refers to a god of ancient mythology; capitalize the names of specific ancient gods.

> The Roman god of war was **M**ars.

11. Capitalize the names of months, days of the week, holidays, and special events; capitalize historical events and periods. Capitalize the names of awards and prizes.

> Banks will close on **M**onday, **M**ay 31, for **M**emorial **D**ay.
> The **W**orld **S**eries used to be in **S**eptember, but now it's in **O**ctober.
> The Yorks and the Lancasters fought in the **W**ars of the **R**oses.

Note: The names of seasons are not usually capitalized.

> Crocuses signal the coming of spring.

12. Capitalize the names of school subjects formed from proper nouns or designating a specific course.

> Joanne needed to take a course in biology or chemistry, so she chose **C**hemistry I.

> Take a course in **G**erman history as well as **G**erman 305.

> **H**eroes and **S**uperheroes is a one-semester course with **E**nglish credit.

Note: Usually capitalize nouns followed by a number or letter.

> He told us that **F**light 134 leaves O'Hare at noon.

13. Capitalize the names of political parties and of government agencies, departments, and bureaus.

> Whom will the **R**epublican party nominate for President?
> The **F**ood and **D**rug **A**dministration has not approved that product.

14. Capitalize the names of specific ships, trains, planes, and spacecraft.

> Will the **S.S.** *France* sail again?
> Did *Apollo 11* land on the moon?

15. Capitalize brand names of specific products.

> Georgio drives a great 1931 **H**udson.
> Please buy some **F**astfoam cleanser to scour the sink.

16. Capitalize the first word and each noun in the salutation of a letter. Capitalize the first word in the closing.

> **M**y good **F**riend,
> **D**ear **M**s. **M**ayez:
> **S**incerely yours,

17. Capitalize the pronoun *I* and the interjection *O*.

> Where should **I** meet you?
> Whatever you say, **O** noble leader.

18. Capitalize the first word of each topic of an outline.

> I. **S**trokes in tennis
>   A. **T**he forehand
>   B. **T**he backhand

Exercise 5

Write out the following sentences, using capital letters wherever necessary to conform to Edited Standard English. Underline the words you capitalize and be prepared to explain your reasons for using capital letters.

Example

a. The letter began, "dear dr. walters, Here i am, sailing on the s.s. *stockholm*."

a. *The letter began, "*<u>Dear Dr. Walters</u>*, Here* <u>I</u> *am, sailing on the* <u>S.S. Stockholm</u>*."*

1. i know, oh i know, o my friend, how hard you worked between thanksgiving and hanukkah.

2. Martha, i think that "fondly yours," is an inappropriate closing for a letter that begins, "dear occupant."

3. Julio dubbed his boat *the silver sailor*, put on his wear-rite jacket and his boat-rite sneakers, and on saturday, june 12, set sail. he hoped all he had learned in his course, "sailing for beginners," would get him through.

4. i don't know many warships, but i do know the *monitor* and the *merrimac*; something from my course on the civil war (history 412) sunk in.

5. Pamela, i suggest that you take one of these courses: calculus 111, which meets on friday at 10 o'clock in room 777; or geometry 123, wednesday at 1 o'clock, room 44.

6. The department of the interior announced on monday, january 15, that all national parks would have special family rates on independence day (july 4), memorial day (may 31), and labor day (september 4).

7. Lindbergh's plane, i believe, was *the spirit of st. louis*.

8. Professor Carlton holds all her courses in room 305: introduction to political science, soviet foreign policy, and advanced political theory.

9. In which old testament book can i read about the battle of jericho?

10. The civil aeronautics board (cab) is investigating the crash of flight 405 that occurred last monday, january 14.

Review Exercise B

Write out the following sentences, using capital letters wherever necessary to conform to Edited Standard English. These sentences cover all the rules regarding capitals that you have learned. Underline the words you capitalize and be prepared to explain your reasons for using capital letters.

1. "didn't the musical *hair*," i asked, "have a song about jupiter and mars? didn't it also have a song called 'let the sun shine in'?"

2. there used to be a famous train—the *city of new orleans*—that ran between new orleans and chicago. i don't think it runs anymore.

3. last wednesday, march 4, juan's aunt maggie sang at the music box theater. her first song was "first time ever i saw your face," which roberta flack had popularized.

4. professor alameda's first assignment for american literature 312 was to read and outline chapter 1, "the puritan tradition," in *sources of american fiction*.

5. "did you hear governor lewis' speech last night at town hall?" consuela asked. "good news. he's going to ask the president for money to build housing in greenwood lake park."

6. "i tell you, governor, i saw a flying saucer last night at 11 p.m.," bertha insisted. "it hovered over east park lane, sailed north on oakwood drive, blinked its lights by eastman tower, and then took off toward mars!"

7. according to dr. hidalgo, who's a dentist in encino, the ancient etruscans made false teeth around 700 b.c.

8. when the english monarch queen elizabeth II visited new york, she went to bloomingdales—a store that sells everything from irish tea to persian rugs.

9. what costume will you wear to the mardi gras parade, uncle byron? i'm going as king louis XIV, who ruled from versailles before the french revolution.

10. "it's not so easy to do a movie," leslie explained. "i had to go to hollywood, spend monday through friday at paramount studios, go on location near fairbanks, join the screen actors' guild, and learn to speak italian—all between july 15 and september 1."

11. after the candidates from the democratic and republican parties had spoken, two other people spoke: dr. joanne rankling of the socialist party and captain don ling from the u.s. navy.

12. on wednesday evening my brother pablo heard the soprano leontyne price perform in the *barber of seville* at the metropolitan opera company.

13. some science fiction, like bradbury's *the martian chronicles*, seems odd now that we have actually left the earth and traveled to mars.

14. the first book i had to read for anthropology 101 was margaret mead's *coming of age in samoa*, a classic study of life in the south seas.

15. after spending months at st. agnes hospital in ames, iowa, rev. jakes is coming home; he says that faith in god and trust in his will was a great source of strength.

16. marcy's cousin lee sung has written a television movie for warner bros. called *to jupiter and beyond: journey toward the edge of the universe.* it will be shown on thursday, october 17, at 8 o'clock p.m.

17. david yen, who is president of acme advertising agency, needs a name for a new brand of dungarees. he's tried "denim dudes," "rancho wear," and "longhorns."

18. maury's first listing under the outline topic "native american dwellings" was *hogan,* the traditional navaho dwelling.

19. last spring—it was either in april or may—i went to philadelphia, one of the oldest cities in the east. independence hall, the liberty bell, and the betsy ross house were great.

20. because of an enormous blizzard on valentine's day, february 14, new jersey schools were closed in bergen county, morris county, union county, and somerset county.

Mastery Exercise A

Write out each of the following groups of words, using capitals where necessary to conform to Edited Standard English.

1. the school on main street

2. a county in southern florida

3. the main street in decorah, iowa

4. dr. langdon, a doctor in the midwest

5. a delegate to the united nations

6. bernice abbott, who photographed manhattan

7. lake arrowhead lodge and restaurant, a popular inn

8. thor and odin, two gods of norse mythology

9. st. paul's cathedral, a church in london

10. zubin mehta, the director of the new york philharmonic orchestra

11. lake hopatcong, a lake in the east

12. uranus and neptune, two planets far from the sun

13. *bury my heart at wounded knee*, a book by dee brown

14. the atlantic coast south of south truro, massachusetts

15. harriet tubman, who led many slaves to the north and freedom

16. "with a song in my heart," a song from the movie *the jane froman story*

17. chris evert, who competed at madison square garden

18. professor leon l. rudolph, a professor at the university of wisconsin, a large university

19. san juan, puerto rico, a major caribbean resort and port

20. an amish market near lancaster, pennsylvania

Mastery Exercise B

Write out the following paragraphs, adding all necessary capital letters. Underline the words you capitalize.

on december 17, 1971, ramona a. banuelos was sworn in as united states treasurer under president richard nixon. her achievement was particularly distinguished, since she was the first mexican-american and only the sixth woman to hold this high government post.

born in arizona, banuelos and her family moved to mexico during the depression of the 1930s. she returned to the united states, however, and in 1949 began her career in business by investing in a tortilla stand, which she turned into a multimillion-dollar business: ramona's mexican food products, inc. today, having returned to the world of private business, she serves as president of that still-expanding california firm!

banuelos first entered the banking field in 1964 and helped found the pan-american national bank in los angeles. her background in business and banking made her well qualified for her government post.

this outstanding businesswoman and citizen has been rewarded for her achievements. among the awards she received are "outstanding businesswoman of the year (los angeles county)" and the "national award of achievement from the office of minority business enterprises." her story is a classic american tale of success and hard work rewarded.

22 Punctuation

The Uses of Punctuation

In general, punctuation separates, links, encloses, and shows omission. For example, a period (.) *separates* one sentence from another; a hyphen (–) *links* parts of a compound word; quotation marks (" ") *enclose* a speaker's exact words and *separate* them from the rest of the sentence; and an apostrophe (') shows that letters have been *omitted* from a word.

The Period

The *period* is used as an end mark following a sentence or an abbreviation.

A declarative sentence makes a statement.

1. Use a period after a declarative sentence.

> Jogging is hard on your heels.
> It's important to wear good running shoes.
> Silver dollars are becoming rare.

An imperative sentence makes a request or gives a command.

2. Place a period after a mildly imperative sentence.

> Please mail your taxes early.
> Have a good time.

3. Place a period after many abbreviations.

Dr.	doctor	P.M.	*post meridiem*
Mr.	mister	Inc.	incorporated
Thom.	Thomas	ft.	feet

Some abbreviations (such as *Ms.* and *Mrs.*) cannot be spelled out. Some other abbreviations are not followed by a period: metric units *(5 ml, 10 kg)*, postal abbreviations for states in addresses *(VA, PA, TX)*, and most government agencies *(NASA, CIA, TVA).* In addition, some large corporations abbreviate their names without periods *(CBS, HBJ, IBM).* Some other common abbreviations do not use periods *(TV, FM, AM, mph).*

Exercise 1

Write out each of the following sentences and place periods where needed. Capitalize the first word of each new sentence you form. Circle the punctuation marks you insert and underline the words you capitalize.

Example

a. "Take 500 mg of vitamin C," Dr Bishop advised "you need it."

a. *"Take 500 mg of vitamin C," Dr⊙ Bishop advised⊙ "You need it."*

1. Warren J Murdoch, Jr, runs Carlyle Advertising, Inc, in St Louis the agency handles the CBS account

2. Please type that report on the new IBM, send a carbon to Dr H L Gomez, and call the patient, Mrs Ross, at 10 o'clock AM tomorrow

3. Capt N Remo, who used to be in the US Navy, won a cruise on the *SS Fairborn* from Luxury Cruises, Ltd, a new travel agency

4. Mr Wm Ahern, Prof J Yen, and J J Stokes will speak on inflation on tomorrow's 9 PM broadcast of "Newswatch"

5. Send your guarantee to this address, Ms Miller:
   Marchi Calculator Co
   15 St James Rd
   Ft Lauderdale FL 33581

6. Sgt Fairford, Capt Porter, Col Washington, and Lt Richardson were at Ft Dix yesterday genl Morris saw them there at 3:30 PM

7. Mileage signs on Rte 1 are changing to the metric system signs that used to read *6 miles* now read *10 km*

8. Prof Adams explained that the average person living on Crete in 2000 BC was only about 5 ft, 2 in tall as a result the doorways and ceilings are lower than ours

9. "The CIA doesn't work in the US," Ms Alens explained "the FBI works here"

10. Now, Mr. Jaust, name the literary figures who have these initials: H L M, G B S, R L S, and L M A.

The Question Mark   A *question*, also called an *interrogative sentence*, ends with a question mark. The question mark separates that sentence from the following one.

Where's the key? I can't find it.

Who took this message? It's illegible.

Note: When a question is *indirectly* stated, it is followed by a period.

Where is State Street?	[direct question]
Ethel wondered where State Street was located.	[indirect question]

The Exclamation Point

1. Place an *exclamation point* after a strongly imperative sentence.

   Hurry! Call the police!

   Shut the window!

2. Place an exclamation point after an exclamation.

   Look out! The shelf is collapsing!

   How much I love New England!

Note: A mildly imperative sentence can end with a period. A mild exclamation at the beginning of a sentence can be followed by a comma; but use an exclamation point, rather than a period or a comma, when you wish to convey stronger feeling.

Exercise 2

Write out each of the following sentences, using periods, question marks, and exclamation points where necessary. Circle the punctuation you insert.

Example

a. Whose jacket is this It's not mine

a. *Whose jacket is this(?) It's not mine(.)*

1. Hurry We'll miss the train
2. When does the movie begin I wonder if we'll have time for dinner first
3. Ouch Who put that chair here
4. Call home, Marc Does your family know you're here
5. Oh no Julio forgot the car keys Do you have your car
6. What a wonderful surprise When did you arrive
7. Do you have tickets Please wait in that line
8. Hooray We won
9. Congratulations How much did you win
10. Do you know if this show is sold out Alicia wondered if she could still buy a ticket

---

The Comma

The *comma* separates words, phrases, or clauses within a sentence.

1. Use a comma to separate words or word groups in a series.

Barbara Chen plays the piano, the flute, and the guitar.

Drive across the railroad tracks, past the school, and straight into town.

You have to wash the dog, fix the faucet, and paint the porch before you can go out.

When items commonly go together, such as *bacon and eggs* or *bread and butter,* they can be paired as one item.

For breakfast we had juice, eggs, and bread and butter.

Note: When the last two items in a series are joined by a coordinating conjunction *(and, or, but),* a comma precedes the conjunction. When all the items in a series are joined by a conjunction, do not use commas.

We drove to Daytona, Palm Beach, and Miami.
We've lived in Boston and in Las Vegas and in Chicago.

2. When two or more adjectives precede a noun, use a comma between the adjectives.

An old, dented, blue Edsel drove past us.
June tried to comfort the lost, terrified, little child.

Note: Do not use a comma between the last adjective and the noun that follows it. Do not use a comma between adjectives unless the word *and* makes sense in its place.

She loved to cook with her grandmother's four new pans.
[no commas between the adjectives]

The stalled train was filled with tired, hungry, irritable passengers.
[An *and* would make sense between each adjective; therefore, use commas.]

3. Use a comma to separate independent clauses that are joined by the coordinating conjunctions *and, but, or, nor, for, so,* or *yet.*

Georgette loves to roller-skate, but she doesn't like to ice skate.
Leila has had many years of working experience, so she decided to open her own company.
I love to ski, and I plan to take a vacation in the Rockies next winter.

Note: In placing commas, watch out for compound subjects and predicates. Be certain that the sentence actually has two independent clauses.

Exercise 3

Write out each of the following sentences and place commas where necessary. Circle the commas you insert.

Example
a. Maria and José bought a couch a rug two chairs and a piano.
a. Maria and José bought a couch, a rug, two chairs, and a piano.

1. Atlantic City Wildwood Ocean City and Cape May are four resorts on the New Jersey coast.

2. Sharks live in the Atlantic in the Pacific and in the Caribbean. Don't be afraid to swim in the ocean but you should always be alert.

3. Joe's car used too much gasoline so he traded it in for a smaller car that got better mileage.

4. I. M. Pei is an innovative architect and he is currently designing buildings both in the United States and in China.

5. The serious flood left people without drinking water without food and without homes.

6. Four furry gray frisky kittens peered out from their box then jumped onto the floor and scattered about the room.

7. Rome's ancient monuments have stood for centuries but now the city's air pollution is destroying the marble.

8. The Red Sox must win tomorrow's game or they will be out of the race for the pennant.

9. The restaurant advertised these healthful specials: yogurt topped with fresh fruit yogurt topped with honey and yogurt with sunflower seeds.

10. At one time it was more expensive to live in the United States than in Europe but a change in the world's economy has made many European countries more expensive than the U.S.

4. Use a comma to separate introductory adverb clauses, introductory participial phrases, and long introductory prepositional phrases from the rest of the sentence.

Adverb clauses are discussed on pages 474–475.

Participial phrases are discussed on pages 455–456.

Prepositional phrases are discussed on pages 453–454

INTRODUCTORY ADVERB CLAUSES
When the railroad workers went on strike, commuters formed car pools to get to work.
Before the war had ended, thousands of people died.

INTRODUCTORY PARTICIPIAL PHRASES
Working all weekend, the Parkers finished painting their house.
Clapping loudly, the audience yelled, "Encore."

LONG INTRODUCTORY PREPOSITIONAL PHRASES
Behind the cabinet in the bedroom, the cat curled up and went to sleep.
During the first half of the game, neither team played well.

Note: Short introductory prepositional phrases need not be followed by a comma unless the comma is needed to make the meaning of the sentence clear.

Under the table sat the dog.
[no comma]

Near the fire, hoses filled the streets like giant snakes.
[Use a comma to avoid confusion.]

5. Use a comma to separate some short introductory elements from the rest of the sentence.

Use a comma after mild interjections and words such as *yes*, *no*, *well*, *why*, *still*, and *now* when they introduce a sentence or an independent clause.

> Yes, I'll be back at work on Thursday.
> Well, cats like to eat fish.
> No, the shop is closed on Sunday.

Note: When these words are used as adverbs, they should not be followed by commas.

> Now the play will begin.

Use a comma after a noun of direct address when it introduces a sentence or an independent clause. (When a noun of direct address is at the end of a sentence, it is preceded by a comma.)

> Ken, where are the books?
> Dr. Landers, I'll tell you my symptoms.
> Please lock the door, Mitchell.

Use a comma after introductory transitional and parenthetical expressions such as *however, accordingly, thus, consequently, therefore, besides, in fact, on the one hand*, and *by the way*. (If any of these expressions are at the end of a sentence, they are preceded by a comma.)

> Nevertheless, jumping rope is good exercise.
> Besides, success requires hard work.
> Life is unpredictable, however.

6. In general, use a comma with any introductory expression that would be followed by a pause if you were speaking.

Use a comma to separate contrasting words, phrases, and clauses introduced by the word *not*.

> I like chicken, not fish.
> Mishiki lives in Dallas, not in Houston.

Exercise 4

Write out each of the following sentences and use commas where necessary. Circle the commas you insert. (Your teacher may ask you to explain why you placed commas as you did.)

Example

a. Yes Mario believes in the supernatural; however he also thinks that many events have scientific explanations.

a. *Yes⊙ Mario believes in the supernatural; however⊙ he also thinks that many events have scientific explanations.*

1. At 10 o'clock on the morning of his stage debut Walter panicked and forgot his lines; however he soon recovered his poise as well as his memory.

2. After training for the Olympics for four years Kim caught the flu and had to withdraw from competition.

3. Preparing for a long wait in line Carmen packed a good book and a sandwich.

4. When the weather is sunny Margot walks to work; thus she saves money on transportation and gets exercise.

5. From medieval times until the present people have sought a way to turn other metals into gold; well they've finally figured out how to do it!

6. By the way the post office is now open until 2 P.M. on Saturdays Herman.

7. Used mostly for entertainment television cameras are also effective for surveillance; for instance banks are monitored by these cameras.

8. Dr. Mendoza the pain is in my right arm not in my left.

9. Carried by the ski lift skiers soared to the top of the mountain.

10. Doctors advise that too much exposure to the sun can be dangerous not healthful; those who are determined to get a tan are actually harming their skin.

Review Exercise A

Write out the following sentences, using periods, question marks, exclamation points, and commas where necessary. Circle the punctuation marks you insert.

Examples

a. Elaine what have you done with the car keys

a. *Elaine⊙ what have you done with the car keys⊙*

b. After working all night at the hospital Dr Lopez went home hid the alarm and went to sleep.

b. *After working all night at the hospital⊙ Dr⊙ Lopez went home⊙ hid the alarm⊙ and went to sleep.*

1. Prof Alexander did Roberto Clemente play baseball for the Pirates the Red Sox or the Cardinals

2. What a fabulous calculator It computes numbers gives the time and has an alarm.

3. Sgt Myers I've looked in my desk in my car and at home for the missing report; still I can't find it anywhere.

4. Well why haven't you called me Pedro I was beginning to think you'd gone away for a year not a month.

5. In a long well-written well-organized letter to the FDA Dr J Barnes complained about the cold remedy he'd taken He described his reaction to the medicine enclosed some of the tablets and asked for an explanation.

6. No we never received your application Prof Langdon; as a result we've offered the job to someone else.

7. Because Rebecca was an experienced teacher she immediately recognized her student's exceptional talent; accordingly she recommended him for a specialized program of study.

8. All the ski resorts had a poor season for there was hardly any snow.

9. Mrs Alvarez do you remember some of the famous comedy teams like Amos and Andy the Marx Brothers and Abbott and Costello?

10. The reclusive eccentric multimillionaires made no public appearances; consequently most people would not recognize them.

11. Determined to reach Nashville by morning Col Jervis left immediately and drove all night.

12. Ms Patricia Gaines Rev M Morton and L C Davis wrote a book on positive thinking sold it to a publisher and will donate the profits to charity.

13. Yes Dr C V Walker, Jr, still works at the following address:
    Meridan Research Labs, Inc
    14 Ft Worth Rd
    S Hadley, MA 02111

14. Michael watch the animals but you shouldn't feed them or put your arms near the cage.

15. In the bottom of the pocket of her old dungarees Melanie found the tarnished broken silver ring.

16. The early conventions of NOW (National Organization for Women) attracted a moderate number of women but later meetings drew larger crowds.

17. While teaching at MIT Prof Duggan did independent research published a book and married Ms Lucy Jones.

18. In ancient Crete people wrote in a script called *Linear A* but scholars still have not deciphered it; as a result artifacts have been discovered but not translated.

19. Linda the play that recently ran on Broadway was *The Wiz* not *The Wizard of Oz* They both have basically the same theme however.

20. Stop that Jason I can't sleep or think with you blasting your radio dancing around the room and singing.

When words of direct address or transition begin or end a sentence, separate them from the rest of the sentence with a comma. Sometimes, these words, phrases, and clauses appear within the sentence. When this happens, place a comma both before and after the expression. Paired commas enclose these words and separate them from the rest of the sentence.

7. Use paired commas with nouns of direct address when they interrupt a sentence.

> Where, Carlos, did you park the car?
> Why, Sir, have you canceled my contract?

8. Use paired commas with transitional or parenthetical expressions that interrupt the sentence.

> We decided, therefore, to cancel our vacation.
> I decided, by the way, to accept the job.

9. Use paired commas with contrasting expressions when they interrupt the sentence.

> Portuguese, not Spanish, is the national language of Brazil.
> You play paddle ball, not tennis, on that court.

Note: Be certain that the word or words that you separate with commas are really interrupters.

> Martha, I believe, is Dutch.
> I believe that Martha is Dutch.

Exercise 5

Write out the following sentences, using paired commas where necessary. Circle the commas you insert.

Example

a. Zaire I believe was previously called the Belgian Congo.

a. Zaire ⊙I believe ⊙was previously called the Belgian Congo.

1. I hope that Jeffrey not Howard wins the election.
2. Jumping rope I suppose is one way to exercise.
3. Did you know Ilene that dogs and cats see only in black and white?
4. A plane not a ship is the fastest means of crossing the Atlantic; the time spent aboard ship however can be a vacation in itself.
5. The sulfur water from springs at that spa I believe is therapeutic; the drinking water on the other hand is terrible.
6. Will you summon the National Guard Mayor if the transit workers strike?
7. Palm Springs not Palm Beach is in California; Palm Springs as a matter of fact is in the desert.
8. I believe Doctor that ragweed not goldenrod is the cause of my allergy; I could however be allergic to both of them.
9. Kansas City in fact is actually in Missouri; West New York by the way is in New Jersey.
10. Chicago's Sears Tower and New York's World Trade Center I believe both have 110 stories; the Sears Tower however is still taller.

10.   Use paired commas to enclose nonessential phrases and nonessential clauses, thus separating them from the rest of the sentence.

Nonessential phrases and *clauses* are those that could be omitted from a sentence without changing its meaning. They are not essential to the thought conveyed by the sentence.

> Barbara Jordan, who is from Texas, is an eloquent speaker.
> [nonessential adjective clause]
>
> Larry Rivers, speaking quickly, explained his painting technique.
> [nonessential participial phrase]

Essential phrases and clauses are necessary to the meaning of a sentence and are not set off with commas.

> The woman who speaks so eloquently is from Texas.
> [*Who speaks so eloquently* identifies the woman and is essential to the sentence.]
>
> The artist now exhibiting at the Marlboro Gallery just published a book.
> [*Now exhibiting at the Marlboro Gallery* identifies the artist; it is an essential participial phrase.]

Note: When a nonessential phrase or clause appears at the end of a sentence, use only one comma preceding it.

> Pablo is from Tijuana, which is near the Mexico-California border.

11.   Use paired commas to enclose nonessential appositives that interrupt a sentence.

When an appositive merely explains the meaning of the noun or pronoun to which it refers and could be removed without changing the meaning of the sentence, it is nonessential and should be set off by paired commas. When an appositive distinguishes the noun or pronoun it explains from other people or things, it is essential and is not enclosed by commas.

> Carl Sagan, an astronomer, is popular with many nonscientists.
>
> Lenny Marks, our neighbor, just bought a new car.
> [The appositives in both the preceding sentences are nonessential.]

The appositives in the following two sentences, however, are essential to the meaning of each sentence.

> Jake's friend Mike inherited $1 million.
> [*Mike* identifies which friend.]
>
> The dance *Cry* was choreographed by Alvin Ailey for the dancer Judith Jameson.
> [*Cry* identifies which dance; *Judith Jameson* identifies which dancer.]

Note: When a nonessential appositive appears at the beginning of the sentence, it is followed by a comma.

> A prolific writer, Janet Devlin publishes one book a year.

Exercise 6

Write out the following sentences and place commas where necessary. Circle the commas you insert. (Your teacher may ask you to explain why you inserted the marks you use.)

Example

a. Mary McLeod Bethune a pioneer in the education of Black men and women founded a school for girls in Daytona Beach.

a. *Mary McLeod Bethune ⌒a pioneer in the education of Black men and women ⌒founded a school for girls in Daytona Beach.*

1. There are many jokes about George Washington who was our first President and his false teeth.

2. Yosemite Falls which is only a thin trickle of water in the summer thunders over the mountain in the spring.

3. Did you know that Daphne du Maurier wrote "The Birds" a short story made into a film by the director Alfred Hitchcock?

4. The Salk vaccine the first effective vaccine against polio has been replaced by the Sabine vaccine which is more effective.

5. The family who bought the Barth Mansion which is one of the oldest houses in Cincinnati will turn the house into a museum.

6. A terribly violent storm Hurricane David did millions of dollars' worth of damage to Santo Domingo an island in the Caribbean.

7. Because the crime rate was higher on streets that were poorly lit, the city installed sodium street lights which give off a very bright light.

8. The man who directed *The Turning Point* a movie about ballet also directed *Nijinsky* which tells the story of this famous Russian dancer who performed with the Ballet Russe.

9. Daniel's best friend Carlotta and her sister Diane went to Caracas the capital of Venezuela to open a branch office of their company Mandrack Industries, Inc.

10. Jackie Kramer bored with living in a town that had only one movie theater moved to Hollywood home of the film industry.

Commas are also used to separate a variety of items that may or may not occur within a sentence. These conventional uses of the comma are dictated by custom and tradition.

12. Use a comma to separate parts of dates and geographical names.

The Wright brothers made their historic flight at Kitty Hawk⌒ North Carolina⌒ in 1903.

The museum in Lincoln⌒ Nebraska⌒ will have its grand opening on Saturday⌒ November 15⌒ 1982⌒ at 8 P.M.

After graduation there will be a reception at Inwood High School⌒ 1400 Lynbrook Lane⌒ Hewlitt⌒ New York 10112.

Note: In addresses do not use a comma between the street number and the street name, nor between the state and the ZIP code. In dates do not use a comma between the name of the month and the day. A comma is not necessary when only a month and a year are given in a date *(August 20, 1984; August 1984)*. When a date or geographical name is used in a sentence, use commas to set off the complete name or date from the rest of the sentence.

13.   Use a comma to separate a person's name (or a company's name) from the degree, title, or affiliation that follows it.

Glenda Hart**,** M.D.
Jack Jales**,** D.D.S.
Parker Industries**,** Inc.

Note: When used in a sentence, the degree or title is also followed by a comma.

Yesterday John Jones**,** Jr.**,** went to Canada.

14.   Use a comma after the greeting and the closing of a friendly letter.

Dear Nancy**,**
Fondly yours**,**

Exercise 7

Write out the following sentences and use commas where necessary. Circle the commas you insert.

Example

a. There are towns named Plainfield Vermont and Plainfield New Jersey.

a. There are towns named Plainfield ⊙ Vermont ⊙ and Plainfield ⊙ New Jersey.

1.   Louis Kantor M.D. studied cardiology in Geneva Switzerland and in Frankfurt Germany.

2.   Because Seattle Washington had a terrible snowstorm on December 29 1979 Amy canceled her party.

3.   Basketball was first played in Springfield Massachusetts in 1891; I think it was in February 1891.

4.   Juanita Pakez R.N. works at Maxwell General Hospital 7700 Sherman Road Atlanta Georgia. She began working there on May 1 1984 and will be there until May 1989.

5.   The office of Paul Strakes D.D.S. will be closed on Friday October 12 and on Monday October 15.

6.   After July 26 1983 the Marchers' address will be 1337 Skyline Terrace Pasadena California 91401.

7. Anita began her letter "Dear Aunt Jill I'm sorry I took so long to write." She signed it "Your loving niece Anita" and addressed the envelope to Jill Porter, M.D. 153 Glendale Avenue Philadelphia PA 19118.

8. Albert Sanger Jr. usually spends his vacation in either Provincetown Massachusetts or Montauk New York or San Francisco California.

9. Mail your letters to Toyland Inc. 410 Maple Drive Louisville Kentucky 44455 before Friday December 20.

10. Frances Mullen M.A. and Ruth Gole Ph.D. have rented offices at 2300 Doheny Boulevard Baltimore Maryland; the lease runs from August 15 1980 until August 15 1990.

Review Exercise B

Write out each of the following sentences and use commas where necessary. Circle the commas you insert.

Examples

a. I'm sure that Labor Day not Veterans Day is in September; I think in fact that it's September 4.

a. *I'm sure that Labor Day⊙ not Veterans Day⊙ is in September; I think⊙ in fact⊙ that it's September 4.*

b. Save the Whales a national organization to protect that mammal will hold a convention on Friday June 19 at the Lincoln Hotel 1400 Orca Road Monterey California.

b. *Save the Whales⊙ a national organization to protect that mammal⊙ will hold a convention on Friday⊙ June 19⊙ at the Lincoln Hotel⊙ 1400 Orca Road⊙ Monterey⊙ California.*

1. I think Denise that Carter's Bakery 133 Main Street Wayside New Jersey bakes fresh bread every day; Martin's Bakery on the other hand bakes fresh bread three times a week.

2. You need not have your gall bladder an organ near the liver to live; you cannot live however without your liver.

3. Well I would rather vacation in Venice Italy than in Venice California; I would rather live I suppose in Venice California.

4. Mario Palmos Ph.D. stopped smoking I think on April 24 1976 when Dr. Laureen Davis M.D. hypnotized him at her clinic at the Medical Arts Building Marcato Plaza Indianapolis Indiana.

5. You know Rev. Marchand that our neighbor Jorge Patron Jr. is moving to Tallahassee Florida on Wednesday April 20.

6. Kew Gardens which is near London England has beautiful flowers; in fact the place is breathtaking when the roses are in blossom.

7. A friend who wants to be a photographer just moved to Rochester New York to do research at George Eastman House which has a huge collection of photographs.

8. Did you know Denis that Harvey Stern who is a photographer just published a book on twins? The pictures as a matter of fact show twins from all over the country.

9. No I have never been to Peking China or to Osaka Japan; I did however visit Tokyo Japan on a business trip for International Importers Inc. on July 25 1983.

10. Fond of animals Lynn Lau works at the San Diego Zoo which is one of the largest in the world. The zoo's main attraction is its primates not its big cats.

11. The house that was used in the movie *Psycho* Hitchcock's suspense masterpiece is on the Universal Studio's back lot in Burbank California; tourists who visit the film company can also visit the house.

12. The architect who designed the home at 222 Beechwood Lane studied with Philip Johnson a well-known American architect; Johnson by the way built a house that is made almost entirely of glass.

13. There is a festival in Pacific Grove California to honor the monarch butterfly which migrates annually to the town. Yes the whole town is filled with butterflies!

14. Marcia Lewis a friend of my mother's has a parrot Max that speaks three languages; the parrot I'm sure speaks French as well as my best friend Doris who lived in Paris for two years does.

15. Amanda Martina's father Carlos Martina Sr. will speak on inflation which is his field of expertise at a panel discussion on Tuesday October 17 at the Economists Club 212 Madison Avenue New York NY 10016.

16. The health food restaurant that is on Market Street in Duluth Minnesota serves a dessert made from carob which is similar to chocolate; carob without doubt is better for you than chocolate.

17. Do you know Margaret that Larry Hagman who became well known as J.R. in the TV series *Dallas* is the son of Mary Martin the musical comedy star?

18. Mark Tilleli who was born in Rome Italy cooks delicious Italian food; accordingly he is opening a restaurant.

19. The photographs that Inge Morath took in China were exhibited at the King Gallery 1360 Eighth Avenue Lexington Kentucky from December 15 1981 until February 1982. Morath who is married to the writer Arthur Miller is an excellent photographer.

20. I'm sure that Puccini not Verdi wrote the opera *La Boheme;* Verdi of course wrote *Aida* a dramatic and tragic opera set in ancient Egypt.

The Semicolon

The *semicolon* is a stronger mark of punctuation than the comma, but it does not signal as strong a break in thought as the period. You might think of the semicolon as a cross between a comma and a period.

Independent clauses are discussed on page 469.

1. Use a semicolon to separate related independent clauses not joined by a coordinating conjunction.

> The quickest route between San Francisco and Los Angeles is the inland highway; the most scenic route is the coastal highway.

> All the stores in our neighborhood used to be closed on Sunday; now they're open all day and sometimes even on Sunday evening.

2. Use a semicolon between independent clauses when the second clause begins with a transitional expression such as *still, furthermore, otherwise, therefore, however, besides, in fact,* or *for example.*

> Marissa loves cats; in fact, she has fourteen.

> The city has adjusted its traffic regulations to accommodate bicycles; for example, most avenues now have clearly marked bike lanes.

3. Use a semicolon to separate items in a series when one or more of the items contain commas.

> Each team's uniform was a different color: the Mavericks, blue; the Bulldogs, red; the Sharks, green.

> The appointment calendar listed Ms. Alvarano, 10:15; Mr. Barks, 11:00; and Mrs. Low, 11:45.

4. Use a semicolon between independent clauses when commas appear within the clauses.

> American television broadcasts nearly twenty-four hours a day; but British TV, on the other hand, does not televise nearly as much.

Exercise 8

Write out the following sentences and use semicolons where necessary. Circle the semicolons you insert.

Example

a. Marta has lived in Springfield, Illinois San Antonio, Texas and Denver, Colorado.

a. *Marta has lived in Springfield, Illinois; San Antonio, Texas; and Denver, Colorado.*

1. Because there was heavy fog, the airport was closed many travelers were delayed all night.

2. Bernie was depressed about his fortieth birthday his spirits improved, however, when he opened his presents.

3. Drivers must always remain alert it's hard to predict, I think, what people will do when they get behind a wheel.

4. The suite of offices was shared by Raoul Alano, M.D. Carla Moran, M.D. and Nate Sharp, D.D.S.

5. If you like to travel, you will probably enjoy Paul Theroux's books he is a master of description.

6. Every year more and more Americans move to the Sunbelt the climate there, it seems, is irresistible.

7. The space program has always generated controversy some people believe that the money could be better spent on earth.

8. Caracas, Venezuela, and Los Angeles, California, share a common traffic problem both cities, I know, have complex freeway systems and enormous amounts of traffic.

9. During the last half of the decade, the price of meat soared as a result, Americans buy less meat than they once did.

10. Raimondo Cavazos, who is the school's top basketball player, enjoys sports in addition to basketball, he plays tennis, baseball, and football.

The Colon   A *colon* calls attention to the word, phrase, or list that follows it.

1. Use a colon to separate a list of items from an introductory statement, which often contains the words *as follows*, *the following*, *these*, or a number.

> The movie plays at these times: 8:15, 10:30, and midnight.
> John has three dogs: Pat, Mike, and Jill.

Note: The introductory statement preceding a colon should be a complete sentence. Do not use a colon between a verb and its direct object or after a preposition.

An asterisk (*) denotes a sentence with a feature that is not part of Edited Standard English.

> *We saw: a maple, an oak, and a spruce.
> We saw three trees: a maple, an oak, and a spruce.

2. Use a colon to separate an introductory statement from an explanation, an appositive, or a quotation.

> The band has this name: "Blondie."
> Remember these words: ". . . a government of the people, for the people, and by the people."

The colon should also be used in the following three conventional situations.

3. Use a colon after the salutation of a business letter.

> Dear Ms. Prince: Dear Dean Lowell:

4. Use a colon to separate hour and minutes in expressions of time.

> 9:24 A.M.   1:00 tomorrow

5. Use a colon to separate chapter numbers from verse numbers in references to Bible chapters.

Matthew 4:12   Isaiah 66:3

Exercise 9

Write out the following exercises, using colons where necessary. Circle the colons you insert.

Example

a. The recipe for real Texas barbecue began as follows dig a large pit in the ground.

a. *The recipe for real Texas barbecue began as follows* () *dig a large pit in the ground.*

1. The tour offered a choice of three hotels the Excelsior, the Regency, and the Empire.
2. Unfortunately all three courses met at 900 Spanish, French, and Russian.
3. What is the source of this quotation "It is better to have loved and lost than never to have loved at all"?
4. Is *Dear Sir* or *Dear Department of Public Relations* a better salutation for my letter?
5. This is his nickname Stoneface.
6. The bus travels on these streets Maple Avenue, Park Lane, Dover Drive, and Lake Court.
7. Marge offered three reasons for taking the job good salary, interesting work, and convenient hours.
8. Four students have won scholarships Meg Cluny, Pam Washington, Helga Lomar, and Beth Castolano.
9. Bart suggested this name for the new graphics firm Visual Engineering.
10. Janine has had the following birds as pets two parakeets, three canaries, and a parrot.

The Dash   The *dash* is similar to the colon. However, you might think of the dash as calling attention to the word or word group that precedes it.

1. Use a dash to separate an introductory series or thought from the explanation that follows.

New York and Paris — those are two exciting cities.
Singing at the Met — that is Meg's dream.

2. Use a dash to separate a sudden change in thought.

> According to the recipe — now, where did it go?
> Let's drive to the beach — no, let's get some food.

3. Use a dash to show the omission of words or part of a word in dialogue.

> "Where's that calcula — ?" Abby asked.

When the elements separated by a dash occur within a sentence, use paired dashes to enclose the word or group of words and separate them from the rest of the sentence. Use paired dashes to enclose a phrase or clause that shows a break in thought or to enclose a parenthetical appositive phrase. Use paired dashes for parenthetical phrases that contain commas.

> People applauded when Lynn Silver — a Miss America candidate — walked on stage.

> Disorders of the nervous system — multiple sclerosis, for instance — are hard to diagnose.

Exercise 10

Write out the following sentences and use dashes where necessary. Circle the dashes you insert.

Example

a. Surely there's a way wait, I found it!

a. *Surely there's a way⊖wait, I found it!*

1. Freezing that's the way to describe Alaska in winter.

2. Do you know Carolyn Janow not Carolyn Baker who's Bert's cousin?

3. "Help, something's fal" Julio shouted.

4. New Wave music it's replaced disco in popularity just sounds like old-fashioned rock to me.

5. Will I catch my train where are my keys to Baltimore?

6. Watermelon that's my favorite fruit.

7. The concert it's next week should be filled with surprises.

8. Dedicated to her cause that's the only way to describe Mother Teresa.

9. Paper Moon Graphics they're a firm on the West Coast makes greeting cards.

10. Did you know that airbrush art it's popular now was used by package designers in the 1930s?

Parentheses *Parentheses*, like commas and dashes, are used to enclose elements that interrupt a sentence. Parentheses indicate a stronger break in thought; words in parentheses, in fact, are really additional information. If omitted, these words would in no way affect the meaning of the sentence.

We all grew up in the same town (Lexington, Kentucky).

The banks will be closed tomorrow (Tuesday).

Review Exercise C

Write out the following sentences, using colons, semicolons, dashes, and parentheses where necessary. (In some instances you could correctly use more than one mark of punctuation.) Be prepared to explain your reason for using each mark of punctuation. Circle the punctuation marks you insert.

Example

a. Happy that's the only word to describe my mother Susan Johnson when she received her degree.

a. *Happy⊖that's the only word to describe my mother (|Susan Johnson|) when she received her degree.*

1. The Bank a rock-and-roll group played two Chuck Berry songs "Sweet Little Sixteen" and "Johnny B. Goode."

2. Reggae music I heard it in Jamaica has been popular here for example, musicians such as Peter Tosh and Bob Marley performed to sellout crowds.

3. Although Mary Cassatt 1845–1926 lived and worked in Paris, she is an American painter she was born, in fact, in Allegheny City, Pennsylvania.

4. Citrus fruits lemons, oranges, limes are rich in vitamin C however, they are also acidic and can be hard on your stomach.

5. Are any of the following flights convenient for you a flight to Chicago, 930 A.M. a flight to Detroit, 1100 A.M. or a flight to Milwaukee, 1130 P.M.?

6. A week on the ski slopes that's what I need in addition I'd like another week just to sleep!

7. George Washington Carver 1864–1943 did research on the peanut as a matter of fact he discovered hundreds of products that could be derived from it.

8. The following people I can't remember any of the schools where they teach will be present tonight at 800 Julia Chang Donald Juarez Professor of Economics and Lois Dales M.D.

9. Find the following cities listed under their original names on the map Izmir, Turkey formerly Smyrna Istanbul, Turkey formerly Constantinople Leningrad, Russia formerly St. Petersburg.

10. Having missed the last shuttle, Max had to spend the night in Boston thus, he checked into a hotel the Concord, went out for dinner The Lobster Pot, and caught a 1030 movie.

11. A Himalayan cat a cross between a Persian and a Siamese has long fur unfortunately it requires a lot of care.

12. The Bartons' party they planned it for weeks was a success everyone, I hear, had a great time.

13. Here are the directions for the sauce combine 4 oz. 112 g of bouillon with 8 oz. 224 g of water add melted butter, flour to thicken, and stir.

14. The manufacturer said that the perfume its scent was floral had a base of jasmine and lilac however, I suspect it contained at least one more floral scent roses.

15. "Whenever I begin reading, the phone interr," Rosalie complained. "Well, there's one solution taking the phone off the hook."

16. Diana and Mitzi Chang were fraternal that's the right word, I think twins as a result, they had similar gestures and features but weren't identical in appearance.

17. The following quotations are from the Bible "Thou shalt have no other gods before me," Exodus 20 3 "Let my people go," Exodus 7 16 and "Our days on the earth are as a shadow," First Chronicles 29 15.

18. The bright flash I'm still seeing spots startled me the picture, however, was wonderful.

19. Both these words are really formed from initials *radar* Radio Detecting and Ranging and *scuba* Self-Contained Underwater Breathing Apparatus.

20. Neologisms new words that are added to the language keep English alive and changing for instance, words such as *teleplay* a script written for television and *computer* were unknown a century ago.

The Hyphen

The *hyphen* is used to link the parts of some compound words. It also links the parts of a word begun on one line and finished on the next. Consult a dictionary if you are unsure about how to hyphenate any given word.

1. Use a hyphen to link the parts of compound nouns that begin with the prefixes *ex-*, *self-*, *all-* and *great-* or that end with the suffix *-elect*.

    ex–partner   self–esteem   president–elect

2. Use a hyphen to link the parts of compound nouns that include a prepositional phrase.

    son–in–law   man–of–war   jack–in–the–box

Note: Many compound nouns are not hyphenated. Some are two separate words (tennis court); some are written as a single word (basketball).

3. Use a hyphen to link prefixes with proper nouns or adjectives.

   pro–American   post–impressionist

4. Use a hyphen to link the parts of a compound adjective when it precedes the noun.

   coal–mining equipment   grease–stained jeans

Note: Do not use a hyphen if the adjective follows the noun or if the first modifier is an adverb ending in *-ly (quickly heated soup).*

5. Use a hyphen to link parts of a fraction used as an adjective.

   two–thirds empty   one–half finished

Note: Omit the hyphen if the fraction is used as a noun.

   One half of the bus was empty.

6. Use a hyphen to link the parts of a compound number between twenty-one and ninety-nine.

   forty–five seats   thirty–four years

7. Use a hyphen when a word is divided at the end of a line. Place a hyphen only between syllables. Do not hyphenate a word if doing so would leave just one letter on either line. If a word already contains a hyphen, divide it only at the hyphen.

   Mr. Cortez is a famous collector of ancient Greek arti–
   facts.

   The crowd was happy to see the ex–
   chairperson.

The Apostrophe

The *apostrophe* is used to show the omission of letters or numbers, to form the plurals of letters or numbers, and to form possessive nouns.

1. Use an apostrophe to show that letters have been omitted from contractions.

   won't [*will not*]   couldn't [*could not*]

2. Use an apostrophe to show that the first two numbers have been omitted from a year.

   '80   '20

3. Use an apostrophe to form the plural of letters, numbers, and words.

   I used a lot of *I mean*'s when I was in my 20's.
   How many *e*'s are in *Mindee?*

Note: No apostrophe is needed when making centuries and decades plural: 1880s, 1400s.

4. Add an apostrophe and an -s to make a singular noun possessive.

> Jake's coat   Alice's restaurant

5. To show possession, add an apostrophe and an -s to a plural noun that does not end in s. When a plural noun ends in s, add only an apostrophe to show possession.

> women's dresses   boys' team

Note: The possessive forms of personal pronouns do not have apostrophes.

> its [possessive]   it's [contraction]
> their [possessive]   they're [contraction]

6. To show possession in hyphenated words and in words showing joint possession, add an apostrophe and -s only to the last word.

> sister-in-law's car
> Harcourt Brace Jovanovich's office
> Bob and Betty's house

Note: When two or more people each possess something separately, make each of their names possessive. You will make your meaning clear by your placement of the apostrophe and -s.

> Joel and David's idea
> Joel's and David's ideas

(For a more complete look at the possessive forms of nouns, see pages 318–320.)

Exercise 11

Write out each of the following sentences and use hyphens and apostrophes where necessary. Circle the punctuation marks you insert.

> **Example**
> a. My brother in laws house doesnt have an attic.
> *a. My brother⊝in⊝law⊙s house doesn⊙t have an attic.*

1. The Waynes beach house is a half hours drive from Daves office.
2. The all star players well deserved trophy sits on its shelf in her den.
3. The gas shortage of the 80s affected everyones well planned vacations.
4. Deedees name has four *es*, which was the popular spelling in the 50s when she was born.
5. Its hard to believe that three weeks work could accomplish so much.

6. Felices great grandmother, whos in her 90s, is a relatively self sufficient woman.

7. The twenty five cent bus fare is a thing of the past; it ended with the 60s, and well never see it again.

8. Didnt Mikes sixty five yard run win yesterdays game and secure the Cougars place in the all star game?

9. Barnum and Baileys circus has a three month run in the East, according to Nellies aunt, whos their publicity agent.

10. "Yesterdays news wraps todays garbage"—thats a trite saying, but Im sure its true.

Quotation Marks

Quotation marks, which usually occur in pairs, enclose a word or group of words and separate them from the rest of the sentence.

1. Use quotation marks to enclose a speaker's exact words.

   "If I can help, I will," Josie offered.

   "I hope," Janis whispered, "that this movie is over soon."

In the preceding sentence the words *Janis whispered* interrupt the direct quotation, so the second part of the quotation does not begin with a capital letter. Use a capital letter to begin each new quotation and each new sentence within a quotation. (For more information on the use of capital letters with quotations, see pages 486–487.)

Note: Use quotation marks only to enclose a speaker's exact words. Do not use quotation marks in an indirect quotation.

   "I like the Dallas Cowboys," Lee declared. [direct quotation]

   Lee declared that he liked the Dallas Cowboys. [indirect]

Commas often separate a direct quotation from the rest of the sentence. Sometimes, however, another mark of punctuation is used with quotation marks. The following rules will tell you how to place other marks of punctuation when used with quotation marks.

2. Always place commas and periods inside closing quotation marks.

   Paula advised, "Wear a sweater. It's freezing."

   "I've never been to Miami," Don admitted.

3. Place colons and semicolons outside closing quotation marks.

   The sign read, "Welcome to Lynn's Inn"; unfortunately, there was no inn in sight.

   Martin meant only one thing when he said, "You need not look further": he was the man for the job.

4. Place question marks and exclamation points inside closing quotation marks if just the quotation is a question or an exclamation. Place the

marks outside the closing quotation marks if the whole sentence is a question or an exclamation.

> Bert asked, "Who won the election?"
> Do you know who wrote "Jingle Bells"?
> The audience yelled, "Bravo!"
> How I hate to see the sign "Closed for Vacation"!

5. Use quotation marks to enclose the titles of short stories, essays, short poems, songs, individual television and radio programs, magazine articles, and parts of a book.

> I read "The Sculptor's Funeral," a short story by Willa Cather, last night. [Notice that the comma goes inside the closing quotation mark.]
>
> Tony Bennett sang, "I Left My Heart in San Francisco."

Note: The titles of books, plays, works of art, long poems, television and radio series, magazines, newspapers, ships, trains, and so on are underlined in writing and *italicized* in print.

In your own writing, you would underline the italicized title.

> "Finding the Right Light" is the first chapter in the book *Care of House Plants*.

6. Use quotation marks to enclose nicknames and slang expressions.

> Mike "Lucky" Malone always hits the jackpot.
> "Far out" is an expression with a variety of meanings.

Exercise 12

Write out the following sentences, using quotation marks where necessary. Circle the quotation marks you insert.

Example

a. One baseball player is nicknamed The Man: Stan Musial.

a. One baseball player is nicknamed ⊙The Man ⊙: Stan Musial.

1. Helene saw three short stories on television in the series *The American Short Story:* The Man Who Corrupted Hadleyburg, Paul's Case, and The Jilting of Granny Weatherall.

2. The performer Bette Midler has kept her nickname: The Divine Miss M.

3. Do you know which book ends with this line: So we beat on, boats against the current, borne back ceaselessly into the past?

4. Cecilia said that she read in an essay, Helping House Plants Survive the Winter, that most people overwater their plants.

5. Because Mario has had good luck finding people apartments, people have dubbed him Best Bet in the West.

6. Which Beatles' album contained the songs Lucy in the Sky with Diamonds, A Little Help from My Friends, and When I'm Sixty-Four?

7. Remember the popular expression Get into it? Then the expression changed to Get behind it!

8. I'll vote, Manuel said, because I think that everyone should take advantage of that right. He added, However, I don't like any of the candidates.

9. Did you know that Yankee Stadium is called The House That Ruth Built? (Ruth, of course, is George Herman Babe Ruth.)

10. Just between you and me, Lou confided, I haven't begun to study yet. He whispered, I know that if I study every night from now until the exam, I'll do well!

Single Quotation Marks

Use *single quotation marks* to enclose a direct quotation or title that occurs inside another quotation.

Pamela said, "I love the saying, 'He who laughs, lasts.' "

Ralph asked, "Who wrote 'On the Sunny Side of the Street'?"

Notice that in the preceding sentence the direct quotation is a question; the title within the direct quotation is not a question. Therefore, the question mark is placed outside the single quotation mark and inside the closing quotation mark of the direct quotation.

Writing Dialogue

When you write *dialogue*, you write the words said by two or more people who are having a conversation. The exact words of the speakers are enclosed in quotation marks. Usually the speakers are identified by phrases, such as *Lilly said, Dick asked, Benny shouted*. These "words of saying" are not enclosed in quotation marks and are often separated from the quoted material by commas.

"When does your job begin?" Myra inquired.
Kim bellowed, "Hang on! This will be a bumpy ride."
"Send in the application," reminded Jo, "by the end of the month."

1. When you write dialogue, begin a new paragraph each time the speaker changes.

"I wonder which job I should accept," Lynn sighed. "Each has its advantages."

"Well," Leroy said, "which one seems more interesting? Which one has more opportunity for advancement? I'd choose the job that offered a better chance of moving into a higher position."

Lynn, still confused, answered, "That's the problem. They're both about equal. I'll have to think about it some more and weigh all the options!"

2. Sometimes, a direct quotation runs for more than one paragraph. In this case use quotation marks at the beginning of the quotation, at the begin-

ning of each subsequent paragraph, and at the end of the entire quotation. (Notice that this is one situation where quotation marks are not used in pairs.)

"I went to a family reunion," Melissa said, "and it was an amazing experience. I never knew I had so many aunts, uncles, and cousins!

"Over the years our family has spread all over the country, so we decided to try to collect everyone in one place. Relatives came from all over, and the house reverberated with the excited chatter of five generations talking to each other. Some of the people, of course, had never even met.

"The reunion was a wonderful experience for everyone. In an era when people can so easily relocate, families often separate and people lose touch. Gathering together gave everyone a sense of continuity and a sense of their own family tradition."

Mastery Exercise A

Write out the following paragraphs, adding all necessary punctuation. In some cases you might choose more than one mark of punctuation, so be prepared to explain your choices. Circle the punctuation you insert.

In the second half of the twentieth century Americans lives are filled with gadgets and inventions imagine living without paper towels rubber bands and TV which are usually taken for granted Who invented these items

Of course the origin of many items is unknown in contrast other items TV for instance are the result of years of research and development. The following three examples however give some idea of American ingenuity.

We owe the convenience of toothpaste in a tube to Dr Washington Wentworth Sheffield who produced a tube for toothpaste in 1892. Dr Sheffield a dentist in New London Connecticut didnt like using toothpaste from a jar the practice of the day so he furthered the march of progress by marketing toothpaste in a tube.

We can thank Walter Hunt a man in need of a money making idea to repay a debt for the safety pin. Quickly producing a sketch for a safety pin Hunt got a patent then he sold his idea for $400 paid his debt but unfortunately never made any more profit from his invention. His story proves this well known adage Necessity is the mother of invention. The necessity in this case was Hunts need for money a time proven stimulus to the imagination not the need for a safety pin!

In 1858 Hyman L. Lipman patented a pencil with an eraser attached to the top. A seemingly simple idea the pencil with eraser was nonetheless new for its day.

23 Spelling

Improving Your Spelling

Many thousands of English words can be learned by mastering a few simple spelling rules. Learning these rules and using the following suggestions will greatly improve your spelling skills.

1. Proofread your writing.

Proofreading for spelling errors is often easier if you begin at the bottom of the page and read upwards, focusing briefly on each individual word. Using a ruler to mark the line you are reading will also help you concentrate. Whenever you find a spelling you are unsure about, circle the word lightly in pencil.

2. Get the dictionary habit.

Always look up a word when you are uncertain about its spelling. If the word is not listed as you have written it, try alternate spellings until you locate the correct one. If you keep a small dictionary handy and become familiar with its use, you will find this process takes only a moment.

3. Record and analyze your own spelling errors.

The best way to understand your spelling problems is to keep a written record of your errors in a notebook. The following example shows one way to do this.

readiness	read·i′·ness	Change the *y* in *ready* to *i* when *ness* is added.
lightning	light′·ning	There is no *e* sound between the two syllables.

The first column shows the word's correct spelling; the underlining indicates the part of the word the student is misspelling. In the second column, the word is divided into syllables with the accent shown. Finally, in the third column the student has written a brief note explaining why the word was misspelled.

Spelling Demons

The word groups in this section are called *spelling demons* because they are used frequently but are also often confused. Some of these demons, *aisle* and *isle*, for example, sound similar but have different meanings and spellings. Other demons, such as *desert* and *dessert* look similar, but have different sounds and spellings. If you learn the distinctions between these confusing words and work on those that cause you problems, you will eliminate many careless errors.

1. accept

Learning to *accept* criticism gracefully is a sign of growing up.
Accept, a verb, means "to receive with consent."

2. except

Except on stormy days Ms. Rodriguez walks to work through the park.
Except, a preposition, means "excluding."

3. advice

Jiro often went to his grandfather for *advice*.
Advice is a noun.

4. advise

The function of the cabinet is to *advise* the President on important issues.
Advise, a verb, means "to recommend or suggest."

5. affect

Celia refused to let her classmate's prejudice *affect* her own opinion.
The verb *affect* means "to influence or change."

6. effect

Because administrators planned carefully, the budget cuts had no *effect* on school services.
The noun *effect* means "the result of an action"; the verb *effect* means "to accomplish."

7. aisle

Ushers at the large country-western concert worked hard to keep the center *aisle* clear of fans.
An *aisle* is a passageway.

8. isle

Alberto fantasized about sailing away to a deserted *isle* in the South Pacific.
An *isle* is a small island.

9. allowed

For wilderness training the scouts were *allowed* to carry only their knapsacks and canteens.
Allowed, a verb, means "permitted."

10. aloud

"Which suspect is the guilty one?" Roy asked, thinking *aloud* about his mystery novel.
Aloud, an adverb, means "with sound."

11. all ready

The class was *all ready* to go, but the principal refused to dismiss them until they were quiet.
All ready means "all prepared" or "in readiness."

12. already

Since Dinar had *already* toured the China exhibit, we decided to visit another museum.
Already means "previously."

13. all right

Chris asked her brother if it was *all right* to read his journal.
All right is the only acceptable spelling for this phrase.

14. all together

Because he kept his source cards *all together*, Tom had no trouble writing the footnote and the bibliography.
All together means "all in one place."

15. altogether

Altogether devoted to scientific and medical research, Ernest Just wrote two books and over sixty scientific papers.
Altogether means "entirely."

16. altar

To signify mourning, the *altars* in many churches are draped with purple or black cloth on Good Friday.
An *altar* is a table for religious ceremonies.

17. alter

Dr. Percy Julian *altered* the structure of soybeans to develop a material that relieved inflammatory arthritis.
Alter, a verb, means "to change."

18. angel

The Zen riddle asked how many *angels* could be placed on the head of a pin.
An *angel* is a supernatural being.

19. angle

Mariko had to shoot from an awkward *angle* to capture the waterfall's beauty with her camera.
Angle refers to a corner or the meeting of two straight lines.

20.	ascent	The dirigible's slow, graceful *ascent* was exciting to watch.
		The noun *ascent* means "a rise or climb."
21.	assent	"I told you last week about this party," protested Kiyo, turning to his father for *assent*.
		Assent means "consent or agreement."
22.	brake	The driving instructor showed me how to use the *brakes* on an icy road.
		A *brake* is a device used to stop a machine.
23.	break	John was so angry he wanted to *break* something, but he restrained himself.
		The verb *break* means "to split into pieces."
		The noun *break* can be a fracture or a rest period.
24.	capital	Although Chicago is the largest city in Illinois, it is not the *capital* of the state.
		The writing is hard to read because the *capital* letters look just like the small letters.
		The noun *capital* refers to the city where a state legislature meets or money used to start a business. The adjective *capital* means "important" or "excellent."
25.	capitol	Luisa has been chosen to work as a page in the state *capitol* next month.
		Capitol refers to the government building in which a legislature meets.

Exercise 1

Write out the following sentences and insert the correct word from the choices in parentheses at the end of the sentence. Use the sentences in the previous section to aid you. Underline the word you choose.

Example

   a. Twelve of Dr. Naismith's original thirteen rules for basketball are still in _____ . (affect, effect)

   a. *Twelve of Dr. Naismith's original thirteen rules for basketball are still in <u>effect</u>.*

1. Before the campaign began, teens in our neighborhood had _____ raised $200 dollars to plant trees in the new city park. (all ready, already)

2. There are no right _____ in an equilateral triangle. (angels, angles)

3. Jennifer will be here as soon as she finishes repairing the _____ on her bicycle. (breaks, brakes)

4. Mrs. Alvarez showed us photos of the ancient stone _____ she uncovered on the archaeological dig. (altar, alter)

5. The editorial in the school paper suggested that portable radios should not be _____ in the cafeteria. (aloud, allowed)

6. Although it was often too chilly to swim, we enjoyed camping at ____ Royale on Lake Superior. (Aisle, Isle)

7. This magazine article definitely suggests that the violence on television _____ children's behavior. (affects, effects)

8. My cousin, who has muscular dystrophy, has _____ the scholarship in computer programming from Blaketon College. (accepted, excepted)

9. This pamphlet from the fire department contains good _____ on how to check a home for fire hazards. (advise, advice)

10. With the ingredients _____ on the kitchen counter, Mr. Santori began showing me how to prepare the Italian casserole. (all together, altogether)

11. Without the _____ of the city council, the mayor feels she will be unable to cut the budget. (ascent, assent)

12. When the director arrived, the young musicians were _____ to audition for the city's youth symphony. (already, all ready)

13. The snow completely _____ the city's landscape, turning the streets of the _____ into a white wonderland. (altared, altered) (capital, capitol)

14. Mary McLeod Bethune was asked to _____ President Roosevelt on issues relating to youth and education. (advice, advise)

15. _____ for a brief dinner _____ , I spent the whole evening reading a Langston Hughes novel. (Except, Accept) (break, brake)

26.	clothes	Henry's parents put him on a *clothes* budget so he would learn how to manage his money. *Clothes* refers to wearing apparel.
27.	cloths	Lisa's aunt saves *cloths* for making quilts. *Cloths* are small pieces of material.
28.	close	It is customary to *close* a political convention with a prayer. The verb *close* means "to conclude" or "to shut"; the adjective *close* means "near."
29.	coarse	The *coarse* bread and strong cheese made a delicious sandwich. *Coarse*, an adjective, means "rough, crude."
30.	course	Akira was interested in art and in computers and couldn't decide which *course* to follow. *Course*, a noun, refers to a path, a series of studies, or part of a meal.

31. council
The town *council* meets Monday morning to discuss a neighborhood recycling plan.
Council, a noun, is a group that meets together for some purpose.

32. counsel
"As your lawyer I *counsel* you not to discuss this case before it comes to trial," said Mr. Ortega.
Counsel, a verb, means "to advise."

33. des'·ert
The Sahara is a *desert* region in Africa that extends over 3,500,000 square miles.
Desert, a noun, is a dry, sandy region.

34. de·sert'
Despite their greatly outnumbered position, the soldiers refused to *desert* their posts.
Desert, the verb, means "to abandon."

35. dessert
For *dessert* Ricardo served cheese and fruit.
Dessert, a noun, is the final course of a meal.

36. dyeing
Before commercial dyes were invented, people used plants for *dyeing* fabric.
Dyeing changes an object's color.

37. dying
There was nothing they could do to save the *dying* fawn.
Dying means "losing life."

38. formally
Everyone was requested to dress *formally* for the large dinner party.
Formally means "properly" or "with dignity."

39. formerly
Formerly with the Oakland Athletics, Reggie Jackson now plays for the New York Yankees.
Formerly means "previously."

40. hear
Mrs. Nielson couldn't *hear* the phone ringing over the noise of her daughter's stereo.
Hear means "to perceive sounds."

41. here
"*Here* are the results of the science experiments from last week," said Mr. Okano.
Here means "in this place."

42. hole
Every week Lana put a new *hole* in her socks during track practice.
A *hole* is an opening or gap.

43. whole
The class voted as a *whole* to elect new officers twice a year.
Whole means "complete" or "as one unit."

44. its
The door opened noisily, *its* hinges creaking loudly in the darkness.
Its is the possessive form of *it*.

45. it's
Some people believe *it's* no longer possible for

the United States to ignore human rights issues in other parts of the world.

It's is a contraction of *it is* or *it has*.

46. knew

Hector *knew* that if he could memorize the vocabulary words, he would pass the French exam.

Knew is the past tense of the verb *know*.

47. new

The *new* teacher looked at the rowdy class with apprehension.

New means "recent in origin."

48. later

"Why don't you come over *later*, when you finish studying?" asked Rosa.

Later means "after some time" or "more late."

49. latter

The *latter* part of the book discussed the Great Depression.

Latter refers to the second of two.

50. lead

Mrs. Sewell attached several *lead* sinkers to her fishing line.

Lead is a heavy metal.

51. lead

Jessica agreed to *lead* the others to the beautiful hiking trail she had found.

The verb *lead* means "to go first" or "to be the leader."

52. led

Alexander the Great *led* his followers from Macedonia through Asia Minor and Egypt to India.

Led is the past tense of the verb *lead*.

53. loose

Kanji's German shepherd left the yard through a *loose* board in the fence.

Loose means "not securely or tightly attached."

54. lose

When you read, it's easy to *lose* track of time.

The verb *lose* means "to suffer loss."

Exercise 2

Write out the following sentences and insert the correct word from the choices in parentheses at the end of the sentence. Refer to the sentences in the previous section if you need help. Underline the word you choose.

Example

a. Ms. O'Neill _____ her client for several days before the trial began. (counciled, counseled)

a. Ms. O'Neill counseled her client for several days before the trial began.

1. After learning of the Italian earthquake, the student _____ collected old _____ and blankets to send to the survivors. (counsel, council), (clothes, close)

2. Irrigation has transformed some _____ regions into productive farmland. (desert, dessert)

3. After the school assembly the new members were _____ inducted into the National Honor Society. (formally, formerly)

4. Ms. Montez checked her client's contract carefully for legal loop-_____ . (wholes, holes)

5. Sixty years ago my grandparents began this business with a _____ of only $5,000. (capital, capitol)

6. Unless a safe glaze is used, some forms of pottery can cause _____ poisoning. (led, lead)

7. At the time of his death, Herman Melville was a relatively unknown writer; only much _____ would his masterpieces be understood and appreciated. (later, latter)

8. After their picnic the children placed all their _____ papers and trash in the waste container. (loose, lose)

9. Although she worked as a pharmacist for many years, Ann Petry _____ she really wanted to write. (new, knew)

10. As part of their weaving _____ , students learned several techniques for _____ yarn. (coarse, course), (dying, dyeing)

11. In 1951 Dr. Ulysses Dailey toured several Asian nations, _____ them on medical questions. (counciling, counseling)

12. Although Rob cannot _____ his instructor's lectures, he lip-reads fluently and takes very complete notes. (hear, here)

13. I understood the point of John's essay, but _____ lack of specific detail left me unconvinced. (its', its)

14. In the address to Congress, the President stressed that inflation is a problem the _____ nation must work at solving. (whole, hole)

15. My mother, who was Ralph Bunche's next-door neighbor _____ in Detroit, _____ he would one day accomplish extraordinary things. (hear, here), (new, knew)

55. miner — The newspaper story on the rescue of the trapped *miner* was very moving.
A *miner* is a worker in a mine.

56. minor — Jennifer's orthodontist told her she had a *minor* problem with her bite.
Minor means "less important."

57. moral — Deciding which countries receive foreign aid is a *moral* as well as a political issue.
The adjective *moral* means "good or right"; the noun *moral* means "a lesson in conduct."

58. morale

The team's *morale* was high after their six-game winning streak.
Morale refers to one's mental condition.

59. passed

"I think we *passed* the turnoff," said JoAnn in a worried voice.
Passed is a form of the verb *to pass.*

60. past

During *past* holidays Damar's family have gone to a family reunion, but this year they are staying home.
Past means "ended, bygone," or "beyond."

61. peace

The ambassador issued the plea that his nation desired *peace.*
Peace is a "state of security or quiet calm."

62. piece

Janice wrote her message on a crumpled *piece* of paper and passed it down the row.
A *piece* is a part of something.

63. personal

I have been a *personal* friend of Mrs. Cortez for several years and recommend her highly for this position.
The adjective *personal* means "private, individual."

64. personnel

The company liked extra *personnel* for the busy season.
The noun *personnel* refers to the employees of a business.

65. plain

Jim's teacher urged him to write his essay in clear, *plain* English and save the embellishments for his short stories.
The adjective *plain* means "clear" or "simple."
The noun *plain* refers to a flat area of land.

66. plane

The *plane* was delayed for takeoff due to engine problems.
The noun *plane* may refer to an airplane, a tool, or a flat surface.

67. presence

With her austere face and piercing eyes, Georgia O'Keeffe is an imposing *presence.*
Presence can mean "an imposing appearance" or "the opposite of absence."

68. presents

Ms. Fong spent the last weekend before the holidays buying *presents* for her family.
Presents are gifts.

69. principal

The new *principal* gave a humorous speech on the first day of school.

The noun *principal* refers to the head of a school. The adjective *principal* means "primary" or "most important."

70. principle

Our coach is dedicated to the *principle* of fair play.
A *principle* is a belief or rule of behavior.

71. quiet

Ricardo liked to practice the piano after school when the house was *quiet*.
Quiet means "without noise."

72. quit

Many techniques, such as hypnosis, are used to help people *quit* smoking.
Quit means "to stop."

73. quite

In his new suit and tie, he looked *quite* elegant.
Quite means "wholly, entirely."

74. right

Freedom of speech is a *right* guaranteed by the Constitution.
Are you sure you have the *right* address?
The noun *right* can mean "ownership," or "a basic privilege," or it can indicate a direction.
The adjective *right* means "correct" or indicates location.

75. write

Sylvia Plath is famous for her poetry, but her ambition was to *write* prose.
The verb *write* means "to form words or letters."

Exercise 3

Write a separate sentence for each of the following spelling demons. Underline the word in the sentence you write and use the explanations in the previous section to check that you have spelled and used each word correctly.

Example

a. personnel
a. *Because the company is so large, Ms. James finds her job as personnel director demanding.*

1. presence
2. principle
3. minor
4. quit
5. morale

6. write
7. passed
8. plain
9. personal
10. piece

76. shone

An eerie light *shone* from the gloomy marsh.
Shone is a form of the verb *to shine*.

77. shown

The visiting dignitary was *shown* all around the capitol.
Shown is a form of the verb *to show*.

78. stationary

Advancing from the desert, Lawrence of Arabia succeeded in taking the port of Aqaba because its cannons were *stationary* and faced the sea.
Stationary means "fixed, unmoving."

79. stationery

Jeanne bought her father monogrammed *stationery* for his birthday.
Stationery is paper used for letters.

80. straight

Before her mechanical-drawing course, Alicia couldn't draw a *straight* line.
The adjective *straight* means "not crooked."

81. strait

The *strait* of Bosporus separates Europe from Asian Turkey.
The noun *strait* refers to a narrow passage between two bodies of water.

82. their

Jules and his sister walked along the river bank but avoided getting *their* feet wet.
Their means "belonging to them."

83. there

"*There* is the culprit," said Mr. Svenson, pointing to the raccoon in the garbage pail.
There refers to a place.

84. they're

"*They're* not as plump as they were last year," said Mrs. Tabor, as she examined the poultry.
They're is a contraction of *they are*.

85. threw

The umpire *threw* the player out of the game for his rude language.
Threw is a form of the verb *to throw*.

86. through

The moon burst *through* the clouds.
Through means "by means of" or "in one side and out the other."

87. to

Yvonne decided she should go *to* study hall the morning of the big exam.
To is a preposition.

88. too

"If it isn't *too* dark after school, we can go on a nature walk," said Hassim.
Too, an adverb, means "also" or "more than enough."

89. two

Two horses stood pawing the ground in their stall.
Two is a number.

90.	wait	"If I have to *wait* for this bus much longer, I'll freeze," said Angela. *Wait* means "remain, stay."
91.	weight	The swimming coach insisted that each team member maintain proper *weight*. *Weight* is a quantity of heaviness.
92.	waist	The dress had tiny tucks at the *waist*. The *waist* is the middle part of the body.
93.	waste	Improper disposal of industrial *waste* is a major pollution problem. The noun *waste* means "unused material." The verb *waste* means "to squander."
94.	weak	After her illness Kim was too *weak* to continue on the volleyball team. *Weak* means "feeble, lacking in force."
95.	week	The *week* before spring vacation seemed to last forever. A *week* is seven days.
96.	weather	"Everyone complains about the *weather*," said Mark Twain, "but no one does anything about it." *Weather* refers to atmospheric conditions.
97.	whether	Suzanne couldn't decide *whether* or not to try out for the school play. *Whether* indicates doubt or an alternative.
98.	who's	"*Who's* interested in going to the concert tonight?" asked Sheila. *Who's* is a contraction of *who is* or *who has*.
99.	whose	"*Whose* paper is this without a name on it?" asked Mr. Mendoza. *Whose* is the possessive form of *who*.
100.	your	"You must make *your* own decision," Ivan's father told him. *Your* is the possessive form of *you*.
101.	you're	*You're* sure to enjoy Langston Hughes' novel *Not Without Laughter*. *You're* is a contraction of *you are*.

Exercise 4

Write out the following sentences and insert the correct words from the choices in parentheses at the end of the sentence. Use the examples in the previous section to aid you. Underline the word you choose.

Example

   a. I always buy this _____ because it is made from recycled paper. (stationary, stationery)

   a. I always buy this stationery because it is made from recycled paper.

1. The _____ boys organized a large reception for _____ grandparents' fiftieth wedding anniversary. (to, two, too), (their, they're, there)

2. Since she hates to _____ time _____ in the dentist's office, my sister always takes a book with her. (waist, waste), (waiting, weighting)

3. The first person ever to swim the eighty-nine mile stretch between Florida and the Bahamas, Diana Nyad waded ashore _____ but exhilarated. (week, weak)

4. Because she backs her _____ with determination, Margaret Thatcher, elected Britain's Prime Minister in 1979, has earned the nickname "the iron lady." (principals, principles)

5. In 1943 _____ _____ after her high school graduation, my aunt enlisted in the WAVES. (to, two, too), (weaks, weeks)

6. Meteorologists study and analyze the _____ conditions. (whether, weather)

7. Mrs. Kim, _____ house is heated by solar energy, explained the process _____ our consumer economics class. (who's, whose), (two, too, to)

8. _____ is the typing room _____ ahead of you on the left-hand side of the corridor. (They're, Their, There), (strait, straight)

9. We will run _____ program _____ the computer tomorrow. (your, you're), (through, threw)

10. _____ Rev. Jesse Jackson speaks or not, _____ sure to find the school assembly valuable. (Whether, weather), (you're, your)

11. Alice Puerala, _____ labor in the steel mills goes back to the fifties, has _____ us that women can handle heavy work. (who's, whose), (shone, shown)

12. Our _____ , Ms. Noburo, believes it is still _____ early to evaluate the success of the new civics program. (principle, principal), (to, two, too)

13. Because the bookcases were _____ , my grandmother didn't have _____ move them when she installed the new carpet. (stationery, stationary), (to, two, too)

14. Most of the world's oil tankers travel _____ the _____ of Hormuz several times a year. (threw, through), (Straight, Strait)

15. The mayor _____ the switch, illuminating the tall pine tree that now _____ with the brilliance of a thousand small white lights. (through, threw), (shown, shone)

Review Exercise A

The following sentences contain many of the spelling demons discussed in this chapter. Write out each sentence, correcting all the spelling errors involving these words. Underline the words you correct.

Example

a. Weather they're chemical formulas worked or not, the chemistry teacher said she new the students' experimentation would be a valuable learning experience.

a. *Whether their chemical formulas worked or not, the chemistry teacher said she knew the students' experimentation would be a valuable learning experience.*

1. Whose the representative from you're congressional district?

2. Robert Abbot sold 300 copies of the first issue of the *Chicago Defender;* much latter, circulation rose to more than a quarter of a million.

3. Most of the class felt Richard Wright's autobiography had a powerful affect on there attitudes.

4. If your sure the course wool in this sweater will be itchy, then don't buy it.

5. In 1890 the United States government formerly declared the American frontier closed.

6. Barbara Jordan has always impressed me as a woman of quit strong principals.

7. With a little over five dollars in capitol, Mary Bethune set out to build a neighborhood cleaning service into a business.

8. In her talk the personal director emphasized that in a small company its especially important to keep up employee moral.

9. Quickly Rosaria past the ball to Liz who was all ready standing under the basket.

10. Threw the entire Presidential campaign, even when it was clear she would loose the election, Shirley Chisholm's moral never wavered.

11. One peace of equipment designed by Garrett Morgan has saved thousands of trapped minors who otherwise would have suffocated weighting for rescue.

12. Tina's eyes shown with satisfaction as she finished the hand-painted stationary she planned to give for presence.

13. During the winter and in bad whether, the waist recycling center closes early.

14. Anita, who's hole concentration was necessary, noticed the absolute quite that spread through the audience.

15. The small straight created a narrow passage between the wood-covered aisles of the Canadian lake.

Basic Spelling Rules

The *basic spelling rules* will help you avoid the most common spelling errors and guide you in determining the spelling of unfamiliar words. Although there are exceptions to some of them, taking time now to learn the rules will help you to write more accurately later.

1. In words containing an *ie* or *ei* combination that sounds like the long *e* in *feet*, use *ie* except after *c*.

   ie sounded as long *e:* f**ie**ld, retr**ie**ve, n**ie**ce
   Exceptions: prot**ei**n, **ei**ther, n**ei**ther, l**ei**sure, sh**ei**k, s**ei**ze
   ei after *c:* conc**ei**ve, c**ei**ling, dec**ei**tful
   Exceptions: financ**ie**r, spec**ie**s

2. In many words containing an *ei* or *ie* combination not sounded as long *e*, especially words with a long *a* sound as in *weigh*, use *ei*.

   ei sounded as long *a:* fr**ei**ght, n**ei**ghborhood, v**ei**n
   ei not sounded as long *e:* sl**ei**ght, forf**ei**t, th**ei**r
   Exceptions: fr**ie**nd, misch**ie**f, handkerch**ie**f, sc**ie**nce, p**ie**r
   And words with a schwa (ə) sound: quot**ie**nt, suffic**ie**nt, profic**ie**nt, consc**ie**nce.

3. Words containing a syllable pronounced like the word *seed* are spelled with one of the following forms.

1	2	3
supersede	exceed	accede
	proceed	concede.
	succeed	intercede
		precede
		recede
		secede

The only word in the English language spelled with the *-sede* form is *supersede*. Three very common words use the *-ceed* form: *exceed, proceed, succeed*. All other words with a *seed* sound have the *-cede* form.

Exercise 5

Write out each of the following sentences, adding the correct *ei* or *ie* combination or *-seed* sound that is missing. Underline the word you complete in each sentence.

   Example
   a. Over the summer Jorge became profic__ nt at operating a small computer.
   a. *Over the summer Jorge became <u>proficient</u> at operating a small computer.*

1. Anita and her fr__ nd waited for the tide to re__ .
2. The pat__ nt's recovery ex__ ed everyone's expectations.

3. The w___ rd sound in the basement turned out to be our n___ ghbor's escaped canary.

4. *Fahrenh___ t 451*, a novel by Ray Bradbury, describes a repressive soc___ ty that burns books.

5. After I showed him the price tag, the cash___ r con___ ed that he had made a mistake.

6. Using a p___ ce of muslin for a s___ ve, Lee strained the red currant jelly.

7. They bel___ ved that the new data on predicting earthquakes would super___ the old studies.

8. In the qu___ t of the evening, he would walk to the end of the p___ r and watch the sunset.

9. The fossil showed an anc___ nt spec___ s of flying insect.

10. She exper___ nced a great sense of rel___ f as she turned in her final term paper.

11. With a conc___ ted air he pulled out his handkerch___ f and sniffed loudly.

12. In sc___ nce class we studied a diagram of the v___ ns and arteries in the human body.

13. Ms. McDonald asked for a rec___ pt for the for___ gn currency she pur-chased.

14. The th___ f tore the br___ fcase from the surprised courier.

15. The soil in the f___ ld is defic___ nt in nitrogen.

Prefixes are discussed on pages 223–224.

4. When a prefix is added to a root word, the spelling of the root word does not change.

un- + specified	Please fill in the exact cost, as I will not sign for an *unspecified* amount.
re- + construct	Inspector Moriarity and her assistant tried to *reconstruct* the crime from the few clues at hand.

Suffixes are discussed on pages 224–225.

5. When a root word ends in an *e*, drop the *e* before adding a suffix beginning with a vowel.

admire + *-ation*	As his sister received her award, Carl's face shone with *admiration*.
virtue + *-ous*	Painfully, I learned that my *virtuous* friend had deceived me.

Exceptions: *noticeable* (notice + -able), *courageous* (courage + -ous), *peace-able* (peace + -able). In these words the final *e* is needed to create the soft *c* or *g* sound.

Some words retain the final *e* for clarity: *canoeing, singeing, dyeing, acreage.*

6. Do not drop the final *e* from the root word when the suffix begins with a consonant.

live + *-ly*	After her *lively* speech on soil conservation, Ms. Sanders answered questions from the audience.
excite + *-ment*	Nothing can dim the *excitement* in my grandmother's voice when she talks about football.

Exceptions: *argument* (argue + -ment), *judgment* (judge + -ment), *ninth* (nine + -th), *truly* (true + -ly), *introduction* (introduce + -tion), *production* (produce + -tion).

Exercise 6

Use your dictionary for help with spelling or definitions.

On a separate sheet of paper, write the correct spelling for the words in the following list. Then use each word in an interesting sentence. Underline the correctly spelled word in the sentence you write.

Example
a. *rate* with the prefix *under-*
a. *underrate*
    Ricardo, I think you <u>underrate</u> your talents in the kitchen.

1. *reserve* with the suffix *-ation*
2. *fame* with the suffix *-ous*
3. *appropriate* with the prefix *in-*
4. *courage* with the prefix *dis-*
5. *historic* with the prefix *pre-*
6. *ridicule* with the suffix *-ous*
7. *argue* with the suffix *-ment*
8. *waste* with the suffix *-ful*
9. *interfere* with the suffix *-ence*
10. *tease* with the suffix *-ing*

7. When a root word ends in a *y* preceded by a consonant, change the *y* to *i* before any suffix not beginning with *i*.

ready + *-ness*	Constantly cleaning equipment and adding supplies, the nurses kept the emergency room in a state of continual *readiness*.
hardy + *-er*	Which of these two tomato plants is *hardier*?
joy + *-ful*	The children's *joyful* cries rang out across the snow-covered streets. (The *y* does not change to *i* because it is preceded by a vowel.)

Exceptions: *drily* (dry + -ly), *gaily* (gay + -ly)

When a suffix begins with *i*, do not drop the *y*.

modify + *-ing*	If they keep *modifying* the blueprints for the library, it will never be built.

Exercise 7

Write out the following sentences, inserting the correctly spelled combination of the root word and suffix in parentheses. Underline each word you form.

Example

a. Mr. Lee called to get the name of a _____ baby-sitter. (rely + -able)

a. Mr. Lee called to get the name of a <u>reliable</u> baby-sitter.

1. As the final bell rang, Lamont _____ grabbed his books from his locker. (hasty + -ly)

2. Former President Nixon _____ guilt in the Watergate scandal. (deny + -ed)

3. Ruth looked through the yellow pages to find a _____ of tropical fish. (supply + -er)

4. Thousands of mourners attended _____ services for slain civil rights leader Martin Luther King, Jr. (bury + -al)

5. Constant rain made the November day seem even _____ . (dreary + -er)

6. In his letter to her, Hamlet called Ophelia "most _____ ." (beauty + -fied)

7. Marina's doctor advised her to move to the Southwest, where the _____ of the climate would improve her health. (dry + -ness)

8. We planned a huge celebration for our grandparents' _____ wedding anniversary. (fifty + -th)

9. Ramon presented a _____ _____ for starting a teen center in our neighborhood. (force + -ful), (argue + -ment)

10. The cat's yowling in the alley sounded so _____ that my brother brought it a bowl of milk. (pity + -ful)

8. Double the final consonant before a suffix beginning with a vowel when both of the following conditions are met.

   a. The root word has one syllable, or the accent is on the last syllable.
   b. The word ends in a single consonant preceded by a single vowel.

hot + *-er*	The water must be much *hotter*—boiling, in fact—to seal the lids of these canned vegetables. [one-syllable word]
con·trol′ + *-er*	Anita finds her work as an air traffic *controller* both demanding and rewarding. [accent on the last syllable]

If both of these conditions are not met, then the final consonant is not doubled before a suffix.

roof + *-ing*	The woman from the *roofing* company said we can save some money by doing the work ourselves. [a single consonant preceded by a double vowel]

ben'·e·fit + -ed   Many young artists and poets *benefited* from the support given them by W. E. B. Du Bois, editor of *The Crisis.*
[accent on first syllable]

The accent on the following words sometimes shifts from the last syllable when a suffix is added.

re·fer'   de·fer'   pre·fer'

con'·fer + *ence*   Maria was selected for the *conference* all-star basketball team.

Exercise 8

On a separate sheet of paper, write the correctly spelled word formed from each root and suffix combination. Then use that word in an interesting sentence, underlining the correctly spelled word. A dictionary will help you find the accent in words of more than one syllable.

Example

a. *forgot* with the suffix *-en*
a. *forgotten*
    Thomas Jefferson's contribution was so great that he will never be forgotten.

1. *shop* with the suffix *-ed*
2. *bat* with the suffix *-er*
3. *hop* with the suffix *-ing*
4. *rob* with the suffix *-ery*
5. *differ* with the suffix *-ence*
6. *crash* with the suffix *-ing*
7. *propel* with the suffix *-er*
8. *appear* with the suffix *-ance*
9. *develop* with the suffix *-ment*
10. *rebel* with the suffix *-ion*

Mastery Exercise A

The following short essay on African art includes thirty-six words formed from prefix, suffix, and root combinations. Rewrite the paragraphs, inserting the correctly spelled words for the combinations given in parentheses. Underline the words you form.

    The origins of African art seem to stretch backward almost to the (begin + -ing) of time. Paintings and (engrave + -ings) discovered all over the Sahara provide the (early + -est) evidence of African art. These (compel + -ing) primitive works are (illustrate + -ions) of Africa's (continue + -ous) (develop + -ment) in the arts over the past fifty (century + -es). The (old + -est) paintings, which show wild animals (run + -ing) through tall grass, are (un- + deny + -able) (indicate + -ions) of a (civilize + -ation) in which hunting was prevalent. The horses, cattle, and camels in more recent works are (rely + -able) signs of the change to an (agriculture + -al) society.

    The oldest sculptures (un- + earth + -ed) in Africa are the pottery heads (date + -ing) to 500 B.C. crafted by the Nok culture. Long (bury + -ed) in the earth until their recent (re- + move + -al) by (archaeology + -ists), these (forgot + -en) but (value + -able) works suggest African artists possessed (admire + -able) (technology + -cal) skill at an early date.

The Niger delta region is (fame + -ous) for the (beauty + -ful) bronze castings produced by Benin artists. The (excavate + -ion) of bronze (ceremony + -al) objects (date + -ing) to the (nine + -th) century (dis- + proves) the theory that the Portuguese introduced bronze casting to the Benin. However, the Benin people's (profit + -able) (trade + -ing) with the Portuguese influenced their art by increasing the amount of brass available to (in- + divide + -ual) artists. Most of the Benin brass (create + -ions) were fashioned exclusively for the (glorify + -cation) of their rulers.

Mastery Exercise B

Many of the words discussed in this chapter are misspelled in the following sentences. Rewrite each sentence, correcting and underlining all the spelling errors you find.

Example

a. Carryed by balloon, the first airmail letter went from Dover, England, to Calais, France, in 1785.

a. *Carried by balloon, the first airmail letter went from Dover, England, to Calais, France, in 1785.*

1. I wash all my cloths so I want too be quiet sure the trim on this wasteband is colorfast.

2. On December 16, 1773, participants of the Boston Tea Party siezed 342 chests of tea and depositted them in the sea.

3. Ann's grandfather whose an expert on foreign coins beleives this one is counterfiet.

4. William Still was a fameous and energytic leader of the Underground Railroad.

5. Runing one of the busyest and most efficeint railroad stops in Pennsylvania, Still aidded 649 slaves seekking freedom.

6. Jazz musicians must often work carefully two produce there themeatic elaborateions.

7. Ragtime, a noisey but pleasing combination of West African rhythm and European musical form, was popular until 1910.

8. Believeing firmly in her own principals, Sojourner Truth spoke out against laws that denyed women the right to vote.

9. This small anceint peace of brass was used as a wait for measureing grains and other goods.

10. At America's earlyest automobile show in 1900, skilled drivers competed in contests involveing starting, stoping, and turning between obstacles.

Speaking/Listening

24 Improving Your Speaking and Listening Skills

Developing Discussion Skills

Some people feel it is easier to accomplish goals alone than to rely on others. However, it is not always practical to work alone, because some tasks can only be executed through people's combined efforts. Moreover, working with others does not have to be a fruitless, dissatisfying endeavor. Anyone who has experienced the unity behind a team's winning effort knows better.

What makes some groups succeed while others fail? The answer to this question often boils down to the type of interaction, or communication, that is established by group members working together. To understand how to use group communication skills, you need to know how groups work and how people within groups work.

The Nature of Groups

Before you can analyze a group's interaction, you need to recognize the difference between being "a part of a group" and being in "a bunch of people." You may think, for example, that you are a part of a group when you are at a pep rally or when you go to a dirt bike race. A rock audience must be a group, since the purpose of listening to music is shared by the audience members. The communication at these crowd functions, however, is quite different from the communication that takes place when there is direct, eye-to-eye contact between speaker and listeners. You may not have trouble roaring your approval at a concert, whereas saying exactly what you mean before ten people takes more time and effort on your part.

The first characteristic of a group, then, is that it is small enough so that members can interact with each other freely and directly.

Second, a group by its very nature means that its members are in control of it. Everyone can and should contribute to the group's plans and decisions.

There may be leadership within the group, but it is still all of the group members who suggest and control the group's actions.

Third, all group members realize that they share some common ground, goals, interests, and purposes that cause the group to exist in the first place.

For example, there may be private reasons as to why different people join a prom committee. However, the purpose of putting on a prom is shared by all committee members and is the unifying reason for the committee's existence.

You will also find that a group is characterized by its members' sense of belonging to the group. Members identify with each other because they identify with what the group is and stands for. If you do not find a sense of belonging by group members or even by just a few group members, then you will find a group that does not function very well.

Finally, you have a group when its members make discussion the pivotal point for its actions. A group exists because people are communicating verbally and nonverbally with each other about what they want to do and what they feel about different ideas. Discussion, then, becomes the glue that holds the group together.

Activity 1

(For this activity each group should be provided with either a sheet of poster board and crayons or some modeling clay.) Divide the class into groups of four or five people and give each group either the poster board and crayons or the modeling clay. If members have the poster board and crayons, then they are to make a team drawing. If clay is provided, then the groups are to design a sculpture. The following set of directions is to be read to the entire class.

1. Each group is either to draw a team picture or design a team sculpture that somehow represents the individual personality of each member but that is also one unified picture or sculpture.

2. Ideas about the picture's composition or the sculpture's design must be provided by each member. Also, each member must actually do part of the drawing or design.

3. The end product must be given a title, and somebody in the group must be able to explain the art project to the rest of the class. Your group's spokesperson should also be able to defend your project, telling why it is a good representation of your group.

4. Take twenty minutes to complete the drawing or design.

After the groups have completed the task, as a class discuss the following questions.

1. Why did the following items either hinder or help the group in completing its task?
    a. A small number of people

b. Members who are in control of what happens

c. A common purpose (In this task you may have found that there was not much common ground or purpose among members. Did this have any effect? Why?)

d. A sense of belonging to the group or a lack thereof

e. The ability to discuss what should be done and how it should be done

2. How would this group be different if everyone really knew other members quite well?

3. Would this group task be different if membership were voluntary? How?

4. Did the group members work well together? Why or why not?

5. Did the group provide equal opportunity for everyone to participate? Why or why not? Is it necessary to do so?

6. Does the art project really represent each personality within the limits of one drawing or design? If it does, is it because of the way the group members worked with each other?

7. What do the end project and title say about the group's ability to discuss and communicate?

The Types of Groups

Once you find yourself involved with different groups of people, you become aware of the various purposes and procedures these groups have. The "Let's-Get-Together-at-Lunch" group may differ greatly in its agenda, format, and interaction from the "Let's-Get-Down-to-Business, It's-Time-to-Plan-the-Fall-Play" group.

A group's purpose often dictates the way people behave and communicate within the group.

If the group consists of good friends, the members may be informal, flexible, and spontaneous about what they do and say. If the group is meeting for the first time to establish a new student discipline code, the group atmosphere may be more formal and structured. This atmosphere will in turn affect the way people interact.

Group purposes can be plotted on a continuum, or line, that ranges from *task-oriented groups* on one end to *social-oriented groups* on the other with task/social-oriented groups falling directly in between.

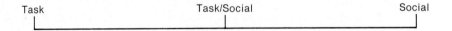

Task   Task/Social   Social

Task-oriented groups are formed when there is a problem to be solved or a goal to be achieved that can only be accomplished with a group effort.

Social-oriented groups, on the other hand, originate because the members just enjoy being with each other.

Even though group members may be influenced by one purpose more strongly than another, somewhere in between these two ends are all of the groups that are influenced by both purposes. A student council, for example, may be mostly task-oriented, even though its members socialize, too. In comparison, your softball buddies play mostly for fun except for the task they undertake when they organize a game against their parents.

These group labels can help you understand that different groups demand different types of discussion skills. The organizational skill needed to make a task-oriented group work may never be needed in a social-oriented discussion, yet people who know how to make supportive statements are needed in all group types.

In the rest of this section on discussion, you will learn about many discussion skills and specifically about those that pertain to task-oriented groups.

Activity 2

On a sheet of paper, label three columns with the words *GROUP*, *TYPE*, and *PURPOSE*. Under the *GROUP* heading, list all of the groups to which you belong. Some may actually have names like *Wrestling Club* or *Band*. Even within these groups, however, you might be in subgroups that you will need to label. You may even find that the number of different social groups to which you belong is greater than you realize. Under *TYPE* determine whether the group is *task*, *task/social*, or *social*. Under *PURPOSE* try to describe exactly why the group exists.

Activity 3

Describe in writing two groups to which you belong by comparing the differences between the two. You might want to compare the atmosphere, interaction among group members, and the expectations for behavior. Finally, describe why you think these differences exist and why you belong to both groups.

The Needs of a Task-Oriented Discussion Group

Task-oriented discussion groups are started because a problem exists that can only be solved by a meeting of minds. If you have ever been on a committee, however, you may be painfully aware that the group can cause more problems than it solves. The group's solutions may be poorly planned or enacted. Bad feelings sometimes arise among group members during discussions, and people occasionally become angry. Some people become defensive and refuse to participate, while others use every means possible to dominate the group's proceedings. What was once labeled as a meeting of minds can now be better described as "World War III."

A good discussion takes place only when people work together to create a climate that encourages members to share ideas openly, freely, and without fear of reprisal or embarrassment. This is easier said than done. Many people charge head-on into task groups, thinking they know how to make groups work only to be discouraged when the groups fail.

Becoming skilled in task-oriented discussion techniques can make the difference between group success or failure.

Learning about the seven basic needs of a task-oriented group is the first step toward developing this skill.

1. Develop an attitude of cooperation.

Before a group can ever succeed, each member must cultivate a cooperative attitude. This means that each member must realize that the group's functioning and decisions are more important than each individual's belief. You may have your own beliefs, and you may share those beliefs within the group, but for the sake of the group, you must cooperate and compromise with the group's needs and desires. Remember that you are involved in a group project, and that you are only one of many working on that project. Therefore, your ideas are no more or no less important than everyone else's.

2. Work to establish an open-channel network.

Many times certain communication patterns will form that tell a great deal about who has good communication with some people but not with others, who talks a lot and who talks very little, and who will talk to the whole group and who will only talk to a few members.

Every group develops a communication network within itself, and those lines of communication can affect the way a group works.

If you have a network where all communication is channeled through just one person, you may get things accomplished quickly, but you might not have a unified group that feels good about itself.

The best kind of communication network for discussion groups is known as the *open-channel network*.

All lines between people are completely open, and all group members feel free to speak up whenever they so desire. Communication flows freely from one member to another with all comments directed to the group as a whole rather than to a selected few.

This type of network does not magically just happen. Group members have to work at making certain that everything they say is group-centered and that they are allowing others the same opportunity to speak and be heard as they claim for themselves. The minute you find yourself in a group speaking only to one other person is the minute you are creating a different type of network. Not every group can develop an open-channel network one hundred per cent of the time during the discussion. If it is not the predominant network most of the time, however, a group will find itself facing problems that undercut its effectiveness.

Activity 4

Have everyone in the class copy the form found at the end of these instructions on a sheet of paper and then complete it. Next break the class up into groups of five or six persons and have all group members discuss the way they marked the worksheet. After all views are aired, each group must come to a consensus, or total group agreement, as to how the group should mark the form if the group as a whole had to make a decision. Share your group results with the other groups.

After you complete this discussion, you might want to discuss as a class whether or not the element of cooperation was present in your group and why or why not.

Female and Male Roles

Instructions: The following are twelve statements to which you should respond. If you strongly agree with the statement, mark it with a *1*; if you agree somewhat, mark the statement with a *2*; if you are neutral, write in a *3*; if you disagree somewhat, identify with a *4*; and if you strongly disagree, mark the statement with a *5*.

_____ The most important job for a female is to care for all of the males in her life—father, brothers, friends, husband.

_____ Females can only be truly happy if they marry, establish a home, and have children.

_____ Many jobs are beyond the capabilities of females.

_____ Today's females are too concerned about personal fulfillment and growth and are not concerned enough about the family structure.

_____ Females should not be forced to choose between career or family.

_____ Females should never date more than one male at a time.

_____ Males should spend most of their time and energy providing for the females in their lives—sisters, mother, wife, friends.

_____ Males should hold the ultimate responsibility for making major decisions in a family.

_____ Males should spend most of their time trying to make career advancements.

_____ If there are a male and female with equal qualifications for a job, the male should be hired.

_____ Males should never date more than one female at a time.

_____ A husband should stay home to care for the family if his wife wants to work.

3. Determine the leadership needed by the group.

Groups do not function well if everyone in the group goes off in a different direction. Somehow a group must be encouraged to stay with the task at hand until it is completed. This need for direction is often fulfilled by a person who becomes group leader, although in small groups it is often possible for members to share leadership duties without having to single out any one person.

When a leader emerges, it is because the group needs someone to help guide the discussion. The leader may be appointed by someone from outside the group, may be elected by the group members, or may naturally emerge as the discussion calls for one.

Encouraging members to participate and making certain that all members have an equal chance to speak are two of a leader's major responsibilities.

Asking questions, resolving disagreements, clarifying and summarizing ideas, promoting good feelings among members, listening to all contributions, being tactful, and avoiding the tendency to dominate a group make a leader's job difficult. Yet these skills of the democratic leader are what helps a group to stay group-centered and cooperative.

What will hinder the group's functioning is having an *autocratic or a do-nothing* leader in charge.

The *autocratic leader* is the total take-charge type of person.

This leader dominates the group and totally determines all group decisions. The autocrat may actually bully people or may try to manipulate them into accepting his or her ideas.

The second kind of leadership that will cause problems is that of the *do-nothing leader.*

Because this leader provides no guidance in a group, the do-nothing has very little in common with either the democratic or the autocratic leader. When the group needs help in clarifying ideas, in resolving conflicts, in encouraging people to speak, the do-nothing does not exercise the leader's power to overcome these stumbling blocks. The group can then flounder and accomplish very little.

4. Choose a group-centered decision-making process.

Closely related to the idea of leadership is the idea of decision-making. In a group there has to be some process or method that determines what the group will and will not do, what it will accept and will not accept, what it will discuss and what it will not discuss. When a group has an autocratic leader, that leader is the group's decision-maker. When a group has a democratic leader who promotes cooperation and an open-channel network, the group usually will use one of two decision-making processes: majority vote or consensus.

When a group is split over what should be done, often a simple show of hands is used. The side with the most votes determines what the group as a whole will do. *Majority vote* can be very beneficial in helping a group to arrive at decisions quickly, especially when there are a variety of opinions and a lack of compromise. Its drawback, though, is that the group is left with a minority that may not feel totally committed to the group's decision.

A better group-decision-making process is *consensus.* Very simply, consensus means that everyone agrees to the group's decision on an issue. That decision can be a very strong one since it is fully supported by all group members. Consensus, however, is not easy to reach and often is very time-consuming. To reach a consensus the group must work out compromises that in some way satisfy everyone at least a little. For a consensus, group members must remember to approach a decision on the basis of logic and to avoid stubbornly arguing for their own way.

Activity 5

Read through the following problem.[1]

> You are in a space crew originally scheduled to rendezvous with a mother ship on the lighted surface of the moon. Mechanical difficulties, however, have forced your ship to crash land at a spot some 200 miles from the rendezvous point. The rough landing damaged much of the equipment aboard. Since survival depends on reaching the mother ship, the most critical items available must be chosen for the 200-mile trip. The fifteen items left intact after landing are in the following list. Your task is to rank them in terms of their importance to your crew in its attempt to reach the rendezvous point. Copy the list on a sheet of paper and then complete it. Place number *1* by the most important item, number *2* by the second most important, and so on through the least important, number *15*.

_____	Box of matches
_____	Food concentrates
_____	50 feet of nylon rope
_____	Parachute silk
_____	Portable heating unit
_____	Two .45 caliber pistols
_____	One case dehydrated milk
_____	Two 100-pound tanks of oxygen
_____	Stellar map of the moon's constellation
_____	Life raft containing CO_2 bottles
_____	Magnetic compass
_____	5 gallons of water
_____	Signal flares
_____	First-aid kit containing injection needles
_____	Solar-powered FM receiver-transmitter

After you have done the individual ranking, break up into groups of five to seven people. As a group rank the fifteen items and record your answer on a separate sheet of paper. You should arrive at your answer by using the consensus method of decision-making. In other words do not make a final decision about each item's ranking until *every* group member agrees to that ranking.

Next compare your group's ranking to the answers determined by the space survival unit of the National Aeronautics and Space Administration found at the end of this chapter. Score your group's answer by finding the difference between NASA's ranking and the group's ranking. For example, NASA may say that an item's rank is *15* while the group's rank for that item is *10*. Subtract the difference between *15* and *10* (*5*) and record that number. Then total up that group of numbers. The lower the total, the better the group did.

After all of the groups have completed the task, discuss as a class the following questions.

---

[1] "Lost on the Moon Game" by Jay Hall from *Learning Discussion Skills Through Games* by Gene and Barbara Dodds Stanford, copyright © 1969 by Scholastic Inc. Reprinted by permission of Scholastic Inc. Originally published by Citation Press, 1969.

Was there a sense of cooperation in the group? Why or why not?

Was there an open-channel network? Why or why not?

Was there a leader in the group?

How was this leader chosen?

What type of leadership was displayed? Democratic? Autocratic? Do-nothing?

What actual things were said or done that indicated that a certain style of leadership was used?

How did the group resolve conflicts and disagreements?

Were there any group members who had trouble giving in for the sake of the group? How did this affect the group?

Were there any group members who just gave in to get on with it? Was this giving in good or bad?

Would the majority vote method of decision-making have been easier? Would it have been better for the group to have used majority vote? Why or why not?

5. Get organized.

A universal complaint about group discussion is that people become sidetracked and disorganized too easily. Outward symptoms of the disorganized group can range anywhere from group members talking all at once because they lack direction to no group members talking because they lack direction. The most common symptom, though, is the helter-skelter effect where the talk is excited and spontaneous but often unrelated. Members do not respond to each other's comments, and there may be no carry-through of an idea before another idea is introduced. Time is wasted; topics are not explored completely; the same material is raised over and over again as people spin their wheels; and meaningful discussion is never achieved.

If your discussion group is plagued by any of these symptoms, you need to develop a plan for discussion. The best plan for a task-oriented discussion group to follow is known as the problem-solution format of discussion.

Step One: *Diagnose the group's problem or task.*

Before group members can achieve a meaningful solution to a problem, they must first clearly understand all sides of their problem—or task—the obvious sides as well as the not-so-obvious sides. They must be able to completely diagnose the symptoms before they can suggest a cure. This diagnosis begins when members first try to gain information by discussing among themselves questions like the following ones.

Can we define exactly what we are supposed to do?
Are there issues raised by this task that are not so obvious?
Who seems to be most affected by this problem and why?
How does this problem affect people?
What causes this problem to exist in the first place?
Is the cause so obvious?

How widespread and serious is this problem?
What information do we need to know to solve this problem?
How can we get this information?
Has there been anything already done toward solving this task?

Step Two: *List all possible solutions.* Once everyone has a clear under-standing of the problem, the group members then begin to seek answers. Discussing what might be done to solve the problem should be your next organizational step. At this point in the discussion, group members should be inventing as many solutions as possible without discussing them. Your purpose is to suggest all possible treatments. The actual prescription will come later.

Step Three: *Discuss the pro's and con's of each suggested solution.* Eval-uation is implied in this step because you will take each listed solution and decide its good and bad points. You will be judging how well each solution will solve the problem you discussed at the beginning. For instance, if your committee is responsible for selecting an off-campus prom site, then your committee must discuss the merits of each possible site. To do so you might consider the initial problems you discussed—money, decorations, space, time limit, traveling distance—to see which place best suits your needs.

Step Four: *Select a solution.* Step Four is a natural outgrowth of Step Three. If your group has weighed all of the information concerning the prob-lem and solutions, then it must come to an agreement about what to do. Maybe group members will choose only one idea, or maybe they will opt to combine several ideas for their final recommendation. In any case the group is ready to prescribe a remedy because it has examined all aspects of the topic in an organized, thoughtful manner.

Step Five: *Put the solution into effect.* Sometimes, it is necessary to discuss who will do what and when. A plan for action must be drawn up by the group that ensures that the solution is carried through. The group's task is not completed until the group has carefully considered these details, too.

Activity 6

Again, divide the class up into small groups of five to seven people to solve the following task. Your group should follow the five steps of the problem-solution format and should appoint a secretary to take notes about what your group discusses under each step. These group notes should be handed in with your final decision to your teacher.

C.H.S. Senior Slam Day

Senior cut day is not officially recognized at Capital High School, even though it is tolerated every year by the administration and faculty. This year, however, major problems existed that make it necessary for the administration to take action and stop senior cut day once and for all. It seems that over $300 worth of damage was done to the school and the surrounding community as seniors "cut" the entire day, and community residents have had enough. The school and community homes were egged and toilet-papered, air was let out of car tires on the school parking lot, and ruts were made in lawns as some seniors jumped curbs with their cars. No one was hurt during this day, and all of the damage was of a prankster nature. This day was dubbed "Senior Slam Day."

Facts in the Case

1. Community members were able to identify some of the seniors who were hot-rodding around the neighborhood.

2. Four members of the senior class were obviously the ringleaders. Even though all four of them tend to be class clowns, they have never gotten into serious trouble before. Tom, JoAnn, Michelle, and Ross are all above average students, but their primary concern is always to have fun. They are well-liked by everyone in the school.

3. When questioned about Senior Slam Day, Tom, JoAnn, Michelle, and Ross admitted to their leadership role in the day's activities. They readily accepted their guilt, but they did not mean any harm. Everyone just got carried away.

Your Group's Task

1. Your committee is responsible for a decision that would be fair and just, but that would also punish the offenders and pay for the damage.

2. Your committee is also responsible for coming up with a plan to eliminate Senior Slam Day once and for all.

3. Your solution should be written out.

Activity 7

Select a problem that your school or community now faces and provide a solution to it by organizing your discussion around the five-step method discussed on pages 550–555. You may want to break down into smaller groups, or you may want to hold the discussion with the entire class participating.

6. Avoid self-centered behavior.

When you join a group, you display a certain behavior that characterizes your place in that group. Your behavior might type you, for example, as the group's intellect, as the group's doer, or as the group's energizer. Your typecasting may also change within the group, depending on how you feel at any given moment on any given day.

Some behaviors that people display either momentarily or full-time are destructive to group discussion and should be avoided if you want to be a good group member. The first step to avoiding such behavior is to identify the characteristics of certain self-centered or attention-getting roles. The next step is to compare your group behavior against these self-centered characteristics so that you can avoid their destructive influence. Some of the most common self-centered behaviors are in the following list.

a. *The Blocker*. This person objects to everything the group wants to do and constantly returns to the same topic even if the group has already gone on.

b. *The Clown*. This person does not become involved with the group because he or she would rather play.

c. *The Take-charge Person*. Take-charge people assume that they are the only ones in the group with abilities, so they try to run the whole show.

d. *The Rover*. This group member is more interested in what goes on in other groups. He or she displays a general lack of commitment.

e. *The Soapbox*. This person is never quiet.

f. *The Follower*. *Yes* is this person's favorite word. If you are a follower, you just go along with the group, seldom, if ever, expressing your own opinion.

g. *The Cutter*. This person is mostly joking at the expense of others. He or she tries to gain attention by deflating the egos of others.

7. Learn to use group-centered behaviors.

Where self-centered behaviors may undermine the group process, group-centered behaviors actually promote it.

Some of the group-centered behaviors that members can assume at various times during a discussion are in the following list:

a. *The Initiator*. This member proposes new ideas, raises new questions, starts the group down a yet-to-be-explored path.

b. *The Supporter*. When you say "I agree," nod your head, or indicate in some way your praise for another member's ideas, you are helping to establish group cohesiveness.

c. *The Clarifier*. Anyone who asks for facts, who asks for additional information, or who tries to clearly define issues or ideas is acting as the group's clarifier.

d. *The Gatekeeper*. This person brings in members who have not spoken and makes certain that all members get a fair chance to speak.

e. *The Mediator*. When differences of opinion do arise, someone needs to act as a go-between.

f. *The Energizer*. This person tries to keep the group on track during the discussion by gently urging on group members.

g. *The Summarizer*. This group member helps the group to stand back for a minute to see what has been accomplished. The summarizer may give the group a progress report, may point out the areas that still need to be discussed, or may summarize areas of agreement and disagreement.

Activity 8

Divide the class into small brainstorming groups. (You may want to form new groups or use the same groups you have had for previous discussions.)

Using the list of seven self-centered behaviors and seven group-centered behaviors, each group should list as many statements and actions as it can for each behavior. For example, a group may find that a blocker is a person who with folded arms keeps saying, "That's dumb!" Drawing from your own experiences, develop a profile for each behavior by considering what statements that type person may make, what body language he or she may use, and what tone of voice he or she may have. Share your profiles with the rest of the class.

Answers for Activity 5, pages 553–554

1. Two 100-pound tanks of oxygen (fills respiration requirement)
2. 5 gallons of water (replenishes loss by sweating, etc.)
3. Stellar map of moon's constellation (one of principal means of finding direction)
4. Food concentrates (supplies daily food requirement)
5. Solar-powered FM receiver-transmitter (distress signal transmitter, possible communication with mother ship)
6. 50 feet of nylon rope (useful in tying injured, help in climbing)
7. First-aid kit containing injection needles (oral pills or injection medicine valuable)
8. Parachute silk (shelter against sun's rays)
9. Life raft (CO_2 bottles for self-propulsion across chasms, etc.)
10. Signal flares (distress call within line of sight)
11. Two .45 caliber pistols (self-propulsion devices could be made from them)
12. One case dehydrated milk (food, mixed with water for drinking)
13. Portable heating unit (useful only if party landed on dark side)
14. Magnetic compass (probably no magnetized poles, thus useless)
15. Box of matches (little or no use on moon)

9

Testing

25 Preparing for Tests

Tests of Vocabulary, Reading, and English Composition

Are you planning to get a job after you finish high school? Will you be going on to college? Do you perhaps plan to join the military or take a specialized training course? Whatever your plans, it is very likely that somewhere along the way you will be asked to take a test. There are two general categories into which such tests may be divided.

Achievement tests measure specific skills and knowledge that you have been taught in school.

In some ways achievement tests are similar to the standardized tests you have been taking all through your school years.

General aptitude tests measure more general skills of learning: abilities to comprehend, think clearly, organize ideas, and express yourself with logic and conviction.

Tests labeled "aptitude" are generally given to assess or predict your probable success in more advanced study. *Specific aptitude tests* may also be given to predict your ability to learn a particular skill (like typing or computer programming or mechanics, for example).

Among the most commonly administered tests for college entrance are the tests of the American College Testing Program (ACT) and the tests of the College Entrance Examination Board: the SAT (Scholastic Aptitude Test) and the English Composition Test, known as the "English Achievement" test. Many colleges that do not require tests for entrance do administer placement tests to help determine which courses are most appropriate for your program. The military services and many employers also require applicants to take tests—of vocabulary, reading, or grammar and usage—when those skills are important to success in the job.

Preparation for Testing

Keeping up with your schoolwork during the year will best help you to prepare for tests. Cramming at the last moment is *not* usually very helpful in improving your scores. Some common-sense rules about test-taking, such as the following ones, are also good to know:

A. Attitude toward the test
   1. Do not panic. You may be nervous, of course, but keep as calm as possible. Try to do your best, but do not be upset that you cannot answer every question. Tests of the kind discussed in this chapter are usually built so that the average student will answer about half of the questions correctly.
   2. Do not be surprised if you "block" on a question. Go on to the other questions and come back to the item that is giving you problems if you have a chance later.

B. Approach to the task
   1. Read the directions carefully. Even if you are certain you understand the task, do the sample questions to be sure you are on the right track.
   2. Be certain you know what the question is asking you to do before marking an answer. Read all the choices before picking one. Many questions ask for the "best" choice, so be sure to compare the alternatives given to you before making your choice.
   3. The answers are usually coded with letters, as is the answer sheet. Be certain you are marking your choice in the correct space for the item and answer you intend. Check at least every fifth item to be sure you are in the right place.
   4. If you change your mind about an answer, be certain you erase your first choice thoroughly. The answer sheet is "read" by a very sensitive electronic scanner that will read both your answers unless the first is well erased. If the machine reads two marks, it will count the answer as wrong.

C. Planning your time
   1. Work rapidly but carefully. Answer questions you find easy first, skipping questions you find difficult. When you have gone all the way through the test (or a section of a test, since you sometimes cannot go back to earlier sections), go back and try those harder questions. Unless you are told otherwise, all test questions have equal value.
   2. Plan your time. Be aware of the length of the test and the amount of time you have to work. Try to be certain you are about halfway through the test when half the time is up. (Do not spend too much time watching the clock, however.)
   3. If you finish before time is called, go back and check the answers you have marked.

D.   Practice
   1.   One of the best ways to prepare for tests is to take practice tests. Some of your homework exercises are good practice tests. Set a time limit and have someone time your work. Tests your teachers give you are also good practice.
   2.   It is also wise to become familiar with the types of tasks you may be asked to do on various kinds of tests. One purpose of this chapter is to give you a brief overview of some of these question formats so that you will find them familiar when you meet them on a test.

Tests of Vocabulary

The vocabulary on which you will be tested is not so much the "everyday" words you use in conversation or informal writing, as it is the more sophisticated vocabulary of formal writing—both literature and informational nonfiction. Your familiarity with this vocabulary is one indication of your present level of reading ability and experience; it is also considered a good predictor of your ability to learn (and use) new vocabulary in advanced study.

There are four commonly used formats to test vocabulary: *vocabulary in context, synonyms, antonyms,* and *verbal analogies.*

Vocabulary in Context

Vocabulary-in-context questions are usually posed in the form of an incomplete sentence that you complete by selecting one of several (usually four or five) possible answers, or options. Often the completion you choose will be a synonym for a word in the incomplete phrase. In other questions, the incomplete sentence will be a descriptive phrase that you complete by selecting the one word that is defined by that phrase. A third possibility is the reverse of the previous one—that is, the option you select will define a term in the incomplete sentence. The following is an example of vocabulary-in-context questions.

Answers to sample questions are marked with an asterisk (*). All other answers are on page 573.

EXAMPLE   A.   Someone who is loquacious is—
   a   reticent
   *b   talkative
   c   fervent
   d   polite

EXERCISE 1. Read the beginning of each sentence below and the choices that follow it. Choose the answer which best completes the sentence.

1.   Handwriting that is abominable is—
   a   barbaric
   b   cursive
   c   legible
   d   atrocious

2. If someone's behavior is ignominious, it is—
   a ignorant
   b disgraceful
   c awkward
   d tempestuous

3. A jocund company is one that is—
   a bankrupt
   b melancholy
   c moribund
   d merry

4. A succinct statement is one that is—
   a descriptive
   b vague
   c concise
   d insincere

5. If someone speaks pejoratively, he or she is speaking—
   a disparagingly
   b falsely
   c appreciatively
   d optimistically

Synonyms

Two or more words or phrases that have essentially the same meaning at least in one sense are *synonyms*. English is a rich language, and there are sometimes several words that have fairly similar meanings, though there are not many instances where two words are truly identical in meaning, tone, or "feel." The "correct" answers in questions of this type are usually more accurately described as "best" answers. Careful reading will help you find the choice that is better than the other choices.

Answers to sample questions are marked with an asterisk (*). All other answers are on page 573.

EXAMPLE   A. <u>abate</u>
  a release
  b increase
  c shrink
  *d subside

EXERCISE 2. For each of the following questions, choose the synonym (word most similar in meaning) to the underlined word.

1. <u>ostensible</u>
   a pretentious
   b vibrant
   c apparent
   d imaginative

2. <u>scrounge</u>
   a cadge
   b whip
   c flatter
   d hoard

3. <u>derelict</u> a resigned
           b barren
           c deserving
           d negligent

4. <u>impute</u> a describe
           b transcribe
           c inscribe
           d ascribe

5. <u>panache</u> a hodgepodge
           b verve
           c cure
           d summit

Antonyms

Words that have almost opposite meanings are called *antonyms*. Antonyms require even more careful reading, as there are very few true antonyms in English. Again, you must look for the best answer. Most options will have some element of negation, but negations are not always antonyms. For example, something that is "*not* light" (negative) is *not necessarily* "dark" (antonym). By the same token, something can be "not dark," yet not be "light."

Answers to sample questions are marked with an asterisk (*). Answers for all exercises are on page 573.

EXAMPLE A. <u>acute</u> a mild
               *b chronic
                c habitual
                d occasional

In the preceding example, note that two options—*chronic* and *habitual*—are synonyms, but they are not both antonyms for *acute*.

EXERCISE 3. For each of the following questions, choose the word *most nearly opposite* in meaning (antonym) to the underlined word:

1. <u>intensify</u> a militate
            b mitigate
            c vitiate
            d aggregate

2. <u>enervating</u> a debilitating
             b nerve-racking
             c terrifying
             d invigorating

3. <u>flagrant</u> a inconspicuous
            b egregious
            c gregarious
            d unflagging

4. <u>restrained</u> a efficacious
              b effulgent
              c efflorescent
              d effusive

5. <u>spurious</u> a meretricious
              b authentic
              c specious
              d gushing

Verbal Analogies

In the other vocabulary formats discussed in this section, it is necessary to understand relationships between a pair of words—either synonyms or antonyms. In analogies, the test taker is asked to match two pairs of terms to demonstrate understanding of the relationships among those terms. Usually you will be given one pair of words or phrases. You must judge the relationship between those two terms and then find another pair of words with the same relationship between them. Sometimes, you will also be given the first word of the second pair, and you have only to select the fourth term. The following is one example:

Answers to sample questions are marked with an asterisk (*). Answers to all exercises are on page 573.

EXAMPLE   A. Pride is to lion as gaggle is to—
                  a bear
                  b eagle
               *c goose
                  d hawk

    In this case *pride* is the term used for a company of lions. *Gaggle* is a parallel term applied to geese.

    Sometimes, the terms are given with colons and double colons, as shown in the following example:

EXAMPLE   B. QUARRY:STONE::
                  a rock: mineral
               *b mine: ore
                  c soil: field
                  d oil: drill

EXERCISE 4. In the following items, choose the pair of words whose relationship is most similar to that of the first pair given.

1. WALK: LIMP::
    a speak: stutter
    b shout: whisper
    c jump: hop
    d flutter: fly

2. RECKON: CIPHER::
    a ponder: wonder
    b conceal: muffle
    c bungle: misunderstand
    d calculate: compute

3. WISDOM: OWL::
   a lion: heart
   b light: feather
   c pride: peacock
   d speed: molasses

4. EPHEMERAL: EVERLASTING::
   a omniscient: universal
   b equable: equitable
   c transient: permanent
   d cogent: trenchant

5. ROPE: STRING::
   a chain: link
   b cable: wire
   c thread: yarn
   d raffia: fiber

Reading Comprehension

Much of what you are expected to learn in many post-secondary courses is presented in written form. Thus your ability to read with accuracy and comprehension is usually assessed on tests used for selection or placement in such courses. Typically you will be asked to read a passage of some length—several hundred words, perhaps—and then to answer questions regarding what you have read. Do not be surprised if the subject matter is unfamiliar, since the examiners are not interested here in your previous knowledge about the subject. Rather, these tests are designed to measure how well you can derive information from the passage itself and how well you draw appropriate inferences from the facts given to you.

Some questions may ask for specific information embedded in the passage—literal detail or factual data. Some may ask for the meaning of a term in the context in which it is being used. More often, however, the questions will require you to draw conclusions, synthesize a number of details, or evaluate the author's intent, point of view, and so forth.

One of the best ways to prepare for tests of this sort is to turn your regular reading assignments into practice tests. Read a few paragraphs in your social studies or literature textbook, and then do the following:

1. State the main idea or thrust of that paragraph.

2. For each important idea stated in the passage, try restating the idea in other words.

3. Look for words in the passage that have multiple meanings and define each word in terms of its use in the paragraph.

4. Identify statements that are expressions of opinion. Are they well-founded, based on facts given?

5. Look for and identify value judgments, expressions of bias or prejudice, exaggerations, understatements.

6. Try to identify the author's intent or purpose in including this particular passage. What is its tone? Is it descriptive, persuasive, argumentative?

7. What inferences can be drawn from what is stated?

English Mechanics and Usage

Tests of English mechanics and usage are designed to test whether you have learned some of the most basic skills of English composition. Although you may also be asked for a writing sample when you are being tested, you will more frequently be given a multiple-choice test that may include sections on spelling, grammar, and usage, as well as exercises designed to determine your sensitivity to language and your ability to organize thoughts into a logical whole. In the test items that follow are some of the more common methods of testing composition skills in multiple-choice formats.

Spelling

Test questions usually assess basic rules of spelling or offer misspellings of frequently used words. The most common format is to present several words, one of which is misspelled. (Sometimes, one option is "no error.") Another format derives from misuse of *homophones*—words spelled differently but sounding the same—such as *peace* and *piece* or *two* and *too*.

EXERCISE 5. For each of the following questions, choose the one word that is misspelled. If no word is misspelled, mark *N* for "no error."

1. a changeable
   b desicate
   c vacuum
   d temperament
   N

2. a accommodation
   b fulfill
   c superceed
   d penicillin
   N

3. a ruse
   b vengeance
   c strategic
   d complection
   N

4. a irrelevant
   b maintenance
   c prevalent
   d hygiene
   N

5. a outragous
   b allegiance
   c mischievous
   d diligence
   N

6. a beggar
   b acknowedge
   c debacle
   d referred
   N

7. a biscuit
   b prophesy
   c espionage
   d nurotic
   N

8. a edible
   b innoculate
   c mediocre
   d vinegar
   N

9. a ice floe
   b playwright
   c knave of a church
   d scout troop
   N

10. a idle gossip
    b hoarse throat
    c copyright
    d filet of soul
    N

Error Recognition

Questions in the error recognition category require you to detect errors in short written passages. Sometimes, you may be asked to specify the nature of the error. Other formats require only that you indicate the *presence* of an error. The following are examples of both these types:

EXAMPLES   TYPE 1.

Mark your answer sheet:
a-if the sentence contains an error in diction (choice of words)
b-if the sentence is verbose or redundant (wordy)
c-if the sentence contains a cliché or mixed metaphor
d-if the sentence contains an error in grammar
e-if the sentence is correct as it stands

EXAMPLE   A. The young man was fit as a fiddle. (c)

TYPE 2

Mark the letter of the line containing an error in spelling, punctuation, capitalization, grammar, or usage. If there is no error, mark N for "no error."

Answers for sample questions are marked with an asterisk (*). Answers for other questions are on page 573.

EXAMPLE   B. *a the canadian flag has
                b a red maple leaf on a
                c ground of white.
                N

EXERCISE 6.   TYPE 1.

Mark your answer sheet:
a if the sentence contains an error in diction (choice of words)
b if the sentence is verbose or redundant (wordy)
c if the sentence contains a cliché or mixed metaphor
d if the sentence contains an error in grammar
e if the sentence is correct as it stands

1. Thousands of foreign tourists come to the United States from other countries each year to visit the American national parks.

2. Having partaken of a game of chess, the girls decided to take a brisk walk.

3. Bats are the only mammals living today that are able to fly.

4. There is no doubt that he plays tennis like the professionals do.

5. The final agreement had to be made between three parties.

6. News of the impending truce had a strange affect upon the troops.

7. Mirages are very common over bodies of water, where they are regularly confused with reflections.

8. The mayor viewed with alarm the impending fiscal crisis of the city.

9. Angered by the public reaction to the slight tax increase, the assemblyman was irritated to think his constituents had not appreciated his efforts to keep the increase to such a small minimum.

10. If the earth was closer to the sun, the average temperature would be higher, and it is possible that life might never have begun.

EXERCISE 7.   TYPE 2

Mark the letter of the line containing an error in spelling, punctuation, capitalization, grammar, or usage. If there is no error, mark N for "no error."

1. a Nathan had to be told of his defeat,
    b but his teacher felt badly that she
    c was the one who had to tell him.
    N

2. a Each of the boys have a special
   b assignment to be completed
   c before the term is over.
   N

3. a We were particularly gratified when
   b Mrs. Smith gave both him and us
   c some complementary tickets to the concert.
   N

4. a The air was magically clear, the sky
   b burnished blue, the clouds, here and
   c there, of purest white.
   N

5. a Being as the president was called
   b away, he appointed an assistant to
   c handle any emergencies that might arise.
   N

6. a Medical research on humans has advanced
   b considerably, yet only recently has attention
   c been given to the roll diet plays in health.
   N

7. a An hour before the operation was scheduled
   b to occur, the nurse was asked to lie each of
   c the surgical instruments on the table.
   N

8. a Harry although tired worked
   b late into the summer evening
   c editing his latest manuscript.
   N

9. a The best of these stories is
   b imaginative and quite descriptive
   c without being either silly or unbelievable.
   N

10. a Her unkind remarks inferred
    b that the science fair winner
    c had been chosen unfairly.
    N

Organizing Paragraphs

Your ability to organize thoughts and present them logically may be indirectly assessed by exercises involving scrambled paragraphs. In this format you are given a passage with sentences in random order, which you must organize into a paragraph.

Before answering any questions, try to order the paragraph in your mind. Look for clues within the sentences, such as pronouns referring to something in another (and therefore earlier) sentence. Note transitional words and phrases. If necessary, jot down the order of the sentences on scrap paper. Then answer the specific questions you are asked.

EXAMPLE   P   Myths, on the other hand, are born, not made.
          Q   A fable is a story, made to order, intended for instruction.
          R   They owe their details to the imaginative efforts of generations of storytellers.
          S   A distinction must be made between myths and fables.

1. Which sentence did you put first?
   a   sentence P
   b   sentence Q
   c   sentence R
   d   sentence S

2. Which sentence did you put after S?
   a   sentence P
   b   sentence Q
   c   sentence R
   d   None of the above. Sentence S is last.

The correct order of these sentences is S, Q, P, R. S is a topic sentence and really makes sense only as the first sentence. As a final sentence, it would be silly unless it included *therefore* or *thus* or *in summary, then,* or some such phrase. Sentence P needs to come after Q because of the phrase *on the other hand.* The *they* in sentence R refers to myths, not fables, so the order is established.

EXERCISE 8. Each group of sentences in this section is actually a paragraph presented in scrambled order. Each sentence in the group has a place in the paragraph; no sentence is to be left out. You are to read each group of sentences and decide the best order in which to put the sentences so as to form a well-organized paragraph.

          P   These are questions every child and every savage must ask.
          Q   Myths that attempt to unveil the mysteries of existence—for example, the creation myths mentioned above—may be categorized as explanatory myths.
          R   The stories devised to answer such questions gradually evolve into myths of creation.
          S   On the other hand, myths such as those of the *Iliad* are called aesthetic myths—having their origin not in the need to explain, but merely in the universal desire for a good yarn.
          T   What is man, and what is the world?

1. Which sentence did you put first?
   a   sentence P
   b   sentence Q
   c   sentence R
   d   sentence S
   e   sentence T

2. Which sentence did you put after sentence P?
   a sentence Q
   b sentence R
   c sentence S
   d sentence T
   e None of the above. Sentence P is last.

3. Which sentence did you put after sentence Q?
   a sentence P
   b sentence R
   c sentence S
   d sentence T
   e None of the above. Sentence Q is last.

4. Which sentence did you put after sentence R?
   a sentence P
   b sentence Q
   c sentence S
   d sentence T
   e None of the above. Sentence R is last.

5. Which sentence did you put after sentence T?
   a sentence P
   b sentence Q
   c sentence R
   d sentence S
   e None of the above. Sentence T is last.

Writing Samples

In the past few years it has become relatively common to include a writing sample in tests of English composition—usually in addition to the kinds of multiple-choice questions discussed in this section. Because writing samples cannot be scanned by a machine or graded with complete objectivity, they are far more difficult to evaluate than are the objective tests with which you are familiar. However, the best possible test of whether you can write well is to ask you to write something and then to judge how well you accomplished the task.

There are two common approaches to marking writing samples used for this purpose. One is known as *holistic scoring*. Using this system, the trained reader/scorer reads your essay or paragraph quite rapidly and gives it a rating—perhaps on a scale of 1 (low) to 5 (high). The rating is based on an *overall* impression of the piece (hence the term *holistic*) rather than on any quantitative or even qualitative evaluation of its various elements. Spelling, punctuation, grammar, usage, organization, tone, even handwriting probably "count" to some degree, but they are not assessed or tallied separately. When writing samples are scored holistically, at least two readers will rate each sample independently. When the readers disagree, a third reader is often called on to make a final assessment.

A second method of scoring involves multiple readings of your sample with separate ratings made for various elements such as ideas, organization, wording, flavor, mechanics, and presentation (penmanship, neatness, spacing, etc.). When this approach is taken, each element may be rated 3 (excellent), 2 (average), or 1 (poor) and the ratings averaged to come up with a total score. If you have not had experience in writing short descriptive or persuasive pieces, you might want to practice writing "on demand" in preparation for this kind of test. The following is a short list of topics similar to those you might be asked to address in a writing sample.

1. Describe your favorite house/garden/landscape.
2. Explain how to make something you know well.
3. Discuss your views on television.
4. Discuss your views on why families quarrel.
5. Explain how to plan a party.
6. My Life Ten Years From Now
7. On Being Popular
8. High School Slang
9. Conservation and the Energy Shortage
10. Traits I Wish I Had/Didn't Have

KEY

Exercise	1	2	3	4	5	6	7	8
Item 1.	d	c	b	a	b	b	b	e
2.	b	a	d	d	c	a	a	b
3.	d	d	a	c	d	e	c	c
4.	c	d	d	c	N	d	N	b
5.	a	b	b	b	a	a	a	a
6.					b	a	c	
7.					d	e	b	
8.					b	c	a	
9.					c	b	c	
10.					d	d	a	

Glossary of Terms

Achievement test A test that measures specific skills and knowledge taught in school

Action In the *Pentad*, any physical or mental activity that has happened or is happening and any creative work or product resulting from those activities

Actors In the Pentad, those people (or other forces) involved in the action

Adjective A word used to modify a noun or a pronoun

Adjective clause a subordinate clause that modifies a noun or pronoun

Adverb A word that modifies a verb, an adjective, or another adverb

Adverb clause A subordinate clause that modifies a verb, an adverb, or an adjective

Affix A syllable or word that carries meaning when joined to a root or to a word

Alliteration The repetition of sounds at the beginnings of words

Almanac A reference book published annually containing lists, statistics, and facts subject to change

Analogy A comparison in which two dissimilar things are shown to have at least one quality in common

Antonym A word with the opposite meaning of another word

Apostrophe Punctuation mark used to show the omission of letters or numbers, to form the plurals of letters or numbers, and to form possessive nouns

Appositive A noun or pronoun that identifies or explains a nearby noun or pronoun

Argument A logical presentation of ideas

Assonance The repetition of vowel sounds in the words of a poem

Atlas A reference book of maps

Autobiography A writer's own account of her or his life

Begging the question A fallacy in which the conclusion is the same as the premise

Bibliography A list of the sources used for a research paper

Biography An account of a person's life written by another

Body All the paragraphs between the introduction and conclusion of a composition

Brainstorming The process of trying to arrive at a new idea by letting one's thoughts wander freely over a subject

Call number The number used to identify and locate a book filed under the Dewey decimal system

card catalogue A file of cards listing books and other reference materials in alphabetical order

Characters Persons written about in a narrative

Chronology Order in time

Classifying a topic Looking at a topic from a specific point of view

Clause A group of words containing a subject and a predicate and functioning as part of a sentence

"Clincher" sentence A sentence that sums up a paragraph

Coherent paragraph A paragraph in which all the sentences follow an orderly progress, with connections between sentences made clear to the reader

Colon A punctuation mark that calls attention to the word, phrase, or list that follows it

Comma The punctuation mark used to separate words, phrases, or clauses within a sentence

Commentary The writer's direct comments, reflections, and observations in a personal narrative

Comparison Pointing out ways in which items are the same and ways in which they differ

Complement A word or group of words that completes the meaning of the verb and the subject

Complex sentence A sentence containing one independent clause and one or more subordinate clauses

Compound sentence A sentence containing two or more independent clauses with no subordinate clauses

Compound-complex sentence A sentence containing two or more independent clauses and one or more subordinate clauses

Conflict The struggle between opposing forces

Conjunction A word that connects other words or groups of words

Connotative meaning   The feeling or tone associated with a word

Context   Words, phrases, and clauses that surround a word

Data   Facts, figures or statistics, and dates—information that has been proven to be true

Declarative sentence   A sentence that makes a statement

Deductive reasoning   Reasoning from a general or universal statement to a specific, more limited statement

Denotative meaning   The meaning of a word as given in a dictionary

Descriptive details   Specifics about people, places, feelings, and states of mind that help the reader share in the writer's experience

Dewey decimal system   A method of dividing nonfiction works into ten categories

Dialect   A variation of a language

Dialogue   Conversation between characters

Direct object   A word or group of words that receives the action of the verb

Either-or fallacy   An argument that ignores the possibility of alternative choices or solutions

Encyclopedia   A reference book containing information in all branches of learning

Euphemism   The substitution of a more agreeable term for one that might be offensive

Exclamatory sentence   A sentence that expresses strong feeling

Explication pattern   Presentation of a main idea and supporting details, or definition and explanation of a concept or term

Expository writing   Writing that presents and explains information

Fallacy   An error in reasoning

Formal outline   An outline using Roman numerals, capital letters, and Arabic numerals to show the order, relationship, and relative importance of ideas

General aptitude test   A test that measures general skills of learning—abilities to comprehend, think clearly, organize ideas, and express oneself with logic and conviction

Generalization   The conclusion in an inductive argument

Gerund   A form of the verb that is used as a noun

Glittering generality   A word or phrase with a powerful positive connotation used to persuade

Hasty generalization   A fallacy in which the conclusion is based on insufficient evidence

Hyphen   Punctuation mark used to link the parts of compound words or to divide words at the end of a line

Illustration sentences   Sentences that develop the main idea of a paragraph by giving examples, reasons, data, or descriptive details

Imperative sentence   A sentence that gives a command or makes a request

Independent clause   A clause that can stand on its own as a sentence

Indirect object   A word that tells to whom or for whom the action of the verb is done

Inductive reasoning   Reasoning from specific facts to a conclusion based on evidence

Infinitive   A form of the verb usually preceded by the word *to*

Interjection   A word that shows strong or sudden feeling

Interrogative sentence   A sentence that asks a question

Letter of adjustment   A letter written to convince a company to replace damaged merchandise, refund money, or correct an error in billing

Letter of application   A letter written to apply for a job

Limiting the subject   Narrowing the subject to a specific topic

Metaphor   A figure of speech stating a comparison, without using the words *like, as, than, seems,* or *appears*

Meter   The pattern of repeating rhythm in poems

Method   The way in which the action of a narrative is brought about

Mood   In grammar, the speaker's attitude toward what is being expressed

Narrator   One who tells, or narrates, the events of a story

Noun   The name of a person, place, thing, or idea

Noun clause   A subordinate clause used as a noun

Noun phrase   A noun and its modifiers

Objective complement   A noun or adjective that completes the meaning of the verb and refers to the direct object

Observation   Paying attention to events, people, places, and appearances

Omniscient narrator   The narrator of a story who is an unseen observer able to relate information about the activities, thoughts, and feelings of all the characters, and to describe the setting

Order letter   A letter requesting a company to send merchandise

Outline   A guide or plan to follow in writing a composition

Overview   A general idea of what is involved in a research topic

Paper of classification   An expository composition that presents and explains the topic by sorting it into smaller groups

Paragraph   A group of related sentences

Paraphrase   To rephrase a word or a phrase

Parentheses   Marks of punctuation that enclose elements that interrupt a sentence

Participle   A form of the verb that is used as an adjective

Pentad   A set of five questions (about action, actors, scene, method, and purpose) that help in gathering information

Period   An end mark following a sentence or an abbreviation

Personal journal   A daily record of events, impressions, and ideas, sometimes private like a diary, and at other times written to be shared

Personal narrative   A form of personal writing in which the writer relates and comments on an incident in his or her own life or focuses on a single theme in the life of the writer

Persuasive writing   Writing whose purpose is to change the way the reader thinks or behaves

Phrase   A group of words that functions as a single part of speech and that does not contain a subject and a verb

Plot   A plan of action that involves conflict and is brought to a conclusion

Point of view   A way of looking at someone or something in a story, the way information is given to the reader

Population   The whole class of events, objects, or persons being studied

Précis   A written summary

Predicate   That part of sentence that says something about the subject

Predicate adjective   An adjective that follows a linking verb and that modifies the subject of the verb

Predicate nominative   A noun or pronoun that follows a linking verb and renames or identifies the subject of the sentence

Prefix   A syllable or syllables attached to the beginning of a root or word and modifying its meaning

Premise   A general or universal statement asserted to be true

Preposition   A word that shows the relationship of a noun or pronoun to some other word in the sentence

Prepositional phrase   A preposition, its object, and any modifiers of the object

Primary sources   Firsthand documents

Pronoun   A word that takes the place of a noun

Proofreading   Reading and correcting a manuscript before submitting it to another reader

Proposition   The thesis statement of a persuasive essay

Purpose   The reason for the action in a narrative

Quotation marks   Punctuation marks used to enclose a word or group of words and separate them from the rest of the sentence

Regional dialect   A variation of a language shared by people living in a particular region

Research paper   A long, formal essay that presents specific information from a variety of sources

Restriction sentence   The sentence in a paragraph that limits the general topic to the specific idea to be developed

Revision   The process of making changes to improve a piece of writing

Rhyme   The repetition of sounds at the ends of words

Root   A core of meaning that cannot be further analyzed

Rough draft   The first writing of a paper

Run-on sentence   Two sentences joined into one, either separated by a comma or run together with no punctuation

Sampling   Specific cases out of the entire population

Scene   The time and place where the action of a narrative occurs

Secondary sources   Documents written about some aspects of the primary source

Sentence   a group of words that expresses a complete thought

Sentence fragment   A group of words written incorrectly as a complete sentence

Sequential pattern   Organization of information by using time relationships

Simile   A figure of speech stating a comparison, using the words *like*, *as*, *than*, *seems*, or *appears*

Simple sentence   A sentence containing one independent clause with no subordinate clauses

Sound reasons   Reasons that can be supported with evidence

Stereotype   A fixed idea about the characteristics of certain groups of people

Subject   That part of a sentence about which something is said

Subjunctive mood   The mood used to express wishes, possibilities, or statements contrary to fact

Subordinate clause   A clause containing both a subject and a verb but not expressing a complete thought

Suffix   A syllable or syllables attached to the end of a word or a root to modify its meaning or change its part of speech

Syllogism   The three-part form of deductive reasoning—major premise, minor premise, and conclusion

Synonym   A word or phrase that has essentially the same meaning as another word or phrase

Syntax   Word order

Theme   One particular incident or idea of a narrative

Thesis statement   The main idea, or thesis, of an expository composition

Time line   A vertical or horizontal line with demarcations or marks showing the occurrence of events

Topic sentence   The sentence in a paragraph that states the general topic

Transition   A word or phrase that helps to link the sentences of a paragraph

Transitive verb   A verb that takes a direct object

TRI pattern   A method of paragraph development using *Topic, Restriction, Illustration*

Unabridged dictionary   A larger and more extensive version of the standard dictionary found in most classrooms

Unified paragraph   A paragraph in which each sentence develops the topic

Verb   A word that expresses action (physical or mental) or a state of being

Verb phrase   A main verb with one or more helping verbs

Vivid details   Details that recreate sights, sounds, tastes, textures, and smells for readers

Index of Authors and Titles

Index

Skills Index

E 7
F 8
G 9
H 0
I 1
J